Darius in the Shadow of Alexander

DARIUS

IN THE SHADOW OF

ALEXANDER

PIERRE BRIANT

TRANSLATED BY

JANE MARIE TODD

Harvard University Press

CAMBRIDGE, MASSACHUSETTS
LONDON, ENGLAND
2015

First printing

Publication of this book has been aided by a grant
from the French Ministry of Foreign Affairs
and the Cultural Services of the French
Embassy in the United States.

First published as *Darius dans l'ombre d'Alexandre* by Pierre Briant
World copyright © Librairie Arthème Fayard, 2003.

Library of Congress Cataloging-in-Publication Data

Briant, Pierre.
[Darius dans l'ombre d'Alexandre. English]
Darius in the shadow of Alexander / Pierre Briant ;
translated by Jane Marie Todd.
pages cm
Includes bibliographical references and index.
ISBN 978-0-674-49309-4 (alkaline paper)
1. Darius III, King of Persia—330 B.C.   2. Iran—Kings and rulers—Biography.
3. Iran—History—To 640.   4. Alexander, the Great, 356 B.C.–323 B.C.   I. Title.
DS284.7.B7513 2015
935'.705092—dc23
[B]
2014018170

Contents

III

RELUCTANCE AND ENTHUSIASM

IV

DARIUS AND DĀRĀ

V

A FINAL ASSESSMENT AND A FEW PROPOSALS

Acknowledgments

I would like to thank all those who offered me their help, especially in the fields of Persian and Arabo-Persian literature and iconography, during the four years I spent preparing and composing this book. Philippe Gignoux (Paris) was kind enough to share with me a manuscript, unpublished at the time, on the Sassanid texts that refer to Alexander (the book appeared in 2007 under the title *La démonisation d'Alexandre le Grand*); Marina Gaillard (Centre National de la Recherche Scientifique, or CNRS, Paris) allowed me to use her French translation of Abū Tāher Tarsusi's *Dārāb-nāmeh*, since published in *Alexandre en Iran* (2005), and was no less generous in sending me unpublished translations of Ibn' Bakhlī and Dīnawarī. In various ways, Francis Richard (Department of Oriental Manuscripts at the Bibliothèque Nationale de France, or BnF), Dominique Gerin (Coins, Medals, and Antiques Department, BnF), Marjan Mashkour (CNRS, Paris), and Marie-Françoise Clergeau (Collège de France) assisted me in collecting images and illustrations: F. Richard guided me in the discovery of manuscripts and their illustrations; D. Gerin gave me her careful attention during my research in the Coins, Medals, and Antiques Department; M. Mashkour showed me information and illustrations concerning the coffeehouse paintings of Iran; and I am indebted to M.-F. Clergeau for allowing me to publish here her remarkable original drawings of an exceptional painting (Fig. 40). My thanks as well to the colleagues who provided me with bibliographical information: Massumeh Fahrad (Freer Gallery of Art, Washington, D.C.), Charles-Henri de Fouchécour (Paris), Robert Hillenbrand (University of Edinburgh), Mary Subtelny (University of Toronto), Maria Szuppe (CNRS, Paris), Gilles Veinstein (Collège de France), and Yuriko Yamanaka (Osaka). The librarians at the Collège de France, the Institut d'Études Iraniennes (Université de Paris III), and the Institut

Français de Recherches en Iran (Tehran) assisted me in gaining access to valuable collections. Finally, my partner read and reread various drafts and, through her constant encouragement and pertinent suggestions, helped me to see this venture to its conclusion.

Editorial Note

With the exception of Chapters 11–12, endnotes in this book have been reduced almost entirely to source references. The reader may consult more extensive notes in "Thematic Notes by Chapter."

Preface to the English-Language Edition

Some ten years after the publication of the French edition of *Darius dans l'ombre d'Alexandre,* I am particularly happy that Harvard University Press is introducing it to anglophone readers, because studies and reflections on Alexander in English-speaking countries have traditionally been so plentiful and so stimulating. With the passage of time, it would appear useful to explain to new readers what my project was and to place it within the context of Achaemenid history as it is now being written, but also within the context of the reflections that have multiplied on the relationship the historian maintains with his or her sources and documentary materials.

The text itself has not been modified, apart from some adjustments in wording here and there and a few updated bibliographical references and explanatory notes. That might seem surprising, given the flood of publications on Alexander that have appeared in the last ten years, including an abundance of studies on the *Alexander Romance* (chap. 10).[1] The reason is simple: since 2003 the subject I deal with here—the construction of images of Darius III in the Greek and Latin literature of the Roman period and in the Persian and Arabo-Persian literature, in all its chronological diversity—has not been the occasion for any specific articles, with the exception of the reviews of the French edition of this book published in various journals. The motivations that led me to undertake that vast inquiry, unprecedented at the time, therefore remain fully valid. The process of reconstituting in detail the personality and reign of Darius III remains an insurmountable challenge, despite a few recent documentary discoveries that enhance both the history of the Macedonian conquest and the history of the transition from Darius to Alexander.[2] This book is therefore not a biography of the last of the Great Kings, and there is nothing about the last sentence of my introduction that I would change: "The objective of this book is instead to explain why Darius, along with so many others, is condemned to haunt the realm of historical oblivion."

The French version was generally well received, especially with respect to the method of analysis I applied to the texts.[3] I do not intend to go on at length about these reviews or to engage in polemics: rather, I would like to initiate a dialogue. Some of the reservations and criticisms the reviewers expressed are worthy of attention and sparked methodological reflections on my part that I believe it would be useful to share with readers. This will also be an opportunity to explain more clearly my way of thinking, just as my book is becoming available to a broader audience.

Reviewers regularly pointed out the continuity between this book and an earlier one I wrote, devoted to the history of the Persian Empire. I myself had remarked on this, referring readers to the chapter in which I had attempted to reconstitute Darius's strategy between 334 and 330.[4] Although I would like to remind readers that this new book has a different object, I also wish to add that the kinship and continuities between the two books go well beyond that simple observation, and that my inquiry really makes sense only when it is placed within an even broader time frame.

The nature of the documentary materials collected for this book made it inevitable that, willingly or not (because the historian cannot choose his documents), I would focus on an analysis of the Greco-Latin sources. Unsurprisingly, therefore, my reflections developed within the larger context of a problematic well known to historians of the Achaemenid Empire: How and to what extent can one write Achaemenid history on the basis of the classical sources? I have continually contended with that question since the early 1970s and attempted to give a preliminary and provisional response to it in a 1982 article.[5] Without going into detail about the discussions (sometimes pointlessly polemical) that continue to take place on that issue, I observe simply that my book constitutes a new contribution to the debate, in the form of a completely individualized and identified set of issues.

At the same time, the context within which research is now being conducted has been profoundly transformed by the unearthing and/or publication in the last forty years of a large number of corpora originating in different regions of the Achaemenid Empire. From Bactriana to Egypt and from Asia Minor to Persia proper (Fārs), the new documentation and our new knowledge are extremely impressive.[6] Apart from ancient Macedonia, few historical fields have undergone such a radical upheaval over such a brief period of time. The change is not only quantitative but also qualitative: these new documents have sometimes radically changed the makeup of the materials that historians of the empire collect and use. In particular, it has not escaped anyone's attention that the new archaeological and iconographical documents, and the multilingual written corpora, sometimes from the central administration (Persepolis, Susa) or the administration of the satrapies (western Asia Minor, Egypt, Idumea, Babylonia, Bactriana), provide a remarkable new perspective on the contributions of the classical sources. These primary sources allow the historian to study the empire from the inside and no longer simply through the classical authors' interpretive grid.

The Greco-Roman sources, however, are not thereby eliminated from research on Achaemenid history. In some cases (and the example of Darius III's reign is not the most extreme), the scarcity or even nonexistence of primary sources requires that we use the Greco-Roman texts.[7] Still, we must do so methodically and lucidly: the writings of Herodotus, Ctesias, Quintus Curtius Rufus, and so many others are not merely sets of data we can draw on at will to fill in the narrative and explanatory lacunae of the primary sources. These preoccupations, which I spelled out long ago, were constantly on my mind as I was preparing and writing this book.

I return now to the reviews of the French edition. In the conclusion to his review, the late Xavier Tremblay, a first-rate Iranist and linguist, clearly alluded to the same problem and made a proposal both heterodox and constructive. I yield to the temptation to quote it in full: "Since, therefore, the histories that [the historians of the Achaemenid Empire use] are adulterated through and through, I have dreamed of a history that would bracket them and would trust only the primary sources, as if we possessed only them: Old Persian, Elamite, Babylonian, Aramaic, Egyptian, Lydian, Lycian, the epigraphy from Greek Asia, a few fragments of direct accounts like those of Parmenion, and so on— and last but not least, the results of excavations. A heuristic effort of that kind could not yield such polished or even definitive results, but perhaps it would be salutary, at least temporarily" (2007, 383).[8]

The proposal is based on a disputable postulate.[9] It remains appealing, however, at least within the very specific context Tremblay was imagining, that of an experiment. I confess that I myself have had that thought (which I sometimes expressed publicly): not to exclude the classical sources from the documentary materials of the historian of the Achaemenid Empire but, as a heuristic exercise (in the form of "gray literature"), to write a history based on the primary sources alone. That would be the most reliable way to give an assessment of our acquired knowledge (sometimes recently acquired, and often provisionally) and of the persisting lacunae. I see no better way to propose new directions for research, *including on the use of the classical sources.*

It is rather surprising, however, that Tremblay makes this suggestion concerning a book that could not have been constructed on the primary sources alone. I imagine he wanted to express a sense of cognitive frustration, because (to borrow my own words), "at the end of our journey, we still do not know who Darius was. And our uncertainty about the 'real' Alexander has also increased." As for Tremblay's claim that "it is a book of Greek history devoted to the legend of Alexander, seen from the other side" (ibid., p. 381), that amounts to confusing the (Greco-Roman) origin of the sources and the (Achaemenid) object of research. I am of course altogether aware that the book is as much a book about the images of Alexander as about those of Darius (in Alexander's shadow), given that it is dedicated to an analysis of the construction, parallel and antithetical at once, of both series of images. But I wish to insist once again that my approach is that of a historian of the Achaemenid Empire, who, in this particular instance, is *constrained* to make use of suspect Greco-Roman sources. That being the case, the key question remains unchanged: How to speak of the last Achaemenid king by means of sources that are essentially devoted to constructing the (contradictory) images of his adversary? In that sense, though the "factual" results may appear scanty, this book is also a contribution, albeit minor, to Achaemenid history.[10] As M.-F. Baslez rightly understood (2006, 515), over the long term the book is part of the project to "find and set in place appropriate approaches to Achaemenid history. This impossible biography therefore stands as an exhaustive inventory and a critical assessment of these approaches."

The guiding thread of this book is directly related to a question that has hounded me for many years—namely, What was the state of the Achaemenid Empire at the moment Alexander and his army disembarked in Asia Minor? Because of the absence of any structural analysis in the classical literature, efforts to reply to that question have always appealed to the personality of Darius III and to his decisions. For a very long time, one theory reigned supreme: that of "Achaemenid decadence"—defined as a drastic weakening of imperial power, generally believed to have begun with Xerxes and to have become only more pronounced throughout the fourth century. In the elaboration of that doctrine, the texts about Darius's confrontation with Alexander had great evidential value, given that the Persian defeat was traditionally attributed to "decadence," even as the Persian defeat "confirmed" that theory. I therefore believed it essential to conduct a systematic deconstruction in an effort to understand on what stereotypes and models the figure of Darius had been constructed "in the shadow of Alexander."

Such is the objective I set for myself throughout this book. To that end, the words and concepts used by the "Alexander authors" have been placed within a broader perspective. They were already a pervasive presence in authors of the classical age steeped in the *Iliad* (that is particularly true of Xenophon), to such a point that these words and concepts were erected into universal explanatory models organized around a few hegemonic themes (the cowardice and flight of the Great King, his luxurious habits even when on a military campaign, and so on). These analyses lead us to consider with a great deal of skepticism the documentary foundations of the images that have circulated about Darius III and his empire, from the ancient world to modern Europe.[11] But the aim is not to postulate (adopting a typically postcolonial approach) that, on the contrary, "the Achaemenians were noble and strong until, quite suddenly, they weren't."[12] It is to free ourselves from the images imposed by the literature of antiquity, in order to conduct afresh the examination (or reexamination) of the existing primary documents.

The doubts I have put forward about the credibility of the classical sources for the historian of the Achaemenid Empire have sometimes caused confusion. Throughout the review Maria Brosius (2006) wrote of this book, she displays her uneasiness with an approach that, she said, tends "to deny any historical element in these stories," or believes that "mere literary motifs [are] devoid of any historical truth," or implies that "much of the history of Alexander [is] literary fiction." Hence this formulation, which tends to establish an opposition between literary analysis and historical research: "If we reduce the history to a literary construct, we avoid the real issue, namely to address the question why the Persian army was defeated and why the death of Darius is synonymous with the end of the Achaemenid empire" (p. 430). In a certain sense, the author develops an argument parallel to the one A. B. Bosworth made in 2003 against P. McKechnie, though without referring to it. McKechnie supported the view that Curtius's narratives are strongly marked by fiction.[13] Bosworth lamented that "it has become fashionable to question the veracity of the historians of antiquity. . . . What is more, if we accept that the addition of bogus 'facts' was a standard historical technique, we are left with very little. There are few criteria to distinguish what was the 'hard core' of authentic material and what was the superimposed fiction" (pp. 167–168).

These fears are at once excessive and a little surprising. Everyone has always known that the sources on the history of Alexander are extremely elaborate literary constructions and that, for this very reason, they must be subjected to an uncompromising critical reading. What is true for the history of Alexander is also true for the history of Darius, and to an even greater degree. Such a statement, based on a carefully constructed argument, ought not to surprise or shock anyone. It is precisely by isolating the stereotypes and the invariant *exempla* that we can conduct a reexamination of the sources of Alexander, seen from the angle of the representations of Darius. Far from excluding the Alexandrian sources from the historian's case file, I wish rather to define the methodological conditions of their use. As I have often explained, though a particular interpretation provided by one of the Alexander authors (Arrian, Curtius, and so on) may be considered suspect, the classical sources are not devoid of all informative value, provided we know how to extract and set forth what I customarily call "the Achaemenid informative kernel."[14] Under such conditions, they can perfectly well be used alongside the primary sources, even to reconstitute (albeit very partially) the reign of Darius III.[15]

That is why, in my mind, the last chapter of this book ("Darius in Battle: Variations on the Theme 'Images and Realities'") occupies an essential and strategic place. It represents both a counterpoint to the deconstruction of the literary sources and a successful conclusion to my reflections, a response to the question that I myself ask: "What is to be done?" In that chapter, I show how comparative history makes it possible to use the information sometimes embedded in the classical sources. To put it succinctly: *Yes,* Darius hastily left the battlefields of Issus and Gaugamela, leaving behind his soldiers, still in combat with the Macedonian army; and *yes,* to that end, he made use of a horse prepared for that very purpose (*ad hoc,* to borrow the expression of Curtius 3.11.11). But *no,* that does not mean that the Great King was a "coward," an interpretation dating to antiquity and complacently borrowed by a dominant current of modern historiography. Rather, Darius was obeying rules of the Persian monarchy, which stipulated that the survival of the king and of the state had to be ensured first of all. In other words, the information provided by Curtius, once disengaged from the hostile view of Darius that pervades it, is perfectly credible and offers the present-day historian an alternative explanation.

It is therefore clear that my reasonable doubts about the classical sources do not have the aim or the consequence of leaving the historian completely incapacitated. On the contrary, a rigorous critical reading opens up paths for methodically constructing documentary materials and for integrating "Achaemenid information" into them, information that is *also* drawn from the classical sources. There is no contradiction between literary analysis and historical inquiry: the first is a preliminary to the second, or rather, the two are inseparable.

Translator's Note

For the Alexander authors—Arrian, Quintus Curtius Rufus, Plutarch (*Life of Alexander* and *On the Fortune of Alexander*), Justin, Diodorus Siculus, Pseudo-Callisthenes, and the anonymous author of *Alexander's Itinerary*—and for a number of other Greek and Latin authors, I quote from standard published translations. These are listed in the Greek and Roman sources at the end of this volume. I have sometimes adapted a translation to conform to the French version and have occasionally made slight modifications for the sake of fluency, accuracy, and consistency of vocabulary. No effort has been made to standardize proper names or to Americanize British spellings.

For many other Greco-Roman authors, quoted at less length, I provide my own translation, based on the version in the French edition of Pierre Briant's book. To distinguish these from published English-language sources, I give the Latin title (even for Greek texts) in the endnote.

With the exception of a few inscriptions (as indicated in the endnotes or in the body of the text) and the *Letter of Tansar,* quoted from M. Boyce's English translation (1968a), passages from Pahlevi, Persian, and Arabo-Persian sources are my translation from the French. For French editions, see the endnotes, the additional notes to Chapter 10, and the general bibliography.

For quotations from texts originally written in modern languages other than French, I have used published English translations whenever these were available. These too are indicated in the endnotes. A complete list of these sources appears in the general bibliography.

A passage from Montaigne's *Essais* is taken from D. Frame's English translation (1965); all other quotations from French sources are my translation.

Darius in the Shadow of Alexander

∾ But the great and most undoubted victory which
Darius lost was this, that he was forced to yield to virtue,
magnanimity, prowess, and justice, while he beheld with
admiration his conqueror, who was not to be overcome
by pleasure or by labor, nor to be matched in liberality.

—PLUTARCH, *The Fortune of Alexander,* 2.7 (= *Moralia*, 339B)

∾ O you who hold your head up high, who know the
traditions of the thrones of the Great Kings, behold what
remains of those powerful kings. . . . Who sings the praises
of their justice now? Heaven has ceased to turn around
them, and no memory remains of these kings except the
words of men, who say that one had nobility of soul and
that the other did not, who blame one and celebrate the
other. In our turn we too shall pass away.

—FERDOWSĪ, *Shāh-nāmeh (Book of the Kings),* book 35, lines 583–589

Introduction

Between Remembering and Forgetting

The History of Darius and the History of Alexander

Historians and their readers have always been fascinated by the history of the great empires, and especially by their emergence and disappearance. In the case of the philosophy of history, we need only recall Jacques-Bénigne Bossuet's pages on "the rise and fall of empires" (1681), the comte de Volney's "meditations on the revolutions of empires" (1791), or G. W. F. Hegel's reflections on the structural reasons behind the fall of the Persian Empire to Alexander the Great, as Hegel developed them in his public lectures (1826–1829). The theory of the five empires—Assyrian, Median, Persian, Macedonian, and Roman—has been put forward since antiquity. The introductions to Polybius's *Histories* and to Dionysius of Halicarnassus's *Roman Antiquities* show that this theory was used primarily to convey the idea of the Roman Empire's superiority over every previous entity, including the Persian Empire, which could not withstand the offensive Alexander launched in the spring of 334. After a four-year war, Darius III, the tenth Great King to succeed the founder, Cyrus (ca. 557–530), was assassinated by members of his own close circle (July 330).

The ancient authors liked to record the vanishing of an empire and to hold forth on its intrinsic fragility. But they had little fondness for explaining the precise causes and modalities of its disappearance—except by regularly pointing out the flaws and vices of the last sovereigns. Contemporary historians have also inquired into the apparent suddenness of the disappearance of certain ancient empires. The formulations may have evolved, but the fundamental questions have hardly changed: Should structural causes be privileged over circumstantial ones? What importance ought to be granted to personal factors? As Jacques Le Goff rightly insists in his *Saint Louis,* "the supposed opposition between the individual and society" is a false aporia. "A knowledge of the society is necessary if we are to discern an individual figure constituting himself and living within it."[1] When considering the monarchies of antiquity, a historian who knows the importance of structural analysis must also learn the tools that allow him to apprehend the last ruler's personality, to understand his political vision, and to assess his aptitude for conducting a strategy or for leading armies.

That is why, as I completed my analysis and overview of the Persian Empire in *Histoire de l'empire Perse* (1996), I was already planning a study on Darius III specifically, a sequel and complement of sorts to the earlier book. At the time, I had the impression that I had taken the structural analysis as far as it was possible to go, in light of the sources and the questions a historian needs to ask. That was a fleeting impression, of course; it is well known that no book is exhaustive, that new documents can surface, that interpretations solid in appearance at the moment they are proposed can later be called into question, and that the author can even change his mind. Nevertheless, my careful perusal of recent publications has assured me that, overall if not in the details, the interpretation I gave of imperial history in my 1996 book has held up well under critical scrutiny.

That book includes not only an analysis of the Achaemenid monarchy and an inventory of the empire at the dawn of the Macedonian invasion but also an attempt to reconstitute the strategy Darius conducted against Alexander.[2] I therefore needed a different angle of attack. I was strongly tempted to devote a book to the last of the Achaemenids, particularly because it would be a first. Darius III, of course, is not absent from works reconstituting Persian history in its dynastic continuity or from those dealing specifically with the conquests of the young Macedonian king; and, at least in the best cases, these books evoke Alexander's early adversary with relative accuracy and fidelity. But though publishers' catalogs and bookstore shelves in many countries attest eloquently— sometimes repetitively and oppressively—to the lasting and even increasing popularity of biography as a genre, and though they illustrate "the return of the event," no book has ever been dedicated to the history of Darius.

That observation may surprise a few readers, though the weight of evidence has surely persuaded others, whether they consider the gap detrimental or, on the contrary, see no reason to object. After all, some may judge that the Persian enemy of Alexander does not justify the same considerations as the Macedonian conqueror himself, given the absence of documentation on Darius and his lack of charisma.

Such an imbalance raises a problem that merits special attention. The Darius file is neither very thick nor particularly coherent. It would be simplistic, however, to attribute the lost memory of that individual solely to the lacunae in the documentation. The choices made by historians have reflected and still reflect an era and a vision, and these choices are both a result and an expression of a method and a problematic. I am altogether convinced that the persistent lack of interest in Darius III and his empire is also a particular manifestation of a general and enduring undervaluation of the Achaemenid phase within the history of the ancient Middle East. Apart from Cyrus and Darius I, the Persian kings have never elicited much interest on the part of historians and biographers.

And aside from the now-commonplace, even ritualistic declarations of principle regarding the misdeeds of a Hellenocentric and Alexandro-maniacal view, specialists on Alexander have been unable to take full advantage of the recent evolution in Achaemenid studies. Yet Michael Rostovtzeff had already opened new avenues in his many studies published from the first years of the twentieth century on, and they ought to have profoundly modified the approach to the Hellenistic world and to the structural and genetic relations it maintained with the Achaemenid world. The introductory chapter of his monumental *Social and Economic History of the Hellenistic World* (1941) does not omit discussion of the empire of Darius III. The logic of his exposition did not require that he spend much time on the person of the Great King, but his editorial choice expressed his deep-seated conviction: the Hellenistic kings did not build on the ruins of the Achaemenid Empire. Rather, they laid their foundations on the living legacy of Darius's empire, conquered by Alexander. Although a number of historians of the Hellenistic world drew inspiration from Rostovtzeff's writings, the same has not been true for the historians of Alexander, who apparently did not find that view enlightening. During the 1970s, historians of the Achaemenid world took up the torch: within the last thirty years or so, there has been spectacular progress in that field of research. But it is regrettable that its impact on the history of Alexander, though not insignificant, has been relatively limited.

For various reasons that need not be analyzed here, many specialists in Alexander still maintain that their research belongs to a field that has only occasional connections to the history of the Middle East under the domination of the Great Kings. It is self-evident that the history of Alexander ought to be included within the framework of the history of Macedonia and of the Greek city-states. But the historian of Alexander also ought to acknowledge that a reflection on the conquest of the countries from the Middle East to Central Asia and India, and on the policy the Macedonian king conducted there toward the different populations, requires a certain familiarity with—an assimilation of—research done specifically on the organization and evolution of the Achaemenid Empire.

That has not really happened, if we are to judge by the articles and books that have appeared in recent decades on the history of Alexander. Paradoxically, the Persian Empire is now sometimes presented in a more cursory manner than it was in works published in the nineteenth century. That is not to say that research on Alexander has undergone a regression since Johann Gustav Droysen's *History of Alexander the Great* (1833). Indeed, Droysen's description of the Persian Empire often appears rather conventional today. But in his time, it was at least considered indispensable to devote part of the introduction to Darius and his empire. Such an approach was long de rigueur in historical studies. How is it possible to explain fruitfully the war between Macedonia and the Persian Empire, while taking no interest in Darius and his entourage or even in the countries and populations he ruled? No one can now doubt that research on Darius III must assume that the two realms, Achaemenid and Hellenistic, intersected to such an extent that they constituted a single realm at the time of the political and cultural shift inaugurated by the confrontation between Darius and Alexander.

That is the real reason I argued—in a book on Alexander first published in 1974—for an approach to Alexander that was less "psychologistic" and more "rational." It was my view at the time, and it remains my view even now, that a corollary of the focus on the young Macedonian king's personality is that one too often neglects his adversary, "as if Alexander were all alone on his personal adventure."[3] And that is also the reason I devoted a chapter in that book specifically to "resistance to the conquest."[4]

The Biographical Impasse

In a deliberately provocative gesture, I began that book by declaring: "This book is not a biography." The page limit imposed by the series in which the book was to be published partly guided my choice: I decided at the time to devote my remarks to "the examination of the big questions that quite naturally arise." I wanted to "set forth the principal aspects of a historical phenomenon that cannot be reduced to the person of Alexander, whatever the acknowledged importance of the personal element." Clearly, that formulation also indicates a certain distrust of biography as a genre, or rather, certain reservations—which have never left me—about the often exclusive focus on the "great man," which the genre has long assumed and favored. It is quite possible that my intimate familiarity with works devoted to Alexander the Great has greatly contributed toward my constant critical vigilance in this area. Indeed, from antiquity to our own time, a large number of biographies devoted to Alexander have maintained unusually close ties to the genre of the paean, which shows little respect for the "opposing camp" and even less for the historian's craft.

Such reservations have been kept in check, however. But if, as Jacques Le Goff rightly repeats in his *Saint Louis*, "a biography is not only the collection of everything one can and must know about an individual," and if, here as elsewhere, the historian must scrupulously and methodically assess the reliability of the sources available, he must at least have at his disposal a full and coherent set of documents. That is the situation of the biographer of Saint Louis, who "(along with Saint Francis of Assisi) is the thirteenth-century figure about whom we have the best firsthand information." And if, again according to Le Goff, the historian's obligation is to recount a life "solely with the aid of the original documents, those of the period" (p. 313), then the book that follows cannot be called a biography. For we do not possess any actual Achaemenid documentation. How can I claim to be writing the life of an individual who makes only a fleeting appearance in the documentation at the age of forty-four and who dies six years later, with no heir and no memorial, his last moments immediately exploited by his enemies for their own advantage?[5]

The nature of the documentation and the way it was constituted have created a paradoxical situation. Although rooted in the *longue durée* of Achaemenid history, Darius and his decisions can be grasped only through the texts about Alexander that originated in the Macedonian camp, sometimes even in the "Western camp." That explains why I have intentionally expatiated in this book on the methods, backgrounds, styles, and assumptions of the authors of the Roman period who discussed the history of Alexander, whether in Greek or in Latin. That is the real reason this book, dedicated to rediscovering and weaving together the threads of Darius's memory, is also a book on Alexander.

One cannot speak of "Greco-Roman sources on Darius," because no author from antiquity believed it useful to make the last Great King the protagonist of a narrative or of a Life. The authors wished first and foremost to speak of Alexander, either to overpraise him or to condemn his vices and excesses—in any event, to relate his career and exploits. In various discursive contexts, however, they were all led to evoke Darius III, or more exactly, a man who was nothing more than the adversary of the young Macedonian hero and who was often distinguished from his glorious namesake, Darius I, with the unflattering designation "Darius, the one who was defeated by Alexander."

That situation is well known for the last phase of Achaemenid history, particularly the fourth century B.C.E. Because of the rarity—or nonexistence—of Achaemenid sources proper, the historian is led to read the Greco-Roman sources "between the lines," that is, to bring to light what can be considered the Achaemenid kernel embedded in a Greco-Roman interpretive shell. Such a method, if conducted rigorously and with caution, is able to extract important information about the Achaemenid Empire that Alexander conquered, an empire whose remnants were fought over by his successors.

So it is that military and logistical concerns, which predominate in a number of Hellenistic accounts, led ancient authors to provide information, explicitly or implicitly, about the bridges, mountains, and passes that the armies had to cross, the irrigation projects that prevented the movements of warships on the Tigris, the granaries and storehouses where the Macedonian troops were likely to find fresh supplies, the villages where they had their winter quarters, the cities and palaces where they found rest and booty, the names and duties of the administrators of the satrapies they seized, but also about the rules of the Achaemenid court, whose rites and rituals Alexander made his own. In a way, the records of the booty amassed when a city or camp was taken, even when they exist only as fragmentary literary excerpts, are for the historian of antiquity the equivalent, albeit modest, of what posthumous inventories are for historians of the modern period. What would we know about the wealth of equipment in the royal camp if, after the Persian defeat at Issus, so many Hellenistic texts had not described the capture of Darius's tent, then Alexander's entry into the sumptuous apartments of the defeated enemy, and finally, the seizure of the immense treasures the Great King had left in Damascus before the battle, which the specialized services of the Macedonian supplies office meticulously counted and recorded?

For anyone setting out in search of Darius the individual as seen through the Alexander sources, the interpretive method is comparable in principle. But it also raises specific problems. It is less difficult to decipher the documents regarding the state of the empire than those concerning the figure of Darius. In addition, investigations of a region can be supplemented by local supporting documentation; but similar documents do not exist for a biographical inquiry, at least in the case of Darius III. Furthermore, because of the ancient authors' personal investment in Alexander and their overwhelming support of the cause of the Macedonian conquest, it is an infinitely more delicate matter to shed light on the personality of his adversary. These authors, even when they mention Darius, are really still speaking about Alexander. It is therefore risky, even impossible, to reconstruct with complete certainty the "reality" of a Persian Darius, which these same authors relegate to the background or evoke unconsciously with words or expressions that transmit the Achaemenid kernel. In my view, that is because these authors often knew nothing or next to nothing about the Great King, his thoughts and strategy, even though some feigned to speak from the Persian camp, even attributing thoughts, feelings, and words to Darius. Not only was their attention completely monopolized by the Macedonian king, but they were also not historians in the sense in which we understand that term today.

Images, Memory, History

I would have liked to use, as an epigraph to this book, the beautiful eulogy that Gautier de Châtillon gave for Darius in about 1180 in his *Alexandréides (Alexandreis)*: "But you, o Darius, if people someday give credence to what we are writing, France will rightly consider you equal in glory to Pompey."[6] The realities of my profession, however, quickly reduce the historian's ambition to more modest dimensions.

The Great King Darius III is of course no Louis-François Pinagot, the eponymous antihero of a book in which the French historian Alain Corbin, not without panache and not without risk, attempts to perform a paradoxical task, that of "bringing to life a second time an individual whose memory has been obliterated," in order to "to re-create him, give him a second chance—a rather strong chance at the moment—to become part of the memory of his century."[7] In explaining his approach, Corbin says he was not seeking to write a biography, "no doubt an absurd undertaking in the case of a nineteenth-century peasant. I sought . . . to bring to life a fragment of the lost world, the fragment that may have presented itself to an inaccessible subject."[8]

It is clearly possible to reject the very principle of methodological comparison, on the seemingly admissible grounds that the situation of Darius is

not as dramatically inaccessible as that of Louis-François Pinagot, and that
the last of the Persian kings is not, strictly speaking, unknown to history.
Nevertheless, it should be noted that what we "know" about him and his life
can be summed up in a few words: the names of his parents; the names of his
wife, mother, daughters, and son; the name he bore before becoming king
(though there are two divergent traditions); scraps of information on his status at court before his accession; the names of battles he lost; the date of his
death; and his age at the time.[9] Almost nothing else—or, more exactly, the "rest"
is indistinguishable from the history of Alexander and his conquests. True,
historians learned long ago not to give in to fear of the documentary void: their
task is also to write the history of what is not known. But in the present case,
the void reaches such vast proportions that it would be unreasonable to aspire
to make it an ally.

One critic, speaking very favorably of Corbin's *Pinagot,* wrote that, in the
end, "we do not know a great deal more about the man after we have finished
the book."[10] I have every reason to fear that the reader will feel the same way at
the end of this book, because, ultimately—assuming we want to place Darius
within the expansive category of "the great men of antiquity"—among those
who held supreme power and led armies, the last of the Achaemenid kings remains an "unknown."

And yet, Darius certainly spoke, wrote letters, sent written orders, and
even perhaps personally led a campaign in some part of his empire before 334
B.C.E. And he undoubtedly loved, conspired with others, and nurtured friend-
ships. But of that public and private life we have no direct trace. It is accessible
only through the Greek and Roman authors. The partial quotations they happen to provide of royal letters, speeches, or written documents are either very
suspect or are presented in such an allusive form that any reconstitution of the
original is impossible. Let me take a simple example from Arrian, who reports
on the deployment of the Achaemenid contingents for the Battle of Gaugamela:
"According to the statement of Aristobulus, the written scheme of the [battle]
arrangement drawn up by Darius was afterwards captured."[11] That formulation clearly shows that Arrian did not have the document before his eyes, even
in the form of a paraphrase that Aristobulus might have provided. And in accordance with a practice well known in antiquity, Aristobulus may have made
reference to a document simply to give his description some authority. In short,
the present-day historian is quite incapable of stating with certainty that Aristobulus had such a document in his hands or that the reference authenticates the

details of Arrian's later discussion. The contemporary historian is justified in postulating only that the Achaemenid general staff had meticulously prepared its battle line, but he might have been persuaded of such an obvious fact even without Arrian's incidental remark.

Above all, these authors wish to present only one hero of the story, Alexander, even if that means attributing to Darius traits and words so stereotypical that they do not allow the contemporary historian to reconstitute a biographical identity of the Great King. In many ancient sources, but also in medieval and modern dramaturgy and historiography dealing with Darius's death, it is fairly clear that, though the depictions may vary in their details, the primary function of these narratives is to exalt Alexander's "chivalrous" attitude toward his enemy. And that enemy is in short order attributed all the virtues associated with the "good loser." Similarly, the many appearances of Darius's mother, wife, and daughters serve less to express the feelings that guided or troubled the Great King than to depict Alexander's "filial attachment" and "admirable self-control," by attributing the appropriate role to each of the figures. That explains the extraordinary success that such scenes have had among painters, enthusiastic admirers of antiquities, and bards vaunting the heroic grandeur of the young Macedonian king. These poets and artists were themselves usually identified with the patron who employed them and commissioned works from them.

It has not escaped anyone's attention that the reason *The Queens of Persia at the Feet of Alexander* (Fig. 47) is one of the scenes from antiquity most often represented is that it illustrates the great generosity of Alexander (and of Louis XIV), and not that it praises the memory of a Great King.[12] Darius is absent, in fact, and is implicitly condemned for having allowed, through his defeat, women of such noble blood and with such noble hearts to fall into the enemy's hands. And in the scene where Alexander throws his mantle over the body of Darius, so ignominiously assassinated by his own men (Fig. 48), it is once again the Macedonian king who is unambiguously set up as the positive hero. In each of these cases, Darius is introduced less as an actor in his own story than as a bit player in the saga of Alexander.

Given that situation, the novelist or fiction writer may choose the path set out by Chevalier Andrew M. Ramsay. In 1727 he published a curious book inspired by the *Cyropaedia* and destined to become a best seller: "In the *Cyropaedia*, Xenophon does not speak of anything that happened to Cyrus from his sixteenth to his fortieth year. I have taken advantage of antiquity's silence about the youth of that prince to allow him to travel, and the account of his travels provides me with an opportunity to paint the religion, the customs, and the politics of all the countries he passed through, as well as the principal revolutions that occurred in his time in Egypt, Greece, Tyre, and Babylon."

Laying claim to the combined privileges of *inventio* and *imitatio*, Ramsay justifies his intermingling of source references and fictional characters: "I have attributed nothing about religion to the ancients that is not authorized by very conclusive passages. . . . I have diverged as little as possible from the most accurate chronology. . . . The only liberty I have allowed myself was to toss into my historical episodes situations and characters to make my narration more instructive and more interesting."[13]

The author is eager to embrace the scholarship of his time. To mark even better his attachment to a form of historical reality, he reproduces in an appendix a letter from Nicolas Fréret, which, he says, justifies his chronology of Cyrus on the basis of the consensus among specialists on that historical period.[14]

That is the approach regularly followed by authors of historical novels. For example, in *Creation* Gore Vidal takes his reader from Pasargadae to Athens and on to India, in the footsteps of his storyteller hero, Cyrus Spitama, grandson of Zoroaster and Xerxes's childhood friend and ambassador. And in *The Persian Boy,* Mary Renault brings to life Darius III and especially Alexander, seen through the eyes of a young eunuch, Bagoas, the favorite of the Great King and then of his Macedonian conqueror. All in all, it makes little difference that, of these two Persian narrators, Cyrus Spitama is a creation by a present-day novelist, and Bagoas is introduced by Quintus Curtius Rufus in the course of narratives and descriptions that belong mostly to the realm of romance and fiction.

As a historian of Darius III, I find it difficult to justify using the "silence of antiquity" as a way to embark on an improbable reconstitution of the last of the Achaemenids. Furthermore, unlike the specialist in "Pinagotic research," or more generally, unlike historians who deal with recent and contemporary times, I cannot consult cadastres or public records where I might have found the precise date of the king's birth and of his accession, and many other pieces of information that would have allowed me to fill, albeit partially, the void of the first forty-four years of a man who lived to be fifty.

The biographer of Saint Louis, amply provided with original documents, could choose not to study the king's life after his death, could opt not to offer his readers "a history of the historical image of the holy king," because such a "subject, though fascinating, would have belonged to a different problematic." On the contrary, as a historian of the final years of the Achaemenid Empire, I am inclined to privilege that approach, that is, to conduct research on the images of Darius III through literature and iconography or, more precisely, on the phases and modalities in the construction of a plural memory of the Great King. It is in fact rather surprising that neither historians of the Persian Empire nor historians of Alexander have, to my knowledge, ever attempted systematically to clear such a path. The only ones who have traveled it and who continue to travel it in every direction are specialists in the romances and legends of Alexander. These studies and this research are altogether robust and extremely fruitful, whether they focus on versions stemming from Pseudo-Callisthenes's *Alexander Romance,* created and disseminated in Western countries during the Middle Ages, or on Persian or Arabo-Persian versions, which constructed and transmitted contrasting images of Iskandar and Dārā.

Here again, however, a lacuna exists, in addition to the silence of the historians. Although the specialists in romances and legends analyze with intelligence and perspicacity the ways and means by which a mythical, legendary, and fictive memory of Alexander was constructed, they too have little motivation to study what the images of Darius may have been in these same ancient and medieval Alexander romances.[15] The absence of any study of that kind based on the Persian and Arabo-Persian texts is particularly detrimental. Indeed, that literature and the oral recitation of the "books of kings" by itinerant bards did much to shape the representations that the Iranians constructed of their past, beginning in about 1000 c.e., when the *Book of the Kings (Shāh-nāmeh)* of Hakīm Abu'l Qāsim Firdowsī Tūsī (Ferdowsī) first appeared. It recounts, among many other episodes, the moving story of Iskandar and Dārā, their battles and their fraternal reconciliation when the king of Iran was breathing his last. That is why, despite my inexperience in that specialized field, I found it indispensable to go in search of Dārā as well. A parallel inquiry became all the more imperative in that the Persian version is partly derived from Pseudo-Callisthenes's Greek romance.

An analysis of the Greco-Roman, Persian, and Arabo-Persian traditions may provide keys for understanding why, when, and how the words and images that began to construct a memory in antiquity came into being, at the end of a process of creative selection and elaboration. On certain points the inquiry will open the way for a biographical reconstitution, which, however, will remain forever partial, incomplete, uncertain, and impressionistic—in a word, kaleidoscopic. The objective of this book is instead to explain why Darius, along with so many others, is condemned to haunt the realm of historical oblivion.

I

THE IMPOSSIBLE
BIOGRAPHY

❦ 1 ❦

A Shadow among His Own

Before examining in detail the Greco-Roman tradition on Darius and the historiographical currents to which it gave rise, I should like to survey the documentation that I shall call "Achaemenid." Consisting of documents (written, iconographic, archaeological, or numismatic) that originated in the empire itself, they should in principle shed an Achaemenid light on the Great King, on the early part of his reign, and even on the decisions he made when facing the Macedonian invasion. To properly assess the challenge, consider the following question: What would a history of Darius elaborated solely on the basis of the contemporary evidence coming from Persia and from the various countries of the empire look like? However hypothetical the exercise might appear, the answer turns out to be particularly enlightening and instructive.

Meditations on Ruins

Hail to you, solitary ruins, holy tombs, silent walls! It is you I invoke; it is to you that I address my prayer. . . . How many useful lessons, how many touching or forceful reflections, do you not offer the mind that knows to consult you! . . . O ruins! I shall return to you to learn your lessons! I shall place myself once again in the peace of your solitude; and there, far from the distressing spectacle of the passions, I shall love men on the basis of recollections.

So writes the Comte de Volney in his introduction *qua* invocation to *Les ruines* (*The Ruins*, 1791), a reconstructed memory of his journey to the Orient in 1784. The author wanders sadly through the scant vestiges of Palmyra, of which barely a "lugubrious skeleton" remains. The book is conceived as a melancholic reflection on the great civilizations of the past, now reduced to dust, victims of the "slow consumption of despotism." Astounded by the scale of the ruins he surveys, Volney provides the reader with his "meditations on the revolutions of empires," greatly aided by the declamation of a garrulous pedagogue, a "Genie of the graves and of the ruins," who has unexpectedly but conveniently appeared beside him: "And the history of past times took vivid shape in my mind. I remembered those ancient centuries when twenty famous nations existed on these lands, . . . [among them] Persia, ruling from the Indus to the Mediterranean, . . . [which] collected tributes from a hundred nations. . . . Where are they, those ramparts of Niniveh, those walls of Babylon, those palaces of Persepolis, those temples of Baalbek and Jerusalem?"

Meditating on the ruins of the Orient and contrasting them to wealthy Europe, Volney comes to fear that the same will someday be true for "the banks of the Seine, the Thames, and the Zuiderzee"—unless, of course, the roots of despotism are extirpated from Europe's deepest substance.

Such evocations, in which precise descriptions intermingle with flights of romanticism, are also found, in scarcely less discreet form, among travelers sent on missions—or among those who went on their own—to discover the great civilizations of the past. In 1817–1820, for example, Sir Robert Ker Porter completed a grand tour of Georgia, Persia, Armenia, and Babylonia, and in 1821 published a report filled with reflections, descriptions, and illustrations. Although intent on producing and distributing accurate surveys of the monuments and images, he too was captivated by the majestic reminiscences emanating from palaces reduced to giant skeletons made of doors, windows, and sculptures in hard black stone: "With a head full of these recollections of Cyrus, who had planted this empire, and of Alexander, who had torn it from its rock, I turned from the tenantless tombs, and as desolated metropolis. All were equally silent; all were alike the monuments of a race of heroes" (*Travels*, 1:683). A short time later, Hegel, who had read Porter, also made note of that abrupt and complete disappearance. "The Persian Empire is one that has passed away, and we have nothing but melancholy relics of its glory. Its fairest and richest towns—such as Babylon, Susa, Persepolis—are razed to the ground; and only a few ruins mark their ancient site" (*The Philosophy of History*, p. 198).

From that moment on, reflections on the sudden and incomprehensible engulfment of Achaemenid civilization and its reduction to a few scattered material remnants would become a commonplace among historians philosophizing about the tumultuous history of the "Eastern empires."

European travelers made the discovery by reading the ancient authors: "There is nothing easier to learn from the descriptions of Arrian, Curtius, and Diodorus Siculus than the situation of Persepolis, and it is a very great pleasure to travel that country with the ancient authors in hand." These are the words of Chevalier Jean Chardin (1711, 9:48), one of the best-known travelers to visit Persia in the seventeenth century. In his reports of his travels, meditations on the inexorable flight of time go hand in hand with a desire to situate the ruins in history. Referring to two tombs located above the terrace he has just described, Chardin evokes the vague and indistinct memory of Darius but manifests a great deal of skepticism about local traditions.

Two and a half centuries later, on May 3, 1902, Pierre Loti viewed the palaces and tombs through the prism of the glorious figures (already well known at that time) of Darius the Great and Xerxes. There is nothing surprising about the romanticism of his words, which is somewhat reminiscent of Volney's "ruinism": "Supreme peace, the peace of worlds forever abandoned, hovers over these April prairies, which have known in their time sumptuosities worthy of Sardanapalus, then conflagrations, massacres, the deployment of great armies, the maelstrom of battles. As for the esplanade we have just climbed, it is at this hour, the approach of evening, a place of inexpressible melancholy. . . . It was Xerxes who had the notion to give the starring role to the two winged giants that, posted on the threshold of these palaces, welcome me. And they reveal intimacies about their sovereign that I was never expecting to chance upon. In contemplating them, more than by reading ten volumes of history, I gradually conceive how majestic, hieratic, and superb was the vision of life in the eyes of that half-legendary man" (*Vers Ispahan,* p. 130).

About to continue their journey, Loti and his companions returned the next morning, May 4, "to bid farewell to the great palaces of silence" and to take photographs. The ruins, reemerging in the wan gray light of dawn, assumed a more run-down and sinister aspect. In that way, Loti immerses the reader in a climate favorable to the evocation of "the Macedonian horde" and Alexander's torch. To that end, he does not hesitate to make use of the most conventional literary tricks:

While treading that old mysterious ground, my foot stumbled over a piece of wood, half-buried. I pulled it out to get a look at it. It was a fragment of a beam that must have been enormous, made of indestructible cedar of Lebanon and—without a doubt—coming from Darius's complex. . . . I pick it up and turn it over. One of the sides is blackened, crumbling into ash: the fire set by Alexander's torch! . . . The trace of that legendary fire survives, it is there in my hands, still visible after more than twenty-two centuries! . . . It is as though a magic spell were sleeping in that block of cedar. . . . And a passage from Plutarch comes back to my memory, a passage translated long ago when I was in school, in sullen boredom under the iron rule of a teacher, but which suddenly comes to life and becomes clear: the description of a night of orgy in the sprawling city, here, around these esplanades. . . . And then the great cries of drunkenness and horror, the sudden blaze of the cedar frame, the crackling of the enamel on the wall, and finally, the collapse of the gigantic columns, toppling down upon one another, reverberating against the ground with a thunderous noise. . . . The piece of beam that still exists and which I touch with my hands was charred on that night. (p. 143)

Loti, like his predecessors on the site, was certainly informed by modern works, but he is careful to maintain toward them the reserve befitting a traveler to the ruins. He was also armed, however, with reminiscences of his readings of Greek authors, especially Diodorus Siculus, who transmitted the first literary description of the ruins during the Roman period. Loti recalls that it was "the passing of the Macedonian's armies [that] revealed their existence to the Western nations." That remark tends to emphasize Alexander's influence on the memory of Persepolis and, consequently, to eclipse the memory of the Great Kings (only Darius the Great and Xerxes are named).

Half a century earlier, in 1841–1842, the painter Eugène Flandin, in the company of the architect Pascal Coste, had gone to Persia on a mission for the French government to study and collect antiquities. The two returned with plans and drawings of an astonishing accuracy, which even today constitute a remarkable source of architectural and iconographic documentation. In addition to the joint publication of these plans in three folio volumes, Flandin wrote a personal report on his own. In it he reveals the substance of his mediations on the ruins of Persepolis. He takes issue with an already hegemonic thesis, namely, the lack of inventiveness in Persian art. He says that, on the contrary, "nothing in these palaces of the Achaemenid princes is savage or barbarian" (*Relation de voyage* [1851], p. 148). He also seeks to connect explicitly the pitiful end of the last Great King to his own meditation. If "the antiquarian evokes the great shadows of the Persians of Xerxes," he writes, he will also "pay homage to the combatants betrayed by fortune at Arbela." Flandin describes "the remains of those magnificent palaces from which Darius escaped, defeated and in flight,

1. *Investiture relief of Ardašir in Naqsh-e Rustam.*

only to die by a traitor's dagger" (p. 269). Expressed in very literary form, that image again places Persepolis within the context of Achaemenid history, instead of
abandoning it entirely to the traditional "Orientalist" vision. But is it really possible to perceive, even indistinctly, the silhouette of Darius III on the terrace of
Persepolis or nearby sites?

Some travelers thought so, wondering about the identity of the protagonists on the reliefs engraved on the cliff of Naqsh-e Rustam, at the foot of the
tombs of the Achaemenid kings (Fig. 1), and about the date of their creation.
One of these reliefs depicts two horsemen, dressed as one might imagine two
kings to be dressed. The horseman on the right holds a ring in his outstretched
right hand, while the one on the left (followed by a parasol-bearer) also extends
his right hand, as if to seize hold of the ring. The illustrious Dutch traveler Cornelis de Bruyn, publishing the account of his travels in 1711, did not omit to
provide a drawing. It is easy to compare his drawing to those of three other
travelers—Chardin, Carsten Niebuhr, and James Morier—given that they were
all collected on a single plate (Fig. 2) by the Russian statesman A. N. Olenin. In
a letter of August 4, 1817, Olenin, "in the name of Sacred Antiquity," urgently asked
Robert Ker Porter to do a precise survey, so as to dissipate all doubts once and
for all. The learned traveler did not fail to do so, providing his readers with a

2. *Investiture relief of Ardašir in Naqsh-e Rustam.*

detailed description (1:548–557) and a drawing (pl. 23), which he characterized as more faithful than those of his predecessors but just as beautiful (Fig. 3).

Chardin and de Bruyn gathered information on-site about the meaning to be given to the relief. Chardin learned "from the people of the country" that it depicted a king of India and a king of Persia (Rustam), "who, after a long and bloody war, agreed to end it with a single combat. This combat consisted of seizing an

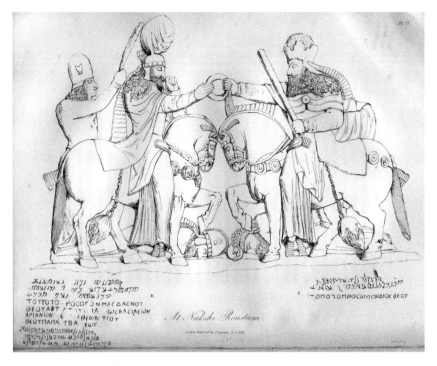

3. Investiture relief of Ardašir in Naqsh-e Rustam.

iron ring and wresting it away from the adversary . . . and the king of Persia
defeated the king of India" (16:182). De Bruyn too inquired into the identity of
the figures represented and reported one of the versions communicated to him:
"It is claimed that the first figure is Alexander and the second Darius, who by
that action handed over the empire to him. Others say that these figures represent two powerful princes or generals, who, after long waging war without either gaining the advantage, agreed that the one who would snatch the ring from
the hands of his competitor would be victorious over him and would be acknowledged as the winner" (*Voyages de Corneille Le Brun*, 2:282).

A nice story, one that could easily be linked to rumors of a single combat
between the two kings, reported by several Greco-Roman authors, during the
Battle of Issus and/or Gaugamela. In reality, as the illustrious A. I. Sylvestre de
Sacy pointed out in 1793 in his *Mémoire sur diverses antiquités de la Perse (On Various
Antiquities of Persia;* pp. 14–16), that was not at all the case. The difference in style
demonstrates that the relief is clearly post-Achaemenid (produced five centuries
after Darius I) and, as the inscriptions reveal, the scene depicts the royal investiture of the Sassanid king Ardašir (horseman on the left) by the god Ahura Mazda

(horseman on the right). But Silvestre de Sacy is overly harsh with de Bruyn, who—like Chardin—had actually expressed the most profound reservations about the story he had heard. De Bruyn concludes: "But there is nothing on which to base such tales." The tradition, then, attested to a form of "Achaemenid" memory among the Persians who welcomed and guided European travelers—except that the local guides must have been referring implicitly to the romance of Dārā and Iskandar rather than to the history of Darius and Alexander.

A King without a Palace

If the modifications and destructions that occurred in the post-Achaemenid period are disregarded, the Persepolis one visits today is the same one that Alexander pillaged and partially destroyed in 330. It is therefore also the Persepolis of Darius III. When one reads the accounts of the Greco-Roman authors, it is easy to superimpose one or another of their descriptions onto the site, as it became known through the excavations and restorations conducted by the American mission and then through the public works projects pursued by the Iranian archaeological services (Fig. 4): the terrace and the two royal tombs above it; the palaces; the fortifications in unbaked clay, now sagging; perhaps as well the arrowheads and weapons found in the city's military district. But even if one pays no heed to the silence of the written sources about some supposed stay there by the last Persian king, has the work done on the structures and on the reliefs ever brought to light the slightest positive trace of Darius's presence? Or are these merely the remnants of the fire, which, though certainly uncovered by the archaeologists, reveal more about Alexander's active presence than about his adversary's obsessive absence? In other words, does the historian of Darius explore Persepolis filled with the joy of discovery, or is he too overcome by an irrepressible brooding melancholy?

Ever since the program Cyrus launched in Pasargadae, one of the qualities that the Great Kings themselves liked to praise in themselves was that of being builder-kings. From Darius I to Artaxerxes III, that trait appears without interruption in royal inscriptions that, in other respects, are extremely spare in their narration of events. Devoid of all reference to foreign wars or even domestic troubles—with the sole exception of the inscription and relief that Darius I engraved in Behistun—royal inscriptions generally put into words the legitimacy of the royal bloodline. They exalt the characteristics touching on the very essence of the monarchy and the dynasty, repeatedly mentioning the genealogy of the living king and insisting on the privileged relationship he maintained with

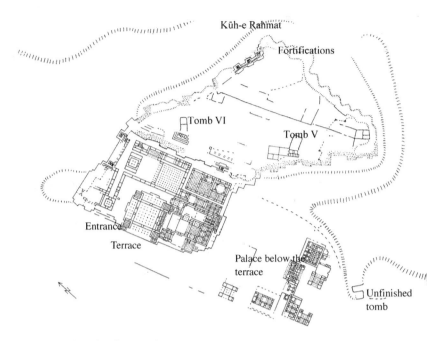

4. *The royal tombs of Persepolis in context.*

Ahura Mazda, the great god of the dynasty, who from Artaxerxes II on is invoked jointly with Mithra and Anahita.

The king's actions take place both on the battlefield and in the palace. In addition to being an elite warrior, a king worthy of the name builds and erects prestigious monuments in his capitals; he completes, and possibly restores, projects begun by his predecessors. Plutarch, wishing to contrast Alexander's generosity to the postulated avarice of the last Achaemenid kings, claims that "many of the Persian kings came but seldom to Persis, and . . . Ochus [Artaxerxes III] never came at all."[1] In reality, after the first building projects were inaugurated in Susa and Persepolis during Darius I's time (522–486 B.C.E.), the construction and restoration of the large royal residences went on uninterrupted. What was true for Xerxes and Artaxerxes I remained true for the fourth-century kings: they built and they restored. Consider, for example, an inscription by Artaxerxes II in Susa: "Artaxerxes, the Great King, King of Kings, king of nations, king on this earth, son of King Darius, Darius son of King Artaxerxes, Artaxerxes son of King Xerxes, Xerxes son of King Darius, Darius son of Hystaspes the Achaemenid, declares: Darius my ancestor made that *apadana* [ceremonial hall], then, at the time of my grandfather Artaxerxes, it burned down; then, thanks to Ahura Mazda, Anahita and Mithra, I had that *apadana* rebuilt. May Ahura Mazda, Anahita and Mithra protect me from all evil" *(A²Sa)*.

In Persepolis, Artaxerxes III's stamp is particularly evident in the south-west corner of the terrace. His contribution is certified by an inscription in his name, of which several exemplars exist. After an invocation to Ahura Mazda and an enumeration of his genealogy from Darius I on, Artaxerxes III had the follow-ing engraved: "This stone staircase was built by me in my time" *(A³Pa)*. Meticu-lous research has shown that the king erected a palace whose front staircase was adorned with reliefs, some of them simply transferred from a former palace of his ancestor Artaxerxes I. On the west façade of Darius's palace, moreover, Artaxerxes installed a staircase decorated with reliefs representing twelve nations come to pay homage to the Great King. They are constructed on the model of the delegations of nations represented on the east and north façades of the *apadana* of Darius and Xerxes, except that those delegations have fewer members.

If the choice of the number twelve was deliberate (and not imposed by spa-tial constraints), it is tempting to hypothesize a relationship between these re-liefs and a detail about the disposition of Darius III's royal procession, as trans-mitted by Curtius. After the chariots dedicated to the gods, then ten other richly adorned chariots, came "the cavalry of twelve nations of different cultures, vari-ously armed."[2] But apart from that possible connection between Persepolitan iconography and a Latin literary source, it must be conceded that, unlike Artax-erxes III, neither Darius III nor his immediate predecessor seems to have left the slightest trace in Persepolis (or in any other of the royal residences). In addition, the inscription of Artaxerxes III just cited is the last specimen from the corpus of royal Achaemenid inscriptions. The current state of our knowledge indicates that Darius III never spoke in Persepolis or anywhere else.

A King without a Sepulchre

The first literary description of the city dates to the same era. It was transmit-ted by Diodorus, who probably got his information from a companion of the Macedonian king. In addition to the citadel and the ramparts, Diodorus men-tions the existence of the royal tombs: "At the eastern side of the terrace at a distance of four plethra [123 meters] is the so-called royal hill in which were the graves of the kings. This was a smooth rock hollowed out into many chambers in which were the sepulchres of the dead kings. These have no other access but receive the sarcophagi of the dead which are lifted by certain mechanical hoists."[3]

Diodorus's description is not free from error or approximation. He seems to have confused somewhat the tombs of Persepolis with those of Naqsh-e Rustam, located four kilometers north of Persepolis (Figs. 5–6). Questions arise in particular about the hoisting devices. According to Ctesias, some of Darius I's relations sought one day to visit the funerary monument that the king was having built on the mountain of Naqsh-e Rustam: "When the priests who were hoisting them up saw [some snakes?],[4] they were frightened and let go of the ropes; the king's relations fell and were killed. Darius was greatly grieved and ordered the decapitation of the forty men responsible."[5]

Although it makes sense that a moving platform hauled up with ropes and pulleys would have existed at Naqsh-e Rustam, because of its sheer cliff, such is not the case for the tombs located above the terrace of Persepolis, which are accessible without any major difficulties.

There, two tombs were dug into the rock on the slope (Fig. 7), one toward the northeast (tomb VI), the other toward the southeast (tomb V). Both are adorned with a carved cruciform façade, on the exact model of the four royal tombs of Naqsh-e Rustam (Fig. 8). One of the tombs of Naqsh-e Rustam is formally identified by the inscriptions engraved on it as the tomb of Darius I. Although the other three do not bear any distinctive marks, it is generally agreed that they once contained the remains of his three immediate successors, namely, Xerxes, Artaxerxes I, and Darius II. For reasons that are poorly understood (there was in fact still room on the cliff of Naqsh-e Rustam), the fourth-century kings apparently chose the mountains of Persepolis for their tombs and had them dug there on the same model. Both sets of tombs display representations of throne-bearers, and on one of them, the south tomb (V), each of the thirty throne-bearers is identified by a short trilingual inscription, as are the thirty porters depicted on Darius I's tomb (*DNe* 1–30): "This is a Persian . . . a Mede . . . etc." That tomb and the inscriptions have sometimes been attributed to Artaxerxes II (*A²Pa*), sometimes to Artaxerxes III (*A³Pb*), with several authors preferring not to choose (*A³P*).

In any case, neither Arses/Artaxerxes IV nor Darius III seems to have been supplied with an individual sepulchre. Although the short duration of Artaxerxes IV's reign and the tragic conditions surrounding his physical elimination by Bagoas may constitute plausible (though not fully convincing) explanations, the case of Darius III raises a much more complex problem. That is because, according to both the Greco-Roman and the Persian traditions, Alexander decided to give a "royal sepulchre" to his defeated enemy in the royal necropolis, which Arrian locates in Persia, precisely where his predecessors were buried.

5–6. *The royal tombs of Naqsh-e Rustam.*

7. *Persepolis, royal tomb VI seen from the terrace.*

8. *Persepolis, royal tomb V, central motif.*

This is certainly the reason it was long accepted that Darius III was actually buried in Persepolis, or at least that, during his lifetime, construction projects for a specific tomb had been undertaken. But where exactly? Jean Chardin writes: "The inhabitants of Persepolis, I mean the curious folk in the region, believe by tradition that Nimrod, whom we call Nemeroth, was buried in the first tomb, and Darius, whom they call Darab, in the second; but they give no proof other than their tradition. . . . It is apparently this baseless tradition of the sepulchre of Darius in that place that gave rise to an even more baseless and ridiculous tradition, namely, that the sumptuous building is the palace of Darius. The Europeans who have settled in Persia call it nothing else. . . . [Our sources] say quite uniformly that 'Alexander had [Darius's] body embalmed and returned it to his mother, with instructions for her to bury it in the tomb of his ancestors'" (16:161–162).

The name Dārā(b) is attributed to two kings in Ferdowsī's *Book of the Kings* (Darius III and his father).[6] It appears that the Persians whom the traveler questioned were referring in this case to Alexander's adversary. They were convinced that their king was buried in one of the tombs located above the terrace. Chardin does not grant any value to that "baseless tradition." He professes strange theories on the history of the site and the nature of the monuments, which he thinks are temples and not royal palaces, and which he dates to the first mythic Iranian kings and not to the Achaemenids (17:18–34). Rather surprisingly, he also concludes, based on his idiosyncratic reading of his sources, that Darius was buried in Ecbatana.

Over the course of the three visits he made to Persepolis, Chardin learned, or saw with his own eyes, that there were remnants of buildings in the surrounding area (see 16:147). But he seems not to have ventured beyond the terrace and the area close to it. If you leave the terrace, however, and walk due south about 500 meters, you come to a low spur. When you go around it, you discover another tomb (called tomb VII), oriented due south, that is, with its back to the terrace (Fig. 9). Because the surface area available for the ornamental sculptures was not adequate, the architects added three layers of closely fitted carved blocks. That extension upward made it possible to reproduce in identical form the motifs arranged on the façades of the other tombs (Fig. 10). In the center, perfectly recognizable, stands the king on a three-step podium, equipped with his bow and facing the fire altar. The representation, supposedly of Ahura Mazda, was carved in the upper register, on the rubble stone layers. The figures of the guards, merely roughed out on the sides (Fig. 11), show that the work was

9. *Persepolis, the unfinished tomb, overall view from the south.*

10. *Persepolis, the unfinished tomb, central motif.*

11. *Persepolis, the unfinished tomb, silhouette of the guard.*

12. *Persepolis, the unfinished tomb, quarry at the entrance.*

interrupted or abandoned: hence the name "unfinished tomb" currently given
to the monument. The appearance of what may have been the esplanade that
provided access to the tomb seems to confirm it: it is still "planted" with rocks
of all shapes, which, it seems, ought to be interpreted as the residual evidence
of a leveling project that was never completed, and/or of a quarry from which
the rubble stone blocks were extracted and carved (Fig. 12). Furthermore, there
is no door and no internal cavities, in short, no tomb in the strict sense, just a
roughed-out façade without means of access or egress.

   Although Chardin said not a word about it, other travelers have not failed
to describe it. A rather imprecise description is found in de Bruyn, within a
context that is also not altogether clear. Reporting on his stay in Persepolis in
November 1704, he describes the two tombs above the terrace. He too judges
that there is no reason to think that Darius III was buried there: "One cannot
state that King Darius's body lies in one of these tombs, since the authors do
not speak of him; and even Curtius, who wrote of the life and deeds of Alexander the Great at some length, says merely that the prince sent the body of
Darius, assassinated by Bessus, to Queen Sisygambis, the monarch's mother,
to have him buried in the tomb of his ancestors" (*Voyages de Corneille Le Brun*,
p. 277).

Then, in a thematic chapter, de Bruyn is led to speak of another tomb, "carved in the rock, close to Persepolis," which bears the image of a "king in front of an altar on which the sacred fire is burning." The king "holds in his hand a half-twisted snake," unless, the author adds (pp. 288–290), it is a bow. Although he does not include a drawing and does not propose any identification, he seems to be referring to what is now called the unfinished tomb.

It was Carsten Niebuhr, who stopped in Persepolis in March 1765, who provided the first truly faithful account. Having given a description of the two tombs above the terrace, he then describes the third and offers, in preliminary form, a few avenues for interpretation, without ever mentioning the hypothesis of a tomb of Darius III: "A quarter league farther south on the same mountain, the rock and the crag have similarly been carved perpendicularly, because here too it had a downward slope. The stones that were removed here were first placed on the top of the façade, to make it higher, and these figures were also first carved in the rock itself; but that work did not progress very far. By way of figures, only two are complete: the one that moves through the air, a round body, which most likely represents the sun, and the one that is in long clothing with a bow in his hand, standing in front of the altar. A few figures to the side are half-finished. So that perhaps it remained a work in progress, either because the contractor died, or because another religion was introduced into Persepolis, or for some other reason. In the interim, several large stones have been detached from the rock but not carried off" (*Voyage*, p. 125).

James Morier also describes the tomb in his *A Journey through Persia* (1818). He wonders especially about the stone blocks that remain in place in front of the façade. He is persuaded that they were put there on purpose, so as to create a sort of labyrinth, formerly covered by large stones and earth. He concludes that only a secret subterranean entrance allowed the initiated to penetrate the tomb. A few years later Sir John Ousley, following Niebuhr, returned to more realistic analyses and also asserted that the monument was never finished. In addition, he proposed that the tomb was older than the other royal tombs (*Travels*, pp. 271–272 and n. 56).

Flandin and Coste, in the famous account of their journey to Persia published in 1841, also devote a few lines and two drawings to the monument, including a general drawing of what they call "Tomb 12" (Fig. 13). They observe that it "displays the characteristic of the [other] two tombs" but maintain a cautious attitude. They remark that "this monument has all the appearances of an interrupted labor" (3:132), adding: "It is impossible to anticipate what its pur-

13. Persepolis, the unfinished tomb (E. Flandin and P. Coste).

pose was supposed to be." In 1892 Lord Curzon, recalling the observations of Niebuhr and Flandin and Coste, also remained very cautious. Although tempted to attribute the tomb to Arses or to Darius III, he was astonished that such a site could have been chosen, because, had the tomb been completed, it would hardly have risen above ground level: "This seems to indicate a relaxation in the earlier ideas of impracticability of access" (*Persia and the Persian Question*, pp. 183–185). Finally, during the same period, Georges Perrot and Charles Chipiez, largely basing themselves on the drawings of Flandin and Coste, were also reserved and imprecise: "Three other tombs have been carved in the massif on which the terrace of Persepolis rests. One of them is only roughed out; we need consider only the other two" (*Histoire de l'art*, 5:633).

The attribution of the tomb to Darius III did not become commonplace until the twentieth century. In 1923–1924, Ernst Herzfeld spent six weeks in Persepolis, taking photographs, surveying the monuments, and drawing maps. His report, published in French and Persian and accompanied by thirty plates and a map, was submitted to the government in Tehran, to urge it to preserve the site and to authorize undertaking excavations there. Plate 13 (a photo of the tomb) bears the legend: "Unfinished tomb of Darius III." The monument is presented as follows: "Finally, not far from the far limit of the suburb, marked at that place by the remains of the enclosing wall, the third royal tomb is carved in the south face of the projecting tip of the mountain that forms the boundary of the district south of the terrace. The work has remained incomplete: it is undoubtedly the tomb of the last Darius, which was not yet finished at the time of Alexander's conquest. Only the upper part, the image of the king worshiping in front of the fire altar, was executed. All the rest is merely a quarry. The sculpture, modeled on other tombs, nonetheless shows evidence of the decadence of art" ("Rapport," pp. 32–33).

Herzfeld's self-assurance may seem surprising, given that he did not add any really new elements to a well-known subject: the reference to "the decadence of art," based on a very subjective aesthetic evaluation, is in fact hardly convincing.

That identification was adopted by A. T. Olmstead in his posthumously published book *History of the Persian Empire* (1948). He also thought, wrongly, that Darius III had overseen construction projects on the terrace (pp. 493–494, 517). His information came from the excavators themselves, with whom he was in close and constant contact and whom he was able to encounter frequently: they were in fact part of a mission of the Oriental Institute of Chicago. It is therefore not surprising that Eric Schmidt, Herzfeld's successor as head of the American mission, expressed his conviction in an authoritative formulation that leaves no room for doubt: "We do not hesitate to assign the unfinished tomb to Darius III" (*Persepolis*, 3:107). He adds that the king's body was clearly not buried there but was placed in one of the two tombs that already existed above the terrace, each of which had sufficient room (probably tomb VI, in his view). According to that interpretation, the project for the unfinished tomb was undertaken on the orders of Darius himself. Henceforth the identification was considered reliable in many scholarly publications and in guidebooks.

Yet many uncertainties remain, and when that identification is accepted today, it is accompanied by a question mark at least. The difficulties in dating the tomb were set out by two German archaeologists, W. Kleiss and P. Calmeyer, following a field investigation conducted in 1973 and published in 1975. While proposing a theoretical reconstitution of what the original plan might have been (Fig. 14), they came out against the date commonly accepted at the time, arguing on the basis of a meticulous archaeological, stylistic, and iconographic analysis. According to them, the tomb clearly does not date from the 330s B.C.E., because the construction technique is very close to that of tomb V. They concluded that it was the first tomb to have been built after the site of Naqsh-e Rustam was abandoned. But the labor ended in a technical fiasco, which led to the choice of the cliff above the terrace. Their conclusions were not unanimously accepted: a few years later (1983) another archaeologist, M. Roaf, without conceding it was Darius III's tomb, maintained that the engraving on it is in

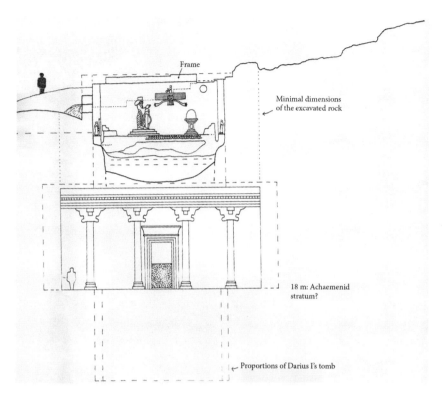

Frame

Minimal dimensions
of the excavated rock

18 m: Achaemenid
stratum?

Proportions of Darius I's tomb

14. Persepolis, the unfinished tomb: theoretical reconstitution of the original plan.

the late style and that "a date in the second half of the Achaemenid period is probable" (*Sculptures and Sculptors*, pp. 146–147).

In addition to the archaeological uncertainty, there is the ambiguity of the Greco-Roman literary tradition. The authors declare that Alexander made the decision to have Darius buried in the tombs of his ancestors, in Persepolis, in accordance with Persian traditions.[7] It is clearly the existence of that information that justified the excavators' certainty that a tomb of Darius existed. But did the funeral ceremonies mentioned ever actually take place? That is disputable. The ancient authors, who were completely focused on following Alexander's campaigns day by day, say nothing about any practical application of the royal declaration. As is too often the case, one is therefore reduced to arguments of plausibility.

This is not the first time that Alexander, in his desire to make an impression, took care to treat the mortal remains of his adversaries with honor. In burying Darius's wife Stateira, "he observed every honour in performing the funeral rites in the native manner of the Persians."[8] After Issus, he permitted "the mother of Darius to bury such as she chose, according to the manner of her country. Sisygambis exercised the privilege in the sepulture for a few of her relatives."[9] The repeated reference to Persian customs illustrates Alexander's desire to show how much he respects his enemies. In that sense the burial of Darius in accordance with Persian royal customs would have been in keeping with a consistent policy. Furthermore, the aim was to demonstrate that, in conformance with a wish that Darius expressed before his death, Alexander intended to succeed the Great King in observance of a clear dynastic continuity. Among the Achaemenids, but also among the Macedonians, overseeing funeral ceremonies was the first opportunity the heir had to prove his legitimacy. But Alexander, preoccupied with pursuing Bessus in Bactriana, could not in fact have led the funeral procession.

Parallels can also be cited. The most evocative is the treatment of the remains of Mithridates, who was betrayed and handed over by his son: "Pompey provided for the expenses of the funeral of Mithridates and directed his servants to give his remains a royal burial and to place them in the tombs of the kings at Sinope, because he admired his great achievements and considered him the first of the kings of his time."[10]

Terms and expressions recur from one example to the next, but it should be noted that parallels are not in themselves conclusive. Alexander's position after Darius's death was not comparable to that of Pompey after the death of Mithridates. At a time when Alexander had to face resistance from Bessus and a number of Iranian populations, Darius's burial in Persepolis, perhaps desirable for the political message it would convey, might also been fraught with danger. Seventy years earlier, when Cyrus the Younger had pronounced a death sentence on Orontas—a member of his close circle suspected of treason—he had taken care to make all traces of the body disappear: "No one, of his own knowledge, could declare the manner of his death; though some conjectured one thing and some another. No tomb to mark his resting-place, either then or since, was ever seen."[11] Darius III was not a rebel, however, and there is therefore no reason to suppose that his remains were scattered. But because Alexander may not have completely won over the Persian population by that time, he may have deemed it dangerous to create a *lieu de mémoire* at the historic heart of Persian-Achaemenid power.

One detail provided only by Plutarch may assume new importance.[12] He said that Alexander sent Darius's remains to his mother, Sisygambis, who we know was being held in Susa at the time. According to that hypothesis, Darius's funeral would have been more private than public in nature. The passage from Plutarch also belongs to a codified system of Greek images concerning the relation between (authoritarian, even abusive) mothers and (weak) sons among the Achaemenids: witness Parysatis's fierce desire to collect the remains of her son Cyrus and to give him a sepulchre (despite a few attempts, it has also never been discovered).[13]

Other silences, finally, leave a nagging doubt. We know that Alexander, upon his return from India, went to Pasargadae and Persepolis.[14] Stories about his time there are full of violated tombs and punishments inflicted on the guilty (real or presumed). In Pasargadae, the king subjected the magi charged with guarding Cyrus's tomb to torture, and Orxines was accused of having plundered the temples and royal tombs. Arriving in Persepolis, Alexander expressed regrets about the decision he had made in 330 to destroy part of the royal palaces and took care to designate a Macedonian satrap, Peukestas, who was himself anxious to assimilate the language and culture of the Persian population. But a tomb where Darius III could have been buried or before which Alexander might have meditated is never mentioned.

In short, an examination of the literary sources does not provide a solution to the problems raised by an analysis of the archaeological evidence. Only one thing is clear: whatever the date of the unfinished tomb, Darius was not buried in it, and no one can prove that he was buried in one of the other two tombs, which would have had to be reopened for the occasion. Even if one assumes that the decision attributed to Alexander was acted upon, any hypothesis is permissible, including the postulate that Darius was buried "in Persia" but not in Persepolis itself: other locations could be proposed, but again without documentary proof.

In any event, this example provides a further illustration of the extraordinary contrast between Alexander and Darius with respect to the transmission of royal memory. Alexander is certainly buried in a tomb that has never been found; Darius, by contrast, certainly never lay in the tomb whose construction was long attributed to him. Everyone is looking for Alexander's tomb, and many have claimed to have discovered it; no one thinks to look for Darius III's tomb, and "the unfinished tomb" is only a place without memory (*lieu sans mémoire*). That is undoubtedly why, even today, meditations on the ruins of an anonymous monument—unfinished and abandoned, sometimes even ignored by guides and tourists—are so moving.

A Faceless King

If we limit our search to the Persian-Achaemenid documentation, we also come up with no notion of the king's physical appearance. Royal coins do exist from the reign of Darius I, gold darics and silver siglos (Fig. 15, a and b). Invariably the obverse depicts a royal figure in the attitude of a warrior in

15a. Daric, type III.b.

15b. Siglo, type II.C.

action (standing, kneeling, running). Wearing a crown and dressed in his royal robe, he faces an invisible enemy with his bow and spear. In 1760 T. Hyde was one of the first to provide a (rather fanciful) drawing of a Persian royal coin (Fig. 16).

At the start of the twentieth century, Ernest Babelon—a specialist in numismatics whose work is still worthy of respect—defended the thesis that the faces on the royal figures were individualized portraits of the different Persian monarchs. He took issue with the opposing thesis that it is impossible to distinguish one figure from another. To support his view, Babelon argued that a portrait of Cyrus really does exist in Pasargadae (it is now conventionally called

16. A royal coin.

the "winged genie," Fig. 17), and that various kings are recognizable on the bas-reliefs of Persepolis: "You will easily recognize the particularities proper to them, characteristics imputable neither to fashion nor to the genius of different artists. The same must be said for the images of kings engraved on cylindrical and conical seals made of semiprecious stones. Despite the small faces and the difficulties inherent in this type of engraving, the portraits of different princes can be distinguished. A specific, significant result would be achieved in comparing these monuments with one another and in comparing them all to the coin types" (*Traité*, vol. 2, part 1, col. 258).

According to Babelon, the same is true of the coins: "On cannot expect a rigorous precision, an adequate resemblance from these iconic figures. . . . But

17. *Winged genie of Pasargadae (Dieulafoy drawing).*

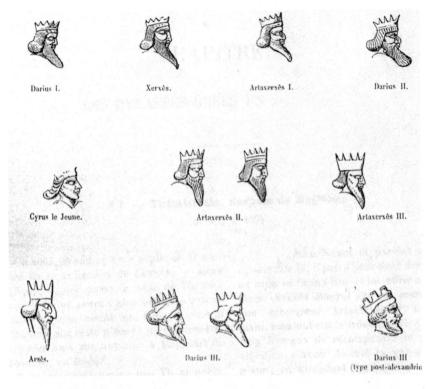

18. *"Royal portraits" (Babelon).*
    Top row: Darius I, Xerxes, Artaxerxes I, Darius II
    Middle row: Cyrus the Younger, Artaxerxes II, Artaxerxes III
    Bottom row: Arses, Darius III, Darius III (post-Alexandrian type)

we do claim that the engravers of the coin dies did not limit themselves to a vague and abstract image of the king of kings: such a conception, in fact, would be at odds with natural logic, which stipulates that one proceed from the concrete to the abstract and not vice versa. . . . At the beginning of each reign, a royal style was adopted, with traits as close as possible to those of the new prince; and that type, once created, was immutable, or varied only slightly throughout the duration of the reign" (col. 259).

Babelon, beginning with a treasure discovered on the Mount Athos peninsula, endeavored to distinguish the coins struck under Darius from those minted during the reign of Xerxes, and more broadly, to construct a chart of the individualized royal portraits (Fig. 18). It is worthwhile to read some of the reasons he advances for identifying one king or another. Of Darius II, he writes, for ex-

19. Late-type daric, obverse.

ample: "This king is also recognizable by his large Semitic nose, and on this matter we may note that his mother was a Babylonian." Exactly the opposite was true for Cyrus the Younger, who had "a straight nose, and his face was of a gentle and intelligent character befitting a Greek more than an Asian" (vol. 2, part 2, cols. 50–51). These are very suspect physiognomic criteria, associated with an ancient historiographical current, which was fond of presenting Cyrus the Younger as a "quasi Greek" and which made the "Babylonization" of the dynasty one of the causes of "Achaemenid decadence."

As for the "portrait" of Darius III, which was apparently more difficult to isolate, Babelon leaves it to C. Lenormant, who presents a very specific daric type hypothetically dating to the reign of Darius III. Here is Babelon's comment on the royal figure represented on the obverse (Fig. 19): "The bearded head of the archer depicted there is a man of mature age, and it is known that the last

Darius did not wear the crown until he was forty-five. Although, on the Pompeii mosaic, Darius's beard is concealed under the fanons of the tiara, there are enough points of resemblance between that full portrait of the king of Persia and that of the prince who can be clearly made out on the medal of M. le duc de Luynes. The face has a virile appearance with an aquiline nose and deep-set eyes, and the half-length beard extends perceptibly forward" (vol. 2, part 2, col. 68).

The weakness of the arguments that Lenormant advances and that Babelon adopts is glaringly obvious, and the draftsman's skill cannot mask the pointlessness of the exercise. The "winged genie" of Pasargadae is not a portrait of Cyrus the Great, and neither the faces, nor the attitudes, nor the crowns of the royal figures of Persepolis make it possible to distinguish them one from another. It is not particular kings who are represented in Persepolis and elsewhere but rather kingship in all its glory, accompanied by impersonal and intangible attributes. And though the debate about the first portrait's date of appearance has never ended, it has proceeded on the basis of coins other than royal coins.

Recent studies have shown that coin types evolved between Darius I and Darius III, but they have also proven that these iconographic adaptations never coincide with a change of reign. It is also easy to postulate that royal coins were struck in great numbers under Darius III's reign, as a means of financing the needs of the armies and fleets. There is not even any doubt that the coins struck under his reign belong to type IVb, in the typology usually accepted today (Fig. 20). But that type was struck from about 380 B.C.E. on and continued to be minted in Babylon after Alexander's death: it bears the royal archer holding a spear in his right hand (Fig. 21). All in all, it is impossible to distinguish the coins struck under Darius III from all the darics and siglos belonging to type IVb. Even if it were possible to establish that some royal coin really was struck during one of Darius's regnal years, it would not follow that the royal figure on it is that of the reigning king. In short, we must resign ourselves: there is no Persian portrait of Darius III.[15]

Regnal Years and History of the Reign

Let us now leave the center of the empire for the provinces and begin with what may seem a surprising question: If we set aside the accounts transmitted by the Greek and Latin authors, how are we to know that a Great King has begun his reign? In the absence of chronicles and narrative-type archives, we do so through the mention of the regnal year in private documents or at the top of public

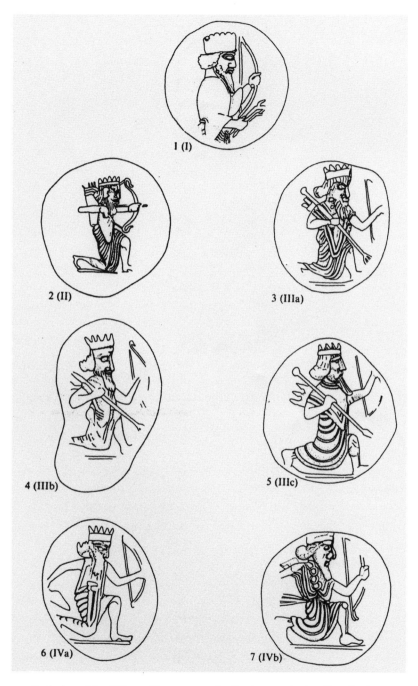

20. *Evolution of the different king types on the Persian royal coins (drawing by Stronach).*

21. Double daric struck in Babylon in Alexander's time.

documents—whether Babylonian tablets, demotic or Aramaic papyri, or inscriptions from Asia Minor in Greek or various local languages. The tablets or other private documents dating to a Darius or an Artaxerxes raise a well-known problem: in the absence of any other marker, it is often difficult to ascertain which Darius or Artaxerxes is at issue. As a general rule, the king's name appears alone, without any indication of his father's name. In principle, mention of the regnal year may make it possible to decide, but that is not a sufficient criterion in all cases.

Take the now-famous example of the trilingual inscription from Xanthos, in its Aramaic version: "In the month of Sivan of year 1 of King Artaxerxes." Which Artaxerxes is in question here? Only the context makes it possible to say that it cannot be Artaxerxes I or Artaxerxes II. The editors have concluded it was Artaxerxes III, in the year 359/358. But this hypothesis has also been disputed, because the date raises nearly insoluble chronological and historical problems within the context of the history of Asia Minor in the fourth century.

That is why it is now agreed that this is the first official mention of the king who, until that time, had been known under the name "Arses," in Greek accounts of the bloody struggles during the last days of the Achaemenid dynasty. In all probability this king, like his predecessors, took the reign name "Artaxerxes (IV)." In that hypothesis, the Xanthos inscription gives the reign of Arses/Artaxerxes an unexpected administrative reality: the life of the empire continued, even during a period that, to believe the classical sources, was entirely taken up with sordid and bloody palace conspiracies, dominated by the figure of the sinister Bagoas. The king is also mentioned or evoked in several Babylonian texts: a fragment fixes the date of Artaxerxes III's death and the accession of his successor; a chronological compilation from the Hellenistic period clearly evokes him under the name "son of Artaxerxes"; and a very fragmentary narrative text mentions his name and that of Alexander in the context of restoration work done on the Esangil of Babylon.

Darius III was not so fortunate. His name rarely appears except as part of a date on documents of little import. In Egypt, for example, a papyrus is dated "year two, third month of the *akhet*-season of Pharaoh Darius": prosopographical cross-references have determined that this must be Darius III. Other documents mention more noteworthy events but do not really provide any earth-shaking information. Consider the Bucheum stela at Memphis dating to year 4 of Alexander the Great, which recalls that the bull buried at that time was born (?) under the reign of the "king of [Upper] and Lower Egypt, Darius who lives eternally," clearly Darius III. This is one illustration among many others of Egyptian continuities beyond the political ruptures. It is also Darius and his predecessor who serve as chronological referents on an Aramaic papyrus of Wadi Daliyeh that records a slave sale: "On the 20th day of the month of Adar, year 2, year of the accession of Darius the king, in the city of Samaria, which is in the province of Samaria." The date was therefore March 19, 335, which is both year 2 of Arses/Artaxerxes (whose name is not given and who was dead by that time) and the year of Darius's accession.

The new lot of papyri and parchments recently put into circulation, written in Aramaic and originating in ancient Bactriana, provides something truly unprecedented. They date to reigns extending from Artaxerxes III to Alexander and include several documents dating to the rule of Darius III. But their novelty lies more in the disputed status of Bactriana in the Achaemenid Empire than in any new knowledge they might provide about the reign of Darius strictly speaking.[16]

Of the Babylonian administrative tablets, very few date with certainty to his reign, and these are of no historical interest, even indirectly. One of them, not particularly original, is a list of rations distributed to the staff of the temples of Babylon and Borsippa, in year X of Darius, most likely Darius III. Another, from Ur, probably dates to March 331. And a third, from Larsa, dating to the same time, shows that business went on as usual, without giving the slightest glimpse of the effects caused by the grave events unfolding at the time in Babylonia (the mustering and training of the royal army).

The King's Names

Another set of Babylonian documents has supplied new information. These are customarily called the "astronomical diaries." Although long known, they were published only recently. They include a small lot of twenty-seven tablets dating to the Achaemenid period, between 464 and 331. These tablets are not chronicles: they contain astronomical observations recorded day after day by Babylonian specialists, whom the Greeks called "Chaldeans." The name of the tablets in Babylonian means "regular observations." Other types of information are sometimes added, but not regularly or systematically: meteorological observations (a little rain, a clear or cloudy sky, torrential rains, and so on); the water level of the Euphrates in Babylon; the market price of five staple commodities (barley, mustard, dates, sesame, wool); and sometimes the mention of a noteworthy event related to the day in question.

Before considering the narrative information to be found in them, I shall simply examine the supplementary data they may provide about the identity of the Great King himself. A tablet dating to 333 indicates: "[Year] 3 of Artašatu [who is called King] Dariyamuš." Darius III, then, before becoming king, bore the lovely Persian name Artašata ("full of the felicity of truth"); and, in accordance with a custom attested many times by the classical sources, he took a reign name, "Darius," at the time of his accession. The choice of reign name sheds light on the new king's notion of his power and of the place he wanted to attribute to his reign over the *longue durée* of the Achaemenid dynasty. Note that, like his two namesake predecessors, Darius III came to power following long and sanguinary struggles that had nearly bled the dynasty dry. Artašata may have decided on that reign name to express the idea that his ascension to the throne would mark the end of anarchy and the beginning of a dynastic renaissance. When considered in terms of his reign name, Darius's political program was not modest.

Royal names originally known in their Persian or Babylonian form were converted into Greek in the Western sources; but once the resulting distortions are taken into account, the information in the two traditions generally corresponds quite closely. Such is not the case for Darius III, however. The adoption of a reign name is confirmed by the classical sources, particularly by Justin (10.3): "On the death of Ochus, he was chosen king by the people out of regard for his former merits, and, so that nothing might be wanting to his royal dignity, honoured with the name of Darius." Like Diodorus, Justin devotes a passage to a stunning feat performed by the future Darius during one of the Cadusian wars waged by Artaxerxes III. But at that point Justin gives him the name "Codomannus," which is completely different from "Artašata" as indicated in the Babylonian diaries.[17] This may be a third name, or rather a nickname, whose etymology specialists continue to ponder.

In any event, the information provided by the diaries is not negligible: it reintroduces Darius, albeit very modestly, into the continuity of the Achaemenid dynasty and monarchical traditions. In some sense it makes him more ordinary, because it does not reduce him to the role of Alexander's unlucky adversary. There Darius has an Achaemenid reality, which the weight of the Greco-Roman tradition tends to obliterate. I should have liked to pursue and refine the Persian portrait of the Great King, but unfortunately the context of the documentation does not really allow it.

An Egyptian Campaign by Darius III?

Because the information that the Greco-Roman sources provide about Darius's activities and policies at the start of his reign and for the years 334–330 is in equal parts elusive and doubtful, any reconstitution of the Persian operations raises tricky problems. From time to time the astronomical diaries provide more or less indirect indications about the wars waged by a Great King (Artaxerxes II), some of which are not mentioned in the classical sources. It is therefore possible that Darius too led his troops on a campaign before Alexander's arrival, even though the Greek and Latin authors do not tell us about it. The problem is that the documents that might have attested to such a campaign are not only rare but also vague, when they are not downright obscure and unclear in their meaning.

A particularly eloquent illustration of that situation appears in an Egyptian document, a hieroglyphic text traditionally called the Satrap Stela (Fig. 22). Since its discovery in 1870, it has stirred a great deal of debate, which continues to this day. Unlike the other documents used in this chapter, the stela does not

22. *Satrap Stela.*

date to the reign of Darius or even to the Achaemenid period: it dates to year 7 of the young king Alexander IV, son and successor of Alexander the Great, that is, to November 311 B.C.E. It is one of the many documents from Lagid Egypt that mention the prior period of Achaemenid rule. They are almost uniformly unfavorable toward that rule and instead praise the Ptolemies, including, in this case, Ptolemy I, at a time when he was merely the governor of Egypt (hence the name given to the stela), and when "His Majesty" (Alexander IV) was in Persia. Originally placed in the Buto sanctuary located in the Western Delta, the document praises the "pharaonic" qualities of Ptolemy, both an elite warrior against the "Asian" enemies and a benefactor of the sanctuary: "He is a youthful man, strong in his two arms, effective in plans, with mighty armies, stout hearted, firm footed, who attacks the powerful without turning his back, who strikes the face of his opponents when they fight, with precise hand, who grasps to himself the bow without shooting astray, who fights with his sword in the midst of battle, with none who can stand in his vicinity, a champion whose arms are not repulsed, with no reversal of what issues from his mouth, who has no equal in the Two Lands or the foreign countries."[18]

The main reason the last years of Achaemenid history are at issue in this document is that, of the heroic deeds that the clergy attributes to Ptolemy, one is acknowledged to have been identical to an action performed by three of his successors. A certain stock phrase raises many questions: "As he brought back the sacred images of the Gods which were found within Asia, together with all the ritual implements and all the sacred scrolls of the Temples of Upper and Lower Egypt, so he restored them in their proper places." Then, after hearing of recent episodes in the sanctuary's history, transmitted by "those who were beside him together with the grandees of Lower Egypt," he rendered a particularly notable service to the Buto sanctuary and to its deities: he guaranteed a donation of lands at the request of the priests of Pe and Dep, the two districts of Buto. They are said to have presented the story to him as follows: "The northern marshland, whose name is The Land of Edjo, it formerly belonged to the gods of Pe and Dep, before the enemy Xerxes revoked it. He did not make offerings from it to the gods of Pe and Dep." Hence Ptolemy's decision: "Then this great Prince said: 'Let a written command be made at the record office of the royal accounting scribe saying: "(By order of) Ptolemy the Satrap. The Land of Edjo, I shall give it to Horus, the protector of his father, Lord of Pe, and to Edjo, Lady of Pe and Dep, from today forever, together with all its towns, all its villages, all its inhabitants, all its acreage, all its water, all its cattle, all its flocks, all its herds and everything that derives from it and which has been part of it previously, together with whatever is added to it, together with the donation made by the King of Upper and Lower Egypt, Lord of the Two Lands, Khababash, living forever."""

Ptolemy's decree appears to be the renewal of an ancient donation, eliminated by Xerxes. Ptolemy made that decision only after his informers had reminded him that the "marshland" had already been given to the gods of Pe-Dep by the "King, Lord of the Two-Lands, Khababash." That king had therefore decided "to make a circuit of the marshland that is its entire territory, going into the interior of the swamps and examining each Nile branch which goes to the sea, in order to repel the ships of Asia from Egypt."

The royal name "Xerxes" provides a means for determining the era in which Khababash ruled and in which he confronted the Persian invasion forces in the Delta. It was long believed that the text was alluding to one of the Egyptian revolts that Herodotus situates at the end of Darius I's reign, and which, he says, was quashed by his successor Xerxes.[19] According to that hypothesis, Khababash was the leader of the rebellion: he made a donation in Buto, and Xerxes, in retaliation, declared it void. The interpretation was especially appealing in that it fit well with the disastrous image that the classical texts give of an "intolerant" Xerxes and that Achaemenid historiography so long used for its own purposes.

But it turns out that such an interpretation is untenable. On one hand, it would be strange if, in 311, Khababash's donation, confiscated by Xerxes in about 484, had not been renewed in the meantime by one of the independent pharaohs who ruled Egypt between 404/400 and the reconquest by Artaxerxes III in 343. More important by far is a set of seven or eight Egyptian documents now at our disposal, which attest without any possible doubt that the reign of Pharaoh Khababash, recognized in both Upper and Lower Egypt, occurred slightly before Alexander's arrival. It must therefore be supposed that a few years after 343 (no document makes it possible to establish a chronology absolutely), Khababash again drove out the Persians and reigned for two years, before yielding to a last Persian counterattack—given that Egypt was ruled by a Persian satrap from 334 until Alexander's arrival.

The reference to an inspection Khababash may have conducted in the Delta at the same time as the donation in Buto seems to belong to that very context. The constant anxiety on the part of fourth-century pharaohs, then on the part of Ptolemy himself, in the face of attacks from Syria by land and sea, is apparent here. To prevent the advance of the enemy fleet and armies, they fortified all the mouths of the Nile, true "gateways" to the Delta and to the capital at Memphis, "being a region crowded with towns, and, besides, intersected by walls and ditches."[20]

There is still the matter of the designation "Xerxes" given to the enemy. Because this cannot be the son of Darius I, another hypothesis is required. Perhaps, as in certain Greek texts, "Xerxes" had become a kind of common noun in Egypt, used to designate the Persian Great King in general. But then, which of the last Persian kings was at issue, Artaxerxes III, Arses/Artaxerxes IV, or Darius III?

Several historians of Alexander's conquests have adopted a date during Darius III's reign for this episode, because they think it provides an explanation for what may appear to be a persistent riddle regarding his war strategy: Why did Darius III's fleet, so superior in number and in skill to the Macedonian fleet, not seek to prevent Alexander from passing through the Straits in the spring of 334? If the Great King's fleet had been immobilized in the Delta or in a poor state of preparation after an expedition into Egypt, that might explain why the Persian military staff was incapable of committing all its forces at the time. Other historians even see the episode as an illustration of what they present as the completely disorganized state of Darius's empire in 334, or as a sign of "Achaemenid decadence." Some do not hesitate to declare that, in the early days of Darius's reign, revolt was brewing not only in Egypt but also in Babylonia, and that it kept the Great King from calmly preparing the defense of the western front. In short, just as the Egyptian revolt of 404 probably favored Cyrus the Younger's offensive from Asia Minor against his brother, King Artaxerxes II, so too Khababash's revolt in the Delta may have allowed Alexander to move into Asia Minor without interference and then to challenge the armies of Darius's satraps there.

It is not surprising that each of the possible dates has been defended and that uncertainty continues to reign, and it would be pointless to enumerate the plausible arguments in favor of one or the other. Some have even postulated that, given the interest the Greek authors always showed in the revolts in the Nile Valley, they would not have remained silent about such an expedition. But given the lack of certainty with respect to the documentation, we must banish all arguments based on the silence of the sources. Let me state quite clearly: there are no truly solid grounds for choosing one of the three dates over another. What we have here is a typical node of hypotheses that apparently support one another. It is well known, however, that even a clever combination of two hypotheses that have been declared plausible does not miraculously create a valid argument. Other explanations have been advanced to explain how Alexander could have landed without interference, but none has won unanimous support and none is wholly convincing. As for Babylonia, the interpretation of the text generally used (the Uruk King List) to promote the idea that Darius must have been fighting against a usurper at the same time is too doubtful to substantiate the hypothesis. How, then, could the

Satrap Stela and the Uruk King List be used in combination? Regrettably, we must resign ourselves: in the current state of our knowledge and reflections, neither the hieroglyphic stela nor the cuneiform tablet can provide reliable and verifiable information about Darius III's situation on the brink of war.

The War through Coins: Echoes and Uncertainties

The state of the documentation on the operations conducted against Alexander is not quite so bad, but it remains discouraging nonetheless.

It is well known that war requires enormous cash resources and that coins must be minted continuously and at a rapid pace. The problem, already mentioned regarding siglos and darics and the so-called royal portraits, is that it is practically impossible to date a minted coin with precision and to establish a direct link between an event and the issuance of coinage. Even when a special coin type or a particularly original legend is in evidence, the coin cannot speak for itself. Any potential narrative link must be made through a comparison hypothetically established with an episode known through the Greco-Roman literary texts.

Consider the reverse of the isolated daric whose obverse appears in Figure 19, and which bears a royal image that unquestionably links its issuance to type IVb in the fourth century. Without a doubt, the reverse poses a riddle. In contrast to an absolutely universal practice, it does not simply depict an incuse square but rather the image of a warship, whose prow bears a Carian letter (Fig. 23). The use of the theme of the royal hero on Carian coinage was not rare. There is even a Carian gold coin with the name of the satrap Pixodarus on it, but it is a special case, only a single exemplar being known. Since the first publication of the coin in 1856, the assumption was that it was made in Halicarnassus in 334, at a time when the city was besieged by Macedonian troops. It is attributed more precisely to Memnon—whom Darius had just named commander in chief of the coast and of the royal fleet—because of the role he played at the time in the mustering of forces within the city and in the preparations for the siege. It could also be a coin struck after Memnon and Orontobates had decided to leave the city and to retreat to fortified sites.[21] In any event, this would have been the first time that a strategos, even one assigned a general command, received the king's authorization to strike a coin of a royal type and to add on the reverse an image that would establish a connection with his post as an admiral. Or could Memnon have decided on his own to take such an initiative? It is clear that, barring the discovery of other exemplars, too much uncertainty remains for it to

23. Prow of a war vessel on the reverse of a late-type daric.

be possible to elaborate further on what is merely a hypothesis or a suggestion, and which must remain so.

The same caution is required with respect to coins, struck in Sinope, that bear names in Aramaic identified with Persians: Hydarnes, Orontobates, and Mithropastes. These could have been coins minted by generals who, after Issus, participated in the Persian counterattack in Asia Minor, known particularly through Diodorus and Curtius.[22] That is an appealing hypothesis, inasmuch as the Persian leaders certainly needed to strike coins to raise troops and to conduct their operations; but it also leaves crucial questions hanging. Of the three names identified (though problems of reading remain), only one "Hydarnes" is cited by Curtius. This may have been a son of Mazaeus/Mazday, a well-known high dignitary active in Darius's immediate entourage, but it is not possible to say with certainty that it was not someone else with the same name. As for "Orontobates," this cannot be the Persian satrap of Caria by that name, known through the texts and coins issued in Caria. A Persian by the name of Mithropastes is also known: the son of Arsites, satrap of Hellespontine Phrygia, he preferred to commit suicide rather than face dishonor after his defeat at the Granicus. We have learned by chance that when Nearchus's fleet was heading back up the Persian Gulf (325), a Mithropastes found refuge on an island of the gulf.[23] But we know nothing about the when or the why. Clearly, the support that the literary sources and the numismatic documents seem to lend to each other is too shaky to allow us to ascribe any faith to such a link, which, in any event, does not offer anything earthshakingly new.

The Persian noble Mazday, attested through many passages in the Greco-Roman literary sources, is relatively well known. Under Artaxerxes III, he was named satrap of Cilicia and was later "in command of the regions beyond the river and of Cilicia," as indicated by the Aramaic legend on a coin minted in his name at the time.[24] He also played a prominent role under Darius III. He was given the assignment of slowing the progress of the Macedonian army, which had just crossed the Euphrates. During the Battle of Gaugamela, he represented a danger to the Macedonian camp, even after Darius had left the battlefield. Having taken refuge in Babylon with his surviving soldiers, Mazday agreed a few weeks later to surrender to Alexander and, by way of compensation, received the title and duties of satrap of Babylonia. The first Iranian satrap to be named by Alexander, he also enjoyed the unique privilege of minting coins.

More recently, in 1995, a new coin type in Mazday's name came to light. The coins in question were minted in the Syrian city of Membig, which was famous under the name "Hierapolis" in the Roman period, thanks especially to the renowned sanctuary of the "Syrian goddess." Dating to Alexander's reign and to the Hellenistic period, well-attested coins there bear the legend "Abdha-dad priest of Membig" on their reverse (Fig. 24). The recently published coin has the same legend on the reverse and, on the obverse, the name Mazday is combined with the words (in Aramaic): "who is (governing the lands) beyond the river [Euphrates]" (Fig. 25). In comparing it with the coins already known, some have been tempted to think that, at a given moment, Mazday lost Cilicia and his command was reduced to Syria. That is why one commentator concluded that the coin was minted after Alexander's conquest of Cilicia in 333, and that until 331 Syria was still part of the territories controlled by Darius and continued as in the past to be ruled by Mazday. But for a number of reasons that it is pointless to detail here, that hypothesis remains very controversial. Differ-

(a)   *(b)*

24. *Priest-type coin from Membig.*

(a)   *(b)*

25. *Coin from Membig in Mazday's name.*

ences in the legends do not necessarily indicate a modification in the political
and administrative situation. It may also be that the coin was minted under
Artaxerxes III or in the first years of Darius III. Unless there are more decisive
discoveries, it is still more reasonable to think that Darius lost the territories
beyond the Euphrates just after the defeat at Issus and the fall of Damascus.

The fourth and last numismatic subset is also the one best situated in the
last years of Achaemenid history. According to Arrian, one of the Persian leaders who died at Issus was "Sabaces, satrap of Egypt."[25] By means of a (small)

(a1)   (a2)

(b1)   (b2)

26. Coins struck in Egypt in the name of the last satraps: Mazakes (a 1 and 2, obverse
     and reverse) and Sabakes (b 1 and 2, obverse and reverse).

number of statements, we know that Darius did not give up after the battle and
that, not satisfied to make ready a new army in Babylon, he also encouraged
the Tyrians to resist Alexander and gave identical instructions to the governor
of Gaza. Tyre and Gaza were supposed to keep Alexander from reaching Egypt.
The Nile Valley was also not abandoned to its fate: Arrian tells us that a new
satrap by the name of Mazakes was named there by the Great King.[26] Silver
tetradrachms and a few bronze coins, all inscribed in Aramaic, have been discovered in Egypt (Fig. 26). They bear the names "SWYK" (Sabakes) and "MZDK"
(Mazdakes). The coins therefore confirm the information provided in the classical texts, and we may surmise that some of the coins issued were used by Sabakes to raise troops from the satrapy on the Great King's orders.

The "Memoirs" of an Egyptian Doctor

Only the Egyptian and Babylonian texts include written accounts of the reaction of the local populations. There is a biographical inscription of an Egyptian noble by the name of Semtutefnakht, who composed it during the time of Ptolemy I. Intended to be read by future generations, that type of funerary inscription necessarily presents the life of the deceased noble in positive terms. Addressing the god Herishef-Re, "god of the Two Lands," the individual evokes one phase of his life that unfolded before and during Alexander's conquest:

> You distinguished me before millions,
> When you turned your back on Egypt.
> You put love of me in the heart of Asia's ruler.
> His courtiers praised god for me.
> He gave me the office of chief priest of Sakhmet, in place of my mother's
>   brother,
> The chief priest of Sakhmet of Upper and Lower Egypt, Nekhthenb.
> You protected me in the combat of the Greeks,
> When you repulsed those of Asia. They slew a million at my sides,
> And no one raised his arm against me. Thereafter I saw you in my sleep.
> Your majesty saying to me: "Hurry to Hnes, I protect you!"
> I crossed the countries all alone, I sailed the sea unfearing,
> Knowing I had not neglected your word, I reached Hnes [Heracleopolis],
> My head not robbed of a hair.[27]

It therefore appears that, when Egypt returned to the bosom of Persia, this individual received a favor on the part of the "Prince of Asia," that is, the Great King, who in this case may have been Artaxerxes III, Arses, or Darius III. Then, when Darius confronted Alexander and the Greeks, Semtutefnakht was in the Persian camp, probably part of the cohort of doctors in the rear. Although he did not fight, he witnessed a battle and was threatened by the victorious Greeks: that is why he thanked the god for protecting him at the time. Perhaps taken prisoner (the terminology is too vague to decide the matter), he was fortunate enough to have a dream in which the god instructed him to return to Egypt. It is possible to imagine several different scenarios, depending on whether the battle mentioned is believed to be that of Issus or that of Gaugamela, but any reconstitution of that type is inevitably built on sand.

Babylon in the Face of Darius's Defeat

The Babylonian astronomical diaries are more informative. Many events that the compilers chose as chronological reference points are obscure to us—for example, the mention of wonders (the birth of a three-legged bird) or bad omens ("a wolf entered Borsippa and killed two dogs; it did not go out, it was killed [on the spot]"; -567). From time to time, an event belonging more clearly to narrative history may be included: an allusion to Salamis in Cyprus, probably to Artaxerxes II's campaign against Cyprus in 372, known through the classical sources (-441); another allusion to the king and the king's son (?) (-378); a reference to a military expedition against Razaundu, a distant land (-369). Other events are even more suggestive: one tablet, dating to the first year of Philip (III) in the month of Airu (-322), notes: "The 29th, the king died." Here, dry and without emotion, is an almost notarial mention of Alexander's death on the night of June 10, 323. Although the insertion of these notations within the narrative context is not always so clear, the interest of these tablets lies in the Babylonian light they shed on events known solely through the Greek and Roman sources, or even on episodes not noted anywhere else.

Three of the tablets extant date to the reign of Darius III (-333, -332, -330). The first two, from year 2 or 3, give only the positions of the planets and a few meteorological observations. Despite breaks and lacunae, the text written at the bottom of the obverse of the third tablet and then on its reverse is of incomparably greater interest for the subject at hand. It is not a day-by-day record but a tablet recapitulating observations that unfolded over a period of more than a month. After indications on a series of troubling meteorological phenomena, dating to between September 13 and 30 (total lunar eclipse, accompanied by "deaths and plague?," "a fall of fire" visible in the Nabu temple district), comes a reference to the following contemporaneous event:

> That month [Ululu], on the 11th [September 18, 331], panic broke out in the camp of the king. [. . .] On the 24th [October 1, 331], in the morning, the king of the world [. . .] the standard? [. . .] They fought with each other, and a severe? defeat of the troops of [. . .].
> [. . .]The troops of the king deserted him and to their cities [. . .].
> They fled [to the l]and of the Gutium [. . . .]
> *(reverse)* That month [Tashritu], from the 1st [October 8, 331] until [. . .]
> [. . .] came to Babylon saying: "Esangil[. . .]
> and the Babylonians for the treasury of Esangil. [. . .]

> On the 11th [October 18, 331], in Sippar, an order of A[lexander . . .] as
> follows
> [. . .] One [. . .] shall not enter your houses." On the 13th [October 2, 331],
> [. . . Sikil]la-gate, the outer gate of Esangil, and [. . .]. On the 14th [Octo-
> ber 21, 331]: these Ionians[, . . .] short [. . .] fatty tissue. [. . .].
> [. . .][. . .][. . .][. . .][. . .].
> [. . .]. Alexander, king of the world, entered Babylon [. . .][. . .]
> horses and equipment of [. . .] and the Babylonians and the people [. . .]
> a letter on parchment to [. . .] thus.
> [. . .][. . .][. . .][. . .][. . .][. . .][. . .]²⁸

Clearly, the document is so lacunary that it would be difficult even to assign
it a date, were it not for the mention of Alexander and of the lunar eclipse. Because the text refers in succession to a battle between "the troops of the king"
and Alexander, to the defeat of the troops and the entry of Alexander, "king of
the world," into Babylon, it can only be about the Battle of Gaugamela and its
consequences. The tablet now makes it possible to date the battle with certainty to October 1, 331 (the 24th of the month of Ululu in year 5 of Darius). The
reasons for panic in the Persian camp on the date of September 18 are not
spelled out: perhaps it was the news that Alexander's army had crossed the Tigris, though that could not have taken Darius totally by surprise, given that he
was waiting for the Macedonian on a battlefield painstakingly chosen and prepared long before. Or did another natural phenomenon occur, spreading fear
among the Great King's soldiers? It is impossible to say.

Darius's defeat is obviously well known through the Greco-Roman sources:
after a short war council at Gaugamela on the same evening as the battle, the
king decided to leave open the road to Babylon and to retreat toward Ecbatana,
hoping to raise a new army there. That is what the Babylonian compiler means
by the use of the archaic term "Guti," which for Babylonians clearly evoked the
mountain regions to the north and east.

The tablet, however, does not simply clarify what was already known
through the accounts of Arrian, Curtius, and Plutarch. It also supplies original
information about the progress of Alexander's march to Babylon and provides
the occasion for reflections on the relationship between the Macedonian and
the Babylonians. In contrast to a long-held canonical view, which resulted from
reading Arrian and Curtius at face value, Alexander's march to Babylon was
not, strictly speaking, a triumphal march culminating in the enthusiastic welcome of the Babylonian population, jubilant at the idea of being rid of the

Persian yoke. The cuneiform text leaves no doubt remaining about something that a different reading of the Greco-Roman sources might also bring to light, namely, that Alexander's triumphal entry was also the result of negotiations between the Babylonian authorities and Alexander, undertaken just after the Battle of Gaugamela. To conclude his negotiations, Alexander had to officially proclaim in Sippar, on October 18, that his troops would not molest the population and would not attack the sanctuaries; there is mention of a sacrifice two days later in which "Ionians" took part. These were very likely Alexander's lieutenants, dispatched as an advance guard. It was therefore subsequent to a true pact that the new master was greeted with the title "king of the world," and that, on October 21 or shortly thereafter, he made his entry into Babylon.

The importance of the document clearly lies in the new information it provides. But its foremost historiographical interest lies in its very existence and in the identity of the compilers. Apart from the very laconic inscription of the Egyptian Semtutefnakht, this is the only narrative text that recounts a moment in the Perso-Macedonian War from the perspective of representatives of the local elites, in this case Babylonian literati closely associated with the temples and sanctuaries. Let me mention in passing that an extremely lacunary Babylonian chronicle mentions a battle against the Haneans, a term used in several Hellenistic Babylonian documents to designate the Macedonian army. The battle was led by one "Darius, King of King[s]" (šar šarr[ani]), very probably Darius III. The beginning of the paragraph seems to refer to the deposing of a king, but the lacunae and uncertainties prevent me from proposing, even hypothetically, a credible narrative reconstitution.

As a result, only the astronomical tablet remains. The narration in that case is limited to a dry enumeration of "facts" listed day by day—a form of zero-degree writing. Yet for the first time, it is truly possible to compare the Greco-Roman sources and the Babylonian sources on a precisely dated and identified event. Furthermore, the cuneiform text, merely a chronological outline written as the events were unfolding, has the notable advantage of not overtly distilling any message or bias in favor of one or the other of the warring parties, though it is of course clear that Darius was defeated and dead, and that Alexander was the victor and was welcomed into the city.

One king of Babylon succeeded another within the continuity of Babylonian history, and the compiler did not express the slightest sense of a sudden catastrophe—for the simple reason that, from the Babylonian point of view, this was more a matter of succession than of upheaval. Let me note that Alexander's recognized titulature, "king of the totality" (šar kiššati), widely attested for the

Neo-Assyrian period, had by then almost disappeared and was rare in the Baby-lonian period. We have recently learned of a single mention dating to the Ach-aemenid period, on the Cyrus Cylinder (in 539 B.C.E.), and of another, dating to the Hellenistic period, under the Seleucid king Antiochus Soter, on the Borsippa Cylinder, more than two and a half centuries later (in 268 B.C.E.). These occur-rences appear in two texts compiled in accordance with purely Babylonian norms and on an archaic model, just as, on the astronomical tablet, "the land of the Guti" designates the mountainous region of Media, to which Darius fled. The texts on the cylinders were also compiled under special circumstances, when two kings (Persian in one case, Macedonian in the other) were integrated into the continuity of Babylonian royalty without losing their specificity. It is neverthe-less a delicate matter to assert that the Babylonian elites, in conferring on the Macedonian conqueror a titulature that is supposed to express the idea of uni-versal kingship, intended to articulate, with particular symbolic force, their desire to reject the domination of Darius, who for his part simply bore the title "king." In fact, Persian trusteeship had disappeared throughout Babylonia. Furthermore, that titulature obviously has nothing to do with what Plutarch says about Alex-ander being proclaimed "king of Asia" after the victory at Gaugamela.[29]

In any case, in the administrative texts dating to 330 (Babylon and Larsa), Alexander bears the title "king of the countries," which had been Darius's a few months earlier (February–March 331) on a tablet from Larsa. The mention of the king, reduced to the function of a chronological point of reference, has no effect on the apparently immutable facts of Babylonian history. It is therefore easy to understand why Alexander's death, narrated and depicted at such great length by the Greek and Roman authors, deserves no more than a brief men-tion in a very long astronomical diary dating to year 1 of King Philip (Alexan-der's half-brother and successor), which gives extremely precise and abundant details on the position of the planets during the period under consideration.

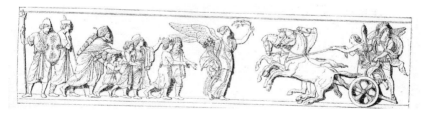

27. *Mazday and his children, preceded by Peace, welcoming Alexander to Babylon.*

It is clear that the political horizon of the compilers of the astronomical tablet does not extend beyond that of the interests of the Esangil, the great temple of Marduk in Babylon. It is probably because of the measures Alexander took in favor of the temple that we possess such a precise reference to Darius's defeat, and especially such a detailed mention of the relationship the new king was able to define and establish with the Babylonian aristocracy. By contrast, the tablet does not breathe a word about an agreement concluded between Alexander and the Persian authorities of Babylon (Mazday and Bagophanes)—an agreement that did not directly concern the sanctuary and that only the Greco-Roman sources and the numismatic documents allow us to bring to light. According to Curtius, Alexander was received by Mazday, "who had taken refuge in the city after the battle. He came as a suppliant with his grown-up children to surrender himself and the city."[30] It is this surrender that Bertel Thorwaldsen sought to depict in a well-known relief (Fig. 27).[31]

When collated with what the Greco-Roman texts tell us and with comparable reflections on the attitude of the Egyptians, the tablet confirms that the Persian defeat cannot be explained simply in terms of a visceral hostility on the part of Babylonians or Egyptians toward Darius and Persian rule. In concluding an accord with the Babylonian sanctuaries, Alexander was only adopting a traditional Achaemenid policy, and there is nothing to indicate that Darius ever distanced himself from it.

All in all, the results garnered from examining the "Achaemenid" documentation on Darius are rather disappointing. The material evidence (archaeological and numismatic) is either absent or very unclear, and in any event it does not really provide new and original elements. The Egyptian coins confirm the accuracy of the names of the satraps appointed by Darius, but they do not radically change our approach to that moment in history. Although the inscription of Semtutefnakht is moving and original, it too tells us nothing about Darius or about his policy. Even the information to be drawn from the Babylonian astronomical tablet is less conclusive than it appears: although it felicitously clarifies the conditions of investiture for Alexander, "king of the totality," by the city's great deity and the authorities of the sanctuary, it does not enlighten us about Darius's policy and strategy after Gaugamela. At best these documents can simply be inserted into a body of evidence built first and foremost on the Greco-Roman sources. Although the two histories are closely linked, in the end the "Achaemenid" documentation does not so much shed light on Darius's reign as enrich the history of Alexander's conquest and the reactions it elicited in various countries.

❦ 2 ❦

Darius Past and Present

To bring to light the major tendencies that have governed judgments of Darius III and his empire, I will need to explain how the individual and his actions have been approached since the early decades of the nineteenth century. At that time, research on antiquity began to develop on documentary and philological foundations, which, within the context of a "science of antiquity" *(Altertumswissenschaft)*, sought to be solid and rigorous. Some of the judgments and interpretations expressed very early on have practically never been called into question, either in their validity or in their formulation.

Although the figure of Darius has attracted infinitely less attention than his conqueror, it is possible to say, as is regularly said of Alexander, that every historian has imagined his own. Just as, since antiquity, there have been two images of Alexander—one positive, the other negative—there are also two antithetical portraits of Darius, elaborated both by specialists in Greek history and by specialists in the history of Persia. First, there is the image of a king endowed with many good qualities, whom destiny brought face to face with an invincible enemy; and second, there is the image of a cowardly and unworthy king who proved incapable of defending his honor and that of the Persians.

Before History

For anyone seeking to write the history of a theme or image, it is always a delicate matter to decide on a starting point. In the case at hand, I am tempted to go back to the fourteenth century and to mention a minor work by Boccaccio (1313–1375), published in Latin under the title *De casibus virorum illustrium* and translated into French by Laurent de Premierfait under the title *Des nobles malheureux*

(On Unfortunate Nobles). Boccaccio does not omit to present Darius III as one of these fated individuals (bk. 4, chap. 8: "De Dario Persarum rege").

Erroneously introduced as the son and successor of Ochus (Artaxerxes III), Darius is portrayed as the most powerful man of his time.[1] Boccaccio can then organize his narrative around the particularly unhappy fate that befell the Persian king. Beaten twice in pitched battles, twice having taken flight, the Great King seeks refuge in Babylonia and attempts to negotiate the return of the blood princesses, who have been taken prisoner. Faced with the impossibility of concluding an agreement with Alexander, Darius prepares an army and, for the third time, faces the Macedonians. Beaten once again, he wants to kill himself but is prevented by his entourage and takes flight with a few companions. He heads for Parthia, more as prisoner than as king: bound in gold shackles, he is transported in a cart. He is soon mortally wounded by Bessus, "the foremost of his Companions." Dying of thirst, he is aided by an anonymous Persian soldier, to whom he confides his last wishes. "So ended the life of such a great, such a powerful, such a rich king." He is not left without a sepulchre, however. Alexander, persuaded by the Persian soldier, comes to meditate on his enemy's mortal remains and orders that Darius be given a "solemn and royal funeral in accordance with Persian custom."

It is clear that the different episodes from the life of Darius were directly borrowed from Orosius, who, on the advice of Augustine of Hippo, had composed a history *(Against the Pagans)* in the early decades of the fifth century. In it Orosius paraphrases earlier works, particularly Justin's *Epitome of the Philippic History of Pompeius Trogus.* The reigns of Philip and of his son Alexander are presented very negatively: "Alexander was a mire of misery and the most horrid of cyclones for the entire Orient. . . . He was insatiable for human blood, whether of his enemies or of his allies. . . . He died in Babylon, when, still bloodthirsty, he drank poison with immoderate greed as a result of a servant's treachery." Alexander is responsible for the catastrophes that befell Darius and his kingdom. It is also from Orosius that Boccaccio borrows the judgment of Alexander's decision to have his enemy buried: "A hollow act of pity," writes Orosius, who, in stark contrast to Justin's intention, wants to establish an opposition between that decision and what he presents as "the cruel captivity in which the Macedonian king kept not only, dare I say, Darius's mother and wife but also even his two little girls."[2] The violently hostile view of Alexander's exploit gives a tragic cast to the image of his enemies, particularly Darius but also some of his friends, such as Callisthenes, to whose pitiable fate Boccaccio devotes another chapter. Orosius's history was widely disseminated and used well before Boccaccio—for example, in the very popular *Histoire ancienne jusqu'à César (Estoires Rogier),* published between 1206 and 1230.

That theme of fickle fortune can be found in a number of other authors from the time of Boccaccio, some of whom were influenced by him—John Lydgate in *Fall of Princes,* for example. These authors had sometimes also been marked by their readings of Curtius and Valerius Maximus. Such was the case for Petrarch in his devastating portrait of the Macedonian conqueror in *De viris illustribus.* Boccaccio was widely read in France, and his *De casibus* was one of the inspirations for the work of a young playwright named Jacques de La Taille. Perfectly well-educated in Greek and Latin, he died at the age of twenty in 1562. Slightly more than ten years after his death, in 1573, two of his works, *Daire (Darius)* and *Alexandre,* were published by his brother. The first centers on the tragic fate of the last Persian king and is set during the short interval between his defeat at Gaugamela (October 331) and his death (July 330). The unfortunate king and the Persian chorus appear in other tragedies, such as Sir William Alexander's *Tragedy of Darius,* first published in Edinburgh in 1603, and J. Crowne's *Darius, King of Persia,* performed at the Theatre Royal in 1688. Darius-Codomannus is also the hero of Thomas Corneille's play *Darius* (1659).

In Jacques de La Taille's play, the king delivers a long monologue, which constitutes act 1, scene 1. He bemoans his fate while addressing a fictive interlocutor:

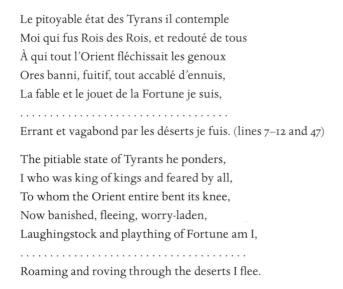

Le pitoyable état des Tyrans il contemple
Moi qui fus Rois des Rois, et redouté de tous
À qui tout l'Orient fléchissait les genoux
Ores banni, fuitif, tout accablé d'ennuis,
La fable et le jouet de la Fortune je suis,

. . . .

Errant et vagabond par les déserts je fuis. (lines 7–12 and 47)

The pitiable state of Tyrants he ponders,
I who was king of kings and feared by all,
To whom the Orient entire bent its knee,
Now banished, fleeing, worry-laden,
Laughingstock and plaything of Fortune am I,

. . . .

Roaming and roving through the deserts I flee.

Darius evokes his Macedonian conqueror, who is now corrupting his soul and undermining his strength by savoring delights that were until recently Darius's own:

> Las! tu es maintenant en mes royales villes,
> À prendre tes plaisirs, and tandis que tu pilles
> Mes biens et mes trésors, et que tu t'effémines
> En pompes et en jeux entre mes concubines. (lines 43–46)

> Now are you, alas, in my royal cities,
> Taking your pleasures, and as you plunder
> My riches and treasures, you turn soft as a girl
> In pomp and in play with my concubines.

Conversations follow with those in Darius's entourage who have remained faithful, such as Artabazus, the eunuch Bubaces, and the Greek Patron. There are also many exchanges between the conspirators, Bessus and Nabarzanes, while the "chorus of Persian civil guards" sings of Persia's splendors and denounces the infamy of the conspirators. At the end of the play, Daire/Darius converses with Polystratus, who brings water to his thirsty master. Alexander makes his entrance in act 5. The chorus, in its last appearance, bestows the term "Great" on him: because of his virtue, he deserves to "govern the Universe."

A number of the situations and images that would mark historiography for a long time were in place from that time onward. Although the title role in Jacques de La Taille's tragedy falls to Darius, the Great King is not really the protagonist. The purpose of the scenes in which he acts, soliloquizes, or speaks to others is not to rehabilitate him or even to laud his virtues. Rather, Darius is a symbol, an eloquent witness to the vicissitudes of fortune and to the way that men of antiquity accepted or failed to accept their tragic fate. As M. G. Longhi points out, the one true hero is Alexander: "The character . . . dominates the work in the aura of his full power: his entrance in act 5 is in reality set in motion from the beginning of the play. Darius continues his monologue, using striking images to lament his fate and that of his mother and children—who have fallen into the enemy's hands—and the death of his wife, Alexander's prisoner" (p. 279).

Equally noteworthy are the ancient sources used by these authors. Aside from Orosius, the favorite author is Curtius, whose *History of Alexander the Great* had an extraordinarily broad diffusion, especially from the fifteenth century on, thanks to the French translation by Vasque de Lucene (1468). It was very

popular nearly two centuries before Claude Favre de Vaugelas's French translation was published posthumously in 1653. In accordance with certain moral and
literary assumptions, Curtius is the only one to take the reader into Darius's
camp between the Battle of Gaugamela and the king's death.[3] And, like Justin
and Plutarch, he gives a moving description of the death of Darius. Justin and
Diodorus are the only authors to attribute a heroic military feat to Darius, a victorious duel with a Cadusian warrior, performed under the name "Codomannus"
(according to Justin) before his accession.[4] The duel is mentioned, for example, in
Thomas Corneille's *Darius* (act 1, scene 3), which introduces the "Cadusians
beaten in so many wars":

> Codoman est toujours le soutien de nos armes . . .
> Depuis qu'un bon destin aux Persans favorable
> Arrête parmi nous ce Héros indomptable,
> Nos plus fiers Ennemis et battus et défaits
> Semblent de tous côtez, n'aspirer qu'à la paix.
>
> Codomannus is still the support of our arms . . .
> Since an auspicious fate, favoring the Persians,
> Has kept among us that invincible Hero;
> Our proudest Enemies, beaten, in defeat,
> Seem on all sides to hope only for peace.

Then, not without a certain bombast, Codomannus himself describes the
services he rendered to King Ochus: "De trois Sceptres voisins j'ai fait votre
conquête, / Sur cent peuples par moi vous régnez aujourd'hui, . . . / L'Égypte,
l'Arménie en rendront témoignage, / De mes nobles travaux en sont les dignes
fruits" (act 2, scene 3) (Three neighboring Scepters I have conquered for you /
Today a hundred nations you rule thanks to me . . . / Egypt and Armenia will
both stand as witness, / Of my noble labors they are the worthy fruit).

In Jacques de La Taille's *Daire,* Darius's lines and speeches, and those of his
companions, are almost word-for-word translations of speeches found in Curtius. It was in Curtius, Justin, and Plutarch that La Taille found the character of
Polystratus, one of Alexander's soldiers who discovers a mortally wounded
Darius. La Taille barely deviates from his models, except that, in imitation of
Boccaccio, he makes Polystratus a Persian soldier, perhaps simply because that
allows the two characters to speak a common language.[5] That tradition held
sway in the view of Alexander and Darius existing at the time.

Arrian's *Anabasis,* translated into Latin in the 1430s by Pier Paolo Vergerio at
the urging of Emperor Sigismund, was the object of long reflection by Sultan
Mehmed the Conqueror in the 1460s and was belatedly rendered into French by
C. Vuitard in 1581, then by Nicolas Perrot d'Ablancourt in 1646. It is much more
critical toward Darius's memory, but it was not used in La Taille's time. In his
preface Perrot d'Ablancourt points out what he considers to be Arrian's superiority over Justin, Diodorus, and Curtius, especially for readers interested in the
history of the great military leaders. Such was not the focus of such writers as
Jacques de La Taille, who preferred to consider the life, and even more the death,
of a tragic hero.

The hegemony of the tradition called the Vulgate (Diodorus, Curtius, and
Justin, as opposed to Arrian) and of Orosius, or more broadly, of a moralizing
historiography dating back to antiquity (particularly Valerius Maximus), explains
why Darius's image was organized around the theme of the caprices of fortune.
That was already Curtius's favorite theme, which he treated with deliberate
pathos. It is therefore clear why, when the first books of ancient history were
written and published in Europe, the dominant image of the last Persian king
was a "romantic" figure, strongly marked by a garrulous pathos intended to
move the reader. That trait was easily integrated into a whole current of moralizing history that developed in the seventeenth and eighteenth centuries, and
which did not hesitate to condemn vigorously the grave flaws that Alexander
displayed after his adversary's death. That "pathetic romanticism" would be denounced by nineteenth-century historians, who believed it more seemly to adopt
an "impartial" viewpoint.

From Droysen to Bossuet and Back Again

Among modern historians of Alexander's conquest, J.-G. Droysen can be acknowledged as the founder of the tribe.[6] Born in Prussia in 1808, he devoted part
of his life to reconstituting and interpreting a historical period that had until
then been very misunderstood, even held in disdain, namely, the era that began
with the defeat of Athens by Philip II (338) and continued through Alexander's
exploits. Droysen saw it as a period of considerable import with respect to the
clash and conflict between the West and the East. The advent of what is now
known in historiography as the Hellenistic period occurred with Droysen. A first
book of his devoted to Alexander's life and conquests was published in 1833, followed by his magnum opus, *Die Geschichte des Hellenismus (The History of Helle-*

nism), which appeared in German between 1836 and 1843. A revised edition of this book (1877–1878) was translated into French in 1883 under the title *Histoire de l'hellénisme.* The first volume of that work is also devoted to Alexander the Great.

Choosing a very classic structure for his book, Droysen first presents the protagonists. He dedicates some twenty pages to the history of the Great Kings from Cyrus onward and to the state of the empire upon the accession of Darius III. Although the last of the Great Kings does not have a major place in the account that follows, and though Droysen criticizes Darius's indecisiveness on the brink of war, the royal portrait that emerges is indisputably positive. It is worth quoting the judgment in extenso, because it was so closely followed by generations of historians, sometimes in its slightest details:

> The kingdom's reins were in the hands of a king unlike any the Persians had had for a long time. Handsome and grave, as the Asiatic readily imagines his sovereign, gracious toward all and honored by all, endowed with all the virtues of his great ancestors, free from the hideous vices that had debased the life of Ochus [Artaxerxes III] and had led the empire to its doom, Darius appeared destined to cure it of its wounds, having arrived without the need for crimes or blood. No revolt occurred to trouble the beginning of his reign. . . . United under the noble Darius from the Ionian coast to the Indus, Asia seemed safer than it had been in a long time. And yet that king was to be the last of Cyrus's descendants to rule Asia, as if an innocent head were needed to expiate what could no longer be healed. . . . Already gathering on the horizon was the storm that would annihilate Persia. . . . Darius wanted to avoid that war at all cost; he seemed to have a presentiment that his colossal empire, torn apart from within and languishing, needed only an external jolt to be broken apart. In that indecisiveness, he allowed the last deadline for preventing that dreaded attack to pass. (1883, 1:67)

The judgment and its formulation enjoyed a great deal of success. This was not a great historiographical innovation, however. On the contrary, the debate about the personality of the last Great King had been active for a very long time. In an essay on the Iranian peoples of antiquity (1839), M. de Saint-Félix provided what was already a canonical description of the Persian Empire upon the death of Artaxerxes III: "The last years of Ochus [Artaxerxes III] had made everyone forget the triumphs at the beginning of his reign, and had laid bare the hideous deformity of his soul. Always hated, he was from that time on scorned, and the decadence of his kingdom, whose seeds had already existed, made rapid progress. The satraps clearly aspired to be independent; discipline was lost amid troops gorged on wine and drunken on pleasure; finances were depleted, and the populations—pressured to supply the ruinous prodigalities of a corrupt and ostentatious court—lost all national spirit and all affection for their government" (pp. 359–360). What could Darius do? Not much, despite his positive qualities: "Brave, active, and generous, Darius was able to repair the kingdom's internal ills and elevate its glory; but Alexander ascended to the throne of Macedonia, and his conquest of Persia lay in store" (p. 359).

Had Saint-Félix read Droysen's *Alexander*, whose first German edition appeared in 1833? The hypothesis is conceivable but in no way necessary. The model was already well in place in the writings of Charles Rollin, who between 1730 and 1738 published the first real textbook in ancient history. Born in 1661, Rollin was professor of rhetoric at the Collège de France (1688), then rector of the Université de Paris (1694), a post he lost as a result of his fidelity to Jansenism.

His work was titled *Histoire ancienne des Égyptiens, des Carthaginois, des Assyriens, des Babyloniens, des Mèdes et des Perses, des Macédoniens et des Grecs (The Ancient History of the Egyptians, Carthaginians, Assyrians, Babylonians, Medes, and Persians, Macedonians, and Grecians)*. The history of the Persians and that of the Greeks are presented in alternating chapters. Book 15 is devoted to the history of Alexander. Rollin, it should be said, was not an adulator of the Macedonian king. His is a moralizing history, intended for the education of princes, which "presents them with illustrious models for all the virtues befitting them . . . [but also] with the base and ignoble defects that tarnished the brilliance [of] good actions and dishonored [the] reigns of Philip and Alexander his son." Indeed, though the author praises certain "brilliant actions" by Alexander, especially his conduct toward the Persian princesses taken prisoner after Issus ("that was Alexander's finest hour"), he goes on to denounce a king who in his view does not deserve the title "Great." In the tradition of one current of antiquity but also for his own reasons—related to the moral and religious idea underlying the entire book—Rollin maintains that, already with the taking of Tyre but even more upon the death of Darius, Alexander was waging an unjust war: "He was no longer a conqueror or a hero but a usurper and a brigand. . . . There was never a more foolhardy ambition, or rather, a more furious ambition than that of this prince. . . . [Of the illustrious men in Plutarch's *Lives*] . . . Alexander is one of the least admirable." The author goes on to reflect on the survival of the myth of Alexander, which he regrets was still being used in his time by "all the orators who undertake to praise a prince."[7]

Darius does not have a prominent place in his account. Rollin acknowledges that the Great King was not without a few positive qualities. Paraphrasing Curtius, Diodorus, and Plutarch, he says of Darius, for example: "He was gentle and accommodating. . . . Naturally gentle and full of humanity . . . He was the most handsome of all the princes, and the tallest and most majestic." Then the author asks a rhetorical question: "But what natural disposition does fortune not corrupt?" He forcefully condemns, as so many others would do, the execution of the Athenian Charidemus, who defended a strategy repudiated by the king (4:42–44). And then, though tall and handsome, Darius did not have the qualities of a soldier that the situation demanded: "The Persians defended themselves courageously, until they saw Darius fleeing and the Greeks routed by the phalanx" (4:55).

Rollin himself leads us back to an earlier time, by naming the one who inspired him (4:286–291). Speaking of Darius III and his empire, he returns to 1681, half a century earlier. He quotes and paraphrases the "Reflections of Mr. Bossuet, Bishop of Meaux, on the Persians, Greeks, and Macedonians" contained in the *Discours sur l'histoire universelle (Discourse on Universal History)*, and more precisely, part 3, on empires, whose "revolutions are governed by Providence." "That universal history of sorts" was addressed to Monseigneur le Dauphin. It is important, in fact, to "have princes read history."

According to Bossuet, the Persian Empire had its proper place between the Egyptians, "the first to have known the rules of governance," and the fall of the Roman Empire, primarily because Cyrus gave permission to the Judeans to return to Jerusalem and to rebuild the temple there. In part 1, titled "The Epochs," the eighth epoch is called "Cyrus, or the Jews Reestablished." Introducing the figure of Darius III for the first time, Bossuet has rather kind things to say about him: "By virtue of his valor, he merits our coming around to the opinion, in fact the most plausible, that he descended from the royal family." Anxious to present to his pupil (the Dauphin) what he calls "the spectacle of history," anxious as well to carefully stage his effects, Bossuet links Darius and Alexander, but not in a way unfavorable to the Great King, at least at this point: "And so two courageous kings began their reigns together, Darius, son of Arsames, and Alexander, son of Philip. They watched each other with a jealous eye and seemed born to compete for world domination."

Another portrait of Darius appears in the account of Alexander and the fall of the empire. Here too, Bossuet chooses positive words: "Darius, who ruled Persia in his time, was just, valiant, generous, beloved of his people, and he lacked neither the spirit nor the vigor to carry out his designs" (pp. 564–565).

But it would be misleading to isolate that sentence from its context. Before it, Bossuet has probing pages on Persia, which may allow his readers, Monseigneur le Dauphin first and foremost, to discover "both what ruined the Persians' empire and what raised up Alexander's." Although Darius is not denounced as an individual, he is devalued by a discourse that places him within the inexorable continuity of the decadence of an empire doomed to disappear, confronted by an Alexander who had inherited from his father "Macedonians who were not only battle-hardened but also victorious." The comparison cannot fail to show Darius in an unfavorable light: "But if you compare him to Alexander: his spirit to that piercing and sublime genius; his valor to the loftiness and firmness of that invincible courage, spurred on by obstacles; that enormous zeal to increase his renown every day, which made him feel deep within his heart that everything had to yield to him as to a man whose destiny made him superior to the others; the confidence he inspired not only in his leaders but also in the least of his soldiers, whom he elevated by that means above the difficulties and above themselves—then you will be able to judge to which of the two the victory belonged. And if you combine with those things the advantages that the Greeks and the Macedonians had over their enemies, you will admit that Persia, attacked by such a hero and by such armies, could no longer avoid a change in masters" (p. 565).

Bossuet had a marked influence on Rollin but also, for example, on Richard, sieur de Bury, who in 1760 published his *Histoire de Philippe et d'Alexandre le Grand, rois de Macédoine (History of Philip and Alexander the Great, Kings of Macedonia)*. De Bury presents the Persian Empire and the succession of kings, "before going into detail about the events that contributed to [its] destruction." He expresses admiration for the private and public mores of the Persians and quotes at length from M. de Meaux's *Histoire universelle (Universal History)* (pp. 224–226). He does not forget to mention the Cadusian exploit of the future Darius, then discusses the conditions surrounding his accession and his character: "Darius was a courageous prince, he had once shown proof of that under the reign of his predecessor, when he saved the army from defeat, but he had never commanded as leader. The power to which he found himself elevated filled him with pride and vanity, and he believed that, along with the scepter, he had acquired the qualities necessary to a king. . . . It is said that Darius was of a gentle and moderate character but that fortune and flattery corrupted his mores. . . . He sent [Charidemus] to his death" (pp. 259–261).

The combined influence of Bossuet and Rollin has been lasting and profound. In the second edition of his famous book on the ancient historians of

Alexander (1804), the baron de Sainte-Croix cites in extenso "the illustrious Bossuet" in introducing Darius (p. xxxii). The influence of the *Discours sur l'histoire universelle* is also acknowledged and embraced by George Rawlinson in his *Ancient History from the Earliest Times to the Fall of the Western Empire* (1900). Rawlinson presents his book as the most up-to-date manual of its time, intended to replace A. H. L. Heeren's *Handbuch der Geschichte der Staaten des Alterthums (Manual of Ancient History)*, whose first edition dates to 1799. He considers Bossuet's *Discours* (in the English translation of 1728) as among the "modern works embracing the whole range of ancient history" (p. 6). Rawlinson also cites Rollin, whose *Histoire ancienne* was enormously successful and had had a profound influence, as C. Grell and C. Michel have rightly pointed out: "The importance of Charles Rollin's *History ancienne* has not been adequately emphasized in our time. Voltaire, in any case, was clear-sighted about it and continued to put many of its passages to his own purposes. Before the publication of that book, there was no handy survey of the history of classical Greece in current use in France. . . . Until the mid-nineteenth century, [it] was in fact regularly reprinted, which means that Rollin ruled as lord and master for more than a hundred years" (1988, p. 82).

The audience for the work extended beyond national borders. It grew to be enormous in a number of European countries, where translations were published one after another. Translated into French in 1768, the book came out in a fifteenth English edition in 1824, based on a French version revised by the illustrious Jean Antoine Letronne in 1821. It is to this edition that Rawlinson refers his readers.

It may not be beside the point to add that Rollin also influenced painters and other artists in search of "good subjects." Take the case of Jacques Gamelin (1738–1803), a talented draftsman and painter who, after a nine-year stay in Rome, moved back to his native Languedoc. He had a vast range of interests and was in particular deeply marked by antiquity. Several of his paintings and drawings depict scenes from "Persian history," in which the figures of Cyrus, Darius the Great, and Ochus (the future Artaxerxes III) can be distinguished, but also scenes drawn from the history of Alexander. When the artist provides a reference to the book from which he drew his inspiration, it is inevitably Rollin's *Histoire ancienne,* cited by volume and sometimes even page number.[8] The selection of highly emotional scenes, rendered as such (Darius's family before Alexander, an ill Alexander saved by his doctor, Alexander consumed by thirst, Alexander's entrance into Babylon, and so on), constitutes a kind of collection of exempla, which Rollin himself recommended compiling.

From George Rawlinson to Mary Renault

George Rawlinson, brother of the man who deciphered the inscription of Darius in Behistun, can be considered Droysen's counterpart in the field of Persian history. In his famous *Fifth Monarchy, Persia,* published in 1867 and reprinted in 1871, Rawlinson shares some of Droysen's judgments. He explicitly takes issue with the disastrous portrait transmitted by Arrian in the form of a funeral oration:[9] "Codomannus, the last of the Persian kings, might with some reason have complained, like Plato [*Epistle* 5], that nature had brought him in the world too late. Personally brave, as he proved himself into the Cadusian war, tall and strikingly handsome, amiable in temper, capable of considerable exertion, and not altogether devoid of military capacity, he would have been a fairly good ruler in ordinary times, and might, had he fallen upon such times, have held an honorable place among the Persian monarchs. But he was unequal to the difficulties of such a position as that in which he found himself" (p. 515).

Rawlinson uses a comparable turn of phrase elsewhere: "Superior morally to the greater number of his predecessors, Darius III did not posses sufficient intellectual ability to enable him to grapple with the difficulties of the circumstances in which he was placed" (1900, p. 93).

But though authors may agree on the essential, they do not necessarily adopt the same judgment on every facet of the king's personality. Serious differences are sometimes discernible even between those whose approach to the Great King is relatively positive—for example, between Droysen and Rawlinson. Droysen denounces Darius, who at Issus "sought his salvation through flight instead of seeking it in battle among his faithful." And after Gaugamela, instead of gathering together his people to defend the heart of the empire, "he sank into an incredible confusion," because he was "ready to do anything to save something."

Rawlinson's view is completely different. Engaged in a controversy with one of his predecessors (G. Grote), he argues that the Great King behaved with good reason and wisely, and that a malicious interpretation has too often been given of his flight from the battlefield, "which was the effect rather than the cause" of the Macedonian victories. When Darius fled after Issus, it was not "simply to preserve for a few months longer his own wretched life," but rather, in the first place, to reconstitute his armies and reconquer what he had lost (1871, p. 528). As for his behavior at Gaugamela, though we may not approve of it, that does not compel us to "withdraw from him that respectful compassion which we commonly accord to great misfortunes." It is true that, had the king been killed on the battlefield, "a halo of glory would have surrounded him." But after all, adds Rawlinson, citing the examples of Pompey and Napoleon, he was not the only king or great general not cut out to be a hero (p. 538).

In any event, the portrait would enjoy lasting success. In 1879, in his *Geschichte des alten Persiens (History of the Ancient Persians)*, F. Justi wrote of the last Great King: "He was a strong and handsome man. . . . He had demonstrated his courage in a war against the Cadusians and was then named satrap of Armenia. One must not belittle that prince; if he had not been obliged to test his mettle against Alexander, he would have made an excellent leader in other respects. He was a courageous man, determined to do battle to the end, but he was betrayed" (p. 130).

Like many others, A. M. Curteis sympathizes with the unhappy fate of a man who was "hurled in [a] short time from the height of human grandeur to the depths of misfortune—a man who might have adorned more peaceful times with the gentler graces of a benevolent despot, but too feeble and apathetic to cope with so tremendous a crisis—a king who would have been happier had he never reigned" (*Rise of the Macedonian Empire* [1886], p. 150).

Similar remarks can be found in General Percy Sykes's *A History of Persia*, the first edition of which appeared in 1901:

> The last member of an illustrious line, he excites a certain amount of sympathy. He had gained a reputation for bravery in the Cadusian campaign by slaying a gigantic tribesman in single combat, and had been appointed Satrap of Armenia as a reward. He appears to have been in character more generous and less vicious than any of his immediate predecessors, and had the circumstance of his reign been normal, he might have ruled with credit. Unfortunately for him, a new power, led by the greatest soldier of all time, had arisen in the West, and Darius, although backed by all the resources of the Persian Empire, quailed and fell before the fiery onset of Alexander the Great. . . . He was certainly more capable than many of his predecessors. (pp. 233, 245)

That assessment, almost unchanged, rapidly made its way into the ancient history manuals, such as Georg Weber's volume of *Weltgeschichte (Universal History)* devoted to the Greeks, translated into French in 1883: "Darius Codomannus, a man of a gentle nature, distinguished by his bravery and his domestic virtues, was adorned with the royal bandeau. He freed himself from the cruel Bagoas . . . and then governed with as much moderation and justice as the difficult circumstances allowed; so that many notable Greeks, to escape Macedonian despotism, served in the Persians' army. But the end of the great monarchy was about to overtake him. Darius had to expiate the crimes of his predecessors" (p. 238).

Then came Gaston Maspéro's *Histoire ancienne des peuples de l'Orient classique (Ancient History of the Peoples of the Classical Orient)*, published in 1889. In a general overview sustained by a reflective reading of the nineteenth-century authors considered authorities in their fields, Maspéro presents the views in fashion, which he dresses up in splendid prose. Like so many others, he begins his portrait of Darius with a reference to his heroic deeds among the Cadusians, then adapts for his own use a comment tirelessly transmitted from generation to generation: "Brave, generous, mild, endowed with an enormous desire to do good, he was better than all his immediate predecessors and deserved to reign in a time when the empire was not so threatened" (p. 808).

That position seems to have acquired canonical status by that time. In his memorable *History of the Persian Empire* (1948), A. T. Olmstead also recalls the future Darius III's feats during one of the Cadusian wars and writes: "He might have proved to be a good ruler had conditions been normal" (p. 490). A few years later, Roman Ghirshman made the same claim in his *Iran des origines à l'Islam (History of Pre-Islamic Iran, 1951)*: "That courageous man might have been able to save his country had his adversary not been, for the first time in the history of his country, all of Greece united in a coalition . . . led by a military genius. The great mistake of Codomannus, caused by his pride as a powerful monarch, was to have had contempt for the young Alexander and to have underestimated the valor of his troops" (p. 200).

F. Schachermeyr's *Alexander der Grosse* (1949; 2nd ed. 1973), whose subtitle, *Ingenium und Macht (Genius and Power)*, makes explicit the author's Herculean view of his hero, belongs to the current that considers Darius a man possessing indisputable royal qualities, though he suffers by comparison to the "superhuman" figure of his Macedonian adversary:

> By nature, he was irreproachably princely in bearing, a noble incarnation of the decadence of the late Achaemenid period. At the age of forty-four, he is depicted as a man tall of stature and handsome. As a prince, he had distinguished himself by his personal bravery and had even appeared as a

heroic participant in a single combat "between two armies," in which he was the victor. In that we can recognize the horseman of austere habits. But we then learn that he was the offspring of a brother and sister—as they existed in Persia, and who were particularly meritorious in their behavior—but also that his wife was his blood sister and that he fathered her children. . . . The many authors of antiquity and of today are wrong to reproach him for being inferior to Alexander. In reality, the intelligent actions that had to be taken against the Macedonian offensive, Darius had already taken many times, with a breadth of vision and always without delay. It is not surprising that he was not prepared for an Alexander, since the West had never produced a phenomenon of that kind. That is why we must not heap reproaches on him, since failure was inevitable, given the superiority of his adversary. Because of the circumstances at the time, decisions in the West did not lie with the Great King but with his Greek general, Memnon. (p. 131)

One last work, belonging in principle to a different genre (the historical novel), also merits a look. In 1972 the famous American novelist Mary Renault published *The Persian Boy,* which was translated into many languages. The eponymous hero is also its narrator. His name is Bagoas, and he is one of two figures bearing that name known through the Greco-Roman sources to have lived in the time of Darius III and Alexander. The other Bagoas is portrayed as a kingmaker, by Diodorus Siculus especially: called a eunuch, he occupied the very high post of chiliarch (commander of a thousand) under the reign of Artaxerxes III, and it was he who assassinated that Great King. He then had Arses, the murdered king's son, ascend to the throne, before eliminating Arses in turn, along with his children. He chose Codomannus/Artašata as Arses's successor under the reign name Darius (III). That Bagoas died soon thereafter, under melodramatic circumstances, which Mary Renault skillfully introduces into the novel: Darius compels Bagoas to drink from the poisoned goblet he has just handed to the Great King.

The second Bagoas is a young eunuch in the service of a master and he goes on to have a personal and intimate relationship with the king. He learns by hearsay of Darius's accession. Renault's portrait of the new king takes a positive approach: "While I lay at the dealer's, the new King had been proclaimed. Ochos' line being extinguished, he was royal only by side descent; but the people seemed to think well of him. . . . Darius, the new King, [the Chief Eunuch] said, had both beauty and valour. When Ochos had been at war with the Kardousians, and their giant champion had challenged the King's warriors, only Darius had come forward. He stood six feet and a half himself, and had transfixed the man with a single javelin, living ever since in the renown. There had been consultations, and the Magi had scanned the skies; but no one in council had dared cross Bagoas' choice, he was too much dreaded. However, it seemed that so far the new King had murdered no one; his manners were reported gracious and mild" (p. 14).

As usual, Renault has done her research. She faithfully adopts the point of view elaborated by Justin, Diodorus, Curtius, and Plutarch, and by an entire historiographical current that followed in their wake.

The Other Model: The Cowardly and Unworthy King

It would be wrong to believe that the "positive" interpretation of the last Great King was adopted by the majority of historians. That was not at all the case, not even in Droysen's time. Within the political current favoring the unification of the Germanies, which inspired Droysen and in which he was an active militant, Philip of Macedon's achievement provided an example and a precedent. His empire stood in sharp contrast to the minuscule republics incapable of greatness. It was an entirely different matter among the "liberals" (especially in England), who were deeply committed to opposing despotic systems. The visceral hostility of the liberals and of others to Napoleonic imperialism, the source of catastrophe for a number of European countries, must also be taken into account. In that context, Philip of Macedon, Alexander, and the "Asiatic despots" (including Darius) were presented and interpreted as particularly deplorable counterexamples.

This is apparent in Barthold Georg Niebuhr's works, including one of his first, a German translation of Demosthenes's *First Philippic* (1805).[10] Niebuhr dedicated the book to Tsar Alexander I and in it the anti-Macedonian inspiration and the anti-Napoleonic symbolism are clear and clearly expressed. The public lectures Niebuhr delivered at the University of Bonn in 1825–1826 and in 1829–1830 also speak volumes. Referring to the "unfortunate Darius," Niebuhr took issue with what he called "the general opinion" and pronounced a very critical judgment:

> In his private station, Darius had acquired a great reputation in the Persian army . . . and the general opinion in history is favourable to him.

But I cannot see that he did anything to justify that reputation: he did
not know how to use the resources of his immense empire against Alexander. In the battle of Arbela, he is said to have been brave; but this is a
very insignificant quality, which he shared with thousands of others, and
the absence of which is only a disgrace. A fallen prince always leaves behind him a feeling of sympathy, and this is increased in the present case
by the fact that Darius was a man of a humane disposition. Not a single
act of cruelty is recorded of him, though cruelty is generally found even
in the best Oriental rulers, who rarely regarded men as anything more
than mere insects. He must have been a man of gentle, mild, and humane
disposition. . . . Had Darius come to the throne in consequence of great
personal qualities, had he descended from his palace to the provinces to
see the state of things with his own eyes, had he entrusted Memnon, in
whom he had confidence, the unlimited command, and had Memnon
been able to maintain himself against the personal jealousies of the satraps, Alexander would have been lost to a certainty. (1852, 2:377 and 431)

During the same period, the many British historians who published books
on Greek history regularly discussed Alexander from a vantage point very different from that of Droysen, sometimes in explicit opposition to him. In 1786
John Gillies remarked that the conduct of the last representative of the dynasty
clearly proved that he was "neither brave nor prudent." On the basis of the obituary written by Arrian, Gillies adds that the king can be credited only with the
absence of any act of cruelty (*History of Ancient Greece*, 2:623–624).

In 1818 W. Mitford deemed that, at Darius's accession, "the court and the
central provinces . . . remained evidently in a trouble state" (1835, 7:211). He argued that, though Arrian's systematic bias against Darius can be condemned,
all in all Arrian's judgment of Darius's military incompetence is altogether
merited (7:211). Connop Thirlwall, overtly disputing Droysen's position, recalls
that at his accession Darius was "a popular and honoured prince," because "he
had acquired some reputation for personal courage, chiefly through an exploit
which he had performed in one of the expeditions against the Cadusians." And,
in having the eunuch Bagoas killed, he "had freed the throne from a degrading
subjection, and was thought well-qualified to defend it." But soon events proved
that such was not the case at all. "His pusillanimity on this occasion [the Battle
of Issus] seems to belie the reputation which he had acquired for personal courage" (*A History of Greece*, 6 [1845]:189–190). Hence this judgment, which already
constituted a historiographical refrain: "One of the many kings who would have

been happier and more honoured if they had never mounted the throne. Yet if he had reigned in peaceful times he would probably have been esteemed at least as well able to fill it as most of his predecessors" (p. 297).

The most determined of Droysen's adversaries was another very talented British historian, George Grote. Like B. G. Niebuhr, whose writings he admired, Grote criticized the figure of Alexander and called into doubt his project of Hellenization, which Droysen had elaborated and lauded in his book. Grote maintained that, "instead of hellenizing Asia," the Macedonian "was tending to Asiatize Macedonia and Hellas" (*A History of Greece,* 12 [1856]: 359).[11] His judgment of Darius also differed greatly from Droysen's. Called "a prince born under an unlucky star," Darius is judged harshly: his culpable inaction at the start of the war but also his "personal cowardice," "timidity," and "incompetence," made the Persian defeats inevitable (12 [1856]: 170–172, 226–228). It is therefore understandable why the nobles sought to depose him: What else could they do?

Also believing that Arrian was the most reliable of guides, Grote, taking him as a model, wrote an overall assessment of Darius's activities and of his reign as they appeared just after his death. He forcefully disputed the romantic image that had long dominated one vein of historiography, with its emotional, even tearful accounts of the conditions under which the Great King had died:

> The last days of this unfortunate prince have been described with almost tragic pathos by historians, and there are few subjects in history better calculated to excite such a feeling, if we regard simply the magnitude of his fall, from the highest pitch of power and splendour to defeat, degradation, and assassination. But an impartial review will not allow us to forget that the main cause of such ruin was his own blindness; his long apathy after the battle of Issus, and abandonment of Tyre and Gaza, in the fond hope of repurchasing queens whom he had himself exposed to captivity; lastly, what is still less pardonable, his personal cowardice in both the two decisive battles brought about by himself. If we follow his conduct throughout the struggle, we shall find little of that which renders a defeated prince either respectable or interesting. (12 [1856]: 252–353)

In the field of "Persian history," several authors—with widely varying levels of professional competence—also pronounced very negative judgments of the Great King. In 1869 Joseph-Arthur de Gobineau published his *Histoire des Perses (History of the Persians).* A steadfast proponent of the thesis of the empire's moral decay, he preferred to base himself on the Persian and Arabo-Persian authors, including Abū Tāher Tarsusi's *Dārab-nāmeh.* But he also quoted a text from the Sassanid period, the *Letter of Tansar*. It was from the Iranian writings that he forged his vision of the last Persian king, whose harshness alienated his subjects and greatly facilitated the Macedonian's conquest. Gobineau's method, long adopted, had already been vigorously challenged by those historians of ancient Greece and of Alexander who sought to base themselves exclusively on the classical sources.[12] Such was the case for the baron de Sainte Croix who, after a review of the Oriental authors (1804, pp. 167–192), unceremoniously concluded: "I have said enough to show and to allow readers to assess how the Arabs and Persians represented in writing, or rather, how they misrepresented, the known actions of Alexander. The true story is found only in the accounts of the Greek and Latin writers, who will be the object of my discussion" (p. 192). J. Gillies maintains that, given the "futility of the Oriental traditions," Arrian must be preferred at every turn (1786, p. 624n56). Similarly skeptical declarations appear in Mitford (8 [1835]: 18) and in Thirlwall (6 [1845]: 142n1). Ernest Renan, in a review of Gobineau's book published in the *Journal Asiatique,* was very harsh regarding the use that author had made of the "Oriental" sources.[13]

The problem is that, whether seen through the Arabo-Persian sources or through the Greco-Roman authors, especially Arrian, the memory of Darius bears the same negative charge. Consider the other portrait of Darius in Gobineau, who, while expressing doubts about the credibility of the Greco-Roman sources (*Histoire des Perses,* 2:404), also makes good use of them. During the first review of the troops, "the king and his courtiers were swept up in national vanity. . . . Darius remained so entranced by his powerful army that he resolved to command it in person and to hand Alexander certain defeat" (p. 37). Soon, however, "he leapt onto a horse, cast aside his bow, his shield, and his mantle, and escaped, not taking time to give an order or to say anything to anyone, thus showing what a prince in decline can be" (p. 380). Similarly, at Gaugamela, "Darius, losing his head, suddenly took off" (p. 389). He sought refuge in Ecbatana, "making no effort, trembling at the future, powerless to fend off events, no doubt hoping for unknown eventualities, and waiting" (pp. 393–394).

As a scholar, T. Nöldeke, nicknamed "the Nestor of Orientalism," was of a completely different caliber. He forcefully took issue with those who wanted to paint a favorable, or at least indulgent, portrait of Darius, and he did so in vigorous terms that obviously owe a great deal to his reading of Grote:

> Misfortune has shed a romantic light on the last prince of the entire empire, but an objective analysis may simply reveal him to be one of those

incompetent despots as the Orient had so often produced. It may be true that he had demonstrated personal courage in the past during the war Artaxerxes III waged against the Cadusians, and that he was rewarded for that heroic deed with the satrapy of Armenia, but as a king he always proved cowardly in the face of danger. Great fervor and dishonorable escapes, a soft—or rather, a sluggish—nature combined with a boastful pride, a lack of clear-sightedness, particularly in the conduct of war: these are the traits that fully justify the comparison Grote makes between him and Xerxes. No one can criticize him for not measuring up to the man who may have been the greatest general of all time, but Ochus [Artaxerxes III] would no doubt have considerably complicated Alexander's task and would have not committed the folly of ordering, in a fit of pique, the decapitation of a man as useful as the old mercenary captain Charidemus, who on the whole understood very well how to wage war against the Macedonians. (1887, p. 81)

As for the works on Alexander, many adopted a very hostile point of view toward the Great King. Such is the case for Helmut Berve's "Dareios," an entry in *Das Alexanderreich auf prosopographischer Grundlage* that in fact constitutes the first "biography" of Darius (1926, p. 129, no. 244). And H. Fuhrmann, in the name of Arrian's superiority over Cleitarchus (the postulated source of Justin and Diodorus for these passages), decides to reject as "fictionalized" the accounts of the Cadusian feat by the future Darius III. He prefers the very negative portrait bequeathed by Arrian and offers a very critical interpretation of the Persian monarch's ignoble attitude in battle, as represented on the Naples Mosaic (*Philoxenos von Eretria* [1931], pp. 143–144 and 323n85). The famous mosaic, discovered in 1831, had already given rise to a flood of publications, with much disagreement among authors on the interpretation to be given to Darius III's conduct.

One of the most influential works was W. W. Tarn's *Alexander the Great*, published in Cambridge in 1948. Dedicated wholly to the glory of the Macedonian hero, it sheds only brief light on Darius III. The final word on the king is very critical: "Darius 'great and good' is a fiction of legend. He may have possessed the domestic virtues; otherwise, he was a poor type of despot, cowardly and inefficient" (1:58).

Later, Tarn disputes the credibility of the sources (Curtius and Diodorus) on the basis of which a more sympathetic portrait of the king could be conceived (2:72).

The idea that Darius was at best a good father had already been developed by Georges Radet in his *Alexandre le Grand* (1931) and in several earlier articles devoted to the negotiations between the two kings. Radet attempts to reconstitute the torments that assailed the Great King after the capture of his immediate family following his defeat at Issus, and which led him to begin negotiations with Alexander. The author argues that Darius's reaction, in the face of an Alexander driven by an insatiable ambition, was consistent with postulated "Oriental" norms. Rather than confront the enemy, he preferred to bargain:

> Were we to imagine the Achaemenid monarch irremediably overcome by his setbacks and resigning himself to bow to the enemy whatever the cost, we would be judging matters with ideas alien to the Iranian world. The motives that impelled him to try his method [to obtain the freedom of the princesses captured after Issus] did not stem solely from political or military necessities; they were also and perhaps to a greater degree familial in nature. . . . His chief subject of anxiety was the fate of his loved ones. In Darius, the virtues of the private man greatly prevailed over the qualities of the head of state. . . . He felt an intimate anguish, more difficult to bear than that of public misfortunes. The worst disgrace for an Oriental sovereign is to lose his harem. Hence that initiative, in which emotional obsession and passionate jealousy played as great a role as reason of state, if not, indeed, a greater one. (pp. 74–75)

In general, Radet resolutely positions himself in the tradition of Darius III's detractors. This is clear in the scathing portrait he draws of the king shortly before his death at the hands of conspirators from his own camp:

> Darius was by no means capable of warding off such a crisis. Endowed with moral decency, he lacked talent and character. In his youth, he had displayed a remarkable vigor, so that, when his talents brought him glory, he appeared to be the one most worthy of the scepter. But he succumbed to the infirmities of age, and his physical bravery faltered. In that diminished fifty-year-old, willpower was weakening. Could he reflect without shame that he, the former hero of the Cadusian saga, had twice deserted the battlefield and abandoned his loves ones to the enemy? So many disasters befell him. Officially, he remained the Great King. In reality, he was now an autocrat in name only, and his lack of intelligence, his senile cowardice, his bending to the winds of defeat stripped him of the prestige attached to his title. (p. 202)

Radet, motivated by an almost compulsive desire to prefer multiple charges against Darius and caught up in the thrall of his own writing, is the only one ever to have advanced the argument of senility! It may have been after reading Radet that the novelist K. Mann drew a rather surprising portrait of the Great King, that of a weak, ugly man, sapped of energy and worn down before his time:

> Darius had a melancholy idyllic disposition, but however, when it mattered, was not squeamish or sentimental. . . . He consoled himself with flowers and educated conversations. . . . He was attached to and very much in awe of his mother Sisygambis, an energetic old woman, who for her part somewhat despised him; and he was also attached with chivalrous tenderness to his pretty and melancholy young wife, who had given him two daughters. . . . The Great King was not a majestic figure, somewhat stocky and almost small, with too huge a head, which he held at an angle when thinking; also he had thoughtful yet empty eyes of a beautiful brown. . . . The mountain people called the Cadusians had become a nuisance to him. As his power of resistance was not very great, the forty-year-old already felt tired; . . . [Upon the death of Memnon,] he just continued to sit there and shook his head, with tears running down his big cheeks. (*Alexander, a Novel of Utopia*, pp. 52, 73)

Darius in the Royal Portrait Gallery

To better grasp whatever individuality Darius may have had, it is imperative to compare his portrait to the judgments given of his predecessors. George Rawlinson, a proponent of dynastic history, argued that the best approach to writing Persian history was to organize it into a gallery of royal portraits. That precept was faithfully followed by generations of historians. Droysen had already put it into practice, though he did not aspire to offer his readers a history of the Persian Empire.

In Droysen, the favorable portrait of Darius III is part of an overall vision, which tends to trace a continuous decline beginning with Darius I, and especially, with the first defeats to the Greeks under his successor, Xerxes: "After Darius, after the defeats of Salamis and Mycale, signs of stagnation and decadence began to come to light . . . At the end of Xerxes' reign, the weakening of despotic power and the influence of the court and harem were already visible. . . . [As a result], the satraps of the interior provinces . . . were further emboldened

to seek their own self-interest and endeavored to acquire independent and he-
reditary powers in their satrapies" (pp. 53–54).

The flaws in the system increased at a dizzying pace in the following century, under the long reign of Artaxerxes II, marked by the revolt of Cyrus the
Younger and especially by the accelerated decomposition of aulic mores: "The
history actually written by Greeks still gives us a sadder portrait of the weakness of old Artaxerxes within his court, where he was tossed back and forth like
a ball from his mother to his harem to his eunuchs" (p. 58). The portrait of Darius is favorable, but it stands as a counterpoint to the critical judgment of the
reign of Artaxerxes III. Granted, that king reconquered Egypt, which had been
independent for two generations: "The empire of the Persians was now as powerful as in its best days." But the hatred Artaxerxes inspired at the time threatened the empire's stability and even its survival over the medium term: "The
tradition depicts Ochus as a true Asiatic despot, bloody and cunning, robust and
pleasure-seeking, and all the more terrible in that the decisions he made were
calculated and cold-blooded. His character allowed him to reassemble the scattered fragments of the empire, which had been shaken to its foundations, and give
it an appearance of strength and youth. He could force rebel peoples and insolent
satraps into submission, accustom them to being silent spectators of his whims,
his bloody instincts, his insane sensual pleasures. . . . The king governed with
frenzied capriciousness and cruelty. Everyone feared and hated him" (pp. 59, 66).

From Droysen's viewpoint—that is, in terms of the internal coherence of
the empire in the face of the Macedonian offensive about to be undertaken—
Darius's accession represented progress: "No revolt troubled the beginning of
his reign. . . . Asia, united under the noble Darius from the Ionian coasts to the
Indus, seemed safer than it had been in a long time."

Nöldeke, a fervent admirer of the reign of Artaxerxes III and a ferocious
detractor of Darius III, has an opposing point of view: "Artaxerxes III was a
completely different sort [from Artaxerxes II, an effeminate king] . . . He is one
of those despots who are able to rebuild an Oriental empire that has been in
decadence for some time—despots who fearlessly spill blood and are not fussy
in the choice of methods, but who habitually contribute to the health of the
state. . . . He was the first king since Darius [I] to have conducted in person a
major victorious military expedition, and thus to have raised up the empire
once again" (1885, pp. 75, 80).

S. G. Benjamin's *Persia* (1888) situates the succession from Artaxerxes III to
Darius III and the reign of the last of the Achaemenids within the *longue durée* of

the dynasty that extends from Cyrus to Alexander. He sees both kings in an even darker light:

> Persia had arisen, as it were, from her ashes. The genius of Artaxerxes Ochus had renewed her splendor and power, and given the empire a new lease of life, which would have insured its continuance for ages if he had been succeeded, as was Cyrus the Great, by rulers of similar talents. But destiny had willed otherwise, and when Persia had to meet in the field one of the greatest generals in history, her fate was confided by Providence to one of the most incompetent sovereigns who ever sat on a throne. Darius Codomannus may not have committed as many crimes as some of his predecessors, but neither was he impelled by their energy and genius. He had the spirit of a coward, and a weakness amounting nearly to imbecility. . . . [After Gaugamela], another monarch or general, with the least spirit and with such forces operating in his own country, might easily have continued to offer resistance to Alexander and his moderate-sized army that might have at least brought them to ruin. But Darius was of the stuff of which they are made who throw away what their fathers have accumulated. The founders and the losers of great empires are cast in different moulds. (pp. 141, 146)

Nöldeke and Benjamin were not the only ones to exalt the memory of Artaxerxes III. Justi reluctantly acknowledges that, though of an "immoral" character, Artaxerxes was a great king: "His last years show a powerful rule and a fastidious administration; he was intelligent enough to leave a few remarkable and trusting men to perform the most important duties, which is not always the case in Oriental courts." He also grasped the Macedonian danger (1879, p. 139). For Olmstead, "bloodthirsty as Ochus [Artaxerxes III] had shown himself to be, he was an able ruler, and it is not too far wrong to say that, by his murder, Bagoas destroyed the Persian Empire." "The assassination of . . . Ochus changed the whole international situation" (1948, p. 489). Ghirshman paraphrases the analysis as follows: "Fate seemed to offer Persia one last chance for salvation, by bringing to the throne a man who was, to be sure, cruel and ferocious but who was endowed with an iron will and had the force of a statesman [Artaxerxes III] . . . The empire was reestablished in its integrity. It seemed to be stronger than it had ever been since Darius [I]. . . . [But] Artaxerxes III died of poison, and that murder struck not only him but also the Persian Empire, which would survive him by only a few years. . . . The assassination radically altered the global political chessboard, where a new force, Macedonia, came into play" (1951, pp. 197, 200).

Finally, A. Toynbee's *Some Problems of Greek History,* which the author presents as a *"jeu d'esprit"* but with a "serious purpose" (1969, p. vi), ponders the role of historical personalities.[14] Toynbee imagines the world as it might have been if three prominent personalities, who died in the space of fifteen or sixteen years, had gone on living. These were Philip and his son Alexander but also Artaxerxes III, whom Toynbee presents as infinitely more energetic than "the lackadaisical Artaxerxes II." In the author's speculative history, Artaxerxes III does not succeed in blocking the invasion of the empire conducted by Philip II in 333 and agrees to conclude a treaty that establishes the demarcation line at the Euphrates; the Macedonian king, meanwhile, gives him several elite corps that allow him to reestablish Achaemenid power over Central Asia. Thanks to the contraction of the empire, the king manages to cure the ills that had considerably weakened it after the defeats of Xerxes in Greece. He dies in 325 of natural causes, surrounded by universal esteem. What is interesting is that Toynbee chose Artaxerxes III to wage war against Philip in 333, as if he were the only one of the last Great Kings who could have played such a role. It obviously did not occur to Toynbee to imagine what might have happened "if Darius had lived on."

All in all, it is obvious that the revival under the reign of Artaxerxes, unanimously acknowledged even by those who denounce his bloody violence, conferred on that "restorer and maintainer of imperial power" a special place within the royal portrait gallery—a place that, implicitly or explicitly, devalues even more the place Darius occupies. Darius, whether or not he possessed the qualities befitting a king, was in fact crushed between two powerful personalities with indisputable imperial achievements. Granted, no one considers placing them on equal footing or even of hazarding the slightest comparison between Artaxerxes III and Alexander. Nevertheless, even when presented positively, Darius plays the role of foil, because he did not manage to preserve the imperial legacy of Artaxerxes III and had no luck in preventing Alexander from seizing it for his own advantage.

Therein lies the historiographical problem of Darius versus Alexander: as M. de Saint-Félix says, what can be done against "one of those geniuses who appear rarely, when the Eternal God wants to change the face of the world"? "Persia, attacked by such a hero and by such armies, could no longer avoid a change in masters" (Bossuet). "Unfortunately for him, a new power, led by the greatest soldier of all time, had arisen in the West" (Sykes), "since the West had never produced a phenomenon of that kind" (Schachermeyr). And so on. Even a critic as virulent as Nöldeke recognizes the extenuating circumstances: "No one can criticize him for not measuring up to the man who may have been the greatest general of all time." In contrast to the Macedonian hero, Darius— attributed by some with virtues and positive qualities—must be measured by the yardstick of ordinary men: "He would have been a fairly good ruler in ordinary times" (Rawlinson); "if he had not been obliged to test his mettle against Alexander, he would have made an excellent leader in other respects" (Justi); "one of the many kings who would have been happier and more honoured if they had never mounted the throne" (Thirlwall). And so on.

The Asiatic Despot

Although generally distinguished from Artaxerxes III, whom Droysen characterizes as "a true Asiatic despot, bloody and cunning, robust and pleasure-seeking," Darius possessed one of the foremost characteristics of the Great Kings: he too was an "Oriental," an "Asiatic." In Radet's words, that is what led him to prefer palaver to battle, because "diplomatic maneuvers were a realm in which the Orientals had always proven to be the masters," thanks to the "headstrong pliability of their fruitful duplicity." Tortured by "emotional obsession and passionate jealousy," Darius was led to negotiate because his own family was captured. Indeed, "the worst disgrace for an Oriental sovereign is to lose his harem." Was not Darius II, whom Rawlinson calls "weak and wicked," already under the deleterious influence of "Parysatis, his wife, one of the most cruel and malignant even of Oriental women"? But the "weakening of despotic power" actually dates back to the end of Xerxes's reign, when "the influence of the court and harem were already visible." Radet's Darius III is truly the heir to Droysen's Xerxes and Rawlinson's Darius II.

To explain the traditions and institutions of the Persians of antiquity, Richard de Bury had already established connections with the Persia of his time, whose essential aspects he knew primarily through the accounts of Tavernier's journey: "In comparing what the travelers of the last two centuries report about contemporary Persians to what the ancients wrote of their ancestors, it is clear that their character, but for a few slight differences, is the same as it was in the time of Cyrus and Alexander" (1760, pp. 224–225).

In the case at hand, the comparison emphasizes the continuity of the virtues recognized in the Persian people both by the Greek authors and by Bossuet and Tavernier. But generally the connections established with the "Orientals" will foist on the Persians of antiquity the particular "Orientalist" vision that developed in Europe from the nineteenth century onward.[15] Thus, Niebuhr makes systematic reference to modern Asian history to explain what the empire of Darius III may have been like. To understand Artaxerxes II's reign, he says, one need only "read the history of the Sufi kings and of the Mongol kings." The decadence of the reign greatly resembles that of Turkey in the late eighteenth century (1856, p. 362). "The king was not a tyrant; but since he was a typical example of an Oriental despot, his history is full of the greatest cruelties, which were committed in the normal course of events" (p. 360). The reign of Artaxerxes III experienced "the normal development of an Oriental state": the prince is pleasure-loving, afflicted with total indolence and hopeless incompetence; the position of the eunuch Bagoas is comparable to what was known about the Persian court in the late eighteenth century. Here, in conclusion, is Niebuhr's explanation for Alexander's victories over Darius's armies: "Battles against barbarians are very different from those waged against civilized nations. . . . The battles against the Persians and other Oriental peoples all have the same character and are, in a certain measure, contemptible. . . . The Battle of Gaugamela was easy; it was a victory over Asian cowardice and barbarian disorder . . . because of the superiority of the Europeans over the Asians: that was always the case, except during the time of the caliphs and the Turkish conquest, when the Europeans had themselves become half Asian" (1856, pp. 423, 439, 445).

A proponent of extremely suspect theories about Alexander's policy toward the Iranians, Berve advances practically identical parallels and formulations. To explain what he considers Darius's grave shortcomings in battle, Berve argues that "only a comparison with the nature of the Oriental sultans" makes it possible to assess Darius's inadequacies. He gives two other examples of such "sultans," taken from antiquity, Tigranes of Armenia and "to a certain extent, Antiochus III, since the Orientals were incapable of displaying that lucid energy known only to Westerners." "From that standpoint in particular, Darius, when compared to Alexander, was the representative of a different world, which the Macedonians violently shattered but which had gradually fallen into decay on its own" ("Dareios" [1926], p. 129).

Whenever the authors evoke "Persian decadence," they repeatedly make comparisons to the sultans. Speaking of the sumptuousness of court life in the age of Xerxes, Justi writes that "the shah's daily life in antiquity was identical to that of today." He sees a striking illustration of that Oriental consistency in the existence of a harem and in the political role played by women: "Women have had a much more important role in the history of the world than is usually believed, and the house of women of the last Achaemenids was not simply the scene of love affairs and bloody quarrels; it was also the point of origin of political actions and of many crimes" (1879, pp. 125–126). And he writes of "harem life" under Xerxes: "Such is the usual evolution of Oriental empires" (p. 123).

It is therefore easy to understand why, for Nöldeke, Darius is nothing but "one of those incompetent despots as the Orient had so often produced." Following Grote, he compares the last Achaemenid king to Xerxes, who, he writes, "conducted himself in wartime as the very model of the Oriental despot." Rawlinson's description of Xerxes is even more apocalyptic: "Weak and easily led, puerile in his gusts of passion and his complete abandonment of himself to them—selfish, fickle, boastful, cruel, superstitious, licentious—he exhibits to us the Oriental despot in the most contemptible of all his aspects. From Xerxes we have to date at once the decline of the Empire in respect of territorial greatness and military strength, and likewise its deterioration in regard to administrative vigor and national spirit. With him commenced the corruption of the Court—the fatal evil, which almost universally weakens and destroys Oriental dynasties" (1871, pp. 470–471).

Droysen writes that Darius was "handsome and grave," only to immediately add a precision that relativizes his admiration: "as the Asiatic readily imagines his sovereign." In Schachermeyr's eyes, by contrast, the comment serves as a compliment. It is true that, just as Gobineau denounces the deleterious influence of the Greeks, "a race over which reason and beneficence have never held sway" (2:131), and regrets that under Artaxerxes II "the Iranian race was now the dominant race in name only" (2:300), Schachermeyr, a proponent of "Aryan purity," is violently opposed to "Levantine" intermixing, which for him signifies "degeneration." That explains his proclaimed admiration for a Darius entirely reconstructed by his racist obsessions: "He has nothing to do with any of those Westernized and Hellenized Persians. It is in no way astonishing that, as a ruler, he remained an Iranian knight above all and added as well the self-importance of an Oriental pasha. Fundamentally Oriental as Darius was, it is surprising to note how quickly he endeavored to adapt to the conditions of a Western policy that increasingly occupied center stage" (p. 131).

These "Westernized and Hellenized Persians" immediately bring to mind Rawlinson's ostensibly favorable portrait of Cyrus the Younger: "Cyrus, though he had considerable merits, was not without great and grievous defects. As the

Tartar is said always to underlie the Russ, so the true Oriental underlay that coating of Grecian manners and modes of thought and act. . . . Again, intellectually, Cyrus is only great *for an Asiatic*" (pp. 495–496, emphasis in the original).

The reference to the Tartars clearly shows that the term "Oriental" is a category that transcends the centuries. Radet does not fail to place Darius and his taste for complicated negotiation within a very long series: "So many unexpected acts of revenge, from the age of Tissaphernes to our own, procured [for the Orientals] the headstrong pliability of their fruitful duplicity" (p. 74). And when he sententiously claims that "the worst disgrace for an Oriental sovereign is to lose his harem," it is clear that Darius is being included within a broad category of kings and sultans or, as Droysen says several times, of "Asiatic despots." Here again is one of the postulates of "Orientalism," as formulated by James Darmesteter in *Coup d'oeil sur l'histoire de la Perse (A Brief Glance at the History of Persia)*, his inaugural lecture at the Collège de France in 1885. Darmesteter embraces the entire history of Persia, from the Achaemenids to the Sassanids: "Despotism is the tradition in Persia." That is also the sole, paltry conclusion to be found a century later in John Manuel Cook's *Persian Empire* (1983), based on a comparison between, on one hand, the tent camps of Xerxes and Darius III and, on the other, the Persian court as the Venetian ambassador Pietro della Valle described it in the seventeenth century: "Despotisms come and go, but there is a stability as old as the Achaemenids underlying the continuity in Persian history" (p. 231).

Stagnation, Decadence, and Development

When Darius III is situated within the very *longue durée* of "Asiatic despots," it becomes clear that, beyond the judgments of his character and of his abilities as a statesman and general, he is being viewed in the first place in terms of a hegemonic theory considered strictly indisputable: that of the uninterrupted decay of the Achaemenid Empire, itself considered a particular example of a phenomenon judged ineluctable, namely, the stagnation inscribed within the heart of any despotic government. From that standpoint, Darius can be located at a key moment in that process. And all the authors agree on the nature of the process, though they may differ from time to time on the capacity Darius III may have had to remedy it.

Within the tradition of the theory of the five empires, which dates to antiquity, Bossuet had already pondered not only "the rise and fall of empires but

also the causes of their advancement and of their decay." What better set of examples could Bossuet have placed before his illustrious pupil's eyes? For indeed,
"where can one receive a finer lesson in the vanity of human glories"?

As Bossuet ends chapter 4 (on the irresistible rise of Macedonia under Philip
II's leadership) and is about to begin chapter 5, "The Persians, the Greeks, and
Alexander," he anticipates his conclusion about the fall of the Persian monarchy: "But to understand its downfall, we must simply compare the Persians and
Cyrus's successors to the Greeks and their generals, especially Alexander." After the conquests of Cyrus the Great, the Persian Empire experienced the same
evolution as all Oriental empires, but at lightning speed. Referring implicitly
but transparently to the famous opposition Plato develops in his *Laws* (3.693c–
698a), between the sons of kings (such as Cambyses and Xerxes) reared by women
and palace eunuchs, and kings born of private individuals and raised under harsh
conditions (Cyrus and Darius I), Bossuet argues that "Cambyses, son of Cyrus,
was the one who corrupted mores." Within the *longue durée* of historiography,
Heeren is really the only one since Plato to have drawn conclusions favorable
to Darius III: "Not having been educated, like his predecessors, in the seraglio,
Darius gave proof of virtues which entitled him to a better fate" (1854, p. 88).
Bossuet, conversely, adopts "the most plausible opinion," which is that Darius
was actually descended from the royal family.

Despite the short restoration period that occurred under Darius I, the harm
was done: "Everything degenerated under his successors, and the luxury of the
Persians knew no bounds." The judgment Bossuet attributes to their eternal
enemies is therefore understandable: "When Greece, thus elevated, looked at
the Asians with their delicacy, their finery, and their beauty, similar to that of
women, it felt nothing but contempt." Consider the lesson, followed by generations of historians, that Bossuet drew from the venture of the Ten Thousand:
"In the universal collapse" of Cyrus the Younger's army, they alone "could not be
broken."

In the same vein, Rollin theorizes that the reasons for the defeat must not
be sought solely in Darius's personal flaws. He puts much greater emphasis on
the idea of the Persian Empire's decadence, to which he devotes several discussions. First, in considering the death of Cyrus, he expatiates on the "causes of the
decadence of the Persians' empire and of the changes that occurred in their mores" (1:566–578). He returns to the question at the end of the reign of Artaxerxes
II, wondering about "the causes of the uprising and revolts that occurred so
frequently in the empire of the Persians" (3:481–485). Rollin goes on to discuss

Darius's death, at which point he explains his views of "the vices that caused the decadence, and finally, the ruin of the empire of the Persians" (4:144–148). His argument begins with the following consideration: "The death of Darius Codomannus can be regarded as the moment, but not the sole cause, of the destruction of the Persian monarchy." Placing Darius within the continuity of the dynasty, Rollin maintains that it "is easy to recognize that that decadence had been under way for a long time and that it proceeded to its end by degrees, in anticipation of total ruin." The statement is categorical:

> So many causes of weakness, gathered together and publically sanctioned, destroyed the ancient virtue of the Persians within a short time. Unlike the Romans, they did not succumb by means of an imperceptible decline, long anticipated and often combated. Cyrus was barely in his grave when a different nation and kings of an altogether different sort appeared. . . . It can be said that the empire of the Persians, almost from its birth, was what other empires became only as the years passed, and that it began where the others left off. It bore within its bosom the principle of its destruction, and that internal vice only grew from one reign to the next. . . . The [princes] abandoned the ambition of conquest and indulged in idleness, softness, and indolence. They neglected military discipline. . . . [The empire therefore had] weak or depraved princes, [driven] by laziness and the love of pleasure, softened by the charms of a voluptuous life. (4:144–148)

Rollin is one of many authors to use the image of a giant deprived of real strength: "The dazzling splendor of the monarchy of the Persians concealed a real weakness. That enormous power, accompanied by so much pomp and haughtiness, had no other purchase on the people's hearts. The first blow struck to that colossus toppled it." The famous expression "giant with feet of clay" is not far off. One explanatory principle later developed by Droysen, then by Maspéro and many others, can be traced back to Rollin, namely, that the incapacity of the Persian Empire to survive lay in the end of conquest: the princes "abandoned the ambition of conquest."

In 1839 M. de Saint-Félix also argued that the collapse of the empire could not be attributed solely to "the influence of Alexander's genius. It must have had internal causes of destruction." The author goes on to enumerate them: the excessive power of the satraps, "the weakening of the royal house, its decimation by Ochus, its abasement under Bagoas," but also "the most monstrous unions."[16]

"That appalling breach, bringing with it disorder in the family, became a fertile source of corruption and no doubt contributed mightily to the abasement of that sovereign people of Asia." All things considered, he argues, "if Persia had not been subjugated by Alexander, it would have split up into several states, a revolution that was merely delayed by the conquest" (pp. 443–445).

In the first pages of his book, Droysen raises the question that provides the rationale for the first chapter (p. 3): "How is it that the empire of the Persians, the one that had conquered so many kingdoms and so many countries, the one that had been able to rule them for two centuries . . . collapsed under the first blow from the Macedonians?" After a digression on the evolution of Greece and Macedonia, he answers the question: Alexander was destined to do in the East what his father had begun to do in Europe. Hence the connection Droysen makes between his discussion of Greece and his remarks on the Persian Empire, which are utterly unambiguous and harsh. "Just as, in Europe, everything was in place for a definitive resolution, in Asia the vast empire of the Persians had reached the point where it had exhausted the elements of power that had been the source of its success; it now seemed to be sustaining itself only through the inertia of a fait accompli" (p. 48). Using the technique of fictive indirect discourse, he attributes the diagnosis to Darius himself: "He seemed to have a presentiment that his colossal empire, torn apart from within and languishing, needed only an external jolt to be broken apart." That formulation, introduced by Rollin, then taken up and adapted by successive generations, was long in vogue. In 1869 Gobineau characterized the empire at the time of Darius II's accession as "an enormous mass sustained only by its own weight" (2:352).

That evolution had begun much earlier, but according to Droysen it accelerated with the transition from Darius to Xerxes, especially after the defeats to the Greeks: "Signs of stagnation and decadence began to come to light. That empire, incapable of internal development, would succumb as soon as it ceased to grow by its victories and conquests." Stagnation was inherent in the system: decadence set in as soon as the structural stagnation was no longer masked by the felicitous consequences of the conquests—that is, by the influx of booty, tributes, and gifts. The model that Droysen develops is that of an empire that lives solely on war and conquest: because it has no endogenous development, it has to go to war to find the wealth it is not producing. Consequently, once the empire loses territory as a result of defeat, it necessarily succumbs to stagnation and decadence.

As Rollin had already seen, such a view lightens the burden of Darius's responsibility. His was an "an innocent head . . . to expiate what could no longer be healed" (Droysen, p. 67); "Darius had to expiate the crimes of his predecessors" (Weber 1883, p. 238). The fall of the empire was thus attributable less to the king's personality than to historical developments stemming from a kind of "despotic fatality." In a last section, which bears the programmatic title "The End of the Old Eastern World," Maspéro develops the idea that Darius's reign marked the final stage of the decomposition process, namely, death:

> With Assyria dead, the Iranians had collected its inheritance and had built an empire unique among all the states that had preceded them on Asian territory. But decadence had come at lightning speed for them, and, having been the master for under two centuries, they seemed already to be slipping into extreme decline. . . . From the first Darius to the last, the history of the Achaemenids was an almost uninterrupted series of internal wars against provinces in revolt. Greeks of Ionia, Egyptians, Chaldeans, Syrians, and tribes of Asia Minor rose up one after another. . . . They depleted Persia by this game, but Persia ultimately used up what had remained vital in each of them: when Macedonia came on the scene, subjects and masters both were in such a state of prostration that their imminent end was predictable. (pp. 813–814)

Maspéro also puts to use Droysen's theory, already introduced by Rollin, on the link between the end of conquest and imperial decadence: "Oriental empires stay alive only on the condition that they are always on the alert and always victorious. They cannot confine themselves within defined borders or restrict themselves to the defensive. Rather, from the day they suspend their movement of expansion, their inevitable ruin begins: they are conquerors or they are nothing" (p. 726).

According to Maspéro, the quality of the sovereign may make the difference: "And that activity, which . . . saves them from decline, like the conduct of affairs, belongs to the sovereign alone, when he is [not] too indolent or too inept to lead." Such was not the case for Xerxes: "With the hostilities shifting from place to place, Greece's maneuvers led to the dismemberment of the empire. So what did Xerxes do? He consumed in languor and debauchery the little energy and intelligence he had originally possessed. . . . The king's incompetence and the sluggishness of the government were soon so clearly on display that the court itself was disturbed by it." The same was true for his successors, each less fit than the one before him to bear the responsibilities of kingship. Even the blood lust of Artaxerxes III was powerless to change anything: "The empire had to be reconquered, then established again piece by piece, if it was to exert in the world the influence that was its right by virtue of its enormity. But would the elements it contained lend themselves to being reorganized and refurbished in a lasting manner?" The answer, clearly contained within the question, is the same for all the authors: "The empire Alexander would attack had long been close to ruin" (Duruy 1919, p. 300). Another author, expressing the same view, makes it a point of pride to discuss Persian history on the basis of the royal inscriptions (Ahl 1922, pp. 93ff.).

That type of declaration about "Oriental empires" long enjoyed great popularity among historians. In a delusional passage on "Persian decadence," F. Altheim, assuming a disarming authority intended to confer a form of empirical verification by the grace of a peremptory judgment, has no hesitation in writing: "In Asia, greatness rarely survived two generations, and the Achaemenids were no exception to that rule" (p. 77). Within that context the author wishes to give major importance to what he arbitrarily postulates to have been the promotion of Babylon as capital of the Achaemenid Empire.[17] He believes that the city itself oozed decadence and communicated it to the conquerors: "What made for the renown of the big city were the pleasures and temptations it offered, its immorality and its feasts. The very name of Babylon evoked the delights of sexuality and decadence, a beauty whose charm came only from its morbid quality. Highly refined forms of pleasure developed in a swampy climate where everything bloomed more quickly but also withered faster. The city resembled a hetaera greedy for young people in whom to take her pleasure and whom she would drag with her to ruin" (*Alexandre et l'Asie* [1954], pp. 76–77).

One can only be struck once again by the extraordinary recurrence of certain turns of phrase and representations. Two centuries earlier, Rollin had given exactly the same explanation, within an already canonical argument about the "decadence of the Persian monarchy": "The conquered Babylon inebriated its conquerors with its poisoned cup and enchanted them with the charms of its voluptuousness. It provided them with the ministers and instruments fit to promote luxury and to sustain pleasure with art and delicacy" (4:144).

Not surprisingly, then, the conclusion Altheim reaches also belongs to the *longue durée*: "The crowning of Darius III Codomannus seemed to presage the arrival of better days. But the hour of death had already sounded" (p. 78).

Colonial Alexander and the Colonized Orient

The simplicity and flexibility of this model explain its success. It was possible to preserve the architecture and meaning of the model, adapt it to new needs, and at the same time add new embellishments. To return to Maspéro's judgment of the decadence of the Achaemenid Empire: its corollary is the affirmation of the necessity of foreign intervention. "The old Oriental world was in its death throes: before it died on its own, Alexander's luck and audacity summoned Greece to claim its inheritance." Maspéro's declaration is directly indebted to Droysen, who in turn bases himself on Plutarch's *De fortuna Alexandri*. Droysen interprets this minor work of Plutarch's in terms of his own vision, largely inspired by Hegel, of the "fecund" encounter between Europe and Asia. Among Droysen's illustrations are the decisions that, he claims, the Macedonian king made to spur production and trade. In view of these decisions, Droysen suggests the following general assessment: "That suffices to indicate the importance of Alexander's successes from an economic standpoint. In that respect, the influence of one man may have never produced since that time so sudden and so profound a transformation over such an enormous expanse of territory. . . . [This was truly] a transformation . . . desired and pursued with full cognizance of the goal" (pp. 690–691).

Praise of Alexander's construction projects casts into even sharper relief the image of Achaemenid stagnation. The measures taken by Alexander had the effect of "awakening the populations of Asia from their torpor," thanks, for example, to "the restoration of the Babylonian canal system."

A related idea can be found among other historians of Alexander, with reference to the works projects conducted on the Tigris. Following Droysen, Wilcken (1931) and Altheim (1953, p. 143) develop two ideas that had already been introduced by Hogarth in 1897 (p. 191). The first idea is that Alexander was a great economist, the second that he proved it by developing irrigation farming in Babylonia: "He had removed the defenses that the Persians had set up in the bed of the [Tigris] to prevent sea attacks. . . . The Persians, having no fleet, had built barriers to protect themselves from an attack coming from the sea; these barriers fell." It is easy to find the origin of that thesis in certain passages from Arrian and Strabo, which were taken at face value. In fact, however, these passages are devoted entirely to exalting the Macedonian king. By 1850, however, F. R. Chesney had placed the defensive nature of the construction projects in doubt: "The destruction of these walls may have been favorable for navigation but detrimental in other respects, particularly since they lowered the country's production rate, to whose growth the Assyrians had dedicated so much successful effort." In 1888 Delattre also advanced commonsense arguments: "It seems incredible that, as Arrian and Strabo claim, the Persians ever feared the invasion of their empire by fleets coming from the Persian Gulf and up the rivers. Where would they have left from? Why, according to that hypothesis, place sea walls so far from the sea?" But it was no use: these comments were not read or adopted, and the same story continued to be endlessly repeated. No one returned to the texts and contexts. The reason for such lasting blindness is simple: what Droysen had baptized "Alexander's economic successes" had become an integral and constitutive part of the canonical presentation of the conqueror, a "colonial hero" in every European country.[18]

Droysen, himself very involved in the political battles of his time, was eager to establish a link between his research and contemporary concerns, because in his view "the events of the Hellenistic period do more than simply [offer] fodder for the laborious leisure of scholarship." In bluntly denouncing "the appalling monstrosities attributable to the systems of colonization at which the Christian nations of Europe have tried their hand for the last three centuries," he proposed that "the truly grandiose system of Hellenistic colonization" be seen as a possible model for the generous colonization he desired (3:774–777). It is therefore not at all surprising that, against their author's intentions, Droysen's interpretations were so easily enlisted by the recruiting officers of colonial ideology. In France that ideology developed greatly after the defeat of 1870: the idea of colonialism had to be imposed on the public, which was for the most against it. An analysis of the textbooks and mainstream publications for the period 1850–1950 yields utterly clear results. Even as the analysis, explicit or implicit, of Darius's empire remained extremely negative, the image of Alexander that had been in force since the seventeenth and eighteenth centuries rapidly changed. Granted, textbook authors continued to deplore the changes in the conqueror's attitude: "The magnanimous and generous Alexander might have served as an example had not vice corrupted him. . . . That prince . . . abandoned himself entirely to money, anger, luxury, intemperance, and debauchery. . . . He attacked, with no right at all, the Scythians and the Indians."[19] And so on. But in 1890–1900, these moral judgments began to be set aside in favor of an exaltation of Alexander's achievement as a reformer of the East.

Theorists, publicists, historians, and geographers looked to the history of antiquity for the precedents that were supposed to prove that France too ought to embark on a colonial venture if it wanted to preserve its status as a great power. Because of the history of the countries that France conquered in North Africa, French authors tended to refer to the Roman precedent, preferring to develop the idea that French soldiers and colons came to restore agricultural prosperity, which had been created by Roman colonization but destroyed by the Arab invasion. But Alexander too was enlisted as a glorious precedent. To cite only one example: on the eve of World War I, a certain Major Raynaud set out to laud the continuity between Alexander's colonization policy and the protectorate system that France intended to impose on Morocco: "We shall ask the Macedonian hero for a lesson in colonization that, though more than two thousand years old, is nevertheless a matter of urgency for us, especially today. . . . Of all the European peoples, we alone are going to put [that example] into practice in Morocco."[20]

The historiographical consequences were heavy and long-lasting, both for the history of the empire and for the figure of Darius. The history of the last days of the Achaemenids was hijacked by historians who had disembarked with Alexander in countries they knew only through the classical authors, too often taken at face value, and through those who were still misleadingly called "the ancient historians of Alexander." Given Darius III's image as the defeated party, the last Achaemenid king had no chance of acquiring an autonomous life within the historiography of that period, particularly because many historians attributed the defeat to the cowardice of an "Asiatic despot" who had gorged himself on power and riches. Even the few moral and domestic qualities that others recognized in Darius did not increase his stature, because the portrait also implied that his positive qualities were largely inadequate to restore his own people's energy and to repel the assaults of the hero from Europe. The unanimously acknowledged excuses—his adversary's unheard-of valor, for example— led him to be mercilessly dismissed as an ordinary king, without greatness or genius.

Colonial historiography also cast Darius as a bad administrator who left the roads in a state of neglect, hoarded the yield of tributes instead of investing in commerce, and took no interest in maintaining the networks of rivers and canals that sustained Babylonia: in short, someone who kept his countries under an unjust subjection and in "Asian stagnation." Hence Duruy, following Droysen, presents the economic transformation of Asia as an indirect consequence of Alexander's conquests.[21] It is not difficult to read between the lines the negative image of Darius's kingdom: "Commerce, the bond between nations,

[was] extensively developed. Commerce saw before it the roads, whether new or pacified, that Alexander had opened to it, the ports, the construction sites, the places to seek refuge or to stop and rest that he had prepared for it. . . . Industry [was] excited by the enormous riches in the royal treasuries, previously inactive and sterile but now put into circulation by the conqueror's generous hand" (1889, p. 314).

Seen within a resolutely teleological perspective, only Alexander, the first victorious conqueror from Europe and a "soldier of civilization," was able to offer a historical solution for the countries in Darius's empire. That is the view A. T. Olmstead presented in 1948 in his famous book on the history of the Persian Empire. From his standpoint, excessive tax levies account for the disintegration of an empire whose history was for that reason punctuated by a growing number of revolts by the native peoples (p. 289). And, positioning himself near the start of Darius III's reign, he denounces the convoluted financial measures imposed by the Achaemenid military leaders on both subjects and mercenaries. He reaches an irrevocable conclusion that attributes in advance the role of the positive hero to Alexander, liberator of an empire crushed under Darius's despotism: "The Near East was being prepared to accept any invader who offered a firm and efficient administration" (p. 487). The thesis appeared so obvious that it was adopted by Reza Pahlavi, former shah of Iran, even though he was anxious to exalt the greatness of Iranian history: "Achaemenid decadence led to a unique phenomenon, Alexander of Macedon" (1979, p. 18).

Final Assessment and Perspectives: Return to the Sources

In the overall image of Darius as it is presented in the historiography of the last quarter century or so, the continuities greatly prevail over the innovations. For many authors—at least those who consider it useful to present the Persian Empire in a few words (which is still rare)—that empire had long since entered a spiral of hopeless decadence. Some continue to maintain that, as a consequence, the Macedonian conquest allowed the Near East to finally experience real economic and commercial development. Artaxerxes III is considered "the last great Achaemenid," or "the most aggressive and victorious monarch during the fourth century," and his reign is seen as an imperial revival before the final catastrophe. When the figure of Darius is introduced otherwise than by allusion—which is only rarely the case—the judgment of him remains mixed, even wavering and uncertain. Historians are fond of recalling that "he was handsome and tall and had accomplished a heroic feat against the Cadusians," but his reign is not necessarily judged more positively as a result. Some argue that "despite the very harsh judgment of posterity, he was not an opponent to be underestimated," while others maintain on the contrary that Alexander's victories can be explained first and foremost by "the mediocrity and incompetence of his adversary." Still others claim that, all things considered, "because of the lack of documentation, no judgment can be made on his abilities." There is also no hesitation, even in studies devoted specifically to the last Great King, in reverting to a platitudinous evaluation, well established since Bossuet, such as: Darius had many positive qualities, but he could do nothing against a man as extraordinary as Alexander.

Over the last quarter century, a historiographical movement to reassess Darius III has also been developing, however. Although the other version still has its proponents, it is now fairly common for historians to adopt the "positive" version. They tend to agree that neither at Issus nor at Gaugamela did the king behave like a stupid strategist or a cowardly soldier. Nevertheless, the monographs, few in number, have proposed neither new avenues of research nor new methods. The reassessment of Darius as a combatant is especially fragile and paradoxical: given the deplorable state of the documentation, any reconstitution of the battles between Alexander and Darius remains and will remain within the realm of contradictory hypotheses. The Battle of the Granicus is exemplary in that respect, because the two most detailed versions, by Arrian and by Diodorus, disagree in every particular. The problems persisting about the battles of Issus and Gaugamela remain so acute that it seems difficult to draw any clear conclusions about Darius's qualities as a warrior vis-à-vis Alexander, in the melee or away from it. The only conclusion that can currently be put forward with great probability is that Darius conducted a conscious strategy between Issus and Gaugamela, a strategy that allowed him to exert control and to draw Alexander to the place where he had decided to confront the Macedonian army. But once again, because of the contradictions in the sources, the precise role the Great King played during the battle is still a matter of dispute.

As for the rest, the fundamentals of the interpretive disagreements have remained almost unchanged. For generations, historians have continued tirelessly to gloss passages from the Greco-Roman texts that allow them both to highlight Darius's physical appearance and abilities as a warrior and to point out his incompetence and cowardice. The first image is derived from a paraphrase of a few passages from the Vulgate authors and from Plutarch, while the second was created primarily on the basis of Arrian's judgments, which are also found in other ancient authors. As demonstrated by the change in tone introduced into British historiography in the first half of the nineteenth century, the unfavorable portrait of Darius took hold whenever historians came to prefer Arrian over Justin, Diodorus, Curtius, and Plutarch. Since the Middle Ages and Renaissance, by contrast, the image of a handsome, courageous Great King pursued by an adverse destiny had spread through reference to Plutarch and the Vulgate authors. The revival of interest in the tradition of the Vulgate, clearly affirmed in recent times, has led historians to put more trust in the favorable portrait of Darius. Nevertheless, whenever military analysis is at issue, the tendency is still to display a certain preference for Arrian. As noted by his French translator, Nicolas Perrot d'Ablancourt (1646), who himself had a particular interest in all these problems, Arrian "is a man of war" who considers the "wars of a great commander."[22]

At the same time, it is a little troubling that the movement to reassess Darius is linked to a tendency, desirable in other respects, to promote the cultural decolonization of the history of Alexander, and that in recent studies it goes hand in hand with a very critical judgment of the consequences of the Macedonian conquests. That dual tendency poses a serious problem. The debate on a "civilizing" Alexander versus a "destructive" Alexander is nothing but the reprise or continuation of a polemic already explicitly elaborated within an entire current of traditional or Christian Roman literature. The reductiveness of the unchanging "moral" terms of the alternative thus set forth is hardly capable of accounting for the complexity of the historiographical issues. No persuasive case can be made that a devalorization of the person of Alexander and of his conquests automatically leads to a reassessment of his adversary, as if the terms of the comparison simply had to be redistributed. For just as the historian of Alexander must avoid overidentifying with the "Homeric hero," the historian of Darius is not merely an expert witness for the defense at a rehabilitation trial.

To escape that impasse, I cannot merely analyze the historiography of the modern and contemporary periods. I must go directly to the ancient sources to understand how the documentation on Darius III was constituted, especially during the Roman period. That will not entail a preliminary search—generally futile—for the primary sources that, having now disappeared, may have been used by the Greco-Roman authors. And in the absence of the minimal conditions required to carry out a true biographical investigation, my objective also cannot be to choose between a "positive" and a "negative" portrait. Even if the last of the Great Kings has been particularly mistreated in ancient and contemporary history, the primary goal of a book devoted to him cannot be to restore his image: it must rather be to understand why and how the image was constructed over the course of the centuries. It will therefore not suffice to refer endlessly to Justin and Diodorus, in order to assert that Darius was a courageous man (because before his accession to the throne he had won a duel against a Cadusian warrior), or to Plutarch, to conclude or postulate that Darius was handsome and imposing in stature. Nor is it enough to denounce Arrian's partiality vis-à-vis Darius and Alexander. Rather, I will seek to understand what literary models Arrian was working with when he composed his book, and, in general, what the assumptions and objectives of the ancient authors who wrote about Alexander were. To give only one example at this point, it is infinitely more important to understand around what images and mental structures the motif of single combat—a motif also found in the royal legend of Darius and Alexander— was built and disseminated.

After all, the questions that emerge from historiographical inquiry express everyday methodological preoccupations—the relationship that we historians maintain with our documents—which could almost be called banal if the inquiry and the responses were not so decisive. How, in the Roman period, did the authors who mentioned Darius while discussing Alexander proceed, and how can they be used today? If we are to have any chance of answering such a question, we will have to take into account a first reality and reiterate it tirelessly: the authors under study were not historians in the sense in which that term is now understood. They are not "our colleagues," as Nicole Loraux, speaking of Thucydides with talent and perspicacity, pointed out not long ago.[23] It will therefore not suffice, with respect to one episode or another, to conduct a contradictory critical analysis of the different versions, postulating that the sorting process will unfailingly separate the wheat from the chaff—for the simple reason that "wheat" and "chaff" together constitute the text. We must rather immerse ourselves in processes of literary creation and inquire into the genesis and circulation of the recurrent images.

II

CONTRASTING
PORTRAITS

❦ 3 ❧

"The Last Darius, the One Who Was Defeated by Alexander"

Lives as Examples, Examples of Lives

Although it is impossible to fix the birth of biography as a genre precisely in time and place, one can say that people in ancient times, even more than today, were fond of works dedicated to celebrating the actions and the memory of "great men": kings, captains, condottieri. Indeed, what is now called biography developed from the genre of the paean, first in Greece and then in Rome. Even when an author sought to propose examples of vices and failings, he still declared that he wanted to use "great men" and not men unknown to history.[1]

Many collections attest to this—for example, Plutarch's *Parallel Lives* (in which Alexander has his rightful place as Caesar's "parallel"), and Cornelius Nepos's *Book on the Great Generals of Foreign Nations*, itself part of a much more imposing opus called *De viris illustribus*, which is now almost completely lost. Granted, neither Plutarch nor Nepos wrote biographies in the sense in which the contemporary historian understands that term. In a discussion of the virtues and vices of Philip V of Macedon, the Hellenistic historian Polybius, without naming names, had already reproached "other writers" for dealing with "kings and famous men" without placing their remarks within a precise historical context. He then set out the method to be followed: "Unlike the other historians, we will never utter such judgments in preambles but will always present the suitable remarks about kings and famous men on the occasion of the events themselves, adapting these remarks to the situations, because we think that this way of sharing one's observations is most consistent with the interests of both the writers and the readers" (10.26.9).

Diodorus intends to take the same tack. At the beginning of book 17, devoted to Alexander, he announces: "But there is really no need to anticipate in the introduction any of the accomplishments of this king; his deeds reported one by one will attest sufficiently the greatness of his glory" (17.1.4).

Plutarch adopts the same distinction at the start of his *Life of Alexander* (1.1–3), but his approach is completely different from Polybius's. Addressing the reader, he sets out his program as follows: "If he finds any of [Alexander's and Caesar's] famous exploits recorded imperfectly, and with large excisions, [I beg him] not to regard this as a fault. I am writing biography, not history, and often a man's most brilliant actions prove nothing as to his true character." Histories, according to him, consist of reports of "battles" and "great deeds" in minute detail; the authors of Lives, by contrast, seek to delve into "those actions which reveal the workings of [the] heroes' minds . . . some trifling incident, some casual remark or jest, will throw more light upon what manner of man he was than the bloodiest battle, the greatest array of armies, or the most important siege."

The Latin author Cornelius Nepos develops the same point of view at the beginning of the chapter he devotes to the feats of the Theban Pelopidas: "If I recount them in detail, perhaps I shall seem to be writing less his life [*vita*] than the history of an age [*historia*]." An author, remarks Nepos, must therefore avoid two pitfalls: in the first genre, that of misinforming his readers for the purpose of entertaining them; in the second, that of boring his readers on the pretext of instructing them. The fear that the reader will turn away also explains why authors of Lives readily sacrificed accuracy to anecdote, and even outright fiction. In any event, neither Plutarch nor Nepos claimed to be acting as a historian. Ancient biography situated itself within a didactic perspective, which also explains its moralism.

It would have been inconceivable to produce such biographies without the repeated use of the famous examples *(paradeigmata, exempla)* that enlivened them and gave them significance. Plutarch scoffed at "lazy people . . . wishing to receive readymade food that others have taken the trouble to chew up for them."[2] But he himself wrote many works of that kind, which he intended for the emperors, who thereby would not waste too much time. Rather, they would be able to "contemplate in brief the image of so many heroes worthy of memory," as he puts it in the preface to his *Apothegms of Kings and Great Commanders,* addressed to Trajan.[3] In distinguishing the genre of "deeds and say-

ings" from that of Lives, Plutarch explains that these "memorable sayings make
it possible to truly understand characteristics and principles of conduct proper
to leaders," because, as he explains elsewhere, "the souls of . . . kings and po-
tentates betray their conditions and inclinations by their expressions."[4]

Collections of exempla, which began with a patient and tedious act of compilation but resulted in an easy-to-consult and entertaining presentation, were
supposed to instruct statesmen and military leaders through the sayings and
memorable words (apothegms) of famous men and through political, financial,
and military stratagems drawn from the lives of powerful and brilliant generals of the past. In Greece in the fourth century B.C.E., there was Aeneas Tacti-
cus's *Poliorcetica* and Pseudo-Aristotle's book 2 of the *Oeconomica;* in the Roman
period, Polyaenus's *Stratagems* and a work by the same name attributed to Frontinus. Valerius Maximus indicates that he composed his *Memorable Deeds and
Sayings* "based on the famous authors," and organized it by theme "so as to spare
those who want to draw their research from it the effort of a long search."[5] It is
not impossible that he himself borrowed his stories, apart from the Roman
ones, from an already-existing Greek collection of exempla.

Even kings and emperors were not averse to spending their time elaborat-
ing such collections. So says Suetonius about Augustus. Steeped in Greek culture, the emperor read a great deal and took notes: "What he sought above all
in his Greek readings were precepts and useful examples to follow in public and
private life. He copied them out word for word and very often sent the needed
warnings in that form, either to the people of the house, or to leaders of armies
or of provinces, or to the magistrates of Rome."[6]

As the rest of the passage indicates, Augustus, in making his personal collections, himself resorted to an eclectic reading of collections of already-existing
thematic exempla, on subjects ranging from "repopulation" to "the excessive
sumptuousness of buildings."

Suetonius also reports that the advice and examples thus dispensed had authority because the questions addressed had already attracted the attention and
interest of the ancients. The same was true for the choice of precedents, even
legal precedents. For example, one of Cicero's speeches in his prosecution against
Verres contests the validity of the adversary's arguments and of his supporting
examples: "For in such an important affair, when, regarding such a grave accusation, the defense has undertaken to declare that a criminal act has often occurred, listeners expect examples taken from ancient times, from literary monuments and the written tradition, examples absolutely worthy of consideration

and going back to early antiquity. It is such examples that ordinarily have both
the most authority as proof and the most charm for listeners."[7]

Quintilian was of the same opinion. He proposed that students at the schools
of rhetoric collate examples, small deeds from the lives of famous men, which
are "a very powerful means in every particular, since they provide illustrations
from which students will profit at the opportune moment. . . . Everyone rightly
agrees that there is no means more suitable for any subject, since most of the
time the future seems to correspond to the past."[8]

Exempla were thus transmitted from generation to generation. Cicero sought
out examples to illustrate his views on prejudices among many peoples, citing
Egyptian, Persian, and Hyrcanian customs. Although himself a master of the
exemplum, he turned to Chrysippus, who had drawn up a list of bizarre—that
is, non-Greek—funerary practices: "There are a host of other customs that
Chrysippus collected, since he was a researcher who neglected no detail."[9] As
M. Croiset has noted, Chrysippus, a representative of the Stoic school, was in
fact "a great compiler." His method was to lift one example or another from
earlier authors, such as Onesicritus, a companion of Alexander quoted by Strabo.
Onesicritus claimed that Alexander, scandalized by the custom in Sogdiana-
Bactriana of allowing dogs or birds to strip the flesh from the bones of cadav-
ers, banned the practice.[10] Another text attests to the same custom in the age
of Alexander's successors.[11] All in all, Chrysippus's collection must have been
very popular, given that the list of henceforth abolished barbarous practices
(including incest among the Persians) is nearly identical to Plutarch's list.[12]
Indeed, Porphyry was still referring to the Bactrian practice in the third century, and Chrysippus's list is found, almost unchanged, in Eusebius of Caesarea
in the fourth century c.e.[13]

Exempla and Lessons of Political Morality

Moralists sometimes arranged the exempla, transmitted in the form of anthol-
ogies, around different themes and used them for the narratives and anecdotes
in their treatises. The lesson Seneca wishes to dispense in De ira is simple: "Here
are the examples to contemplate in order to avoid them, and here, on the contrary, are the examples of moderation and mildness to live by."[14] That was the
one true aim of a collection of exempla. In Seneca's view, the Persian examples
he gives illustrate "the ferocity of raging barbarian kings, which no instruction,
no literary culture had penetrated."[15] Although directly inspired by Herodotus,

he did not underscore one of the traits of the Persian monarchy that the author of the *Histories* had transmitted: "The king does not put anyone to death . . . for a single flaw; it is only after reflection and if he finds the misdeeds of the guilty party more numerous than the services rendered, that he gives in to anger."[16] Seneca does submit examples of "moderation and mildness" for his readers to contemplate, but no Persian king is cited.[17] And yet the mildness and moderation of Artaxerxes II had become a commonplace in the literature of the Roman period.[18] Curtius, moreover, notes the mildness and moderation of Darius III on several occasions, but without concealing that the Great King was also subject to uncontrolled fits of temper and violence.[19]

Among the authors of collections of exempla, there is clearly no concern for historical research, no aim of exhaustivity or internal coherence. The only thing that matters is the didactic use to be drawn from an anecdote artificially removed from its context. In the treatise Plutarch devotes to the control of anger, there is no mention of a Great King, apart from a very brief and fairly obscure allusion to Cyrus the Younger.[20] And different kings are often confused. Cicero tells an anecdote in which Darius III is the protagonist, whereas in Plutarch the same anecdote concerns Artaxerxes II.[21] Valerius Maximus attributes to Ochus a heroic deed, the "overthrow of the Magi," which is regularly (and normally) associated with the memory of Darius I.[22] Elsewhere, in fact, the exemplum is cited to laud the memory of Darius the Great.[23] In the first case, Ochus is vilified for his betrayal of those who aided him; in the second, Darius is praised for his personal courageous battle against "a sordid and cruel tyranny." It is therefore quite possible that the name of Ochus, whose terrible reputation created the very prototype of the cruel king, was systematically linked to evil and reprehensible actions.[24] This example shows that variations can occur as a function of the thematic chapter in which the author introduces the story: depending on the initial choice, the narrative may undergo modifications to better serve the didactic subject.

Another type of moral has a privileged place in these collections. These are exempla that can explain why and how an empire collapsed. Regular reference is made to the abuses of luxury and good food; and in this context the Great Kings are systematically cited. The custom among the Persian kings of ordering the most sought-after dishes and the most exotic recipes from throughout the world is frequently denounced as if it were an established fact, based (albeit implicitly) on the authority of Xenophon and using incorruptible Sparta as a counterexample. Valerius Maximus (following Cicero, no doubt) concludes with regard to

Xerxes: "But while he indulged in all the excesses, into what disaster did he not allow such a powerful empire to collapse?"[25] Using nearly the same words and making the same accusations, the philosopher Clearchus of Soli assigned the responsibility for the collapse of the Persians' power to Darius III, who "did not perceive that he was defeating himself until others had seized his sceptre."[26]

Contemporary historians need not concern themselves with such a discordance or attribute the slightest heuristic value to it. It is simply necessary to know, first, that the image of Xerxes as seen through the exempla Valerius Maximus collected is particularly despicable; and second, that, given the very simplified memory the Romans had of Xerxes and Darius III, either of them could very well be named responsible for the fall of the empire. Xerxes's defeats in Greece were reputed to have inaugurated a long period of irremediable decline, and Darius's defeats at the hands of Alexander were the definitive downfall of the empire built by Cyrus. As a result, one explanation—the mad pursuit of luxury and pleasure—was tirelessly repeated as self-evident. In addition, many authors attributed that flaw generically to an anonymous Great King, thus transforming, on the model imposed by Xenophon, an individual responsibility into a structural analysis.[27]

Comparable, even analogous, procedures were commonly used in works by "historians." Livy embraces that method in his *Preface*, arguing that "the principal and most salutary advantage of history is to display before your eyes, in a bright frame, examples of every nature." The ancient historians used these collections and also added to them, so much so that many discussions of Alexander or Darius greatly resemble a series of exempla, arranged with greater or lesser skill and logic within a narrative framework. Curtius's account of Alexander's stay in Babylon, for example, uses the same cultural stereotypes about "decadence" that structure Livy's narrative of Hannibal's stay at Capua. The exemplum is everywhere. Although, from our present-day standpoint, the collections of exempla represent a minor literary genre based on a narrowly utilitarian conception of history, it would be wrong to neglect their contribution and to set them aside when gathering our sources.

For neglected or forgotten subjects or personalities, examples and apothegms transmit information that is partial but still useful, especially when a historian is seeking to reconstitute a lost memory. They provide access to information that is often absent from historical works in the narrow sense, and that information frequently comes from works that have themselves disappeared. Hence the interest of Athenaeus's *Deipnosophistae*, which, in the guise of banquet conversations among philosophers, cites a considerable number of passages drawn from authors about whom little is known other than their names. As it happens, the work makes frequent mention of the Great Kings and of the Achaemenid aulic customs adopted by Alexander. That is especially true of book 12, where the exempla tend to be about luxury *(tryphē)* and pleasure *(hedonē)*. The Persians are frequently recognized as masters in that realm, because they were the "first men in history to become famous for their luxurious way of life [*tryphē*]" (513f).

Exempla are supposed to transmit what is "worthy of memory," in the expression used by many historians and writers of antiquity. Such were the true foundations on which the history of Alexander was conceived in ancient times, even by its protagonist. According to Arrian, Alexander was distressed at not having someone near him who could have been, as Homer was for Achilles, the "herald of his fame."[28] When Alexander was preparing what would later be represented as an unparalleled feat during the siege of an Indian fort, he chose the posture most likely to serve his reputation and to foster his memory: "He therefore perceived that if he remained where he was, he would be incurring danger without being able to perform anything at all worthy of consideration [*logou axion*]." If he had to take risks, "he would die not ignobly [but] after performing great deeds of valour [*megala erga*]."[29] It is therefore clear why Diodorus introduces the action as follows: "The king was left alone, and boldly took a step which was as little expected as it is worthy of mention [*mnemēs axia*]."[30]

Such a conception reduces the field of history to the "great man." The authors of collections of exempla allowed ancient statesmen to "contemplate in brief the image of so many heroes worthy of memory [*axioi mnemēs*]."[31] And in a work that is now unfortunately lost, Cornelius Nepos devoted a number of his discussions to "leaders of the Greek people who were judged worthy of memory [*memoria digni*]."[32] Hence the feigned embarrassment of Lucian, when, appealing to Arrian's precedent, he gives his rationale for taking an interest in the life of the imposter Alexander of Abonoteichus and for devoting a book to him: "I blush . . . to think that the memory of a man thrice execrable is worthy of the memory of history."[33] Conversely, Valerius Maximus sets out these criteria of selection: "I do not like to take examples from the history of obscure figures [*ab ignotis*], and moreover, I am reluctant to speak of great men [*maximi viri*] only to reproach them for their vices."[34] The notion persisted over the centuries. Thus Voltaire, convinced that history is made at least in part by the energetic actions of "great men" (kings assisted by philosophers), used terminology directly inherited from antiquity, claiming: "The history of a prince is not everything he has done but only what he has done that is worthy of being passed on to posterity."[35]

Needless to say, contemporary historians have their own criteria and their own imperatives. The very idea of being obliged to select deeds and "memorable" actions and to distinguish them from others, destined to be forgotten, clashes head-on with the historian's notion of history, even the history of "great men." Above all, a historian who is attempting to speak of a king who never had a herald or a memorialist by his side does not have a choice of sources. He must rush to and fro, pace back and forth, and by his methods attempt to make fertile the sandy soil of documentary islets, those, in fact, that his methods have delimited, and to save them from being engulfed by oblivion. Under such conditions, collections of exempla, if considered both systematically and methodically, constitute documents that, within their specificities and limits, serve to bolster the historian's case. They do so not only through the anecdotal information they provide but also through the interpretation—"the lesson of history"—in which that information is embedded and that gives it its meaning.

The Legacy of Antiquity

It may be useful to note that, as a literary genre, the exempla have had a vast number of descendants. In the works of medieval theorists and in those of the modern age, the situations depicted, the commentaries proposed, and the apothegms invented seem extraordinarily similar to those found in the Greco-Roman authors. These later writers easily found, in the writings of their ancient colleagues, material to bolster and illustrate the courage and feats of their modern monarchs.

These are not mere coincidences. The phenomenon occurred at the very moment when the Greek and Latin classics were being translated, read, and imitated, and when new collections of exempla, written on a model that had been highly developed in antiquity, were multiplying. In a literary and cultural context dominated by the concern to imitate the ancients, that type of literature was destined to thrive and proliferate. *L'institution du prince (The Institution of the Prince)*, composed by Guillaume Budé between 1515 and 1522 and dedicated to Francis I, first appeared in print in 1547. It bore no title at the time, but in 1907 Delaruelle gave it the name *Le recueil d'apophtegmes offert à François Ier (The Collection of Apothegms Offered to Francis I)*. Budé borrowed from Plutarch his structure and a number of his "notable sayings, maxims, and deeds of the great princes . . . the kings of Assyria, of Media, of Persia, of Egypt, and of Macedonia, and Alexander the Great, his father, Philip, and the successors of Alexander throughout the land of Asia." He invokes the authority of his model, "who was a domestic servant of Trajan the good emperor," and begins the work by imitating Plutarch's address to his illustrious dedicatee. Whenever Budé wishes to make known "things worthy of memory in times past," he abundantly quotes "the Greeks, very diligent and industrious in the field of history" (Budé 1965, p. 10r). He believes that, thanks to him, the great deeds of the kings will not fall "into oblivion" (p. 24v). Budé puts to his own use the first courtly exemplum, which depicts "the great Artaxerxes, king of Persia," praised for his benevolence toward those who offered him even modest gifts. Francis I is similarly praised, for his "very accessible humanity and gentle and mild gaze" (2v–3r). The story of the simple peasant coming to offer Artaxerxes water collected in his own hands, recounted twice by Plutarch and also by Aelian, had already been included in several collections of exempla from the Byzantine era.[36]

Perrot d'Ablancourt, in publishing his translation of Plutarch's *Apothegms* in 1663, recalled the precedent of Erasmus's *Apophthegmata*, published in 1500 under the title *Adagiorum collectanea* and continually revised and augmented by the author in the following years.[37] Perrot also mentions a publication by the Alsatian humanist Lycothenes (Conrad Wolfhart), which he judges too scholastic (it "smacked too much of his school"). Nevertheless, the Latin lexicon of apothegms, compiled by Lycosthenes in 1555 and organized by theme, had enjoyed phenomenal success.[38] Thirty years later (1576), Innocent Gentillet published a comparable work in which several anecdotes and apothegms about Alexander and his entourage, taken from the ancient authors, were enlisted to support the author's argument. In it Gentillet "complacently displayed his erudition, drawing from all the collections of exempla and indulging in interminable digressions."[39] Gentillet also devotes a long chapter to flatterers, informed by references and exempla from Plutarch and other ancient authors. He includes the moment when "Alexander, the great king of Macedonia . . . left his country to make war on that great ruler Darius." Montaigne's *Essais,* first published in 1580, then augmented in 1582 and again in 1588, also belongs to this context: the author drew hundreds of his sayings and deeds from collections of exempla, Lives, and historical works from Greek and Roman antiquity.[40]

The genre remained very popular in the following period. The programmatic declarations of Valerius Maximus, as well as Quintilian's exhortations to make lists of exempla, irresistibly bring to mind a remark made by Rollin, himself a master pedagogue. He forcefully urged students to compile their own excerpts: "These sorts of collections, when they are made by a skillful hand, spare one a great deal of trouble and provide a writer with marks of erudition that cost him little and which often continue to do him much honor."[41] In the footsteps of M. de Tourreil, Rollin offers his readers a little collection of "Philip's memorable deeds and sayings," so as to "paint the character of that prince." The rationale he gives for that exercise is very similar to Plutarch's—namely, that "some deeds and words are better able to shed light on [great men] than their most brilliant actions" (*Histoire ancienne* [1817], 3:603). From antiquity to the modern age, the genre has been marked by a dialogue between the prince and the philosopher and by the precedence given to didacticism.

Shards of Memory and Fragments of Life

It is an understatement to say that Darius III holds a modest place in the Lives of illustrious men and in the collections of words and stratagems passed on to posterity as examples worthy of being compiled, transmitted, and meditated upon. He was clearly not among the men "worthy of memory." Two authors do present an overview of the Achaemenid dynasty and its representatives. Strabo, after the chapters in which he describes Persia and its inhabitants, points to the importance of Cyrus and of Darius, then skips to the last kings, Arses and Darius III, for whom he declares no great admiration. He claims that Darius III did not belong to the royal family.[42] And Nepos, after passing in review "almost all the leaders of the Greek people who are judged worthy of memory," begins a laudatory chapter on the Persian kings:

> But of those who combined with their title a boundless power, the most remarkable in our view were the kings of Persia, Cyrus and Darius, son of Hystaspes, who were both ordinary citizens [*privatus*] when their merit [*virtus*] earned them kingship. The first fell to the Massageteans on the battlefield. Darius died of old age. There were also three from the same nation: Xerxes and the two Artaxerxes, nicknamed Long Hand (Macrocheir) and Great Memory (Mnemon). What especially made Xerxes famous was that, leading the most powerful armies that history has kept in its memory [*post hominum memoriam*], he attacked Greece by land and sea. As for Long Hand, he owed his chief renown [*laus*] to his imposing aspect

and physical beauty, to which he added an astonishing military courage [*incredibili virtute belli*], since of all the Persians he was the one who had the greatest personal valor. Great Memory, by contrast, found glory through justice; for, since his mother's criminal acts had taken his wife from him,[43] he was clever enough to make a sacrifice of his suffering to the duty of filial piety. These two kings by the same name, laid low by illness, paid their debt to nature; the other [Xerxes] died at the hand of the prefect Artabanus. (*De regibus,* 21)

Darius III is not at issue here, though the precision "Darius, son of Hystaspes" is an implicit reference to another Darius, with whom the informed reader must not confuse the first. It is difficult to draw the slightest inference from that silence, particularly because Darius II is also not cited and Artaxerxes III and Arses are similarly ignored. Apparently none of them belonged to the category "kings worthy of memory." Nepos does not explain the reasons for his choices, but it is clear that their absence casts into relief the portrait of an ideal king: born an ordinary citizen, he distinguishes himself by his physical qualities and extraordinary personal valor in battle, and also at times by human qualities belonging to the private sphere (Artaxerxes II's filial piety). All these are mere commonplaces: strictly speaking, there are no individualized portraits. But then, the passage is only a rapid summary of a lost work devoted to the "kings of foreign peoples," to which Nepos explicitly refers his readers.

For obvious reasons the overwhelming majority of these works are dedicated to Greek and Roman leaders and generals. Only one of Plutarch's Lives is devoted to a Great King of Persia, namely, Artaxerxes II. It is a very odd Life, the only one Plutarch wrote that is not on a Greek or a Roman, and one of only four that are not accompanied by a parallel. The choice of Artaxerxes II can probably be explained, at least in part, by the abundance (if not the high quality) of the information Plutarch found in Ctesias, Dinon, Xenophon, and a few others; and also to the renown of Datames, satrap of Cappadocia, who revolted against Artaxerxes II.

The situation is no different in the collections of exempla. Datames is the only Persian to appear in the gallery of famous generals whose financial and military stratagems Cornelius Nepos collected from the author of the *Oeconomica* and from Polyaenus. Several Great Kings do appear in another of Plutarch's works, the collection of apothegms attributed to kings and famous men. The memory of Artaxerxes II opens the collection and serves as a model for Plutarch's fawning and laborious dedication to Trajan. Also appearing are Darius I, Xerxes, Artaxerxes I, Cyrus the Younger and his mother, Parysatis, as well as two fourth-century generals, Orontes and Memnon. Memnon was one of the military leaders most heeded by Darius III, but the Great King himself is never cited, except as a counterpoint to stories intended to vaunt the merits of his conqueror.[44]

By contrast, Darius appears fleetingly in the *Varia historia* by Aelian of Praeneste, another author of collections of moralistic stories during the Roman period. The Great King is included on a list of twenty individuals reputed to be of obscure origin but who reached the pinnacle of power. Two Persian kings are listed: Darius I, who also appeared in that context in Nepos and in Herodotus's *Histories;* and Darius III, who is called, both inaccurately and unflatteringly, a "slave."[45] Aelian also mentions Darius III twice in his other collection, *De natura animalium,* each time to praise the loyalty of the Great King's domestic animals. In the guise of sentimental histories about the bond between master and beast, the anecdotes illustrate in stark terms the deplorable fate of a Great King constrained in one case (6.48) to hastily flee the battlefield (with the assistance of his mare), and forced in the other (6.25) to die in the most pitiful solitude (attended only by his dog). These exempla lie on the borderline between two types of thematic collections: "deaths of famous men" and stories about animals watching over their masters or even saving them from death. Another well-known story was that of Darius I saved by the camel carrying his provisions.[46]

In Valerius Maximus's *Memorable Deeds and Sayings,* Darius appears only in stories about the exploits of Alexander, conqueror of the Persians, or about the courage of the Macedonians, from which the author draws the following moral: "If that genius had been placed before Darius's eyes, he would have known that soldiers of that race could not be defeated; he would have realized the robustness with which they were endowed from their earliest childhood."[47]

Polyaenus's *Stratagems,* written in the second century C.E. and addressed to emperors Antonius and Verus, is identical in that respect. Of the 900 exempla patiently collected by the author, a not insignificant number of stratagems attributed to fifth- and fourth-century Greek generals are explicitly placed within the context of wars and conflicts with the Persians. Several Great Kings are depicted—Cyrus, Cambyses, Darius I, Xerxes, Artaxerxes I, and Artaxerxes III—but not Darius III. Generals and satraps of the Great Kings appear as well. The author, not surprisingly, also presents a series of thirty-two examples drawn from the history of Alexander the Great.[48] There the name Darius appears five times, generally as a referent, nothing more. He was the one commanding the

Persians against Alexander; it was that king whose armies were several times defeated.

In an extraordinarily informative passage on the practices of the Achaemenid court, Polyaenus includes a list of products used by the Great King's cooks. He claims, however, that the text was found by Alexander's soldiers in Persepolis in 331/330, inscribed on a bronze column, and attributes the authorship of the regulations to Cyrus (§ 32). A Byzantine abridger known as Leo the Emperor wisely understood that their real subject was Darius III's royal dinners. Furthermore, when Polyaenus cites an episode that, in other sources, reveals a skillful stratagem employed by Darius and his advisers prior to Gaugamela (placing metal traps in the ground to put the Macedonian cavalry out of commission), it serves solely to illustrate the lucid and far-sighted skill of Alexander, who is able to save his soldiers from the traps cunningly laid by his adversary (§ 37). In short, it is difficult for Darius to lead a satisfying historiographical life, because he is eclipsed by the looming shadow of a hero of history who is fearless and beyond reproach.

Darius versus Alexander

How, then, did Darius fare among those conventionally called the "historians of Alexander"? These are authors from the Roman period who wrote in Greek (Diodorus, Plutarch, Arrian) and Latin (Curtius, Justin). They made use of works that are now lost or that survive only in fragments, sometimes minuscule ones. These authors sought to provide a continuous account of the life and actions of Alexander, either in a book or a chapter written with that particular aim in mind (Arrian, Curtius, Plutarch), or in one part of a work of universal history (Diodorus, Pompeius Trogus as summarized by Justin).

Curtius, Justin, Diodorus, and Plutarch represent a specific tradition, called the "Vulgate," which is generally believed to be derived from Clitarchus, who worked in Egypt in the time of Ptolemy. The term "Vulgate" is in many respects disputable and misleading. In placing the emphasis on the supposed common source, it tends to subordinate historical reflection to an interminable and often futile investigation into the identity of that source (or sources). Furthermore, it confers a unity on these authors, each of whom has his own personality and, first and foremost, his literary personality, that is, his freedom to create a work from the materials he has collected and/or set aside. Under such conditions, a reflection on the literary models the authors used is incomparably more fruitful.

For a long time the Vulgate was viewed rather condescendingly. Arrian was considered a serious, precise, and conscientious historian, whereas the tradition stemming from the Vulgate was judged fictional and fanciful. Such an opposition is no longer accepted, even though, explicitly or implicitly, a certain preference for Arrian continues to hold sway. And yet Arrian's method is no more reliable in assessing Alexander and Darius than the methods of other Roman-period authors. In reality both Arrian's work and the Vulgate constitute documents that need to be read, decoded, and interpreted with the same level of attention and the same keen critical eye. The question is whether the treatment of Darius varies appreciably between Arrian and the Vulgate authors.

In terms of the overall literary composition, the death of Darius holds a specific place in both sets of texts. The presence and even the length of the funeral oration that Arrian devotes to the Great King mark the end of one cycle in his narrative.[49] The oration concludes the first part of his book, which is much shorter than the second, devoted to the years 330–323. In Curtius's *History of Alexander,* the two parts are even more sharply distinguished, but they are much closer in length, with each comprising five books. It is known that Pompeius Trogus also devoted a special section, book 11, to the "acts and deeds of Alexander, up to the death of the king of the Persians."[50] In faithfully summarizing Pompeius Trogus's work, Justin adopts the same structure.[51] So too, in the Hellenistic chronology called the Parian Marble, the death of Darius constitutes a point of reference, along with the accession and death of the Macedonian kings and of the other Persian kings.

That is not only because Darius's death was in itself an important moment for the conception of universal history held by all these authors, inasmuch as it marked the end of the Persian Empire and the transition to Macedonian hegemony. His death also assumed a special meaning within the more limited context of the history of Alexander, because it was seen as the first clearly identifiable stopping place in that history. For many ancient authors, Darius's death and the manner in which Alexander assumed his succession constituted a sort of theatrical ending to the conflict between the two kings, the end of their race to the high countries, during which one king advanced and the other retreated. Their first and last encounter—one king was still alive, the other dead (or dying)—was represented as a highly dramatized scene in the different traditions. Soon after, Alexander began to adopt the practices of Darius's court, a choice that met with the ancient authors' disapproval. In short, for each of the traditions, but to varying degrees, the death of Darius represented an important element in the narrative composition. From the standpoint of the history or fate of the last of the Achaemenids, the years 334–330 constituted a drama in the theatrical sense.

It would certainly be overreaching to believe that the first part of these ancient works represents a "history of Darius." But even in Arrian's intentional amnesia, Darius represents the only royal figure who might have been able to rival the Macedonian conqueror he faced. In a sense the two kings are considered side by side, all the more so in that they ascended the throne at roughly the same time. For the authors who were not interested solely in Alexander's fate, it was thus tempting to produce a synoptic history—a choice that sometimes raised problems of composition. For example, at the beginning of book 5, which is to say after the account of the Battle of Gaugamela, Curtius gives clear reasons for not including any discussion of Greek affairs: "As for contemporaneous operations in Greece or in Illyria and Thrace under the supreme command of Alexander, if I intended to record these in accordance with strict chronology, I should be obliged to interrupt my Asian narrative. There seems to be good reason for presenting this as a whole, especially up to Darius' flight and death, and for preserving in my work the coherence of the actual events. I shall therefore begin with the occurrences connected with the battle at Arbela."[52]

He returns to the events of Europe only at the beginning of book 6, explaining: "So ended the war. It had started suddenly, but it was concluded before Darius' defeat by Alexander at Arbela" (6.1.21).

Diodorus takes the opposite approach, alternating between the affairs of Europe and those of Asia and introducing an excursus on European affairs.[53] It is therefore not surprising that book 17 opens with a programmatic declaration: "In this book we shall continue the systematic narrative beginning with the accession of Alexander, and include both the history of this king down to his death as well as contemporary events in the known parts of the world [*oikoumēnē*]. This is the best method, I think, of ensuring that events will be remembered, for thus the material is arranged topically, and each story is told without interruption" (17.1.2).

A comparable declaration appears at the start of each of the books: Diodorus specifies the period he will be considering, while recalling the period(s) discussed in the previous book(s). The next book logically begins: "The preceding Book included all the acts of Alexander up to his death" (18.1.6). The focus is clear: Diodorus is writing an account devoted to Alexander. At the same time, however, the author—as elsewhere in his work—will move from one historical front to the other. After summing up in a few chapters the first years of the reign of Alexander (17.2–4), he declares: "Now that we have described what took place in Greece, we shall shift our account to the events in Asia" (17.5.1). This is a particularly easy transition to make, given that a Macedonian military corps had been operating in Asia Minor since the end of the reign of Philip II. Diodorus gives some information about that army, then turns resolutely to the situation in the Persian Empire, thereby establishing an explicit link to the discussions he had devoted to it in the previous book (16).

It is here in particular that, in the course of a long account of Artaxerxes III's expedition in Syro-Phoenicia and Egypt (16.42–51), Diodorus presents the "odious" figure of Bagoas (16.49–51), destined to play a prominent role in Darius III's ascension to the throne. "As our narrative is now to treat of the kingdom of the Persians, we must go back a little to pick up the thread."[54] He then reports the conspiracies and dynastic struggles that had left the court awash in blood, from the assassination of Artaxerxes III to the accession of Darius III. There follow two diverging accounts of that event, plus a very positive portrayal of Darius himself, then a report on the military measures the king took at the time against the looming Macedonian threat (17.5–6).

The same story appears in book 10 of the *Philippic Histories,* which Pompeius Trogus devoted to the history of the Persian kingdom between 380 and 335, up to Darius III, who "maintained a long war . . . against Alexander the Great."[55] Unfortunately that work has been lost, except in the form of a summary transmitted by Justin at the end of his book 10, devoted to the troubled and bloody history of the Achaemenid family and dynasty, between the accession of Darius II and that of Darius III (ca. 425/424–336). Only Diodorus and Justin present an original version of Darius III's accession to the throne. These chapters are unique in ancient literature, by virtue of the concern they express to present, albeit in outline form, the man who would wage war against Alexander. Regrettably, the first two books of Curtius's *History of Alexander* have disappeared: they too almost certainly had a few chapters on Darius before Alexander's arrival.

The excursus assumes its full meaning within the fabric of the larger literary piece into which it is inserted, which consists of nothing less than contrasting portraits of the two kings. Both Justin and Diodorus have already introduced Alexander in a very laudatory light. After giving an overview of the difficulties that await the young man after his father's death, Diodorus presents, in anticipation, the efforts he will make to stabilize his throne: "But, for all the problems and fears that beset his kingdom on every side, Alexander, who had only just reached manhood, brought everything into order impressively and swiftly. Some he won by persuasion and diplomacy, others he frightened into keeping the peace, but some had to be mastered by force and so reduced to submission."[56]

It is clear that, particularly in Diodorus and Justin, the discussions of the Persian Empire and of the Macedonian kingdom are conceived and constructed as parallels. Alexander, in fact, had accused the Persian king of having had a hand in Philip II's murder.[57] Diodorus is fond of noting that Alexander and Darius began their reigns at about the same time.[58] Although the Great King is alleged to have been initially misled by the new Macedonian king's youth, "Dareius took warning and began to pay serious attention to his forces. He fitted out a large number of ships of war and assembled numerous strong armies, choosing at the same time his best commanders."[59] In short, the mobilization of men and means proceeded apace on both sides.

Diodorus's synoptic view allows him to be even more economical. He is able to conclude the chapters that present the two kings, in Europe and in Asia, at the moment when Alexander is about to undertake his expedition against Darius. Having emphasized the eminent qualities of both men, he has no difficulty introducing the war about to get under way as a game of winner-takes-all between two men who had already shown proof of their valor, one in Europe, the other in Asia. Arrian also develops that agonistic view of their conflict, this time in a polemical and accusatory mode, in the invented letter Alexander supposedly sent to Darius in response to the Persian king's overtures after his defeat at Issus: "And if you dispute my right to the kingdom, stay and fight another battle for it; but do not run away. For wherever you may be, I intend to march against you."[60] Diodorus and Justin have a very different perspective: they openly declare that Darius's qualities as a combatant and war leader unquestionably made him an adversary worthy of Alexander, who came to settle the quarrel over sovereignty. The victor in that duel would quite simply be awarded the "supremacy"—which would entail the death of one of the adversaries and the birth of a power that would unite Europe and Asia.[61]

A Fictionalized Darius

Alongside the writings of Arrian, the Vulgate authors, and Plutarch, a fictional or fictionalized history of Alexander and his conquests was elaborated at about the same time in Hellenistic and Roman Alexandria. The principal representative of that current is the *Alexander Romance*. Some Byzantine copyists attributed it to Aristotle's nephew Callisthenes. It must be conceded, however, that, as the text is known to us today—through several recensions from different eras—it is the work of an unknown author. Probably in the third century C.E., that author was able to make use of the many versions that were circulating at the time. The image of Alexander that the author of the Romance intends to elaborate is set out clearly: "The best and most noble of men, for he did everything in his own way. . . . We are now going to speak of the deeds of Alexander, of the virtues of his body and his spirit" (1.1.1–2, Stoneman trans.). The original text, now lost, was adapted into Latin by Julius Valerius under the title *Res gestae Alexandri Macedonis (Heroic Deeds of Alexander of Macedonia),* which might very well have been the original title of what is customarily called the *Alexander Romance.*

"Many say that he was the son of King Philip, but they are deceivers. This is untrue: he was not Philip's son, but the wisest of the Egyptians say that he was the son of Nectanebo, after the latter had fallen from his royal state" (1.1.3). The pronounced Egyptocentric tone of the Romance is present from the start. Alexander's "father" is introduced against a well-known historical backdrop, that of Artaxerxes III's reconquest of the Nile Valley in 343/342, which resulted in the pharaoh's flight to Ethiopia.[62] In the Romance, Nectanebo, having been driven from his country by the Persian invader, takes refuge in Macedonia. The god of the grief-stricken Egyptians announces that their pharaoh "will return to Egypt not as an old man but as a youth, and he will overcome our enemies the Persians" (1.3.4). Olympias then becomes pregnant by Nectanebo the magician; Alexander is born and is accepted by his "father," Philip; and Alexander becomes the pupil of Aristotle. The author goes on to describe Alexander's remarkable virtues, especially "his intelligence and his warlike prowess" (1.16.4). While his father is away at war, Alexander finds himself facing the Persians for the first time. He receives an embassy from the Great King, who has come to demand payment of the traditional tribute of "one hundred golden eggs each weighing 20 pounds of solid gold" (1.23). Alexander unceremoniously sends the ambassadors back to their master, promising that he will soon come personally to reclaim the tributes that had previously been paid. Before leaving, the ambassadors have time to commission a portrait of Alexander from a famous painter.

So begins the first part of the Romance. It will end with Darius's death. The expedition to Asia follows an itinerary that is original and complicated, to say the least. After defeating the Persian satraps at the Granicus and conquering the coast of Asia Minor, Alexander embarks for Sicily, accepts the surrender of the Romans, then goes to Africa and Libya. He visits the sanctuary of Amun, and the god acknowledges him as his son. Several chapters on the king's stay in Egypt follow: not only does Alexander found Alexandria, he is also officially enthroned king of Egypt during a stop in Memphis, after his lineage is discovered. In front of a statue, which he is told represents Nectanebo and on which the text of a prophecy concerning war against the Persians is inscribed, he immediately decides to levy on the Egyptians taxes that "they had formerly paid to Darius" (1.34). The people readily consent and escort Alexander triumphantly to the country's border. In some ways, instead of being a Greek war of retaliation against the Persians—who are accused of having violated the Greek sanctuary during the Median wars—the conflict undertaken against Darius thus has the aim of erasing the consequences of the Egyptian defeat to the Great King and of making Alexandria "the capital of the whole world."

The itinerary retraces the one Alexander actually followed beginning in the spring of 331, but certain events are necessarily dislocated in time. It is after he goes to Egypt (and not while heading south) that Alexander besieges Tyre, seizes it, and establishes a satrap "to rule over Phoenicia." It is then that he receives the first embassy from Darius, who sends him a whip, a ball, and a chest full of gold. The Great King's letter explains the meaning of that strange present: "That is what suits your age: you need still to play and to be nursed. Therefore I have sent you a whip, a ball, and a chest of gold, of which you may take what you prefer: the whip, to show that you ought still to be at play; the ball, so that you may play with your contemporaries instead of inducing such numbers of arrogant young men to come with you like bandits and terrorize the city. . . . I have enough gold and silver to fill the whole world. I have sent you a chest full of gold . . . to feed your fellow-bandits" (1.36).

The tone of the young Macedonian's reply is easy to guess. He reverses the symbolic meaning of the message. Thanks to the whip, he says, he will subject the barbarians to slavery with his own hands; the ball shows that he will conquer the world; as for the chest, it means that Darius will pay a tribute to his young conqueror.

When the satraps prove hesitant to proceed, Darius himself comes to confront his adversary and pitches his camp "by the river Pinarios." Then Alexander, after leaving southern Asia Minor for Sicily and taking the road from Egypt to Phoenicia, crosses the Taurus Mountains and arrives in Cilicia from the north. All this follows Alexander's actual itinerary. The two adversaries face off again, in the position they occupied in reality before the Battle of Issus. The Persians are defeated, Darius flees, and the royal tent is captured, along with the Great King's mother, wife, and children. As Darius is forming another army, the Macedonian again follows a surprising route, returning to Europe—to Abdera, on the coast of southern Thrace. At that moment the narrator recounts the punishment inflicted on Thebes, an event that in reality dates back to Alexander's departure.

"Then Alexander hastened on through Cilicia to the regions of the Barbarians." Thus begins book 2 (version A), in which the two kings face off. But Alexander veers seriously off course. After recounting a nice story about the king being cured after bathing in the Cydnus River in Cilicia, the storyteller has his hero conquer Greater Armenia. Alexander orders his troops to cross the Euphrates, after building a "bridge with iron arches and bands." Then on to the battle near the Tigris, along whose banks the Great King has set up his camp. The battle is inconclusive. Once again Alexander prepares his troops, the two kings exchange letters, and Darius asks for the aid of Porus, king of India. Alexander reaches Persia, and, in disguise, crosses the frozen Stranga River, then arranges to be received at the Great King's court as an envoy of King Alexander. Soon recognized by one of the Persians who had been part of an embassy to the court at Pella, Alexander hastily leaves the banquet hall and succeeds in recrossing the Stranga, whose ice breaks up just as his pursuers reach the riverbank.

It is that same river, frozen over, that Darius soon crosses on his way to test his mettle against Alexander. He is again defeated. Darius, in flight, manages to cross over the frozen river, but such is not the case for his troops. Desperate, he writes to Alexander, proposing to exchange piles of gold for the members of his family. Soon Alexander and his army reach Darius's palace in Persia. The king orders the palace of Xerxes to be burned down, then changes his mind. During that time Darius has taken refuge in Media, then near the Caspian Gates, where two of his satraps, Bessus and Ariobarzanes, conspire to kill their king. They strike him with their swords: Darius's famous death scene follows. The Great King's assassins, attracted by the false hope of a reward, are soon put to death for their crime.

The composition of the Romance, even more than the historical tradition, clearly divides the story into two distinct parts, separated by the death of Darius. From the moment Darius dies, the narratives takes on a completely different tone. Alexander sometimes adopts the role of narrator, in quotations from letters sent to his mother, Olympias. Apart from the episode depicting the confrontation and duel with the Indian king Porus, the author omits the various stages in the conquest of the Iranian plateau and the countries of Central Asia. This is quite easy, because the traitor Bessus and his accomplice are executed just after Darius's death. The author provides us instead with the initiatory journey of a young man "filled with the desire to see the ends of the earth . . . and to explore and see those places." Alexander encounters wondrous peoples, trees, and fruits, headless men, stout giants with blazing eyes, men who bark like dogs. He even explores the bottom of the sea in a glass diving bell. After entering into contact with legendary princes and princesses, such as Queen Candace and the queen of the Amazons, he returns to Babylon, where he dies. Throughout this section, the hero's actions and desires are completely disconnected from even the idea of taking territories by force. Alexander has embarked on a discovery of the wonders of the world and of himself. In both the Greek legend and the Arab myth, Alexander is "the master of thresholds and passageways," to borrow François de Polignac's inspiring phrase.

By contrast, the first part of the Romance, though fictionalized, deals with conquests, conflicts between one king and another, victories in pitched battles, and the taking of territory, which, despite the inventions and detours, can be followed on a map. Here again the emphasis is on the personal rivalry between the two kings and on the Macedonian king's desire to confront his adversary one-on-one. Even the Great King's brother Oxydelkys (Oxathres) bluntly expresses his doubts about Darius's ability to prevail over his young adversary. The superiority attributed to Alexander is symbolized by the Macedonian king's willingness, before a battle, to put his royal authority in play and thus to win it back personally, against the man fighting him for it: "You must rather imitate Alexander, and in that way hold on to your kingdom. He did not entrust the conduct of the war to generals and satraps, like you, but has always been the first to enter the cities and has fought at the head of his army. During battle he sets aside his kingly nature, and resumes it when he has won. . . . Alexander has been successful in everything because he has not put anything off; he has done everything bravely, as is his nature. Even in appearance he resembles nothing so much as a lion" (2.7.4–6).

Throughout the narrative, Darius will prove incapable of facing his fate.

❦[4]❧

Arrian's Darius

Obituary as Character Assassination

In his *Anabasis,* Arrian follows step by step even the most insignificant episodes in the life of the Macedonian king, without ever concerning himself with Darius. The explanations and justifications he gives by way of introduction, which concern his task of sorting out the false from the true and the plausible, have to do only with the life and person of Alexander. Darius is never even introduced to the readers of the *Anabasis.* Until the moment Darius personally takes command of the army and leads it into Cilicia, where he suffers a major reversal at Issus (November 333), he is almost completely absent, except in distant and indirect evocations. It is not until his death (July 330) that the first discussion is devoted to him and his life, in the form of a retrospective overview. And even the view transmitted in that passage seriously distorts the memory of the last of the Great Kings:

> This was the end of Darius, when Aristophon was archon at Athens in the month Hecatombaeon. He was the softest of men, and the least sensible in warfare; but in other matters he committed no offence, perhaps for lack of opportunity, because the moment of his accession was also the moment of the attack on him by the Macedonians and Greeks.
>
> So even if he had had the will, he was no longer free to play the tyrant to his subjects, as his position was more dangerous than theirs. His life was one series of disasters, with no respite, after his accession. The cavalry disaster of his satraps on the Granicus happened at once, and at once Ionia and Aeolis were in the enemy's hands, with both Phrygias, Lydia and all Caria except Halicarnassus; the loss of Halicarnassus, and then of

all the coast-line as far as Cilicia soon followed. Next came his defeat at
Issus, where he saw his mother with his wife and children taken prisoners; then Phoenicia and all Egypt were lost; and then he himself was
among the first to flee dishonourably at Arbela, and lost the greatest army
of the whole barbarian race; a fugitive from his own kingdom and a wan-
derer, he was at last betrayed by his own escort to the worst of fates, to be
at once a king and prisoner carried off in dishonour; finally he perished by
a conspiracy of his closest connections. These were the tragedies of Darius' life. After death he had a royal burial and his children were brought
up and educated by Alexander as if he were still on the throne, and Alexander married his daughter. At his death he was about fifty years old.
(3.22.2–6, P.-A. Brunt trans.)

The portrait and the narrative are equally sketchy, which allows the author
to accentuate certain traits but at the risk of caricature or at least simplification.
That is particularly clear in the report on Darius's defeats, which takes the form
of a flashback in fast-motion. Arrian, to mark clearly the ineluctability of the
Persian defeat and the overwhelming responsibilities of the last Great King,
punctuates his discourse with temporal expressions and adverbs, which markedly and remarkably speed up and distort the process of defeat. In so doing, he
does not hesitate to take liberties with the chronology, which he reproduced
more faithfully in the first books of the *Anabasis*. The personal accusations are
no less vicious. Darius is portrayed as a colorless and mediocre individual, an
ignominious coward. He is incapable of confronting, with nobility and determination, the fate that awaits him. Even his supposed virtues (moderation, for
example) are called into doubt and transformed into flaws and potential vices:
supposedly the historical circumstances simply did not allow him to exercise
his cruelty toward his subjects. The indictment is particularly impressive in that
Arrian maintains the same tone throughout the account, even in the descriptions of the pitched battles.

Neither a Courageous Soldier nor a Wise General

It is clear that Arrian does not intend to grant any virtue to Darius. On the contrary, he appears to have concentrated in a few lines the reproaches and con-
demnations found scattered among many other authors. Let us examine in
more detail one of the judgments Arrian pronounces. "He was the softest of

men, and the least sensible in warfare."[1] Despite their mundanity, these adjectives were very evocative for Arrian's readers. Speaking of Artaxerxes's situation prior to Cunaxa, Plutarch writes that he had "countless satraps and generals who surpassed Cyrus in wisdom and military skill."[2] That combination of qualities identifies as outstanding those close to the Great King—Mardonius, for example, "one of the foremost Persians for his bravery at war and his wisdom in the councils," or Tiribazes, Artaxerxes's adviser at the time, of whom it was said: "In wars . . . he excelled in valour, and in council his judgement was so good that when the King followed his advice he never made a mistake."[3] And the Persians whom Artaxerxes III selected during the Egyptian campaign are said to have been endowed with both "valour and loyalty."[4] Conversely, Persian generals are sometimes denounced for their "cowardice and inexperience."[5] Parsondas in the Medo-Persian legend, however, is said to be "renowned for his valour and intelligence."[6]

In that respect, everyone seems to model himself on the royal virtues, which Darius I and then Xerxes take pride in demonstrating at every opportunity, "in the palace and on the battlefield" (DNb; XPl).[7] But the framework for interpreting their personalities is not exclusively Persian. In an apothegm Plutarch declares that "Darius [I], singing his own praises, said he was becoming more clear-sighted in battles and in the presence of danger."[8] In the same way, Arrian, in describing (or discrediting) Darius III, makes no reference, even implicitly, to royal declarations. In the early fourth century B.C.E., when a Greek poet composed an epigram in honor of the dynast Arbinas of Xanthos, he also praised "his intelligence and strength." It should not be concluded, however, that the poet was imitating the inscription of Darius. The combination of the qualities of courage and intelligence was obviously not specific to Persian monarchical ideology, and it is infinitely more probable that a Greek poet drew inspiration and turns of phrase from the Homeric poems.

Furthermore, a Greek adviser is sometimes described in the same terms: Charidemus, who fought beside Darius III, was also "a man generally admired for his bravery and skill as a commander—he had been a comrade-in-arms of King Philip and had led or counselled all his successes."[9] He also acted as an adviser to Darius. And a Greek general can be hailed as "distinguished and superior both in valour and in sagacity," even if he is in the service of an enemy of the king.[10]

What Arrian denounces, using terminology easily recognizable to his Hellenophone readers, is Darius's military incompetence. The first qualifier ("effeminate" or "soft") designates more specifically unfitness in battle and even cowardice. The second ("lacking in good sense") also entails an unfitness at devising a strategy and applying it rigorously and consistently. Herodotus uses the same term to explain why and how Cambyses, without having made the necessary logistical preparations, waged a campaign against the Ethiopians, heading "to the ends of the earth." "He lost his wits completely, and, like the madman he was . . . off he went."[11]

In several dialogues between Alexander and Parmenion, Arrian, a specialist in military matters and a military man himself, explains very clearly what it means to be a general worthy of the name, and to that end cites the example of the Macedonian king. He is brave and has an "eagerness for encountering danger."[12] At the same time, he is endowed with sound judgment, that is, with a capacity to judge a given situation and to evaluate the circumstances that permit or rule out an attack at one time or another.[13] "He was very clever in recognising what needed to be done, when others were still in a state of uncertainty; and very successful in conjecturing from the observation of facts what was likely to occur."[14] That quality, which the Greeks called *gnōmē,* is also the opposite of anger: a leader must never make a rash decision, when he is unable, even briefly, to control his drives and passions.[15]

According to Pericles/Thucydides (2.13.2), who may well have influenced Arrian, that foremost quality of a leader, combined with sufficient financial resources, is what allows him to win wars. But intelligence takes precedence over logistics. Even with a good supply of money and soldiers, a leader is a bad general if he lacks *gnōmē:* he is on the road to ruin and takes his army with him. That is the real reason Arrian argues that the successive defeats of the royal armies can be explained by the personal shortcomings of a king who, possessing inexhaustible reserves of armies and treasures, did not have the qualities of a soldier or of a commander in chief.

From One Obituary to Another

The force of the accusation is clearer and crueler when contrasted to the obituary that Arrian devotes to Alexander. Arrian exalts his hero's superhuman virtues and defends his memory against attacks dating to antiquity, which focused on certain character traits and practices:

> He had an extraordinary physical beauty and hardihood and an exceedingly shrewd and courageous spirit; he was unsurpassed in his love of

honor, his zest for danger, and his scrupulous attention to the rites of the
gods. With regard to' bodily pleasures, he enjoyed perfect self-control;
where pleasures of the mind were concerned, he was insatiable only for
men's praise. He was extremely adept at seeing immediately what had to
be done when it was not yet obvious, and was exceptionally good at guess-
ing what was likely to happen based on the available evidence; he showed
outstanding talent for drawing up, arming, and equipping an army. In raising his soldiers' morale, filling them with good hopes, and dispelling their
fear in times of danger by his own fearlessness, he showed himself su-
premely gifted. All that needed to be done openly he did with the utmost
courage, while in situations requiring stealth and speed he also excelled at
getting the jump on his enemies before they suspected what was coming.
He was utterly reliable in honoring promises and agreements, and no one
was less likely to be taken by deceivers. Uncommonly sparing in the use of
money for his own pleasures, he spent ungrudgingly for the benefit of others. (P. Mensch trans.)

As in Plutarch, the physical portrait of Alexander is, to say the least, concise
and stereotypical, perhaps simply because the Macedonian did not have the impressive stature befitting a king.[16] What is particularly disastrous for the memory of Darius, however, is that, contrary to a well-established literary rule, Arrian
does not give the slightest indication of the physical appearance of the Persian
king, even though, according to Plutarch's rather all-purpose formulations, Darius was "the tallest and handsomest man in Asia."[17] Alexander is a paragon of every virtue, as indicated by the rapid-fire succession of superlatives, no fewer
than nineteen in the passage cited. He is the sole hero in the history narrated by
Arrian. Against or beside him are many who are merely adequate, even mediocre: Darius is indisputably their most prominent representative.

The Historical Portrait and Literary Norms: On the Role of Mimesis

I shall frequently have occasion to return, in general terms and in detail, to the
contrasting portraits of Darius and of Alexander, as they are presented or suggested by the different authors. It is important to understand why and how Arrian came to assign such pronounced traits to the Persian king and to adopt a
judgment so lacking in nuance. The question and the response matter, because

many of the traits in these portraits persist even in contemporary historiography. The debate is closely linked to the problem of the literary models that inspired Arrian and the other authors and to the norms they obeyed.

The vast differences between ancient historiography and the historical method as it was constructed in Europe during the nineteenth and twentieth centuries must be constantly kept in mind. Such an introductory declaration may elicit smiles, given that its author would seem to be intent on stating the obvious. But the smiles and irony vanish once we immerse ourselves in the ancient and modern literature that grew up around the figure of Alexander and his exploits. Present-day historiography, still too absorbed in the search to identify the "primary" sources—now lost and known only in fragmented form—used by authors of the Roman period, may continue to overvalue, albeit tacitly, the historiographical contribution of Arrian and other authors, handily but fallaciously categorized as "historians of Alexander." In reality, the literature we are constrained to use in the reconstruction of the contrasting histories of Alexander and Darius has nothing to do with "history" as that term is now understood. In his thought-provoking book *Mimesis* (1963), Erich Auerbach devoted pages of great lucidity to that subject:

> The ancients' way of viewing things . . . does not see forces, it sees vices and virtues, successes and mistakes. Its formulation of problems is not concerned with historical developments either intellectual or material, but with ethical judgments. . . . An ethically oriented historiography . . . is bound to use an unchangeable system of categories and hence cannot produce synthetic-dynamic concepts of the kind we are accustomed to employ today. . . . And this is the second distinctive characteristic of antique historiography: it is rhetorical. . . . The ethical and rhetorical approach are incompatible with a conception in which reality is a development of forces. . . . [The texts used] reveal the limits of antique realism and thus of antique historical consciousness. (*Mimesis*, 38, 40)

The necessary corollary to that approach was an attachment to models of exposition and explanation that had proven themselves throughout antiquity. That may have been even more true in the Roman period, when the works of Greek literature were religiously collected and systematically imitated: schoolchildren learned to copy out selected passages to serve as unsurpassable models. Dionysius of Halicarnassus is known to have written a treatise on mimesis *(On Imitation),* now lost, but, "even before him, the methodical imitation of the great writers was one of the three parts of an orator's education" (M. Croiset).[18] Dionysius's treatise dealt primarily with what ought to be imitated in the great historians of the past (Herodotus, Thucydides, Xenophon, and others).

In another of his treatises, *Ancient Orators,* Dionysius—after many others— took issue with what he called "decadence," which according to him came to afflict the art of oratory after Alexander. It was ruined by a defect called "Asian- ism," defined by characteristics very close to those commonly used to refer to Darius's Persia: opulence *(euporia),* luxury *(tryphē),* lack of dignity *(ageneia),* soft- ness *(malakia),* effemination. In short, Asianism was a courtesan of easy virtue who, "having arrived the previous day, or the day before that, from some filthy hole in Asia, a Mysian perhaps, or a Phrygian, or even some Carian woman of ill omen," took the place of the "freeborn wife." Against such a deplorable devel- opment, Dionysius proposed no more and no less than to restore the ancient order *(hē arkhaia taxis),* that is, ancient rhetoric founded on wisdom (1.2).

To illustrate his thesis, Dionysius used the example of the rhetor Hegesias of Magnesia, who wrote a history of Alexander in about 250 B.C.E. Strabo consid- ered Hegesias the one who, "more than any other, initiated the Asiatic style, as it is called, whereby he corrupted the established Attic custom."[19] Dionysius saw him as the prototype of literary decadence, the alpha and omega of the authors he hated because they considered themselves original enough to break free from the rules of the tradition. He denounced the way Hegesias treated one episode in the history of Alexander, namely, the punishment imposed by the Macedo- nian king on Batis, whom Darius had named governor of Gaza. It is clear that, in recounting this episode, Curtius or his source (as well as a few authors closer to our own time) strove to copy as skillfully as possible a Homeric model, the pun- ishment of Hector by Achilles. Hegesias attempted the same thing, but Diony- sius believed he was unable to carry it off because his Asian manner was "scarcely good even for women or people of lowly station." The debate or polemic did not turn on whether one or another author had attempted to do "historical research," as we would call it: it was simply a matter of judging the literary quality of the work by the traditional rules of mimesis.

Dionysius's judgment of Hegesias—whom Strabo designated by the techni- cal term "rhetor"—tells us a great deal about the "historians of Alexander" dur- ing the Roman period. The debate reflected the intellectual climate in which these authors were working. Authors writing between the principate and the em- pire during the Roman period were primarily "moralists" in the political sense of the term: they granted priority to the social and cultural norms of their time.

In works that are essentially historicized essays on kingship *(peri basileias)* and on the sound balance required in the exercise of power, they used a narrative form frequently augmented and broken up by exempla and apothegms, so as to exalt the "good kings" and denounce the "bad." Arrian does not avoid such heavy-handedness. Consider his introductory declaration: he says he is basing himself primarily on two works, that of Aristobulus, "because he served under king Alexander in his expedition," and that of Ptolemy, "not only because he accompanied Alexander in his expedition, but also because he was himself a king afterwards, and falsification of fact would have been more disgraceful to him than to any other man." That statement may seem to reveal a disarming naïveté, but only when measured against present-day historical methods. In the tradition of the lessons he received from Epictetus, and probably with a bow to the imperial power of his own time, Arrian puts to use and contributes toward conveying one of the accepted characteristics of the "good king": he is duty-bound to tell the truth.

It is essential to observe that, within Arrian's intellectual context (and that of many of the other authors under discussion here), mimesis was a literary norm to which authors readily submitted, because possession of its secrets allowed them to rival the best writers. So it was that, from one author to the next and from one century to the next, typical heroes, typical situations, and typical (invented) speeches were transmitted and tirelessly reproduced, without regard for historical verisimilitude, or rather, without any regard for a historian's concerns. In a famous opuscule, *How to Write History,* Lucian, who was acquainted with Arrian's work, ridiculed all those who, he said, took pride in writing history without taking the trouble to familiarize themselves with the rudiments of the historical method. His aim was to correct their errors and to teach them their craft. In particular, he scoffed at anyone who intended slavishly to imitate the great ancestors: "One copies Thucydides, another transcribes Herodotus . . . all these historians enter into competition with Thucydides" (§§ 18, 26). He denounced the tendency among the historians of his time to devote their books to the praise of the great men whose biographies they were writing: "The historian's only duty is to say what happened. But he cannot do so if he is afraid of Artaxerxes, whose doctor he is, and if he is expecting a purple gown, a gold necklace, a Nisean horse as payment for the praise lavished [on the king] in his history" (§ 39).

Lucian's readers knew that his target in this case was Ctesias, physician in the court of Artaxerxes, but also anyone who agreed to work in the service of a

Great King and to receive tokens of appreciation. An artist or doctor like Hippocrates, who reputedly refused to reply to the Great King's invitation to his court, became a classic literary type.

The problem is that Lucian, though a polemicist and a talented parodist, was not in the best position to dispense lessons on method to anyone, being himself a fanatical and captivating practitioner of mimesis. Praising Thucydides and Xenophon—who is called an "unbiased writer," which may come as a surprise to some—Lucian denounces Aristobulus, who "had described the single combat between Alexander and Porus, and read that selection from his work specially to the king, in the hope that it would win him the prince's favor, because of the lies he had invented to enhance Alexander's glory and the exaggerations he had given of his real exploits" (§ 12). Lucian may have reproached the historian-courtiers out of a desire to mock a contemporary, Arrian, who in his preface had expressed full confidence in Aristobulus. The paradox is that Lucian himself turned these reproaches into a form of kingship fable. Energetically rejecting the witless fawning of Aristobulus, "the king took the book and threw it into the Hydaspes, on which they happened to be sailing." The moral of the story is simple and clear: the ideal king is the friend of truth *(alētheia)*; he hates flatterers *(kolakes)*. Lucian comes close to repeating one of Arrian's justifications in that same preface, used in support of Ptolemy's credibility. Because Ptolemy was himself a king, "falsification of facts would have been more disgraceful to him than to any other man."

It has often been pointed out that the primacy granted to imitation does not rule out creativity, at least in the best writers of the Hellenistic and Roman periods. It might even be preferable not to translate *mimesis* as "imitation." It is not pastiche but rather a "reference to the literary heritage."[20] Such an observation will surely delight specialists in literature and literary creation. Historians are another matter. They must now confront an even more terrifying monster, born of the unlikely but fertile union between imitation and invention. Distinctions must clearly be made between one ancient author and another, but it is not unusual for an ancient "historian" to dedicate himself to imitation and, at the same time, to engage in the most unbridled inventions, against a backdrop that is unverified and difficult to verify by contemporary historians. Following the well-worn method of source criticism, historians of Alexander and Darius are often reduced to weighing the plausibility of the imitation against the implausibility of the invention, at the risk of attributing an immoderate place to the plausibility of their own interpretations.

Arrian and Xenophon: From one *Anabasis* to Another

It is possible to claim, without devaluing his talent in any way, that Arrian, a contemporary of Lucian, also made broad use of the resources of mimesis. There is little doubt that, in the opposition he sets up between Alexander and Darius and in many other passages of his work, Arrian, like a number of his literary contemporaries, used and abused famous models he had borrowed. Photius said that, from the linguistic and stylistic standpoint, Arrian was "unquestionably an imitator of Xenophon." Arrian's admiration for Athens and for Xenophon is well known, as attested by the title he chose for his book on Alexander's conquests: *Anabasis.* In terms of his contrasting portraits of Darius and Alexander, one obvious parallel to Xenophon's book by the same name is unavoidable, namely, Xenophon's sharp opposition between King Artaxerxes II and his brother Cyrus the Younger. Think in particular of the portrait of the young prince, which Xenophon, obeying a norm that Arrian will also follow, introduces just after the description of Cyrus's death on the battlefield of Cunaxa.

This famous passage has its place within a literature of praise that began in courtly circles and that passed into a current of Greek literature that had taken Cyrus's side. In fact, the exaltation of Cyrus the Younger in one current, long hegemonic, of contemporary Achaemenid historiography is purely and simply beholden to that ancient tendency.

As for Plutarch's *Artaxerxes,* it takes its information, and especially its judgments, from Ctesias and other authors of the *Persica.* It constantly hammers away at Cyrus's moral and political superiority to his brother. Xenophon summarizes his view elsewhere, in a fictive dialogue: "'By Zeus,' said Socrates, 'Cyrus the Younger, had he lived, would, I think, have made an excellent sovereign. He showed evidence of that, especially when he marched against his brother in their rivalry for the throne.'"[21] According to Plutarch, Cyrus, "along with much high-sounding talk about himself, . . . said he carried a sturdier heart than his brother, was more of a philosopher, better versed in the wisdom of the Magi, and could drink and hold more wine than he. His brother, he said, was too effeminate and cowardly either to sit his horse in a hunt, or his throne in a time of peril."[22] This passage makes it easier to understand the struggles between the two camps in the court of Darius II, father of Artaxerxes and Cyrus: "Restless and factious men thought that affairs demanded Cyrus, a man who had a brilliant spirit, surpassing skill in war, and great love for his friends; and that the magnitude of the empire required a king of lofty purpose and ambition."[23]

These are all qualities that will also be found lacking in Darius III, when facing Alexander.

Let us now read the funeral oration for Cyrus in Xenophon's *Anabasis* side by side with the funeral orations that Arrian devotes to Alexander and Darius. From Xenophon's first words, it is clear that the objective is to contrast, point for point, Cyrus to his brother Artaxerxes, the legitimate king. Like Arrian, who obviously borrowed a great deal from his model, the portrait is constructed around a series of superlatives (fourteen in the Greek text):

> While [Cyrus] was still a boy and was being educated with his brother and the other boys, he was regarded as the best of them all in all respects . . . the most devoted to horses and the most skilful in managing horses;[24] he was also adjudged the most eager to learn, and the most diligent in practising military accomplishments, alike the use of the bow and of the javelin. Then, when he was of suitable age, he was the fondest of hunting and, more than that, the fondest of incurring danger in his pursuit of wild animals. On one occasion, when a bear charged upon him, he did not take to flight, but grappled with her and was dragged from his horse; he received some injuries, the scars of which he retained visible to all, but in the end he killed the bear; and, furthermore, the man who was the first to come to his assistance he made an object of envy to many. (1.9.2–6)

Arrian borrowed many stylistic features from Xenophon. In particular, his portraits are based on categories that Xenophon used in his different works. In a sense, Artaxerxes facing Cyrus the Younger, and Darius facing Alexander, represent the generic Great King. In a different opuscule *(Agesilaus)*, Xenophon contrasts that type to the Spartan king, a Greek hero steeped in every virtue. Whereas Artaxerxes "believed that it befitted his dignity to allow himself to be seen only rarely, Agesilaus was eager to appear at all times. . . . People scoured the world over in search of what the Persian might take pleasure in drinking; thousands strove to invent something to pique his appetite. . . . Agesilaus, thanks to his love for work, drank with pleasure anything at hand, ate with pleasure whatever food there was" (§ 9). Think of Arrian's Alexander: "With regard to bodily pleasures, he enjoyed perfect self-control; where pleasures of the mind were concerned, he was insatiable only for men's praise." Darius, by contrast, "was in the habit of taking with him" whatever was necessary "for his luxurious mode of living, even though he was going on a military expedition."[25]

Xenophon's book and writing technique were not copied solely as a school exercise. The reason Darius is so rarely mentioned in Arrian's work is, first and foremost, that the *Anabasis* is devoted to celebrating Alexander's heroic deeds. Arrian aptly expresses his view in a long passage, traditionally called the "second preface":

> And, indeed, Alexander was right to account Achilles happy on that score especially; for though Alexander was fortunate in other respects, here there was a void, since his exploits were not published to mankind in a worthy manner either in prose or in verse. Nor were his praises sung in lyric poetry as were those of Hieron, Gelon, Theron, and many others who do not bear comparison with him. Consequently, Alexander's exploits [*ta erga*] are much less well known than the paltriest of ancient deeds. For the expedition of Cyrus' Ten Thousand against King Artaxerxes, and the sufferings of Klearkhos and the men captured with him, and the march to the coast of those same men under Xenophon's command are much better known, thanks to Xenophon, than Alexander's exploits [*ta Alexandrou erga*]. Yet Alexander did not serve under another man's command, nor did he merely defeat those who impeded his march to the coast as he fled from the Great King. One can point to no other man, Greek or barbarian, who performed exploits so numerous and so momentous [*kata plethos he megethos*]. It was this, I affirm, that spurred me on to write this history, and I have not considered myself unworthy to make Alexander's exploits [*ta Alexandrou erga*] known to mankind. That much I have discerned about myself, whoever I may be. I need not set down my name, for it is not unknown to men, nor is my country nor my family nor the offices, if any there were, I have held in my own land. But this I do put on record: that these chronicles are my country and my family and my offices, and have been from my youth. And that is why I do not consider myself unworthy of a foremost place among Greek writers, if indeed Alexander merits a foremost place among warriors. (1.12.2–5; P. Mensch trans.)

Arrian, then, intends to celebrate Alexander's heroic deeds, or *erga*. The repeated use of that term leaves no doubt. It attests as well to an imitation of Herodotus, who set out to highlight and recall the *erga* of the kings—especially the Lydian, Babylonian, Egyptian, and Persian kings—and of the various peoples.[26] There is also no doubt that Arrian sought inspiration in Homer, even more than in Xenophon and Herodotus, particularly for the most heroic aspects of the young Macedonian king.

The preface contains an explicit reference to Cyrus and the Ten Thousand, but in an infinitely less positive context than in the speech attributed to Alexander before the Battle of Issus. As Mogens H. Hansen points out, such pre-battle speeches were composed entirely by the ancient authors, based on apothegms and very short sentences that the general may have uttered as he went from one contingent to another along the battle line, perhaps addressing a soldier or officer.[27]

According to Arrian (2.7.9), in the speech Alexander gave prior to Issus, he "reminded them of Xenophon and the 10,000 men who accompanied him, asserting that the latter were in no way comparable with them either in number or in general excellence. . . . And yet they put the king and all his forces to rout close to Babylon itself, and succeeded in reaching the Euxine Sea after defeating all the races which lay in their way." In the preface, by contrast, Arrian strives to place the two anabases and their respective leaders in opposition. Alexander led the army on his own, whereas Cyrus was flanked by Greek leaders. The Ten Thousand and Xenophon did not face the multitude of the king's soldiers alone: Cyrus led them on the first part of the expedition, as they ascended (*anabasis* in the strict sense) toward the interior. There was no crushing victory outside the walls of Babylon, and that precedent is not judged very positively. It is said that the Ten Thousand fled the Great King, and the victories they subsequently enjoyed were against adversaries who were less than glorious. In addition, these victories occurred when the Greeks were fleeing toward the sea, during the *katabasis* (descent toward the coast). By contrast, Alexander did not undertake any *katabasis;* he did not flee the Great King.

In other words, Arrian exploits the historical precedents for the needs of the argument at hand. In the first instance (the speech prior to Issus), the Ten Thousand are used to exalt the consistent superiority of the Greeks over the Barbarians, on the basis of a well-known topos, the opposition between quantity (Barbarians) and quality (Greeks). In the second instance (the preface), Arrian is motivated by the desire to prove that no one had performed *erga* that could compare to those of Alexander. In that case, the adventure of the Ten Thousand is put forward as a counterexample, because, fundamentally, they behaved in a manner similar to Darius III. Note the reference to a flight from the enemy: Arrian in particular presents these frantic and repeated escapes from pitched battles as a recurrent trait of Darius III's conduct vis-à-vis Alexander, and in contrast to him. It is also clear that Arrian, in accordance with the principles defined in his preface, does not cite any heroic deed *(ergon)* attributable to the Great King, even though one tradition, known to Diodorus and Justin and transmitted by them, claimed that before his accession Darius had performed a memorable feat.[28]

Those who insisted on the cowardice of the Persians, based on long-distance comparisons with the great captains, often made Alexander's victories look less glorious. Lucian is amused by that paradox, fictively attributing to Philip words that are very critical of his son's victories: "You who never fought anyone but cowards *[deloi]* . . . Medes, Persians, Armenians . . . always ready to throw down their bows, their javelins, their wicker shields . . . don't you know that, before you, the Ten Thousand under Clearchus's leadership defeated them, and that the enemy fled without even waiting for the Greeks' arrows?" In another chapter of *Dialogues of the Dead,* it is Hannibal who points out the superiority of his victories, in a formulation that once again postulates the Great King's cowardice: "I fought against the bravest men, not against the Medes and the Armenians, people who flee before they are even pursued and who abandon victory to the bold. . . . As for Alexander, he was victorious over the cowardly Darius."[29]

Alexander's flatterers were perfectly well aware of that rhetorical trap. Merely to avoid the difficulty, they liked to attribute words to Darius, so that he could thereby personally authenticate Alexander's courage. That is quite obvious in the speech attributed to the Great King when he learns, upon the death of his wife, Stateira, of Alexander's magnanimity: " 'Well,' said he, 'I do not yet perceive the condition of the Persians so deplorable, since the world can never tax us now with imbecility or effeminacy, whose fate it was to be vanquished by such a person.' "[30]

Cyrus the Younger, Alexander, Darius, and Their Faithful

Certain characteristics of the "ideal leader" can be identified in Xenophon's work. In some sense they add further weight, if only by way of contrast, to the negative charge attached to Darius III. One particularly convincing example: the leader must have the ability to attract and hold on to the indefectible devotion of his friends and soldiers, by means of his generosity toward them.

Just as Arrian's Alexander "spent ungrudgingly for the benefit of others," Xenophon's Cyrus is particularly praised—as is the Cyrus of the *Cyropaedia*—for the quality of *polydōria.* The term can be translated as "generosity," but etymologically

it refers to the distribution of multiple gifts *(dōra)*. *Polydōria* is the act of reward-
ing services rendered and of showering gifts on those who serve with devotion.
Cyrus, "when he had tasted some specially excellent wine, . . . would send the
half remaining flagon to some friend . . . or, perhaps, . . . the remainder of a
dish of geese."[31] So too Alexander, "when the rarest fruits and fish were sent to
him from the sea-coast, . . . would distribute them so lavishly among his friends
as to leave none for himself."[32] It was thanks to that practice that Cyrus the
Younger was able to rally around him the Persian nobles and, more generally,
all those who should have maintained their allegiance to Artaxerxes II, the legitimate Great King.

In the discourse of legitimation in Xenophon's *Oeconomicus,* Socrates, the
fictive spokesman, explains that Cyrus the Younger would have made an excellent sovereign, presenting the following observation as indisputable proof: "No
deserter, it is said, went over to the Great King from Cyrus, but thousands and
thousands went over to Cyrus from the Great King. Now, in my eyes, it is great
proof of a leader's valor that people readily [*hekontes*] obey him and consent to
remain with him in danger. Cyrus's friends fought with him as long as he lived
and, when he was killed, all except Ariaeus died with him, doing battle on his
body" (4.17–18).

And in the *Anabasis:* "Although Cyrus was a slave, no one deserted him to
join the King, save that Orontas attempted to do so (and he, mark you, speedily
found out that the man he imagined was faithful to him, was more devoted to
Cyrus than to him); on the other hand, many went over from the King to Cyrus
after the two had become enemies (these being, moreover, the men who especially possessed self-respect), because they thought that if they were deserving,
they would gain a worthier reward with Cyrus than with the King" (1.9.29).

The same presentation can be found in Ctesias, court physician to Artaxerxes II, whose *Persica (Persian History)* also displays a flawless commitment to
the memory of Cyrus the Younger: "Many defectors went over to Cyrus from
Artaxerxes, but none went over to Artaxerxes from Cyrus. That is why Arbarios,
who attempted to join with Cyrus and was denounced, was smothered to death
in ashes."[33] In reality, many of the Persian nobles did choose Artaxerxes over
Cyrus, and many more deserted Cyrus than Xenophon and Ctesias want to
admit. But it hardly matters that the initial observation is fabricated: this is the
realm of image making, and ideal kingship is here embodied in a man who the
authors want to show deserved the royal title more than his brother. The emphasis placed on the Persians' loyalty and their unification behind Cyrus be-

longs to a universal discourse of royal legitimation, which favors the hero at the expense of a brother who is reputed to be totally lacking in the virtues that define and authenticate a king.

What is particularly noteworthy, however, is that an absolutely identical discourse can be found in a letter that, according to Arrian, Alexander sent in response to Darius's diplomatic overtures after Issus. The Macedonian king does not merely accuse the Great King and his predecessors of being responsible for the war: he presents himself as a political alternative. To that end, he methodically undertakes to call into doubt the royal and dynastic legitimacy of his adversary, who, he believes, seized royal power in violation of Achaemenid rules and Persian traditions. Among the arguments used by Arrian's Alexander: "Now that I have prevailed in battle—over your generals and satraps, and now over you and your own forces—and the gods have given me possession of the country, I am also responsible for all the men who on your side, survived the battle, and fled to me, and who remain with me not unwillingly, but have joined my campaign voluntarily [*hekontes*]" (2.14.7).

The message, which contrasts two types of adversaries, those who surrender of their own free will and those who surrender following a defeat, could not be clearer. Alexander is claiming that the Persians who were in his camp after the battle were not prisoners of war eager to return to Darius's camp and to participate in reprisals and a counterattack. On the contrary, they had voluntarily rallied behind Alexander and, rather than be the Great King's comrades in arms, they now wanted to face him as the Macedonian's comrades.

That argument provides support for a discourse that leads logically to the following statement: "Come to me therefore—since I am lord of all Asia." From Xenophon to Arrian, from Cyrus the Younger to Alexander, and finally, from Artaxerxes II to Darius III, the discursive connections are unequivocal: after implacable discourses of delegitimation, Artaxerxes II and Darius III were stripped of their status as Great Kings, not simply by their declared enemy but also as a result of an irrevocable choice publicly expressed by their former comrades in arms. Even worse, when the discourse is partly reversed in favor of Artaxerxes, beginning with Cunaxa, the long-distance comparison with Darius will once again work against the memory of the last of the Achaemenids. The argument recurs in the monarchical literature: Ptolemy uses it to denounce the violence and illegitimacy of Perdiccas; and an identical charge, based on the same ideological assumptions, is brought against Darius in the Persian and Arabo-Persian literature.[34]

One of the signs that Socrates considered proof of the indefectible attachment of Cyrus's close circle to his cause and, even more, to his person, was that, "when he was killed, all except Ariaeus died with him, doing battle on his body." There is a striking contrast between Cyrus the Younger's death as recounted by Xenophon and Darius III's demise as narrated by Arrian. The inspiration they share is fairly obvious, at both the literary and the ideological level. First, there is Cyrus in Xenophon's *Anabasis:* "Furthermore, what happened to Cyrus at the end of his life is a strong indication that he was a true man himself and that he knew how to judge those who were faithful, devoted, and constant. When he died, namely, all his bodyguard of friends and table companions died fighting in his defence, with the exception of Ariaeus; he, it chanced, was stationed on the left wing at the head of the cavalry, and when he learned that Cyrus had fallen, he took to flight with the whole army that he commanded" (1.9.30–31).

As an example of the remarkable devotion to the beloved and respected master Cyrus, several ancient authors report the story of Artapates. Here is Xenophon's version: "Of Artapates, the one among Cyrus' chamberlains who was his most faithful follower, it is told that when he saw Cyrus fallen, he leaped down from his horse and threw his arms about him. And one report is that the King ordered someone to slay him upon the body of Cyrus, while others say that he drew his dagger and slew himself with his own hand; for he had a dagger of gold, and he also wore a necklace and bracelets and all the other ornaments that the noblest Persians wear; for he had been honoured by Cyrus because of his affection and fidelity" (1.8.28–29).

What a difference from Darius's death in Arrian! "After this, wandering as an exile from his own kingdom, he died after being betrayed by his personal attendants to the worst treatment possible, being at the same time the Great King and a prisoner ignominiously led in chains; and at last he perished through a conspiracy formed of those most intimately acquainted with him" (3.21.5).

The theme and how it is treated are especially noteworthy in that Arrian is the only one of these authors to develop them within the context of a discourse directed against Darius. The theme is later taken up in collections of exempla. Aelian tells a "lovely story" in which he contrasts the pitiable death of Darius, abandoned by all—except his dog—to the admirable loyalty of Artapates, who preferred to kill himself on his master's body.[35]

Alexander, Darius, and the Homeric Model

To return to Arrian's declarations in the second preface of the *Anabasis*: "One says that Alexander blessed Achilles for having Homer to proclaim his fame to posterity. . . . It was this, I affirm, that spurred me on to write this history, and I have not considered myself unworthy to make Alexander's exploits [*ta erga Alexandrou*] known to mankind." Greek education was based on a constant reading of Homer, especially the *Iliad*. Arrian recalls that Alexander, upon the death of Hephaestion, shaved his own head. Arrian comments: "That Alexander should have cut off his hair in honour of the dead man, I do not think improbable, . . . especially from a desire to imitate Achilles, whom from his boyhood he had an ambition to rival."[36] And Plutarch reports, in an enthusiastic portrait of the young Alexander: "He was likewise fond of literature and of reading, and we are told by Onesikritus that he was wont to consider the Iliad the provisions for his journey, which sustained his military valor [*tes polemikēs aretēs ephodion*], and that he always carried with him Aristotle's recension of Homer's poems, which is called 'the casket copy,' and placed it under his pillow together with his dagger."[37] Dio Chrysostom even claims that the king knew the entire *Iliad* and a large part of the *Odyssey* by heart.[38] The early part of the campaign is full of explicit references to the Trojan War: just as Agesilaus had attempted to do, Alexander, on a completely different scale, conducts his adventure in the footsteps of Achilles and Agamemnon.

On the basis of these references, some historians have reconstructed a Homeric portrait of an Alexander heady with glory, showing no concern for the rationality that befits the leader of an army. That is going too far, however. Alexander's desire to be heroic is plausible, and his wish to capture the imagination no less real. As described by Arrian, the pilgrimage to the tombs of the Greek heroes in Troy indicates an undeniable admiration for heroes of what would now be called mythology, but who were for Alexander heroes near at hand. It also attests to his intent to appropriate their glory and to present himself as their designated successor: "He went up to Ilium and offered sacrifice to the Trojan Athena; . . . he dedicated his full armour in the temple, and took down in its place some of the dedicated arms yet remaining from the Trojan war, which, it is said, the hypaspists henceforth used to carry before him into battle."[39]

It is also beyond doubt that heroic imitation was part of an ancient tradition dedicated entirely to celebrating Alexander's glory. Like everyone who received a Greek education anywhere in the Greco-Roman world, Arrian had a good knowledge of Homer. What could be better than to take inspiration from the *Iliad* to depict Alexander's feats? Heroic and Homeric images are scattered throughout the ancient accounts and in fact organize them. They are presented as Homeric-style narratives and were understood as such by readers. That is particularly true of the accounts of battles and of Alexander's heroic deeds *(erga)*.

According to Arrian's account of the Battle of the Granicus, for instance, Alexander set an example in the attack: "Alexander leaped upon his steed, ordering those about him to follow, and exhorting them to show themselves valiant men," and he repeatedly engaged in feats of single combat.[40] Diodorus depicts a duel *(monomakhia)* between Alexander and a Persian, whose outcome is greeted by cheers from the soldiers in both camps.[41] Diodorus makes direct reference to Homer: he reports that Alexander received many blows, including "three on the shield which he had brought from the temple of Athena" (17.21.2).

What is most interesting is the contrast, whether explicit or merely suggested, between Alexander and the Persian leaders. Before the battle, as the armies mass on either side of the river, Alexander "was conspicuous both by the brightness of his arms and by the respectful attendance of his staff."[42] Not only does he not conceal himself, he has every intention of exposing himself to view before battles and to blows during battle, and "was made a conspicuous figure by his shield and the long white plume which hung down on each side of his helmet."[43] At Gaugamela, "his helmet was of steel, polished as bright as silver."[44] That motif was borrowed directly from the Homeric epic, which presents Hector "of the gleaming helmet" and Achilles, "whose splendid shield, diversely decorated, covers his chest, while on his head his beautiful helmet sways . . . where brilliant golden hair flutters about."

Where were the opposing Persian generals? According to Arrian, Alexander had to lead the charge of his horsemen, in order to flush them out from "the place where the whole mass of their horse and the leaders themselves were posted."[45] That detail immediately evokes what the same author, basing himself explicitly on Xenophon, says of the position Darius would occupy during the two pitched battles to come. Arrian mentions that "Darius himself occupied the centre of the whole army, inasmuch as it was the custom for the kings of Persia to take up that position."[46] That was also the case at Gaugamela, again according to Arrian: "In the centre where King Darius was had been posted the king's kinsmen, the Persian guards carrying spears with golden apples at the butt end, the Indians, the transplanted Carians, as they are called, and the Mardian archers." The information can probably be traced back to Aristobulus, who claimed that, in the reconstitution of the deployments of the Persian army at Gaugamela, he had used "the written scheme of arrangement drawn up by Darius," which was later captured.[47]

Arrian confirms and authenticates the information with the following reference, comparable to present-day footnotes: "The reason of which arrangement has been recorded by Xenophon, son of Gryllus." In fact, in the description he gives of the disposition of troops by Artaxerxes and Cyrus the Younger at the Battle of Cunaxa, Xenophon uses the following expression: "The King held the centre of the Persian army; in fact, all the generals of the barbarians hold their own centre when they are in command, for they think that this is the safest position, namely, with their forces on either side of them, and also that if they want to pass along an order, the army will get it in half the time; so in this instance the King held the centre of the army under his command . . . there was no one in his front to give battle to him."[48]

It is difficult to escape the impression that, within Arrian's narrative logic, that explanation adds even more weight to the negative judgment of a Great King who, for reasons of safety first and foremost, rejected one-on-one combat. That is how Callisthenes presents it: the Great King, having initially planned to place himself at the center of the army, supposedly slipped into a different position to avoid directly confronting his adversary.[49]

On the opposite side, by contrast, Alexander made himself seen; everyone was looking at him. There is even the impression that the armies stopped to better admire the young king's personal exploit. Described as a painter would represent it, Alexander's position is the opposite of the one that the classical texts regularly attribute to the Persian kings. Most often, such kings do not take part in skirmishes; they stand to the side and watch the battle unfolding before their eyes, as if it were a spectacle.[50]

The Homeric view is not specific to Arrian. In the description Diodorus gives of the Battle of the Granicus, the Persians conduct themselves very courageously, but Alexander's stance is heroic. He is the only one to fight against the multitude: "The Royal Kinsmen[51] now pressed in a solid body about the two fallen men; at first they rained their javelins on Alexander, and then closing went all out to slay the king. But exposed as he was to many and fierce attacks he nevertheless was not overborne by the numbers of the foe. Though he took two blows on the breastplate, one on the helmet, and three on the shield which he had brought from the temple of Athena, he still did not give in, but borne up by an exaltation of spirit surmounted every danger" (17.21.1–2).

Many narrative and literary elements also appear in the accounts Diodorus gives of the assaults on Tyre:

> Alexander addressed the Macedonians, calling on them to dare no less than he. . . . Now he performed a feat of daring which was hardly believable even to those who saw it. He flung a bridge across from a wooden tower to the city walls and crossing by it alone gained a footing on the wall, neither concerned for the envy of Fortune nor fearing the menace of the Tyrians. Having as witness of his prowess the great army which had defeated the Persians, he ordered the Macedonians to follow him, and leading the way he slew some of those who came within reach with his spear, and others by a blow of his sabre. He knocked down still others with the rim of his shield, and put an end to the high confidence of the enemy. (17.46.1–2)

Similarly, Curtius writes: "Conspicuous in his royal insignia and flashing armour, he was the prime target of enemy missiles. And his actions in the engagement were certainly spectacular." And in Gaza, "he did put on his cuirass, which he rarely wore."[52]

Homeric mimesis is everywhere. Curtius also describes the punishment inflicted on Batis, head of the garrison, as follows: "The king gloated at having followed the example of his ancestor Achilles in punishing his enemy."[53] This is a reference to book 22 of the *Iliad*: "Achilles committed a grave offense against divine Hector. He pierced the tendons of his feet from the heels to the ankles, then bound them to his chariot, letting his head drag on the ground. He climbed into the chariot, took up the illustrious weapons, and with a crack of the whip made away with the horses, which fervently flew off."

Several histories of sieges in India confirm the heroic bent of the ancient sources. According to Arrian, Alexander, facing enemies who had taken refuge in a citadel, "was seen to be the first man to scale the wall and get hold of it. The other Macedonians seeing him were ashamed of themselves and mounted the ladders in various places."[54] A few days later, he faced a new rampart and a new siege, which would become one of the Macedonian king's most celebrated claims to fame.

> Thinking that the Macedonians who were bringing the ladders were laggard, Alexander seized a ladder from one of the bearers, set it up himself against the wall, huddled under his shield and mounted up; next went

Peucestas, carrying the sacred shield, which Alexander had taken *from the temple of Athena of Ilium* and always kept by him. . . . Standing as he was upon the wall, Alexander was shot at all round from the neighbouring towers (for none of the Indians dared approach him). . . . *Conspicuous as Alexander was* both by the splendour of his arms and by his extraordinary audacity, he decided that by remaining where he was he would be in danger, while not even performing any *deed of note,* but that if he leapt down within the wall he might perhaps by this very action strike the Indians with panic but, if not and danger was inevitable, he might do great deeds [*megala erga*], *worth hearing to men of later generations,* and that glory would attend his death. On this decision he leapt down from the wall into the citadel. . . . Alexander himself was struck . . . and fell there bending over his shield. Peucestas stepped astride him as he lay there, and held over him *the sacred shield from Ilium.* (6.9.3–5; 10.2; Brunt trans., my emphasis)

Other authors give the same account: "The king was left alone, and boldly took a step which was as little expected as it is worthy of mention. It seemed to him out of keeping with his tradition of success to descend from the wall to his troops without accomplishing anything. Instead, he leapt down with his armour alone inside the city."[55] Diodorus adds that Alexander, gravely wounded by an arrow that had struck him under the breast, continued to defend himself and even to attack. He killed a barbarian with his sword and "defied the Indians to come forward and fight with him."[56] A heroic and Homeric motif if ever there was one, that type of challenge is extremely common in the *Iliad.* The desire for renown is also borrowed from the epic: "No, I will not die without a fight or without glory, or without a great exploit that will be recounted for posterity," says Hector.

Alexander's conduct, both at Issus and at Gaugamela, is presented and judged in the terms of that heroic war ethos, particularly in Arrian. Such a reference can only accentuate the negative portrait of Darius. On each occasion, Alexander personally led his army with youthful verve. Already at the Granicus, he rejected Parmenion's advice to be cautious, and he was the first to set off into the river. The Persians, who recognized him "by the brightness of his arms and by the respectful attendance of his staff," massed their cavalry squadrons in front of him.[57] Surrounded by valorous enemies, Alexander fought them off and took three blows "on the shield which he had brought from the temple of Athena."[58] In Justin's account of the Battle of Gaugamela, "Alexander . . . made the most hazardous efforts; where he saw the enemy thickest, and fighting most desperately, there he always threw himself, desiring that the peril should be his, and not his soldiers'. By this battle he gained the dominion over Asia" (11.14.5–6).

That technique of mimesis, combined with the use of invention, has clear implications for the present-day historian, in terms of the credibility that ought to be granted to Arrian. The acknowledged similarity between one *Anabasis* and the other raises many doubts, both about the idealized portrait Xenophon presents of Cyrus the Younger and about the disdainful portrait Arrian transmits of Darius, not only in the funeral oration but also more generally, in all the chapters that relate the first years of the war Alexander waged against the Achaemenid Empire.

Arrian's Darius is less a historical figure with a distinct and clearly analyzed individuality than a historiographical phantom created through the use of stereotypes. Systematically positioned as a foil, he is destined on every occasion to enhance the brilliance of the young Macedonian conqueror. The cursory portrayal of him is the result less of historiographical observation than of a literary elaboration that, though creative, conveys Greco-Roman representations that exclude every other point of view. Arrian, even while challenging the works of courtiers and flatterers, which he judges harmful, in reality places himself very clearly within an encomiastic logic: from the standpoint of the image of Alexander it seeks to transmit, his *Anabasis* belongs in the first place to the genre of the paean.

Darius, Alexander, and Porus

Of all the adversaries the Macedonian encounters, a single king stands out, and the traditions that arose about him cast into even greater relief, by implicit or explicit contrast, Darius's terrible reputation. All the ancient authors emphasize repeatedly the imposing physical presence of King Porus of India, "equally distinguished for strength of body and vigour of mind."[59] "Most historians are agreed that Porus stood four cubits and a span high."[60] But Arrian and Diodorus claim he was even taller. It is even said that he was properly proportioned to ride an elephant, and that "his javelins were flung with such force that they were little inferior to the darts of the catapults."[61] Hence the reflection that Curtius attributes to Alexander: "At last . . . I behold a danger that is a match for my courage—I must take on extraordinary beasts and extraordinary warriors together."[62] This is one way to suggest that Alexander was himself tall, which was not the case.

According to Lucian, the king threw into the Hydaspes pages that Aristobulus had read aloud to him, and which attributed mad exploits to Alexander during his single combat with Porus. In particular, Aristobulus claimed that Alexander had killed elephants with only his javelin.[63] That excellent exemplum is intended to illustrate everything that separated a king enslaved to his flatterers from a king who bowed to the imperative of truth. All these passages elaborate a well-known discourse on ideal kingship, in which Alexander is presented as the indisputable protagonist, even when he agrees to share the stage with a "partner" he has chosen for himself.

The account of Porus's resistance makes him out to be a hero. Although wounded in multiple places, he wants to do battle to the end. According to one version, he was ultimately placed in a cart, and, when Alexander came to see him, Porus acknowledged that the Macedonian was stronger than himself, adding: "Even so, being second to you brings me no little satisfaction." Hence Alexander's decision: "Alexander made him one of his friends and, shortly afterwards, bestowed on him an empire larger than he had formerly held."[64]

The same ingredients can be found in Arrian, accompanied by a few distinctive and interesting comments. After the battle, Alexander arrived on horseback with a few companions to meet his adversary, as if to pay homage to a king whose authority, or in any case moral distinction, he had recognized. "He admired his handsome figure and his stature, and the appearance he gave of a spirit not yet tamed; but one brave man meeting another brave man, after an honourable struggle against another king for his kingdom."[65]

A contrast can immediately be drawn between that statement and the way the ancient authors present Darius's ultimate decision to do battle with Alexander, at a war council reported by Diodorus: "He searched for a competent general to take over Memnon's command but could find no one, and finally felt constrained to go down himself to take part in the contest for the kingdom."[66] Conversely, the encounter between Alexander and Porus is between two brave men, two kings in the fullest sense of the term. Furthermore, when Alexander asks Porus how he wants to be treated, the Indian simply responds, "like a king," and Alexander "treated the brave man like a king, and from that time found him faithful in all things."[67]

The opposition set up between Porus on one hand and Darius and the other Persian kings on the other is not only suggested by the phraseology; it is also explicit at the beginning of Arrian's discussion. "When Porus, who exhibited great talent in the battle, performing the deeds not only of a general but also of a valiant soldier, observed the slaughter of his cavalry, and some of his elephants lying dead, others destitute of keepers straying about in a forlorn condition, while most of his infantry had perished, he did not depart as Darius the Great King did, setting an example of flight to his men; but as long as any body of Indians remained compact in the battle, he kept up the struggle" (5.18.4–5).

That says it all. The "royal" treatment that Alexander grants to Porus stands in contrast to his response to Darius after Issus. The Great King had (supposedly) written: "And now he, a king, begged his captured wife, mother, and children from a king."[68] Alexander's reply is scathing: "Come to me therefore—since I am lord of all Asia. . . . Whenever you send to me, send to me as the king of Asia, and do not address to me your wishes as to an equal. . . . Speak to me as to the man who is lord of all your territories. . . . And if you dispute my right to the kingdom, stay and fight another battle for it; but do not run away. For wherever you may be, I intend to march against you."[69] For Arrian, the opposition between Darius and Porus is perfectly clear-cut. Porus shares with Alexander the royal virtues—the "chivalrous" virtues, so to speak—that find such clear expression on the battlefield. In both cases, the discourse makes Alexander a perfect king, whether he stands in contrast to Darius or whether he himself recognizes that Porus possesses the same virtues that make Alexander a hero.

❦ 5 ❧

A Different Darius or the Same One?

In the Great King's Camp

No funeral oration, favorable or unfavorable, appears in the works of the Vulgate authors for the last of the Achaemenids. But the overall tone of these writings, especially with respect to their judgments of Darius, does have certain particularities when compared to Arrian's work.

It is clear, for example, that Curtius's choice is different from Arrian's: instead of following Alexander step by step, he prefers to give the impression that he is taking readers into the heart of Darius's camp and is making the Great King and his intimate circle speak and react before their eyes. That is why he describes a war council in the spring of 333, the marching order of Darius's troops as they left Babylon, and the scene of the Great King torturing the eunuch Tyriotes.[1] Such points of view are particularly common in book 5, where Curtius chooses to follow events leading up to the death of Darius, without interrupting them with a report on European affairs. The reader is therefore "present" at the war council that gathers at Arbela after the defeat of Gaugamela and at the meetings marked by interminable speeches. The reader then witnesses the plot Bessus and his lieutenants hatch against Darius, not to mention his death scene, which is unfortunately truncated by a lacuna in the manuscript.[2]

Should the present-day reader, however, be taken in by procedures that usually allow the author to present moral considerations—very commonplace, moreover—on the exercise of power and the fragility of all things human? In analyzing such narratives, we must always keep in mind the technique of the apothegm, as it is set forth by Plutarch and as it is applied on a grand scale in the works devoted to Alexander: "Some casual remark or jest . . . will throw more light upon what manner of man he was than the bloodiest battle."[3] That is exactly why Arrian expresses reservations in reporting the anecdote of the Persian princesses brought in to Alexander and Hephaestion: "This I record neither being sure of its truth nor thinking it altogether unreliable. If it really occurred, I commend Alexander for his compassionate treatment of the women, and the confidence he felt in his companion, and the honour bestowed on him; but if it merely seems probable to historians that Alexander would have acted and spoken thus, even for this reason I think him worthy of commendation" (2.12.8). In other words, *se non è vero, è ben trovato!* (even if it's not true, it's a good invention). In Arrian's eyes, all that matters is the nuance he can thereby add to Alexander's moral portrait.

On literary grounds alone, it was certainly gratifying to make the Great King himself one of the speakers, to have the reader learn of the death of the king's wife from the eunuch who had just fled Alexander's camp, or, after the battle, to see Darius assembling his councillors and delivering an interminable speech, "reproduced" in direct or indirect speech. It was also tempting to report the words of a Greek soldier in Darius's immediate entourage: for example, Patron, leader of the Greek mercenaries, to whom Curtius attributes a number of exchanges with his master. But in that case the soldier in question is only Curtius's mouthpiece or the author's creation pure and simple, and his presence in no way authenticates the account. In addition, in the case of the (supposed) conversations between Darius and Porus, Curtius, intent on depicting an exchange that supposedly remained absolutely secret and confidential, without witnesses, claims that the king "had some knowledge of Greek."[4] By contrast, in a passage that is at least as suspect, in which Justin depicts Darius on the brink of death, entrusting a soldier with the mission of transmitting a message to Alexander, the author clearly suggests that the king is unable to speak any language but his own.[5] And it would be utterly pointless to assess the relative credibility of each of the two texts, with the aim of determining the reality of Darius's language skills. Neither Curtius nor Justin cares about that, and they probably have no information on the subject. All that matters to them is the coherence, and therefore the effectiveness, of their literary devices.

Treason and Loyalty

From time to time Curtius also seems to be analyzing one political situation or another from the point of view of Darius's interests. Consider the use of the term "traitor" *(traditor)* applied to Persians who went over to Alexander's camp. The case of Mithrenes, who handed over the citadel of Sardis without a fight in exchange for a place within the Macedonian king's aulic hierarchy, is altogether interesting. After the Battle of Issus, when Alexander wanted to send an emissary to reassure the Persian princesses, held captive and overcome with anxiety about Darius's death, he considered dispatching Mithrenes, "the man who had surrendered Sardis . . . since he knew the Persian language." Then the king changed his mind, because "he became concerned that a traitor might only rekindle the captives' anger and sorrow."[6] Mithrenes is also called a traitor *(proditor)* when he receives a satrapy after the taking of Babylon. In that case he is linked to two other Persians, who have just handed over the city to Alexander. In both cases, then, they seem to be rewarded by the Macedonian king for their act of treason: "On the deserter [Alexander] conferred the satrapy of Babylon, and he instructed Bagophanes, who had surrendered the citadel, to accompany him. Armenia was assigned to Mithrenes, the man who had betrayed Sardis."[7]

The example of the (anonymous) military governor of the city of Damascus is also worthy of note. After Issus, Alexander sent Parmenion to take possession of Damascus and the enormous riches Darius had left there before the battle. The Macedonians seized an Achaemenid soldier, a Mardian, who was carrying a letter that the governor of Damascus had sent to Alexander: "In it Alexander was told to send one of his generals quickly with a small detachment so that the governor could surrender to him everything the king had left in his keeping. Parmenion accordingly gave the Mardian an escort and sent him back to the traitor [*proditor*], but the man gave his guards the slip and entered Damascus before dawn" (3.13.3–4).

In the end, the governor ordered men, beasts, and treasures to leave Damascus: "He feigned flight," because "his real purpose was to offer the treasure as plunder to the enemy." The ploy was successful. Curtius's judgment of the traitor is irrevocable: "The man who betrayed his huge fortune was quickly visited by the avenging deities with a well-deserved punishment. One of his confidants—I suppose out of respect for the king's station, even in these sad circumstances—murdered the traitor and took his head to Darius, providing him with a timely consolation for his betrayal: for now he had both taken revenge of an enemy and was also aware that the memory of his former majesty had not disappeared from the minds of all his subjects" (3.13.17).

It certainly cannot be said, however, that Curtius systematically takes Darius's side against Alexander. He condemns those who betrayed Darius, but not because he regrets that they facilitated Alexander's task or because he is using a Persophile source. His words express a view that is less historical than dramatic. The Latin author is a legitimist and a moralist: he praises those who remain faithful to their pledges and condemns those who rise up against the established authorities and betray the trust the king has placed in them, whether that king is Darius or Alexander. Indeed, those close to Alexander must also show proof of their loyalty at every opportunity, including and especially when they receive a letter from the Persian king urging them to betray or even assassinate their leader. Such is the case for Sisines, "one of his loyal associates," and for the Greek soldiers on whose attachment and loyalty Alexander thought he could count.[8] For Curtius, it matters very little that Sisines is actually in the service of Darius and that Arrian characterizes him as "one of his own faithful Persian court-iers."[9] Only the exemplum of monarchical morality really interests Curtius. That also explains the remarkable popularity of a story that, shortly thereafter, depicts Alexander suffering from a violent fever after a bath in the icy Cydnos; the physician Philip, though suspected of treason, cures his king and thereby gives stunning proof of his loyalty. Curtius draws the moral of that monarchi-cal fable: "The Macedonians have a natural tendency to venerate their royalty, but even taking that into account, the extent of their admiration, or their burn-ing affection, for this particular king is difficult to describe."[10]

When we move from Alexander's camp back to the camp of Darius, the reconstituted speeches and declamations are no less numerous, prolix, and rhe-torical, and the exempla and lessons proposed vary but little: again and again, the aim is to exalt what the author obviously considers the supreme virtue, namely, monarchical loyalty. That is particularly true in this part of Curtius's work, where he juxtaposes the king and his faithful on one hand, and, on the other, the traitorous satraps Bessus and Nabarzanes and the Bactrian troops. He especially praises the Greek mercenaries and their leader, "whose loyalty to the king remained unshaken to the end."[11] So too Artabazus, "the oldest of Dar-ius' friends," though exiled to Macedonia under Artaxerxes III's reign, demon-strated toward Darius a loyalty "right to the end."[12] More generally, the author says, the Persians believed that "to desert a king was an act of sacrilege."[13] In fact, "among those peoples the king commands extraordinary respect: his name itself is enough to make them assemble, and the veneration he enjoys in prosperity remains with him in adversity."[14]

Such formulations proliferate in Curtius, who claims that, after Issus, Alex-ander "was unable to discover" where Darius had gone, "because of the Persian custom of concealing the secrets of their kings with an amazing degree of loyalty. . . . The ancient code, enforced by the kings, had ordained silence in these matters on pain of death, and disclosure meets with more severe punishment than any crime."[15] In this context, Curtius argues that the person who punished a traitor and brought his head to Darius showed "respect for the king's station" and that Darius himself could therefore believe he had not lost the loyalty of his subjects.[16] That is why the author also praises Batis, governor of Gaza, "a man of impeccable loyalty," he says approvingly—and why he condemns the Homeric but barbarous treatment inflicted by Alexander, now a follower of "foreign modes of behaviour."[17]

Batis's loyalty is given particular emphasis because the author has just denounced Bessus, satrap of Bactriana, to whom Darius had appealed to ready a new army, when the Great King returned to Babylon after the defeat of Issus. "His loyalty was suspect and he was restless in his position as a second-in-command; he had regal ambitions, and treason was feared on his part since it was his only way to fulfil them."[18] All these individuals resurfaced in Ecbatana after the defeat of Gaugamela. Against the king and his faithful, Bessus and Nabarzanes had a plan to betray Darius and hand him over to Alexander, but they were afraid that the Macedonian king, himself a natural defender of monarchical loyalty, would punish them for their treachery.[19] In the words Curtius puts into Darius's mouth, the king, to better convince those close to him to remain faithful despite their reluctance, vilifies these men, who are called "parricides"—a term also used for the physician Philip, suspected of poisoning Alexander, and for the young page Dymnus, suspected of conspiracy against his king.[20] Darius provokes his own men, suggesting that the only alternative to continuing the war will be "to follow the example of Mazaeus and Mithrenes and govern a single province at another's whim."[21] In fact, he tells them, "traitors and deserters are now rulers in my cities so that the rewards given to them might tempt your support away from me."[22]

Using the same expressions repeatedly throughout these chapters, Curtius also attributes an important role to Patron, leader of the Greek mercenaries, who accompanies Darius to Ecbatana with the little band of survivors. Curtius likes to single out for high praise the Greeks' indefectible loyalty to Darius, particularly that of Patron, "ready to resort to any means to prove his loyalty"; Patron himself "followed the king's carriage, looking out for a chance to talk to him, for he sensed treachery on Bessus' part."[23] Then Patron is granted a private interview with Darius to denounce the conspiracy of Bessus and Nabarzanes.

Curtius attributes these words to him: "Your Majesty . . . we few are all that remain of 50,000 Greeks. We were all with you in your more fortunate days, and in
your present situation we remain as we were when you were prospering, ready
to make for and to accept as our country and our home any lands you choose.
We and you have been drawn together both by your prosperity and your adversity. By this inviolable loyalty of ours I beg and beseech you: pitch your tent in
our area of the camp and let us be your bodyguards. We have left Greece behind" (5.11.5–6).

Despite the art of rhetoric Curtius deploys here, the long discussion set in
the Persian camp, combined with a series of speeches from the protagonists
(Darius, Artabazus, Patron, Bessus) and their conversations among themselves,
raises many doubts for present-day readers. The emphasis placed on the decisive role of the Greek mercenaries is very suspect. The story of Patron and his
men is only one illustration of a proven theme long used by the ancient authors.
Curtius, speaking of the contingents of Greek mercenaries that came to Darius
before the Battle of Issus, comments that it was in them that "the king had most
confidence. . . . They were his main hope, and virtually his only one."[24] But the
use of that topos is attested much earlier and is constantly driven home during
accounts of the wars the Great Kings waged throughout the fourth century. It
is on the basis of these texts that the questionable theory of the "military decadence of the Persians" was elaborated—they were incapable, it was said, of
holding onto their empire without the decisive role of Greek mercenaries, hired
at a steep price on the Aegean market.[25] Although under totally different conditions, the place Curtius attributes to Patron—alongside Darius, surrounded by
dangers and traitors—brings to mind the excessive importance that all the
Greek sources grant to the Greek leader Memnon in the Great King's plan of action at the start of the war. Learning of Memnon's death but reluctant to take
command of the army himself, Darius seeks a possible successor within his close
circle, but to no avail.[26]

Even the composition of these chapters attests more to Curtius's desire to
construct a drama around the eternal themes of treachery and reversals of fortune: "I am living proof of fortune's capriciousness," exclaims the king before
his entourage (5.8.15). The unlucky hero's solitude is the emblematic representation of such vicissitudes. An exile in his own kingdom (5.8.11), Darius has only
a few loyal men left (Artabazus, Patron, and their Persian and Greek soldiers),
whereas the Bactrian contingent is completely devoted to the traitor Bessus
(10.5). Then, soon convinced "of the truth of the charges made by the Greeks"

(12.3), the king himself urges Artabazus to leave his personal service and go over to the Greek camp. He once more finds himself completely alone, except for a few eunuchs, who "had nowhere else to go." "The men forming his customary bodyguard slipped away (men who ought to have risked even their lives to protect their king) because they thought they would be no match for all the armed men they believed to be already approaching. A deep solitude fell on the tent." Upon entering, Bessus and Nabarzanes "were informed by the eunuchs that the king still lived; they ordered him to be arrested and bound. The king who a short time ago had ridden in a chariot and received divine honours from his people was now, with no interference from without, made a captive of his own slaves and set in a squalid wagon" (5.12.9, 15–16).

These chapters prepare the reader for what follows: Darius's assassination, the death scene, the mission the dying king entrusts to his conqueror to avenge the "parricide," and finally, Alexander's pursuit of Bessus.[27] The capture of Bessus, and therefore the expedition to Bactriana, appear to be a logical and necessary sequence: every crime must be punished, every traitor must suffer the punishment he deserves.

Darius and the Cadusian Giant

More surprisingly, passages from Diodorus and Justin recount a story that supposedly depicts Darius's extraordinary courage, which is said to have earned him the right to wear the Persian crown. The singularity of this tradition raises a problem.

Diodorus Siculus devotes a discussion to Persian dynastic history centered on the loathsome personality of the chiliarch Bagoas, "a eunuch in physical fact but a militant rogue in disposition," whom he had already introduced in the previous book. The author tells how that high-ranking individual assassinated Artaxerxes III and placed the young Arses, the deceased's younger son, on the throne. About to be eliminated himself, Bagoas had the king and his children killed and entrusted supreme power to "a member of the court circle," the one called Darius, before being eliminated in short order by the new king.[28] That discussion does not project an unequivocally positive image of Darius: like his predecessor, he is more or less a plaything in the hands of Bagoas, to whom he is even more indebted given that he was named king when "the royal house was . . . extinguished, and there was no one in the direct line of descent to claim the throne." Endlessly repeated, that version portrays Darius as a usurper. Alexander could therefore legitimately contest his power. He tells his adversary:

"After slaying Arses with Bagoas's assistance, you unjustly seized the throne contrary to the law of the Persians and ruled your subjects unjustly."[29]

Only the end of the story gives a positive coloring to Darius's personality. Not content to resist the chiliarch's intrigues, "the king, calling upon Bagoas, as it were, to drink to him a toast and handing him his own cup [already poisoned by Bagoas] compelled him to take his own medicine."[30] The new king thus gave proof of his ability to act, albeit by ruse and in combination with a masked violence.

The next episode is much warmer, even frankly laudatory:

> Dareius's selection for the throne was based on his known bravery [*andreia*], in which quality he far surpassed the other Persians. Once when King Artaxerxes [III] was campaigning against the Cadusians, one of them with a wide reputation for strength [*alkē*] and courage [*andreia*] challenged a volunteer among the Persians to fight in single combat [*monomakhēsai*] with him. No other dared accept, but Dareius alone entered the contest and slew the challenger, being honoured in consequence by the king with rich gifts, while among the Persians he was conceded the first place in prowess. It was because of this prowess that he was thought worthy to take over the kingship. This happened about the same time as Philip died and Alexander became king. Such was the man whom fate had selected to be the antagonist of Alexander's genius, and they opposed one another in many and great struggles for the supremacy [*peri tou prōteiou*]. (17.6.1–2)

In book 10 of the *Philippic Histories,* now lost, Pompeius Trogus recounted the history of Persia between the reign of Artaxerxes II and the accession of Darius III, apparently devoting a large place to the revolts by the satraps. The prologues that survive indicate that the author dealt with the reign of Arses, then with that of Darius, who "maintained a long war . . . against Alexander the Great"—the usual periphrasis that allowed ancient authors to distinguish that Darius from his homonymous predecessors.[31] Fortunately, Pompeius Trogus's work was summarized by Justin, who transmits a fragment of its history of Darius: "[Thus Ochus] made war upon the Cadusii; in the course of which one Codomannus, followed by applause from all the Persians, engaged with one of the enemy that offered himself for single combat, and, having killed his antagonist, regained the victory for his fellow soldiers, as well as the glory which they had almost lost. For this honourable service Codomannus was made governor of Armenia. Some time after, on the death of Ochus, he was chosen king by the people from regard to his former merits [*virtus*], and, that nothing might be wanting to his royal dignity, honoured with the name of Darius. He maintained a long war, with various success, but with great efforts, against Alexander the Great. But being at last overcome by Alexander, and slain by his relations, he terminated his life and the kingdom of the Persians together."[32]

The two passages, which certainly come from a common, intermediary source, give a homogeneous image of Darius, that of a heroic warrior and an active, energetic, and effective ruler. That tradition was followed by an entire current of European historiography, which since Bossuet had wanted to emphasize the great valor of Alexander's adversary: "Darius, who ruled Persia in his time, was just, valiant, generous, beloved of his people, and he lacked neither the spirit nor the vigor to carry out his designs" (*Discours sur l'Histoire universelle*, pp. 564–565). Texts relating his courage during a Cadusian war were obviously the source of that sympathetic portrayal.

Diodorus seems to give two opposing versions of Darius's accession, placed one after the other, without really grasping that they are not easily reconcilable. In one version, Darius is an intimate friend, even an obligee, of Bagoas, and the chiliarch puts him on the throne to better retain his own hold on power. In the other, Darius owes his accession to his personal courage, which was recognized and rewarded by King Artaxerxes III himself (in the form of a provincial governorship) and by the Persians as a whole (in his accession to the throne). In the first version, Darius is only the last avatar of a royal line, as unremarkable as Arses had been, promoted and then eliminated by Bagoas. He is even somewhat less glorious. It is pointed out, in fact, that he does not belong to the royal Achaemenid bloodline. In the second version, by contrast, Arses is not even named, and Darius succeeds Artaxerxes III without any break in continuity.

The Tradition of the Duel before the Two Armies

The tradition transmits a story built on a model that is extremely widespread in many societies. Valerius Maximus, in an enumeration of the victories of one Lucius Siccius Dentatus, explains that he participated in 120 pitched battles; that "thirty-six times [he] returned with spoils from the enemy, and of that number, eight times they were taken from those he had provoked in a duel, in the presence of both armies."[33] This passage demonstrates that ritualized duels need to be carefully distinguished from single combats, which can unfold during pitched battles. A number of man-to-man combats appear in the battles described in the

Iliad, and the pitched battles Alexander waged are often depicted on the Homeric model.

As Arrian notes, speaking of the Battle of the Granicus, "though they fought on horseback, it seemed more like an infantry than a cavalry battle; for they struggled for the mastery, horses being jammed with horses and men with men."[34] Curtius makes a comparable remark about the personal conflicts at Issus: "Obliged to fight hand-to-hand, they swiftly drew their swords. Then the blood really flowed, for the two lines were so closely interlocked that they were striking each other's weapons with their own and driving their blades into their opponents' faces. It was now impossible for the timid or cowardly to remain inactive. Foot against foot, they were virtually engaging in single combat, standing in the same spot until they could make further room for themselves by winning their fight."[35]

At the Granicus, the Persian Spithridates, "a man of superior courage," accompanied by a troop of elite horsemen, swooped down on the Macedonians, "as if this opportunity for a single combat was god-given. He hoped that by his individual gallantry Asia might be relieved of its terrible menace." Alexander decided to go up against him and "drove his lance squarely into the satrap's chest. At this, adjacent ranks in both armies cried out at the superlative display of prowess." This remark, introduced to draw the reader's eyes and imagination to the king's heroic deed, does not imply that the duel occurred in isolation.[36] In declaring that "Fortune brought together in one and the same place the finest fighters to dispute the victory," Diodorus is being true to his model. To hail Alexander, he repeats an expression he had used a few chapters earlier in evoking Darius's prestige after his Cadusian victory: "Thus the king by common consent won the palm for bravery and was regarded as the chief author of the victory."[37] In reality, however, the combat between Alexander and Spithridates, accompanied by many parallel combats, did not decide the fate of the battle.

A parallel example immediately comes to mind. Known through Diodorus and Curtius, the scene takes place during one of Alexander's campaigns in Aria, a region of Iran. The satrap of Aria, named by Alexander, was Satibarzanes, "distinguished both for generalship and for personal bravery," who took up arms against the Macedonians. The king sent an army to oppose him. A pitched battle ensued, and, according to Diodorus, its outcome was indecisive: then "Satibarzanes raised his hands and removed his helmet so that all could see who he was, and challenged any of the Macedonian generals who wished to fight with him alone. Erigyius accepted and a contest of heroic nature ensued, which resulted in

Erigyius's victory. Disheartened at the death of their commander, the Iranians sought their safety in surrender, and gave themselves up to Alexander."[38]

Curtius's account is very similar. It simply clarifies that Erigyius responded to the challenge "though well advanced in age" and proudly displayed his white hair. The scene of single combat is presented canonically: "One might have thought an order to cease fighting had been given on both sides. At all events they immediately fell back, leaving an open space, eager to see how matters would turn out not just for the two men but for themselves for, though others fought, the decision would encompass them all."[39]

Interestingly, Curtius presents the final outcome of the duel as follow: "Alexander . . . was met on the road by Erigyius, who carried before him the barbarian's head, his trophy of the war."[40] In using typically Roman terminology, Curtius reminds us that Rome also had a tradition of single combat: when a Roman killed the enemy leader before the battle, he seized his weapons, which he would place in the sanctuary of Jupiter Feretrius as rich spoils *(spolia opima)*—at least under certain circumstances.[41] Apart from Romulus himself, the most famous example is certainly Marcellus, "a skillful man of war; his body was robust, his hand swift, his character bellicose. . . . He outdid himself in single combat. He never refused a challenge and killed all who provoked him." His most brilliant feat was performed during a battle against the Gauls at Clastidium: "At that moment, the king of the Gesates caught sight of him and guessed by his insignia that he was in command of the army. The king urged his horse on, far ahead of the others, and rushed to meet him, challenging him with loud cries and brandishing his spear. This was a man whose stature surpassed that of the other Gauls, and he was distinguished by the brilliance of his armor, dazzling as lightning and resplendent with silver, gold, and splashes of several colors. . . . Marcellus dashed toward the man, transfixed his cuirass with his spear, and, assisted by his horse's momentum, knocked him down, then, with a second and third blow, killed him on the spot."[42]

The Roman traditions also tended to recall the memory of Maximus Valerius Corvinus, who fought Gauls as well: "The leader of the Gauls, of an extraordinary size and height, his weapons gleaming with gold, strides quickly forward, swinging his javelin on his arm. Contemptuously and arrogantly looking about from on high, he demands that whoever in the Roman army dared fight him should come out to meet him. Then, as the others were paralyzed by fear and shame, the tribune Valerius, having first obtained permission from the consuls to fight such a monstrously arrogant Gaul, advanced with courage and discretion; they march toward each other, they stop, and already they were upon each other. . . . And so the tribune, before the eyes of both armies . . . defeated that fierce leader of the enemies and killed him."[43]

Another well-known combatant was Manlius, who took the nickname "Torquatus," supposedly because "of a gold necklace, plunder he had taken from the enemy he had killed": "A Gaul advanced. . . . Silence suddenly descended: he shouted in his loudest voice that whoever wanted to do battle with him should come forward. No one dared, because of his monstrous stature. Then the Gaul began to jeer and stuck out his tongue. All at once, Titus Manlius, a man of the most noble birth, took offense that such a great shame should come to the city. Manlius, I say, advanced and did not allow Roman valor to become the shameful booty of a Gaul. Girded with an infantryman's shield and a Spanish sword, he took his position opposite the Gaul. . . . When he had knocked him down, he cut off the head, removed the necklace, and placed it, still bloody, around his neck."[44]

A recurrent trait in these duels—particularly notable in the biblical battle between David and Goliath and in the confrontation between Alexander and Porus, but also in the examples of Marcellus, Maximus Valerius, and Manlius Torquatus—is the immoderate size of the "barbarian" leader.[45] This is also evident in the single combat in Sicily, where Pyrrhus defeated the leader of the Mamertines: "Pyrrhus advanced alone, ahead of the battle line, to repel them. He exposed himself to great dangers, attacking trained and courageous men. . . . Then one of the enemies, running far ahead of the others—a giant of sorts, splendidly armed—challenged the king in an arrogant voice to come out if he was still alive. Pyrrhus, exasperated, retraced his steps in spite of his squires. Filled with rage, his face wet with blood, terrible to behold, he rushed through his own men, caught up with the barbarian, and struck his head with a sword. Pyrrhus's arm was so strong and his weapon of such well-tempered iron that it split the body from top to bottom, and the two parts fell to either side at the same moment. That feat stopped the advance of the barbarians. They admired Pyrrhus for his superior nature and remained dumbstruck."[46]

The same trait is found in a fragment from the poet Alcaeus, quoted by Strabo. The story is set in the Near East during the Neo-Babylonian period (late seventh century B.C.E.): according to Alcaeus, "his brother Antinemides . . . won a great struggle when fighting on the side of the Babylonians, and rescued them from their toils by killing 'a warrior, the royal wrestler' (as he says), 'who was but one hand short of five cubits in height'" (about 6 foot 7 inches). For this feat he was awarded an ivory-handled sword.[47]

Darius, Codomannus, and the Cadusians

Precisely because of the diversity of cultures (from the Mediterranean to the Pacific) represented in the examples ordinarily used to illustrate the practice, the feat attributed to Darius cannot be associated specifically with the Iranian world. Even the challenge issued by Satibarzanes does not prove it was a practice confined to the satrapy of the Iranian plateau. In fact, the Macedonian leader Erigyius immediately understood the meaning of the challenge his adversary issued and responded to it without delay, quite simply because the practice was not unknown in Macedonia. That does not rule out the possibility, however, that it was also an Iranian tradition.

Although the Achaemenid documentation does not attest to the practice, illustrations of it can be found in Iran at a later time. In his *Persian War,* Procopius provides an excellent example when he describes a confrontation between the Sassanid Persians and the Byzantine army under the command of Belisarius and Hermogenes. The battle was slow getting under way, and an anonymous young Persian emerged from the ranks, rode up to the Roman battle line, and issued a challenge. The episode that follows greatly resembles accounts we have already seen: "No one of the whole army dared face the danger, except a certain Andreas, one of the personal attendants of Bouzes, not a soldier nor one who had ever practised at the business of war, but a trainer of youths in charge of a certain wrestling school in Byzantium." Without asking anyone's opinion, Andreas advanced and killed the Persian. The Persians, vexed, sent another horseman with the same aim, "a manly fellow and well favoured as to bodily size." This time, it was not a young man but an already elderly one, as attested by his white hair. Once again, no one responded to his challenge except Andreas. The first blow sent both fighters to the ground: accustomed to wrestling, Andreas was able to gain the advantage over the Persian, who was handicapped by his size. A roar from the Roman army greeted the feat, and the two armies separated.[48]

Duels are also common in Ferdowsī's *Book of the Kings,* where they unfold in accordance with an immutable ritual: a fighter issues a challenge, no one dares respond to it except a soldier distinguished by some quality or characteristic (an old man with white hair, for example, a motif that appears in the story of Satibarzanes and Erigyius and also in the story of Andreas the Byzantine).[49] One of the most famous accounts depicts Sohrab coming to the doors of King Kaous's tent to issue his challenge. No one dares respond except the famous Rustam, who, it is soon learned, is Sohrab's father. The two men face off in a specially delimited place, "a place two parasangs long between the two armies, where no one dared venture."[50] Then Rustam mortally wounds Sohrab.

The story of the Cadusian battle can easily be inserted into this system: when armies cannot decide the winner, a single combat is initiated by means of a provocation, issued aloud by a fighter from the "barbarian" army; the combat unfolds in a space left open by the soldiers, who are its spectators. In this case, a particularly impressive Cadusian soldier advances and provokes Artaxerxes's soldiers. The future Darius is the only one in the entire royal army to accept the challenge, and both camps acknowledge that his victory in single combat marks the end of the battle and the war. The Cadusians are considered collectively conquered, and the Great King is the conqueror. Darius/Codomannus has saved his camp and the king's prestige.

One of the constitutive elements of the narrative places it well within the imperial Persian tradition: the context of a war that the king is waging against the Cadusians. The classical authors mention several expeditions—under Darius II, Artaxerxes II, and Artaxerxes III—launched by the king against that people, whose territory extended north of Iran to the region surrounding the Caspian Sea. The primary aim of these periodic "visits" was to renew the treaty of "friendship and alliance" that linked Great Kings and Cadusian petty kings. By the terms of that alliance, the Cadusians were in principle supposed to provide tribute and military contingents.[51] It was in that capacity that Darius III, after Gaugamela, intended to demand that the Cadusians and the Sacians provide soldiers to the army he was proposing to reconstitute in Ecbatana.[52]

It is tempting to assume that the relationship between the central power and the Cadusians illustrates what Marcel Mauss defined as "regulated hostility." An accord could be concluded between two communities following a complex series of reciprocal services "of the agonistic type" *(potlach),* which might include single combat: "Clans, tribes, and families clash and confront one another, either in groups facing one another on the field or through their leaders, or both at once. . . . The principle of rivalry and antagonism predominates in all these practices. It extends even to battle, to the killing of the leaders and nobles who confront each other in that way."[53]

A recurrent element in accounts of these expeditions, which sometimes caused great difficulties for the Great Kings, was the repetitive character of the single combats between Roman and Gallic leaders: a Persian warrior displays extraordinary qualities, which leads to his being noticed and singled out by the king. The first example is Datames, who at the time belonged "to Artaxerxes [II]'s military corps assigned to guard the palace." The son of Camisares, "him-

self brave, an excellent soldier, whose loyalty the Great King had often had occasion to test," Datames received his first promotion: "For the first time, he
showed his mettle in the war the Great King was pursuing against the Cadusians, in which he played an important role. As a reward, since that war had
caused the death of Camisares, he succeeded his father in his government."[54]

During a different expedition conducted by Artaxerxes II, also against the
Cadusians, Teribazus extricated the army and the king from difficulties. He managed to fool the two Cadusian kings, persuading each of them that the Great
King wanted to make him his privileged ally: "And a peace was ratified with both
kings; whereupon Teribazus, now a great and splendid personage, set out for
home with the king."[55]

It is therefore not surprising that the Cadusian context and the theme of
single combat were purposely chosen to construct, a posteriori, a heroic biography favorable to the new king. It is easy to imagine that, in Persia as well, royal
legitimacy was indicated by the warrior function, a function clearly affirmed in
Darius's "mirror of the prince," that is, the inscription he had engraved on his
future tomb. The Greek authors were fond of courtly legends built around the
theme of the warrior king. Herodotus, for example, gives this explanation for
why Cambyses eliminated his brother Smerdis: "He was jealous of him for being the only Persian to succeed in drawing—though only a very little way, about
two fingers' breadth—the bow which the Fish-Eaters brought from Ethiopia."[56]
And the Greek writings that discuss the opposition between Artaxerxes II and his
brother Cyrus are filled with anecdotes and bons mots illustrating the theme of
the younger sibling's military superiority over the elder.

It is also interesting that, in the Cadusian context, Ctesias had already developed the motif of the hero who becomes king. Before Cyrus conquered the
empire, Ctesias says, the Cadusians were bitter enemies of the Medes. Under
the leadership of the Persian Parsondes, who had been exiled from the Median
court, they enjoyed a great victory over the Medes: Parsondes "was so admired
by the people of the land that he was chosen king."[57] Strabo can also be cited,
though the connection may be more tenuous in his case. He declares that "choosing the most courageous man to be king is a custom proper to the Medes, but it
is practiced only by the mountain peoples and not everywhere."[58]

The emphasis on an individual's personal courage and his promotion by
virtue of a royal act of favor is quite consistent with another canon of fictionalized biographies: Darius, being the son not of a king but rather of a private individual (idiōtēs), was particularly deserving of the crown. That is Cornelius Nepos's judgment of Cyrus and Darius I, "the most remarkable of kings, both of

whom were ordinary citizens when their merit earned them the crown."[59] As Valerius Maximus shows (3.4), studies of private individuals who became kings, or at least very powerful men, were an obligatory chapter in collections of exempla. Darius III appears alongside Darius I on such a list drawn up by Aelian.[60] In his manual on ancient history (1836), Heeren took a positive stance toward Darius, no doubt basing himself on Aelian and on Plato's theory: "Not having been reared in the seraglio like his predecessors, Darius displayed virtues that made him deserving of a fate better than the one that awaited him" (p. 119).

That legend, moreover, completely effaced another, infinitely less positive version, which made Darius a mere puppet in Bagoas's hands. It also eliminated Arses's reign, given that Justin claims that the royal proclamation occurred upon the death of Artaxerxes III, precisely because of the distinction the deceased king had granted Codomannus. It was the "Persian people" (again according to Justin) who, in a burst of spontaneous enthusiasm, brought Codomannus to the throne because of his remarkable virtues and conferred on him the illustrious name Darius.

There is little doubt that minstrels and storytellers of all kinds widely circulated such legends of legitimation. A passage from Dinon, father of Clitarchus, tells of a famous bard in the court of Astyage who alerted the king, through song and metaphor, of the danger posed by the Persian Cyrus.[61] As also attested by Xenophon and Strabo, it was through the "wise men," that is, the magi, that the founder's legends were committed to memory and then transmitted to young Persians from one generation to the next.[62] That means of transmission is eloquently attested in an extant fragment of Chares of Mytilene's *History of Alexander*. The author was a Greek who held an important post at the court of the Macedonian king. He tells of a lovely Iranian romance, in which the heroes are the beautiful princess Odatis and Prince Zariadres. Chares gives interesting details about how the story circulated among the Persians and Iranians: "This love affair is held in remembrance among the barbarians who live in Asia and it is exceedingly popular; in fact they picture this story in their temples and palaces and even in private dwellings; and most princes bestow the name Odatis on their own daughters."[63]

This is a concrete illustration of the transmission of stories in societies that, by preference, do not use the written form. Rather, they transmit the deeds of great men through the voices of bards—the memories and inventions they convey—and through the colorful and vividly rendered images of painters. It is therefore perfectly conceivable that an author during Alexander's time could have similarly collected and put in writing the version of the heroic duel won by Darius, adapting it for Greek readers, whose own mythic and historical memory was full of such stories of ritual combat.

Nuances and Contradictions

All in all, there is no doubt that ancient authors, in all their diversity, transmitted portraits or character traits of Darius that differed noticeably one from another. Not only are the Vulgate authors alone in recording a single combat between the two kings, but they also give unique information about the king's location during the major battles. Arrian, in a reference to Xenophon, specifies that Darius was at the center of the army, whereas Curtius notes that at Issus the Great King was situated on the left wing, where he "intended to fight."[64] Similarly, at Gaugamela, "Darius was positioned on the left wing with a large crowd of his men."[65]

Referring to Darius's conduct during battles, the Vulgate authors commonly use somewhat or even very positive expressions and formulation. Plutarch is the only one to give a "royal" physical portrait of Darius, calling him "the tallest and handsomest man in Asia. . . . Alexander had already noted the conspicuous figure of this tall, handsome prince, as he stood in his lofty chariot, surrounded by the royal body guard."[66] Justin underscores the king's steadfastness in military conflicts: "He maintained a long war, with various success, but with great efforts, against Alexander the Great."[67] The Great King's personal bravery is cast into relief: "Riding high in his chariot, Darius cut a conspicuous figure."[68] "The Persian king received their attack and fighting from a chariot hurled javelins against his opponents, and many supported him."[69] Diodorus and Curtius also report that it was not the Great King who gave the signal for the retreat at Gaugamela: "Persians and Macedonians alike were convinced that it was the king who had been killed, and though the fortunes of the battle were, in fact, still even, Darius' 'kinsmen' and squires caused consternation almost throughout the battlefield with their mournful wailing and wild shouts and groans."[70]

A tradition that Curtius and Justin transmitted about Gaugamela also merits attention. Referring to anonymous sources ("it is said"), Curtius reports that "Darius drew his sword and considered avoiding ignominious flight by an honourable death, but highly visible as he was in his chariot, he felt ashamed to abandon his forces."[71] The temptation of suicide brings to mind the attitude of Arsites, whom Darius named to the command of the armies of Asia Minor in 334. After his defeat at the Granicus, "Arsites fled from the battle into Phrygia, where he is reported to have committed suicide, because he was deemed by the Persians the cause of their defeat on that occasion."[72] That portrayal, originating in Pompeius Trogus as followed by Orosius, is also transmitted by Justin: "Darius, when he saw his army repulsed, wished himself to die"; Justin adds that he was "compelled by his officers to flee."[73]

Curtius and Justin also introduce a particularly significant monarchical motif, which tempers somewhat the very negative judgment generally made of the Great King's flight. The remnants of the royal army, hastily leaving the battlefield of Gaugamela and heading toward the city of Arbela, had to cross the Lykos (Little Zab) River. Royal advisers expressed the view that the bridge ought to be destroyed, to cut off the pursuers. At that time Darius refused to make such a decision: "He could see that destroying the bridge would make the thousands of his men who had not yet reached the river an easy prey for his enemy. We have it on good authority that, as he went off leaving the bridge intact, he declared that he would rather leave a road to those chasing him than take one away from the Persian fugitives."[74]

That is very different from the attitude of his distant successor Khōsrau, who under similar circumstances gave his soldiers three days to cross a bridge on the Euphrates: "When the appointed day was come, it happened that some of the army were left who had not yet crossed, but without the least consideration for them he sent the men to break up the bridge."[75]

It should be added that Diodorus and Justin are the only ones to mention any awareness on Darius's part of the Macedonian danger when he acceded to the throne.[76] Curtius and Diodorus also give information on logistical measures taken by the Great King at the start of his reign and between the battles of Issus and Gaugamela.[77] They are also the only ones to report a Persian counterattack on Alexander's rear guard after the Battle of Issus.[78] Diodorus, and especially Curtius, also seem to have had a particular interest in the "ancestral customs" of the Persians, to which they refer on several occasions. It is therefore beyond doubt that, overall, the view transmitted by Curtius, Diodorus, and Justin is less unfavorable than what is found in Arrian throughout the first part of the *Anabasis,* and in certain cases even displays a marked originality.

A "History of Darius"?

Are we to infer that Diodorus, Curtius, and Justin had access to a single and specific source that was based on information coming from inside Darius's own camp? Was there ever a Persian, or at least a Persophile, version of Darius?

The British historian W. W. Tarn defended that very thesis. A spirited proponent of Alexander's unequaled greatness, he could not admit even the partial reality of the positive notations about Darius found here and there: "Darius 'great and good' is a fiction of legend. . . . He was a poor type of despot, cowardly and inefficient," he wrote with great self-assurance (1:58). He attributed the positive portrait to the lost work of an unknown author, whom he calls "the mercenaries' source," and which, he postulated, was written from the point of view of the Greek mercenaries in Darius's service. It is this source that Diodorus supposedly followed up to the Battle of Issus and that Curtius employed until the death of the Great King (2:71–75, 105–106). Diodorus and Curtius, Tarn believed, borrowed the portrait of "Darius the brave" from that source, even though, according to him, "he was really a coward" (2:72).

Tarn went even further, proposing to identify, at least hypothetically, the origin of the information abundantly used by Diodorus and Curtius. According to him, Patron, leader of the mercenaries in Darius's service, was certainly the principal inspiration, or even the author, of the book in question. But the scenes and anecdotes set in Darius's camp in book 5 of Curtius's history do not necessarily prove that there were privileged informants there who later revealed their exclusive recollections. These scenes are closer to a skillful weaving of exempla than to a historical reconstruction founded on indisputable and verifiable eyewitness statements.

Several studies, relying primarily on the accounts of the first years of the war, have convincingly demonstrated that this "mercenaries' source" is nothing but a figment of the imagination. Although it is perfectly conceivable that mercenaries, after the war or after being captured, recounted what they had witnessed in the Persian camp (or what they had heard from where they stood), the existence of a book by Patron or someone else seems highly improbable. It would be better to consider the possibility of oral witnesses, who are by nature impossible to identify. In accordance with that plausible hypothesis, the most one could add is that the Persians who surrendered to Alexander between 334 and 330 might have spoken as well and might have transmitted memories to their friends and families. That may be how the accounts of the Cadusian exploit by the future Darius were collected.

It is often difficult, moreover, to draw firm conclusions on the basis of a comparison between Arrian and the Vulgate authors on a single episode. Take the example of Darius's location during the two pitched battles: he was on the left wing according to Curtius and Diodorus, whereas Arrian, basing himself on Xenophon, declares that his place was in the center, both to attend to his safety and to allow him to communicate with the right wing and the left.[79] Arrian, is not the first who, basing himself on Xenophon, mentions it. In a transparent allusion, Plutarch introduces the motif in one of the many versions of the famous (but most likely apocryphal) conversation held in Pella between Alexander and the Persian king's ambassadors. Anxious to garner information useful to the expedition he is contemplating, the young prince wants to know "in what part of the army the king fought."[80] At almost the same time Nicholas of Damascus also mentioned that central position, in recounting a battle between Cyrus the Younger and the Median king Astyages: "Cyrus was in the middle with the most noble Persians."[81] The author does not cite his source, though it may have been Ctesias. And in Arrian's time, Lucian even makes that detail an element of farce in his parody of Alexander's expedition: "The center for me, declares Samippos, as is the custom among the kings of Persia when they assist in operations," all the while assigning the right and left wings to his two companions.[82] Because Xenophon does not use the term *nomos,* it must have been in Arrian that Lucian found and copied it.[83]

The authors of the Roman period introduced the "king at the center" as a constitutive element of the narrative. For Lucian, in a tone of pure mockery, the central position of each of the two kings (Samippos and the Persian king) introduces the motif of single combat. That is already suggested by Xenophon's account of the Battle of Cunaxa, during which Cyrus the Younger supposedly wanted to go one-on-one against his brother. Situated within its context, Plutarch's comment also suggests that, several years before 334, Alexander was already thinking of the place the Great King would occupy, with the intent of fighting him in single combat. It is probably for the same reason that Aristobulus notes the presence of Darius III at the center during the Battle of Issus—a portrayal and interpretation that would elicit this ironic criticism from Polybius: "How did Alexander and Darius each know the other's position in the army?"[84]

References to Persian customs are common in the Greek and Roman texts, even among authors from the Byzantine period. Agathias devotes several chapters to the religious and social customs of the "Persians of today" (Sassanid era), using some information drawn from classical authors such as Herodotus and Ctesias, which allows him to mention several times Persians of times past (Achaemenid period).[85] References to Persian customs are also common in narrative texts, not only among authors who deal with Alexander's expedition but also in Procopius, who devotes a long discussion of his *War* to the conflict between the Byzantine and Sassanid armies.[86]

It is often difficult to determine the authenticity (or lack thereof) of the customs the Greco-Roman authors thereby introduce. The problem is to distinguish between a real custom, a custom invented to justify or adorn an Orientalist discussion of Persia, and a custom cited by an author from the Greco-Roman or Byzantine period on a model borrowed through mimesis from an author of the classical age. For example, the customs that the Greek authors cite in the context of the succession of kings are founded on a legalistic and almost constitutional view of the Persian monarchy, which in no way corresponds to reality. Within one historiographical current of antiquity, these same customs were integrated into a very suspect discourse, whose aim was to contest the dynastic legitimacy of Darius III.[87]

All things considered, nothing indicates that there was ever a "history of Darius" that could have inspired the Vulgate authors and from which, for example, they could have extracted original information on the "traditional customs of the Persians." At most it may be postulated that Clitarchus could have had privileged access to specific information through his father, Dinon, author of a work on Persian history *(Persica).* But that work is now lost, and it is not known at what moment in Darius's career Dinon ended his narrative.

One Alexander, Two Dariuses

Furthermore, these authors did not have a well-thought-out plan to rehabilitate the Great King. Depending on the needs of the narrative or argument, a single author may develop diametrically opposed theses from one work to the next and even from one chapter to the next, or, more exactly, he may transmit portraits that differ in every respect. Within the space of a few lines, for example, Diodorus offers two contradictory versions of Darius's accession. Plutarch is another case in point: although Darius is treated fairly well in the *Life of Alexander,* in *De fortuna Alexandri* he is violently denounced as a plaything of Fortune, a mere puppet in the hands of the vile eunuch Bagoas, and an undeserving and illegitimate Great King. Is it necessary to repeat that, despite the generous designation "historians of Alexander," granted purely for the sake of convenience, the authors we use—for lack of anything better!—are not historians in the sense we understand that expression?

Similarly, after showing Darius courageously doing battle, these authors do not hesitate to vigorously denounce the desperate flight on which he embarks as soon as the situation becomes a bit thornier. For example, Curtius forcefully condemns the decision Darius made in the grip of fear, taking flight and even shamefully "throwing off his royal insignia."[88] In a few words, the author completely destroys the favorable impression produced by the previous account. As for the theme of single combat, the conclusion drawn once again serves to exalt the bellicose zeal of Alexander, who constantly heads to the front lines and provokes his adversary.

It is therefore clear that the assessments favorable to Darius are presented concurrently with very negative judgments and are inserted into an account that always turns to his adversary's advantage. Admiration, in the form of Homeric mimesis, for the personage of Alexander and his incomparable feats is not specific to Arrian. Here, for example, is how Diodorus introduces his book devoted to the conquest: "Alexander accomplished great things in a short space of time, and by his acumen and courage surpassed in the magnitude of his achievements all kings whose memory is recorded from the beginning of time. In twelve years he conquered no small part of Europe and practically all of Asia, and so acquired a fabulous reputation like that of the heroes and demigods of old. . . . On his father's side Alexander was a descendant of Heracles and on his mother's he could claim the blood of the Aeacids, so that from his ancestors on both sides he inherited the physical and moral qualities of greatness."[89]

This passage confirms, were there any need to do so, that Curtius, Diodorus, and Plutarch also made broad use of many heroic and Homeric motifs.

In Plutarch's two very rhetorical discourses collectively titled *On the Fortune of Alexander,* the author is keen to develop the theme of the wounds Alexander received during the assaults he conducted in command of his troops, particularly during sieges, and not in individual exploits pure and simple. The stories about the feat performed during the siege of "an inconsiderable fortified town in a barbarous land" (India) occupies a prominent place, for "to what can you compare it but to a gleam of lightning violently flashing from a cloud?"[90] The king, bearing wounds over his entire body, displays a superhuman courage in the face of suffering: "wounded by the enemy, mangled, battered, bruised, from the crown of his head to the soles of his feet, *With spears, and swords, and mighty stones.*"[91] "Nor can we otherwise believe but that he himself gloried in his own wounds, which every time he beheld them called to his remembrance the conquered nation and the victory, what cities he had taken, what kings had surrendered themselves; never striving to conceal or cover those indelible characters and scars of honor, which he always carried about him as the engraven testimonies of his virtue and fortitude."[92] In this instance Plutarch gives a Roman interpretation of the warrior's scars, truly "signs acknowledging his manly courage," which, he says elsewhere, candidates for the consulate in earlier times had to display before all eyes, as unimpeachable evidence of their civic virtue.[93] The authors had a fondness for citing the famous example of the 120 pitched battles in which Lucius Siccius Dentatus had participated. They were eager to point out that, though his body was marked by forty-five wounds, "his back was free of all scar," because obviously only scars from "wounds received from the front" *(adverso corpore)* were honorable.[94] In the eyes of the Roman Curtius, the wounds Alexander and his generals received were also clearly "testimony of their valour."[95] And because the Vulgate authors liked to salute the courage of the Persian nobles as well, they sometimes used the same image to that end. Curtius is quite capable of distinguishing, among the Persians, between those Alexander wounded in the face and those who were run through from the back as they fled.[96] He hails the courage of the first group in the following terms: "Around Darius' chariot lay his most famous generals who had succumbed to a glorious death before the eyes of their king, and who now all lay face-down where they had fallen fighting, their wounds on the front of the body."[97]

The same author returns on several occasions to the theme of the Macedonian king's scars: "Though the scab had still not formed on his first wound, [he] kept fighting in the front line."[98] Even more explicitly, he says that the king, to instill courage in his troops before the Battle of Gaugamela, would himself set an example of bravery: "He was going to fight before the front standards. All his scars were testimony to his courage."[99] Plutarch's emphasis on the wounds Alexander received belongs, then, to a code that signifies the hero's incomparable courage and endurance. The king's body, transformed into a book of "engraven testimonies," becomes a witness to history: Every part of his body "called to his remembrance a conquered nation."[100]

In that respect, Plutarch says, Alexander was a counterexample to the Persian kings and especially to Darius. They are expressly characterized as "kings that never felt a wound nor ever saw a finger bleed; for they were fortunate, it is true,— your Ochi and your Artaxerxes." That includes Darius III, a "Sardanapalus . . . comber of purple wool."[101] For what is there to say about a man who, like Darius I, Xerxes, or Oarses (Darius III), ascended the throne "free from wounds, without loss of blood, without a toilsome expedition," and who, thanks to the intrigues of Bagoas, "had only to throw off the garb of a messenger [*astandēs*] and put on the tiara that ever stands erect"?[102]

Plutarch's *Life of Alexander* takes the form of an apologia, defending his memory against accusations that had been made against him in antiquity. The exposition of the virtues of the future king from his early youth speaks volumes in that respect. Using a common—even banal—literary device, Plutarch seems to suggest that these extraordinary propensities were publicly confirmed by the enemies the king was already preparing to face, in this case the ambassadors King Darius sent to Pella. Plutarch turns them into spokesmen for the incomparable greatness of the young Macedonian prince: "The ambassadors were filled with admiration, and declared that the boasted subtlety of Philip was nothing in comparison with the intellectual vigour and enlarged views of his son"—so much so that they "were astonished, and said, This youth is a great prince, but ours only a rich one."[103]

In the end, from Arrian to the Vulgate authors, whichever adversary is contrasted to Darius, either explicitly (Alexander, Porus), implicitly (Cyrus the Younger), or by subliminal mimesis (Artaxerxes), the Great King is doomed to lose the battle of memory, both under the weight of the weapons brandished by his adversary and through the cumulative effect of the literary devices the Greco-Roman authors use to sing the glory of the Macedonian king. It is altogether clear that the Persian king's conduct is described and conceived as a function of ethical norms for which Alexander serves as the sole paragon: the Great King cannot acquire or hold on to the devotion of his intimates; he lacks the mark of a great strategist, namely, an understanding of situations; he does not fight on the front lines; he does not take cities by storm; and his body is not covered with glorious scars. Within the logic of the history thus reconstituted and transmitted, he remains fundamentally "the Darius who was defeated by Alexander."

From Arrian to the *Alexander Romance*: The Solitude of the Great King

The central themes that the author of the *Alexander Romance* develops in his portrayal of Darius are identical to those Arrian elaborates. Unable to take up the challenge issued by his adversary, Darius unquestionably comes to look like a bad king. His faults are clearly depicted, beginning with the first embassy he sends to Alexander, who is in Phoenicia at the time. Darius is contemptuous of his adversary, whom he considers a child who still needs "to play and to be nursed"; a little later he orders his satraps to capture Alexander and bring him to Darius, "so that I may . . . send him back home to his country to his mother, Olympias. I shall give him a rattle and knucklebones, such as Macedonian children play with." Hence the haughtiness of Darius's response: "Even if the whole world becomes united under a single ruler, it will not be able to bring down the Persian Empire. I have so many troops that one might as well count the sand on the seashore as attempt to number them. I have sent you a chest full of gold, so that if you are unable to feed your fellow-bandits you can now give them what they need to return each to his country. But if you do not obey these orders of mine, I shall send my soldiers to pursue you until you are captured. Then you will not be treated like a son of Philip, but crucified like a rebel" (1.36).

The Macedonian king's reaction is understandable: he calls his adversary a braggart and compares him to those "dogs which, though weak in body, bark very loudly as if they could make an impression of strength by their barking."

With the first exchanges between the two kings, a recurrent theme is introduced, that of the betrayal by Darius's intimates. Struck by the young Macedonian king's strength and charisma, they are tempted to join him. Even the Great King's ambassadors are eager to explain to Alexander how to capture Darius "in an ambush." Alexander refuses but enjoins them to keep quiet about their conversations: Then "the messengers of Darius made many laudatory remarks, and the whole army joined in the acclaim."

Darius, who is himself soon struck by Alexander's self-assurance, orders his "generals beyond the Taurus" to seize the Macedonian. They refuse, fearing the Macedonian king and his army, and urge Darius to come personally to their assistance with a large army. A theme often repeated in the "historical" texts is thus introduced in an original form: the Great King takes command of the army and directly confronts Alexander only when forced to do so by his generals' failings. He soon demonstrates his inferiority, and the same words and expressions recur repeatedly to denounce his flight: "In the end there was a great rout of the Persians, who fled precipitately. . . . When evening came, the terrified Darius was still in fast retreat. Because his commander's chariot was too conspicuous, he dismounted and fled on horseback. But Alexander considered it a point of honour to capture Darius, and made all speed to catch up with him, for fear someone should kill him first. After pursuing him for six hundred stadia Alexander captured Darius' chariot and weapons, as well as his wife, daughters and mother; but Darius himself was saved by the onset of darkness, and because he had obtained a fresh horse. And so he escaped."[104] During the final battle King Darius exhibits the same behavior, not hesitating to trample the bodies of his own soldiers to get away: "Darius in terror pulled round the reins of his scythed chariot; as the wheels whirled, he mowed down a multitude of the Persians, like a harvester cropping the stalks of corn." Instead of being concerned for the fate of his soldiers in flight, instead of ordering the bridges to be left in place, Darius crosses the frozen Stranga. When his fleeing soldiers reach the river, the ice is breaking up, and "the river bore away as many as it engulfed.

The remaining Persians were killed by the Macedonians" (2.16.8). Then comes the conspiracy led by Bessus and Ariobarzanes, who hope to be pardoned and rewarded by Alexander.

Another Latin work customarily included among the writings in the literary vein from the Roman period is *Alexander's Itinerary*, which dates to about 338 or 340 C.E. It is addressed to Emperor Constantius II. On the eve of the expedition the emperor will lead against the Sassanid Persians, the narrative recalls the Macedonian's heroic deeds (and those of Trajan). Sometimes attributed to Julius Valerius (the hypothesis is debatable), the *Itinerary* seems to have been greatly inspired by Arrian, and its image of Darius is not fundamentally different from that author's. Facing a hero full of courage and daring in battle, one who shares the hard life of the common soldiers and is always ready to personally take command of his troops, the Great King resorts to trickery in his attempt to physically eliminate his adversary, and uses money to try to dissuade Alexander from continuing the fight. He leaves behind his royal insignia when he flees. At Gaugamela "he saw his men scattering in confusion, and his longing for safety made him neglect his reputation and turn in flight, with his chariot, too, deeming this the nobler course. Without difficulty the rest voted with their feet, followed their king's example, and shared his decisions" (§ 62; I. Davies trans.). Alexander's pursuit fails because "Darius had flown by like a veritable bird of passage" (§ 64).

Some sections of the *Itinerary* are clearly inspired by the Vulgate vein, however, including the flight of the eunuch Tyriotes after the death of the Great King's wife Stateira, a story particularly well developed in Curtius. In the *Itinerary*, the eunuch is anonymous and, instead of being brought to Darius's tent and tortured (as in Curtius and Plutarch), he makes his appearance in the form of a deus ex machina, as Darius is lecturing his troops before the Battle of Gaugamela. Without making explicit reference to Stateira's death, the eunuch delivers a long speech in which he praises Alexander's sexual continence and the respect he has shown toward the captive princesses. It is then that "Darius prayed to the gods, in front of the whole parade, that if he himself were no longer allowed by fate to rule over the Persians, Alexander might do so" (§ 57).

The treason of the Great King's intimates, insistently pointed out by Arrian, is also a prominent theme in another fictionalized history of Darius.[105] Long erroneously attributed to Plutarch, this curious minor work bears the title *Greek and Roman Parallel Stories*. Its author, pastiching Plutarch and using examples from the lives of illustrious Romans, seeks to show that stories and legends can actually be based on historical facts. To that end, Pseudo-Plutarch cites a parallel episode from the life of someone who belongs to what the author terms a more recent past. In that way Darius III is placed side by side with the Etruscan king Tarquin the Proud (§ 11). Both kings, the author claims, had to suffer betrayal to the enemy at the hands of a son. He mentions the first defeat of the Great King at the Granicus, where he supposedly lost "seven satraps and five hundred and two scythed chariots." Pseudo-Plutarch's "seven satraps" reappear in the *Itinerary:* "They govern the whole of Asia," declares the author: it was against them that Alexander supposedly sent Parmenion and Attalus as an advance guard, to weaken the Persian resistance (§ 19). These are Darius's "satraps and generals" in the *Alexander Romance* (1.28.4), whom the author also calls "generals" or "satraps" "from beyond the Taurus," the guards of Darius's kingdom (1.39.8). In any event, according to Pseudo-Plutarch, Darius decides to attack again the next day. But his son Ariobarzenes, particularly well disposed toward Alexander, vows to betray his father. Outraged, Alexander orders his head cut off.

The anonymous author cites his sources, whom he calls "men devoted to the writing of history" (in this case, an obscure "Aretades of Knidus," the presumed author of a work on Macedonia). But the anecdote is obviously only remotely related to the history of the battles between Darius and Alexander. Nevertheless, it further blackens the terrible reputation of the last Great King.

Freeze-Frame: Darius in the Naples Mosaic

Distinguished from the literary texts but not unrelated to them is a well-known iconographic document, which also bolsters "the history of Darius." This is the famous mosaic discovered in the "House of the Faun" in Pompeii on October 24, 1831, and called ever since the "Alexander Mosaic," the "Battle of Issus Mosaic," or the "Naples Mosaic" (Fig. 28). That last designation indicates merely that the mosaic is currently held in the Museo Archeologico Nazionale. The first two titles, by contrast, allude to particular, but disputed, interpretations of the figure considered to be the principal actor in the scene and to the historical circumstances that may have inspired the artist.

Composed of more than two million tesserae of naturally colored limestone and measuring 512 by 271 centimeters (16 feet 9 ½ inches by 8 feet 10 ¾ inches)—with its frame, 582 by 313 centimeters (19 feet 1 inch by 10 feet 3 ¼ inches)—the mosaic depicts a battle between two armies. From the very first hours of the mosaic's discovery, these were identified as the armies of Darius III and Alexander (Fig. 29). The right part of the composition comprises nineteen figures (Fig. 30). The Great King is recognizable in his chariot (Figs. 31–32): holding a bow in his

28. *Naples Mosaic, discovery and first surveys (drawing by Niccolini).*

29. Naples Mosaic, general view.

30. Naples Mosaic, Darius group.

31. Naples Mosaic, Darius on his chariot (drawing by Niccolini).

left hand, he leans forward and extends his right hand, while the driver whips
the beasts to get off the battlefield in a hurry. Next to the chariot, a Persian
thrown from his horse holds the animal by the bit (see Fig. 43). To the right and
behind the chariot, groups of horsemen can be clearly made out, most of them
identifiable as Persians, by virtue of their headgear and clothing. In the background, dominating the entire group, long spears point toward the sky. This
creates the impression that the Great King's army is moving left to right. Only
the spears in the background stand askew. One of the horsemen in that group
holds a standard with a barely recognizable motif. In front of the chariot, a Persian horseman can also be distinguished. His mount has collapsed onto the
ground and his own body is pierced by a spear, held by the horseman coming

32. Naples Mosaic, Darius on his chariot.

from the left (Fig. 33). That horseman, dashing forward (from left to right), is Alexander. He wears a rich breastplate decorated with a gorgon (Fig. 34). In the background, a bare tree, with a very long spear above it, unites and balances the two parts of the composition at the vertical point of contact, clearly located in front of the Great King's chariot.

It is easy to understand why this discovery sparked the enthusiasm of archaeologists, art historians, and more broadly, members of the general public versed in the ancient world. For the first time, Darius was seen represented on his chariot facing Alexander—a scene Le Brun had imagined in composing his painting *The Battle of Arbela* (Fig. 35). With his bow in his right hand, seated on a giant chariot-throne, a terrified Darius sees his young adversary on horseback gathering the laurels of victory, which is symbolized by the flight of an eagle over the scene.

Interpretive debates have continued since the first day, and publications have multiplied in recent years. Although I shall summarize the principal points and arguments, I do not intend to embark on a detailed analysis. I leave to others the task of analyzing the composition, the colors, and the perspectives within the context of an overall reflection on Hellenistic painting, in conjunction with

33. *Naples Mosaic, Persian horseman run through by Alexander's spear.*

34. Naples Mosaic, Alexander (drawing by Niccolini).

the discoveries in Vergina, Macedonia. Indeed, no one has ever doubted that the mosaicist used a model that was originally the work of a painter: what remains in dispute are the identity of the artist, the date of the canvas, and the meaning conveyed.

As a function of the date assigned to the mosaic—the end of Alexander's reign or just after his death, or, on the contrary, much later—critics have argued either that the artist created a motif that was widely copied or that he was inspired by an already-existing cartoon. In any event, the mosaic is not the only example of a "battle of Alexander." In particular, vase paintings from southern Italy have been attributed to the studio of the "Darius Painter" (about 330–320?). They too represent Darius's defeat and flight in his chariot, pursued by Alexander on horseback, spear in hand, setting off at a gallop on his adversary's heels (see Fig. 44). The Great King, reduced there as well to the position of the vanquished, is making a gesture with his right hand in the direction of his adversary, comparable to the one the mosaicist attributes to him. The battle of Alexander is

35. Charles Le Brun's The Battle of Arbela: *Alexander on horseback.*

also one of the motifs on the famous sarcophagus of Sidon, known as the "Alexander Sarcophagus" (Fig. 36a). The same motif is found on several Italiote works. On a relief discovered in Rome, the Roman emperor on horseback is stabbing a barbarian (Germanic) horseman in the belly with his spear, following a model identical to that used by the mosaicist. The theme of the horseman stabbed by an attacker's spear is also illustrated on a Roman sarcophagus from Isernia, and on an Etruscan funerary urn (Fig. 36c), and also on a cup inscribed with the name "C. Popilius" (Fig. 36b), where it is linked to the motif of the vanquished man in flight on his chariot, pursued by his enemy on horseback. There is therefore no doubt that the diffusion of the motif in Roman Italy was part of a cultural and political phenomenon well known at the time: the imitation of Alexander *(imitatio Alexandri)*. That is probably one of the reasons that the owner of the House of the Faun had the mosaic installed there.

One problem is that the mosaic itself is not in very good condition. It was undoubtedly damaged while being transported to Naples in 1843, but it had also been damaged earlier, in antiquity, as indicated by the clear traces of restorations done at that time. The left part (the Alexander group) is very incomplete. It is probably missing a piece in the center of the motif, in the contact zone between the Alexander group (coming from the left) and the Darius group (coming from the right). Certain lacunae are particularly unfortunate, given the interpretive function that is attributed to one detail or another, particularly the design that originally appeared on the raised standard at the extreme right of the representation (Fig. 30, no. 13).

Disputes abounded from the start, given the scarcity of information available in paintings that took a battle of Alexander as their theme. Pliny cites a work by Philoxenus of Eretria, whose patron may have been Cassander (one of Alexander's successors). According to an author from the late first century c.e., a certain Helen of Egypt supposedly produced a painting representing Alexander during the Battle of Issus. A fragment refers as well to a certain Aristides of Thebes, who made a painting of Alexander (?) in battle against the Persians.[106] At present, it is the Philoxenus hypothesis that recurs most often, but the Apelles hypothesis, proposed by Quaranta back in 1832, has been developed again in a recent book (Moreno 2001). Others, by contrast, find it unlikely that no ancient text would have mentioned that an artist so close to Alexander had composed such a work.

The debate on the lost masterpiece's paternity, though important in the eyes of art historians, must not be considered a prerequisite for reflections on the ways and means by which the images of Darius were constituted and diffused.

36. Charles Le Brun's The Battle of Arbela: *Alexander on horseback charging Darius.*

36a. The "Battle of Alexander" on Alexander's sarcophagus.

36b. The "Battle of Alexander" on C. Popilius's cup.

From that standpoint as well, different interpretations have been advanced and continue to be the subject of acrimonious debate. In brief, is the image conveyed by the mosaic positive or negative? Did the artist want to show a courageous Great King worthy in adversity, or a cowardly king abandoning his troops on the battle line? The discussion began in the first days of the discovery.

36c. The "Battle of Alexander" on an Etruscan funerary urn.

During a trip to Italy in 1787, Goethe had visited Pompeii, including the house where the mosaic would be discovered—that is why the designation "house of Goethe" was used at the time. Less than five months after the discovery, the archaeologist W. Zahn completed a first drawing and sent it to Goethe, who received it on March 6, 1832, sixteen days before he died. Dazzled and overwhelmed by "such a wonder of art," Goethe immediately replied to the archaeologist who had consulted him. He was delighted to see Alexander as "the victor" of a Darius who was not so much terrified by danger as profoundly moved by the sacrifice of one of his own, struck dead by the adversary.

Since then, many have attempted in observations and arguments to reconstruct what the painter's intentions might have been or what instructions he might have received. In 1931, H. Fuhrmann argued at length that Philoxenus was the artist responsible for the original painting. He developed the thesis that the painter had wanted to depict a Darius without greatness or courage: "His only concern was for his own fate. . . . Alexander appears utterly different, steadfast and sure of his objective." As evidence in support of his thesis, Fuhrmann noted the horse held by the bridle in front of the chariot (see Fig. 43), a horse, he thought, that was intended to facilitate the Great King's flight (*Philoxenos von Eretria,* pp. 143, 148). Using a common method, he interpreted the painting with help from the ancient texts, which report the presence of such a horse, provided "for this very purpose," to borrow Curtius's expression.[107] Fuhrmann also believed that it was impossible to determine which of the two battles was at issue. The painter, he said, intended to represent "the" battle of Alexander against Darius and not to offer a snapshot of a definite moment in a particular battle.

Another school of thought has interpreted very differently the intentions and achievement of the artist (whoever he may have been). One of that school's most notable and influential representatives has been and remains Carl Nylander, who, in "The Standard of the Great King" (1983), bases a large part of his interpretation on the identity of the standard brandished by one of the Persians on the right side of the composition. Using old drawings, he seeks to demonstrate that this standard is not the peace flag *(phoinikis)* used in Greece and Macedonia but is actually the Persian royal standard. Furthermore, he maintains that the length of the spears does not imply that the Persian troops have been turned back by Alexander's soldiers, equipped with long Macedonian spears *(sarissas).* The author recalls that, prior to the Battle of Gaugamela, Darius had adopted Macedonian weapons. As a result, any intention to depict the rout of the Persian army, supposedly caught in a stranglehold after the Macedonian contingents turned them around, vanishes from the painter's plan. On the contrary, Nylander thinks that the Great King's army remains in perfect battle formation.

Nylander, adopting an interpretation previously proposed by several other exegetes, also argues that it is not Alexander who dominates the scene but Darius, occupying a high position on his chariot. Darius is shown not as a coward but as a king concerned about the sacrifice of the noble who has thrown himself in front of the chariot. The Great King's gaze, not fearful in the least, is directed toward the nobleman and not toward Alexander. The painter thus wanted to show the Persians' devotion toward their king: far from abandoning him at the moment of danger, they were ready to give their lives to save him. In "Il milite ignoto" (1982), therefore, Nylander argues that it is not impossible that the painter's patron was a noble who, after the conqueror's death, firmly supported the policy of Irano-Macedonian rapprochement advocated by Alexander. Another indication of that view would be the precise details in the rendering of the clothing and jewels worn by the Great King and by the Persians around him, as well as of the arms and equipment of the horses and horsemen. Nylander's argument, as it appears in "Darius III—The Coward King" (1993), is part of a clearly expressed desire to rehabilitate Darius's memory.

The orientation that Nylander defines so clearly (including his identification of the Battle of Gaugamela) was favorably received by some commentators. E. Badian maintains that the work ought to be called the "Darius Mosaic" and even argues that the posture of Alexander's horse gives the impression that it is refusing to advance. According to him, the precision of the painting implies that the artist "must at least have worked from a very detailed description of Darius, whose depiction seems as realistic as that of Alexander (if more sympathetic)," and that therefore "Darius III is the only Achaemenid King whose features we actually know" ("Note," [1999], p. 85).

When all the exegeses and commentaries are considered, however, the least that can be said is that the differences in interpretation remain profound, and that many of the recurrent arguments on which they are based are weak. To take only one recent example (*Untersuchungen,* 1998), M. Pfrommer argues that the Persian details are often inaccurate or, more exactly, that their accuracy must be evaluated in terms of the Persianizing representations persistent in the Hellenistic period. For that and other reasons, Pfrommer concludes that the painting may have been produced several decades after Alexander's death, perhaps in an Egyptian political context. Whereas Nylander suggests that the work was commissioned by the circle of Seleukos I, Pfrommer proposes that the painter, in depicting a triumphant Alexander against a fleeing Darius, sought to laud the superiority of the Lagid kings over the "Asian" monarchs, in this case the Seleucids, who fought them in the "Syrian wars." Situated in that particular context and instrumentalized, Darius is characterized as a cowardly man, ready to profit from the sacrifice of his own men by embarking on an uninterrupted flight. In conclusion, Pfrommer trenchantly identifies the scene as the Battle of Issus, an interpretation that in turn gives rise to a few questions.

Many of the arguments advanced on both sides can in fact be turned inside out. Despite what Nylander and his followers have proposed, it seems far from certain that the person who commissioned the painting wanted to give an absolutely positive image of Darius. For the present-day historian, determining the patron and inspiration for the painting would also seem a delicate matter. Did the painter choose not to attribute the onus of the defeat to Darius alone? Did he want to suggest instead that it was the chariot driver who took the initiative to retreat? That interpretation, though possible, is not at all self-evident. Is it really certain, as Goethe suggested, that Darius's gaze is directed exclusively toward the nobleman struck dead by Alexander's spear, and does it express compassion alone? Is not the Great King looking rather at his immediate adversary, Alexander? Is Darius not fearful in the face of the impetuous and victorious assault of Alexander, who, energetically and willfully handling his spear and driving his horse, will soon reach the Persian king in his chariot, unarmed and unable to resist, preferring to avoid direct confrontation with the young Macedonian king? Is it truly possible to read in Darius's eyes the feelings that moved him at the time? The diversity of the graphic renderings of the mosaic attests clearly to the subjective nature of the exegetical exercise (see Figs. 31–32).

Strictly speaking, Darius is not being denounced: the bow he holds in his hand and the empty quiver on his left flank clearly imply that he has personally done battle. Nevertheless, the overall meaning of the composition could have left no doubt in the minds of beholders during the Hellenistic and Roman periods. Taken in at a glance, the movements of the different groups make the artist's intention clear. He renders the very moment when, in the face of the impetuous assault that the Macedonian king, astride his horse, is mounting from left to right, Darius beats a retreat. Despite the sacrifice of the Persian who has thrown himself in front of him, the Great King is abandoning his army, still in battle formation, as indicated by the movement of his cavalry and the angle of the spears, which tilt from right to left. The painter rendered with remarkable force and eloquence the living metaphor of the transition from one rule to another, brought about by victory and defeat. The image of Darius, even in the form given him by the artist, that of a "tragic hero," remains that of a defeated man who, for reasons that the iconography does not allow us to determine, is leaving the battle site instead of risking everything, including his life, for the fate of the empire and of Persia.

Words and Images

The representation, conceived and produced around that guiding idea and transformed into images, necessarily has a limited narrative and documentary value. Was the Great King painted from a model, as Badian would have it, and did the painter render Darius's face realistically? In the absence of any external confirmation, it is impossible to decide. After all, neither the headgear nor the clothing Darius is wearing on the mosaic corresponds exactly to the "upright tiara" and "royal robes" (kandys) that were supposed to be part of the "royal insignia."

At the same time, it is easy to establish correspondences between the texts and the image. For example, the Persian horseman struck dead by Alexander in

front of the royal chariot immediately brings to mind the description Curtius
gives of the Battle of Issus:

> Alexander was as much a soldier as a commander, seeking for himself the
> rich trophy of killing the king. Riding high in his chariot, Darius cut a
> conspicuous figure, at once providing great incentive to his men to pro-
> tect him, and to his enemies to attack him. His brother, Oxathres, saw
> Alexander bearing down on Darius and moved the cavalry under his
> command right in front of the king's chariot. Oxathres far surpassed his
> comrades in the splendour of his arms and in physical strength, and very
> few could match his courage and devotion to Darius. In that engagement
> especially he won distinction by cutting down some Macedonians who
> were recklessly thrusting ahead and by putting others to flight. But the
> Macedonians . . . burst with Alexander himself into the line of Persian cav-
> alry. Then the carnage took on cataclysmic proportions. Around Darius'
> chariot lay his most famous generals who had succumbed to a glorious
> death before the eyes of their king, and who now all lay face-down where
> they had fallen fighting, their wounds on the front of the body. (3.11.7–9)

Diodorus, certainly relying on the same source, also emphasizes the mad
courage of Oxathres:

> When [Oxathres] saw Alexander riding at Dareius and feared that he would
> not be checked, he was seized with the desire to share his brother's fate.
> Ordering the best of the horsemen in his company to follow him, he threw
> himself with them against Alexander, thinking that this demonstration of
> brotherly love would bring him high renown among the Persians. He took
> up the fight directly in front of Dareius's chariot. . . . The fighting qualities
> of Alexander's group were superior, however, and quickly many [Persian]
> bodies lay piled high about the chariot. . . . [Dareius] himself, in extreme
> peril, caught up the reins, being forced to throw away the dignity of his
> position and to violate the ancient custom of the Persian kings. (17.34.2–6)

The scene and characters are reintroduced with the same words and images
at Gaugamela: "Darius was riding in his chariot, Alexander on horseback. . . .
Each man thought it a noble fate to meet his end before the eyes of his king." It
is then that Curtius inserts a variant: "Darius' charioteer who drove the horses,
seated before the king, was run through by a spear."[108] Similarly, Diodorus
writes that Alexander, "with the royal squadron and the rest of the elite horse

guards . . . rode hard against Dareius. The Persian king received their attack and fighting from a chariot hurled javelins against his opponents, and many supported him. As the kings approached each other, Alexander flung a javelin at Dareius and missed him, but struck the driver standing beside him and knocked him to the ground" (17.60.1–2).

Nevertheless, Curtius's and Diodorus's colorful descriptions and evocations, centered on the motif of the "duel between the two kings," do not serve to "confirm" what the painter showed on his canvas and what present-day observers may read on the mosaic. It may be assumed with good reason that the painter himself was inspired by the version that these authors adopted and that he in fact combined the two images of Darius: a fighter who does not hesitate to make contact with Alexander and even to take him on, but also one who despairs and/or takes flight once the enemies become too threatening. It is for the most part the second, less commendable phase that the artist illustrated; the first (Darius as fighter) is simply suggested by the bow and quiver.

In comparing the attitude attributed to Darius during the pitched battles to what is known about the actions of Great Kings in such circumstances, one cannot fail to be surprised by some profound differences and to wonder whether Darius ever fought in his chariot. As far as can be determined from sketchy information, none of the Great Kings ever took part in battles, either on horseback or in a chariot. More exactly, the only scenes that evoke Darius as a fighter are also constructed on the motif of the duel between pretenders to the throne (Cyrus the Younger and Artaxerxes II at Cunaxa).[109]

The royal virtues of the warrior, so exalted in official inscriptions, especially the "mirror of the prince" engraved on the façade of Darius I's tomb in Naqsh-e Rustam (DNa), are not lauded in the royal residences, except in the form of a "royal hero" confronting hybrid monsters, which he overcomes with his bare arms and short sword (Fig. 37). The scene recurs endlessly on seals (Fig. 38), which also show the motif of the king holding a line of prisoners attached to one another by a rope (Fig. 39). From that standpoint, the scene on the mosaic is an exception: it does not render a Persian view of the king at war but illustrates a Greek agonistic vision.

The only parallel to the mosaic and the original painting is another painting, supported by wood beams and now held in a Munich museum.[110] One of the painted scenes represents a battle between the Persians and the Scythians, who are particularly recognizable by their tall red tiaras. If one adopts the first publisher's claim that this is a representation of the war Darius I waged against

37. *The "royal hero" in Persepolis, throne room, west*
    door (drawing by Ghirshman).

38. The "royal hero" on a Persepolis seal.

39. Seal of Artaxerxes I (?).

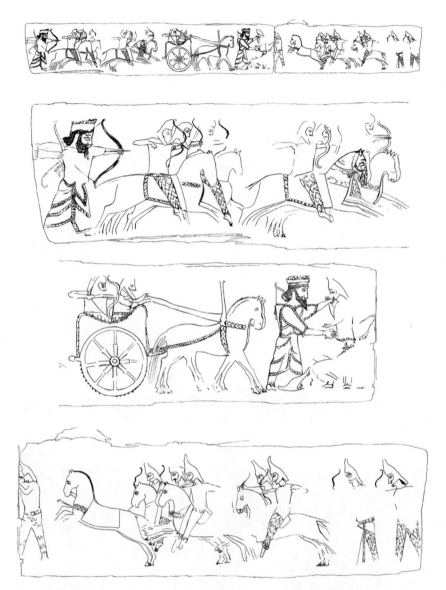

40. *War scene on a painting on wood from the Achaemenid period (drawing by M.-F. Clergeau).*

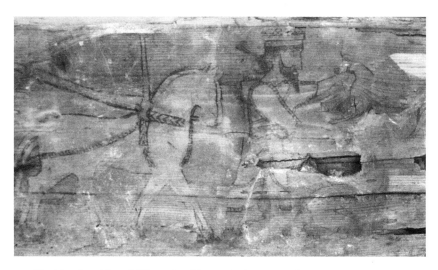

41. The king/royal hero killing a Scythian: painting on wood.

the Scythians of Ukraine, the painting may date to about 500 B.C.E. In any event, on the left side of the image (Fig. 40) a first royal figure is clearly distinguishable. He has his bow drawn and is shooting arrows at Scythian horsemen. In the foreground, in front of a chariot, it is possible to discern even more clearly a Great King wearing the long Persian robe (the *kandys*) and a crenellated crown. He is seizing a Scythian by his beard and is plunging his short sword into his foe's body; under his feet lies another enemy (Fig. 41). Rather than a realistic scene, what we have before our eyes is one of the articulations of the "royal hero."

In some sense, if the painting serves to illustrate the qualities of a warrior associated with the person of every Great King, it does so in the form of an ideal representation; it does not render a real battle or its unfolding. It therefore does not serve to "confirm" that the Great King, during wars and battles, was supposed to take part in battles directly. Even in its specific iconographic expression, the same is true for the Naples Mosaic. There is no doubt that, during official processions but also at the start of battle, Darius III, "in his usual manner," was in his chariot, "towering above all the others."[111] That accounts for the political meaning that Macedonian propaganda attached to the capture of Darius III's chariot, from which the king's robe and bow are reputed to have been taken as well. By contrast, nothing proves that the Great King, from his chariot, threw javelins and shot arrows, even less that he ever faced Alexander one-on-one.

❦ 6 ❧

Darius between Greece and Rome

From the Persians to the Parthians

Darius, when compared to Alexander, would retain his negative image even after death. The reason is to be sought in the context, both historical and literary,
of the transmission of power from Darius to Alexander. What is conventionally
called "the Orientalization of Alexander" began at that time. Contemporary
historians analyze that process in terms of Alexander's Iranian policy, which
consisted of rallying the defeated to his cause. He was well aware, in fact, that he
could not realize his forthcoming expedition without the cooperation of the Iranian aristocracy, which had been the real backbone of the Great Kings' empire.

For ancient authors, the outward mark of that policy was the adoption of
Achaemenid aulic customs. That shift was deeply resented by some members
of Alexander's entourage, advisers and generals who accused their king of abandoning the "pure and rough" customs of his Macedonian ancestors. The indictment was deeply rooted in Greek representations: Oriental kings were ruined
by luxury and lust; they were effeminate, incapable of displaying virile robustness and military energy. These were contradictory representations, because
luxury *(tryphē),* denounced by many as both a symptom and a cause of "moral decadence," was considered by others to be the splendid mark of power and wealth.
Polemics raged on the matter. In a famous passage, Plutarch took issue with his
contemporaries and defended Alexander's adoption of Achaemenid ceremonial
dress. To that end, he used the metaphor of animal taming, which was hardly
flattering for the Iranians and the "barbarians" in general:

> They who hunt wild beasts clothe themselves with their hairy skins; and
> fowlers make use of feathered tunics; nor are others less wary how they

show themselves to wild bulls in scarlet or to elephants in white; for those creatures are provoked and enraged at the sight of these colors. But if a great king, in taming and mollifying stubborn and warlike nations, took the same course to soften and allay their inbred fury which others take with wild beasts, and at length brought them to be tame and tractable by making use of their familiar habits and by submitting to their customary course of life, thereby removing animosity from their breasts and sour looks from their countenances, shall we blame his management; or rather must we not admire the wisdom of him who by so slight a change of apparel ruled all Asia, subduing their bodies with his arms and vanquishing their minds with his habit?[1]

It is therefore clear why, in works of the Roman period, the figure of Alexander came to have a dual valence. Embraced by a series of leaders and emperors as an illustrious precedent who legitimated their conquests and political ambitions, the memory of Alexander also bore a negative charge in a number of Roman historians and moralists. According to them, the Macedonian king had appropriated despotic power for himself. The authors had already condemned the despotism of Darius and the Great Kings in general, and they condemned it in Rome as well.

The similarity between Alexander and Darius, stated explicitly or slyly suggested, had an obvious corollary. Even after his death, Darius continued to be exploited as a negative example of the exercise of supreme power, as extolled by Alexander's Greek and Macedonian opponents and, later on, by those Romans who dreamed of a return to the sources of ancient morality, during the time of the principate especially. Behind the Roman moralists' invocation of traditional Macedonian customs, which they claimed had been forgotten, lay a denunciation of some of their own generals who had also succumbed to the deleterious charms of the Orient and who were accused of abandoning the old Roman traditions. The contrasting portraits of Caesar and Alexander in Velleius Paterculus, one of the representatives of that moralist current, are a case in point. He judges that, with respect to the personality and heroic deeds of the two men, Alexander could compare to Caesar only before the Macedonian's disastrous evolution, before he was given to drink and when he was still in control of his passions. Caesar was never overtaken by sleep and he never overindulged at mealtime. He was governed not by pleasure but by life.[2]

The theme of Alexander's moral decadence under the corrupting influence of the Orient became a veritable topos of Roman literature. There is no doubt

that the topos was based both on a Roman value system, which seemed to lie at
the opposite extreme of the conduct Alexander adopted at the time, and on a
reference, implicit or explicit, to contemporary events. When they spoke of the
Persians—about whom they knew very little—authors of the Roman period
were often thinking of the Parthians. Military leaders and emperors had to
wage many hard and murky wars against the Parthians, who sometimes dealt
them bloody defeats. Lucan, who can hardly be suspected of sympathy for Alexander, uses the term "Parthian" to describe the Persians of Darius's time, so as
to mark even more cruelly the opposition he sets up between Macedonian successes and Roman defeats: "Alexander fell into his Babylon, revered by Parthia.
O shame! The peoples of the Orient feared the *sarissa* more than they now fear
the *pilum*. . . . We shall yield in the Orient to the master of the Arsacids. That
Parthia, so fateful for the Crassi, was only a peaceful province for little Pella!"[3]

The Parthian Wars were the subject of many works by Romans. Did not
Lucian deride all those authors who suddenly discovered within themselves
the vocation of historian?[4] Arrian, a contemporary of Lucian, was not only the
author of the *Anabasis of Alexander,* he also composed the *Parthica,* which nar-
rates in detail Trajan's expedition against the Parthians. During the same time
period the Persians occupied a significant place in Polyaenus's *Stratagems,* but
for circumstantial reasons having to do with the dangerous threat the Parthians posed for the eastern borders of the empire. In 161 C.E., in fact, the Romans
had suffered humiliating defeats in Armenia. In addition, the author himself
claims to be of Macedonian stock and shamelessly presents himself as heir to
the virtues of those men who, led by Alexander, were powerful enough to sub-
jugate the Persians by force of arms. He explains that, unable to enlist in the
army himself, he was offering Emperors Antoninus and Verus a collection of
strategical exempla filled with lessons for waging their campaigns. That was
also the intent of the dedication that the anonymous author of *Alexander's Itinerary* addressed nearly two centuries later (in about 338 C.E.) to Emperor Constantius II, who was preparing to face the armies of the Sassanid Great King.

The identification between the Persians and the Parthians was all the easier
in that Parthia had been one of the countries subject to the Great Kings and, combined with the nearby region of Hyrcania, constituted a satrapy. It held a strategic
place on the "Khorasan road" that reached Central Asia via Ecbatana and Rhagai.
The entire region had played a prominent role during the revolts that erupted in
Central Asia when Darius I took power. In January 521 B.C.E., Ecbatana had become the headquarters for the new king, and his father, Hystaspes, was called

upon to restore order in Parthia-Hyrcania. That same road was taken by his distant descendant Darius III in the spring of 330, when Alexander's arrival was announced. With his army, Darius took that route to Rhagai and the Caspian Gates, before being assassinated in the Parthian region, as he was heading toward the future Hecatompylos (Šahr-e Qumis). Like every subject country, Parthia sent contingents to the royal armies: a Parthian contingent was part of Darius III's army at Gaugamela.[5] When Alexander took over, he assigned the post of satrap to the Parthian Amminapes.[6] Polybius has no doubt that the country was part of the Great Kings' domains "when the Persians were the lords of Asia."[7]

Justin therefore has no difficulty making explicit the perceived continuity in Rome between the Persians and the Parthians ("Alexander . . . was then in Parthia"), when he sets out the new court etiquette, a symbol of "barbarization" that led to its decay.[8] Darius died in Parthia, in the village of Thara. Justin draws this sententious conclusion: "The immortal gods, I suppose, ordain[ed] that the empire of the Persians should have its termination in the country of those who were to succeed them in dominion."[9] Curtius makes many references to the Parthians, once Alexander has reached these regions: "The Parthyaei [are] a race living in the areas which are today populated by Parthians who emigrated from Scythia. . . . The Macedonian kings took up residence in other cities, which are now occupied by the Parthians. . . . Media . . . is now inhabited by the Parthians, who use it as their summer residence. . . . From here they marched into Parthiene, land of a people little known at that time but now the most important of all regions situated beyond the Euphrates and Tigris and bounded by the Red Sea."[10]

The continuity between the Parthians of Alexander's time and the Parthians of the Roman period is also clearly marked in Dio Cassius's *Roman History*. Speaking of the beginning of the Roman wars against the Parthians, Dio Cassius provides a flashback:

> These people dwell beyond the Tigris, for the most part in forts and garrisons, but also in a few cities, among them Ctesiphon, in which they have a royal residence. Their race was in existence among the ancient barbarians [*oi palai Barbaroi*] and they had this same name even under the Persian kingdom; but at that time they inhabited only a small portion of the country and had acquired no dominion beyond their own borders. But when the Persian rule had been overthrown and that of the Macedonians was at its height, and when the successors of Alexander had quarreled

with one another, cutting off separate portions for themselves and setting up individual monarchies, the Parthians then first attained prominence under a certain Arsaces, from whom their succeeding rulers received the title of Arsacidae.[11]

In his excursus on Persia, Ammianus Marcellinus also indicates that continuity and, following Justin, recalls the dynasty's legendary origins in notably imprecise terms: "When Alexander had closed his eyes in Babylon, the Persians received the name 'Parthians of Arsaces,' Arsaces being an obscure man who started out as the leader of bandits and, through a series of exploits, became the glorious founder of a dynasty."[12]

The ancient authors also note, or merely serve as witnesses to, the borrowing or survival of Achaemenid customs. Pliny ascribes to the Parthian kings the custom of reserving the water of the Choaspes for the king's consumption, a custom well known for the Great Kings through a whole series of texts.[13] Strabo mentions that the Parthian kings changed residences seasonally, spending the winter in Ctesiphon.[14] Athenaeus makes the link to the Great Kings, claiming that the Persian kings, the "first men in history to become famous for their luxurious way of life [*tryphē*]," were therefore the first to move from one residence to another: "Similarly, the Parthian kings lived in Rhagai in the spring, but they wintered in Babylon and spent the rest of the time in Hecatompylos."[15] Curtius, referring to Darius III's arrival in Ecbatana, writes matter-of-factly that it is now "the capital city of Media . . . inhabited by the Parthians who use it as their summer residence."[16] And it is rather difficult to decide, on reading Dio Chrysostom, whether he is evoking the memory of the Great King's travels or of those of the Parthian kings.[17] It is therefore easy to understand why Lucian, in a parody that imagines a new conquest of Alexander led by an ambitious Athenian, combines obvious reminiscences of Xenophon's *Anabasis* and the ancient Alexander authors (probably Arrian in the first place) with clear references to the Parthian king, whose capital was Ctesiphon.[18] Lucian, like his contemporaries, did not have the slightest interest in historical accuracy: he could unproblematically attribute to the Arsacids the famous golden plane tree of the Achaemenid court, so renowned among the Greeks.[19]

Darius's Satrap, or the Image of a Perverted Monarchy

Given the circumstances, Darius, the Persians, and the Parthians, all living in luxury and lust, would be lumped together for political and moral ends, as would

Alexander, Darius, and the Persians, particularly after Alexander had entered Parthian country. In Roman historiography, Alexander, in seizing Darius's power, in presenting himself as his avenger, and in adopting the customs of the Achaemenid court, would himself be transformed into a Great King, a Darius.

A very famous instance of political fiction occurs in Livy, who also makes a comparison between the Parthians and Alexander. Their renown and power, he asserts harshly, are put forward indiscriminately by "Greeks anxious to extol even the glory of the Parthians at the expense of the Roman name." The author himself was an experienced user of exempla and a representative of moralizing history. As he puts it so well in his preface, he intends to "follow, by means of thought, the imperceptible weakening of discipline and that first relaxation of mores, which, soon slipping down a slope more rapidly every day, precipitated their fall even until recent times, when the remedy became as unbearable as the ailment." According to Livy, the ailment indisputably came as a result of the foreign conquests, particularly after the victories of Manlius Vulso and his triumph upon his return to Rome in 187 B.C.E.: "The luxury of foreign nations entered Rome with the Asian army; it was the army that introduced into the city beds adorned with bronze, precious carpets, loosely woven veils and fabrics. . . . It was at that time that singers, harp players, and street performers were invited to feasts for the amusement of the guests; . . . that cooks, who for our ancestors were nothing but the lowest and least useful of slaves, began to be very expensive, and a lowly trade was passed off as an art."[20]

The excursus on Alexander is strongly marked by these representations of the past. Livy seeks to show that, if Alexander had attacked Italy, he would have had no chance of victory, quite simply because he would have found himself facing Romans who were not spoiled by Asian luxury. In other words, contrasting memories of Alexander and of Darius were put to use within the framework of a reflection on what was judged to be the negative change in Roman mores.

To conclude his demonstration, Livy considers two Alexanders in succession, the one before Darius's death and the one after it. He does not deny that Alexander, before succumbing to Persian mores, was a great general *(egregius dux);* furthermore, he remarks, Alexander, the sole commander, could attract all the glory to himself, and he had the good luck to die young, before the unpleasantness of old age and care. By contrast, he writes, the young king, had he attacked Rome, would have had before him Roman generals of exceptional valor, who certainly would have prevailed. The expected comparison follows: Alexander would not have been pitted against a mere Darius, who, for the needs of the demonstration, Livy presents as a caricature. "A king dragging behind him an army of women and eunuchs, encumbered by his purple and gold, laden with all the impedimenta of his greatness, looking much more like prey than like an enemy, whom Alexander conquered without any resistance, with no other merit than to have successfully dared brave a mere hobgoblin. He would have found Italy very different from India, which he passed through at the command of a drunken army in continual debauchery."[21]

Having denigrated the Macedonian's victories against the Persian Darius, a "mere hobgoblin," Livy finds it even easier to denounce the Oriental Alexander: "And I speak of Alexander before he was inebriated by wealth, to which no one was ever more susceptible than he. Given the state of mind that his new fortune had introduced in him and the new character that victory had given him, he arrived in Italy with a much stronger resemblance to Darius than to Alexander and with an army that no longer remembered Macedonia and that, having adopted the Persians' mores, had fallen into decadence. It is with regret that I recall, in such a great king, the disdain that made him change his costume, the adulation he wanted the people to pay him, prostrating themselves on the ground, homages that would have been unbearable for the defeated Macedonians, and which were all the more so for the victorious Macedonians."

The image is simple and strong: Alexander turns into a Persian king, a Darius—a transformation marked by the term *degenerare,* so often found in the Latin texts that refer to the loathsome Orientalization of Alexander. Spoiled by the enemy's pleasures and turpitude, the Macedonian army and its leader become incapable of waging war, just as Darius and the contingents levied in "effeminate Asia" had been, by virtue of their very structure.

Diodorus reports that, following Darius's death, Alexander continued his march toward Hyrcania. For all the ancient authors captivated by the picturesque quality of the Orient, one of Alexander's greatest exploits was his romance with Thalestris, queen of the Amazons, with whom he spent thirteen days and thirteen nights of love. For Diodorus, that sensual episode illustrates Alexander's unbridled indulgence in the lifestyle of his defeated and dead enemy, whether that meant royal robes or royal concubines:

> It seemed to Alexander that he had accomplished his objective and now held his kingdom without contest, and he began to imitate the Persian luxury and the extravagant display of the kings of Asia. First he installed ushers of Asiatic race in his court, and then he ordered the most distinguished persons to act as his guards; among these was Dareius' brother

Oxathres. Then he put on the Persian diadem and dressed himself in the white robe and the Persian sash and everything else except the trousers and the long-sleeved upper garment. He distributed to his companions cloaks with purple borders and dressed the horses in Persian harness. In addition to all this, he added concubines to his retinue in the manner of Dareius, in number not less than the days of the year and outstanding in beauty as selected from all the women of Asia. Each night these paraded around the couch of the king so that he might select the one with whom he would lie that night. Alexander, as a matter of fact, employed these customs rather sparingly and kept for the most part to his accustomed routine, not wishing to offend the Macedonians. Many, it is true, did reproach him for these things.[22]

The image of a Macedonian king ruined by the luxury and lust typical of Darius can be found among all the ancient authors. According to Justin, for example, "soon after, Alexander assumed the attire of the Persian monarchs, as well as the diadem, which was unknown to the kings of Macedonia, as if he gave himself up to the customs of those whom be had conquered. . . . That he might imitate the luxury too, as well as the dress of the Persians, he spent his nights among troops of the king's concubines of eminent beauty and birth. To these extravagances he added vast magnificence in feasting; and lest his entertainments should seem jejune and parsimonious, he accompanied his banquets, according to the ostentation of the eastern monarchs, with games; being utterly unmindful that power is accustomed to be lost, not gained, by such practices."[23]

Hence the indignation, noisily manifested by the entire army, that Alexander "had so degenerated from his father Philip as to abjure the very name of his country, and to adopt the manners of the Persians."[24] Philip, in fact, "was more inclined to display in war, than in entertainments; and his greatest riches were means for military operations. . . . The father was more inclined to frugality, the son to luxury. By the same course by which the father laid the foundations of the empire of the world, the son consummated the glory of conquering the whole world."[25]

Arrian pursues a comparable politico-moral discourse, in a long digression placed between the punishment of Bessus (Darius's murderer) and the scandal involving the pages and Callisthenes. Arrian disapproves of the punishment inflicted on Bessus after his capture in Sogdiana, because, he believes, it was borrowed from reprehensible Persian practices: "Then Alexander summoned a council of those present, brought Bessus before them, and accusing him of treachery towards Darius, commanded that his nose and ear-laps should be cut off, and that he should be taken to Ecbatana, to be put to death there in the assembly of Medes and Persians. For my part, I do not approve of this excessive punishment of Bessus; I regard the mutilation of the extremities as barbaric, and I agree that Alexander was carried away into imitation of Median and Persian opulence and of the custom of barbarian kings not to countenance equality with subjects in their daily lives. . . . Not one of all these things is any contribution to man's happiness, unless the man whose achievements are apparently so great were to possess at the same time command of his own passions" (4.7.3–5; P.-A. Brunt trans.).

Arrian also does not approve of the Macedonian king's innovations in banquet arrangements and in his new habits of dress: "Nor do I at all approve the facts that, though a descendant of Heracles, he substituted the dress of Medes for that traditional with Macedonians and that he exchanged the tiara of the Persians, whom he himself had conquered, for the head-dress he had long worn. . . . In fact, Alexander had already taken to new and more barbaric ways in drinking" (4.7.4; 4.8.2).

In replying harshly to the sophist Anaxarchus, an enthusiastic supporter of such innovations, Callisthenes recalled that Macedonian monarchical traditions were totally different from Persian norms and, to make his message utterly convincing, he chose, by way of counterexamples, two Persian kings with the worst reputations among the Greco-Roman authors: "You should rather have remembered that you are not attending nor advising a Cambyses or a Xerxes, but a son of Philip . . . whose forefathers came from Argos to Macedonia, and have continued to rule the Macedonians not by force [bia] but in accordance with custom [alla nomōi]" (4.11.6).

A despotic power founded on the prince's arbitrary wishes was contrasted to a power tempered by the "customs of the ancestors": no example but that of the Persian kings could illustrate the remarks with greater force.

Curtius notes that the Macedonian king tended to adopt deplorable foreign practices after the taking of Gaza.[26] But he dates the real beginning of Alexander's negative evolution, and that of his men, to the long stopover in Babylon after the Battle of Gaugamela. Diodorus is sober, almost technical, regarding the episode: "Alexander refreshed his army from its private labours and remained more than thirty days in the city because food was plentiful and the population friendly." He is less sober when speaking of the troops' second entry

into the city, on their return from the Indian expedition: "As on the previous
occasion, the population received the troops hospitably, and all turned their attention to relaxation and luxury, since everything necessary was available in
profusion."[27] Roman ideas about luxury, moral decadence, and the weakening
of military discipline, which Diodorus evokes in transparent terms, are complacently adopted by Curtius.

On the evening of the defeat, Darius, the author's designated spokesman,
introduces what will come next. He says he has chosen to leave the Babylon
road open, because luxury and women will corrupt his adversaries.[28] That also
explains why, a short time later, Curtius pretends to think that, when the satrap
of Susa voluntarily surrendered to Alexander, the order might have been given
by Darius himself, "so that Alexander would be delayed by taking plunder."[29]
The description of Babylonian amusements is an accumulation of conventional
images: "Alexander's stop in this city was longer than anywhere else, and here
he undermined military discipline more than in any other place. The moral
corruption there is unparalleled; its ability to stimulate and arouse unbridled
passions is incomparable. Parents and husbands permit their children and
wives to have sex with strangers, as long as their infamy is paid for. . . . After
thirty-four days of revelling in such dissipation, that army which had conquered Asia would doubtless have been weakened for any subsequent confron-
tations, if it had had an adversary."[30]

This passage is nothing but a particular variety of the Roman literature of
exempla. As the first words and moral of the story show, "Alexander's stop in
Babylon" could have easily been integrated into the chapters in Frontinus's and
Valerius Maximus's collections titled "On Military Discipline" or "The Institutions of Times Past." For Valerius Maximus, as for Livy and so many other authors, the terrible "taste for luxury" was introduced into Rome following the
victories in Macedonia and Asia.[31] They forcefully condemned it, because it
perverted individuals and nations, more particularly the Romans, as it had previously perverted the Spartans. For example, "no sooner had Pausanias, who
had performed the greatest feats, indulged in the customs of Asia, than he was
not ashamed to let his courage grow soft under the effects of the effeminate life
lived there."[32] Like one Roman literary current, which aspired to be the standard-
bearer of traditional values, Curtius, even without using the word here, denounces "idleness" (otium) as contrary to the rules of life that allow an army to
remain united, strong, and powerful.[33] In this case, idleness has made the army
too weak (debilior), and only the absence of any enemy worthy of the name

made it possible to conceal the evidence. That is Curtius's true subject, and he uses every possible cliché about decadence to announce the change to come in Alexander's character.

Precisely because of the very Roman inspiration and stereotypical character of Curtius's history, it is easy to find parallels. The most striking example is clearly Livy. Here is his description of the stopover in Capua by Hannibal and his army:

> He went to take his winter quarters in Capua. For most of that time, he kept his troops—long tempered and hardened against all suffering, so unaccustomed and alien to comfort—lodged in the houses of the city. The surfeit of ills had found them invincible; but they were defenseless against the delights of immoderate sensual pleasures, all the more intoxicating in being unknown to them. They rushed to them in a fury. Sleep, wine, feasts, debauchery, baths, and rest, made more attractive daily by force of habit, enervated them so much that they defended themselves afterward more by their past victories than by their present strength. . . . Hence it was clear that Hannibal no longer had the same army when he left Capua. Almost all the Carthaginians returned with women of easy virtue in tow; and when they began once again to live in tents, when they returned to the marches and fatigue of the soldier's life, strength failed them, along with courage. Later, throughout the summer, they escaped in droves, leaving their ensigns without permission; and it was in Capua that the deserters took refuge.[34]

This exemplum, for that is what it is, is also used by Valerius Maximus in the chapter devoted to luxury and the pleasures of the senses (luxuria et libido): "The softness of Capua was very favorable to our republic's interests. By the power of its charms, it chained Hannibal, whom weapons had been unable to defeat." He was defeated "by the abuse of good food, wine, sweet perfumes, and sensual pleasures, which lulled them to delightful sleep."[35]

Like all the other authors, Curtius returns to the question after Darius's death: "As soon as he was free of these worries that beset him, he yielded to dissipation, and the man whom the arms of Persia had failed to crush fell before its vices. There were parties early in the day; drinking and mad revelry throughout the night; games; women by the score. It was a general decline into the ways of the foreigner. By affecting these, as though they were superior to those of his country, Alexander so offended the sensibilities and eyes of his people that most of his friends began to regard him as an enemy."[36]

Oriental singers were brought to the banquets—a novelty that Curtius denounces as "artless songs which grated on the ears of foreigners." The prudish
Curtius feels compelled to apologize to his readers for being obliged to give sca-
brous details, especially about the immodesty of the women, who "finally throw
off their most intimate garments" (5.1.38).

A little later, he also mentions the romance with the queen of the Amazons:
"It was at this point that Alexander relinquished control of his appetites. His self-
restraint and continence, supreme qualities at the height of good fortune, degenerated into arrogance and dissipation."[37] Reporting the introduction of Persian
aulic customs, Curtius does not omit to mark their opposition to "the traditional
ways of his people, the healthy, sober discipline and unassuming demeanour of
the Macedonian kings. . . . He began to ape the Persian royalty."

Even more noteworthy in this passage are the explicit similarities that the
author establishes with Darius. Alexander "wore on his head a purple head-band
interwoven with white, like the one Darius had once had." On letters he sent to
Asia, he "set the seal of Darius' ring. . . . The royal quarters had a complement of
365 concubines, the number Darius had possessed."[38] All of which explains the
discontent of the Macedonians, "a group inexperienced in sensuality. . . . Their
king resembled one of the conquered rather than a conqueror—demoted from
king of Macedon to satrap of Darius."[39] Introduced at this point only by Curtius, the story of the love affair with the young eunuch Bagoas, whom Darius
too had loved, further blackens the portrait of a Macedonian king who, from
that time on, never ceased to "degenerate," to the point of relying on "a male
whore's judgement to give some men kingdoms and deprive others of their
lives."[40]

It is clear that the condemnation of Alexander for having attempted to turn
the "rugged" Macedonian monarchy into a despotic power corrupted by luxury and lust also applies to Darius the corruptor. He is the epitome of the Asian
despot who, leading enormous armies but without any real strength, is under
the sway of the effeminate luxury that, as Arrian points out, follows him everywhere, even in wartime.[41] After Darius's death, his memory and his legacy are
taken over by Alexander. Darius is even reputed to have designated his adversary as his avenger against the regicide Bessus, who had proclaimed himself
king in Bactra, had dressed himself in royal robes, and had taken the reign
name "Artaxerxes." In Macedonian propaganda, however, that was in the first
place a justification for continuing the war. It was also a legitimation of the new
power, which intended to recast itself in the dead man's clothing.

Even after his death, Darius does not obtain what the entire tradition refused him during his lifetime, at the time of his open opposition to Alexander.
In the unanimous view of the authors of the Roman period, Darius is considered, not an example worthy of imitation, but rather a precedent to contemplate
and dismiss. When Plutarch, in his two minor works collectively called *On the
Fortune of Alexander,* defends the policy his hero conducted toward the Persians
and Iranians, the figure of Darius does not benefit at all: on the contrary, the
image conveyed is particularly disastrous for his memory.[42]

To return to the last sentences of Arrian's funeral oration for Darius: "These
were the tragedies of Darius' life. After death he had a royal burial and his children were brought up and educated by Alexander as if he were still on the throne,
and Alexander married his daughter."[43] A cursory reading creates the impression that Darius obtained a sort of posthumous rehabilitation. But that is not at
all the case. The logic of the oration shows rather that Arrian wants to prove
once again Alexander's virtue: it is thanks to the conqueror's generosity and
kindness that Darius is not pitifully left without a sepulchre, that his children
receive an education worthy of their rank, and that one of his daughters attains
the honor of being wife to a king (thanks to Alexander's marriage to her several
years later). In other words, the Persian king was unable to assume his public
and private duties to the very end.

The Five Empires

Although the preceding analysis provides part of the answer, it also leads to a
necessary question: In the Roman literature, is the judgment of Darius III's royal
conduct directed at him specifically, or is it part of an overall assessment of the
Persian monarchy?

As a temporal notion, what is known as the "Achaemenid period" is one
stage in the political evolution that led inexorably to Rome's domination of the
world. That theory is very clearly expressed in the introduction to Polybius's
Histories and in Dionysius of Halicarnassus's *Roman Antiquities.* Polybius wishes
"to take an interest in the question of how and by means of what government
the Roman state could do something unprecedented, namely, extend its domination to almost the entire earth, and in less than fifty-three years." He therefore cites "the most famous empires of the past, those that have held the attention of historians," those "for which a parallel is admissible." The empires
mentioned are the Persian, the Peloponnesian, and the Macedonian. Dionysius

is more inclusive, referring by turns to the Assyrians, the Medes, the Persians, and then the Macedonians.

Such considerations recur like a refrain in the allusions the authors regularly make to the development of political societies up to the establishment of Rome's global dominion. Velleius Paterculus, for example, evokes the shift in the "sovereignty of Asia" from the Assyrians (Sardanapalus) to the Medes (Arbakes), and cites a Roman chronology by Aemilius Sura: "The Assyrians were the first of all races to hold world power, then the Medes, and after them . . . the Macedonians. . . . The world power passed to the Roman people. . . . Ninus, king of the Assyrians, . . . was the first to hold world power."[44] Later (in the late fifth century C.E.), Zosimus, the "Polybius of decadence," borrowed from Polybius's explicit model the view of the succession of Persian, Macedonian, and Roman rule.[45] In the early fifth century C.E., Orosius, on the other side in the battle between Christianity and paganism, also adopted the imposed model. He begins with Ninos—the first Assyrian king—and Semiramis, ending with Sardanapalus, under whom "power passed from the Assyrians to the Medes" and then to the Persians, to whom Orosius devotes several chapters. He then discusses Alexander, "that mire of misery," followed by the Hellenistic kingdoms and the Roman conquest.[46]

It is that theory of the succession of empires that Arrian mentions in a prognosis *post eventum* of the Battle of Issus: "For it was already decreed by fate that the Persians should be deprived of the rule of Asia by the Macedonians, just as the Medes had been deprived of it by the Persians, and still earlier the Assyrians by the Medes."[47] The same was true of the people of India, whom Alexander conquered: "Those people were formerly subjects of the Assyrians, then, after the Medes, they were subject to the Persians, and they carried to Cyrus, son of Cambyses, the tributes from their land as he established them."[48] Hence the prestige of Cyrus, whom Darius invokes before the Battle of Gaugamela: "By the immortal memory of Cyrus, who first wrested the empire from the Medes and Lydians and transferred it to Persia."[49] In a dialogue by Lucian, Cyrus is presented as follows: "Cyrus, son of Cambyses, transferred the empire of the Medes to the Persians. He has just defeated the Assyrians and has seized Babylon. He is preparing at this moment an expedition against Lydia to defeat Croesus and thereby become master of the world."[50]

Considered from the standpoint of universal history *(koine historia)*, as Dionysius of Halicarnassus conceived it, the Romans belonged to a long line of conquerors. At the same time, however, they were distinguished from the earlier conquerors by the incomparable splendor and unmatched results of their achievements—for example, the prestige attached to the conquests of Pompey: "The Iberians had never been subject either to the Medes or to the Persians; they had even escaped Macedonian domination, since Alexander rapidly departed from Hyrcania. Nevertheless, Pompey routed them in a great battle."[51] That is the thesis Plutarch develops in his rhetorical opuscule *On the Fortune of the Romans*:

> Fortune and Virtue[52] have likely made a truce to form an alliance and, once joined, have together realized and achieved the finest of human works. . . . So long as the greatest powers and empires of the world went forward and clashed following the whims of fortune, because there was no supremacy established and because each yearned for it, there was nothing but ruination, vagaries, and universal instability. Finally, when Rome had assumed its full might and expanse and had bound to itself not only all the peoples and nations of its own region but also the foreign kingdoms located beyond the seas, supreme power came to be stable and fixed. Then, in a world of peace, hegemony unerringly followed its course in a single orbit.[53]

The Greek term *arētē* must be understood in the strong sense: it is virtue in the sense of *virtū*—force, courage, and intelligence, conscious and organized—in opposition to the uncontrollable whims of blind fortune *(Tychē)*. The unheard-of successes of the Romans, says Plutarch, were the result of the unique conjunction between their own will and the choice of *Tychē*. By contrast, Alexander owed his success only to his *arētē*, while the Persian kings owed their power solely to *Tychē*. This is typical of a recurrent discourse of universal harmony and the "end of history," conceived and spread by a hegemonic power that has just put an end to division. Plutarch's two discourses titled *De fortuna Alexandri*, in making reference to a previous endeavor, present Alexander as the one who unified a divided world and inspired universal harmony. The different peoples were now united under Greek cultural norms: "They whom Alexander vanquished were more greatly blessed than they who fled his conquests. For these had none to deliver them from their ancient state of misery; the others the victor compelled to better fortune."[54] In the fourth century C.E., Eusebius of Caesarea adopted the same discourse in his *Praeparatio evangelica*, this time within an eschatological vision imposed by Christianity. His references, though implicit, are clearly drawn from Thucydides and Plutarch: "What had never before taken place in history, what no illustrious man of the past had ever achieved, came into being solely through the words of our Savior. . . . The customs of all nations are equitable, they that were formerly brutish and barbarous. . . . And so, now that they have become His followers, the Persians no longer wed their mothers, and the Scythians renounce cannibalism. . . . The other races of barbarians no longer commit incest with their daughters or sisters. . . . That was in former times; it is no longer the same today. The law of redemption alone dissipated the brutal and inhumane leprosy of all those practices."[55]

Such discourses necessarily restore to their "rightful place" previous attempts at hegemony: for Polybius, Plutarch, Dionysius of Halicarnassus, Dio of Prusa, and many others, Rome's predecessors, including the Persian Empire (mentioned fleetingly but inevitably), can be considered merely rough sketches for a harmonious painting that only Rome was able to achieve to perfection:[56] "Fortune left behind Persians and Assyrians, traversed Macedonia on light wings, and soon cast down Alexander, traveled through Egypt and Syria, sweeping up thrones here and there, then, turning away, more than once exalted the Carthaginians; finally, having arrived at the Palatine Hill, as it was crossing the Tiber it apparently put down its wings, removed its sandals, left behind its unsettled and capricious sphere. So it is that it has arrived in Rome, resolved to stay there."[57]

Although times had changed by then, in 400 C.E. Claudian tirelessly delivered the same discourse, as if to convince himself that he concealed within himself a sort of magical and reinvigorating value, at a time when the old Roman Empire was experiencing extreme troubles: "Roman rule will never have limits; the other empires crumbled, victims of the vices engendered by luxury or the hatred inspired by pride; so Sparta overthrew the fragile greatness of Athens, only to succumb in its turn to the superiority of Thebes; so Media stole supremacy away from Assyria, only to have it taken by Persia, which was later conquered by Rome. But Rome had the oracles of the Sibyl to sustain it, the religion of Numa to propel it."[58]

In Plutarch's view, one of the signs of the remarkable superiority of Rome was its ability to move beyond its own domestic space and to seize foreign kingdoms "beyond the sea." Crossing an arm of the sea seems to have been perceived as a founding act of victory and hegemony. The expression *terra marique,* "on land and sea," which appeared in Rome in about 67 B.C.E., best conveys the difference in scale when compared even to Alexander's conquests. Plutarch's declaration is also discursively in harmony with the observation of both Polybius and Dionysius of Halicarnassus, namely, that the Persians, for their part,

never succeeded in crossing the maritime limits of Asia or in bringing time and
history to heel. Hence the limitations imposed on their hegemonic will: "Every
time they attempted it, they placed in peril their domination and their very existence" (Polybius). "The Persians . . . continued in power not much above two
hundred years. . . . The supremacy of the Romans has far surpassed all those
that are recorded from earlier times, not only in the extent of its dominion and
in the splendor of its achievements . . . but also in the length of time during
which it has endured down to our day."[59]

Such is also the mutilated image of the glorious Achaemenid past that survives in Ammianus Marcellinus:[60] "It is quite well known that the vast conquests of that people extended their rule to the Propontis and to Thrace, when
they had conquered with brute force a very large number of countries, but that
the pride of their ambitious leaders, whose attacks continued without restraint
in distant lands, led to their being weakened by significant reversals, beginning
with Cyrus's act: he had crossed the Strait of Bosphorus with a fabulous multitude, then was annihilated by the queen of the Scythians, Tomyris, bitter avenger
of her sons. Then Darius, and later Xerxes, attacked Greece, turning land into sea
and sea into land. And after watching as nearly all their troops on land and sea
were swallowed up, they themselves only barely escaped."

Despite his declared ambition to correct the errors of his predecessors, Ammianus clearly plays fast and loose with his sources: he partly confuses Xerxes's
expedition beyond the Bosphorus with Cyrus's expedition to Central Asia
against the Sakas (Scythians).[61] For Herodotus and later authors, Cyrus's expedition is punctuated by a mythical confrontation with Tomyris, queen of the
Amazons.[62] There is also some confusion between the expedition Darius sent
to Greece and the one Xerxes led there in person. But accuracy is not the author's foremost concern: for him all that matters is to construct an appealing
discourse using the largest possible number of exempla.

Strabo, in the captivating abridgment he gives of the history of the Persians
from Cyrus to Darius III and beyond, does not omit to point out their sad fate.
"The hegemony of the Persians over Asia lasted about two hundred and fifty
years," but they were then conquered by the Macedonians, before falling under
the yoke of the Parthians.[63]

Accepted by all, such an established fact did not require long hours of meticulous scholarly research on the history of the Persian monarchy. The example of
Strabo shows that the dynastic succession of the Great Kings was known, and
that there was also information about many aulic customs. These were transmit-

ted by the authors of *Persica* and by Alexander's companions and were assembled into collections of exempla, including specialized collections such as "Particularities of Persia," attributed to one Heraclides of Alexandria and now lost.[64]

In their newly conquered territories, moreover, Rome's leaders had to deal with problems associated with their position as the successors, albeit remote, of the Persian Empire. Tacitus reports, for example, that in the time of Tiberius, a senatorial commission conducted an inquiry in Asia Minor to decide whether the privileges that the temples and cities were claiming deserved to be ratified.[65] Several of the local leaders noted charters granted by Achaemenid kings, particularly Cyrus and Darius I. During the imperial Roman period, ingenious forgers invented a completely fabricated document in Greek, engraved on stone, that supposedly reproduced a letter from Darius I to one of his subordinates in Asia Minor by the name of Gadatas: it established the fiscal privileges that the sanctuary of Apollo was claiming under Roman rule.

It is also possible (but far from certain) that, in response, the Parthian and Sassanid kings claimed to be the legitimate heirs of Achaemenid greatness. According to Dio Cassius, Ardašir aspired to "win back everything that the ancient Persians had once held, as far as the Grecian Sea." And according to Herodian, the Sassanid king invoked his ancestors, from Cyrus—"the first to have transferred the empire of the Medes to the Persians"—to Darius III, "their last king, overthrown by Alexander the Macedonian."[66] Not without good reason, some historians have called into doubt the thesis of such a deliberate continuity, judging rather that the declaration, known only through the Greco-Latin sources, was Roman propaganda. It may perhaps be identified as such by its reference to the theory of the succession of empires and the typically Greco-Roman epithet used to designate Darius III. According to that hypothesis, the Romans had not forgotten the past of the Persian-Achaemenid Empire or the scope of its territorial domination. But that is not surprising: after all, the lands between the Mediterranean Sea and the Euphrates, over which Roman dominion extended, were indistinguishable from the western satrapies of the Great Kings.

Finally, the Roman generals had to fight dynasties in Asia Minor that claimed to descend from Cyrus and Darius, such as the dynasty of Pontus. In the procession marking Pompey's triumph over Mithridates, "the sixteenth in descent from Darius, the son of Hystaspes, king of the Persians," "the couch of Darius, the son of Hystaspes" even made its appearance.[67] Among Mithridates's closest collaborators were his sons, bearing the names Artaphernes, Cyrus, Oxathres, Darius, and Xerxes.[68] Pompey had also conquered "Darius, king of the Medes."[69]

One "Darius the Arsacid" can be found in the triumph of Gaius.[70] The Romans were also familiar with the dynasty of Commagene, which, through writings and images, meant to link itself to Darius, son of Hystaspes. But these more or less fictive relics neither presupposed nor created a body of precise knowledge about the era of the Achaemenid Persian domination.

The Persian Kings in the Roman Literature of Exempla

Overall, what the Romans knew of the Persian past came primarily from the very partial and often distorted, even polemical, echoes found in the Greek classics, especially Herodotus but also Plato, Ctesias, Xenophon, and the courtier-chroniclers of Alexander's campaigns. The Great Kings held a small, even incidental place in the works of Roman-period authors. In reality, the only ones to escape oblivion were Artaxerxes II and some close to him: his brother Cyrus the Younger; his mother, Parysatis; and satraps such as Orontes and Datames, thanks especially to Plutarch and Cornelius Nepos. Of the other kings, the ones most often cited are Cyrus, Darius, and Xerxes. Thanks to Herodotus, Plato, and especially Xenophon in the *Cyropaedia,* Cyrus was erected into a model of a good king from the classical age on, and he still had that status in the Roman period.

Darius and Xerxes have a significant place in anecdotes and apothegms, primarily within the context of moralizing stories about the Median Wars. A parodic passage from Lucian's *The Rhetorician's Vade Mecum* (§ 18) shows that certain episodes of the Median Wars were systematically included in collections of anecdotes, set against a historical backdrop: "May all your discourses end with the names Marathon and Cynegire. Without them, no one could do anything. Sail constantly past Athos and traverse Hellespont on foot, let the sun be obscured by the arrows of the Medes, and let Xerxes take flight. May Leonidas be admired, and the inscription of Orthraydes deciphered; may Salamina, Artemision, and Plataea recur in your discourses at every moment."

It is therefore clear why Xerxes's disastrous reputation persisted among the writers of the Roman period. In Valerius Maximus, all the vignettes that depict Xerxes are placed within the context of his Greek expedition. Except when he is presented as the man who welcomed his conqueror, Themistocles, as the latter was being pursued by Athenians, the exempla about Xerxes are all damning: he does not pay heed to miracles or to the advice of specialists (the magi); he carries off statues stolen from Athens; and though he is the "leader of all Asia," it is only through treachery that he can prevail over a small troop of resolute Spartans.[71] He is met with catastrophes on the sea, which he madly attempted to put in chains; he is responsible for the loss "of the youth of all Asia, united under arms."[72] Shamefully defeated, he is overtaken by fear and takes flight.[73] Not only is he without good sense, he is mentally deranged.[74] He is also puffed up with pride and, as his name implies (sic), intemperate.[75] His defeat and the collapse of his empire result from his love of luxury and pleasures.[76]

There is no doubt that the Median Wars were still perceived as a signal event and that they had an undeniable operative value within the ideological and political framework of the confrontation with the Parthians. Furthermore, Xerxes's arrogant desire to turn the sea into a continent by means of bridges over the Bosphorus and his ultimate failure—so often evoked as a counterexample in the panegyric literature of the Roman period—constituted exempla particularly well adapted, for anyone so inclined, to the exaltation of Rome's uniqueness. For Rome was the only power ever to have ruled the known world "on land and sea."

Depending on the era and the circumstances, the precedent was used in different ways. In the early fifth century c.e., Claudian argued that Stilicon's enormous army, marching against the Barbarians, had only one precedent, which, oddly enough, he seemed to consider encouraging: "Never had such considerable forces, possessing such a variety of tongues, obeyed the same command. . . . Thus, it is said, did the army Xerxes had assembled at the ends of the world make the rivers it encountered run dry, the brightness of day turn dark with its arrows, while its fleet crossed reefs and built a bridge across the sea, to defy it by crossing without getting wet."[77]

Claudian might just as easily have referred to Darius III's armies, whose numbers were regularly inflated to the point of absurdity by Greek and Roman authors. These authors too mentioned the problems caused by the diversity of languages that the different contingents used.[78] Once again, this is the register of the exemplary commonplace, not of historical analysis.

Several Great Kings are also cited in Seneca's De ira, in which the author appropriates examples drawn directly or indirectly from Herodotus's Histories. Cambyses is a particular target: he overindulges in wine; he puts a young Persian aristocrat to death as a joke, at a banquet where the wine is flowing particularly freely; he embarks on an absurd military expedition, during which his soldiers die by the thousands.[79] Darius is condemned for having killed Persians who did not want to take part in an expedition.[80] Xerxes acts similarly in a comparable situation: "He therefore met the fate he deserved: defeated, routed, seeing on all sides the collapse of his fortune, he marched amidst the corpses of his men."[81] Within the logic of Seneca's own argument, Cyrus does not escape an occasional negative judgment. He flies into a rage against a river and for that reason is accused of fury *(furor)*: "He squandered his time, a grave error under the circumstances; and the fervor of the soldiers, whom he broke down through pointless labor; and also the opportunity for a surprise attack, by waging against a river the war declared on an enemy."[82]

Generally speaking, it is not difficult to grasp how the ancient authors selected and constructed their moralizing tales. Using a proven rhetorical technique, they were inclined to invoke the authority of "ancient documents" *(antiqui libri)*.[83] But their information-gathering was usually limited to a quick reading of Greek works (Herodotus, in the case of Seneca's Persian anecdotes). Sometimes, indeed, they simply consulted collections of exempla already in circulation.

The Persian Kings in the Histories of Alexander

The Roman authors who inserted references to the Persian kings in their histories of Alexander's expedition did not proceed any differently. A clear illustration occurs in the discourse attributed to Callisthenes, who opposed the innovations Alexander had introduced into his court after Darius III's death, and who sought to demolish the arguments Anaxarchus put forward in defense of the king's policy. The negative references that the philosopher introduces in reply are unambiguous. They are intended to cast into relief the opposition between the haughtiness of absolute despots and their military negligence, even against enemies reputed to be weaker than they. From Cyrus to Darius III, each of the Great Kings is targeted for abuse: "You are not associating with and giving advice to Cambyses or Xerxes, but to the son of Philip. . . . We ought to bear in mind that the Scythians, men poor but independent, chastened that Cyrus, that other Scythians again chastened Darius, as the Athenians and Lacedaemonians did Xerxes, as Clearchus and Xenophon with their 10,000 followers did Artaxerxes; and finally, that Alexander, though not honoured with prostration, has chastened this Darius."[84]

In that indictment of the Persian kings and of Alexander, the ideological burden falls especially on Cambyses and Xerxes, both reputed among the Greeks for their cruelty and intolerance. But it is clear that Cyrus is also stigmatized for his defeats, as are Artaxerxes II and Darius III. In general, however, Cyrus enjoys a particular status and prestige, for reasons that are easy to fathom. He was the founder of the empire and "established the Persians in their hegemony"; "Cyrus . . . first wrested the empire from the Medes and Lydians and transferred it to Persia."[85] He was "the most enterprising of the monarchs of Asia," as attested by his expeditions against the Scythians and in Central Asia, where he founded the city of Cyropolis.[86] Thanks to his victories, the riches piled up in the royal residences that Alexander took over, including Persepolis:[87] Treasure "had been accumulated from the state revenues, beginning with Cyrus, the first king of the Persians, down to that time, and the vaults were packed full of silver and gold."[88] His power and renown could be measured by the splendor of the capital, Pasargadae, which he had founded. His tomb—described at length by Alexander's companions—was located there, and the magi continued to make the traditional sacrifices before it.[89] His renown was such that, in an expression typical of the rhetor Curtius, Alexander was astonished "that so famous a king who possessed such great wealth should have received no more expensive a burial than if he had been one of the common people."[90] Cyrus's renown is associated not only with his victory but also with his intelligence and sagacity (phronēma): that is the reason Plutarch cites him first on a list of famous men (Agesilaus, Themistocles, Philip, Brasidas, Pericles) from whom Alexander was said to have inherited particular virtues.[91]

Another reason Cyrus holds a place apart in the accounts of Alexander's campaigns is that the Macedonian conqueror consciously sought to appropriate Cyrus's memory by presenting himself as his successor. As the "first king of the Persians and founder of their hegemony in Asia," Cyrus was in fact the holder and dispenser of royal legitimacy. The kings put on Cyrus's robe at the investiture ceremony held in Parsargadae.[92] They constituted an uninterrupted line of Cyrus's successors, with the exception of Darius III, who was accused of having usurped the glorious founder's throne.[93] It is therefore understandable why, "as soon as Alexander had conquered Persia," according to Arrian—who describes at length the measures taken by the Macedonian king in Pasargadae—he "was very desirous of entering the tomb of Cyrus."[94] The ancient authors do not hesitate to maintain that Alexander translated an inscription on the tomb into Greek. It said: "I am Cyrus, who won the empire for the Persians."[95] Strabo says that Alexander was "fond of Cyrus" (philokyros), and the king intended to spare Cyropolis despite its revolt only because "no other king of those lands inspired more admiration in him than Cyrus and Semiramis."[96] At the same time, Alexander was competing with a model that he intended both to imitate and to surpass: "No one else had invaded the country of the Indians to wage war there, not even Cyrus, son of Cambyses, though he advanced as far as the Scythians and was the most enterprising of the monarchs of Asia."[97] In fact, according to Arrian, Cyrus had not gone beyond Gedrosia: "He had come to that region with the intention of invading the territory of India; but before he could reach it, he had lost almost his entire army, which fell victim to the desert and the insurmountable difficulties of the route; these facts reported to Alexander are said to have sparked his emulation of Cyrus and Semiramis."

Alexander meant to preserve for himself alone the brilliant renown of the "first king of the Persians." Hence his exasperation with Orxines, who had seized the governorship of Persia during the Indian expedition. Curtius presents him as follows: "Descended from one of the seven Persians," he also "traced his line back to the renowned King Cyrus."[98] He was "pre-eminent among all the barbarians for his nobility and wealth."[99] Darius himself sought Cyrus's protection and, before Gaugamela, invoked his tutelary memory: "By the immortal memory of Cyrus who first wrested the empire from the Medes and Lydians and transferred it to Persia."[100] From Alexander's standpoint, such a claim was intolerable, as he asserts in a discourse Curtius attributes to him: "Even Darius did not inherit his rule of the Persians; he owed his succession to the throne of Cyrus to the benefaction of the eunuch Bagoas."[101]

As for Darius and Xerxes, they rarely appear, except in references to the Median Wars. Alexander declared that he was waging a war of reprisal against these kings. Hence, in the speech Alexander delivered prior to Issus, "Approaching the Greeks, he would remind them that these were the peoples who had inflicted wars upon Greece, wars occasioned first by Darius and then Xerxes, when they insolently demanded water and earth from them. . . . He reminded them that these were the men who had demolished and burned their temples, stormed their cities, violated all the laws of gods and men."[102] The king also made accusations against them in the letter he sent to Darius: "The Darius whose name you have assumed wrought utter destruction upon the Greek inhabitants of the Hellespontine coast and upon the Greek colonies of Ionia, and then crossed the sea with a mighty army, bringing the war to Macedonia and Greece. On another occasion Xerxes, a member of the same family, came with his savage barbarian troops . . . so that he could destroy our cities and burn our fields. . . . The wars you Persians undertake are unholy wars."[103] Persepolis was targeted for destruction because it was from that place that the armies of Darius and Xerxes had set off for an unholy war.[104] Despite their power, Darius and Xerxes failed to make the Greeks slaves of the Persians.[105]

It is especially clear that Xerxes's memory is omnipresent in the accounts of Alexander's landing and his Trojan exploits, even when he is not named. Curtius denounces the traitors who made false claims, like the Branchidae: "To please Xerxes, they had violated the temple called the Didymean."[106] Some Boeotians had also followed him and had settled in Babylonia, where they were still living when Alexander arrived.[107] Xerxes had taken statues from Greece and had installed them in Babylon.[108] The sacrileges he committed in Greece were avenged with the aid of a courtesan, the infamous Thais, reputed to have led the procession that set fire to the palaces of Persepolis.[109] Alexander points out that the Persians "would have suffered a more grievous punishment at the hands of the Greeks had they been forced to see him on Xerxes' throne and in his palace."[110] Plutarch even invents a mute dialogue between Alexander and the Great King during the sack of Persepolis, which in fact attests to an ambivalent view of the Persian monarch: "Alexander, observing a large statue of Xerxes which had been thrown down and was being carelessly trampled upon by the soldiers as they pressed into the royal palace, stopped, and addressed it as though it were alive. 'Shall we,' said he, 'leave you lying there, because of your invasion of Greece, or shall we set you up again because of your magnificence and greatness of soul?' He then stood musing for a long time, till at length he roused himself from his reverie and went his way."[111]

If Xerxes, like Cambyses, was believed to typify the impious despot, it was because his evil deeds too were directed against his own people:[112] Alexander, upon entering Babylon, "commanded the Babylonians to rebuild all the temples which Xerxes had destroyed, and especially that of Belus, whom the Babylonians venerate more than any other god."[113] Arrian again refers to the temple of Belus with regard to Alexander's second stay in Babylon: "This temple had been razed to the ground by Xerxes, when he returned from Greece; as were also all the other sacred buildings of the Babylonians."[114] The terrible image of Xerxes and his enormous armies date back in part to stories peddled in Greece since the Median Wars; but the story of the destruction of the temples of Babylon seems to have been invented either upon Alexander's arrival or in the years following his death. By the Roman period, it was perfectly canonical. Arrian returns to it once, when he cites the stories circulating in his time about the measures Alexander had taken in Ecbatana after the death of Hephaestion: "Others again affirm [but I by no means believe] that he ordered the shrine of Asclepius in Ecbatana to be razed to the ground; which was an act of barbarism, and by no means in harmony with Alexander's general behaviour, but rather in accordance with the arrogance of Xerxes in his dealings with the deity, who is said to have let fetters down into the Hellespont, in order to punish it."[115]

The reference to Xerxes also appears in Plutarch's two minor works collectively called *On the Fortune of Alexander*. In what is a book of pure rhetoric, Plutarch intends to demonstrate, against the Roman current that opposed the conqueror, that Alexander was a philosopher king the like of which the world had never known. His victories cannot be explained by the intervention of Fortune (*Tychē*) but only by his own qualities (*aretē*). To make his argument, Plutarch is often led, quite naturally, to compare Alexander's success to those of other monarchs, including the Persian sovereigns. Of these, Xerxes is called "barbarous and stupid": "How vain was all your toil to cover the Hellespont with a floating bridge! . . . Wise and prudent princes . . . join and fasten nations together not with boards or planks, or surging brigandines, not with inanimate and insensible bonds, but by the ties of legitimate love, chaste nuptials, and the infallible gage of progeny."[116] This is an obvious reference to the marriages between Macedonian men and Iranian women that Alexander promoted. To make it clear that Alexander owes everything to his personal qualities and feats and nothing to the goddess Tychē, Plutarch will contrast the conditions surrounding his accession to those in place when the Persian kings took the crown. The passage inserts Darius III into a long line of kings who, unlike Alexander, had none of the requisite qualities of kingship: "But now I shall return to the beginnings of his advancement and the early dawnings of his power, and endeavor to discover what was there the great work of Fortune, which rendered Alexander so great by her assistance. First then, how came it to pass that some neighing barb did not seat him on the throne of Cyrus, free from wounds, without loss of blood, without a toilsome expedition, as formerly it happened to Darius Hystaspes?[117] Or that some one flattered by a woman, as Darius by Atossa,[118] did not deliver up his diadem to him, as the other did to Xerxes, so that the empire of Persia came home to him, even to his own doors? Or that, like Oarses, thanks to the intrigues of the eunuch Bagoas, he had only to throw off the garb of a messenger [*astandēs*] and immediately put on the tiara that ever stands erect?"[119]

Plutarch, like all Greeks a faithful reader of Herodotus, drew from that author the examples of Darius and Xerxes, but, in contrast to Herodotus, Plutarch uses them ironically and polemically. As for those "kings that never felt a wound nor ever saw a finger bleed," it is once more a question of Persian kings, the "Ochi and Artaxerxes,—who were no sooner born but they were established by you on the throne of Cyrus."[120] And Plutarch characterizes Darius III, confus-

ing him with Arses, as "a servant and the king's courier." Whereas Alexander
was a self-made man and had to fight enemies each more formidable than the
last, men such as "Artaxerxes the brother of Cyrus" were proclaimed kings by
their fathers "in their own lifetime; they won battles which no mothers wept
for; they spent their days in festivals, admiring the pomp of shows and theatres;
and still more happy, they prolonged their reigns till scarce their feeble hands
could wield their sceptres."[121] Here again is one of the favorite themes of Hellenistic political philosophy: Is the best king the son of a king, or the son of a private individual? That is why Plutarch cites, in addition to Artaxerxes II, both
Antiochus, son of Seleucos, and Ptolemy Philadelphus, indicating thereby that
these sons painlessly reaped the benefits that their fathers, Alexander's comrades in arms, had attained gloriously.

It is within this context that Darius, "the one who was defeated by Alexander," is cited in a passage from Aelian's *Varia historia*. The Persian king, called
the son of a slave (along with Darius I, "Cyrus's quiver-bearer"), is on a list of leaders and kings who had become powerful even though they were reputed to
have emerged from nowhere.[122] Valerius Maximus also devotes a chapter to the
problem: "Men of Humble Origin Who Became Illustrious."[123] The Persian kings
are not included, but the author, who had read his Herodotus, does not omit to
recall an anecdote featuring Darius I when he was merely a private individual.[124]
The topos is taken up by Nepos, who judges that "Cyrus and Darius, sons of
Hystaspes, are the most remarkable of those who attached an unlimited power
to their title. They were both private individuals when their merit earned them
the crown."[125] In fact, as Plato had already argued, because they were not the
sons of kings, they were free from all the flaws and vices associated with the
soft life of the palaces.[126] But this time, in contrast to Alexander's heroic destiny,
the supposedly obscure origin of the king does not work in his favor: all that
remains is the epithet "the Darius who was defeated by Alexander."

Alexander, directly addressing the goddess Tychē, adds to this denunciation a comparison that further devalues his adversary: "Darius was a product of
your own rearing, who of a servant and the king's courier was advanced by you
to be monarch of all Persia. So too was Sardanapalus, who from a comber of
purple wool was raised by you to wear the royal diadem."[127] For Plutarch, as for
many other ancient authors, Sardanapalus had become the emblematic figure of
the Asian despot ruined by luxury and vice. Plutarch contrasts him to the conquering Semiramis: "Sardanapalus, . . . though born a man, spent his time at home
combing purple wool, lying among his harlots in a lascivious posture upon his

back, with his heels higher than his head. After his decease, they made for him a statue of stone, resembling a woman dancing alone like the barbarians, who seemed to snap with her fingers as she held them over her head, with this inscription,—*Eat, drink, indulge thy lust; all other things are nothing.*"[128] Plutarch's comparison does not, to say the least, increase the stature of Darius, already discredited as a plaything of Fortune. The (invented) epitaph on the tomb of Sardanapalus contrasts markedly with the epitaph (no less fabricated) that the ancient authors, following Onesicritus, claimed to have read on the tomb of Darius the Great (or Cyrus?): "I was a friend for my friends. As a horseman and archer, I proved superior to all others; I was the best of hunters."[129]

From One Darius to Another: Greatness and Decadence

In keeping with the very favorable tradition he presents upon Darius III's accession, Justin states that the new king, placed on the throne by the people, was "honoured with the name of Darius," so that "nothing might be wanting to his royal dignity."[130] Although that choice of names may reveal his great ambitions and his awareness of the Achaemenid past and of his own value, it is a cruel comparison, at least in terms of imperial history: one King Darius expanded and organized the empire, the other lost it. Not only did that mundane observation not escape the ancient authors, they even made it the nexus of their historical vision.

In a passage from Aelian, Darius III and Darius I are included in the category of men who emerged from (albeit relative) anonymity to become kings, and the contrast is clearly marked. One "was defeated by Alexander," the other was universally known by his ancestry—"Darius, son of Hystaspes"—and by another recurrent expression, which recalls the best-known heroic deed of his reign: "Darius, the one who killed the magus and gave dominion to the Persians."[131] In contrast to that glorious namesake and predecessor, Darius III bears the blame for allowing the empire of the Persians to pass into the hands of the Macedonians. That is clear in the cavalier view Strabo gives of Persia's dynastic history: "The man who established the Persians in their hegemony was Cyrus. Cyrus was succeeded by his son Cambyses, who was deposed by the Magi. The Magi were slain by the Seven Persians, who then gave over the empire to Dareius, the son of Hystaspes. And then the successors of Dareius came to an end with Arses. Arses was slain by Bagoüs the eunuch, who set up as king another Dareius, who was not of the royal family. Him Alexander deposed, and reigned himself for ten or eleven years. And then the hegemony of Asia was divided amongst his several successors and their descendants, and then dissolved. The hegemony of the Persians over Asia lasted about two hundred and fifty years."[132]

That paragraph concludes the last part of book 15, which Strabo devotes to the geography of Persia and to the history and traditions of the Persian people and dynasty. The following book covers Babylonia and Assyria.[133] Describing Assyria, it gives the location of the village of Gaugamela. Strabo speaks of it as a "notable settlement," because it recalls the memory of Darius I, who had given it "as an estate for the maintenance of the camel which helped most on the toil-some journey through the deserts of Scythia."[134] To designate the king, Strabo uses the well-known expression "Darius, the son of Hystaspes." But a few lines earlier, he does not fail to recall, with respect to Gaugamela, the battle that un-folded there in 331. It is there, he says, that "Dareius was conquered and lost his empire."[135] From one Darius to another, Strabo effectively evokes the memory both of the pinnacle of a powerful empire and of its fall.

III

RELUCTANCE AND ENTHUSIASM

⚜ 7 ⚜

Upper King and Lower King

Up Country, Down Country

The ancient authors have little to say about Darius's activities after Alexander's arrival. Diodorus alone gives some information on the royal preparations, the aim of which was to conduct an offensive against the expeditionary corps Philip II had sent to Asia Minor, or even to push it back into the sea. Diodorus then jumps ahead to Alexander's landing and the Battle of the Granicus, asserting simply, without explanation, that "the Persian satraps and generals had not acted in time to prevent the crossing of the Macedonians."[1] The only one to present an explanation—based on an ethical conception that is more Greek than Persian—is Justin, who claims it was Darius's choice: "King Darius, . . . from confidence in his strength, abstained from all artifice in his operations; observing that 'clandestine measures were fit only for a stolen victory.'"[2] That sentence and the one that follows indicate, albeit imperfectly, how the chain of command functioned: "The first engagement, in consequence, was fought on the plains of Adrastia." The "in consequence" *(igitur)* leaves little doubt: the satraps of Asia Minor waged battle in Phrygia under the direct orders of the Great King. And who could have doubted it?

Overall, the negative charge associated with the portrait of Darius becomes increasingly strong throughout the first year of the war, when Alexander pushed the satraps back to the Granicus (spring of 334), then seized the coast of Asia Minor, including Sardis, and then Gordium (spring of 333). This may appear paradoxical, because during that time Darius is practically absent from the ancient accounts. But the paradox is only apparent. It is precisely because of his distance from the theater of operations that Darius is so ill treated—not so much in overt denunciations as through the narration's focus on his adversary. His absence is interpreted as inaction, because the ancient authors analyze Darius through a Macedonian interpretive grid, that of a heroic war of movement, described and written in accord with a pervasive literary model, the Homeric model.

Arrian's choice of the title *Anabasis* clearly reveals his debt to Xenophon, but it also inscribes Alexander in the *longue durée* of Greek expeditions to the Achaemenid Empire. In the Greeks' conception of maritime and continental spaces, the regions bordering the sea bore the designation "down country." Upon leaving the coast to march toward the interior of the continent, one "ascended" or went "up country." When traveling in the reverse direction, one "descended" or went "down country." The upward march was the "anabasis," the downward march the "katabasis." The adverbial expressions could also be used in the comparative or superlative, the notions being understood in relative terms. As seen from Susa or Persepolis by the Greek authors, the countries of western Asia Minor were "low countries," and the satrapies of the Iranian plateau and Central Asia were systematically called "High Satrapies" or "upper satrapies," also translated as "Higher Satrapies."[3]

The comparison is not only valid for the anabasis conducted by Cyrus the Younger. The Greek orators—and Alexander himself, in pre-battle speeches attributed to him—immoderately and unrestrainedly extolled the precedent of campaigns conducted to the very heart of Achaemenid power. But in fact, the war narrated by Xenophon, the *anabasis* in the strict sense (march up country), was waged by a Persian prince in revolt against his brother, the legitimate Great King. Despite the central place that Xenophon unduly attributes to them, Greek soldiers were in the service of a cause not their own. Furthermore, after the death of the one who had hired them, the *katabasis* (march down to the sea) looked more like a flight from the Great King than a victorious expedition into his states—as Arrian does not fail to point out in a different passage.[4]

Within that perspective, the anabasis that the Spartan king Agesilaus attempted in 396–394 took on a completely different symbolic meaning in the Greek imagination. The choice of the port of embarkation, Aulis, makes explicit a direct connection between the war that was about to begin and the expedition that Agamemnon had led to the walls of Troy. The plans that the Spartan king's panegyrists attribute to him are unusually bold and wide-ranging: "He then formed a plan for a campaign into Persia and an attack against the Great King in person"; "he was preparing to go as far as possible, marching against the upper countries, with the idea that all the peoples he put behind him would be lost to him by the king."[5] According to Plutarch, the matter at hand for Agesilaus was actually to drive the Great King out of his upper palaces once and for all: "Then he determined to go farther afield, to transfer the war from the Greek sea, to make the King fight for his person and for the happiness he enjoyed in Ecbatana and Susa, and firstly to rouse him from his idleness, so that he could not be any more able, at leisure from his throne, to play the arbitrator for the Greeks in their wars nor to corrupt their popular leaders" (*Agesilaus,* 15.1).

The canonical portrait of the Great King was the one common in Greece when Alexander set off through the straits, and when he came to honor the Greek heroes of the Trojan War. The attitudes and decisions attributed to Darius would be conceived, described, and explained point for point within the normalized framework of Greek imagery. Here was a Persian sovereign who concealed his indecision inside his palaces and "chose profit and luxury with a life of ease" over the risks, but also the glories, of man-to-man combat.[6] By contrast, Alexander had no intention of "yawning upon the throne of slothful and voluptuous power."[7]

According to one tradition, Alexander, upon his landing in Troas, declared that he was taking possession of the land of Asia: "When they arrived at the continent of Asia, Alexander first of all threw a dart into the enemy's country" "and then leapt ashore himself the first of the Macedonians, signifying that he received Asia from the gods as a spear-won prize."[8] The overall meaning of the declarations attributed to the conqueror leaves no doubt: he was issuing a challenge to Darius. Mirroring Plutarch's Agesilaus, he wanted "to make the King fight for his person and for the happiness he enjoyed in Ecbatana and Susa," that is, for his empire. It is from that agonistic angle that the ancient authors would systematically present the long-distance contacts between the two kings, until Alexander finally stood over the remains of Darius, assassinated by his own men.

Initially, according to Plutarch, Alexander "remained in doubt as to what to attempt next; whether to attack Darius at once and risk all that he had won upon the issue of a single battle, or to consolidate and organise his conquests on the coast of Asia Minor."[9] Then Plutarch attributes a new decision to Alexander, which he situates in the spring of 333, when the king, then in Gordium, learned of Memnon's death: he was "encouraged in his design of proceeding farther up into the interior [*anō*].[10] . . . Darius, too, came down from [*katabainō*] Susa, confident in the numbers of his army."[11] In taking his army to the low country to face Alexander, who was coming up from the sea, Darius in some sense finally responded to the challenge issued by his adversary a year earlier.

The two kings, apart and yet close to each other, would move through the space of the empire as in a ballet, governed by movements up or down country. These movements themselves made visible to everyone the territorial domains of each of the protagonists fighting for hegemony and also determined their expanse. The resulting image, perfectly univocal, is simple and evocative: one of the kings continually advances and builds an empire, the other calculates and waits, then withdraws and flees, losing any chance of holding onto his empire as the days pass.

Such is the storyline. Let us now consider the details of the script.

The King, His Advisers, and the Flatterers

The ancient authors, to reintroduce the Great King into a game that only Alexander seemed fit to play until now, will represent a war council that supposedly took place in the Persian court. Following a proven narrative technique, they let readers take part in the (fictive) debates, which allows them to create an active complicity, to make their readers ipso facto the authenticating agents of their accounts. Contemporary readers, of course, know how to detect the ruse and avoid the trap.

Diodorus presents the council in detail, before his report on the mustering and training of the troops in Babylon. Curtius also alludes to the council but situates it after the assembling of the army.[12] The reasons for that minor discrepancy are purely literary. The occasion for convening the council, which the authors place in the spring of 333, is the announcement of the death of Memnon, who for a year had made life difficult for the Macedonians' rearguard at sea. They considered that loss a fatal blow to the king's affairs.[13] Arrian does not speak of that council. Later, however, during the maneuvers in preparation for the Battle of Cilicia, he evokes in very similar terms a heated discussion between Darius and a Macedonian, Amyntas, who had sought refuge with the king.[14] Curtius also depicts a debate between the king and leaders of the Greek mercenaries who, under Darius's order, had been sent back from the maritime war front by Pharnabazus (successor to his uncle Memnon) to strengthen the royal army.[15]

All these accounts have one point in common: Darius and a Greek or Macedonian adviser are at odds on the best strategy to adopt. Darius asks his Companions a simple question: Should he personally take command of the army and "march down with all his armed forces and fight the Macedonians in person," or should the mission be entrusted to generals? Two positions are put forward: some urge the king to take command, but they are opposed by an Athenian exile, Charidemus, in the Great King's service at the time. He "recommended that Dareius should on no account stake his throne rashly on a gamble" but should send "to the war a general who had given proof of his ability." The king, initially tempted to follow Charidemus's advice, eventually sides with his Companions, who "brought Charidemus into suspicion of wanting to get the command so that he could betray the Persian empire to the Macedonians." Because of the aggressive tone of the Athenian, who places the Persians' courage in doubt, the king, mad with rage, immediately orders him to be executed. Then, too late, he feels remorse for "having made a serious mistake." He is overcome with fear at the military valor of the Macedonians and their king. In the end he decides to take command of the army himself.[16]

For the first time, then, we are introduced into the Persian camp at a decisive moment. It is not surprising that the information is transmitted by two authors, Diodorus and Curtius, who are particularly fond of giving such elucidation. These passages are supposed to provide, or at least propose, answers to many questions that were asked about the Great King's strategy, objectives, and tactics in the face of the Macedonian invasion, not to mention his personal abilities to lead maneuvers not only in staff meetings but also on the battlefield. Should we stop there, at the ponderous mistrust elicited by our reading and first analysis?

Neither this preliminary inquiry nor the conclusion to come implies that no debate took place in Darius's court. It would be surprising, in fact, if that were the case. Strategic initiatives had to be taken upon Alexander's landing. There is no doubt that the decision the satraps of Asia Minor made to oppose Alexander was communicated to them directly by the central power, which named Arsites, satrap of Hellespontine Phrygia, to take command of the army. That no doubt explains why Arsites, feeling responsible for the king's defeat, took his own life.[17] And whatever one might think of the exaggerated role that an entire ancient tradition attributed to Memnon, there is no reason to deny that Darius, after the news of the defeat at the Granicus, assigned him the post of "governor of lower Asia and commander of the entire fleet."[18] It is just as easy to postulate that, at a given moment, a debate took place at the court about what ought to be done in response to Alexander's advances. There is no doubt that Alexander's repeated successes created an entirely unprecedented strategic and political situation: despite the maintenance of very active Persian rearguard naval forces

(Darius's naming of Pharnabazus to replace his uncle Memnon), the leader of a Greek anabasis for the first time had the opportunity to wage a victorious offensive against the high countries.

The matter at hand, then, is not to place in doubt the existence of debates within the court or of decisions by Darius. It is simply to determine in what measure, to what extent, and in accordance with what interpretive grid the historian of today can use texts claiming to speak from Darius's court and often in his name.

The Great King and His Council

To assess the credibility to be granted to that type of situation and discourse, it is necessary to place that council within a long series. The Greek authors love to take their readers behind the scenes of power. It is not without reason that an Italiote painter—known as "the Darius Painter"—represents such a scene, a decade at most after Darius III's defeat at the hands of Alexander (Fig. 42). Beneath a frieze of gods, where the opposition between Greece and Asia is clearly evoked (Asia is associated with Apatē, goddess of deceit), a Great King is on his throne. He is identified by the name "Darius" and is surrounded by soldiers and dignitaries from his court. In front of him, a man on a small round platform, marked with the name *Persai*, is addressing the king and the other advisers. Below, a scene of tributary payment is represented, also in the Greek manner. It is generally acknowledged that the central register represents a council held at court before an expedition against the Greeks. According to one of the com-

42. *The king in his council: painting on the "Darius vase."*

monly accepted hypotheses, the painter had a visual image in his mind of a council in the Greek style, convened by Darius I to assess the situation at the start of the revolt of Ionia. Others believe he was depicting the reflections prior to the first Median War. Because the vase dates to 330–320, other exegetes have believed that it is the war council convened by Darius III upon news of Memnon's death, after which the royal adviser Charidemus was put to death for having given advice that displeased the king.

It is altogether noteworthy that a Greek painter from the beginning of the Hellenistic period in Greater Greece might have drawn his inspiration from known representations of the Persian court. But it is not really surprising. That is because the conquests were widely known, as attested by other vase paintings by the same painter or, in any case, from the same workshop. His choice of the scene of a council assembled around the Great King demonstrates the popularity of that theme, which is also connected to a reflection on the exercise of power and decision making within a political system totally different from that of the Greek city-states. But is the search to identify a precise date really pertinent? Nothing is less sure. In fact, Greek representations of courts "after the Persian manner" were not supposed to be snapshots of events precisely located in time and space. They abound in conventions, which constitute both their underlying framework and their idiom.

The same is true of the texts claiming to introduce the reader into the private circle of the Great King's advisers. Curtius imagines and depicts other war councils assembled around Darius, after the Battle of Arbela and during the court's stay at Ecbatana between October 331 and the spring of 330. He is not afraid to "quote" in extenso endless discussions and oratorical duels that unite and divide Darius's intimate circle.[19] He also likes to "reconstruct" conversations that the king and an adviser held in private.[20] It is perfectly clear that Diodorus and Curtius, or their common source(s), drew a great deal from a conventional repertoire of characters, scenes, and lines.

More generally, the scene of a council convened by a Great King is a classic of Greek literature. One famous scene is the "constitutional debate" held by the conspirators gathered around Darius, those who had just eliminated the "reign of the magus" and who, according to Herodotus, raised questions about the political regime that ought to be established henceforth.[21] Then there is the council, also convened by Darius, to name his successor. Two of his sons, Artobarzanes and Xerxes, are in competition: Xerxes is vigorously supported by his mother, Atossa, and by a Spartan exile, Demaratus.[22] Other councils had to decide whether it was opportune to launch a military expedition. In particular, there is a very long passage in Herodotus in which Xerxes, "on the point of taking in hand the expedition against Athens, called a conference of the leading men of the country," less to leave the decision to them than to allow them to hear his own and to launch a Greek-style rhetorical assault.[23]

These councils are imagined in stereotypical and repetitive form, and the roles are assigned in accordance with an immutable order. At the council convened by Xerxes before the expedition to Greece, for example, two men in the king's intimate circle face off: Mardonius, who pushes for war, and Artabanus, who implores the king not to take such a risk against the Greeks, stressing their valor. Mardonius plays the same part in 479 opposite his colleague Artabazus. Mardonius, of a violent and rash temperament, wants to lead the troops into battle against the Greeks and to that end evokes "the good old Persian way" of engaging in battle. Artabazus, by contrast, "a man of more than average foresight," believed "it would be a mistake . . . to risk another battle." He therefore thinks it wiser to distribute money to the Greek leaders, who would not fail to "give up their liberty."[24]

The arguments exchanged and the human types depicted irresistibly bring to mind the war council of 334 that assembled the Persian satraps of Asia Minor in Zeleia, with an identical agenda: whether or not to do battle with Alexander.[25] The part played by Artabanus in Xerxes's court, then by Artabazus in Greece, is here played by the Rhodian Memnon, who recommends not risking a confrontation. It is better, he says, to adopt a scorched-earth tactic toward Alexander and at the same time to take the war to Europe and force Alexander to turn back. Like Artabazus in 479, Memnon also maintains that a distribution of Persian gold would persuade many leaders to leave the Macedonian camp.[26] And just as Herodotus presents Artabazus as "a man of more than average foresight," so Diodorus says of Memnon that he gave "the best counsel, as after-events made clear." Curtius does a similar analysis. He notes that in Cilicia, Arsames, "reflecting upon the strategy advocated by Memnon at the start of the war, decided all too late to follow a course of action that would earlier have been profitable. He laid waste to Cilicia with fire and sword in order to create a desert for his enemy."[27]

In opposition to Memnon, the Persians around Arsites present an argument similar to that of Mardonius in Greece. Defending the idea of facing Alexander in pitched battle, they invoke a tradition proper to them, a form of *megalopsykhia,* a term that can be understood to mean "proud exaltation" or "high spirits."[28] The expression is oddly reminiscent of "the good old Persian way" of doing

battle put forward by Mardonius, against what he presents as Artabazus's pusillanimity. That is certainly what Justin conveys in attributing to Darius certain
strategic ideas, manifestly based on an ethical view of open and joyful warfare:
"King Darius, . . . from confidence in his strength, abstained from all artifice in
his operations; observing that 'clandestine measures were fit only for a stolen
victory.'" The declaration curiously resembles the line Arrian attributes to Alexander before Gaugamela, in opposition to Parmenion's proposal to resort to
a nocturnal ruse: "It was dishonorable to steal the victory, and . . . Alexander
had to win openly and without stratagem."[29]

In all cases, those who advocate an offensive carry the day; and in all cases,
the Greek author firmly takes the side of the "wise" solution and denounces the
adventurism of those who push the king toward war. The reason is surely that,
in the meantime, events have shown that a dilatory attitude would have made
it possible to avoid a defeat in pitched battle. But in fact the accusation also re-
dounds on the king or leader who has chosen to take a thoughtless risk. For
Artabanus, Artabazus, Memnon, and Charidemus have something else in common, which is that they all warn against any denigration of the valor of the
Greek and Macedonian troops, and, more precisely, against the smug disdain
manifested by Mardonius, by the Persian satraps in 334, and even by Darius III.
Curtius harshly judges the condescending haughtiness Darius manifests toward his adversary: "There was more show than truth in these boasts of his."[30]

Curtius presents the Persian king's feelings after he has passed in review his
vast troops: "But the one thing Darius did not lack was military numbers. The
sight of this assembly filled him with joy, and his courtiers [purpurati] further
inflated his expectations with their usual flattery. He turned to the Athenian
Charidemus" (3.2.10).[31]

The entire passage is constructed on the principle of mimesis. Curtius explicitly copies a famous Herodotean model, comparing the enumeration and
review of the troops in front of Darius to those organized by Xerxes in Abydos
and then in Doriskos in 480.[32] The Great King had come back enthralled by the
spectacle of Abydos: "When he saw the whole Hellespont hidden by ships, and
all the beaches and plains of Abydos filled with men, he congratulated himself,"
considering himself "a lucky man." Herodotus's expression has its clear counterpart in the words Curtius uses to convey, much more flatly, Darius's self-
satisfaction: "The sight of his assembly filled him with joy."[33]

The parallel lies not simply in the description and the mode of counting up
the troops but also in the actors and their lines. According to Herodotus, after

the parade Xerxes brings in a Greek exile, Demaratus the Spartan, to see him and asks for his advice. The Greek does not fail to warn him against the unjustified sense of superiority he seems to feel toward the small number of Greek troops, just as Charidemus will warn Darius III. To be faithful to his illustrious model in every detail, Curtius, unlike Diodorus, places the conversation after (and not before) the assembling of the troops. The most notable variant occurs at the end of the story: "Xerxes burst out laughing at Demaratus' answer, and good-humouredly let him go." This is far removed from the mad rage of Darius, who has Charidemus put to death.

The Great King's Greek adviser is a well-known literary type. Darius the Great promised Histiaeus, whom he wanted to see leave Miletus, that if he came to Susa, he would confer on him the titles of table companion and adviser.[34] The same is true for Demartus vis-à-vis Xerxes, as depicted at another famous council that Darius I called to decide which of his sons would succeed him. According to Herodotus, it was Demaratus who was able to introduce the determining factor in favor of Xerxes. The argument of porphyrogenesis appeared so indisputable that, according to Plutarch, Parysatis attempted to use it again in favor of her favorite son, Cyrus, this time without success.[35] Charidemus, for his part, "had been a comrade-in-arms of King Philip [?]" and then "counselled all [Darius's] successes."[36]

The presence of these Greek exiles, the favorites of princes, leads us to another literary motif, the jealousy they aroused in the Persian nobles. The king questions a Greek adviser, and the Greek's advice is systematically attacked by the Persian nobles taking part at the council. Memnon, in 334, and Charidemus, in 333, were suspected of having the same ambition and of committing the same crime: "The other Persians agreed with Arsites, because they had a suspicion that Memnon was deliberately contriving to protract the war for the purpose of obtaining honour from the king."[37] According to Diodorus, Darius's friends vigorously opposed Charidemus and even brought him under suspicion of "wanting to get the command so that he could betray the Persian empire to the Macedonians."[38] Similarly, the advice and counsel of the leaders of the Greek mercenaries prior to Issus were vehemently opposed by the royal courtiers, who suspected the mercenaries of being ready to sell out to the highest bidder: "The only reason the mercenaries wanted the force divided was so that they could hand over to Alexander whatever part was entrusted to them."[39] Texts and contexts in their turn irresistibly evoke the conflicts that, according to Diodorus, had broken out between Artabazus, the Persian leader of the Egyptian expedition in 373, and the head of the mercenaries, the Athenian Iphicrates: "When Iphicrates demanded that he be given the mercenaries that were on hand and promised if he had them to capture the city, Pharnabazus became suspicious of his boldness and his courage for fear lest he take possession of Egypt for himself."[40]

In each of these cases, the sagacity of the Greek leaders and advisers is praised by the ancient authors, who all judge that the course of history would have been altered had the kings been able to model themselves on the boldness of these leaders and the prudence of the advisers. Concerning Memnon, Diodorus displays a partiality identical to that which he systematically manifests elsewhere for the Greek leaders operating in the Achaemenid armies.

In that respect Memnon and Charidemus had at least one illustrious precedent: Themistocles. Driven from his own country, that Greek had come to reside at the court of Artaxerxes I. Themistocles "learned an adequate amount of Persian and conversed with the king without an interpreter. . . . He took part in his hunts. . . . He was even admitted to see the king's mother, and he educated himself about the magi's doctrine." The rest can be divined: "Themistocles aroused the jealousy of those powerful at court, who believed that he had had the audacity to speak freely against them before the king."[41] The story of Themistocles may itself bring to mind that of Daniel, who obtained an envied post in Darius's court: "Then this Daniel was preferred above the presidents and princes, because an excellent spirit was in him; and the king thought to set him over the whole realm. Then the presidents and princes sought to find occasion against Daniel concerning the kingdom; but they could find none occasion nor fault; forasmuch as he was faithful, neither was there any error or fault found in him."[42]

The King's Wrath: Literary Creation and the Monarchical Fable

There is no doubt that the anecdote about Charidemus fueled images and fantasies about the Persian sovereigns, their absolute power over people and things. Curtius and Charidemus proclaim that "even natural inclinations are generally corrupted" by such power.[43] The different motifs assembled as anecdotes are meant to illustrate a moral, about monarchy in this case.

From beginning to end, Darius demonstrates his weakness of character and of judgment. In fact, these authors express unanimous and unsparing opinions about the king himself. "Wrath blinded him to his advantage," writes Diodorus. According to him, Darius "seized Charidemus by the girdle according to the custom of the Persians, turned him over to the attendants, and ordered him put to death."[44] The scene is directly borrowed from Xenophon's *Anabasis,* which describes in the same terms the judgment of the traitor Orontas in Cyrus the Younger's tent: "After this, at the bidding of Cyrus, every man of them arose, even Orontas' kinsmen, and took him by the girdle, as a sign that he was condemned to death; and then those to whom the duty was assigned led him out."[45] For good measure, Diodorus (who was particularly fond of the expression) adds the words: "according to the custom of the Persians." The parallel does not shine a favorable light on Darius, who, irresolute by nature, belatedly regrets his decision and "admitting the truth of Charidemus' words, ordered his burial."[46] Cyrus, by contrast, decisive and ruthless in pursuing his own interests, makes every trace of the conspirator disappear: "From that moment no man ever saw Orontas living or dead, nor could anyone say from actual knowledge how he was put to death—it was all conjectures, of one sort and another; and no grave of his was ever seen."[47]

The scene and characters could have been included in a collection of exempla devoted to anger, and the comparison could easily have served as supporting evidence for a brilliant sophist wishing to give a lecture on the "good king" and the "bad king." Darius, in fact, could have illustrated both. His weakness of character went hand in hand with violence and cruelty, of which he soon provided a new example: "Egged on by his courtiers, who succumbed to a frenzy of barbarous ruthlessness, Darius had the hands cut off of every one of them and the stumps cauterized. He then gave orders for the men to be taken around so that they could get an impression of his troops and, when they had sufficiently inspected everything, he told them to report what they had seen to their king," that is, to Alexander.[48]

Curtius calls Darius "by nature a sincere and sympathetic person" and even "a man of justice and clemency."[49] The king knows, therefore, not to give in to his impulses. In another exemplum illustrating the "good king," the author says that "he would not commit so heinous a crime as to order the slaughter of men who had taken up his cause and who were his own soldiers."[50] But the expression Curtius uses is probably not as laudatory as it may appear: especially against an adversary of Alexander's caliber, being "sympathetic" might also indicate weakness. That is clear in Plutarch's contrasting portraits of Cyrus the Younger and Artaxerxes, and in the debate they illustrate between two models of kingship: "There was, too, a certain dilatoriness in the nature of the king, which most people took for clemency. Moreover, in the beginning he appeared to emulate the gentleness of the Artaxerxes whose name he bore. . . . Nevertheless, restless and factious men thought that affairs required Cyrus, a man who had a brilliant spirit, surpassing skill in war, and great love for his friends; and that the magnitude of the empire required a king of lofty purpose and ambition" (*Artaxerxes*, 4.4; 6.1).

A third qualifier is also found in Curtius: Darius is "of a mild and placid disposition."[51] "Placid" in this case also means that the king is indecisive and irresolute: "The courtiers themselves were summoned to daily meetings with him and proffered conflicting opinions."[52] Lacking judgment and fortitude, the king is the plaything of his courtiers, who incite him to alter his initial decision,[53] even though Darius finds Charidemus's advice "less objectionable than his courtiers."[54] But "his courtiers inflated his expectations with their usual flattery."[55]

The terminology places Darius III within a long series of kings spoiled by bad advisers and flatterers. Debates on that point were especially keen in Alexander's court.[56] Speaking of Darius and then of Alexander, under very different circumstances of course, Arrian denounces in almost identical terms "those ingratiating courtiers, such as do and will haunt each successive king to his detriment."[57] But according to him, Darius suffers from specific character flaws that make him a disastrous war leader: "All this made Darius waver in his decision. He himself was readily induced to adopt any opinion it was most agreeable to hold. . . . On all sides his courtiers egged him on, telling him that he would trample the Macedonian force underfoot with his cavalry. . . . But the worse counsels prevailed, as they were more agreeable to hear at the time" (2.6.4, 6; Brunt trans.).

The image of the indecisive king, plaything of his advisers, is extraordinarily persistent in the monarchical literature. Reflections on Darius clearly belong to a whole current of Hellenistic philosophy relating to the exercise of royal power. Book 6 of Athenaeus is devoted in great part to a discussion of the banqueter philosophers and focuses on two related loathsome and ridiculous human types, the parasite and the flatterer.[58] Many essays on flattery were published by Aristotle's student Theophrastus, for example, but also by the Stoic Clearchus of Soli. Polybius also devotes many discussions to that theme, because he believed that the influence of advisers was such that they needed to be chosen with care. He does not fail to denounce a number of these royal advisers, particularly at the court of the Lagids. One of Plutarch's moral opuscules is titled "How to Tell a Flatterer from a Friend." Without expressly using the example of the Persian kings, the author stigmatizes many "effeminate kings," who, given over to luxury and pleasure, abandoned real power to the flatterers.[59] He denounces flattery, which, he maintains, can cause "the ruin of great houses and great ventures, and often even the overthrow of monarchies and empires."

A similar formulation is also found in Seneca.[60] Kings who listen to flatterers "bring on pointless wars that will compromise everything. . . . They make empires without measure break apart on their heads and on the heads of their people." This statement comes from a long exemplum built around the relations between Xerxes, the flatterers, and Demaratus. Seneca develops the notion that "those who possess all things" have the greatest need for "someone who will tell them the truth"; otherwise, they will "have their heads turned by the lies of their entourage and by those who flatter them." In the guise of a proof *a contrario*, Seneca cites the council convened by Xerxes, which he had certainly read about in Herodotus, but which he adapts to his own thesis with inventive audacity. "His soul puffed up with pride and oblivious to the fragility of the support on which it placed its trust, the king found nothing but encouragement" whenever he questioned his advisers. As a result, the courtiers who pressed him to go to war "overexcited a man already crazed by presumptuousness." Only one man, the Greek Demaratus, dared call into doubt the validity of the advice lavished on him. Using the future tense—in actuality, the future perfect—Demaratus stresses that the very enormity of Xerxes's armies would be an insurmountable handicap against the Greek armies: "The events confirmed Demaratus's prognosis: the one who overturned divine and human laws . . . the Persian measured the distance that separates a mob from an army. Thus Xerxes, more pathetic for his shame than for his losses, thanked Demaratus for having told him the truth and allowed him to ask for whatever he liked. . . . He had earned the reward before asking for it; but how the people were to be pitied when there was no one to tell the king the truth!"

Granted, Seneca does not mention Darius by name. But the comparison with Xerxes's conduct vis-à-vis Demaratus is clearly evoked by Curtius and, as presented by these authors, Darius acts and reacts just like the anonymous potentate Seneca denounces. "Having arrived at the point of no longer knowing the truth, through the very habit of hearing what is flattering instead of what is right . . . he gives in to fits of temper instead of suppressing them. . . . He punishes unverified acts as if they were real, he believes it is as shameful to let himself be swayed as it is to let himself be beaten."

In the attitudes and feelings they attribute to the Great King—his temporizing, his waffling, his anger, his fear of Alexander and of the Macedonians, and also his violence against those who speak "the language of truth" to him—these texts display a great similarity to popular reflections on the exercise of royal power. In illustrating these attitudes in the form of a particularly eloquent exemplum, the authors further accentuate the disastrous impression created. After the fact, the Great King "promptly regretted his act and reproached himself for having made a serious mistake" in putting Charidemus to death, but it was no use. As Diodorus sententiously comments, "all his royal power was not able to undo what was done."[61]

The irony of power is that, when measured against the respect everyone owes the person of the king, Charidemus's thoughtlessness is also a reason for self-reproach: "Charidemus's prospects had been high, but he missed their fulfilment because of his ill-timed frankness."[62] Readers at the time were certainly aware of the delicate situation of the advisers, subject to the Great King's wrath, as exemplified by Aelian: "If someone intends to give the Great King advice on a secret question that is difficult to decide, to do so he stands on a gold plinth. If he seems to have provided wise advice, before taking his leave he receives the plinth as a reward; he is whipped nonetheless, because he contradicted the king" (*Varia historia*, 12.64).

It is therefore understandable why an intimate or a courtier, before giving advice, generally asked if it would please the king to listen to him.[63] Even so, the king must heed the wise adviser, which, as Curtius laments, Darius did not do. In that context one may savor with particular delight the touching ingenuousness of the line that same author puts in the Great King's mouth. When his courtiers are urging him to put to death the leaders of the Greek mercenaries, accused of disloyal advice, the king rejects the suggestion, replying sententiously that "nobody's life should be forfeit for making stupid recommendations . . . if giving advice involved risk he would run out of advisers."[64]

The Great King and Affairs Below

Having analyzed the set, the actors, the dialogue, and the set design, I now return more precisely to the denouement of the council. Curtius, using the balanced rhetoric for which he is known, presents matters as follows: "Darius was duly distressed by the news of Memnon's death. Abandoning hope of any other option, he decided to take to the field in person; for, in fact, he was critical of all the actions of his generals, believing that most lacked military precision and all of them good luck" (3.2.1).

For his part, Diodorus says that Darius resolved to take command only because he did not have confidence in any of his generals: "He was haunted by dreams of the Macedonian fighting qualities and the vision of Alexander in action was constantly before his eyes. He searched for a competent general to take over Memnon's command but could find no one, and finally felt constrained to go down himself to take part in the contest for the kingdom" (17.30.7).

The accusation of cowardice is not explicit, but it surfaces constantly. According to these authors, the king was tempted to heed Charidemus and, once again, to make war by delegation, that is, to remain behind, waiting, in the high country.

The value of the explanation must once again be measured against the literary precedents. Consider the reign of Artaxerxes III and the situation of the Nile Valley. Egypt, after seceding in about 400, had since that time resisted several attempts at reconquest. "Artaxerxes . . . himself unwarlike, remained inactive," entrusting the armies to his generals, all of whom failed "because of [their] cowardice and inexperience." When the Phoenicians and the kings of Cyprus joined the revolt, the king "became enraged and decided to make war upon the insurgents. So he rejected the practice of sending out generals, and adopted the plan of carrying out in person the struggles to preserve his kingdom."[65] The Persian kings are not the only ones at issue. The same explanation is advanced, also by Diodorus, regarding the indecision of Pharaoh Akoris against the Persian threat: "But having no capable general, he sent for Chabrias the Athenian, a man distinguished both for his prudence as general and his shrewdness in the art of war, who had also won great repute for personal prowess."[66]

From Artaxerxes III to Darius III, the explanations Diodorus gives in stock phrases add further support to the view that he and other ancient authors frequently express concerning the relationship the Great Kings maintained with army leaders sent to fight incursions or revolts, particularly in the low countries. This relationship is presented as rife with conflict, almost by virtue of its very structure. Many court stories were built around the perennial theme of the ingratitude of kings; for example, the story of Datames, as Cornelius Nepos tells it: "That prompt action assured Datames all the Great King's favor but aroused no less envy in the minds of the courtiers, who saw that on his own he had more importance than all of them together. Such a thought led them without exception to join together to bring about his downfall" (Datames, 6.2).

Datames receives a warning from his friend Pandantes, who ends his letter with a sententious expression, rendered by Nepos in indirect speech: "He explained that such was the custom of Great Kings: they attribute their ill fortunes to men and their success to their auspicious destiny, which means that they are easily persuaded to bring about the downfall of generals when told of a defeat" (*Datames*, 5.4).

According to these authors, kings are at once authoritarian and petty. They do not allow the generals to take any initiative, requiring that they not vary in any way from the instructions they received on setting out. According to Diodorus, that explains the incredible length and slowness of an offensive, which often allowed the enemy to repair his defenses and to successfully repel the king's armies.[67] Such strict oversight is also exercised over the funds available to them: the budget is calculated on the basis of a preliminary estimate, and the general can in no case exceed the amount prescribed, unless he draws from his personal coffers.[68] The room for maneuvering that Memnon seems to enjoy is also limited. In fact, he sent his wife and children to the court: "He calculated that leaving them in the king's care was a good way to ensure their safety, while at the same time the king, now that he had good hostages, would be more willing to entrust Memnon with the supreme command. And so it turned out."[69] If the story is accurate, it may have been on the king's order that the wife and children were left as a "security deposit."

Artaxerxes III, in a first phase of his reign, and Darius III before Memnon's death thus correspond completely to the portrait Plutarch sketches of a Great King "at leisure from his throne," playing arbitrator for the Greeks in their wars and corrupting their popular leaders.[70] The royal characteristics in what is reputedly a portrait of Artaxerxes III before Agesilaus's offensive are perfectly generic and can therefore easily slip from one king to another. Until the spring of 333, according to Diodorus, Darius "had counted on Memnon's transferring the impact of the war from Asia into Europe."[71] It seems that, whatever Memnon's real plans may have been, his counterattack in the Aegean raised fears and hopes in Greece, which was preparing for the landing of Persian troops.[72] To that end, Memnon used gold and silver released by Darius: "Memnon distributed bribes freely and won many Greeks over to share the Persian hopes." In the letter he is reputed to have sent to Darius after Issus, Alexander accuses his adversary of having attempted, even before the Macedonian offensive, to bribe "the Lacedaemonians, and certain other Greeks. . . . Your agents corrupted my friends, and were striving to dissolve the league which I had formed among the Greeks."[73]

That complaint, traditionally made against the Great Kings, was based partly on a Greek mistranslation of "gift" as "misappropriation." Nevertheless, the view suggested is truly that of an idle Great King who, from within his luxurious palaces, refuses to go to the war front and prefers to use the corruptive influence of his treasures. Hence the famous rejoinder attributed to Agesilaus when he was forced to retreat from Asia Minor: "Agesilaus said, as he was breaking camp, that the King was driving him out of Asia with ten thousand 'archers'; for that number of darics had been sent to Athens and Thebes and distributed among the popular leaders there, and as a consequence those peoples made war upon the Spartans."[74] In this symbolic image, the upper king succeeds in repelling the Greek anabasis without even having to take up arms.

Another of Alexander's accusations completes the portrait. Reluctant to take command of the army, Darius turns to conspiracies and assassinations. Not only does he owe his throne to the physical elimination of Arses, but also, Alexander writes, he conspired with the assassins of Alexander's father, Philip.[75] And during the first year of war, that same Darius is suspected of having bribed hired assassins and poisoners, a cowardly way to get rid of his enemy. Situating the episode at different moments between the battles of the Granicus and of Issus, the ancient authors mention that Darius, pretending to send a message to the satrap of Greater Phrygia, makes contact with Alexander of Lyncestis, a member of the Macedonian high aristocracy, and promises him that "if he would kill king Alexander, Darius would appoint him king of Macedonia, and would give him 1,000 talents of gold in addition to the kingdom." The messenger, Sisines, is arrested and confesses, as does Alexander of Lyncestis, who is clapped in irons.[76] According to another accusation, this time attributed to Parmenion (and probably a complete fabrication), Darius also approached Alexander's doctor, Philip, promising him a thousand talents and his sister's hand in marriage if he would poison his illustrious patient. The story allowed the ancient authors to laud Alexander's magnanimity and his courage in the face of death, as well as the loyalty of those who served him.[77] It is therefore not at all surprising that the exemplum appears in Valerius Maximus's collection, accompanied by an adapted monarchical moral: "The immortal gods . . . did not let a false report induce him to reject a remedy capable of saving his life."[78]

The Great King resumed his maneuvers shortly before Gaugamela. Although he had made vast preparations for combat, for which he meticulously chose the site, he is once again accused of wishing to avoid pitched battle. On one hand, he seeks to prevent his enemy from advancing by ordering a scorched-earth tactic ahead of him. Hence Alexander's anxiety: "He was afraid Darius would make for the interior of his kingdom and would have to be followed through vast stretches of completely desolate lands."[79] Furthermore, the Great King attempts to find allies in Alexander's camp, and more particularly among the Greek troops, who, it was postulated, were not absolutely loyal: "A letter from Darius was then intercepted in which he tried to suborn the Greek soldiers to murder or betray Alexander. The king wondered whether he should read it aloud in a general assembly since he had sufficient confidence in the good-will and loyalty of the Greeks, but Parmenion deterred him by declaring that such promises as Darius made should not reach the soldiers' ears, for Alexander was vulnerable even if only one man were a traitor, and avarice recognized nothing as a crime. Alexander followed his advice and struck camp" (Curtius 4.10.16–17).

The King Caught in a Trap

During the maneuvers leading up to the battle to be waged near Issus, Darius, facing critical remarks from the Greek leaders of his army, replies with apparent fervor: "Proceeding with a retreat would certainly mean handing his kingdom over to his enemy. Success in warfare depended on one's reputation, he said, and the man who retreated was believed to be on the run."[80] That virile self-assurance recalls the words Justin attributes to Darius, this time upon Alexander's arrival. At the time, the king has deluded himself that he is intentionally allowing Alexander to come onto his lands, before commanding his satraps to stop him in the Adrastes plain (Battle of the Granicus): "King Darius, on the other hand, from confidence in his strength, abstained from all artifice in his operations; observing that 'clandestine measures were fit only for a stolen victory'; he did not attempt to repel the enemy from his frontiers, but admitted them into the heart of his kingdom, thinking it more honourable to drive war out of his kingdom than not to give it entrance" (11.6.8–9).

These are somewhat paradoxical declarations. Diodorus, in fact, also says that Darius, after many hesitations, "felt constrained" to take command of the army and to go down and confront Alexander.[81]

According to Curtius, Darius also justifies his decision by citing his duty to remain faithful to a Persian custom: "Even splitting the troops meant breaking with tradition, for his ancestors invariably brought their forces *en masse* to a critical battle."[82] The meaning of the expression and of the nature of the custom evoked by Darius can only be conjectured: all of a sudden, the Great King appears particularly intent on going into battle. Once again, Herodotus provides the solution. When Xerxes assembles the leading Persians to present them with his plans and listen to their advice, he introduces his speech with these words: "Do not suppose, gentlemen, that I am departing from precedent in the course of action I intend to undertake. We Persians have a way of living [*nomos*], which I have inherited from my predecessors and propose to follow. I have learned from my elders that ever since Cyrus deposed Astyages and we took over from the Medes the sovereign power we now possess, we have never yet remained inactive. This is God's guidance, and it is by following it that we have gained our great prosperity" (7.8).

The similarity clearly reveals mimesis at work. Curtius read Herodotus closely, and, like Herodotus and many ancient authors, is fond of justifying one or another interpretation of Persian attitudes by reference to immemorial customs, whose reality may legitimately be called into doubt. In each case the king finds an argument to explain and justify his decision.

But in calling the king's self-assurance "haughtiness," Curtius is certainly not being complimentary. In the first place, he denounces the senseless disdain that Darius displayed at the time for Alexander, whom Darius accused of having feigned illness in Tarsus, then of having "taken to a hiding-place in the narrow parts of a mountain valley, just like the lowly animals that lurk in the woodland lairs at the sound of people passing."[83] "On all sides they were urging him on, asserting that he would trample down the army of the Macedonians with his cavalry," confirms Arrian.[84] At the same time, Curtius denounces the stupidity of the king, whose choice of tactics (a tight space) leaves him open to defeat, which Arrian judges ineluctable.[85] In recalling that, when the king deployed his army on the plain, Amyntas "advised him not to abandon [his] position," Arrian also observes the Great King's unfathomable fickleness.[86] Darius, explains Curtius, might have added a logistical argument: in any event, he could no longer turn back; his enormous army being "in a country that was now a desert and had been ravaged alternately by his own forces and the enemy, there would be insufficient provisions."[87] Curtius obviously borrowed this all-purpose explanation from Xenophon: it is the same advice Ariaeus had given the Greeks after Cunaxa, to convince them that they could not return to the low country by taking the same route as during their ascent to Babylonia.[88] It is therefore clear that none of these (supposed) royal declarations and none of the ancient commentaries really increase the stature of a king who, praised by his courtiers, appears increasingly self-satisfied with an illusory superiority.

Also surprising, perhaps, is a literary procedure that consists of denouncing a Great King because he is reputed to be reluctant to march against Alexander but, at the same time, gives the starring role to advisers who, precisely, propose that he wait and see, that he be cautious, even that he retreat, and who for that reason are ill treated by Darius. But the contradiction lies merely on the surface of the words and things, because both arguments cast a pall over Darius's portrait and do a disservice to his memory. In the eyes of these authors, Darius— not having been compelled by events—remains guilty because he did not enthusiastically take up the challenge Alexander issued with such spirit and panache. Like Plutarch's Great King, he did not choose on his own to fight to defend his person and his empire; rather, he was wrested from his idleness.[89]

But he is also denounced because he ultimately decided to agree to pitched battle. The reasons are clearly spelled out by the authors' spokesmen. Like Xerxes in 480, Darius in 333 is nursing a misplaced superiority complex. Such is the full meaning of the speech that Curtius, modeling it on the one Herodotus attributes to Demaratus, has Charidemus deliver after the review of the royal army: although Darius's army might be adequate to keep the people of his empire in compliance, it is powerless against a well-trained army whose soldiers are accustomed to the hard life and have disdain for the gold and silver lavished on the Great King's army.[90] Furthermore, Darius chooses an absurd tactic, which assures his irremediable defeat. Under such conditions, it would have been better to listen to his advisers and to wait, even retreat. The memory of the Great King is thus held prisoner within the bonds of an incontrovertible sophism elaborated by extraordinary rhetors.

The trap approaches perfection, when viewed from inside Alexander's camp. There, the role of wise adviser is assigned to Parmenion. Arrian introduces him five times as an old companion of Philip II grown gray in service.[91] The device will allow him to illustrate Alexander's qualities in the heat of action, in keeping with the proven formula of ancient biography: the presentation of remarks about kings on the occasion of events in which they participated.[92] In four of these apologues, the debate centers on the qualities of a leader who is constantly driven to make choices and hence to decide between his love of danger and the necessity of understanding a situation.

Whatever opinion Parmenion puts forward, it is dismissed by Alexander and by Arrian. If Parmenion advises caution (such as before the Battle of the Granicus, or regarding Darius's offers after Issus), Alexander vaunts the virtues of action: "I consider that this would [not] be in accordance . . . with my own eagerness for encountering danger." He therefore opposes his general, who is called fortunate to no longer have future dangers to face. When Parmenion instead proposes that a naval battle be launched outside Miletus, Arrian determines that it is not enough to declare oneself ready to partake of dangers: the most important thing is to show judgment, that is, to take the specific conditions into account. When, on the eve of the Battle of Gaugamela, Parmenion proposes a nocturnal attack, Arrian enthusiastically approves Alexander's refusal: however "fond of encountering danger in battle . . . Alexander ought to conquer in open daylight, and without any artifice." The leader must, in fact, manifest "self-confidence amid dangers" and at the same time use "correct reasoning." On only one occasion does Arrian judge that Alexander should have followed Parmenion's advice—when he counseled not to destroy Persepolis. The reproach is firm but is at the same time considerably mitigated by Alexander's own later view of his decision in the spring of 330. Revisiting Persepolis upon his return from India, Alexander "repented of the errors which he had committed."[93]

The programmatic introduction of fictive dialogues between Alexander and Parmenion thus allows Arrian to praise the complementary qualities that make Alexander an extraordinary leader: his risk taking but also his sound and balanced judgment, his respect for the rules of open warfare, and even his capacity to regret an eventual error. In short, he is the opposite of Darius, who is "effeminate" and "lacking in sense," to borrow Arrian's qualifiers.[94] It is therefore logical that, whatever decision the Great King supports or makes, he systematically emerges devalued from the encounters the authors cleverly set up with his advisers. Strewn with rhetorical pitfalls and sophistic traps, the battle of images is not a fair fight. Darius has absolutely no chance of winning.

Cyrus the Younger, Artaxerxes, and Darius III

Indeed, Darius III is eclipsed not only by Alexander's shadow but also by an unfavorable comparison to his ancestor Artaxerxes II. The introduction of Artaxerxes may seem surprising, because, particularly in Arrian, the images of Darius and Alexander are modeled on the contrasting images of Artaxerxes and Cyrus the Younger, later elaborated and transmitted by Xenophon, Ctesias, and a few other authors. But during the pitched battle at Cunaxa, the two brothers' images will become confused, even inverted in part. Darius, to his greater historiographical misfortune, is not entitled to such favorable treatment: in the Greek gallery of Persian royal types, the correspondences and echoes from one account to another saddle him with the combined errors and defeats of Artaxerxes II and Cyrus the Younger.

In the opposition and then the comparison between an upper king and a lower king, Darius's situation vis-à-vis Alexander is somewhat reminiscent of that of Artaxerxes vis-à-vis Cyrus. Both Darius and Artaxerxes must respond to an offensive launched from the low countries by an adversary who considers himself worthy of being king and who has every intention of ascending to meet the king and to strip him of supreme power. Cyrus and Alexander, moreover, both say they are convinced that they can attract to themselves "the people of the interior."[95] Artaxerxes and Darius must therefore define a strategy.

The debates that took place around Artaxerxes at his general staff meetings, as depicted by Plutarch and by those who inspired him, sound like nearly perfect precedents—but negative ones—for the council in which Charidemus is reputed to have suggested that Darius not take command of the army. At Artaxerxes's council, the role of the royal adviser is here played by a Persian noble: "It was Teribazus, as we are told, who first plucked up courage to tell the king that he ought not to shun a battle, nor to retire from Media and Babylon, as well as Susa, and hide himself in Persia, when he had a force many times as numerous as that of the enemy, and countless satraps and generals who surpassed Cyrus in wisdom and military skill. The king therefore determined to fight the issue out as soon as possible" (Artaxerxes, 7.3).

The matter is clear: following his adviser's counsel, the king decides not to withdraw to the high country but to stop Cyrus in Babylonia, thus taking advantage of the superiority of his soldiers, generals, and advisers. The Great King is able to make such a decision because, unlike Artaxerxes III and Darius III, who are reputed to have complained about the lack of valorous generals, he has a surfeit of choices among his satraps and generals.[96]

The uncertainty and indecisiveness now shift to Cyrus's camp. There, the role of cautious adviser is played by a Greek, Clearchus, who, like Charidemus vis-à-vis Darius, has his master's ear and complete confidence. Cyrus has even brought him into the circle of the seven Persians "among his personal attendants," assembled to judge the traitor Orontas, "due to the position he held among the other generals, in the opinion not only of Cyrus, but also of the rest of the court."[97] Like Charidemus for Darius III, it is Clearchus who advises Cyrus to be cautious, to wait and see. Plutarch is very critical, attributing the defeat to the fearful circumspection of the Greek leader. He believes it is ridiculous for Clearchus to act in that way, when "he had marched ten thousand stadia up from the sea-coast under arms, with no compulsion upon him."[98] It is obvious that the function of the comment attributed to Clearchus is to clear Cyrus of all blame. That is even probably the underlying reason for a change in tone that, though it does not actually concern King Artaxerxes, works to his advantage. Indeed, someone must be held responsible for the disaster, even if that means casting the valorous Clearchus against type.

This example confirms that the ancient authors analyzed all situations in terms of an unvarying structure. Darius's inadequacies vis-à-vis Alexander are initially expressed in identical terms as those of Artaxerxes vis-à-vis Cyrus, but after Cunaxa the pendulum swings in the other direction. Nevertheless, the authors continue to use the same binary scheme: good adviser, bad adviser; Persian adviser, Greek adviser; advance or retreat; ascent to the high country or descent to face the adversary; courage and cowardice; the intelligence of the councils or an incapacity to understand the situation; and so on. As a result, the long-distance comparison between Artaxerxes and Darius, from one author to the next, will turn to the advantage of Artaxerxes. As the victor on the battlefield, Artaxerxes will defile the body of his mortally wounded rival.

Parallels can be found in the judgments the authors make of the protagonists. Initially, these comparisons come at the expense of Artaxerxes and Darius III, whose preparations for battle and mode of waging war are judged harshly. Just as, according to Diodorus, Artaxerxes did not receive the contingents of "Indians and certain other peoples . . . because of the remoteness of those regions," so too "the hurried mobilization" (festinatio) of Darius's army precluded the "Bactrians, Sogdians, Indians and others living on the Red Sea" from being levied.[99] The comparison is supposed to illustrate unvarying Persian combat methods, given that spatial and logistical constraints certainly represent one of the elements in the choice of strategy. Nevertheless, the theme of the slowness of Persian military preparations, which in the fifth century came to constitute a literary motif, evokes instead the weight of mimesis. The motif is also found in Lucian, a contemporary of Arrian. In the parody The Ship: or The Wishes, Samippus, heading the expedition against the Great King, assembles his advisers and asks them their opinions. One of them, Adimantus, represents caution and even cowardice; the other, Timolaos, proposes "to march with all the troops against the enemy, without waiting to reinforce his army by assembling from all parts allies who would come to join him." "While the enemies are still on their way, let us attack them," he concludes. At that moment, in fact, the king has succeeded in assembling only "men from the surrounding area and the outer cities of the empire."[100]

Initially Artaxerxes "decided not to give battle" but to dig a trench and beat a retreat.[101] Xenophon emphasizes the culpable confidence Cyrus manifests at the beginning of the clash with his brother: "But as the king had failed to hinder the passage of Cyrus's army at the trench, Cyrus himself and the rest concluded that he must have abandoned the idea of offering battle, so that next day Cyrus advanced with less than his former caution."[102] Here again the parallel is not far off. Alexander "had resolved that their advance should be very slow," but Darius "made no further advance; he remained on the river bank, which was in many places precipitous, in some part building a stockade, where it appeared more accessible. This made it plain to Alexander and his staff that Darius was in spirit a beaten man."[103]

In other words, Darius chooses to protect himself behind a fortification. Arrian develops the same sort of argument to condemn Persians in Darius's time. According to him, they obstructed the course of the Tigris with a series of *katarraktes*, which are portrayed as actual permanent fortifications. In reality they were lightweight dams made of bundles of sticks and earth, designed to raise the water level at low tide and thus to favor irrigation. According to Arrian, Alexander hastened to destroy them, saying "that such devices were unbecoming to men who are victorious in battle."[104] That reflection is obviously inspired by those of Greek philosophers and orators, including Plato and Xenophon: a commonwealth must not take refuge behind walls but must count first on the courage of its citizens.

Darius combines Artaxerxes's flaws (positioning himself in the middle of his army and taking refuge behind man-made defenses instead of fighting) and those of Cyrus (his arrogance before battle, when he is convinced that Alexander is afraid to advance and face him).[105] Darius demonstrates his inferiority, even declares and proclaims it—not a military inferiority in the strict sense so much as a moral and psychological one. He therefore also refuses to lead the offensive or counteroffensive at the head of his troops, unlike his adversary: "Alexander rode about in every direction to exhort his troops to show their valour. . . . From all sides arose a shout not to delay but to attack the enemy."[106] As had been happening since Alexander's landing, one of the two kings advances, joyful and swaggering; the other remains fixed in place, indecisive, as if paralyzed by what is at stake and by his adversary's youthful alacrity.

The Tradition of the Duel between Darius and Alexander

One tradition, elaborated solely by the Vulgate authors and ignored by Arrian, adds a further stroke to the portrait. It claims that Alexander, on his own initiative, sought to prevail in a personal battle against Darius. Curtius renders the situation with his Roman vocabulary: Alexander sought for himself "the rich trophy of killing the king."[107] The same version can be found in Diodorus: "Alexander cast his glance in all directions in his anxiety to see Darius, and as soon as he had identified him, he drove hard with his cavalry at the king himself, wanting not so much to defeat the Persians as to win the victory with his own hands" (17.33.5).

The wording implies a competition: "No Macedonian had any other thought than to strike the king."[108] Above all, it tends to extol Alexander's desire for personal glory alone, and it is not far from the turn of phrase the author used to explain the initiative of the Persian Spithrobates at the Granicus. The idea is that monomachia can decide the outcome of a pitched battle.[109] Diodorus continues in the same vein, describing the Battle of Gaugamela and attributing the same thoughts to Alexander: "Alexander saw that it was time for him to offset the discomfiture of his forces by his own intervention with the royal squadron and the rest of the elite horse guards, and rode hard against Darius."[110]

Although Arrian says nothing explicit on the subject, the tradition of the royal duel was very well known in his time. Consider the parody written by Lucian. One of the characters, Samippus, fancies himself a new Alexander conquering Asia and going up against the Great King. He is even wounded, as in one version regarding Alexander and Darius: "As for me, as you see, I am going to engage in single combat [monomakhein] against the king: he has challenged me, and hiding would be absolutely dishonorable. . . . I charged him and transfixed him, along with his horse, with a single blow of my spear! Then I cut off his head and took his diadem: now I am king and all bow down before me. May the barbarians bow down!" (The Ship, 37).

Polybius places in doubt the existence of a real duel and, following his habit, develops an extremely rational argument. Among the reasons he puts forward to criticize the description that Callisthenes had given of the Battle of Issus is the following: "He says that Alexander arranged his army so as to do battle with Darius in person, that Darius originally had the same idea about Alexander, but that he later changed his mind. How did Alexander and Darius each know the other's position in the army? Where did Darius go then? Absolutely nothing is said about that" (12.22.2).

The tradition was so widespread that, according to Eratosthenes, single combat was mimicked in camp. Informed that the army varlets, divided into two troops—one commanded by an "Alexander," the other by a "Darius"—had done battle by throwing clods of dirt at one another, then switching to sticks and stones, Alexander "ordered the two leaders to fight in single combat: and he himself armed the one called Alexander, while Philotas armed the representative of Darius. The whole army looked on, thinking that the result would be ominous of their own success or failure. After a severe fight, the one called Alexander conquered, and was rewarded with twelve villages and the right of wearing the Persian garb. This we are told by Eratosthenes the historian" (Plutarch, *Alexander*, 31.4).

As the tradition was transmitted and reelaborated, variants appeared, raising doubts and sparking debate. In reporting a version of the duel attributable to Chares of Mytilene, Plutarch "quotes" a letter from Alexander to Antipater in which the king speaks of his wound but "does not mention the name of the man who wounded him."[111] Curtius, in describing the fight—but without mentioning Darius—also speaks of a wound to the thigh, as does Diodorus, without connecting it to a duel.[112] Arrian too mentions such a wound, but without any reference to a single combat with Darius.[113] In battles where man-to-man combat was so common, it was easy to introduce the motif of a royal monomachia.[114] Furthermore, the wound to the thigh is a motif that recurs frequently in a number of legendary accounts. It is possible that the tradition about that wound (a real one) served as a narratological catalyst.

In reality, a purely factual quest is not the first priority of the present-day historian, who is more interested in the significance to be granted to the genesis and diffusion of a literary and monarchical motif. It is clear that such a motif can be conceptualized particularly well through the idea of the Macedonian challenge. In rejecting Darius's offers after the Battle of Issus, Alexander is said to have written to the Great King: "And if you dispute my right to the kingdom, stay and fight another battle for it; but do not run away. For wherever you may be, I intend to march against you."[115] The line attributed to Alexander, when he refuses the offers Darius supposedly made prior to Gaugamela, belongs to the same thematic: "What he has lost and what he still possesses both remain the prizes of war."[116] The ancient authors frequently claim that the direct participation of the king in battle is required to maintain imperial rule, and in that context they all use an agonistic vocabulary: the king himself must fight to preserve his kingdom or universal kingship.[117] And the tradition relating to Darius's own accession attests that kingship can be the outcome of a victorious duel. Lucian adapted that popular theme: his hero dreams that he is confronting the Great King, because "it is a royal trait as well to be wounded while fighting for one's empire."[118]

It was not only the authors of histories of Alexander who developed the motif; so too did authors dealing with the confrontation between Cyrus the Younger and King Artaxerxes II. Xenophon presents the personal conflict between the two brothers at the Battle of Cunaxa. Cyrus, left alone with his closest friends (known as the "table companions"), "caught sight of the King and the compact body around him; and on the instant he lost control of himself and, with the cry 'I see the man,' rushed upon him and struck him in the breast and wounded him through his breastplate—as Ctesias the physician says, adding also that he himself healed the wound" (*Anabasis*, 1.8.26).

According to Diodorus, "in the centre of the lines, it so happened, were stationed both the men who were contending for the kingship. Consequently . . . they made at each other, being eagerly desirous of deciding the issue of the battle by their own hands; . . . Cyrus was the first to hurl his javelin from a distance, and striking the King, brought him to the ground." The information undoubtedly comes from Dinon, who reported that Cyrus clashed with Artaxerxes and brought him to the ground. At the third assault, the king decided to confront his brother directly: "He attacked Cyrus, who boldly and recklessly threw himself into the midst of the arrows raining down on him. The king struck him with his javelin, and the men in his entourage struck him as well." Ctesias claims, on the contrary, that Artaxerxes was wounded and retreated to a nearby hill, and that Mithridates, a Persian, struck the decisive blow against Cyrus. After the victory, the official version insisted that it was Artaxerxes who had killed his brother.[119] For that reason, two individuals were put to death, each of whom claimed to have accomplished the deed. Obviously, that victory in single combat was supposed to legitimate each one's power.

From Cunaxa to Issus and Gaugamela, mimesis certainly had its way. Although the motif is officially absent from Arrian's report, the single combat Alexander desired is in line with the movement that systematically pushes the Macedonian king forward to confront his adversary. At Gaugamela, for example: "He led them with a quick charge and loud battle-cry straight towards

Darius himself."[120] Or again at Issus, according to Diodorus: "Alexander cast his glance in all directions in his anxiety to see Dareius, and as soon as he had identified him, he drove hard with his cavalry at the king himself, wanting not so much to defeat the Persians as to win the victory with his own hands."[121] Plutarch transmits the story of the duel in recounting the Battle of Issus: "He himself fought among the foremost, and, according to Chares, was wounded in the thigh by Darius himself."[122] The motif is also found in Justin: "Soon after a battle was fought with great spirit. Both kings were wounded in it."[123]

The Vulgate authors express it even more clearly for the Battle of Gaugamela. According to Arrian, Darius quickly takes flight after Alexander falls upon him with his horsemen.[124] Curtius evokes the two kings coming face to face: "With the main bodies almost together the two kings spurred on their men to battle. There were more Persian dead now, and the number of wounded on each side was about equal. Darius was riding in his chariot, Alexander on horseback, and both had a guard of handpicked men who had no regard for their own lives. . . . Each man thought it a noble fate to meet his end before the eyes of his king" (4.15.23–35).

For Curtius, the difficulty in making inroads that the Macedonians encountered is resolved by the intervention of a diviner, who restores the soldiers' confidence, "especially after Darius' charioteer who drove the horses, seated before the king, was run through by a spear. . . . The left wing was routed and abandoned the king's chariot."[125] Diodorus attributes the death of the driver to Alexander, and gives a clear account of the Great King personally taking part in the battles: "With the royal squadron and the rest of the elite horse guards . . . [he] rode hard against Darius. The Persian king received their attack and fighting [agōnizomenos] from a chariot hurled javelins against his opponents, and many supported him. As the kings approached each other, Alexander flung a javelin at Darius and missed him, but struck the driver standing beside him and knocked him to the ground. [The troops thought Darius was dead]. . . . The king himself was alarmed and retreated" (17.60.1–3).

The narrative gives the impression that Darius agreed to a monomachia, then lost it because of a paradoxical and purely accidental success on Alexander's part: having missed his adversary, he unseats the driver and thus causes panic in the Great King. In all cases, the outcome of the duel reinforces and confirms Alexander's royal ambitions. Alexander "fought among the foremost," and only by fleeing did Darius escape his fate.[126]

Combat or Palavers?

Ill at ease on the battlefield, the Great King is also accused of employing delaying tactics. After the Battle of Issus, the Great King's own family (his mother, wife, two daughters, and young son) fell into Alexander's hands. According to the ancient authors, two or three embassies, which each author places at different times, were sent to the Macedonian king. The top priority of Darius, who is reintroduced into the narrative at this point, is reputed to have been to make peace with Alexander, so as to have his family near him again—even if that meant abandoning to his enemy all of Anatolia and even the lands between the Mediterranean and the Euphrates. In some sense that amounted to fixing permanently the situation prevailing at the time: coexistence, this time peaceful, between an upper king and a lower king.

It is easy to understand why historians won over to Alexander's cause, who can hardly be suspected of indulgence toward Darius, were able to make use of the classical tradition. Georges Radet does not hesitate to place the opening of negotiations within the *longue durée* of "Oriental" practices: "Since the fortunes of war had betrayed him, he resolved this time to try his luck with diplomatic maneuvers." The author, closely reading the ancient authors and readily appropriating both their substance and their style, draws unkind conclusions about the Great King. His maneuvers "betray, with the recklessness of blind presumption, the dullness of a brain resistant to the lessons of the facts. They denote a total lack of psychological sense. . . . A dedicated son, a loving father, a tormented husband, Darius slides toward the capitulations of weak souls. The soft influence of familial affection leads him to repudiate the haughty convictions of his political faith" (*Alexandre*, pp. 73–74; 78, 80).

And so was born the image of a Great King who, consumed by domestic sorrow, was ready to sacrifice the empire of his forefathers to obtain the liberation of his loved ones. The British historian Tarn expresses it plainly: "He may have possessed the domestic virtues; otherwise, he was a poor type of despot, cowardly and inefficient" (1:58). And even though historians for the most part now look critically at the content of the correspondence between the two kings, the strange conduct attributed to Darius transmits both the notion of a regrettable political weakness and the touching expression of personal feelings. The two notions merge to construct a recurrent image of the Great King.

The ancient texts have often been scrutinized in an attempt to determine the reality and the substance of these diplomatic overtures. My objective here is not to take up once again the question of when exactly the embassies occurred or what exactly the Persians were offering. There is no reason to doubt the existence of the first two embassies, in 333/332. As for knowing what was said, that is a completely different matter. The discourses and letters attributed to the kings are nothing but literary and rhetorical compositions, more or less skillful, more or less overwrought. They come close to fiction or quite simply merge with it. What these texts primarily convey belongs less to diplomatic history than to the history of representations, in this case the contrasting images of the Great King and Alexander, which these narratives and discourses had created and conveyed since antiquity.

In particular, the manner in which the negotiations were conducted is supposed to illustrate once again the limited abilities of the Great King as a war leader. According to Arrian, the second embassy sought out Alexander during the siege of Tyre, that is, several months after Issus. Informed of Alexander's refusal, Darius "began to make fresh preparations for war."[127] The turn of phrase implies that he had remained inactive for many months after Issus or at the very least that he had suspended preparations during the negotiations. Diodorus, by contrast, certifies that the Great King had lost none of his resolution when he came back to Babylon after Issus.[128] Nevertheless, the same author and others assert that, during a third embassy sent slightly before the Battle of Gaugamela, Darius offered to hand over all the territories west of the Euphrates. The response attributed to Alexander sounds like a moral and political condemnation of his adversary: "He bade them tell Dareius that, if he desired the supremacy, he should do battle with him to see which of them would have sole and universal rule. If, on the other hand, he despised glory and chose profit and luxury with a life of ease, then let him obey Alexander."[129]

The financial proposals advanced in negotiating the fate of the illustrious prisoners further blacken the portrait. Darius intended to ransom the royal princesses and the young prince for money, in the same way that one might redeem ordinary people who had fallen into the hands of bandits and pirates. Alexander, by contrast, who took care not to treat the members of the royal family like mere prisoners, could not fail to receive such proposals as unworthy of him, because he preferred "glory to the gifts which were extended to him."[130] Here again is a well-known motif of monarchical ideology, illustrated by the measures taken by Alexander and his successors. In traveling the road from Susa to Persepolis, Alexander similarly refused to pay the local populations (the mountain-dwelling Uxians) the gifts and tributes that the Great Kings were in the habit of paying to ensure safe passage from one capital to the other. A few years later, one of his successors, Antigonus Monophthalmus, was faced with the same problem, this time while traveling from Susa to Ecbatana by the mountain route. This was the most direct route, and another population, the Cosseans, were attempting to collect gifts and tributes along it: "Antigonus regarded it as beneath his dignity to use persuasion on these people or to make them presents when he had so great an army following him." In view of the unprecedented difficulties he encountered at the time, "Antigonus regretted that he had not . . . purchase[d] the right of passage with money." Nevertheless, in both cases the ardent desire of the Macedonian leaders not to buy a victory with money stands in explicit opposition to the disquieting weakness that the Great Kings demonstrated in the very heart of their kingdom.[131]

It is against that backdrop that the dialogue between Alexander and Darius needs to be analyzed. Defeated in pitched battle, a Great King once again intends to take his revenge, or quite simply to stop his adversary by paying out gold, instead of placing himself at the head of his troops. He acts like one of his predecessors, against whom Agesilaus had wanted to march, to force him to fight for his person.[132] Instead the Spartan king was driven from the kingdom by "the king's archers," that is, by the silver siglos and gold darics distributed in Greece to spread corruption. The message is clear: Alexander does not allow himself to be diverted from the goal he has set for himself. On the contrary, the responses he gives to the Great King adequately express the idea that if Darius wants to recover the princesses and the prince, he can do so only after a victory in open country. Like the territories already lost and those that Darius still controls, the members of the royal family are among the stakes of the continuing war.[133]

Admittedly, the portrait is not simply negative, because Darius ultimately chooses to fight. But the reproach is implicit: he did not make that choice of his own free will; he would have preferred to put an end to the war by diplomatic avenues. In a certain sense he has again been forced to fight, by an adversary much more resolute than he: "Dareius heard Alexander's answer and gave up any hope of a diplomatic settlement," writes Diodorus.[134] Curtius presents the Great King after the failure of the second overture in the same way: "Losing all hope of the peace . . . Darius now concentrated on rebuilding his strength and vigorously resuming hostilities."[135] The rejection of Alexander's demands, though noted in positive terms, remains embedded in a narrative and a semantic logic that point to the Great King's lack of courage or, in any case, to his indecisiveness. In the end, the underlying accusation is really that he preferred secret negotiations and risk-free arrangements to a clear and fair fight, one on one, on the battlefield.

Furthermore, the scenario attributes the most decisive condemnation of Darius to the princesses themselves. Their moans are heart-rending less because they fear death or dishonor than because they are experiencing violent grief. They are persuaded that their son, husband, or father died in battle. They learn of his death, or believe they have learned of it, under conditions that vary only in their details from one author to another. In Curtius, "one of the eunuch prisoners," the bearer of bad news, "happened to be standing in front of their tent when he recognized Darius' cloak in someone's hands (the man had found it and was now bringing it back)—the cloak which . . . Darius had cast off so that his identity would not be betrayed by his dress. The eunuch assumed it had been taken from Darius' dead body and so he brought the false report of his death."[136] According to Plutarch, "the mother and wife of Darius, and his two daughters, who were among the captives, had seen the chariot and bow of Darius, and were mourning for him, imagining him to be dead."[137] In Diodorus, the princesses collapsed in sorrow as soon as they were told that "Alexander had come back from the pursuit after stripping Darieus of his arms."[138] To reassure them, Alexander has Leonatus tell them that he has brought back nothing but the weapons and robe the Great King left behind in his chariot.[139]

Whatever the version, the scenario is perfectly univocal. The princesses' reaction, in expressing the idea that the king's death is an established fact, implies that a king worthy of the name would never have abandoned the "insignia of power" on the battlefield, but, on the contrary, would have died fighting to defend them. The primary function of the anecdote thereby introduced is to show the tragic contradiction existing between the glorious image the princesses have of the Great King and the dishonorable image that the Macedonian view intends to impose. Thanks to the princesses, that view is clearly presented as a factual reality that no one can place in doubt.

Even Darius's very young son is exploited to express a silent condemnation of his father. Curtius and Diodorus recount in similar terms a scene set in the Persian women's tent, when Alexander and Hephaestion come to offer their respects. The king "took Darius' son in his arms, and the child, not in the least frightened at the sight of Alexander (although this was the first time he had seen him), put his arms around his neck. Impressed by the boy's fearlessness, the king looked at Hephaestion and said: 'How I could have wished that Darius had acquired something of his character'" (Curtius, 3.12.26).

Diodorus is even more explicit: Alexander "remarked to Hephaestion that at the age of six years the boy showed a courage beyond his years and was much braver than his father."[140] A little later, another detail expands on that comment. Reporting the arrival of a third embassy from Darius to Alexander, Curtius asserts that the Great King, whose top priority is to find his mother and two daughters, proposed that his adversary keep his son Ochus hostage in exchange.[141] In going so far as to abandon the young prince, "heir to this empire from birth" *(in spem huius imperii genitum),* to the hands of his enemy, Darius gives proof that his personal feelings have prevailed over his duties as king and thereby fully "confirms" the judgment Alexander pronounced in the young boy's presence.[142]

Frantic Escape to the High Country

The image of a coward seeking to postpone a deadline is also bolstered by ancient accounts of Darius's successive escapes, terminated only by his pitiable death in a Parthian town. As soon as the danger becomes too great, Darius retreats and flees; in addition, he personally gives the signal to the army to scatter. Arrian provides a particularly forceful and consistent image of Darius, first at Issus: "The Persians did not give way until they perceived that Darius had fled. . . . Then at last there ensued a decided flight and on all sides. . . . But as soon as the left wing of Darius was terrified and routed by Alexander, and the Persian king perceived that this part of his army was severed from the rest, without any further delay he began to flee in his chariot along with the first, just as he was" (2.11.2,4).

As Darius was escaping, pursued by Alexander, he rid himself of all the marks of his royal rank: "He was conveyed safely in the chariot as long as he met with level ground in his flight; but when he lighted upon ravines and other rough ground, he left the chariot there, divesting himself both of his shield and Median mantle [*kandys*]. He even left his bow in the chariot; and mounting a horse continued his flight. The night, which came on soon after, alone rescued him from being captured by Alexander" (2.11.5).

Alexander can declare himself the victor because he returns to his camp with Darius's chariot, shield, robe, and bow. He soon takes possession of the Great King's tent and of his riches, a striking sign of the transfer of hegemony.[143]

According to Arrian as well, the Great King's conduct was not more honorable during the Battle of Gaugamela. Darius again stood at the center of his

deployed troops, surrounded by elite contingents.[144] Then, in the course of battle, Alexander took the offensive:

> The cavalry with Alexander, and Alexander himself, pressed vigorously,
> shoving the Persians and striking their faces with their spears, and the Mace-
> donian phalanx, solid and bristling with its pikes, had got to close quarters
> with them, and Darius, who had now long been in a panic, saw nothing
> but terrors all around, he was himself the first to turn and flee. . . . Alex-
> ander rested his cavalry till towards midnight, and hurried on again to
> Arbela, to seize Darius there with his treasure and the other royal be-
> longings. He arrived at Arbela next day, having covered in all, since the
> battle, about six hundred stades in the pursuit. However, he did not catch
> Darius at Arbela, as he continued his flight without pause, though his
> treasure and all his equipment was captured and his chariot was seized
> then a second time, and his shield was taken a second time, and his bow
> and arrows too. (3.14.2–3; 3.15.5; Brunt trans.)

Arrian repeats the same image in a ringing paean to the courage that the
Indian king Porus displayed toward Alexander. Here, he sets up a long-distance
comparison that is once more disastrous for Darius. Despite the accumulated
difficulties and the blows the Macedonians dealt his troops, Porus "did not depart as Darius the Great King did, setting an example of flight to his men."[145]
He later returns to the matter in a brief glimpse back at the Battle of Gaugamela, "at which battle [Darius] fled and did not desist from flight until he was
arrested by Bessus and put to death at Alexander's approach."[146]

Although the Vulgate authors provide positive remarks about the Great
King's conduct and attitude during battle, all describe his fear and his flight in
scathing terms: "The result remained doubtful until Darius fled," writes Justin.[147] After describing the ruthless battles that unfolded at Issus around the
royal chariot, Diodorus writes:

> The horses which were harnessed to the yoke of Dareius's chariot were
> covered with wounds and terrified by the piles of dead about them. They
> refused to answer to their bridles, and came close to carrying off Dareius
> into the midst of the enemy, but the king himself, in extreme peril, caught
> up the reins, being forced to throw away the dignity of his position and to
> violate the ancient custom of the Persian kings. A second chariot was
> brought up by Dareius's attendants and in the confusion as he changed

over to it in the face of constant attack he fell into a panic terror. Seeing
their king in this state, the Persians with him turned to flee, and as each
adjacent unit in turn did the same, the whole Persian cavalry was soon in
full retreat. . . . When he knew that he was decisively defeated, Dareius
gave himself up to flight and mounting in turn one after another of his
best horses galloped on at top speed, desperately seeking to escape from
Alexander's grasp and anxious to reach the safety of the upper satrapies.
(17.34.6–7; 37.1)

Curtius, obviously using the same source, also describes the fear of the
horses attached to the royal chariot, then that of the Great King, which spreads
to the fighters around him: "Frightened that he might fall into his enemy's
hands alive, Darius jumped down and mounted a horse which followed his
chariot for this very purpose. He even stooped to throwing off his royal insignia so that they could not betray his flight. The rest of his men now scattered in
fear. They broke out of the fighting wherever they could find an escape-route"
(3.11.11).

The same thing happened at Gaugamela, though Diodorus and Curtius report that, on that occasion, it was not the Great King who gave the signal to
scatter: "The Persian king received their attack and fighting from a chariot
hurled javelins against his opponents" (Diodorus 17.60.2); "Persians and Macedonians alike were convinced that it was the king who had been killed . . . and
though the fortunes of the battle were, in fact, still even, Darius' 'kinsmen' and
squires caused consternation almost throughout the battlefield with their
mournful wailing and wild shouts and groans" (Curtius 4.15.28–29).

It is on this occasion that Curtius even claims that Darius, "it is said," abandoned by his left flank, drew his short sword and wondered whether he could
avoid the shame of fleeing by dying with honor. But, perched on his chariot,
"he felt ashamed to abandon his forces when they were not all committed to
leaving the battle."[148]

Although Darius was not the chief one responsible for the panic and defeat,
he did give up as soon as he saw his flank was exposed: "The king himself was
alarmed and retreated. . . . It was impossible to tell in what direction Dareius
was fleeing. . . . The air was filled with the groans of the fallen, the din of the
cavalry, and the constant sound of lashing of whips. . . . Dareius directed his
course to the upper satrapies, seeking [to put] distance between himself and
Alexander."[149] "It was no longer a battle but a massacre, and Darius also turned

his chariot in flight. . . . But they could hear the sound of reins time and time again lashing the chariot-horses, the only trace they had of the fleeing king" (Curtius 4.15.32–33).

Arrian says that, at Issus, Darius fled in his chariot before abandoning it to leap onto a horse.[150] Curtius introduces a particularly disparaging motif, that of a flight prepared in advance: "Frightened that he might fall into his enemy's hands alive, Darius jumped down and mounted a horse which followed his chariot for this very purpose."[151] Although noting as well that Darius was not the source of the panic and even hailing his courage, Plutarch tells how the royal chariot could no longer maneuver, so obstructed were its wheels by the corpses piled up all around: "Darius, we are told, left his chariot and his arms, mounted a mare which had recently foaled, and rode away."[152] Aelian, an author from the Roman period, develops this theme more fully in a moralizing anecdote included in a collection of animal tales: "It seems that the mare is a good mother and that she cherishes the memory of her foals. The last Darius had taken note of that. That is why he liked to be accompanied on the battlefield with a few mares who had recently foaled but who had left their young behind. Foals who lose their mother are raised on the milk of another mare, just like human beings. So when the battle being fought near Issus turned badly for the Persians, and when Darius was defeated, he mounted on a mare, anxious as he was to escape and save his life as quickly as possible. Remembering the foal she had left behind, the mare is well known to have saved her master, with all the speed and care possible, from such a critical moment of danger" (De natura animalium, 6.48).

Granted, an author of collections of exempla such as Aelian must be used with caution. It is necessary to distinguish what constitutes the substance of the story from the moral commentaries with which he has embellished it. Here his remarks concern the attachment that mares, in his view, maintain with their foals: even when the mother is separated from her young, she does not forget them. The story of the relationship between mares and foals must have been well known, given that, in an entirely different narrative context, it is also found in the *Alexander Romance* and in Nizāmī's *Iskandar-nāmeh*.[153] To make the subject more lively and amusing, Aelian inserts it into a narrative scene representing Darius III's conduct during a battle. It is therefore not surprising that the topos of the cowardly, runaway king recurs, though such terms do not appear in the story. The narration is propelled by that character trait: according to Aelian and Plutarch, Darius, knowing the attachment of mares to their foals,

intentionally chose a mare that had recently given birth. A hasty reader is led to
believe that, even before undertaking battle, Darius had prepared everything
that could be used to ensure his ineluctable flight. Hence Curtius's expression:
"a horse which followed his chariot for this very purpose [ad hoc]." The aim of
the story is clearly to disparage a king prepared to engage in any sort of subter-
fuge and ruse to keep from risking his own life. Commentators have interpreted
the presence of a horse near the royal chariot on the Naples Mosaic (Fig. 43)
in terms of that very tradition: the Persian holding the bridle, they say, is
ready to place it at the Great King's disposal, his chariot having just beaten a
hasty retreat.[154] Is it necessary to add that the iconographical interpretation
also relies on assumptions about the Great King's weakness and cowardice—
assumptions reinforced in this case by the convergence between Arrian and
the Vulgate?

It is clear that the words and expressions used to discredit Darius and to di-
vest him systematically of the universally agreed-upon characteristics of a legitimate king, when taken one by one, correspond to and reinforce one another in associative networks. A legitimate king fights on the front line in a
qualifying ordeal, instead of systematically running from the enemy; he tries
anything to force fate's hand, as is his duty, rather than anticipate defeat; he
protects his soldiers from defeat and humiliation, a moral obligation, instead of
preparing a means of escape for himself even before undertaking battle.

Another motif expresses the notion that, if Darius ultimately escaped Alexander, it was first and foremost because he left the battlefield when the battles
were still raging (particularly at Gaugamela) but also because he took advantage of the darkness of night to conceal his escape. A comparison to one of the
conversations, depicted by Arrian, between Alexander and Parmenion on the
eve of the Battle of Gaugamela is unavoidable at this point.[155] The old general
"urged him to make a night attack on the Persians, saying that thus he would
fall upon them unprepared and in a state of confusion, and at the same time
more liable to a panic in the dark." The response given by Alexander, and especially by Arrian, presents tactical and practical arguments (night can favor the
weaker party) and even political ones: "A furtive and nocturnal attack on the
part of the Macedonians would relieve [Darius] of the necessity of confessing
that he was an inferior general and commanded inferior troops." The argument attributed to the Great King refers, implicitly but clearly, to norms that
both camps accept and that are obviously ethical norms: a battle won at night
does not determine the true victor.

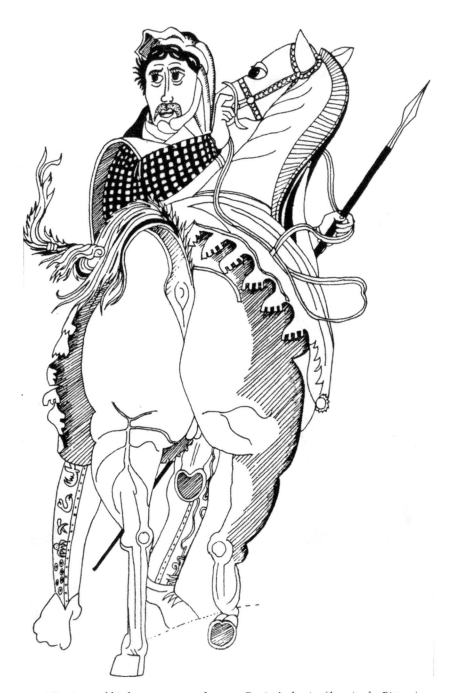

43. *A Persian and his horse represented next to Darius's chariot (drawing by Bittner).*

Whereas Arrian tends to present the practical and tactical arguments, Alexander is more likely to put forward the ethical arguments. He told Parmenion "that it would be dishonorable to steal the victory, and that Alexander had to win his victory openly and without stratagem."[156] That reply is an exact echo of the one Justin attributes to Darius at the start of the war.[157] And it is reproduced by the Arabo-Persian author Tha'ālibī, author of *History of the Kings of Persia*. Without naming Parmenion, he represents the same dialogue: "An attack by night is banditry, and banditry is unbecoming of kings," responds Iskandar (Zotenberg ed., p. 408). The king's reply belongs quite precisely to the traditional mind-set, according to which a soldier wages his battle by day; the night, conversely, is the realm of trickery and disreputable attacks. The opposition between Alexander and Darius thus coincides with the contrast between the pursuer and the pursued, and between the heroic battle the Macedonian king wages on the front lines with his troops in broad daylight, and the shameful flight of a Great King who uses the dark of night to shirk—surreptitiously and shamefully—what, at least by Greek norms, is his duty: to confront the adversary head on, without ruse or artifice.

The Motif of the Great King in Flight

In many respects the image of Darius in flight is indistinguishable from that of Xerxes in 480. The two, moreover, were condemned in almost identical terms for having caused the fall of the empire by their love for luxury, which corrupted them and turned them soft.[158] It also seems fairly likely that one or another episode of the *Alexander Romance* was directly inspired by the apocalyptic descriptions of Xerxes's retreat as they appear in Aeschylus. Just as a portion of Xerxes's army vanished into the Strymon River, which, after freezing, was thawed by the sun's rays, so too, only Darius and his retinue got across the frozen Stranga before it broke up, engulfing "most of the Persians and barbarians."[159] Other comparisons are also noteworthy: Xerxes left behind the chariot of Zeus/Ahura Mazda, which was in his cortege as he departed from Sardis, just as it was in Darius's official cortege upon leaving Babylon.[160]

Notable for their generic quality, the narratives about each of the two Persian kings are especially evocative in that they refer to two closely related themes, that of a defeated king's flight and that of a reversal of fortune. These themes were abundantly treated and elaborated by the classical authors with reference to Xerxes's defeats and then to what they unanimously consider his uninterrupted escape to Asia after the Battle of Salamis: "Xerxes emits a long moan at the sight of that mire. . . . He rends his clothing, emits a high-pitched sob, then suddenly gives an order to his land army and rushes away in a panic" (Aeschylus, *Persians,* 465–470). "Xerxes, when he realized the extent of the disaster, was afraid that the Greeks, either on their own initiative or at the suggestion of the Ionians, might sail to the Hellespont and break the bridges here. If this happened, he would be cut off in Europe and in danger of destruction. Accordingly, he laid his plans for escape. . . . [He] made his way by forced marches to the Hellespont. He reached the crossing in forty-five days, but with hardly a fraction of his army intact. . . . It was at Siris that Xerxes, during the march to Greece, had left the sacred chariot of Zeus, and now he failed to recover it" (Herodotus 8.97,116; *cf.* 9.108).

The portrait Justin draws of Xerxes also displays certain traits usually attributed to Darius, such as his feeling of superiority and even his arrogance and boasting. The author establishes an opposition between the enormity of the army Xerxes has just passed in review and the faults and failings of the king himself: "But for this vast army a general was wanting; for if you contemplate its king, you could not commend his capacity as a leader, however you might extol his wealth. . . . He was always seen foremost in flight, and hindmost in battle; he was a coward in danger, and when danger was away, a boaster; and, in fine, before he made trial of war, elated with confidence in his strength."[161]

In Valerius Maximus, the flight of such a powerful king was naturally erected into a commonplace of cowardice: "That man, who had formed a chain of his ships to surround the sea, became on land a fleeing animal and was obliged to turn around, terror-stricken, and go back to his kingdom" (1.6, ext. 1).

The story also illustrates a no less time-worn theme, that of a reversal of fortune, which is expressed without hesitation via bombastic images: "In proportion to the terror of his entrance into Greece, was the shame and dishonour of his retreat from it. . . . Having found the bridge broken down by the winter storms, he crossed in the utmost trepidation in a fishing-boat. It was a sight worth contemplation for judging of the condition of man, so wonderful for its vicissitudes, to see him shrinking down in a little boat, whom shortly before the whole ocean could scarcely contain" (Justin 2.11.1; 13.9–10).

The images of Persian kings in defeat were so strong and persistent that other authors of the Roman period used them to describe Pompey's frantic flight from the battlefield. Like Darius, Pompey "left behind his insignia of command."[162] And, as Justin's Xerxes had done, he "leapt into a boat incapable of withstanding the winds and the waves . . . which roughly bore him toward the open sea: the man whose oars still beat the waters of the Corcyra and the Gulf of Leucas, the master of the Cilicians and of the Liburnian lands, slipped, a trembling passenger, into a fragile skiff."[163]

It is easy to understand why painters of the Hellenistic period particularly prized the theme of King Darius in flight in his chariot. The motif appears on several Apulian vases. On the Naples amphora (Fig. 44), the king is standing in a chariot drawn by four horses and guided by a driver whipping the team, as a horseman wearing a Corinthian helmet and armed with a spear pursues him from the left; represented on the right is a battle between a Greek and a Persian. As on the Vase of the Persians, which depicts the royal council convened by a king—labeled with the name Darius (Fig. 42)—the narrative scene is surmounted by divine figures: Zeus is ordering Nike (Victory) to crown the personification of Hellas before a humiliated Asia. The motif also appears on three other vases from the same period (one of them now lost). It is now believed that these vases date to the years 330–320. All of them could have come from the workshop of the Darius Painter or from a nearby workshop.

In the same decade that both Darius and Alexander died, seven years apart, the Apulian painters had hearsay knowledge of the principal scenes from the Alexander epic, given that accounts of them had begun to circulate immediately. But the painters' purpose was not to provide information about historical events: they were working from repetitive mythological models. The painting on the Naples amphora makes no more claim to be realistic or documentary than does the one representing the royal council. The human figures are less historical individuals than conventional types, presented as such: the chariot is

44. *The Great King in flight on his chariot, pursued by Alexander on his horse, Ruvo amphora.*

in the Greek style, the Great King wears the costume regularly attributed to Persians—but also to Amazons—in theatrical productions; he is depicted as an effeminate "Oriental" king who shows no sign of resistance, an image very remote from that of the fighter (albeit defeated) on the mosaic. As for the pursuer on horseback, supposedly Alexander, he is bearded, and no consideration is given to his physical traits, though they were well known and widely represented. In addition, the scene implies that Alexander had seized Darius, had even put him to death, which was by far a minority view in the literary tradition. In fact, only the iconographical context makes it possible to postulate that these anonymous figures, brought together by the painter's art, can be nothing other than a representation of Alexander's pursuit against Darius. Whatever the graphic expression, it must be noted that "Darius's flight" early on came to constitute an inescapable image of the Persian defeat and of Alexander's victory, symbolized by the spear with which the Macedonian king is directly threatening his enemy, disarmed and frightened in his chariot.

The Qualifying Heat

The contrast portrayed by the painters, between the fleeing king and the pursuing king, is the essential message of all the ancient narratives. Arrian uses a particularly strong expression: whereas the Macedonian king was in the front ranks of the fighters,[164] Darius was in the front ranks of the fugitives.[165] Then there is the image of the spirited young conqueror who, after landing in the low countries, chooses without hesitation to ascend "farther into the interior" to face the Great King, because "Alexander had now determined to attack Darius wherever he was."[166] Prior to Issus, Amyntas reminds Darius, apparently convinced that Alexander will not dare attack, "that Alexander would certainly come to any place where he heard Darius might be."[167] After the Persians' first diplomatic overtures, the young king provokes his adversary to battle for the crown, warning him: "Do not run away. For wherever you may be, I intend to march against you."[168] That warning is reiterated during the second embassy: "Wherever Darius could run he could follow."[169] According to Plutarch, Alexander was distressed by the delaying tactic his adversary had chosen, which, he said, would detract from his glory, and was delighted to be in a position to face him in pitched battle.[170] For, as he told Parmenion the morning of Gaugamela, "Do you not think we have already won the victory, now that we are no longer obliged to chase Darius over an enormous tract of wasted country?"[171] It is this conviction, according to Curtius, that decided Darius to wage battle: "Then a report circulated from reliable sources that Alexander intended to pursue him in full force into any area he went and so, well aware of the energy of his adversary, he ordered all the forces coming to his aid from distant nations to muster in Babylonia" (4.9.2).

The recurrence of the same expressions in the different authors shows how closely linked the theme of a personal confrontation between the two kings is to that of Alexander's pursuit. Immediately after Issus, Darius, after making the decision to go down personally to face his adversary, in fact continues to flee. By contrast, the Macedonian king is possessed of the firm and constant will to ascend to the high country and to force his adversary to put supreme power in play on the battlefield. The lesson of the two kings' parallel movements through space leaves no room for doubt, particularly because it is easy to make the connection to the diplomatic offers attributed to the Great King. In continually fleeing up country, Darius abandons sovereignty over territories that, in the Great King's still-fresh footsteps, the Macedonian conqueror covers at top speed and appropriates without delay. Curtius attributes the following reflections to Alexander, addressing his troops before the Battle of Gaugamela: "The clearest sign of their desperation was their burning of their own cities and agricultural land, by which they admitted that anything they did not spoil belonged to their foes."[172]

As in any clash of that kind, each camp's objective is to personally seize the opposing leader. On either side, "each soldier sought for himself the glory of killing the enemy king."[173] "No Macedonian had any other thought than to strike the king," and Alexander thought only of seizing his enemy in flight.[174] Such was the case at Issus, where, according to Plutarch, Darius "was four or five stadia ahead"; and where, writes Diodorus, Alexander, "continued on for two hundred stadia and then turned back, returning to his camp about midnight."[175] According to Arrian, Darius, having abandoned his chariot and the insignia of power, resumed his flight on horseback.[176] "The night, which came on soon after, alone rescued him from being captured by Alexander; for as long as there was daylight the latter kept up the pursuit at full speed. But when it began to grow dark and the things before the feet became invisible, he turned back again to the camp. . . . For his pursuit had been too slow for him to overtake Darius, because, though he wheeled round at the first breaking asunder of the phalanx, yet he did not turn to pursue him until he observed that the Grecian mercenaries and the Persian cavalry had been driven away from the river" (2.11.5–7).

Alexander had a comparable failure at Gaugamela: "The victor kept hard on the heels of his fleeing enemy."[177] In some sense, "while the outcome of the fight was still undecided, he conducted himself like a conqueror," for which Curtius congratulates him, judging that, by so doing, he displayed proof of "caution rather than eagerness."[178] But during that time, an offensive led by Mazeus put the Macedonians in the position of having to take flight themselves. In the face of such pressing danger, Parmenion sent a messenger to ask Alexander to turn back and seal off the breaches. It was only after being assured of success that the king could resume the pursuit, which he continued till nightfall. He set up camp after crossing the Lycos River; Darius had left a bridge across it shortly before, according to Curtius, to allow his troops to escape the Macedonians.[179] "After giving his horsemen rest until midnight, Alexander again advanced by a forced march towards Arbela, with the hope of seizing Darius there, together with his money and the rest of his royal property. He reached Arbela the next day, having pursued altogether 600 stades from the battle-field. But as Darius went on fleeing without taking any rest, he did not find him at Arbela."[180]

Alexander's disappointment is understandable: "The king had already covered a great distance in his pursuit of the fleeing Persians when the bad news from Parmenion arrived. His mounted men were told to pull up their forces and the infantry column came to a halt. Alexander was furious that victory was being snatched out of his hands and that Darius was more successful in flight than he himself was in pursuit."[181]

Subsequently, Parmenion was accused of having allowed Darius to escape for the second time: "Alexander was much vexed at the message, but without explaining to the soldiers what his real reasons were, ordered the trumpets to sound the recall, as though he were tired of slaughter, or because night was now coming on."[182]

Nevertheless, the terminology Diodorus uses to describe the taking of Darius's "insignia of power" (skeulenō) suggests that Alexander stripped Darius of his cuirass and weapons, as the Roman victor in a single combat might have done.[183] (The Roman would then place his enemy's armor in a specific sanctuary, as "rich spoils" dedicated to Jupiter Feretrius.)[184] Likewise, Curtius says that, at Issus, Alexander "was seeking for himself the rich trophy of killing the king."[185]

King of the Upper Country and of the Lower Country

According to Curtius, on the evening of the defeat, with Alexander on his heels, Darius held a brief war council in Arbela with his friends. Despite marked reluctance, he chose not to defend Babylonia but rather to retreat to Ecbatana, where he would be able to assemble a new army.[186] Diodorus writes: "Dareius directed his course to the upper satrapies, seeking by putting distance between himself and Alexander to gain a respite and time enough to organize an army. He made his way first to Ecbatana in Media and paused there, picking up the stragglers from the battle and rearming those who had lost their weapons. He sent around to the neighbouring tribes demanding soldiers, and he posted couriers to the satraps and generals in Bactria [Balkh] and the upper satrapies, calling upon them to preserve their loyalty to him."[187]

As planned, Alexander headed for Babylonia and, over the following months (November 331–April 330), devoted himself to taking over the great royal residences and to consolidating his power in Persia. Unlike the situation that had prevailed since the Battle of Issus and the offensive conducted from Egypt, the Macedonian army was no longer marching in the footsteps of the Achaemenid army; each of the two kings followed his own route. That is obviously the reason that, once again, the Great King disappears from the narratives of the ancient authors, whose attention is monopolized by Alexander's actions.

Nevertheless, the two adversaries certainly remained on the alert. Darius continued to be on the Macedonian's mind. In Media, Alexander received news from the Darius camp. As soon as affairs were stabilized in Persepolis (April/May 330), the pursuit resumed, more relentless and intense than ever. Here is how Arrian presents the Great King's hopes and plans:

> Darius had determined, if Alexander were to remain at Susa and Babylon, to wait himself where he was in Media, in case there were any new developments on Alexander's side, but if Alexander were to march straight against him, he proposed to go up country to the Parthyaeans and Hyrcania, as far as Bactra, ravaging all the country and making further progress impossible for Alexander. He sent the women, all the belongings he had still with him and the closed waggons to what are called the Caspian gates, while he stayed himself in Ecbatana with the force he had collected from available resources. (3.19.1–2; Brunt trans.)

The rest of the narrative shows that the information Alexander received at the time was contradictory. Some reported Darius's desire to fight in a pitched battle; then, very quickly, it appeared that the Great King, unable to compel the Scythians and Cadusians to send him contingents, had decided to resume his flight up country. "When he was only three days' journey from Ecbatana, he was met by Bistanes, son of Ochus [Artaxerxes III], who had reigned over the

Persians before Darius. This man announced that Darius had fled five days before, taking with him 7,000 talents of money from the Medes, and an army of 3,000 cavalry and 6,000 infantry" (3.19.4–5).

Arrian later reports the conspiracy against Darius led by Bessus, satrap of Bactriana, and Barsaentes, satrap of Arachosia and Drangiana, who, joined by the chiliarch Nabarzanes, had arrested Darius, henceforth "ignominiously led in chains."[188]

Curtius covers this moment in the history of Darius and Alexander throughout book 5, which goes from the immediate aftermath of Gaugamela to the Great King's death, then continues on to the successive councils and conspiracies in Ecbatana. The author does not hesitate to reconstitute public speeches and private conversations, even in their slightest details. According to Curtius, as soon as it was announced that Alexander had resumed his pursuit, Darius, because "no distance now seemed a sufficient counterbalance" to Alexander's speed, changed "both his strategy and his route." The author adds that the Great King "began to prepare for battle rather than retreat,"[189] and that the king's closest friend, Artabazus, proposed: "We shall follow our king into battle . . . dressed in our richest robes and equipped with our finest armour, mentally prepared to expect victory but also ready to die."[190] But though "all applauded these words," Curtius never lets the reader suppose that a pitched battle was seriously in the offing. On the contrary, Darius "had decided to go from there to Bactria," and "no distance now seemed a sufficient counterbalance" to Alexander's speed.[191] That is clearly because, in the meantime, Bessus and his accomplices had done everything possible to undermine the authority and prestige the Great King still enjoyed.

The context is therefore truly that of an escape. Curtius shows the king, "by nature a sincere and sympathetic person," forgiving the conspirators, then leaving Ecbatana in high style, in accordance with the rules of the court: "Darius gave the signal to march and climbed into his chariot in his usual manner. . . . He had no worries about the impending danger as he hurried to escape the hands of Alexander, his only fear."[192] The least one can say is that the words the author uses do not increase the stature of the king, who for years seemed to be obsessed by a single concern: to put as much distance as possible between himself and his pursuer. Then comes the betrayal, the arrest, and the reflections on reversals of fortune: "The king who a short time ago had ridden in a chariot and received divine honours from his people was now, with no interference from without, made a captive of his own slaves and set in a squalid wagon. . . . To allow the king some mark of respect, however, they bound him with fetters of gold, for fortune kept on devising new kinds of insult for him; and to prevent his being recognized by his royal dress they had covered the wagon with dirty skins" (5.12.16, 20).

Alerted of these events, Alexander went even faster, more resolute than ever to seize the person of the king, who had escaped him since the autumn of 333: "In his person lies our victory," he tells his generals, to instill his energy in them.[193] At the time, in the midst of a scorching heat, he was preparing to double his pace, crossing regions without water resources: "Alexander, therefore, led his force on speedily, racing rather than marching and not even resting at night to compensate for the day's exertions."[194]

> By reason of the speed of his march many of his troops were left behind worn out, while the horses were dying. Still Alexander went on and reached Rhagae on the eleventh day. This place is one day's journey from the Caspian gates for anyone marching like Alexander. . . . Despairing of capturing Darius by close pursuit, Alexander remained there five days and rested his force . . . then he marched towards the Parthyaeans. . . . [Darius is arrested by his satraps.] On learning this Alexander pressed on faster than ever, with only the Companions, the mounted *prodromoi*, and the strongest and lightest of the infantry, carefully selected. . . . Travelling all night and the next day till noon, he rested his troops a short time and then went on again all night. . . . On hearing this, Alexander decided that he must pursue with the utmost vigour. Already his men and horses were growing utterly wearied under the continued hardship; none the less, he pressed on, and accomplishing a great distance during the night and the following day till noon, he reached a village where the party with Darius had bivouacked the day before. . . . [Choosing a shortcut], he dismounted some five hundred horsemen, selected from the officers of the infantry and the rest those who had best kept up their strength, and ordered them to mount the horses. . . . Alexander then started off himself at evening, and led his troops on at full speed; during the night he covered up to four hundred stades,[195] and just at dawn came upon the Persians marching in disorder without arms, so that only a few of them attempted resistance. (3.20–21, Brunt trans.)

Darius, after months of "wandering as an exile from his own kingdom," had reached the end of his desperate trek.[196] He died miserably, abandoned by all—except by his dog.[197] The tragic and romantic atmosphere of this episode may well bring to mind the fate of the last Sassanid king, Yazdegerd: defeated by the Arab armies, he was slaughtered during his flight to Khorasan by the miller Khosrau. His remains were collected by holy men, who buried him "in a tomb rising higher than the clouds," thus marking the end of a history that had begun four centuries earlier with Ardašir.[198] Similarly, Darius's death marked the end of an imperial saga that had begun with Cyrus the Great more than two centuries earlier.

Alexander was the victor, in control of his enemy's remains, which he ordered buried in the royal tombs. Just as Darius had done before the spring of 334, he could finally consider himself king of the low countries and of the high countries. Nevertheless, the victory was not complete, because, in Bactra, Bessus was reclaiming the Achaemenid crown under the name "Artaxerxes." Darius's flight had come to an end, but the chase scene of Alexander, successor to Darius, would continue against his new rival, master of the upper satrapies.[199]

❦ 8 ❧

Iron Helmet, Silver Vessels

On the Great King, His Baggage Train, and His Concubines

For the ancient authors, the reason for Darius's defeat is not to be sought solely in the Great King's personality. Or more exactly, the reactions Darius displayed and the decisions he made are also linked to causes that we would call structural. Given that these authors are not at all interested in conducting in-depth analyses, the original weaknesses in the Persian camp are marked in their discourse by symptoms that in their view are strikingly revealing of what one historiographical current, long hegemonic, has called "Achaemenid decadence." These very symptoms are spelled out in anecdotes and exempla that have been tirelessly recopied since antiquity, or in descriptions that have been interpreted on the basis of an unvarying interpretive grid.

In Charles Rollin's *Histoire ancienne (Ancient History)*, for example, published in the first third of the eighteenth century, the author returns three times to what he obviously considers an acknowledged fact, namely, the accelerating decadence of the empire. From the first assessment done at the end of Cyrus's reign, a firm diagnosis named the unquestionable culprit, the love of luxury: "The most judicious historians and the most profound philosophers all proffer as a clear and incontestable maxim that luxury never fails to bring ruin to the most prosperous states." In Rollin's eyes, the most obvious and incontestable symptom is the habit Persian kings had of trying to maintain the same standard of living under all circumstances, even during their travels and military campaigns: "That splendor and luxury were taken to a point of excess which was true folly. The prince took his women with him, and you can clearly imagine the trappings that followed that band. The generals and officers did the same and in equal measure. The pretext was that they would be motivated to fight better by the sight of what they held most dear in the world; but the real reason was the love of pleasure. . . . A second folly was to want the army's luxury in tents, chariots, the table and good food to surpass even that which reigned in the cities" (1:568).

Bossuet, whom Rollin also read closely, had already insisted on that glaring symptom of Persian degeneration, denouncing "the infinite multitude that the king and the grandees dragged behind them, solely for pleasure. For they were so soft that they wanted to find the same magnificence and the same delights in the army as in the places where the court ordinarily had its residence; so that when the kings marched, they did so accompanied by their wives, their concubines, their eunuchs, and everything that served their pleasures" (*Discours*, p. 550).

Rollin returns several times to the original diagnosis, both in his assessment of Artaxerxes II's reign and in the one presented before Alexander's arrival. He refers frequently to Curtius, particularly to a long passage traditionally used to demonstrate that Darius's army suffered from a fatal lack of mobility. The description begins with a discussion of the Great King's military preparations. Then Curtius provides details about the army's marching order *(agmen)* when the royal forces left Babylon.[1] After describing the chariots of the gods, the king's position, and the clothes he was wearing at the time, along with the different categories of courtiers and the military corps that accompanied him, Curtius presents the chariots at the end of the cortege and the people occupying and surrounding them:

> At a distance of one stade, came Sisigambis, the mother of Darius, drawn in a carriage, and in another came his wife. A troop of women attended the queens on horseback. Then came the fifteen so-called *harmamaxae* [four-wheeled chariots, as opposed to those with two wheels; compare Herodotus 7.41], in which rode the king's children, their nurses and a herd of eunuchs (who are not at all held in contempt by those peoples). Next came the carriages of the 365 royal concubines, these also dressed in royal finery, and behind them 600 mules and 300 camels carried the king's money, with a guard of archers in attendance. After this column rode the wives of the king's relatives and friends [*propinqui et amici*], and hordes of camp-followers and servants. At the end, to close up the rear, were the light-armed troops with their respective leaders. (3.3.22–25)

Logically, Rollin proposes the following lesson: "Does it not seem that this is a description of tournaments and not of an army march? Is it conceivable that sensible princes were capable of such folly, of taking along with their troops such a cumbersome lot of wives, princesses, concubines, eunuchs, and servants of both sexes? The custom of the country required it: that was sufficient. Leading six hundred thousand men amidst that superb throng, which was for him alone, Darius believed himself great and inflated the idea he had of himself with that vain external pomp. Reduced to his proper measure and his personal merit, how small he was! He is not the only one to have thought that way and of whom the same judgment could be made" (4:46).

After the description of Darius's treasure, taken in Damascus, Rollin draws an unsurprising and irrevocable conclusion regarding the reasons for the king's defeat: "A fitting cortege for a king headed toward ruin." The same image is used later to denounce any army rendered incapable of moving quickly by the weight of its baggage train and the number of its carriages.[2]

Rollin borrows moral judgments and logistical remarks from Xenophon and especially Curtius, who enlivened his own description with commentaries. These were intended to illustrate one of his favorite themes—the corruptive effect of wealth along with the opposition that, from his standpoint, ought to be established between an army's appearance and its military capacities. He was particularly fond of noting the discrepancy between the luxury of the attire or ornaments of one or another military corps and its incompetence at war. That is also the reason luxury of attire is often called "feminine." Even as he gives information of the greatest interest about the cortege, Curtius registers a certain uneasiness at seeing bands of eunuchs and royal concubines included. He himself draws the moral of the story, setting up an implacable opposition to Alexander's troops: "The Macedonians, on the other hand, provided a different spectacle: horses and men gleaming not with gold, not with multi-coloured clothes, but with iron and bronze. It was an army ready to stand its ground and follow its leader, and not overloaded with numbers and baggage—an army eagerly watching not just for a signal from Alexander but even a nod. Any location sufficed for their camp, any food for their provisions. Accordingly Alexander was not deficient in troops in the battle while Darius, king of such a teeming host, was reduced by the confined limits of the battlefield to such small numbers as he had disdained in his enemy" (3.3.26–28).

Further on, evoking the pillaging of the Persian camp after the battle, the same author points out "all manner of riches" and comments: "a huge quantity of gold and silver (the trappings of luxury, not war)."[3] Curtius uses nearly the same terms in describing the colorful splendor of the Babylonian horsemen that welcome Alexander upon his entry into the city in November 331: "Their equipment and that of the horses suggest[ed] extravagance rather than majesty."[4] Once again, a rhetorical opposition is set up here, one for which Curtius and many other authors of the Roman period had a particular fondness: that between gold and iron. Even before the battle, putting words into the mouth of Darius's Athenian adviser Charidemus, Curtius gives a glimpse of the battle's outcome: the Persian army "gleams with purple and gold; it is resplendent with armour and opulence," in contrast to the "coarse and inelegant" Macedonian phalanx "behind its shields and lances." Charidemus warns the king: "Don't think that what motivates them is the desire for gold and silver; until now such strict discipline has been due to poverty's schooling. When they are tired, the earth is their bed; they are satisfied with food they can prepare while they work; their sleeping time is of shorter duration than the darkness" (3.2.12–15).

Clearly, such a sharp opposition was well suited to an entire moralizing current, which denounced armies laden with gold, such as the army of Antiochus as described by Valerius Maximus: "His army, imitating his mad and blind sumptuosity [luxuria], generally wore shoes trimmed with gold nails, had silver vessels as cooking utensils, and raised tents decorated with embroidered fabrics. That was booty offered up to the enemy's greed rather than an obstacle to a courageous adversary's victory" (9.2, ext. 4).[5]

Curtius, who also expounds on the vitiating effect of luxury and wealth for empires and individuals, here uses one of his favorite devices: he turns the Great King into a speaker who authenticates his own analyses. In that way, it is Darius himself who "confesses" that such customs constituted a real handicap for his army. That is why, during the "third embassy," supposedly sent to Alexander shortly before Gaugamela, Darius again proposes that his adversary return the Persian princesses, who had been held captive since Issus (Darius's wife, however, had died in the meantime): "Now too, he said, it was his firm opinion that Alexander should take 30,000 talents of gold in exchange for an old woman and two girls who merely retarded the army's progress" (4.11.12).

A little later, Curtius fictively takes his reader into the war council convened in Arbela following the defeat at Gaugamela. The Great King attempts to persuade his advisers that the best tactic to follow is to leave the road to Babylon open to Alexander. The king's harangue is rendered in indirect speech: "[Alexander] and his men were after rich and easily-acquired plunder. In the circumstances, said Darius, this would prove to be his own salvation, since he was going to head for the wastelands with a light-armed detachment—the remote parts of his empire being still intact, he would have no difficulty in raising forces for the war with them" (5.1.4–5).

As Alexander is about to become a Great King, Darius wants to appropriate the logistical and tactical advantages attributed to his Macedonian rival. Here is how he presents to his friends the reasons for past defeats: "As far as he was concerned, the rapacious Macedonians could seize his treasure and glut themselves with the gold for which they had so long hungered—for they were soon going to be his prey. Experience had taught him that expensive furniture, concubines and troops of eunuchs were no more than deadweight and encumbrances, and with these in tow Alexander would be handicapped by the very things which had previously given him victory. . . . War was fought with iron not gold, and by men not city-buildings: and all things come to the man with the weapons. This, he said, was how his ancestors had, after initial reverses, swiftly recovered their old prosperity" (5.1.6).

In this declamation, all the cultural stereotypes about the vitiating effect of luxury and sex recur, evoked through the insistent mention of eunuchs and concubines, and through the repeated reference to the superiority of iron over gold. And when Darius, alias Curtius, gravely explains that "war was fought . . . by men not city-buildings," it becomes clear that Curtius, alias Darius, had read his classics well, particularly Plato expounding on the ideal republic. Plato denounces the tendencies of the city to count on walls to defend itself more than on the courage and spirit of sacrifice of the men who are its citizens.[6] That also explains the prestige, among Roman moralists such as Valerius Maximus, of the original Sparta, pure and hard, which had contempt for any fortification.[7]

As for Rollin's phrase "everything that served only the luxury and magnificence of the court," it merely reproduces a passage from Arrian. The ancient author has just explained that, in Darius's camp captured after the Battle of Issus, though the Macedonians managed to lay their hands on the royal princesses, they were extremely disappointed by the small quantity of money they found there, "no more than 3,000 talents." In fact, he explains, before the battle "the other Persians happened to have despatched their women along with the rest of their property to Damascus; because Darius had sent to that city the greater part of his money and all the other things which the Great King was in the habit of taking with him as necessary for his luxurious mode of living, even

though he was going on a military expedition."[8] Indeed, Curtius's description
of the booty of Damascus has a Hollywood quality to it:

> The royal treasure was now littered throughout the plains: the cash ac-
> cumulated to pay the men (a massive sum), the clothes of so many high-
> ranking men and so many distinguished women,[9] golden vessels, golden
> bridles, tents elaborately decorated on a royal scale, and wagons full of
> enormous wealth, abandoned by their owners. It was a sight to sadden
> even the looters—if there were anything that could arrest greed! For now
> a fortune of amazing and unbelievable proportions, which had been
> hoarded up over many years, was being rooted out by the looters, some
> of it torn by bramble-bushes, some of it sunk in the mud. The looters did
> not have enough hands to carry off their booty. . . . The coined money
> taken amounted to 2,600 talents, and the weight of wrought silver was
> equivalent to 500 talents. Thirty thousand men were also captured, to-
> gether with 7,000 pack-animals and their burdens. (3.13.10–11, 16)

In keeping with the custom of all armies, Parmenion had been assigned to
conduct a meticulous inventory of the booty thus assembled. As chance would
have it, we possess two partial quotations from the report, written in the first
person, as it was sent to Alexander. The passages are from a famous work by
Athenaeus of Naucratis, *The Deipnosophists,* a gold mine of quotations from every king and particularly rich in notations on the luxury *(tryphē)* of the Persian
and Hellenistic kings. These are partial quotations: the author, following the
logic of his own theme, gives only a list of drinking cups and an inventory of
the staff responsible for food service and preparation and for the Great King's
banquets:

> Parmenion, summing up the booty taken from the Persians, in his *Letters
> to Alexander,* says: "Gold cups, weight seventy-three Babylonian talents,
> fifty-two minae; cups inlaid with precious stones, weight fifty-six Babylo-
> nian talents, thirty-four minae."[10] Even princes were often excited over
> flute-girls and harp-girls, as is made clear by Parmenio in the *Letter to Alex-
> ander* dispatched to him after the capture of Damascus, when he came into
> possession of Darius's baggage train [*aposkeuē*]. Having caused an inven-
> tory to be made of the captured stuff, he writes also the following: "I
> discovered concubines of the king who played musical instruments [*pal-
> lakidai mousorgoi*],[11] to the number of 329; men employed to weave chaplets,

46; caterers, 277; kettle-tenders, 29; pudding-makers, 13; bartenders, 17; wine-clarifiers, 70; perfume-makers, 14." (13.607f–608a; C.-B. Gulick trans.)

Even from these scattered, random scraps from lost archives, it is possible to understand the ancient authors' astonishment, and also how easy they found it to make both a moralizing and a polemical use of it, as in Arrian's remark: "The Great King was in the habit of taking with him [everything] . . . necessary for his luxurious mode of living, even though he was going on a military expedition." The presence of women from the royal house in the camp at Issus, and of all the women who accompanied the army and had been left behind in Damascus, also did not fail to elicit comments from the ancient authors. Xenophon clearly alludes to them as well in the *Cyropaedia*. After a victory, spoils were taken from the enemy, as were a great number of "covered chariots, filled with women of the highest rank, wives or concubines, which the enemies took everywhere with them for their beauty." As was his habit, Xenophon makes a comparison to what was done in his own time and comments: "Even today, all the Asians take their most precious possessions on their campaigns; they say they will be better able to fight if they have close to them what they hold most dear, since they will be obliged to defend it with zeal. That may be so; perhaps, too, they do it to satisfy their sensual appetites" (4.3.1–2).

The second interpretation, presented as an alternative suggestion, is in line with a prevailing notion that Xenophon himself develops at length in the last chapter of the *Cyropaedia*, a systematic exposition of the flaws and vices of the Persians "of his time," a notion also frequently found in many other authors of antiquity. As proof of the good fortune the Persian king enjoyed, one of Athenaeus's banqueters cites his propensity for great sexual activity.[12] Aelian for his part points out "the sensuality with which the Median and Persian barbarians abandoned themselves to the pleasures of love."[13] Denouncing the endogamic practices of the Persians/Parthians, Lucan affirms: "Do we not know how those barbarians practice love, which they blindly gulp down with beastly instincts? . . . An entire night spent in the embraces of all those women does not tire one man."[14] Ammianus Marcellinus writes of the same barbarians: "They are more dissolute and more strongly attracted to matters of love than most people, and they have a great deal of trouble satisfying themselves even with a host of concubines."[15]

Instead of seeing the custom of the Great King's 360 concubines as a mark and symbol of royal splendor, the Greek authors regularly maintain or imply that it demonstrates first and foremost the extreme sensuality and unbridled sexual appetites of the Persian king, who every evening personally selected the woman "with whom he would lie that night." Hence the condemnation directed at Alexander, who "added concubines to his retinue in the manner of Dareius."[16] The lesson the philosopher Dicaearchus (one of Aristotle's students) drew in his *Life of Greece* is therefore not surprising. He contrasts the practices of Philip of Macedonia to those of Darius, "the one who was deposed by Alexander." Philip "did not, to be sure, take women along with him on his campaigns, as did Darius, [who,] . . . although engaged in a war in which his entire empire was at stake, took round with him three hundred and sixty concubines."[17]

Such an image tended to become a stereotype. For the Roman authors, the mere presence of concubines in an army sufficed to discredit it, especially if they were accompanied by eunuchs.[18] Livy, with the sole aim of completing his devalorization of Alexander's victories, dresses up his own discourse by using the image of a Darius weighed down by the luxury of his baggage train, in terminology curiously close to that of Curtius (who probably borrowed it from him): "A king dragging behind him an army of women and eunuchs, encumbered by his purple and gold, laden with all the impedimenta of his greatness, looking much more like prey than like an enemy, whom Alexander conquered without any resistance, with no other merit than to have successfully dared brave a mere hobgoblin."[19]

That idea is present, overtly or implicitly, in many episodes of the war between Alexander and Darius, either in the form of narratives or, most often, in that of exempla. The conclusion expressed or implied is always the same: the Great King is reputed to have been defeated precisely because he was simply incapable of doing without the pleasures of the table (chap. 8) and of the bed (chap. 9), even in the gravest of circumstances. On the contrary, he was intent on relishing them to the point of satiety, both in his tent in wartime and in the recesses of his palaces in peacetime.

Kitchens and Outbuildings

Rollin also writes: "The most exquisite dishes, the finest game, the rarest birds, had to reach the prince wherever in the world he happened to set up camp." In support of his indictment, he cites and paraphrases a passage from *De ira,* in which Seneca discourses on the insane luxury of the Great Kings. During a lengthy discussion in which the disastrous image of Persian kings is used as a foil, Seneca tries to show that "fury ravages entire nations, it strikes cities, rivers, and inanimate objects."

In the guise of an exemplum, Seneca refers to Cambyses's famous campaign against the Ethiopians, of which Herodotus spoke at length.[20] Like his model, Seneca conveys the misfortune of the Persian army, which was left without resupplies because of the culpable lack of foresight on the part of a king driven solely by an irrational anger. Barely surviving during a first stop by chewing "tender leaves and buds," then obliged to consume "leather softened by fire and everything that necessity had made into food," having finally reached the depths of despair, "when there were no more roots and grasses in the sands for them, and the desert appeared emptied even of animals, they chose one in ten of themselves by lot and obtained a nourishment worse than hunger." The end of the story is a denunciation by the book of the odious conduct of the king, insensitive to the suffering his troops were enduring: "Rage spurred on the king, even though he had partly lost and partly eaten his army, until the moment he feared that he himself would be selected by lot; only then did he give the signal to retreat. During that time, he was served delicate birds, his dishes were carried along on camels, while his soldiers were drawing lots to know who would perish from a cruel death and who would live an even worse one" (*De ira*, 3.20).

The reference to "delicate birds" and "dishes carried along on camels" shows quite clearly that the one who inspired Seneca knew the rules and practices of the Persian royal table.[21] But in reality Seneca, like every author of collections of exempla, perhaps copying a predecessor in that respect, also took liberties with Herodotus. That author does make clear that Cambyses did not give any "orders for the provision of supplies" (3.25) and that, on the point of death, his soldiers turned to cannibalism, but there is no mention anywhere of the splendor of his table in the very heart of the Western Desert. It was, however, easy to graft onto a Herodotean framework a motif so frequently found in the collections of monarchical conduct, laudable or reprehensible.

In his *Life of Alexander*, in fact, Plutarch intends to show that the practices of the Macedonian king were radically different from those of Darius. Returning from his fruitless pursuit of the Great King, Alexander was welcomed in the following manner:

> The royal pavilion of Darius himself, full of beautiful slaves, and rich furniture of every description, had been left unplundered, and was reserved for Alexander himself, who as soon as he had taken off his armour, pro-

ceeded to the bath, saying "Let me wash off the sweat of the battle in the bath of Darius." "No," answered one of his Companions [*hetairoi*],[22] "in that of Alexander; for the goods of the vanquished become the property of the victor." When he entered the bath and saw that all the vessels for water, the bath itself, and the boxes of unguents were of pure gold, and smelt the delicious scent of the rich perfumes with which the whole room was filled; and when he passed from the bath into the magnificent and lofty pavilion, where a splendid banquet was prepared, he looked at his friends and said "This, then, it is to be a king indeed [*to basileuein*]." (20.11–13)

In Plutarch's mind, the king's response means that he has no intention of identifying with the defeated king: on the contrary, he wants to mark clearly the line of demarcation between Darius's barbarous past monarchy and the one he now embodies. Readers certainly had no doubts about the lesson to be drawn. Consider as well, also in Plutarch, the reflections of Caesar's soldiers as they seized hold of Pompey's camp after the Battle of Pharsalus: "The Caesareans could observe the insane frivolity of the enemies: all the tents were decorated with myrtle and adorned with flowery hangings; the tables were laden with goblets and kraters filled with wine. These were luxurious preparations for a sacrifice and an official feast rather than for warriors taking up arms. That is how intoxicated the Pompeians were on their hopes and, in marching into battle, how full of a mad presumptuousness" (*Pompeius* 72.5–6).

In remarking that "the ground for the tents was covered with mounds of freshly cut grass," Caesar believed he had good reason to be surprised that "it was those people who reproached for its softness Caesar's army, so poor and so tough, and which had always lacked the necessities."[23]

The apologue also brings to mind a passage from Herodotus. The year is 479, the setting, Greece. The previous year, after the defeat of Salamis, Xerxes had departed from Attica for Asia Minor. Upon his departure he left to Mardonius an elite army, along with part of his royal equipment, including his tent. After the victory in Plataea, where Mardonius met his death, the Spartan general Pausanias entered the huge royal tent:

When Pausanias saw it, with its embroidered hangings and gorgeous decorations in silver and gold, he summoned Mardonius' bakers and cooks and told them to prepare a meal of the same sort as they were accustomed to prepare for their former master. The order was obeyed; and when Pausanias saw gold and silver couches all beautifully draped, and gold and

silver tables, and everything prepared for the feast with great magnificence, he could hardly believe his eyes for the good things set before him,
and, just for a joke, ordered his own servants to get ready an ordinary
Spartan dinner. The difference between the two meals was indeed remarkable, and, when both were ready, Pausanias laughed and sent for the
Greek commanding officers. When they arrived, he invited them to take
a look at the two tables, saying, "Gentlemen, I asked you here in order to
show you the folly of the Persians, who, living in this style, came to
Greece to rob us of our poverty." (9.82)

Plutarch also seeks to mark an opposition between Alexander and his soldiers. He extols Alexander's obvious attachment to his simple and frugal living
habits, in the face of the insatiable appetite of the soldiers for the wealth of the
Orient, on which they gorged after the taking of the treasure of Damascus: "All
the camp was filled with riches, so great was the mass of plunder. Then did the
Macedonians get their first taste of gold and silver, of Persian luxury and of
Persian women; and after this, like hounds opening upon a scent, they eagerly
pressed forward on the track of the wealthy Persians. The rest of the army also
had its fill of booty."[24]

Plutarch maintains that, by contrast, Alexander never even allowed anyone
to speak in his presence of the beauty of Darius's wife; and though he had in his
service the "best cooks," he was extremely frugal. "He earn[ed] his breakfast by
a night-march, and . . . an appetite for his dinner by eating sparingly at breakfast. . . . He was less given to wine than he was commonly supposed to be."[25]

The same contrast can also be found in Persepolis, where, according to
Polyaenus, Alexander was able to learn from the inscription on a bronze column the foodstuffs that were to be used in preparing the Great King's lunch
and dinner. The text was fictively attributed to Cyrus, along with inscriptions
of other customs (nomoi), also supposedly on the column. As a document, it
provides helpful information about Persian aulic regulations in the age of Darius III; but it is the moral commentary into which it is inserted that is of more
direct import here. Once again, it establishes a direct connection between the
practices of the Persian kings and the defeats that Darius and his men had suffered on three occasions: "When the other Macedonians saw the list of preparations for the dinner, they admired the opulence to which it bore witness. Alexander, however, made fun of it, seeing it as a bad omen and a great hindrance.
He therefore gave the order to knock down the pillar on which the list was

written, telling his Companions: 'The kings who were raised to dine in such a spendthrift manner drew no advantage from it, for excessive prodigality and great luxury [*tryphē*] necessarily correspond to great cowardice:[26] you can see, moreover, that those who wolf down such lavish dinners have been quickly vanquished in battle'" (4.3.32).

What a difference from Alexander's daily regimen, praised by Plutarch: he did not covet "the golden burden of ten thousand camels . . . the possession of the Median women or glorious ornaments of Persian luxury"; he was not greedy for "Chalybonian wine or the fish of Hyrcania."[27] Although the Great King is not explicitly named, Plutarch's readers understood very well that the remarks were aimed at Darius, known for consuming only wheat from Assus in Aeolis, wine from Syria, and water from the Eulaios.[28]

In the eyes of a moralist from the Roman period, nothing better defined Asian luxury than that frenzied desire to bring the most refined dishes from remote places for one's own pleasure. That is why exempla condemn Harpalus, Alexander's treasurer, and Aesopus, a tragic actor, for bringing in fish at great cost from the banks of the Persian Gulf or from the oceanside.[29] When elaborate dishes, including rare fish, were brought to him from a long way off, Alexander chose to distribute them to each of his Companions, as Cyrus the Younger— whom Xenophon praises for the same reasons and with the same words—had also done.[30] Alexander and Cyrus were frugal and generous both; they were therefore full of vigor and energy as well.

Alexander and His Baggage Train: Rigor and Abstemiousness

Alexander would soon show further proof of his determination not to adopt the practices of Darius and of his predecessors. In nearly identical terms, several authors tell the same story, which they situate either just after Darius's death (Curtius), shortly before the trip to India (Plutarch), or during the Indian campaign (Polyaenus). Here is Plutarch's account: "As Alexander was now about to invade India, and observed that his army had become unwieldy and difficult to move in consequence of the mass of plunder with which the soldiers were encumbered, he collected all the baggage-waggons together one morning at daybreak, and first burned his own and those of his companions, after which he ordered those of the Macedonians to be set on fire. This measure appears to have been more energetic than the occasion really required; and yet it proved more ruinous in the design than in the execution: for although some of the soldiers were vexed at the order, most of them with enthusiastic shouts distributed their most useful property among those who were in want, burning and destroying all the rest with a cheerful alacrity which raised Alexander's spirits to the highest pitch" (*Alexander*, 57.1–2).

Even more than other ancient armies, Alexander's army, because of the length of the expedition, was weighed down by the soldiers' personal possessions, which increased regularly as a result of the unorganized pillaging and the redistribution of the spoils. Furthermore, it was accompanied by a considerable number of noncombatants—merchants, women, servants, vivandiers, and artisans—all lumped together in the ancient texts under the collective term "those who were in the baggage train." There is also no doubt that every leader was concerned about lightening the baggage. According to Frontinus, Alexander's father, Philip, "had forbidden the use of chariots [and] had assigned a single varlet to each horseman and to each group of ten foot soldiers."[31]

In this case it matters little whether, beyond the rhetorical exaggeration and even bombast of the texts that make note of it, Alexander really took such a measure at a given moment. For everything indicates that, throughout the expedition, Alexander's royal tent was on the contrary distinguished by its rich accoutrements, which in all probability were in no way overshadowed by the Great King's tent.[32] Plutarch, for example, reports the wealth of precautions taken by "the chief of Alexander's household servants," assigned to guard the furnishings, as the ground on which the royal tent would be planted was being prepared.[33] Even in the midst of the march through the Gedrosian desert, when animals and common soldiers were falling like flies, Alexander enjoyed a tent equipped with special provisions.[34] It is also possible that long-term logistical and strategic objectives and lofty moral grounds were later put forward to disguise, as a monarchical fable, what had been merely a limited conflagration, decided on by the king for infinitely less noble reasons. In an anecdote reported by Plutarch, in fact, Alexander—in India at the time—gave his slaves the order to burn down the tent of Eumenes, his secretary, as a means of proving he had enormous quantities of hidden silver. But "the tent went up in flames too quickly, and Alexander regretted his decision because the archives located there were destroyed."[35]

In any event, the ancient authors, situating the episode at different dates and in different contexts, conferred on it a status of didactic exemplum, remote from everything that the present-day historian, not without a certain naïveté at times, likes to term "historical fact." Once again, the narration is subordinated to the contextual logic of a monarchical literature devoted entirely to exalting

the merits of the "good king." For Polyaenus, Alexander's objective was to instill the desire in his men to continue the campaign into India: having rid themselves of the booty accumulated from the Persians during the last years, "the
Macedonians, thus deprived of their treasures, immediately become anxious
for more; and, in order to obtain it, are of course ready for new enterprises."[36]
The reasons invoked are roughly the same in Curtius: having just devoted a
discussion to Alexander's "Orientalization," he quite clearly suggests that the
king intended to show his people that he had not turned into a Darius. To that
end, Alexander reacted forcefully against the transformation of his own army
into an army like that of Darius III, one without momentum and without motivation. In fact, "the column could scarcely get moving under the weight of its
spoils and extravagant impedimenta."[37] Based on the same assumptions, Plutarch cites the anecdote elsewhere, to contrast the Macedonian king Perseus to
Alexander: he condemns Perseus for having wanted at all cost to keep his treasures with him, even at the price of defeat, instead of lightening his load.[38]

The reader therefore has no doubt about the meaning to be given to the
story. To order tents and chariots burned, even to set fire to them with one's
own hand, is an act of symbolic power comparable to the (invented) destruction of the (fictive) bronze column of Persepolis. Lovers of exempla could thus
show that Alexander had always challenged the practices of luxury *(tryphē)* and
magnificence *(polyteleia),* considered to be typically Persian and at cross-
purposes with the proper operation of any army worthy of the name. That also
explains the emphasis on the detail that the king's tent and those of the army's
high commanders were destroyed first. Curtius even adds a strong image to
fire the imagination: "All were waiting to see what [Alexander's] next command
would be. He ordered the animals to be led off, put a torch to his own baggage
first and then gave instructions for the rest to be burnt. . . . No one dared lament
the loss of what he had paid for in blood, since the same fire was consuming the
king's valuables."[39] The soldiers' enthusiasm in abandoning their baggage to
follow their leader also constitutes one of the obligatory articulations of the
exemplum.

The fable, attributed to various historical figures, is repeated over and over
again in the collections of exempla. It is elaborated in chapter 4.1 of Frontinus's *Stratagems* (in which he also cites the example of the measure taken by
Philip), titled *De disciplina,* and also in Valerius Maximus, under the same ru-
bric. P. Cornelius Scipio, named commander of the Roman army outside the
walls of Numantia, took the measures required to strengthen his armies and

thus also to secure the surrender of the besieged: "Upon entering the camp, he decreed that everything that had been accumulated to satisfy pleasure [*voluptas*] would be removed and disposed of. For he was sure that a huge crowd of peddlers and camp-followers would then come out, accompanied by two thousand prostitutes. Once it was rid of that rabble, which debased and dishonored it, our army, whose fear of death had only shortly before led it to sully itself with a shameful armistice treaty, recovered and revived its courage [*virtus*], and crushed the famed stamina and zeal of Numantia" (2.7.1).

Curtius takes the same lesson from the victory at Gaugamela. The enormous booty collected after Issus had weighed down the baggage train of Alexander's army. During the battle a Persian counterattack had almost carried off the Macedonian baggage train, including the members of Darius's family detained there.[40] Alexander had to turn around and throw himself back into the melee. Curtius, analyzing the Macedonian success, once again and relentlessly underscores the Macedonian king's moral merit: "The loss of the packs and baggage he very wisely disregarded because he saw that the battle would decide the entire issue."[41] A little earlier, the author had noted that Alexander "was afraid—not without justification—that concern with recovering the baggage might draw his men from the fight."[42] The praise and the glory are for Alexander alone. But the opposition between the baggage train (the rear) and the battle (the front lines) implicitly but clearly entails a comparison unfavorable to Darius.

The King Is Thirsty, the King Does Not Drink!

Many monarchical apologues are set within the context of a famine that strikes the army on the march, following a script as popular as it is repetitive. The soldiers are starving to death: How does the king commanding them react, especially when the king in question is accustomed to wanting for nothing? That was certainly one of the requisite rubrics for any collection of exempla. Frontinus, for example, devotes an entire chapter to leaders who know how to be satisfied with the common soldier's regimen, drinking the sailor's mediocre wine (Cato) or eating the grunt's dry bread (Scipio, Alexander).[43] Following an immutable rule, the apologue condemns the king who cannot do without the trappings of his usual lifestyle (Cambyses or Darius III) and praises the sovereign or general who, in command of his army, is able to be content with little, such as Artaxerxes according to Plutarch.[44] So too, an apologue lauds Alexander, who during a review of the troops in the middle of winter, invites a common soldier to come near the fire, and it contrasts the simplicity of his practice to the Persians' prohibition limiting access to the Great King.[45] The march into a blazing and drought-stricken region offers the author a particularly favorable narrative context, because it allows him to take advantage of highly dramatic and moving circumstances. Lucan tells the story of an exhausting march by Crassus's army across a Libyan desert. Crassus is presented as an admirable leader, refusing to enjoy any of the advantages of which his soldiers might be deprived: "He does not allow himself to be indolently carried on the shoulders of others or drawn in a chariot. He is the most abstemious when it comes to sleep, the last to quench his thirst. If, finally, one comes across a spring, where the men, avid to cool off, repeatedly shove one another aside, he stands there, letting the lowliest varlet drink."

And when the troops arrived at an abundant spring, which the soldiers feared was contaminated by the snakes swarming in it, "he drew out that water, poisoned perhaps, and in all the sands of Libya that was the only spring from which he asked to drink first."[46]

The ancient accounts of Alexander's campaigns did not avoid what was clearly an exemplary monarchical motif and one of the most effective plot mechanisms. On several occasions the soldiers are starving to death and dying of thirst. For example, while crossing Gedrosia on their return from India, they are obliged to kill and eat the horses and other beasts of burden. Arrian devotes a long passage to the motif, insisting on the extraordinary suffering the soldiers endured: "Some were left behind along the roads on account of sickness, others from fatigue or the effects of the heat, or from not being able to bear up against the drought."[47] It is in this context that the author decides to interrupt the narration proper to report what he calls "the most noble deed perhaps ever performed by Alexander":

Alexander himself, though oppressed with thirst, was nevertheless with great pain and difficulty leading the army on foot, so that his soldiers also, as is usual in such a case, might more patiently bear their hardships by sharing the distress equally. At this time some of the light-armed soldiers, setting out away from the army in quest of water, found some collected in a shallow cleft, a small and mean spring. Collecting this water with difficulty, they came with all speed to Alexander, as if they were bringing him some great boon. As soon as they approached the king, they poured the water into a helmet and carried it to him. He took it, and commending the men who brought it, immediately poured it upon the ground in sight of all. As a result of this action, the entire army was re-invigorated to so great a degree that any one would have imagined that the water poured away by Alexander had furnished a drink to every man. This deed beyond all others I commend as evidence of Alexander's power of endurance and self-control, as well as of his skill in managing an army. (6.26.1–3)

As usual, Arrian leaves nothing unsaid, spelling out the lesson that any reader could have drawn on his own: he provides both the entry code and the instructions for use. The anecdote comes to illustrate one of the foremost qual-ities of the good leader: the king must be a leader of men, and to that end he is obliged to set an example in every circumstance.

At the beginning of his account, moreover, Arrian mentions versions that diverge from it, not so much in the content of the story as in the date and place. According to other authors, he says, the episode unfolded earlier, in northern India. Curtius places it during a desert crossing in Bactriana, on the march toward Oxus; Plutarch even a little earlier, in Parthia, during the pursuit of Darius, betrayed by his men; and Frontinus earlier still, in Africa, that is, in Egypt.[48] The context lends itself well to that setting, because dur-ing the march toward the oasis of Ammon, Alexander's soldiers also suffered cruelly from thirst and were saved by divine intervention.[49] Polyaenus, fi-nally, gives no geographical details.[50] As is their habit, the authors introduce the anecdote wherever it will shore up the narrative or even the argument. For Plutarch, it is cited during a long discussion intended to show that, de-spite his successes, Alexander remained a true leader, unlike some of his companions, who "were living in great luxury and extravagance." Alexan-der "risk[ed] his life in the vain endeavour to teach his friends to live with simplicity and hardihood."[51] The same topos is found in all the ancient au-thors, for example, in Curtius, who explains how the king's concern to share his soldiers' way of life and their ordeals had earned him their boundless af-fection and devotion.[52] It is easy to understand why the scene inspired paint-ers and engravers (Fig. 45).

The genre of the exemplum obviously does not rule out the possibility of identifying variants from one author to another. For Plutarch, Alexander asso-ciates with his horsemen, while Arrian has him dismount to more closely share

892-23-236

45. Alexander refuses to drink the water offered by his soldiers (J. Gamelin).

the suffering of his men on foot.[53] One or another author may add a personal embellishment, such as a familial context. In that way Curtius and Plutarch can increase the emotional charge of the narration and present an image of Alexander as a surrogate father: the soldiers who find water "take it to their sons, who they knew were in the same column as the king, and suffering a great deal from thirst." Alexander refuses the water, telling them: "Go quickly and give your sons what you have brought on their account."[54] But beyond these variations from one author to another, the script, the actors, the scene (a blazing desert without water), and the intermediate objects (the water and the helmet) are identical, and the monarchical moral is the same.

The Great King's Silver Vessels

At this point the reader of today is entitled to ask: Why return to an already-dissected monarchical motif—that of the leader of men—when, unlike other stories already presented, the anecdotes about the helmet and water do not explicitly bring in Darius or any other Great King by way of contrast? The answer is simple: in this case, the silence about Persian practices is deafening. In reality, Greek or Roman readers of the past (most likely) and present-day readers familiar with the ancient texts (certainly) would irresistibly establish obvious comparisons between the conduct attributed to Alexander and the well-known practices of the Achaemenid court.

In discussing Cyrus the Great's expedition against Babylon, Herodotus introduces into it a tradition of the Achaemenid court relating to the king's movements during military campaigns: "When the Persian king goes to war, he is always well provided not only with victuals from home [*ex oikou*] and his own cattle, but also with water from the Choaspes, a river which flows past Susa. No Persian king ever drinks the water of any other stream, and a supply of it ready boiled for use is brought along in silver jars carried in a long train of four-wheeled mule waggons wherever the king goes" (1.188).

After Herodotus, that rule was mentioned by many ancient authors, so striking did they find it for its singularity and ostentation. Athenaeus quotes Herodotus as well as Ctesias. "Ctesias of Cnidus also tells how this water for the king is boiled and how it is put into the vessels and transported for his use, adding that it is very light and pleasant."[55] The excellence of the water of the Choaspes was widely acknowledged: the river "reputedly carries fine drinking water," writes Curtius.[56] As for Strabo, he claims that this water was much lighter than all the other waters known.[57]

These technical comments are inserted into a discussion, broached many times in antiquity, on the medicinal and curative virtues of waters. A privileged collector of exempla and learned quotations, Athenaeus associates the Persian custom with a decision of Ptolemy II Philadelphus: "When, too, the second king of Egypt, surnamed Philadelphus, gave his daughter Berenice in marriage to Antiochus, king of Syria, he took care to send her Nile water, for he wanted his daughter to drink of this river only."[58] In fact, the water of the Nile was "very fertilizing and fresh."[59] Pliny also uses the example of the Choaspes in a long discussion on the respective value of different waters, showing that the Achaemenid custom was transmitted to the Parthian kings: "The Parthian kings drink only water from the Choaspes and the Eulaios. That water accompanies them, however far they may go. But it obviously does not please them by virtue of being river water, since they do not drink that of the Tigris or of the Euphrates or of so many other rivers."[60]

Contrary to what has long been postulated, these rules have nothing to do with some sort of alimentary taboo or with the prescriptions linked to the Great King's religious function. The texts just cited abundantly show that the first concern was to ensure the king permanent access to a water whose natural qualities were recognized by all. Herodotus and Ctesias further note that the water was first boiled. That preparation gave it an even greater gustatory value, because water that "heats and cools in a reasonable time, and when poured into a bronze or silver vessel does not tarnish it," is good to drink.[61] In addition, it was believed that the act of heating the water kept it cooler: "It was an invention of Emperor Nero to have water boiled and placed in glass flasks and frozen in the snow. One then had the pleasure of coolness without the disadvantages of snow. In any case, it was agreed that any boiled water was better, and also—a very subtle invention—that water became colder after being heated. Unsanitary water was made clean by boiling it down to half its volume."[62]

It is thus clearer why the Persians boiled the water intended to be consumed by the king and had it decanted into silver receptacles. They wanted thereby to offer the king a water that was at once pure, light, cool, and renowned for its healthful properties.

Such provisions protected not only the king's health but also his life: preserved and transported separately, royal water was safe from attempts to assassinate the king by poisoning him. The same was true of wine. According to Xenophon, the royal cup-bearers had to drink a few drops of the wine they were about to pour into the royal cup, "so that, if they had put poison in it, they drew no benefit from it."[63] According to Diodorus, Darius III was able to escape an attempted poisoning of his designated cup of wine.[64] There was in fact a punishment specially reserved for poisoners: "There is a broad stone, and on this the head of the culprit is placed; and then with another stone they smite and pound until they crush the face and head to pulp."[65] Were there also "water tasters"? No one knows.

There is reason to doubt the accuracy of the numbers mentioned by the ancient authors in their calculations of the respective weight of waters coming from various springs and rivers. But the interest displayed in their specific virtues is not surprising, nor is the importance that the court's services granted to the quality of the water the king would drink. In his *Voyage en Orient (Journey to the Orient)*, Gérard de Nerval, in Constantinople at the time, reported that water was imported there and that "a bizarre industry" existed, that of "vendors selling water by the unit and by the glass."[66] Waters and vintages were compared to one another: "Sold in these boutiques of sorts are waters from various countries and of different years. The water of the Nile is the most highly valued, since it is the only one the sultan drinks; it is a part of the tribute brought to him from Alexandria. That water is reputed to promote fertility. The water of the Euphrates, a little green, a little bitter to the taste, is recommended for weak and sluggish natures. The water of the Danube, laden with salts, pleases men of an energetic temperament. There are waters from several years. The Nile water of 1833 is highly appreciated, corked and sealed in bottles that sell for a high price." The similarities to ancient texts are altogether astounding, especially with respect to the water of the Nile, which, as it had been in Theophrastus's time (fourth century B.C.E.), was reputed to promote fertility. Nerval also reports that it was sent to the sultan as tribute. That immediately brings to mind the information Dinon collected, as transmitted by Plutarch: "Dinon also informs us that amongst other things the Kings of Persia had water brought from the Nile and the Danube, and laid up in their treasury, as a confirmation of the greatness of their empire, and to prove that they were lords of all the world."[67] In this case, the water is not consumed but is rather representative of the Great King's territorial ascendancy, symbolized by the rivers that mark the empire's limits.[68] But was that not also true for the sultans Nerval evokes? It is clear that, in both cases, the administration designated a certain water as being that of the king (or sultan).

It should also come as no surprise that the Officers of the Royal Table were assigned the task of keeping that water cooled and permanently available to the king, wherever he went and wherever he stayed throughout the year, in peace and in wartime. Austen Henry Layard mentions that, when Muhammad Ali conducted a campaign in Arabia, he regularly had water brought to him from the Nile. Nearly four millennia earlier, the kings of Mari had had snow and frost collected and stored in icehouses, and could thus chill and dilute their favorite drinks (wine, for example) during their travels and throughout the kingdom, or they could transport ice to their Mari palace.

Herodotus explains that, in the royal caravan, water itself is one element in a wealth of "victuals." In the description he gives of Xerxes's army, Herodotus describes the Immortals, whose "special food, separate from that of the rest of the army, was brought along for them on camels."[69] The same was certainly true of the Great King's own food: that is how Aelian and Seneca understood the matter.[70] And in an anecdote reported by Plutarch and Strabo, Darius the Great is saved by the camel transporting food reserved for the king.[71]

In general, the ancient authors insist a great deal on the wealth of the food preparation services that followed the king in all his travels, which is also indicated by the incomplete survey of the riches Darius III left behind in Damascus in 333. That wealth of the king's table had become proverbial: in Greek and Roman reflections, it was perceived and used as an outstanding mark of the power the king exercised over the territories and their products, and also as a fateful sign that he was going soft. The dual value of the term *tryphē* is also apparent here: it signifies both ostentatious luxury, which allows kings to indicate their superiority, and effeminate softness, which the Greeks denounce as a typically slave attitude, and which they contrast to "effort," which they call royal.[72] It is in that devalorizing sense that Strabo, among many others, understands luxury, in his excursus on the mores and customs of the Persians. He does not omit to include the famous custom of the king's water: "For their customs are in general temperate; but on account of their wealth the kings fell into such luxury [*tryphē*] that they sent for wheat from Assus in Aeolis, for Chalybonian wine from Syria, and for water from the Eulaios, which is by far the lightest of all waters" (15.3.22).

Plutarch also has a negative view of the custom.[73] Aelian, adopting an identical moralizing vision, judges that the provisions that followed the king, and especially the water of the Choaspes, "served almost exclusively to show his magnificence and luxury."[74] But in pointing out the ostentation of the royal caravan, the authors give one of the keys to interpreting the custom: it impresses the different populations. The reader of today can only imagine these many four-wheel carts, gleaming with the silver vessels that contained the king's water. These carts may have been decorated with tinkling bells, like Alexander's funeral chariot and the sixty-four mules that drew it.[75] This is a long way from the rustic Macedonian helmet that common soldiers used to offer a little water to Alexander, consumed by thirst in the middle of the desert.

The King Is Thirsty, the King Drinks!

Nonetheless, several vignettes also depict Great Kings in a situation of distress, if only for the needs of the authors of collections of exempla. And here again, more direct comparisons can be made to the story about Alexander. The question is always the same, but it is raised in terms specific to the Great Kings: How will a king accustomed to such plenty and luxury, reserved exclusively for him, react if for some reason he cannot have access to them? Seneca condemned Cambyses, who, under the worst conditions of hunger and thirst imposed on his soldiers, continued calmly to enjoy delicacies and the splendor of his precious serving dishes.[76] Another monarchical fable concerns Artaxerxes II:

> Against the Cadusians . . . he made an expedition in person, with three hundred thousand footmen and ten thousand horses. But the country which he penetrated was rough and hard to traverse, abounded in mists, and produced no grains, although its pears and apples and other such tree-fruits supported warlike and courageous populations. Unawares, therefore, he became involved in great distress and peril. For no food was to be got in the country or imported from outside, and they could only butcher their beasts of burden, so that an ass's head was scarcely to be bought for sixty drachmas. Moreover, the king's dinner was not served; and of their horses only a few were left, the rest having been consumed for food. (Plutarch, *Artaxerxes*, 24.2–3)

The phrase Plutarch uses—"the king's dinner was not served"—implies that royal meals had to be prepared by the rules, wherever the king happened to be. But unlike Cambyses, Artaxerxes does not persist in his luxury next to soldiers in abject poverty. On the contrary, he is praised for his qualities as a leader of men, which he demonstrates on the return marches:

> And the king now made it plain that cowardice and effeminacy are not always due to luxury and extravagance, as most people suppose, but to a base and ignoble nature under the sway of evil doctrines. For neither gold nor robe of state nor the twelve thousand talents' worth of adornment which always enveloped the person of the king prevented him from undergoing toils and hardships like an ordinary soldier; no, with his quiver girt upon him and his shield on his arm he marched in person at the head of his troops, over precipitous mountain roads, abandoning his horse, so that the rest of the army had wings given them and felt their burdens lightened when they saw his ardour and vigour; for he made daily marches of two stadia and more. (24.5–6)

Here Artaxerxes could easily be mistaken for Alexander. The virtues of the leader are lauded in the same words that appear in many anecdotes praising the

Macedonian. Like Alexander in Gedrosia, Artaxerxes abandoned his horse and
marched in the lead with the common soldiers.[77] The result is the same: the
king communicates his exemplary energy and enthusiasm to the troops. In this
case, Artaxerxes is presented as a countermodel to the traditional image of the
Persian king, brought down by the luxury of his table and bed, incapable of
leading his soldiers into battle.

Plutarch begins his address to Trajan, placed at the beginning of *Apothegms,*
with the memory of that same Artaxerxes: "O very great Emperor Caesar Trajan:
Artaxerxes, king of the Persians, deemed that it was no less royal and generous
to receive small presents with good grace than to make large ones oneself.
While he was traveling on horseback, a man of the people, an ordinary citizen
who had nothing else to offer him, presented him with the water he had taken
in his hands from the river. Artaxerxes accepted it with pleasure and smiled,
measuring the value of the gesture by the donor's zeal and not by the utility of
what was given" (*Apothegmata,* 172B). There was clearly a collection of monarchical fables built around Artaxerxes II.[78] The same vignette is recounted in
much greater detail by Aelian, who places it within the context of a mandatory
Persian custom: "The inhabitants of the places the king passed through on his
journeys offered him presents, each according to his ability. The plowmen, all
those who generally labored to cultivate the land, and the artisans offered him
nothing superb, nothing precious: one gave an ox, one a ewe, others wine. When
the king came through, everyone set out on the road what he had taken care to
bring. All that was called by the term 'present,' and the king received it under
that name. The poorest folk presented milk, cheese, dates, seasonal fruit, and
the first fruits of the other products of the region" (*Varia historia,* 1.31).

It is then that Aelian illustrates the custom with the story of the poor Persian Sinetes, "troubled by the sight of the king, both out of respect for his person and out of the fear inspired in him by the custom, which he was not in a
position to perform satisfactorily." "Having nothing at hand that he could offer
the sovereign, he saw with distress the advantage that the other Persians would
have over him, and he could not bear the shame of being the only one who had
not made a present to the king. Straightaway he made up his mind, ran as fast
as he could and with all his strength to the Cyrus River, which was flowing
nearby. He leaned over the edge and drew water from it in both hands" (1.32).

The king receives the gift with great benevolence and summons Sinetes to
the next relay point on the route, where the king is obliged to take a rest. To
honor the poor man even more, the king orders the eunuchs to "take Sinetes'

gift. They rushed up and received in a gold bowl [*phialē*] the water he was carrying in his hands." Later the king confers extraordinary gifts on Sinetes— "a Persian robe, a gold *phialē,* and a thousand darics"—accompanied by the following citation: "The king hopes this gold will give you as much pleasure as your attention gave him, in not failing to offer him your present, such, at least, as the circumstances allowed you. He wants you to drink the water from the Cyrus drawn with this very vessel."

Other stories of water portray the Great King in critical situations, as a result of having lost or become separated from his baggage train during an expedition or military march. One such story shows Artaxerxes after the Battle of Cunaxa, which had brought an end to the usurpation of his brother Cyrus the Younger:

> Since the king was almost dead with thirst, Satibarzanes the eunuch ran about in quest of a drink for him; for the place had no water, and the camp was far away. At last, then, he came upon one of those low Caunians, who had vile and polluted water in a wretched skin, about two quarts in all: this he took, brought it to the king, and gave it to him. After the king had drunk it all off, the eunuch asked him if he was not altogether disgusted with the drink. But the king swore by the gods that he had never drunk wine, or the lightest and purest water, with so much pleasure. "Therefore," said the king, "if I should be unable to find and reward the man who gave you this drink, I pray the gods to make him rich and happy." (Plutarch, *Artaxerxes,* 12.3–4)

After the battle, the Caunian is indeed found, and he is one of the beneficiaries of the distribution of royal gifts: the king "raised him from obscurity and poverty to honour and wealth."[79]

Finally, another of Aelian's anecdotes shows Xerxes in a similar situation. It begins with a negative judgment on the excessive luxury and ostentation of the Great King's provisions. The story that follows is supposed to illustrate the thesis: "Xerxes, finding himself tormented by thirst one day in a desert, where the supply services had as yet been unable to reach him, he had a herald proclaim throughout the camp that if anyone had water from the Choaspes, he ought to bring it to him, to give the king to drink. There was a man who had a small quantity of it, but it had gone bad. Xerxes drank some, and bestowed the title of benefactor on the one who had given it to him, because without that water he would have died of thirst" (12.40).[80]

The same schema can be found in all these anecdotes: the king is overcome with thirst, and an ordinary man (a soldier or peasant) offers him a few swallows of water, regularly called meager and bad. Nevertheless, compared to the parallel story of Alexander stricken by thirst, or of Artaxerxes unable to have his usual "king's dinner" during his Cadusian campaign, the tone of the "Persian" vignettes is completely different, and their social and ideological significance equally so.

In the first place, even when the author (Aelian) asserts that the king (Xerxes) is in a place called a "desert," he does not mean that the king is lost with a few companions in a landscape of sand assaulted by the sun, several days' march from any resupply point. In the context in which it is used, the term *ērēmos* (too complacently translated as "desert") must not lead to confusion. It simply means that there is no spring or well or running water in the immediate vicinity. In no case does the king find himself in an urgent situation that could place his life in danger. The reason for his thirst is infinitely more circumstantial and fleeting: the king temporarily finds himself away from the silver vessels that follow him everywhere, either because his march has taken him farther ahead (Xerxes) or because the supply services cannot send the chariots all the way to the battlefield (Artaxerxes at Cunaxa), or because he is peacefully riding on a route between two "royal relay stations" where the supply services have meticulously prepared the royal table (Artaxerxes II in Persia). The personal aspect, so weighty in the story of Alexander and his soldiers, is thus completely absent from these Persian apologues.

Gift and Obligation

These stories, lacking in dramatic tension, are equally lacking in the emotional charge that runs through the story of Alexander dying of thirst but refusing to drink the water offered. Here, in fact, the context in which the soldiers' gesture is recounted is so theatricalized that it authenticates the depth of their affection for the king. And if, in Curtius's and Plutarch's versions, fathers are ready to sacrifice their sons' survival, it is obviously because the relationship they have with Alexander is not merely based on subjection to a king but is also cemented by exchanges of affection. In principle, there is also no calculation on the soldiers' or on Alexander's part, even though Arrian, an attentive observer of military matters, does not fail to note that the episode also conveys the Macedonian king's extraordinary aptitude for commanding.

By contrast, there is no trace of affection in the Persian stories. No spontaneity or generosity between one man and another is expressed by the soldiers
and peasants coming to offer water to their king. Rather, the "donors" respond
to a summons, an order, or a regulation. At Cunaxa it is not the soldiers who go
to Artaxerxes; rather, the relationship is mediated by the eunuch Satibarzanes,
an intimate of the king who takes the initiative, making inquiries among the
soldiers. He is the one who brings to the king the flask he "borrowed" from a
poor soldier of Caunos.[81] There is reason to doubt that the soldier had any choice,
and it is certain that he was not invited to come to the king in person! In the
vignette about Xerxes, the situation is equally clear: the herald issues a proclamation in the camp, inviting (or commanding?) those who might have water
available to give it to the thirsty king.[82]

Even more explicit is the story of the peasant Sinetes offering Artaxerxes a
few drops from the nearby river, cupped in his hands. Aelian himself makes it
an exemplary illustration of a "Persian law" (nomos persikos), whose substance
he has just recalled. That Persian custom is in fact a royal regulation, which
obliges every person living on the king's route to set out an offering by the side
of the road.[83] Aelian's terminology (everyone contributes, based on his ability
to pay) is frequently used in a fiscal context. These are not taxes in the strict
sense: they are gifts, but the interesting explanation the author gives eliminates
any notion of spontaneity. "All that was called by the term 'present,' and the
king received it under that name." There is no better way to say that the gifts are
listed in the empire's ledgers, alongside taxes and fees. The benefit takes on an
equally obligatory character, as indicated concretely by the poor peasant's panic.
The narrative reports the competition between neighbors to offer the "gift most
likely to please the king"; but it illustrates even more Sinetes's frantic anxiety
about being unable to satisfy the nomos. The theoretical difference is that a tax
is set by the administration, whereas it falls to each individual to estimate the
value of the gift. But it is doubtful that any more freedom reigns in the second
case than in the first. Furthermore, the simple peasants of Persia are not the
only ones obliged to pay benefits when the king passes by. The cities are also
compelled, "in proportion to their population," to supply the king's and the satrap's tables.[84]

The donors are rewarded by the king and are generally granted the rank of
benefactor. But however prestigious such a title might be, it has no real value
unless the party in question is part of the court hierarchy, which is certainly not
the case for a destitute peasant from Persia or an obscure soldier from the

ranks. When Plutarch writes that the Caunian soldier was elevated to "honour and wealth," that expression does not mean he was admitted to the highest rank in the imperial hierarchy. His honor and wealth have meaning only in relation to the condition of his former companions in misfortune. There is no doubt that he is now differentiated from the other poor Caunian soldiers in the army, nothing more. In addition, it must never be forgotten that every royal gift, including the bestowal of a distinguished title, is precarious: if one is to hold onto it, complete and definitive loyalty to the king is required. The exchange is therefore structurally unequal: it further increases the dependence of a donor, who in the meantime has been transformed into a donee simply because the king decided to reward him. The same is true for the exemplary ending of Sinetes's story: the water retroceded to him does not, in the strict sense, become his. On the king's order, the eunuchs "received in a gold bowl [*phialē*] the water he was carrying in his hands." Then the king lets him know his mandatory wish: "He wants you to drink the water from the Cyrus drawn with this very vessel," as if the water could be kept only in a vessel made of precious metal, as "royal water." The powerful emotion that an admirer of Alexander could have extracted from such a situation can only be imagined. If the king had decided to drink, he surely would have collected the water thus offered in his own hands and immediately brought it to his mouth.

For the King's Pleasure

The exempla provide material for the well-known genre of the monarchical fable, given that, at least in certain aspects, they are similar to a well-represented series of encounters between kings and ordinary subjects in the countryside. The apologue about a king received incognito in the tumbledown cottage of a peasant, with whom he shares his simple pottage, continued to enjoy enormous success throughout the monarchical literature. In one of Plutarch's apothegms, Antiochus, during a hunting party, "became separated from his friends and servants"; he shared incognito "the meal of poor people in a cabin," who spoke freely with him. When his intimates arrive early the next morning, he boasts that he had "heard words of truth about [himself] for the first time."[85] Here again is a specific illustration of the theme of good advisers and flatterers, so frequently elaborated within the framework of royal councils. Guillaume Budé found the anecdote sufficiently noteworthy and illustrative to include it in his *Institution of the Prince* (58v–604), among the exempla demonstrating the ways and means of good kingship. It is also cited in the late sixteenth century in the writings of Camerarius, who had collected many exempla on wise princes: "Their adventures always began with a long hunt, during which the prince, separated from his companions, became lost and sought refuge during the night in a peasant's cabin, where he was not recognized. Pursuing his advantage, the unrecognized prince questioned his hosts about the events of the time."[86]

The same narrative cliché was also skillfully introduced into Nizāmī's *Seven Wise Princesses*. Dissatisfied with his vizier's methods of government, King Bahram Gūr seeks the distraction of a hunt. Having gone off alone and without provisions, he is soon tormented by thirst: "And he scampered about the land so much that thirst overcame his brain, and he scampered around the land so much, so as to catch sight of some freshwater port: the more he sought, the less he found." He reaches the shack of an old shepherd, who offers him "meat and drink," apologizing for his poverty. The shepherd tells the horseman a story about his dog, which, entirely in the grip of his desire for a she-wolf, betrayed the trust of his master, and as "payment for services rendered," let the she-wolf devour the ewes. The king immediately sees this as an image of his vizier (the dog) and his people (the ewes). Returning to the palace after eating a little bread and drinking a little water, he rejoices that "from that old shepherd lad, I learned kingship."[87]

Also in Iran, several of Saadi's apothegms and apologues are expressly set within that context, particularly in the first chapter of *Bustan,* devoted to the theme "On the Duties of Kings." Inevitably the apologue that depicts "the illustrious king" Dārā is introduced with the formulation: "It is said that the king, while out hunting, became separated from his escort." That gives the king a way to escape the isolation of his closed circle of ministers and courtiers and to enter into contact with the simple people. The king gratefully accepts the lesson of "good kingship" he receives from his humble subjects. In fact, the king must prefer, to the advice of a flatterer or the lessons of philosophers, the advice given by "a simple man who expresses himself sincerely about his shortcomings. . . . Everything is to be feared for the security of a kingdom whose leader has less sagacity than the lowliest of his subjects."[88]

As J. Dakhlia has pointed out, this fable is frequently found in the monarchical literature of Islamic countries: "It is always during an encounter outside the palace walls that the unjust prince, neglectful of his duties, converses with one of his subjects, opens his eyes to his errors, and adopts the path of wisdom," either after a "fortuitous encounter" or "an initiative on the sultan's part." In one frequently repeated anecdote, Antiochus is the hero in Plutarch's version, Bahram Gūr in Nizāmī's: "The sultan accidentally becomes separated from his escort—during a hunt, for example—and finds himself in a position of weakness, hungry, without shelter. This is a complete inversion of the classical dialogue of the petition. He has been stripped of any sign that would indicate he is the sovereign. Absolutely incognito, therefore, he accepts the hospitality of one of his subjects and hears from his mouth a declaration of allegiance or even love. When the ruler's anonymity is stripped away, this declaration is rewarded. Praise of the sovereign's fairness thus also requires a scene of fortuitous truth-telling."[89]

Among the constitutive traits of this story is the hungry and thirsty king's discovery of simple dishes. The king is amazed to have taken pleasure in sampling food that is perfectly alien to his everyday diet. Hence the comment regularly attributed to him: King Artaxerxes "swore by the gods that he had never drunk wine, or the lightest and purest water, with so much pleasure."[90] The same king has to be satisfied with "dried figs and barley bread" upon his return from his Cadusian campaign, "a rout, during which his baggage train had been plundered." Plutarch has him say, clearly in an amused tone, "What pleasure, I had no idea!"[91] This is oddly reminiscent of the reply Cicero attributes to Ptolemy in somewhat similar circumstances: "During a ramble in Egypt, he was not joined by his escort, and in a cabin he was given coarse bread: he found that bread to be a real feast."[92]

These monarchical fables have multiple meanings. They celebrate the good king, who readily accepts the lesson from a mere peasant endowed with common sense; but they also transform mere subjects into admiring agents of the king's pleasure. There is no better way to mark the insuperable boundary that distinguishes the king from an ordinary subject: the encounter between the two only further underscores its inviolability. Kings, at once inflexible despots and spoiled, overgrown children, amuse themselves in a situation that they control from start to finish and that there is no reason to reproduce ever again, except by their own will or on a whim.

The case of Persian kings who receive a little water from common soldiers displays characteristics proper to it. None of the kings thus depicted is welcomed incognito; on the contrary, the king appears in the story ex officio. Furthermore, he never refuses to drink on the pretext that other persons in his entourage might be more thirsty than he. On the battlefield, Artaxerxes drinks all the water offered him, without asking any questions. In essence the kings satisfy their thirst, their desire, and their pleasure. Only one of them (Artaxerxes) gives the water back to the donor (Sinetes). As it happens, however, the gift of water on that occasion is not intended to quench the king's thirst: the apparent simplicity of his conduct is only on the surface of things and words. Alexander is praised for having agreed to bear the hardships of his men on equal footing, and Artaxerxes is shown "undergoing toils and hardships like an ordinary soldier" during the Cadusian campaign.[93] By contrast, when a Persian king shares food with an ordinary subject, no notion of equality is introduced, not even fleetingly, no sense that the two might share the same human condition. The relationship revealed on these occasions between the king and the simple people (soldiers in the ranks, poor peasants) instead belongs to the context of domination and subjection.

The King and the Philosopher

Vignettes and apothegms provided the material for philosophical discussions on power and were at the same time inspired by them. One of the questions under debate was whether the Great King's luxurious lifestyle was enviable. Polyarkhos, whom Aristoxenus quotes in his *Life of Archytas,* believed it an admirable proof of power that the Great Kings were able to order the most delicious dishes on every occasion, brought to them from all over the world.[94] The teachings of Diogenes the Cynic, as Dio Chrysostom presents them in his Sixth Discourse, were completely different. He railed against the habits of senseless luxury among the Persian kings. Not without irony, he asserted that, like the Great King, who went from one capital to another depending on the season, he himself was in the habit of dividing his time between Corinth and Athens. Diogenes maintained that the philosopher enjoyed incomparably superior satisfactions, because the Great King had to travel enormous distances and therefore spent most of the winter and summer on the road. In saying this, "he meant to bring to the attention of those who admired the wealth of the Persian and his reputed happiness that there was nothing in his actual life such as they imagined. For some things were of no use at all and other things were within the reach of even the very poor" (§§ 1–7).

The opposition between the king and the philosopher coincides with the opposition between custom and nature. A free man ought to follow the rhythm of the seasons and not move about during the course of the year, fleeing the heat and the cold, as Persian royal custom dictated. Those who have superfluous wealth cannot really benefit from it: they do not even find pleasure in making love, because they do not wait for their natural desire. The free man must not eat or drink too much, and even more, he must eat and drink only when hunger and thirst make their appearance. Diogenes thus contrasts his regime to that of those who, like the Great King, "never experience a natural thirst [*kata physin*]." The philosopher felt that "hunger was the most satisfactory and pungent of appetizers . . . and enjoyed a drink from a stream of running water more than others did their Thasian wine" (§§ 11–12).

Cicero's critical commentary is directly linked to the "Cynical" current. He in fact mentions Diogenes on several occasions in the *Tusculan Disputations*. There he introduces a Ptolemy "who never waited to be hungry before eating," but also a Darius "who apparently never waited to be thirsty to drink."[95] The function of the royal apothegms he reports is to illustrate a reflection close to that which Dio Chrysostom attributes to Diogenes: "Is it not clear that appetite accentuates the flavor of all foods?" Furthermore, like Chrysostom, Cicero was familiar with the comparison that Diogenes liked to establish between his condition and that of the Persian king: "He maintained that he wanted for nothing, whereas his rival could never get enough; for the pleasures that could never have sated his rival, he himself felt no need."[96] In his barrel, does not Diogenes demand that Alexander not take from him a possession that nature dispenses to all: the light and heat of the sun?[97]

Oddly enough, Dio Chrysostom does not mention the Great King's silver vessels, even though the discursive context would have lent itself perfectly to doing so. That is probably because he was appropriating almost word for word Xenophon's discourse in *Agesilaus,* where the Spartan king's regime is contrasted in every respect to that of the Great King, including his mastery of hunger and thirst.[98] And Xenophon makes no allusion to the Great King's silver vessels. The critical tone of his remarks is nonetheless scathing: "As for the Persian, people roam the whole land in search of what he might drink with pleasure, and thousands of others concern themselves with what will pique his appetite." Many authors and philosophers of antiquity borrowed that image. Athenaeus cites, in addition to Xenophon, Theophrastus, Theopompus, and Clearchus of Soli.[99]

According to a discursive logic that since antiquity has continually pervaded the historiography of the Eastern empires, kings seal their fate by indulging without restraint in banquets and drinking sessions. For example, Justin establishes an opposition between Philip, who was "more inclined to frugality" and "laid the foundations of the empire of the world," and Alexander, guilty of intemperance, who "consummated the glory of conquering the whole world."[100]

It is therefore easy to understand why, within an entire ancient philosophical current, the fall of the Persian monarchy is inserted into a general discourse on the Great Kings' royal luxury, illustrated by the example of the last of those kings. Strabo denounces the depths of insolent luxury into which the Great Kings had fallen: they demanded the wheat of Assos of Aeolides to eat; and, to drink, the wine of Syria and the water drawn from the Eulaios River in Susa.[101] Alexander, by contrast, is reputed not to be interested in luxury and good food, "the golden burden of ten thousand camels . . . the possession of the Median women or glorious ornaments of Persian luxury . . . Chalybonian wine or the fish of Hyrcania."[102] The philosopher Clearchus of Soli, in his treatise *Peri biōn (Lives)*, in which he discusses what he considers the overabundance of the royal table, writes of "the Darius who was conquered by Alexander": "The Persian king gave prizes to those who catered to his pleasures, but brought his kingdom to defeat through all these indulgences, and did not perceive that he was defeating himself until others had seized his sceptre and were proclaimed rulers."[103] A fitting epilogue to a luxury and abundance that were an insult to nature.

Polystratus's Helmet

At least in the excerpt Athenaeus provides, Clearchus does not mention the real end of Darius, which, rather curiously, is connected to several stories of thirst and water, in the combined form of an apologue and an epilogue. In the same passage from the *Tusculan Disputations* in which he holds forth on the notion and reality of desire among the Epicureans, Cicero introduces several historical figures confronted by the need for food and drink. Ptolemy, separated from his supply services, says he was charmed to have "tasted coarse bread in a shack." At this point another king makes an appearance, and Cicero transmits this apothegm about him: "In his flight, Darius drank muddy water [*aqua turbida*] fouled by corpses: he declared that he had never found a more pleasant drink. Apparently, he never waited to be thirsty to drink."[104]

The king's retort is so similar to the one Plutarch attributes to Artaxerxes II upon quenching his thirst on the battlefield at Cunaxa that one may wonder whether Cicero had not simply confused the two kings.[105] That is possible: users of collections of exempla (and Cicero was one) were primarily concerned with illustrating a moral notion or attitude and therefore bothered little with scholarly verification, which in any case would not have altered their certainty. It is also very possible that an author of a collection had previously attached to Darius a remark that others attributed to Artaxerxes. For the army's flight from the battlefield of Gaugamela occurred under extremely difficult conditions, which Curtius reports in a scene of high drama: "Thirst parched the throats of the tired and wounded especially, and throughout the countryside they threw themselves down at all the streams, trying to gulp the flowing water with open mouths. The water became muddy [*aqua turbida*] and they swallowed it greedily, so that their stomachs quickly became distended under the weight of the mud. . . . No pool was too remote or dried up to escape the thirsty Persians" (4.16.12–13).

For an author of the Roman period, the expression "in flight" could designate only Darius III. A comparison of the texts and expressions shows that Cicero places the words attributed to Darius within the context of his flight from the battlefield of Gaugamela, at a time when Darius had not yet reached the depths of despair but was still king.[106]

A few months later the Great King's final moments are marked by another story of thirst and water, this one infinitely more tragic. The stage can be set in a few words. Darius, having left Ecbatana shortly before Alexander's arrival, took the eastern route via Rhagai and the Caspian Gates and advanced by crossing Parthian country toward the future Hecatompylos (Shahr-e Qumis). Betrayed by his intimates, he is soon stabbed by the conspirators, who abandon him as he loses blood and who also "maimed his animals to prevent them advancing any further." Thus the beasts, left on their own, "had left the main road."[107]

The setting is a very rough region in Parthyene—especially rough in midsummer (July)—as also attested by Alexander's forced marches in pursuit of the Great King: "In the forced march which he made, many of his soldiers were left behind, worn out with fatigue, and many of the horses died." Then, when he learns that Darius's camp is nearby, on the other side of the Caspian Gates, he goes even faster, leading a small elite troop, with "nothing but their arms and provisions for two days." The speed becomes almost unbearable: Alexander takes a shortcut "that ran through a country which was desert through lack of water."[108] The difficulty of the route is also noted by Polybius, reporting an expedition conducted on that same road by the Seleucid king Antiochus III against the Parthian king Arsakes: "Arsakes had expected Antiochus to reach that land but did not anticipate that he would dare cross the nearby desert with such a large army, primarily because of the lack of water. There is no surface ground water visible in the region, but there are numerous underground canals, with wells connected to them and distributed throughout the desert, which were not known to those unfamiliar with the country" (10.28.1–2).

Polybius is referring to what are now called the *qanats*, subterranean canals that collect water from the aquifer strata they pass through. They then carry it far away, to the place where a village will be established.[109] In other words, in leaving the "main road," the last royal convoy had cut off its resources of easily accessible water.

To resume Curtius's narrative: "Since they lacked a driver, the animals pulling Darius had left the main road and after wandering around for four stades had come to a stop in a certain valley, exhausted as much by the heat as by their wounds. There was a spring close by. This had been pointed out to the Macedonian Polystratus by people who knew the area, and he now came to it because he was tormented with thirst. While he drank the water from his helmet, he caught sight of the spears stuck in the bodies of the dying animals and, surprised at their being wounded rather than driven off [he was shocked by the cries] of a man only half alive" (5.13.23–25).

Unfortunately, a lacuna in the manuscript prevents us from knowing what follows. We must turn to other authors, all of whom knew one or several versions of Darius's death. Arrian is absolutely silent.[110] But the other Vulgate authors do not fail to provide a narrative of the last Great King's death that aspires to be highly moving. The thirsty soldier is regularly present and will play the part of an intermediary between Darius and Alexander (Fig. 46). Justin does not give him a name: "One of the soldiers, going to a neighbouring spring, found Darius in the vehicle, wounded in several places, but still alive."[111] In Plutarch, the man is called Polystratus. He is one of the soldiers in Alexander's army who is given the task of finding Darius's cart: "At last he was found, lying in his chariot, pierced with innumerable javelins, and just breathing his last. He was able to ask for drink, and when given some cold water by Polystratus, he said to him, 'My good sir, this is the worst of all my misfortunes that I am unable to recompense you for your kindness to me; but Alexander will reward you, and the gods will reward Alexander for his courteous treatment of my mother and wife and daughters'" (*Alexander*, 43.3–4).

In reading Curtius's account alongside Plutarch's, one cannot help but notice that, like Alexander's soldiers in the desert, the soldier holds out his hel-

46. *A thirsty Darius aided by a soldier. Etching by Bernhardt Rode, 1774 © National Gallery of Art, Washington, D.C. 2001.51.1.*

met, filled with water from the fountain. Indeed, it is Plutarch himself who suggests the connection, to increase the drama of the narrative. He inserts the story of Alexander aided by his soldiers in the middle of the account of the pursuit of Darius: "He now set out on a long and toilsome journey in pursuit of Darius, for in eleven days he rode more than thirty-three hundred stadia, so that his men were terribly distressed, especially by want of water. One day he met some Macedonians who were carrying water from a river in skins on the backs of mules. Seeing Alexander faint with thirst, as it was the hottest time of the day, they quickly filled a helmet with water and gave it to him to drink" (42.6–10).

Because the Vulgate authors also juxtapose the Great King's death scene with the infernal pursuit conducted by Alexander, the reader cannot fail to establish the narrative link between the two scenes. Whereas Alexander, in full glory and in full possession of his faculties, intentionally chooses a route lacking fresh supplies of water in order to accelerate his pursuit, and whereas he refuses the water his soldiers offer him in a helmet, the Great King, vanquished, betrayed, stabbed, and consumed by thirst, drinks the water that Alexander's soldier has just drawn into his own helmet.

The End of Empire and the Philosophy Lesson

So goes the last water story concerning a Great King. Unlike Alexander, none of these kings is reputed to have refused the water offered by a soldier or an ordinary subject. But how many differences as well separate the last Darius from his glorious namesake! When his army was about to perish from thirst during a campaign in central Asia, Darius the Great, unlike Cambyses, did not seek merely to safeguard his own well-being by drawing on the provisions set aside for him.[112] He performed his duties as king and interceded with the gods to save his army as a whole: "At sunrise, he climbed a very high mountain and placed his royal robes and tiara on his scepter, which was itself stuck into the ground. He prayed to the god Apollo to send them water from heaven, if it was the fate of the Persians to be saved. The god heard him and a great rainstorm fell."[113]

How many differences as well separate the story of Darius III's last moments from the apologues that depict Xerxes and Artaxerxes, but also from the tale Cicero reports in which Darius, pursued by Alexander after the defeat of Gaugamela, drinks a little water to quench his thirst and jokes about the quality of the potion, collected from a stream polluted by corpses.[114] On the brink of death, there is no longer any point to expressing amazement with a witty remark about the water, which Polystratus offers him when the king is devoured by a raging thirst, caused by the heat and the mortal stab wounds.

This scenario resembles the death scene of Nero, though the images of the two royal personages, separated by a few centuries, are very different. Forced to roam the countryside, "through copses and brush on a path planted with reeds . . . and to draw water from a pond into the hollow of his hand . . . he drank it, saying: 'Here, then, are the refreshments of a Nero.'"[115] There is no amused tone to this comment, only a great deal of lucid despair. Reputed to have introduced in Rome the technique of cooling water by plunging flasks of boiled water into the snow,[116] Nero makes it clear that his time of power and splendor is passing away. Like the poor Persian peasant Sinetes, he does not even possess a receptacle—not even a clay one—with which to draw water from the river. Nero's destitute condition in turn recalls that of Pompey fleeing the battlefield of Pharsalus, near where he had had to abandon a camp abundantly supplied with every comfort and with all the luxuries of the table: "Being thirsty, he threw himself face down on the ground to drink water from the river."[117]

The image of the defeated and fleeing king or general, dispossessed of any vessel from which to drink, forced to drink directly from the pond or river to quench a consuming thirst, or to draw a few drops into his hands, is without a doubt a powerfully evocative representation of a brutal change of fortune, itself marked by the sudden disappearance of a gleaming but passing royal splendor. That image stands in contrast to that of a king "who had never waited to be thirsty to drink," and in whose court a courtier in disfavor was made to drink from clay cups.[118] That representation also marks the moral victory of the philosopher, who by his own choice, without being compelled, declares that he prefers to quench his thirst with a mere trickle of running water rather than drink the best of wines.

Darius's last thirst and his last swallow symbolize a great deal more than they seem to do. Even in the irenic image imposed after the fact, that of a harmonious succession from conquered to conqueror, this is truly a scene marking the end of an empire. Rendered laughable by Aelian, who imagines the Great King's dog watching over his dying master, all alone, the scene is made even more dramatic by the destitution of a despot who until that time had been provided with everything, even superfluity.[119]

"Asiatic luxury" is a distant dream, especially the silver vessels filled with the water of the Choaspes, which in the eyes of the Greek authors were its most striking symbol. Alexander's soldiers, scouring the Persian camp in search of the Great King, "passed over great heaps of gold and silver, and pursued a long line of waggons, full of women and children, which were proceeding along without any driver."[120] The baggage and baggage train, everything "the Great King was in the habit of taking with him . . . even though he was going on a military expedition," are now nothing but abandoned wrecks, and the silver vessel has turned into an iron helmet.

❦[9]❦

The Great King's Private
and Public Lives

The Persian Princesses in Alexander's Hands

The luxurious table maintained in the midst of military campaigns, singled out by the proponents of moralizing history, is not the only sign of the Great King's incapacity to show a manly courage against an adversary such as Alexander. The custom of dragging along troops of eunuchs and women, including royal princesses, is also considered antithetical to a war of movement free from all encumbrances. From Issus to Gaugamela, these women occupy a place of choice in the narratives, so much so that their figures and silhouettes will contribute toward sustaining the image of a Great King who is both there and not there, and of a man prey to every vice.

The different strands of the plot come together on the evening of the battle. To recall briefly the setting, the actors, and the lines in this drama: While marching toward Cilicia, Darius had sent back to Damascus his treasure and his baggage train, which included many noblewomen from the great Persian families. Only the closest members of his family accompanied him to the end: his mother, Sisygambis; his wife, Stateira; his two nubile daughters, Stateira and Drypetis; and his very young son, Ochus.

From that moment on, the ancient authors concentrate on a few women and a young boy, whom Curtius portrays in a style that suggests a group captured in stone by a sculptor's chisel, or on canvas by a painter's brush (Fig. 47):

> It was Darius' mother and his wife, now prisoners, who had attracted to themselves everybody's gaze and attention. His mother commanded re-

IL EST D'UN ROY DE SE VAINCRE SOY MEME.
Alexandre ayant vaincu Darius pres d'Isse, entre
dans une tente ou étoient la mere, la femme, et les
filles de Darius, ou il donne un exemple singulier
de retenüe et de clemence.

SUI VICTORIA INDICAT REGEM.
Alexander Dario ad Isum victo tabernaculum
Reginarum ingreditur ubi singulare clementiæ ac
continentiæ præbet exemplum.

47. The Queens of Persia at the Feet of Alexander, *anonymous painting after Charles Le Brun.*

spect for her age as well as for her royal dignity, his wife for a beauty that even her current misfortune had not marred. The latter had taken to her bosom her young son, who had not yet turned six, a boy born into the expectation of the great fortune his father had just lost. In the lap of their aged grandmother lay Darius' two grown-up but unmarried daughters, grieving for their grandmother as well as themselves. Around her stood a large number of high-born women, their hair torn, their clothes rent and their former gracefulness forgotten. They called upon their "queens" and "mistresses," titles formerly appropriate but no longer applicable. (3.11.24–25)

After the Persians were routed, the Macedonian troops plundered their camp. Everything was taken, brutally ripped away: gold and silver objects, and sumptuous clothes, including the rich accoutrements that everywhere accompanied the women of the royal house, their suite, and their domestic staff. Their tents were sacked and their bodies stripped bare: "Not even their persons were spared the violence of lust . . . the cruelty and licence of the victor swept through the prisoners irrespective of rank or age."[1]

Curtius is particularly fond of that type of description of the captive noble-women. He returns to them again a short time later, when he takes his readers to Damascus, where Darius had sent his baggage train before the battle:

> The royal treasure was now littered throughout the plains. . . . The loot-ers did not have enough hands to carry off their booty. Now they reached those who had been the first to flee. Several women were dragging their little children along with them as they went, and among these were the three unmarried daughters of Ochus, who had been king before Darius.[2] Once before a revolution had brought them down from the lofty station their father enjoyed, but now fortune was more cruelly aggravated by their plight. The same group contained the wife of Ochus, the daughter of Darius' brother, Oxathres, and the wife of Artabazus, Darius' chief court-ier, as well as Artabazus' son, whose name was Itioneus. The wife and son of Pharnabazus (the man whom Darius had given supreme command over the coastal area) were also taken, as were the three daughters of Mentor, and the wife and son of the renowned general Memnon. Scarcely any courtier's household was unaffected by the catastrophe. (3.13.10–14)

During the looting of Darius's camp, only the sumptuous royal tent was spared, "it being their tradition to welcome the conquerors in the tent of the conquered king."[3] Upon his return from his fruitless pursuit, the Macedonian king was ushered into that tent. He performed his ablutions in the luxurious bath reserved for the Great King, then went to the dining hall, where the king's dinner awaited him.[4] During the dinner, the sound of women's sobs and moans could be heard: "Suddenly the diners were alarmed by the sound of lamenta-tion, punctuated by typically barbarian shrieking and howling."[5] Here, the ad-jective "barbarian" is quasi-technical: it refers to the particular vocal mode by which the Persian women, convinced that Darius was dead, expressed their sorrow. Alexander, having been informed of the situation, sent a message to the princesses via Leonatus, reassuring them about Darius's fate and promising to visit them the next morning, which he did. It is there that the best-known scene is set, during which Darius's mother throws herself at the feet of Hepha-estion, mistaking him for the king because of his imposing physical presence. She is soon disabused and bows to Alexander, who immediately displays the utmost respect for her: "He decked her with her royal jewelry and restored her to her previous dignity, with its proper honours. He made over to her all her former retinue of servants which she had been given by Dareius and added more in addition not less in number than the preceding. He promised to provide for the marriage of the daughters even more generously than Dareius had promised and to bring up the boy as his own and to show him royal honour" (Diodorus 17.38.1).

The filial relationship between Alexander and Sisygambis is a recurrent theme until the king's death itself: "One might have thought that Darius was recently lost and that at the same time the poor woman had to bury two sons. . . . [She] withdrew simultaneously from nourishment and the daylight. Five days after deciding on death, she expired" (Curtius 10.5.21).

In his characteristically heavy-handed and bombastic style, Curtius does not fail to improve on the Alexander panegyric, establishing an unambiguous connection to the measures the king had taken in the wake of Issus: "Her end provides firm evidence for Alexander's gentle treatment of her and his fairness towards all the captives: though she could bear to live on after Darius, she was ashamed to survive Alexander" (10.5.25).

Arrian indicates that the story of Alexander and Hephaestion's visit to the tent of the Persian princesses was not communicated to him by his privileged informants—Ptolemy and Aristobulus—but he does not reject it all the same. As he explains, "this I record neither being sure of its truth nor thinking it altogether unreliable. If it really occurred, I commend Alexander for his compassionate treatment of the women, and the confidence he felt in his companion, and the honour bestowed on him; but if it merely seems probable to historians that Alexander would have acted and spoken thus, even for this reason I think him worthy of commendation" (2.12.8).

Arrian returns to the visit later, establishing a parallel with the encounter between Alexander and Roxana, another "fine story." That beautiful young woman, daughter of the Sogdian noble Oxyarthes, made a deep impression on the Macedonian king, and he decided to marry her.[6] The reasons for Arrian's comparisons are easy to understand. Like the Persian princesses, Oxyarthes's wife and daughters—one of whom (Roxana) was of marrying age—were taken prisoner during the fall of their husband and father's fortress. Arrian draws the moral of the story: Alexander "acted with modesty . . . at the same time exhibiting a very proper desire to obtain a good reputation."

The episode thus reconstructed provided further support for the well-worn theme of Alexander's sexual continence and restraint. Plutarch gives many examples in succession, and Arrian returns to the question in his funeral oration: "With regard to bodily pleasures, he enjoyed perfect self-control; where pleasures of the mind were concerned, he was insatiable only for men's praise."[7] Plutarch is fond of contrasting the king's virtue to the vices of his intimates and successors, with "their continual herding among impudent and lawless women, like stallions released among mares."[8] Alexander, the enemy of luxury in all its forms, proponent of physical effort and frugality, haughtily repels the indecent proposals of his courtiers and orders that "two Macedonians of Parmenio's regiment . . . [who] had violently outraged the wives of some of the mercenary soldiers" be put to death "like mere brute beasts that prey upon mankind."[9] Diodorus celebrates his "consideration and generosity," his "exceeding propriety of conduct," and judges that "of many good deeds [*kala erga*] done by Alexander there is none that is greater or more worthy of record and mention in history than this."[10] Plutarch speaks of "kindness" and "honour," and exalts the king's "self-restraint." Alexander, he says, was determined that his self-control "should be as much admired as their beauty, and passed by them as if they had been images cut out of stone."[11] As for Stateira, "he spared her honour, exercising a great amount of chastity."[12]

Such is the conclusion that all the ancient authors reiterate, anxious as they are to absolve Alexander of the faults and vices of which he was frequently accused in antiquity, as Curtius reports. That author foreshadows the corruptive effects of the victory and regrets that Alexander was unable to preserve to the end "this degree of moderation," his "self-restraint and abstinence," "self-control and clemency."[13] Curtius also emphasizes Alexander's kindness in such circumstances to the high-born women who had followed Darius to the end and who surrendered after the Great King's death. In fact, the Latin author remarks, "there yet lingered in the king's heart slight traces of his former qualities." At a banquet where women captives were supposed to entertain the guests by singing, Alexander perceived a young woman whose bearing betrayed her noble origin: "She was asked who she was, and answered that she was the granddaughter of Ochus [Artaxerxes III], the former king of Persia, being the daughter of his son; and that she had been the wife of Hystaspes (who had been related to Darius and who had himself commanded a powerful army). . . . He felt respect for a woman of royal stock who had suffered a reversal of fortune and for so eminent a name as that of Ochus. He not only ordered the captive released but he also had her possessions returned to her and a search instituted for her husband so that he could return his wife to him if he were found" (6.2.6–9).

In this case Alexander's conduct is very close to that he exhibited toward the royal princesses captured after Issus.

From One Stateira to Another

Without denying the historicity of the taking of Darius's camp and the capture of the princesses and the young prince, I must point out that the tone of the narration and the characteristics, attitudes, and reflections attributed to the protagonists belong to a genre and style located on the porous borderline between history and fiction. The literary mode of expression does not necessarily give a detailed or realistic presentation of the princesses. Apart from their names, and a detail in passing about the brother-sister relationship between Stateira and Darius,[14] the young women are primarily symbolic characters in a stereotypical narrative. The exemplum, thus inserted into a fictional framework, gives meaning to a historicized narrative.

Xenophon's *Cyropaedia,* to take a first example, supposedly reports the upbringing of Cyrus the Great and all his conquests over a lifetime. The taking of an enemy camp is a favorite story, because the theme is linked to the author's reflections on the rules for dividing up booty and on the shares set aside for the king and the gods. The description of the camp of an "Asiatic" king is canonical: "Most Asiatics at war take with them those who live under their roof."[15] There are many women, and they are particularly vulnerable in the event of defeat. The conquerors lay their hands "on covered chariots filled with women of the highest rank, wives and concubines."[16] That is why, after Cyrus's army captured the Assyrian camp, "the women of the Assyrians and of their allies, seeing the army already in flight within the camp itself, began to scream and to run about terrified, some carrying their children, others, the younger ones, rending their garments and scratching their faces, begging all they encountered not to flee and abandon them but to defend their children, their wives, and themselves."[17]

The depiction of panic among these high-born women, who rend their garments, scream, and shield their young children, is astonishingly similar to that found in Curtius. So too is the description of the booty attributed to the conquering king. Like Alexander after Issus, "the most beautiful tent" is reserved for Cyrus, which Curtius calls a "tradition."[18] As in the *Iliad,* the most beautiful women captives are the leader's share. Xenophon's Cyrus therefore receives a "woman of Susa who, it was said, was one of the most beautiful [*kallistē*] ever seen in Asia, as well as the two best lady musicians [*mousourgoi*]."[19] That woman is Panthea, wife of Abradatas of Susa. She is assisted by her eunuchs and female servants and has a beauty enhanced by every virtue: "Never had a mortal of such beauty been born or lived in Asia." Cyrus refuses to see her, fearing he would succumb to her charms. He leaves her in the custody of his childhood friend Araspas. When she learns that she is destined for Cyrus, she is distressed, though he is "a man worthy of admiration," for she intends to remain faithful to her husband, Abradatas.

Soon, at her insistence, Abradatas joins Cyrus's camp, finding it all the easier to do so in that his wife is singing the praises of the Persian: "Panthea related the pious virtue, the continence and compassion of Cyrus toward her."[20] Then Abradatas dies. Rather than survive her husband, Panthea kills herself on the sumptuous tomb she had just had constructed in his honor and memory. The fidelity the woman shows her husband is seconded by the fidelity of his eunuch scepter-bearers (skeptoukhoi), who also opt to kill themselves.[21] In this they follow the example of Artapates, the most faithful of Cyrus the Younger's scepter-bearers, who after his master's death "drew his dagger and slew himself with his own hand."[22] Jacques de La Taille found the recurrent image so evocative that, in his tragedy Alexandre (1561), he imagines that Sigambre (Sisygambis), Darius's mother, in complete despair and determined to die, "strangled herself on Alexander's body" (line 1251). Ten years later (1571), Panthea herself had the title role in a tragedy by Caye Jules de Guersens. In act 4, Panthea and her three eunuchs, whom the author names Demartez, Aratis, and Osonoris, speak in turn, all ready to sacrifice themselves on the tomb.

Xenophon's portrayal of Panthea is not at all original. On the contrary, the moving and extraordinary beauty of the female captives is expressed in a stereotypical expression—"the most beautiful ever seen in Asia"—that can be found almost systematically in the Greek authors who write about the women of the Great King's court. For example, Amytis, daughter of Xerxes and wife of Megabyzus, was "the most beautiful woman in Asia"; so too was Timōsa, lady-in-waiting to Artaxerxes II's wife.[23] Cyrus the Younger's companion and concubine Aspasia "was the most beautiful girl in her age, and in her century there was no beauty that could compare to her own; she combined all the graces."[24] As for the famous 365 royal concubines, they were "outstanding in beauty as selected from all the women of Asia."[25] That is also the case for Odatis, the heroine of a famous Iranian romance of antiquity, transmitted by Chares in his Stories of Alexander: "Odatis was the most beautiful woman in Asia," and her beloved, Zariadres, was himself a very handsome man.[26] The women and concubines of the "Asians" are in fact always "beautiful."[27] Darius's wife, for example, was of a "beauty that even her current misfortune had not marred."[28] She was "surpassed by none of her generation in beauty," and the royal princesses "were extremely beautiful."[29] "The wife of Darius is said to have been the most beautiful princess of her age, just as Darius himself was the tallest and handsomest man in Asia, and their daughters are said to have resembled their parents in beauty."[30] Her beauty was particularly notable in that the other female captives were of a remarkable beauty and presence, and that, according to Alexander "quoted" by Plutarch, "Persian ladies make men's eyes sore to behold them."[31] That admiring observation can be found several centuries later in Ammianus Marcellinus: "Persia is renowned for the beauty of its women."[32] In that respect, the only one who could compare to Stateira was Roxana, "who was asserted by the men who served in Alexander's army to have been the most beautiful of all the Asiatic women whom they had seen, with the single exception of the wife of Darius."[33]

It is on the basis of that well-established reputation that Chariton, author of the Hellenistic romance *Chaereas and Callirhoe*, constructed a whole section of his narrative, set in a Persia strongly inspired by the "Orientalist" vision transmitted by Ctesias in his *Persica*. Among the influential participants in court life are many beautiful princesses and powerful eunuchs. When, after many adventures, the Greek heroine, Callirhoe, arrives at the court of the Great King Artaxerxes, her beauty, reputed to be worthy of a goddess, arouses the jealousy of the Persian women. The Great King's wife, also named Stateira (the name became a marker for "Persian queen"), she too "the most beautiful of all women under the sun," attempts to calm them: "Let one of us, when she enters the city, stand next to her, to eclipse that wretched creature, that slave!" They choose the most beautiful among them, "Rhodogune, daughter of Zopyrus, wife of Megabyzus," a fictional character obviously created on the model of Ctesias's Amytis. She is "voluptuous, insolent in her luxury, and provocative" (5.3). The rest can be guessed: "Callihroe's stunning face and splendor dazzled all eyes, as when, in the dark of night, a great light suddenly appears." So beautiful is she that she touches the king's heart, but so virtuous and faithful to her husband that she dares refuse his advances. The king attempts to resist his desire and to maintain control over himself; to do so, he expends his energy on a hunt, but without success (6.3–4).

The revolt of Egypt saves the heroine from the fate awaiting her. With the queen and ladies of the court, she accompanies the expedition, because "the custom was that the king himself and the nobles, when they went to war, took with them their wives, their children, gold, silver, clothing, eunuchs, concubines, dogs, tables, all sorts of riches and luxury articles." Chariton had read the *Cyropaedia* carefully and was also familiar with the narratives relating the campaign of Issus. Like Darius sending his baggage train to Damascus, Artaxerxes, anxious to make the army lighter, decides to leave the women and treasures (including the queen, which Darius had not done) on the island of Arados. The island is soon captured by Chaereas himself, and the women are taken prisoner. Hence Stateira's despair when she is caught off guard, "her head on Callihroe's knees." Callirhoe refuses to hand herself over to the conqueror—who is none other than Chaereas, her beloved husband, from whom she has been separated since the beginning of the romance. In a noble gesture, Chaereas, prompted by Callihroe's pleas, sends Queen Stateira to the Great King and calms Artaxerxes's fears, assuring him that he has respected the queen. We might as well be reading the ancient texts on the captivity of the "real" Stateira, Darius's despair, and Alexander's continence and magnanimity.

For the Alexander authors, the women in Darius's entourage are "beautiful and good." That figure of the Persian princes, which I shall call "type II," is very clearly distinguished from the traditional figure (type I), seen especially in Ctesias. Amytis is not only "the most beautiful of all the women in Asia," she is also "the most licentious."[34] She leads a dissolute life. While her husband, Megabyzus, is still alive, she is accused of adultery, and once a widow "she begins to seek out the company of men," even taking the physician Apollonides as her lover.[35] But the darkest figure is certainly the mother of Artaxerxes II, Parysatis, who is "naturally of a harsh temper and savage in her wrath and resentment."[36] She sows terror around her, causing her enemies to perish in the most horrible agony, even including her daughter-in-law Stateira, wife of King Artaxerxes II (§§ 55–56; 61). Was she not accused of pursuing an intimate relationship with her young son Cyrus? Roxana, the Sogdian wife of Alexander, is a later version of her. Also called "the most beautiful of all the Asiatic women,"[37] she decides, after Alexander's death, to kill Darius's two daughters, one (Stateira) the widow of Alexander, the other (Drypetis) the widow of Hephaestion. Plutarch presents the matter in a narrative that sheds light on the nameless cruelty of the Oriental princesses: Roxana, "being jealous of Statira, . . . sent her a forged letter, purporting to come from Alexander and asking her to come to him. When Statira came, Roxana killed both her and her sister, cast their bodies down a well, and filled up the well with earth."[38]

Cruel, domineering, and licentious, the "Persian princess" (type I) also wallows in an insolent luxury worthy of the Asian despots. Consider a vignette, also set in Damascus in 333, that depicts two women of imperial high society, the wives of Artabazus and Mentor.[39] They are introduced in moralizing discussions directed against the flatterers. Plutarch simply quotes "those flattering women of Cyprus who were called 'step stools' when they went to Syria, because they lay down flat in front of the kings' wives to help them into a chariot."[40] In his *Deipnosophists,* Athenaeus gives a more elaborate version set in the fourth century, in which he discusses women called "Flatterers" *(Kōlakides),* "subject to female despots."[41] Some of these women, from the islands (Cyprus), were summoned to the continent by the wives of Artabazus and Mentor, who changed their names to "step stools" or "Ladder-lasses" because of a certain practice: "In their desire to please the women who summoned them, they made ladders of themselves so that the women riding in carts could mount or dismount on their backs. To such a pitch of luxury [*tryphē*], not to call it abjectness, did they bring these very stupid women through their devices."

Athenaeus is even distressed that these Persian women, taken to Macedonia after a reversal of fortune, had a disastrous influence on the princesses and noblewomen of Macedonia.[42] Valerius Maximus does not fail to include the exemplum in the chapter "On Luxury and Debauchery," concerning two vices introduced into Rome as an indirect consequence of the defeat of Philip V.[43] He enriches the topos by noting the growing effeminacy of the population brought about by their queens: "Had they been men, the people of Cyprus would have preferred to lose their lives rather than obey such an effeminate power."

The princesses (type II) in Darius's suite are certainly rich and covered in jewels, and they travel "in sumptuous chariots," accompanied by a swarm of ladies-in-waiting and domestics. But as the ancient authors describe them, they maintain a reserve that is broken only by defeat and misfortune. Far from being condemned for their mode of life, they arouse pity in their conquerors. Unlike Amytis, Parysatis, and Roxana, they are not simply beautiful, they are also "noble and virtuous."[44] As for Aspasia, the heroine of a beautiful romance set in the Persian court, she is remarkable not only for "her physical beauty" but even more for "the nobility of her soul."[45] Far from wallowing in lust, these princesses travel "without letting any part of their bodies be seen." And when their clothing is torn off during the scene of plunder, and they grovel at their conquerors' feet, it is Alexander's soldiers who are denounced as vile louts who do not respect the modesty of the women imploring them.[46] In fact, as Plutarch writes, "the Barbarian folk are terribly jealous in all that pertains to the pleasures of love, so that it is death for a man, not only to come up and touch one of the royal concubines, but even in journeying to go along past the waggons on which they are conveyed."[47]

Then there is the example of Ochus's daughter, taken prisoner after the death of Darius. In one scene, Curtius portrays her at a banquet during which prisoners are compelled to dance and sing: "The king himself noticed one of these women more downcast than the others and out of shyness resisting those trying to bring her forward. She was exceptionally beautiful [*excellens erat forma*], and her modesty lent further charm to her beauty. With eyes fixed on the ground and her face veiled as far as was allowed, she made the king suspect that she was too highly born to appear among such dinner-table displays" (6.2.6).

This is a classic scene, and the words had often been repeated: the reader is again transported to the world of romantic fiction. To be persuaded of that, one need only evoke the drinking banquet held by Cyrus the Younger, where Aspasia once again makes an appearance. In contrast to her three companions, who play at easy seduction and display loose morals, Aspasia refuses such indulgences and, like Ochus's granddaughter, "keeps her eyes lowered to the ground, barely holding back her tears." As a result, Cyrus "admired a virtue of which the Persians had no notion."[48] The commentary is a reminder that the narrator, like Aspasia, is Greek and is repeating a story that also circulated around the Great King. In reality, Aspasia is the heroine of a romance, a genre that by definition transcends cultures and presents eternal types, in this case that of the beautiful, good, and honorable young lady who, even when immersed in the corrupt world of the men's banquet, knows how to remain true to herself, so much so that she impresses her conqueror.

It would be very difficult to characterize, physically or psychologically, that type II "Persian princess" and to isolate descriptive elements that could confer on her a marked historical identity. In Curtius and Diodorus, neither Stateira nor her daughters seem to have any real existence; nothing is communicated about them, apart from their "beauty." For the contemporary historian, they truly are as Alexander wanted to see them—or rather, to avoid them—namely, "images cut out of stone."[49] In that respect these women from good families are, curiously enough, very close to the heroines of Greek romance, whose beauty is endlessly vaunted in the superlative and usually associated with noble birth, without any real description or portrait of them. Plutarch's term, *agalma*, is not fortuitous. It is the same one Chariton uses in presenting Callirhoe at the beginning of the romance: "She was the idol of Sicily." "That detour through statuary, a classical metaphor for beauty," is significant: "The term *agalma* is particularly interesting: Callirhoe, a true pleasure for Syracusan eyes, is also an object of veneration, another recurrent motif in the Greek romance, since in principle the term designates the statue of a deity."[50] The words evoke the Homeric model of the "beautiful captive" Briseis, "with beautiful cheeks, beautiful hair," comparable to Aphrodite and compared to her.[51] But they also again bring to mind Aspasia, who owes her beauty to "the most beautiful of goddesses," Aphrodite, who appeared to her in the form of a dove and cured her of the unsightly growth she had borne on her chin since her infancy. Here too the Homeric reference is present: "Her legs would have earned her a place among the beautiful women Homer characterizes by the epithet *kallisphyrēs* [pretty feet]."[52]

It is therefore easy to understand how the prototype of the "captive Persian princess" could have been transposed into a romance such as *Chaereas and Callirhoe*. A whole section of the romance is set at the Great King's court under the Persian Empire, and even during a war waged by Artaxerxes. It is not such a great distance from Stateira, wife of Darius, to Stateira, wife of Artaxerxes: both evoke the Panthea of the *Cyropaedia*. Might the reason not lie in the way Curtius (or his source) imagined those young women, and in the context within which they lived? The transition from Curtius to Chariton is not necessarily an abrupt shift from one genre (history) to another very different from it (fiction). Indeed, at least in these episodes Curtius seems to have strived, under the cover of "history," to present characters and scenes from an "Oriental romance." The reader moves smoothly from his Darius to Chariton's Artaxerxes.

The Spinner and the Princess

Traces of the literary exemplum can be discerned not only in the stereotypical description of the princesses but also in certain attitudes or lines attributed to them, via vignettes with perfectly well-codified meanings. When an ancient author wants to illustrate their specific mode of life, as he implies or reports it to be, the depiction is clearly still informed by the literature of exempla. Consider an anecdote that only Curtius transmits:

> Darius' mother and children he also left in the city [of Susa]. As it happened, Alexander had been sent from Macedonia a present of Macedonian clothes and a large quantity of purple material. Since he showed Sisigambis every mark of respect and his regard for her was that of a son, he ordered these to be given to her along with the women who had made

the clothes, and he added the message that, if she liked the clothes, she should train her granddaughters to make them and that he was presenting her with women to teach them to do so. At these words tears came to the queen's eyes, signifying her angry rejection of the gift—for to Persian women nothing is more degrading than working with wool.

Alexander makes his apologies: "Mother, these clothes I am wearing are not merely a gift from my sisters, but also their handiwork. I was led into error by our own customs [nostri mores]. Please do not take offence at my ignorance. I have, I hope, scrupulously observed what I have discovered of your conventions [tui mores]. I know that among you it is not right for a son to sit down in his mother's presence without her permission, so whenever I have come to you I have remained on my feet until you beckoned me to sit. Often you have wanted to show me respect by prostrating yourself before me but I have forbidden it. And the title due to my dear mother Olympias I give to you" (5.2.17–22).

This story belongs within a series of episodes and anecdotes about the Persian princesses that gives the starring role to Sisygambis, Darius's mother. After taking the capitals of Babylonia and Elam, Alexander decided to leave the members of the royal family in Susa, even, according to Diodorus, "providing them with persons to teach them the Greek language."[53] It was there that, a short time later, a kinsman named Madates, commander of a fortress besieged by Alexander, asked Sisygambis to intercede with the king to spare the lives of the citadel's defenders, should they hand over the stronghold to the Macedonians.[54] According to one of the versions extant, it was ultimately to Sisygambis that the king sent Darius's mortal remains.[55] The story thus shores up a recurrent theme, Alexander's appropriation of the Achaemenid royal family: Sisygambis is his "mother," the daughters are his "sisters," and the young Ochus is his "son." It is within that context that Alexander addresses the princesses and that Sisygambis replies to him.

Many stories that circulated through the ancient collections depict spinners and weavers, to mark the opposition between women's work and that of men. In several Roman anecdotes, working with wool at home is reserved for honorable women, such as Lucretia, "busy spinning wool deep within the palace," or "the daughters and granddaughters of Augustus, raised simply and used to working with wool."[56] The wool basket (talaros), regularly designated as the attribute of married women in Greek funerary inscriptions, is called a "sign of the well-managed virtue" of a young woman from Sardis.[57] A robust and belligerent woman, by contrast, would receive weapons as her attribute. Artemisia, for example, because of her valorous conduct during the Battle of Salamis, received from Xerxes "a panoply of arms as the price of valor." The royal admiral, meanwhile, was provided with "a spindle and distaff," because Xerxes had so often seen the men fighting like women and the women like men.[58]

The image of the spinner is particularly significant in that, in Mesopotamian texts, a "spindle" is often bestowed on an effeminate man. The inversion is perfectly realized in Sardanapalus. According to one of the many versions in circulation, that king had the custom of living in the gynaeceum, dressed, bejeweled, and made up like a woman, spinning purple in the company of his concubines.[59] Sardanapalus is one of the emblematic Greek figures of a weak and emasculated Asia, a figure long received favorably by historians meditating on the fall of empires.[60] It is striking to observe that, in a discourse violently hostile to Darius III, Plutarch evokes the image of Sardanapalus, "comber of purple wool."[61]

Another version of that oft-told tale, built on recurrent themes, is found in Herodotus. The heroine is Pheretima of Cyrene who, having taken refuge in Salamis of Cyprus, refuses all the gifts King Euelthon offers her, because she wants to receive the command of an army: "Euelthon ended by sending her a golden spindle and distaff, with wool on it. Pheretima repeated the same words as before, which drew from Euelthon the reply that he had sent her a present which, unlike an army, he thought suitable to her sex."[62] There is also the famous tale transmitted by Herodotus, who embroiders on the incendiary love affairs that arose, first, between Xerxes and the wife of his brother Masistes, and then between Xerxes and his future daughter-in-law, Artaynte. On that occasion, Herodotus writes, "Xerxes' wife Amestris gave him a long robe, of many colours and very beautiful, which she had woven with her own hands." He refuses to give that beautiful garment to Artaynte, who had asked him for it, and instead offers her an army "under her sole command," which is "a thoroughly Persian gift."[63] After the king finally gives in to the beloved's plea, the story ends badly, for one of the characters—Amestris, King Xerxes's own wife—is the type of Persian princess motivated by senseless cruelty.[64]

Are we to conclude that Persian royal princesses (like Amestris—or like Penelope) agreed to weave but not to spin (hence Sisygambis's distress)? Obviously not. The function or purpose of such stories is not to transmit a verified piece of documentary information: they do not bear witness to the everyday life of ladies of the court. One cannot fail to notice that, in the Persian and

Iranian context, a great number of stories depict horsewomen and women warriors rather than princess weavers or spinners. But it would make no more
sense to contrast that tradition to the tale Curtius transmits. It would appear
that Curtius himself did not have an inkling of the existence of such a Persian
custom or, for that matter, of an antithetical Macedonian custom. His concerns
are not those of an ethnologist intent on explaining precisely the Persians' customs and traditions.

The story is simple and simply told. Unusually, Alexander is judged to be at
fault. In contradiction to the marks of esteem and respect he has continually
attested toward the princesses, he does not recognize the prestigious station of
Darius's mother or that of her granddaughters. But he is quickly forgiven because, if one is to believe Curtius, he did not commit a moral offense, merely a
cognitive error, based on a difference in cultures unfamiliar to him. Through
the king's remorse, Curtius strives to demonstrate that Alexander is sensitive
to the specificities of Persian culture and does not wish to go against them. He
therefore does not intend to impose on Darius's daughters a different mode of
life, that of the conquerors.

The Conqueror and the Beautiful Captive

Like Cyrus in the *Cyropaedia,* Alexander is praised for his "continence." According to the version transmitted by Ptolemy and Aristobulus, Alexander refuses
to see the wife of Darius, just as Cyrus decided not to set eyes on Abradatas's
wife: "He never would endure to hear a word spoken in commendation of her
features."[65] Here again is the direct echo of ancient discussions on the birth of
love, codified in romances as the first glance exchanged between two young
and beautiful creatures. That also explains the reserve of the young Persian
captive who keeps her "eyes fixed to the ground" to avoid any possible exchange with Alexander, and, conversely, King Artaxerxes's passionate desire to
continue "to enjoy the adorable sight of Callirhoe."[66] Even in the version that
has the king visit the Persian women in their tent, Alexander's reserve is emphasized. Plutarch attributes this reply to him: "I have never seen, or desired to see
the wife of Darius, and have not even allowed her beauty to be spoken of in my
presence."[67] Similarly, regarding Roxana: "Though he was in love with her, he
refused to offer violence to her as a captive, and did not think it derogatory to
his dignity to marry her."[68]

The conqueror's encounter with the beautiful captive is a recurrent theme
in the ancient monarchical literature. After the stronghold of Maogamalcha

was taken in 363 C.E., Ammianus Marcellinus places Julian in an identical situation: "As for the young women prisoners, pretty as they usually are in Persia (the beauty of women being extraordinary there), he did not want to approach or even see any of them, in imitation of Alexander and Africanus, who refused to do likewise, that those who had everywhere proven themselves invincible in the labors [of war] might not be seen to have been broken by desire" (24.4.27).

The comparison between Alexander and Scipio Africanus clearly invokes one of the most remarkable actions attributed to the Roman during the taking of New Carthage. Here again, the context is the distribution of the booty.

The story was told by many authors, all using a common structure, itself built on the genre of the exemplum. It is elaborated in great detail by Livy and Polybius and is composed of two episodes. In the first,[69] the leading role of captive strangely resembles the one played in the ancient texts by Sisygambis after Issus. In New Carthage, she has no name but is presented "as the wife of Mandonius, brother of Andobales, king of the Ilergetes, . . . who displayed a majestic dignity."[70] She is very elderly. As Scipio is deciding the fate of the hostages, she throws herself weeping at his feet, imploring him to protect the virtue of the young girls in her care. They are her nieces, "Andobales' daughters, in the flower of their youth and beauty, along with several others of the same rank, who all revered her like their mother." "Grasping her right hand, he invited her and the others to take heart, for he would watch over them as over his own sisters and children, and would put trustworthy men in charge of them, in conformance to what had previously been said" (Polybius 10.18.1–15).

Compare that story to the scene Diodorus sets in the tent of the Persian princesses after Issus: "Assuring Sisygambis that she would be his second mother he immediately ratified in action what he had just promised orally. . . . He added many other assurances of consideration and generosity. . . . He gave them his hand as pledge of all this and was . . . showered with praises by those who had been helped" (17.37.6; 38.3).

The story also resembles that of Panthea. Just as Scipio entrusts the young girls to persons whose morality is above suspicion, so Cyrus asks his best friend, Araspas, to protect Panthea's virtue.

The second episode illustrating Scipio's continence, the only one to be elaborated by Frontinus and Valerius Maximus, maintains close narrative ties to the anecdotes circulating about the Persian princesses who had fallen into Alexander's hands. The episode introduces "a princess with a beauty so perfect that, every time she walked by, all eyes were drawn to her."[71] Polybius refers to her as "a young girl in the flower of youth, with a beauty surpassing all other women. . . . Scipio was struck with admiration at her beauty." He resists temptation and returns her to her father. Livy is more detailed and more laudatory. Scipio summons the beauty's fiancé and her parents, and assures them that he has "kept [her] as an inviolable prize," like the young Persian princesses who, in Alexander's camp, "lived unseen and unmolested, more as though they were in some sacred retreat of holy virgins than in a camp."[72] Plutarch praises Alexander for his ability to reject the immoral offers that his close companions made to him; likewise, the ancient authors recount how "Roman soldiers, who had found a maiden in the flower of her youth with a beauty surpassing that of other women, and who knew that Scipio was a connoisseur of women, took her to him and, in presenting her, declared that they were making him a gift of the young maiden."[73]

Scipio and Alexander do not merely respect the captives, they also see to their future. Alexander returns shares of the booty to the princesses, so that they can bury their loved ones, and "allowed them to retain the regal title and state, and even increased their revenues."[74] In addition he promises to "provide for the marriage of the daughters" and arranges "marriages not unbefitting their father's rank."[75] As for Scipio, he rejects any ransom to free the young Iberian and returns her to her fiancé and parents: "He ordered that the gold given to redeem the maiden be added to her dowry."[76] Recall as well Alexander's good deeds toward the granddaughter of Ochus, captured after Darius's death: "He not only ordered the captive released but he also had her possessions returned to her and a search instituted for her husband so that he could return his wife to him if he were found."[77] As for Cyrus, he welcomes Abradatas as a guest. In other words, the just conqueror does not break the bonds of marriage; on the contrary, he reunites husbands and wives whom the war has separated, or at the very least does not violate the conjugal union.

This is typical of the monarchical literature of exempla—even in modern times.[78] It is in that capacity that the story of Scipio and the young Iberian appears in Frontinus's collection, in a chapter on how to "keep those one mistrusts true to their duties."[79] It is also in Valerius Maximus's *Memorable Deeds and Sayings,* in a chapter devoted to "abstinence and continence."[80]

Such edifying stories were sometimes derided, for example, by Aulus Gellius, who offers his readers ironic remarks about such stories repeated by trained rhetors:

> It is therefore possible to have a nice discussion: whether one ought to consider Publius Africanus the most virtuous, he who . . . returned to her

father, intact, a maiden of a remarkable beauty and ripe for love, the daughter of a Spanish noble . . . or King Alexander, who refused to see King Darius's wife and also his sister, taken in a great battle, who, he was told, was
of an extraordinary beauty, and forbad her being brought to him. . . . But
as for that agreeable and contradictory declamation about Alexander and
Scipio, let it be made by those with an overabundance of talent and leisure and verbal ease; for our part, we need only say what is historical
[*quod historia est*]. (7.8.1–6)

In contrast to those tales, Aulus Gellius quotes lines that the poet Naevius
had written against Scipio: "Even that man, who often performed glorious deeds
with his arms, whose actions still have life and force today, and who alone has
prestige among nations—he, clad only in a cloak, was taken home from his beloved's by his father!"

And Aulus Gellius concludes: "I believe it is these lines that led Valerius Antias
to make a judgment of Scipio's conduct contrary to that of all other authors, and
to write that the young captive was not returned to her father, unlike what we
said above, but was kept by Scipio and taken by him in the pleasures of love."

There is no doubt that the edifying stories about the relationship between
Alexander and Darius's wife were also the occasion for many doubts. In the
Alexander Romance (2.17.5), for example, Darius's wife stays alive and, when an
embassy from the Great King comes to propose an exchange, Parmenion urges
Alexander to accept the offer, using words marked by a calm cynicism: "If I
were you, Alexander, I should accept the gold and the land that is offered to
you, and should give back to Darius his mother and his children and his wife,
after sleeping with them." And if, as one tradition has it, Stateira died in child-
birth shortly before the Battle of Gaugamela, it would have to be conceded that
the child's father could hardly have been anyone but Alexander.[81] In any event,
just as the cowardice of the fleeing Darius is condemned with particular force
through the words and attitudes attributed to the princesses, so too the tradition that arose in the footsteps of Alexander would attribute to the Great King
the role of authenticator of his enemy's incomparable virtue.

The scene takes place after the announcement of the death of Stateira, who,
according to another, more politically correct version, was "exhausted by the
unremitting hardships of the journey and her dejected state of mind."[82] Alexander "graced her funeral with such a regal pomp, and bewailed her death so pite-
ously, that his kindness cast discredit upon his chastity, and his very courtesy

incurred the obloquy of injustice."[83] So as to absolve Alexander of all suspicion, the ancient authors once again give Darius a role to play. Using a well-known literary ruse, they transport the action to the Persian camp. The reader, perhaps surprised, even incredulous, but charmed by such a reversal, suddenly learns that "in the grief and alarm, Tyriotes, one of the eunuchs who had attended the queen, slipped out of a gate which was not heavily guarded because it faced away from the enemy. Arriving at Darius' camp, he was received by the guards and taken to the king's tent groaning and tearing his clothes. The sight of Tyriotes upset Darius, who now expected all kinds of bad news and did not know what to fear most."[84] Told of the sorrow Alexander had displayed, and jealous of his adversary's youth, the king postulates that such grief attests to a guilty attachment and thinks that Stateira's conqueror has dishonored her. The eunuch is interrogated. The king must face the incredible facts. Hence his invocation in the form of a prayer: " 'Gods of my country,' he said, 'before all else make firm my rule; but my next prayer, if my career is at an end, is that Asia find no other ruler than this just enemy, this merciful victor.' "[85]

Not only does Darius acknowledge his adversary's unheard-of virtue but also, even though his army is ready to fight, he concedes in advance the legitimacy of Alexander's victory. In addition, according to Justin and Curtius, it is because he is overcome with admiration for the Macedonian king that he decides to send a third embassy: he says that he is ready to abandon all the territories west of the Euphrates to get back his mother and daughters; furthermore, he proposes that Alexander keep Darius's son Ochus as a hostage "as guarantee of his word regarding the peace-terms."[86] Who could doubt Alexander's continence and Stateira's virtue when thus certified by the person most concerned, Alexander's adversary and Stateira's husband?

Just as the pretty story of Sisygambis and her granddaughters does not convey any trustworthy information about the lives of women in the Persian palaces, so too, the story of the eunuch Tyriotes transports the reader to places that are never described, into a royal tent about which nothing is known, and to a Great King who seems to have no specific characteristics. Both stories, however, rendered with particular effectiveness through the use of literary fiction, transmit a clearly expressed political moral: Alexander is a good king, a skillful conqueror, and a good son.

Stateira between Darius and Alexander

As a couple, Darius and Stateira are often evoked but never really portrayed, except in Plutarch's words: "The wife of Darius is said to have been the most beautiful princess of her age, just as Darius himself was the tallest and handsomest man in Asia, and their daughters are said to have resembled their parents in beauty." The terms used to "describe" Darius ("tall and handsome"), which belong to the conventional vocabulary of praise, are just as stereotypical as those that introduce Stateira.[87] When the courage that Alexander himself reads on the face of the very young Ochus is taken into account, the present-day reader may easily imagine she is looking at the photograph of a model middle-class family, taken on the parents' wedding anniversary.[88] Handsome, loving, and close, Darius and Stateira represent the friendly face of the "Achaemenid royal couple."

The only couple comparable to them is Artaxerxes II and another Stateira, as presented in the Life that Plutarch devotes to that king. Artaxerxes, the offspring of an entirely different kind of royal couple, the violent and bloody Parysatis and Darius II, was reputed for his "gentleness and magnanimity."[89] His wife Stateira was almost the sole survivor of a family that Darius and Parysatis had systematically massacred. Called "beautiful and excellent," she obviously belongs to type II of the Persian princess, "beautiful and honorable," like all the other known Stateiras in Darius's family, on down to Chariton. In addition, Stateira was "beloved of the common folk": when the court traveled, "what gratified the king most of all was the sight of his wife Stateira's carriage, which always appeared with its curtains up, and thus permitted the women of the people to approach and greet the queen" (5.6). The celebrity press is not far off.

She will soon find herself facing type I, represented by Parysatis. Artaxerxes, married on his parents' orders, kept his wife "in defiance of them," because Darius "wished to kill her also." But "throwing himself at his mother's feet and supplicating her with many tears," Artaxerxes "at last obtained her promise that his wife should neither be killed nor separated from him" (2.2). Parysatis's hatred did not abate. She was soon "vexed by Stateira," who accused Parysatis of having caused the war by unreservedly supporting Cyrus the Younger's rebellion: "Therefore Parysatis hated Stateira, and being naturally of a harsh temper and savage in her wrath and resentment, she plotted to kill her" (6.8). After Cyrus's death, the mother-in-law thus poisoned the daughter-in-law during a meal.

The hostility between the two women is not so much political as personal, consisting of a rivalry for Artaxerxes's affection: "Parysatis, accordingly,

340 PART III: RELUCTANCE AND ENTHUSIASM

who from the outset had a lurking hatred and jealousy of Stateira, saw that her own influence with the king was based on feelings of respect and honour, while that of Stateira was grounded fast and strong in love and confidence; she therefore plotted against her life" (19.1). The same character and the same motive are also found in the romance of Aspasia. Bound to Cyrus the Younger by a deep love, she also knows how to manage Parysatis and not place the son's relationship with his mother in peril: "Parysatis saw with the greatest satisfaction that Aspasia was using the influence she had over Cyrus to ensure for herself only the second place in his heart, and that she left the first place to the prince's mother."[90]

Cruel and full of twists and turns, the story of Stateira, Artaxerxes, and his mother is not told merely for the reader's or listener's pleasure. Deeply inscribed in a discourse on good kingship, it also holds a political meaning. The "gentleness" that Plutarch and his sources, not without a certain admiration, recognize in Artaxerxes also has negative connotations. Even in Artaxerxes's daily tasks as king, Plutarch believes, that "gentleness" is excessive, and "there was, too, a certain dilatoriness in the nature of the king, which most people took for clemency" (4.4). The rest of the story shows that Artaxerxes lacks energy and vigor and allows his close circle and intimates, including Stateira, too much freedom: he does not apply with sufficient rigor the aulic protocol, which placed an insuperable obstacle between the king and his wife and subjects. Under difficult conditions, in the face of a violent and determined adversary, that "gentleness" was all the more unsuitable for the missions a Great King must perform (4.4). As a result, "restless and factious men thought that affairs required Cyrus, a man who had a brilliant spirit, surpassing skill in war, and great love for his friends; and that the magnitude of the empire required a king of lofty purpose and ambition" (6.1). In other words, "gentleness" is an eminent virtue in the domestic sphere but not in the realm of political action. The same is true for the "gentleness" characteristic of Darius III according to Curtius, who links it to two particularly disastrous flaws in a leader: mental malleability and ingenuous behavior.[91]

It is no different for the love and affection between spouses. Once the husband is king, love is a chain and a shackle that can prevent him from acting in the kingdom's best interests. That is the meaning of the romance between Darius and Stateira, as it was invented and recounted by Hellenistic and Roman authors. At the level of human feelings, the love that Darius the man has for his wife may be moving, but it makes Darius the king lose all control over the political situation: he declares himself ready to exchange half his kingdom for his wife and the rest of his family. The third (fictive) embassy even introduces a further shading in the confusion between family affection and a king's duties. To recover his mother and daughters, Darius offers to hand over to Alexander, as a hostage, his young son Ochus, the one person who is explicitly presented as heir to the empire. In other words, Ochus is disinherited in favor of Alexander. From that moment on, the Great King has accepted as self-evident that, were he to be defeated, power would devolve to Alexander, because of the magnanimity with which the Macedonian king behaved toward Darius's family, especially after the death of Stateira.

In that respect Darius falls short both as a king and as a war leader. In fact, the "continence" displayed by great conquerors is not only an expression of moral virtue, it is in the first place the condition for their freedom to make decisions. Even Chariton's Artaxerxes is tormented by the matter of conscience he must resolve: Can he serenely decide to which husband Callirhoe is to be awarded, when he himself has fallen desperately in love with the "beautiful maiden," the prize in the trial for which he must be the supreme judge? He certifies to his favorite adviser that he does not want to violate the laws that he himself decreed: "Do not accuse me of lacking self-control!"[92] Love, like sleep, is a weakness that must be relentlessly combated: so proclaims Alexander in the face of all the temptations that assail him after the victory over Darius.[93] As for Cyrus, he explains that he does not want to take time away from his "public" duties to satisfy a "private" desire. There can be no question of visiting a woman as beautiful as Panthea is reputed to be: "If . . . I allow myself to be persuaded to go and see her, not having a great deal of time of my own, I fear she will persuade me to return to see her even more often, at the risk, afterward, of neglecting the affairs for which I am responsible, in order to sit there contemplating her."[94] That is also the reason Scipio refuses to relax and take pleasure in the young Iberian captive who has just been brought in to him: "In times of activity, such diversions become cumbersome shackles, both physically and morally, for those who devote themselves to them." He might have accepted the gift, he says, if he had been a common soldier (idiōtēs), but his position as a general (stratēgos) absolutely forbids it.[95] The king or general has obligations and constraints of which the common soldier or subject is free. In fact, in his negotiation with the local elites, Scipio's trump card is that he has preserved the virginity of the "'beautiful captives.' . . . That generosity won over the entire nation to the Roman people."[96] The young fiancé "hastened to solicit collections from his clients and came back a few days later to find Scipio once again in command of fourteen hundred elite horsemen."[97] The narrative reports the extraordinary profitability of the initial investment (that is, "continence").

In the "historical" texts, Artaxerxes II appears in another story of a beautiful captive, Aspasia. After the defeat and death of Cyrus the Younger, she was part of the human booty when the defeated camp was plundered. Already famous far and wide, she was taken by Artaxerxes himself: "Outraged that she had been brought to him in chains, he ordered the irons put on those who had participated in such barbarous treatment. At the same time, he commanded that his captive be brought the most magnificent clothing. . . . The king fell madly in love."[98] Aspasia, however, is a Greek captive, not a Persian princess, and in conducting that love affair the Great King does not put in peril the empire he has just safeguarded through his victory over his brother.

Nevertheless, according to the story reported by all the ancient authors, a major conflict regarding the possession of Aspasia soon erupted between the king and his son Darius, which led to the revolt and subsequent execution of the crown prince. As required by custom, the king had to hand over Aspasia to his son; but, full of wrath at both his son's request and at Aspasia's choice of Darius, he condemned her to chastity, consecrating her like a Persian Vestal to the cult of the goddess Anahita. Once more, history, tale, and fiction merge together, but the lesson is no less clear. The anecdote again illustrates a recurrent Greek vision of the Persian court, within which the private affairs of kings, including love affairs, directly influence political decisions of the greatest importance. In this case, at issue is no more and no less than how to deal with the chief problem raised throughout Achaemenid history, namely, how to ensure a harmonious dynastic succession. In addition, the rest of the story, as related by Plutarch, attests to the devastating consequences of such practices: the last part of Artaxerxes's reign is nothing but a series of plots and murders, conducted by another infernal couple, composed of two of Artaxerxes's children, the "cruel Ochus" and the "licentious Atossa." Indeed, Atossa, already married to her own father (with the consent of Parysatis, the grandmother), was also romantically involved with her brother.[99]

In contrast to such "barbarian" aberrations, Alexander is perfectly capable of distinguishing between the private man and the statesmen within himself. Sizing up "the beautiful captives" of Issus and Damascus, the private Alexander marries Barsine, "after the death of her husband Memnon. . . . She had received a Greek education, was naturally attractive, and was of royal descent, as her father was Artabazus, who was himself the offspring of one of the Great King's daughters."[100] Because she is a widow, she is unattached and, especially, lacks any exchange value. Without remorse or regret, therefore, he can take the captive "distinguished for her beauty."[101] It is very clear, by contrast, that the Persian princesses are first and foremost a major weapon in the hands of Alexander the statesman. According to Plutarch, that is one of the reasons for the heartache Alexander displays when the wife of Darius dies.[102] Plutarch also clearly explains the meaning of Alexander's Perso-Iranian marriages. Alexander married only one woman for personal reasons. "He married Roxana merely for love; but Statira, the daughter of Darius, upon the account of state-policy, for such a conjunction of both nations strengthened his conquest" (Fortune of Alexander, 2.6 [= Moralia, 338D]).

Although Plutarch distinguishes between marriage for love (erasteis) and marriage for reason of state (pragmata), he also expresses the idea that Alexander never sacrificed his political will to his sexual desire or to his private emotional attachments. Although Alexander immediately fell in love with Roxana, he had to curb his violent drives, those of a victorious warrior, so as to obtain all the political advantages he was expecting from marriage to the beautiful Iranian.[103]

The message of all these stories of "beautiful captives" is as follows: love and desire must not be obstacles in the path of statesmen, especially if they are building or maintaining an empire. On the contrary, men in power must use eros within the framework of political action; love must be kept in a secondary and subordinate position. Darius is judged perfectly incapable of adopting such an attitude and is denounced for bringing on his military expedition his wife, his immediate family, his concubines, and all the women of the nobility but also all his riches and luxurious lifestyle. He is portrayed as someone obsessed with the desire to see once more his mother, wife, and children, even though they were abandoned to enemy hands when he himself fled. Once again the scales are not balanced in the comparison between Darius and Alexander, who is free from all romantic or emotional attachments, perfectly in control of his feelings and drives, and contemptuous of "Asiatic luxury." On opposite sides of the mirror, Alexander and Darius are, respectively, the living example and the counterexample of the lesson in political morals that Valerius Maximus presents under the title De abstinentia et continentia: "Families, a state, and a kingdom do not easily maintain perpetual balance, except when they reduce to a minimum the power that the passion for love and money demand of them."[104]

Bagoas between Darius and Alexander

The Great King has just died, and a new element arises to sow discord. It is of particular interest to us because its direct aim is not to sully the memory of the deceased king but rather to pillory the "infamous mores" that Alexander is reputed to have borrowed from Darius at that time. The story appears only in Curtius.

Sometime after the Great King's death, Alexander decides to resume his march and to lead his army northward, toward Hyrcania. One of the first of Darius's high-ranking officers who offers to surrender is the chiliarch Nabarzanes, who participated in the plot against the Great King. Alexander receives a letter in which the chiliarch swears that he did not personally raise his hand against the sovereign and declares he is ready to surrender: "Alexander did not hesitate to give Nabarzanes an assurance, using the Persian conventions, that he would be unharmed if he came."[105] Others then deliver themselves as well: for example, Phrataphernes, satrap of Parthia and Hyrcania, "surrendered both himself and the men who had fled after Darius' death. [Alexander] gave them a courteous welcome."[106] So too, shortly thereafter, the old Artabazus, "together with his children, Darius' relatives and a small contingent of Greek soldiers. As he approached, the king offered him his right hand." Then Artabazus brought his sons "to Alexander's right hand."[107] In writing that the king had given his assurance (*fides*) to Nabarzanes in accordance with Persian conventions, Curtius certainly means that the king had given him his right hand.

It is only after the victorious campaign against the Mardi that, still according to Curtius, Nabarzanes comes to the king to surrender in person, and it is then that, for the first time, the authors introduce the one called Bagoas:[108] "Arriving then at the city in Hyrcania where the palace of Darius stood, he was met by Nabarzanes, who had been given a safe conduct and who now brought Alexander lavish gifts, including Bagoas, an exceptionally good-looking eunuch in the very flower of his youth."[109] "Darius had had a sexual relationship with him [*cui et Dereus adsuetus fuerat*] and presently Alexander did, too [*et mox Alexander adsuerit*]. It was Bagoas' pleas that did most to influence Alexander to pardon Nabarzanes."

Curtius, the only one to report the story, does not go any further. He is probably eager to take his reader to the Amazons to share the thirteen nights of love that Alexander spends with their queen, and then to deliver a long moralizing discourse on the degeneration of Alexander's character and mores.

Bagoas thus disappears from Curtius's narrative as abruptly as he entered it. He makes a reappearance, just as unexpected, when the king and his army return from India. Traveling from Carmania, they arrive at the borders of Persia. Because the satrap whom Alexander had named has died in the meantime, the Persian Orxines is exercising his authority there. Curtius, who introduced him briefly during his account of the Battle of Gaugamela, represents him as a noble of very high lineage: Orxines "was descended from one of the seven Persians and also traced his line back to the renowned King Cyrus."[110] "A man pre-eminent among all the barbarians for his nobility and wealth," "he traced his lineage from Cyrus, the former Persian king, and his wealth was partly inherited from his ancestors and partly amassed by himself during his long tenure of the satrapy" (10.1.22–23).

In accordance with the standard practice, Orxines comes to welcome Alexander and his people and offers precious gifts: "Orsines met Alexander with all manner of gifts, which he intended to give not only to the king but to his friends as well. With him were herds of horses, already broken in, chariots trimmed with silver and gold, expensive furniture, fine jewels, heavy gold vessels, purple garments, and 3,000 talents of silver coin."

It is under these circumstances that a sudden falling-out with Alexander occurs, not because of the gifts strictly speaking but because of the selection Orxines makes from among the possible recipients:

He paid no court to the eunuch [spado] Bagoas, who by now had gained Alexander's affection through putting his body at his service [qui Alexandrum obsequio corpore deuinxerat sibi]. He was advised by certain people of Alexander's strong attachment to Bagoas, but he replied that he paid his respect to the king's friends, not to his whores, and that it was not the Persian custom to regard as men those who allowed themselves to be sexually used as women [qui stupro effeminarentur]. When he heard this, the eunuch directed the power gained from his shameful self-degradation against the life of an innocent man of supreme distinction. (10.1.25–27)

Bagoas spreads venomous denunciations of Orxines, who is soon suspected of being the violator of Cyrus's tomb. To back up his claim, the eunuch does not hesitate to invoke the testimony of the dead Darius, who supposedly confided that a treasure had been buried in the tomb. Bagoas soon manages to instill doubt in Alexander's mind: "Orsines was arrested. Not satisfied with seeing an innocent man executed, the eunuch seized him as he went to his death."[111] In

reporting his cruel end, the Latin author is at pains to point out the moral dignity that Orxines displays: "Looking at him, Orsines said: 'I had heard that
women were once rulers in Asia, but this really is something new—a *castrato* as
king [*regnare castratum*]!' Such was the end of the most noble of Persians, a
man who was not only innocent but who had also shown the king exemplary
kindness."

This relationship between Alexander and Bagoas was certainly discussed at
length in antiquity. Plutarch, also in a negative register, cites Bagoas in a treatise devoted to showing the dangers posed to kings by flatterers, and the differences between the flatterer and the friend. These flatterers, comments the author, brought hatred and disunity to Alexander, who, under their influence, put
to death men of talent, such as Callisthenes, Parmenion, and Philotas. And Plutarch denounces "Hagnon, Bagoas, Agesias, and Demetrius," accusing them of
having "worshiped Alexander on their knees, groomed and reshaped him like a
barbarian idol."[112] The choice of words clearly refers to the same context as in
Curtius, namely, the moment when Alexander adopts Achaemenid aulic customs. The contrast Plutarch highlights between friend and flatterer coincides—
only in part, but clearly—to the distinction made by Orxines (Curtius's mouthpiece) between the king's friends and those he calls prostitutes and whores.

Plutarch presents Bagoas in much more specific terms, evoking grand feasts
that unfolded in Gedrosia upon Alexander's return from India: "At the capital
of Gedrosia, Alexander again halted his army, and refreshed them with feasting
and revelry. It is said that he himself, after having drunk hard, was watching a
contest between several choruses, and that his lover [*erōmenos*] Bagoas won the
prize, and then came across the theatre and seated himself beside him, dressed
as he was and wearing his crown as victor. The Macedonians, when they saw
this, applauded vehemently, and cried out to Alexander to kiss [*philēsas*] him,
until at length he threw his arms round him and kissed [*katephilēsen*] him" (*Alexander*, 67.7–8).

The story is also found in Athenaeus's *Deipnosophists*, in book 13, devoted to
stories about women and love. As usual, these stories are drawn from a large
number of authors. Athenaeus does not fail to mention, on several occasions,
the love of boys and the marked preference among some men for such relationships. The anecdote about Alexander and Bagoas at the theater is cited from
Dicaearchus, a student of Aristotle's: "King Alexander also was madly devoted
to boys [*philopais*]. Dicaearchus, at any rate, in his book *On the Sacrifice at Ilium*
says that he was so overcome with love for the eunuch Bagoas that, in full view

of the entire theatre, he, bending over, caressed Bagoas fondly, and when the audience clapped and shouted in applause, he, quite willingly, again bent over and kissed him" (13.603b).

There has been much speculation about the influence the story may have had on Alexander's reputation. W. W. Tarn, a fierce defender of the Macedonian conqueror's moral and political greatness, was horrified that Alexander could be accused of such sexual depravity. In his famous book, Tarn therefore devotes a separate appendix to that delicate question, while at the same time apologizing to his readers for such a discussion. In this he resembles Curtius, who, on a different occasion, was also solicitous of public and private morality.[113] Tarn seeks to show that Alexander's homosexuality was merely an odious accusation of slanderers, who entirely invented the story to damage the memory of a king they hated. The attacks had supposedly come from a current in the school of Aristotle who were shocked that Alexander had put to death their master's nephew Callisthenes. In an article that has remained famous ("The Eunuch Bagoas," 1958), E. Badian argues, on the contrary, that Tarn's interpretation is the result of moral postulates typical of the Victorian age and that, in reality, within the general context of Greek and Macedonian customs and the history of conquest, the story is perfectly credible.

In terms of historical method, the debate is not without interest, and may lead to reflections on the relationship the historian maintains with his documents.[114] In my view, however, it is still marked by a certain scholarly ingenuousness. It would be easy to produce texts seeking to demonstrate that Alexander found the love of boys repellent, or others, conversely, demonstrating that pederasty was a widespread practice. To make Alexander an icon of sexual morality, however, it is not enough to shield oneself behind apologetic texts; and to establish the veracity of a story ipso facto, it is not enough say that it is credible.

For anyone interested in Darius and his memory more specifically, the question of the historicity of Curtius's discussions of Bagoas is neither of foremost importance nor determining. Similarly, whether such an individual as Bagoas existed is not a problem that ought to occupy our attention. The episode, whether invented or not, adds an element to the image that was reconstituted of the last Great King. In that respect it would be useful and illuminating to bring to light the genesis and narrative structure of the story. That aspect of the question has never attracted reflection, as if the opposition between an "effeminate" Persian monarchy and a "virile" Macedonian monarchy raised interpretive problems only with regard to the accusations against Alexander.

Whatever the source Curtius used, the episode must be read in the first place as an exemplum, used to support an argument on good and bad kingship. Within the documentation, the passages from Curtius have a specific narrative unity. They make it quite clear that the figure of Bagoas and the relationship he established with Alexander are the homothetic transposition of practices already known in the court of Darius: the young eunuch is both the symbol and the vehicle of Alexander's "Orientalization." In Curtius's eyes, Bagoas's very existence is highly representative of the depravity of the "Asian" monarchy, all of whose symbolic attributes Alexander intends to adopt.

Bagoas's first appearance occurs at the moment when, to borrow Curtius's expression, Alexander turned into "Darius's satrap" and adopted the Great King's luxurious and reprehensible personal habits: "He began to imitate the Persian luxury and the extravagant display of the kings of Asia"; "the man whom the arms of Persia had failed to crush fell before its vices."[115] Aside from the Macedonian king's reputation, whether justified or not, the episode gives substance to the representation of Darius. For if one is to believe Curtius, the disturbing nature of the relationship to be surmised between the Great King and Bagoas stands in stark contrast to the kindness and constancy of the filial, conjugal, and paternal feelings that the same author attributes to the Great King, faced with the captivity of his mother, wife, daughters, and son.

The Disturbing Figure of the Young and Beautiful Eunuch

Bagoas, called a eunuch and a castrato, belonged to a class of people within the Persian court that was often cited by the Greco-Roman authors. The authors frequently denounce the vices of this group and their participation in conspiracies, alongside those of another type, just as dangerous, the cruel and perverse princess. In reality, not all those described by these authors by the term "eunuch" were necessarily castrati. Rather, the original designation might even have been a courtly title. There were obviously hierarchical distinctions among all these eunuchs. For example, the chiliarch Bagoas, the "kingmaker" in the era of Artaxerxes III and Artaxerxes IV, and also at the beginning of Darius III's reign, was a very high dignitary of the court. He had next to nothing to do with some insignificant eunuch who, in Darius's court, was responsible for overseeing the staff in a princess's house, and even less with all those anonymous eunuchs, castrated or not, who performed humble tasks as domestics and other servants.[116]

Initially Bagoas is portrayed rather sympathetically. A contributing factor is the physical description of the young boy, in words that, stereotypical in nature, vary little from the terms these same authors use to report the "beauty" of a young female captive: Bagoas was "an exceptionally good-looking eunuch in the very flower of his youth."[117] These words were certainly evocative for Roman readers, who were captivated by the disturbing beauty and sexuality of the *puer delicatus*. In the Roman period, moreover, "Bagoas" was the name given to particularly beloved eunuchs.[118] As the anecdotes unfold, they leave no doubt about the pederastic relationship that was immediately established between Bagoas (the *ērōmēne*) and Alexander (the *ēraste*). The documentation as a whole suggests no less clearly that the same relationship had existed between the young man and Darius.

In all the texts expressing the Greek vision of court life among the Great Kings, only one story presents a parallel with the supposed intimate story between Darius and Bagoas. It is itself merely part of a great love story, whose protagonist is once again Aspasia.[119] A former companion-concubine of Cyrus the Younger, captured by Artaxerxes II after his victory at Cunaxa, Aspasia was compelled by the king to put on the magnificent robe he had given her: "In those new clothes, she appeared the most beautiful of all women. From then on, Artaxerxes was madly in love with her." Cyrus's love was first triggered by another dress: Aspasia, obliged to appear at the banquet of the Persian leaders, had refused to "put on a costly chiton. She had believed it was not worth the trouble to wrap herself in an embroidered mantle and had refused to put up with a bath. . . . She was beaten and, under duress, she put on the clothes and yielded to the orders." It is obvious there was a special costume for the singer-courtesans who provided the amusement at banquets, just as servers at the king's table had first to bathe, then put on a white garment.[120] Aspasia is therefore not wrong to believe that the clothes being imposed on her are a marker of her new status.

Aspasia continues to resist Artaxerxes's advances, remaining faithful to Cyrus's memory, bound by the deep feelings they had for each other. It is at this point that the hopeless love story is linked to another royal love affair, also desperate, with a young eunuch, which Aelian presents as follows: "Some time later came the death of the eunuch Tiridates, the most beautiful and most pleasing in all Asia. His life ended when he was barely more than a child, and it was said that the king loved him passionately."[121]

Once again one finds the words customarily used to designate the extraordinary beauty of the Persian princesses. Other authors clearly evoke the lithe beauty of childhood, which is also that of the young Bagoas, who has fallen into Alexander's hands. Then comes the description of the sorrow of an apparently inconsolable king: "The king was truly very aggrieved by that loss and suffered acute sorrow. There was general mourning throughout Asia, everyone seeking thereby to please the king. But no one dared approach him or try to console him. They believed he was in despair because of the misfortune that had occurred."

Marked by a discreetly expressed but clearly evoked eroticism, the rest of the story will reintroduce Aspasia and, for the third time, will bring to bear a scene that involves dressing, in this case, the wearing of a specific article of clothing:

> Three days having passed, Aspasia put on mourning clothes and, as the king was about to go to the baths, she stopped him, standing before him and weeping with her eyes downcast. He was surprised to see her and asked why she had come. She told him: "I came to console you, Sire, if it please you, since you are suffering and aggrieved. Nevertheless, if it angers you, I will go away." The Persian was very happy with that solicitude and ordered her to go and wait for him in the chamber. She did so. When he entered, he put the eunuch's clothes over Aspasia's black ones. The boy's costume quite suited her, and her beauty shone even brighter in her lover's eyes. At that sight, the king was in her thrall and pleaded with her to continue to come to him dressed that way, until the acute pain of his grief had diminished. She was, they say, the only one of the Asian women, and even of the king's intimate circle, including his sons and kinsmen, to console Artaxerxes. He recovered from his grief by allowing himself to be persuaded by that woman's solicitude and acts of consolation.

It is a marvelous story, in which the transfer of love comes about through the beloved's clothes, which allow the young woman to incite the sexual desire that the king's deceased young lover was so good at sustaining.

There is an obvious narratological kinship between Tiridates and Bagoas, including the Iranian proper names used to designate the two. Whether or not they existed has absolutely no relevance. What interested the ancient authors was the love story, made explicit or intimated with expressions, words, and images that were certainly familiar to readers during the Roman period. We find ourselves deep in the Orientalist courtly and harem romance.

In the absence of any biographical indicator, one is therefore free to imagine Bagoas's life, as Mary Renault did in *The Persian Boy* (1972). She too uses images well established among today's readers. The young Bagoas is presented as the son of a Persian noble, Artembares, "of the Pasargadai, Kyros' old royal tribe" (p. 9). The family lives in a castle not far from Susa. Artembares makes the mistake of supporting Arses and opposing the fearsome chiliarch Bagoas, who has him assassinated by his henchmen. Only the young boy survives, most certainly because of his delicate beauty. It is said of him: "A real thoroughbred, the antique Persian strain, the grace of a roe-buck" (p. 12). He is soon sold to a dealer and later castrated, in a scene that the novelist depicts with a great deal of realism. He becomes the sexual partner of Darius, who, in the absence of his wife—held prisoner by Alexander—divides his nights between the young boy and the young women of the royal harem. Bagoas is witness to all the events at court and their repercussions, from Darius's accession to the moment when Nabarzanes gives the eunuch to Alexander. During the confrontation with Orxines (depicted by Curtius) in front of Cyrus's tomb, Bagoas discovers that Orxines is none other than the man who killed his father ten years earlier. That convenient scene of recognition allows the novelist to exonerate Bagoas and therefore Alexander of the flaws and vices of a "whore" that Curtius had heaped upon him.

The Young Eunuch, the King, and the Persian Noble

Curtius's rendering of Orxines's death is typical of his art of rhetoric. The two Persian protagonists are opposites in every way, and the author firmly chooses in favor of Orxines, "pre-eminent among all the barbarians for his nobility," someone "who traced his lineage from Cyrus." He presents Orxines's unjust and cruel death as follows: "Such was the end of the most noble of Persians, a man who was not only innocent but who had also shown the king exemplary kindness."[122]

By contrast, Bagoas has lost the youthful aura he still had when he fell into Alexander's hands. In Curtius's *History*, eunuchs figure greatly in the negative view of Darius III's court that the author promotes and transmits. In describing the organization of the royal cortege leaving Babylon, he notes that it included "herds of eunuchs," placed near the wives and children in the cortege and just ahead of the "360 royal concubines." With an astonishment clearly marked by disapproval, Curtius adds that they "are not at all held in contempt by these peoples."[123] It is clear that, like Tacitus, Curtius believes that the presence within the army of a "large and effeminate procession of concubines and eunuchs," or of "troops of minstrels and eunuchs," accounts for an obvious weakening in virile and military capacities.[124] And when Curtius recalls that, after Darius's death, Alexander also adopted the custom of possessing "365 concubines," he further explains that "along with them were hordes of eunuchs."[125] He then adds an interpolation that refers directly to the femininity of these individuals: they were, he says, "practised in playing the woman's part."[126]

There is little doubt that, in using the expression, Curtius is not merely evoking the physical appearance of the eunuchs or the feminine nature of their daily tasks within the palace. Rather, he is designating, while at the same time condemning, sexual practices in which eunuchs played the passive role. Seen in light of the episode at Pasargadae, Bagoas's relationship with the king is no longer that of a beloved young man toward his elder, in the purest style of Greek pederasty—as it is in the anecdote of the kiss reported by Dicaearchus and then by Plutarch.[127] He is no longer simply Alexander's intimate (adsuetus), having previously been that of Darius. He is one of those men "who allowed themselves to be sexually used as women."[128] Their relationship now falls within the realm of venal sexuality and perverse complicity in the unbridled exercise of power: "The unconscionable male whore did not forget his scheming even when he was submitting to the shame of the sexual act for, whenever he roused the king's passion for him, he would accuse Orsines."[129]

Confirmation can be found of Curtius's profound revulsion for that type of individual in the view he provides of the intimate relationship between two young Macedonians, Dymnus and Nicomachus: Dymnus "was totally devoted to the boy, whose favours he alone enjoyed."[130] Then the young Nicomachus refuses to join the plot against the king and only with great reluctance promises to keep quiet. To make him yield, Dymnus heaps disparaging insults on him, based on a very "virile" view of male/female relations, "alternately calling him an effeminate coward and a traitor to his lover."[131] In the face of his stubborn resistance, Dymnus even comes to threaten Nicomachus physically. Curtius comments: "Nicomachus possessed the steadfast resolve appropriate to a clean-living man."[132] He thereby indicates that the loyalty the young man displays toward the king is so admirable that it is worthy of "normal" sexuality.

The term mignon ("minion"), used by certain modern translators to describe Bagoas, is an anachronism, but one, it seems to me, that accounts fairly well for the way that Curtius himself represents the triangular relationship among Alexander, the Persian nobleman, and the debauched eunuch. In view of the theory advanced by Perrot d'Ablancourt and his contemporaries, such a translation could legitimately be called a belle infidèle: it interprets the situation and the debate of Pasargadae within the looking-glass of the fierce political polemic directed against Henry III and his *mignons*. At that time the term took on very pejorative connotations within circles hostile to the king and to the nobles surrounding him, who were themselves often accused of sodomy. France was sometimes expressly linked to the Asian nations, as in the satirical tract *France-Turquie*. The French, in that view, were nothing but "shriveled-up eunuchs," "castrated and widowed of their virility," "effeminate servers" of their master: "The effeminate character of the *mignon* is implicitly associated with the vices of avarice, sensual pleasure, and ambition, virility being by contrast the perfect form of virtue." As Nicolas Le Roux has shown in *La faveur du roi* (2000), there as well the accusation targets "the flatterer who makes the prince's government shift from the public to the private sphere."

In an earlier episode, no less invented, Sisygambis teaches Alexander the Persian customs that govern the life and station of the princesses.[133] In this case it is Orxines who, addressing Bagoas in indirect speech, claims that "it was not the Persian custom to regard as men those who allowed themselves to be sexually used as women."[134] Did Curtius invent a story out of whole cloth, or did he get the idea from the debate that had raged, from Herodotus to Plutarch and beyond, about the existence or nonexistence of homosexuality among the Persians? Ultimately it makes little difference. Let me simply point out that the words and notions are typically Roman, as illustrated especially by the all-too-common pejorative "herds of eunuchs" used to describe those who accompanied and organized the debauchery.[135] Curtius openly takes the side of the nobility, which, like Orxines, had preserved its traditional virtues since the early generations. That nobility is violently hostile to a despotic monarchy, which brings to power new men, faithless and amoral. In making a Persian his mouthpiece, he seeks to give his account a stamp of authenticity. But it is a transparent ruse: Curtius, defender of the morality of his milieu and of his time, turns a Persian eunuch into a Roman exemplum. Although apparently targeting Alexander, the moral of the story is actually directed first and foremost at the author's contemporaries.

Its political meaning is very clear and similar to the one to be drawn from the stories of "beautiful captives." In this particular case, the king is unable to control his sexual drives. He therefore allows his new lover exorbitant power: Nabarzanes owes his pardon to Bagoas's intervention with Alexander, and it is the eunuch's twisted and vicious intrigues that cause the unjust condemnation of Orxines.[136] In Curtius's eyes, that is the mark of the profound transformation of Alexander, corrupted by the mores inherited from Darius: "At the end of his life, his degeneration from his former self was so complete that, though earlier possessed of unassailable self-control, he followed a male whore's judgement to give some men kingdoms and deprive others of their lives."[137] The man who, not long before, haughtily and with horror rejected the offer that his companions and flatterers made to purchase "two beautiful young [Greek] boys of an extraordinary beauty" for his pleasure, now gives himself to a debauched and venal Asian eunuch.[138] He thereby turns the social order inherited from the ancestors (whether Persians or Romans) completely on its head.

Then comes the death of Orxines, which Curtius renders by the rules of the genre, which dictated that the dying person utter particularly heartfelt last words.[139] Well informed (by Curtius himself!) of the stories that made into an honored precedent the mythical conquests of Queen Semiramis in the epic of Alexander, Orxines, about to expire, launches a final insult at his tormentor: "I had heard that women once were rulers in Asia but this really is something new—a *castrato* as king."[140] Reduced to a status inferior to a woman, Bagoas is thus transformed into a wicked creature, similar to his namesake, "Bagoas the Elder," "a eunuch in physical fact but a militant rogue in disposition," who, from the reign of Artaxerxes III to that of Darius III, created and manipulated kings, reducing them to puppets.[141] Darius was reputed to have eliminated the first Bagoas, to whom he owed the throne, according to one of the recurrent motifs of Macedonian propaganda.[142] He then abandoned himself to the perverse and exorbitant power of a namesake eunuch, younger but just as contemptible and enterprising, who would inject Asia's vices into the very depths of the conqueror's soul.

IV

DARIUS AND DĀRĀ

⁅ 10 ⁆

Dārā and Iskandar

Between Forgetting and Mythical History

It would be a frustrating venture to conduct research on the images of Darius solely through the Greco-Roman literary sources and thereby reduce studies to the Western view alone. It is indispensable to complement that research with an analysis of how Iranian literature received the history of Darius (Dārā) and Alexander (Iskandar). What images did it construct of that last king of a powerful dynasty and of the man who caused a major upheaval in Iranian history?[1]

From the start, however, the shift from Darius to Dārā and from the Greco-Roman documentation to the Iranian literature of the Sassanid period, and then of the Islamic period, raises particular problems and requires a specific approach—and this despite the narrative connections long acknowledged between the Greek *Alexander Romance* and the works compiled in Iran on Iskandar's adventures. Because Dārā's reign and Iskandar's conquest are placed within a vast continuum of Iranian history, the most decisive question raised by the documentation is the relationship the Iranians established and maintained with their past. One must consider the conception of history and of time that they developed, for it is within that conception that they spoke of their own history and that they transmitted a particular representation of the period during which Iskandar defeated and succeeded Dārā.

The problem can be posed in concrete terms, with reference to the inscriptions that princes engraved on the walls of Persepolis, in Persian and in Arabic, between antiquity and the modern age, and in regard to the representations of the remote past they wanted to express thereby. In a captivating study devoted to them, A. S. Melikian-Chirvani points out that "contrary to an image fairly widespread in the West, the site of Persepolis, along with other sites, never fell into complete oblivion, from which it would supposedly have emerged thanks to European science. In reality, not a century went by from the Buyid period onward when royal travelers did not leave a mark of their passing. Their inscriptions, often calligraphied by great masters, make Persepolis a true Islamic memorial, revealing evidence of a series of reflections, extraordinary in their substance, that the sight of the carved bas-reliefs inspired in Iranian Muslims."[2]

Several inscriptions do attest that, well before European travelers, Iranian princes had come to Persepolis, had stopped there, and had sought to leave a memory of their passing engraved in the stone, in Persian and/or Arabic. Nevertheless, though these "meditations on ruins" attest to the princes' desire to situate themselves within the *longue durée* of the glorious Iranian past, they attest as well that the history was almost entirely forgotten. The reflections most often take the form of an ahistorical meditation on the futility of all things human. In 1335 Sheikh Abū Eshāq contemplated the fragility of life: "To whom does the kingdom belong today? To the One God, the Ruler. / Where are the Khōsraus, the tyrants of earliest times? They buried treasures. Neither they nor their treasures have remained!"

Other inscriptions were engraved in 1423 by Ibrahim Sultan, son of Shahrokh. One of them, in Persian, evokes "the victorious standards of the servants of his imperial Majesty . . . erected in this high place and this fortified site: it has become the empire's tent camp." Himself the descendant of Tamerlane and governor of Fārs, the prince did not omit to reflect on his own fate, in a literary form that could be called "funerary": "Our intent in engraving these characters has been that they should remain after us; for alas! I see that our existence is not of long duration. Perhaps one day some pious soul, touched by a feeling of compassion, will address prayers to the Almighty on behalf of the poor!"

Then there is this inscription in Arabic: "Where are those kings who enjoyed sovereign power, until the cup-bearer of death made them swallow the fateful drink? How many cities were built on the earth's surface that were then destroyed, and whose inhabitants are in death's abode?"

It is clear that these meditations do not entail any specific knowledge of the past. In 955 Prince 'Adud al-Dawla indicated on the stone that men of letters had deciphered the ancient inscriptions at his request. The declaration expresses a naïve vainglory. Above all, however, it shows the prince's desire to place himself within a continuity that was all the more impressive in that he found it perfectly impossible to indicate its limits precisely.

Even earlier, in 311 C.E. (during the pre-Islamic period, therefore), eight centuries after the city was founded by Darius I, the Sassanid king Šapur II (310–379), son of Hormazd II, and some of his dignitaries left inscriptions in Pahlevi (Middle Persian) on the north wall of the south portico of Darius I's palace. One of them runs: "In the month of Spandarmah, in the second year of the reign of His Zoroastrian Majesty Šapur [II], the king of kings of Eran and Aneran, whose origin is from the gods. At that time when Šapur, the king of the Sakae, king of Hindustan, Sakistan and Turan down to the seashore . . . travelled on this road, the road from Istakhr to Sakistan, and graciously came here to *sād-stūn* [100 columns = Persepolis], he ate bread in this building. . . . And he organized a great feast, and he had divine rituals performed, and he prayed for his father and his ancestors, and he prayed for Šapur, the king of kings, and he prayed for his own soul, and he also prayed for the one who had this building constructed" (Wiesehöfer trans. in *Ancient Persia* [1996], p. 223).

Eleven years later Šapur sent one of his subordinates, a certain Seleukos, to inspect the inscription he had ordered engraved there. He demonstrated thereby that he too meant to insert himself into an indiscernible millennial history. But let there be no doubt: when the Sassanid king hailed the builders' work, he did not know or even guess at anything about their identity, even less about the era when they had lived and worked. Furthermore, he did not name them. Similarly, the Sassanid kings' use of the cliff of Naqsh-e Rustam to engrave monumental reliefs in no way proves that these kings were informed about the identity of the ancient rulers who had had their tombs dug out just above.

The term used to designate the terrace and the palaces is worth mentioning: *Sād-stūn,* "The Hundred Columns." At around the same time Ammianus Marcellinus, who knew his classics, cited Persepolis as one of the famous cities of Persia (23.6.42). But the remote descendants of Darius and of Xerxes seem to have forgotten that the site was called Pārsa in Old Persian. A few centuries later, when the first European travelers visited the site, the inhabitants presented it to them under the name Čehel-menār ("The Forty Pillars"). From Sād-stūn to Čehel-menār, the same toponymic logic is at work: in both cases the Persians used a descriptive metonymic expression to designate a site whose history totally eluded them. Others used the name Taxt-e Soleimān, "Throne (or House) of Solomon." That designation recalls the "Tomb of the Mother of Solomon," the name regularly given to the tomb of Cyrus in Pasargadae, which is one in a whole series of "biblical" toponyms widespread in the region. Also attested is Taxt-e Jāmšīd, "Throne of Jāmšīd," even today the preferred term in use in

Iran. Finally, Chardin and others mention that the guides referred to the "House of Darius" (Taxt-e Dārā) as well. Everything suggests that, under that king's name, they were signifying one of the two Dārās known to Iranian dynastic legend, either Alexander's adversary or that Dārā's father. One need only read the pages Chardin wrote about the date of the structures and about the legends and histories he heard during his travels (17: 21–41) to be convinced that, in the representations the Persians made of their past at the time, the site, its builders, and the kings who had lived there were situated indistinctly in epic and legendary times.

In 1423, eleven centuries after Šapur II and nearly twenty centuries after Darius I, Ibrahim Sultan also ordered the engraving of inscriptions:

> Whom therefore do you know among the sovereigns of the Iranians,
> From the time of Feridun, or Zahhāk, or Jam,
> Whose throne and kingdom did not undergo decline,
> Who from the hand of fate did not suffer insult?
> Did it not sail all day on the wings of the wind,
> That throne of Solomon, salvation be upon it?

It is interesting to note that, in hailing the ancient kings, Ibrahim Sultan mentions neither the Achaemenid nor the Askhanian and Sassanid kings. He quite naturally chooses well-known names of mythical kings. The Iranian royal epic, elaborated over the centuries, was given concrete form in about the year 1000, in Ferdowsī's *Book of the Kings*. Persian and Arabo-Persian annalists and poets organized their narratives into four dynasties (and four trimillenniums), based on the mythical divisions of Iranian time. The first dynasty, Pishdadian, is said to have lasted 2,441 years. It was founded by Gayomard, the "first man," who had to defend himself against the evil demon, Ahriman. The second dynasty, the Keyānid, is reputed to have reigned for 732 years. These two dynasties are largely indistinguishable from mythical times, though the last two kings of the Keyānid dynasty, Dārā and Iskandar, represent in principle the two historical figures who clashed between 334 and 330.

The last two dynasties, the Askhanian (Arsacid) and the Sassanid, are situated in a more clearly determined historical era, though the tone of the narrative remains epic, often very remote from historical narrative. In 1335 Sheikh Abū Eshāq evoked the fourth dynasty under the name Khōsrau. There is no doubt that this is the famous Khōsrau I Anuširwan ("of the immortal soul"), who ruled Iran from 531 to 579. He quickly became legendary as a magnanimous and simple king, whose virtues are depicted in a multitude of *adab* (an equivalent of sorts to the exempla, which offer exemplary illustrations of the right way to live). That may explain why the Sassanid king, mentioned by a fourteenth-century prince, is placed within a very misty past, associated with the anonymous and indistinct category of "tyrants of the earliest times."

The kings that Ibrahim Sultan cites belong to the first dynasty. Jam(shid), the fourth king in the succession, is reputed to have brought peace and prosperity and to have organized society into four classes (priests, warriors, farmers, and artisans). But, puffed up with pride, he was dethroned after a "reign of seven hundred years." He was succeeded by Zahhāk, an evil and even monstrous king who "reigned for a thousand years." Serpents coming out of his shoulders devoured the brains of young men. He was in turn defeated by Feridun, heir to Jamshid's glory. Feridun chained Zahhāk to Mount Alborz (Demavend) and succeeded him.

One has only to leaf through Ferdowsī's *Book of the Kings* to realize that the kings most often mentioned are those of the first dynasties. The kings of the Sassanid period invoke the early sovereigns as well, using expressions clearly borrowed from the princes who left traces behind in Persepolis. As Bahram Gūr, one of the most famous Sassanid kings, exclaims: "Where is the master of the throne of Feridun, who was the support of his age? Where are these powerful offspring of the royal race, Key Khōsrau, master of the world, and Key Kobad?" (bk. 34, lines 378–380).[3] In the same way, it is the epic kings that Ferdowsī's Dārā evokes before his valiant knights, despairing at the two successive defeats he had just suffered at Iskandar's hands: "The Rūmi [Iskandar] has become Zahhāk, and we are Jamshid" (bk. 19, lines 212–213). It was, of course, the narrator Ferdowsī himself who directly inspired the authors of the inscriptions in Persepolis. During a melancholic and anxious meditation on the succession of kings, did he not exclaim: "Where are Feridun, Zahhāk, and Jamshid, the princes of the Arabs and the kings of Persia? Where are those powerful Sassanids, from the descendants of Bahram to the Samanids?" (bk. 21, lines 29–30). These are the same three legendary kings who were evoked by Ibrahim Sultan in 1423. And Jamshid and Feridun are linked once again by Nizāmī, who reports Bahram Gūr's royal pretensions. Claiming to be a descendant of Jamshid, Bahram Gūr also declares: "Neither the throne of Jamshid nor the crown of Feridun has lasted until the present."[4]

Bīrūnī, a contemporary of Ferdowsī and a famous specialist on history, chronology, and many other disciplines, did transmit a list of ten "Persian kings who reigned after the fall of the Median kingdom," even mentioning the duration of each of their reigns.[5] There one finds names and a succession well attested elsewhere, from Cyrus to Arses and Darius III. But the author is following not an Iranian tradition but the Greco-Babylonian one, to which he had access through the Syriac authors.[6] This example shows once again the importance of the Greco-Roman and Babylonian sources for reconstituting Achaemenid dynastic history. In Iran, the epico-mythical tradition tends to dominate and to determine representations of the past.

Within that vast fresco of mythical history, composed primarily of accounts of the first two dynasties, it was often believed that the second (Keyānid) dynasty "corresponded" to the Achaemenid dynasty. That is certainly the image that the Iranians of the medieval period formed of a past that was as remote to them as it was incomprehensible. Nizāmī designates as follows one of the princes who came to entertain the king: "The first princess was of high Keyānid stock, that is, of Persian and Achaemenid stock."[7] This is likely the reason efforts were long made (since Bīrūnī himself) to identify one or another of the ten royal Keyānid figures—from the founder, Key Kobad, to Dārā and Iskandar—as a particular Achaemenid king. The enterprise was pointless and hopeless. The names of the kings in one tradition may certainly correspond to those in the other, given that they were never lost: the petty princes of Fārs from the Seleucid and Parthian periods also bore the names of Achaemenid kings, for example, "Artaxerxes" (Ardašir) and "Darius" (Dārev). But because the endeavor was not historiographical in nature, the incoherencies and inventions are too numerous and ponderous to allow us to rehistoricize the narratives of royal legends—whether they concern the ancestry of Darius III/Dārā, supposedly the son of another Dārā(b), or of that Dārā(b), who is said to have succeeded his mother, Homai, or, obviously, of Iskandar, reputed to be the son of Dārā(b). Similarly, the Keyānid king Vištaspa is not a representation (not even a distorted one) of the father of Darius I (Hystaspes/Vištaspa); Ardašir son of Bahman is not Artaxerxes II; and Dārā(b) has nothing to do with Darius I or Darius II.

All the evidence shows that the history of the Achaemenid dynasty was quickly forgotten in Persia, even after the Macedonian conquest. More exactly, it was transmitted orally from one generation to the next as mythical representations. As early as the Achaemenid period, that transmission was one of the duties of the magi, responsible for educating the young men of the Persian aristocracy. These "wise men," as seen in Xenophon, Dinon, and even Strabo, were tasked with memorizing the royal legends and transmitting them to the young.[8] It was these founding myths of collective identity that, at a given moment, were codified as "books of kings." It was also primarily in oral form that the narratives were transmitted in the Sassanid period, by "minstrels" *(gōsān)*, but also later, in the medieval and modern periods and even afterward, by itinerant storytellers *(naqqāl)*. Some of them (the "reciters of the books of kings"), from the reign of Ferdowsī's patron Mahmūd on down, specialized in the recitation of *Shāh-nāmeh*. Different books of kings and also popular romances, transmitted in written and oral form and also as painted images, long exerted a strong influence, determining the conception the Iranians had of their past. Any research on a particular segment of that epic must always take into account these collective representations, which give each segment its meaning. The story of Dārā and Iskandar is no exception to the rule.

From Dārā to Ardašir in Sassanid Literature

Although, overall, the Iranians shared a common vision of the past, after the Arab conquest Islamization did not affect all populations equally. In Fārs, but also in other regions, some groups—those the European travelers called "Guebres"— remained attached to the ancient Zoroastrian religion.[9] Chardin had frequent exchanges with them and provides his readers with long descriptions of their particular customs. He adheres completely to his interlocutors' interpretation of their remote past, including the bitter memory of Alexander's invasion:[10]

> I have found nothing more sensible in their teachings than the ill they speak of Alexander. Instead of admiring him and revering his name, as so many others do, they despise him, hate him, and curse him, considering him a pirate, a brigand, a man without justice and without brains, born to disrupt the order of the world and to destroy part of the human race. Among themselves, they whisper the same thing about Muhammad. They place both men at the top of the list of bad princes, one for having personally been the instrument of so many misfortunes, such as fire, murder, rape, and sacrilege, the other for having been the cause, the occasion for them. They know quite well that their ruin comes from these two usurpers, Alexander and Muhammad, and they are not wrong in that. (17: 8)

Before Chardin (in about 1650), Father Gabriel de Chinon collected similar traditions about Alexander, destroyer of religion and of the holy books: "After his death, a just punishment for his temerity and malice, their doctors—who had run from the carnage and fled to the mountains to save their lives and their religion—gathered together, and seeing they had no books left, wrote one about what they still remembered of those they had read so many times."[11]

That image of Alexander dates back to early antiquity. Although it was long thought that it had originated in Persia, following the destruction wrought in Persepolis, the available documentation indicates that it began to take shape during the Sassanid period. At practically the same time that the *Alexander Romance* was circulating in the West, and that the anonymous author of the *Itinerarium Alexandri* was recalling the exploits of the Macedonian to Emperor Constantius— about to leave on a campaign against the Persians (in about 338)—an entirely different image of Alexander was being elaborated in Iran. Starkly negative, it would gain strength and spread throughout the period, up to the defeat of the last Sassanid king, Yazdegerd III, at the hands of Caliph 'Umar's troops. The educated and religious Sassanid milieus brought two charges against Iskandar: he had ruined the "good religion" *(Dēn)*, and he had destroyed Iran's political unity.

The protagonist of a large portion of the literature dating back to that period is Ardašir I, conqueror of the Parthians and founder of the Sassanid dynasty (224–239/240). He is the hero of the *Book of Great Deeds of Ardašir, Son of Papak (Kārnāmē ī Artakšīr ī Pāpakān).* A legend of the founder, this book consists of initiatory adventures somewhat reminiscent of those attributed to Alexander in his Romance and in Iranian literature. It lauds King Ardašir's restoration of Iranian greatness: the king succeeded in repairing the destruction Iskandar had caused. Supposedly a descendant of the Dārā defeated by Alexander, Ardašir was reputed to be worthy of the glory of the Keyānids.

Special interest should be accorded to another text, known under the title *Letter of Tansar.* The Pahlevi original, attributed to Bahram, son of Xorzād, and to the "learned men of Fārs," was translated into Arabic in the eighth century, then retranslated into Persian by Ibn Isfandiyār in 1216. The first part contains the letter as well as a text titled "Correspondence between Alexander and Aristotle." Tansar is known through other texts, especially the *Dēnkard,* where he is called a "man of the doctrine of the ancients." In the time of Ardašir, Tansar was the high priest charged with restoring the Right Religion and collecting all the lost or destroyed texts of the Avesta. In his famous book, *Meadows of Gold,* al-Mas'ūdī, an Arab author from the late tenth century, introduces him as the king or governor of the province of Persia and as a member of the Platonic sect, "that is, the school of Socrates and Plato."

Tansar's interlocutor, Gušnasp, is the "King of Tabaristān and Pariswăr." When Ardašir creates a new, greater Iranian kingdom at the expense of the last Arsacid king, Gušnasp is reluctant to rally behind him and asks for Tansar's advice. Tansar will persuade Gušnasp to acknowledge the sovereignty of the Sassanid king, using an argument that closely associates politics and religion. Fundamentally, this is a dissertation *peri basileias* (on kingship), intended to answer the questions that traditionally troubled thinkers close to power: How to exercise good kingship? What acts legitimate royal power? Tansar presents four arguments. First, he says that Ardašir, within fourteen years, had succeeded in restoring a country that had been in ruins for four centuries, ever since Alexander's invasion. Second, Tansar addresses the question of the division of society into four classes (religious, warriors, scribes, producers). Third, he deals with the question of punishment. And finally, he notes in detail the grave problem of succession to the throne. Alexander's invasion and its negative consequences are addressed in the first, historical part, in the form of a flashback. The figure of Dārā and his reign are introduced in the discourse on dynastic succession.

Another Sassanid document is closely related to the letter: the *Testament of Ardašir*, known through an Arabic translation. The king writes that testament for Šapur, the son who is supposed to succeed him. The virtues of a sovereign are set down in writing, as is the connection between power and religion: "Know that kingship and religion are twins, neither of which can exist without the other, since religion is the foundation of kingship, and the king is the guardian of religion. . . . Know that the decadence of nations begins when subjects are allowed to concern themselves with things other than their traditional and known activities."[12]

The same topoi are found in the testament and in the letter: in particular, the necessity of every subject to remain bound to his class, and the king's fervent obligation not to divulge the name of the crown prince.

Two Pahlevi encyclopedias, the *Dēnkard* and the *Greater Bundahišn*, may also be cited in this context. Both undoubtedly date back to the end of the Sassanid period and the beginning of the Islamic period. The *Dēnkard*, from the tenth century, is an encyclopedic overview of the Mazdean religion. Book 4 provides a history of the restoration of the Avesta and the Zand (Pahlevi commentary) from Dārā to the Arsacid period. That history includes the destruction of these texts, attributed to Iskandar: "Then came His Majesty Ardašir i Pāpākan, king of kings, for the restoration of the kingdom of Iran, who had this record of the dispersal brought [to where he was] and in a single place. Then appeared Tosar [Tansar], the Ancient Sage, the Just, who was the Herbed. He collated it with this information from the Avesta, and, under orders, completed it in accordance with that information" (3.430).

Other allusions to the Macedonian appear in books 3 and 5, in repetitive formulations. The *Bundahišn,* probably dating to the end of the Sassanid period, is a compilation in Pahlevi of Mazdean cosmology and cosmography. The book gives an account of Iranian mythical, historical, and eschatological times, from the first man to the end of the world; it covers some 12,000 years, divided into four trimillenniums. The fourth trimillennium begins with the appearance of Zoroaster. Historical times are marked by struggles between the farmers and the nomadic peoples, between Iran and Turan (Central Asia), between Iran and Iskandar, and between Iran and the Turks.

One of the most interesting works is the *Book of Arda Viraf (Ardā Vīrāz Nāmag).* The extant edition may date to the ninth century, but, like the other books written in Pahlevi, it must have been set in writing after a long oral transmission. This is a very important text for the study of Iranian eschatology. It gives the account of an initiate, destined to visit paradise and hell after drinking a narcotic. Viraf was chosen by ordeal from a group of "seven men, the most steadfast in divine matters and religion," to take a journey to the next world. There he will consult the Menogs, "the gods and the souls of the righteous." He will have to determine whether acts of worship reach the gods or rather the demons (1.15). At the end of his journey, he comes back to the world of "material beings," having received a sermon from Orhmazd, "the holiest of the Menogs": "Righteous Viraf, tell the Mazdeans of the *gētīg:* the path of justice and the path of the elders' doctrine are one, and all other paths are no path. Take that one path, and do not deviate from it in times of prosperity or in times of distress" (101.7–8).

The Accursed Aliksandar

Beyond its diversity, the literature as a whole transmits a common message: the superiority of the right religion and the connection existing between the establishment and respect for the right religion and the legitimacy of royal power. The king must be the defender and preserver of religion. In short, these writings mark the link between the right religion, good kingship, and the Iranians' power. Political defeat and the destruction of religion go hand in hand. The political meaning of this literature is no less obvious. It reveals a desire on the part of the Sassanids to legitimate their power. The magic word is "revival," the restoration of affairs prior to Iskandar. The great political theme is the shift from the unity of Iran (under Dārā) to its division (from Iskandar on), then a reverse movement—from division to unity—thanks to the achievements of Dārā's true successor, Ardašir. Within such a system of logic, Alexander's personality and achievements can only be seen negatively: he is the destroyer of the unity and glory of Iran, and he is also the destroyer of religion.

In the *Letter of Tansar,* Ardašir's work of restoration is directed against the destruction wrought by Alexander, which caused political disunity and the disappearance of the religious traditions. Dārā is not exempt from all responsibility for the disaster. On the advice of Aristotle, Alexander does not put the nobles to death. To do so would be to leave power in the hands of the "wicked." Rather, Aristotle advises:

> "Divide the realm of Iran among their princes . . . giving none precedence, ascendancy or authority over another, that each may be absolute on the throne of his own domain. . . . There will appear among them so much disunity and variance and presumption and haughtiness, so much opposition and rivalry about power, so much bragging and vaunting about wealth, so much contention over degree, and so much ruffling and wrangling over retainers, that they will have no leisure to seek vengeance upon you, and being occupied one with another will not be free to think upon the past." . . . [Alexander] divided the land of the Persians among their princes, who became known as the "kings of the peoples" [*Mulūk uattvāif*]. (§ 3)

Gušnasp was one of these provincial kings. He had a special status, however, having reconquered the territory from Alexander's successors by force of arms. Moreover, he adhered to the faith and party of the kings of Fārs. That explains the letter Tansar sent him, urging him to rally behind Ardašir. In any case, the invasion culminated in the destruction of religion:

> Know that Alexander burnt the book of our religion—1200 ox-hides—at Istaxr. One third of it was known by heart and survived, but even that was all legends and traditions, and men knew not the laws and ordinances; until, through the corruption of the people of the day and the decay of royal power and the craving for what was new and counterfeit and the desire for vainglory, even those legends and traditions dropped out of common recollection, so that not an iota of the truth of that book remained. Therefore the faith must needs be restored by a man of true and upright judgment. (§ 11)

Alexander's image is not fundamentally different in the *Testament of Ardašir*—
which makes sense, given that the two texts were inspired by the same sources.
Holding forth on the problems of royal succession, Ardašir lists the kings who
preceded him. He distinguishes them from one another, but at the same time
gathers them together in a single formulation: "And these kings succeeded one
another in the same spirit, as if they were a single king. Their souls were like
one soul, the predecessor strengthening [the kingdom] for his successor and the
successor remaining faithful to his predecessor. So that the accounts of their
ancestors, the legacy of their opinions, and the disciplines of their understanding were combined in their descendants after their deaths. It was as if the ancestors came together with the descendants to instruct and advise them" (p. 71).

That admirable continuity of the race, but also of the dynastic ethos, was
shattered by Alexander: "[And all that lasted] until what came to pass on the
head of Dārā, son of Dārā, came to pass, and Alexander took from him what he
wrested from him of our kingdom. Alexander considered it more important to
destroy our power, to divide our people, and to annihilate the prosperity of our
country than to spill our blood" (p. 71).

Then came the restoration of the ancient order, under the leadership of
Ardašir himself. Many other texts show that, in order to achieve that restoration, he had to split apart and then reunite the 240 "tribal kings." These were
the same kings among whom Alexander had divided Dārā's former kingdom,
on Aristotle's advice, rather than put to death the nobles surrounding the conquered king: "When god allowed the [re]unification of our country and state,
and of the nobles, there came to pass what came to pass for us by the grace of
god. By carefully considering this, you will avoid missteps, and those who follow us will be richer in experience than we, when they learn the lesson from
the extraordinary wonders we have known" (p. 71).

In other words, Ardašir reestablished the continuity of good kingship and
good religion; he ended the contemptible digression introduced by Alexander.

Similar, even identical, representations are also found in the *Book of Arda
Viraf*:

> It is said that, once the saint Zoroaster had propagated throughout the
> world the religion he had received, after three hundred years the religion
> was in its purity, and men lived in certainty. But then the accursed bad
> Spirit, the evil one, in order to make men doubt that religion, led astray
> the accursed Aliksandar, the Greek living in Egypt, who came to the

Aryan country with a harsh tyranny, war, and illness. And he killed the
governor [dahibed] of the Aryans, destroyed and ruined the court and the
monarchy. And that religion, all the Avesta and the Zand, written in a
golden liquid on prepared oxhide, was deposited in Staxr-Pāpagān, in the
"Fortress of Writings." And that evil-doing enemy, heretical and wicked,
the maleficent Aliksandar, the Greek living in Egypt, took them and
burned them. And he killed many priests, judges, herbeds, and mobeds,
many faithful, experts, and wise men of the country of Ērān. And after
that, the people of the country of Ērān were in revolt and struggled one
against another, and since they had neither a sovereign [xvadāy] nor a governor [dahibed] nor a priest who knew about religion, and remained in
doubt about divine things, many varieties of doctrines and beliefs, heresies,
doubts, and differences came to the world. (1.1–9)[13]

In the books written in Pahlevi, various themes echo one another. The author of the *Great Deeds of Ardašir* writes, for example: "After the death of Alexander, resident of Rum, there were no fewer than 240 princes in the territory of
Iran" (§ 1). The *Dēnkard* (5.3.3) lists Alexander as one of the evildoers who began
a period of destruction, after Arjasp (enemy of King Vištaspa), and before "the
wild-haired demon. . . . The second was Alexander the Roman, a man of death
and ill repute, and those who were with him." Alexander the destroyer is a
"wretched man" (*dušxvuarrah*: 7.7). In one of the passages that vigorously condemn the invader, the writer recounts that the Mazdean faith was set down
in writing by the illustrious Keyānid ruler Kay Vištaspa: "He deposited all
these fundaments in the royal Treasure [*ganz i shaspikān*] and ordered that
suitable copies be distributed. Then he sent a copy to the Fortress of Writings
[*diz i nipišt*], and it was there that the information was kept. During the up-
heavals that affected the *Dēn* and the monarchy of Iran, by the deeds of the
accursed Alexander, the copy in the Fortress of Writings was lost to fire, and
the one in the Royal Treasury fell into the Romans' hands, was translated
into the Greek language, and was combined with the information of the ancients" (3.420).

Book 4 recalls the history of the holy book from Dārā to Khōsrau I. It is
Dārā who, unusually, is hailed here as the first king to have "ordered two copies
of the entire Avesta and Zand to be set in writing, in the very form that Zoroaster had received them from Ohrmazd, and that these copies be preserved,
one in the Royal Treasury, the other in the country's archive." After the

destruction wrought by Alexander, it fell to the Parthian Vologeses, then to the Sassanid Ardašir, assisted by Tansar, to do the work of restoration.[14]

The *Great Bundahišn* depicts Alexander's maleficent role no differently: "When King Dārā, son of Dārā, exercised kingship, Alexander, caesar of Rum, invaded the kingdom of the Iranians, put to death King Dārā, exterminated all the families of rulers, the magi, and the nobles of the kingdom of Iran, extinguished a great number of fires, seized the Zand of the Mazdean religion [*dēn*], and sent it to Rum. He burned the Avesta and divided the kingdom of the Iranians into ninety family chiefs [petty princes]. In the same millennium came Ardašir son of Pāpāk, who put these dynasts to death, restored [royal] power, and promoted the religion of the Mazdeans."

Beyond the variations in detail (for example, the number of petty princes who succeeded Dārā's monarchy), the context is much the same. That body of literature conveys an eschatological vision of religion and royal power in Iran, in a history reconstituted primarily through very vague memories, themselves resituated within the invariable framework of preestablished representations of the world. It is not actually known what happened in Alexander's time: it would be rather surprising if he really did destroy the religion and the holy books.[15] It seems rather that the Zoroastrians of later eras had to explain why and how the "right religion" had disappeared; they had to designate the responsible parties. Were the holy books even compiled in full at that time? The question is a subject of heated debate, because transmission was exclusively oral throughout the Achaemenid period. Passages from the *Letter of Tansar* (11) and other Pahlevi writings attest clearly to the importance of memorization on the part of wise men and scholars.[16]

In any event, among the Zoroastrians of the Sassanid period, Alexander was regularly denounced as the one who had destroyed the foundations of society, kingship, and the right religion *(dēn)*. Through the dark legend of Aliksandar/Alexander, they express the desire to restore a millenarian state of things, the intangible organization of the world, imposed and protected by the gods and maintained on earth by their lieutenant, the "good king." This is both a concept and a belief, what the royal Achaemenid inscriptions call *arta* (truth, loyalty, order). Every Great King proclaimed himself to be its preserver or even its restorer, against the forces of *drauga* (deception, rebellion, disorder). Aliksandar is placed resolutely on the side of disorder and evil; Ardašir, by contrast, comes to restore the order of the world in all its divine plenitude.

Dārā the Bad King

By contrast, Dārā appears passive most of the time, performing no actions of his own. He is included simply because his reign marks the end of a cycle in Iranian history. Alexander's invasion took place at that time, and the narrative references are clustered around that event. The name of the last of the Keyānid kings is not even expressly mentioned in the *Book of Arda Viraf*: he is recognizable only through the anonymous and generic titulature "leader of the country of the Aryans [Iranians]" (1.4: *Ērān dahibed*).

When the role of Dārā in the country's disaster is addressed directly—which is rare—he is not characterized as a hero of Iran. This is altogether clear in Tansar's reply. In the first place, Dārā was defeated after being betrayed by his intimate circle. Although opprobrium is heaped upon the regicides, a king betrayed by his own men during battle, then murdered, cannot be said have the stuff of a hero—particularly because, though the traitors' conduct is not justified morally, it is so politically. To understand the author's portrayal of Dārā as a bad king, one must consider the logic of his discourse on royal legitimation. Tansar is seeking to reply to one of the objections that Gušnasp had raised about the possibility of rallying behind Ardašir. The "King of Tabaritān and Parišwǎr" was surprised that Ardašir chose not to name an heir. Tansar replies that, in his view, the king showed wisdom in that respect, because his decision allowed and would allow people to live in peace and tranquility: "Since to know the succession holds no advantage for king or people, it is best hidden" (§ 10). The same lesson appears in the *Testament of Ardašir*: "Among the things that cause the perversion of subjects is the disclosure of the crown prince's identity. Here is the corruption that comes of it: a burning enmity begins to pit the king against the crown prince. No two people are so violently opposed as when one is working to destroy the other's desires. That is precisely the case between the king and the heir to the throne. . . . From the moment they separate as a result of mutual suspicion, each chooses his own friends, his own 'faithful,' and his own entourage" (p. 76).

Tansar cites the example of the story of Dārā, son of Sheherazad, the father of the Dārā in question here (§§ 28–39). Dārā the Elder, nicknamed "Toyūlšāh" (the word's meaning is uncertain), was handsome and respected by everyone, "from China to the western lands of Greece." But Dārā, his son, and their people to that day were assailed by "troubles and afflictions." The Persians' defeat at the hands of the "accursed Alexander" is attributed to the modalities of

succession from Dārā the Elder to Dārā the Younger, and more precisely, to the
son's certainty from birth that he would succeed his father: "When the child
had left the time of cradle and swaddling band . . . he had the gates of honour
flung open and the resources of fatherly favour marshalled. He had devoted
servants for his education and for organizing him and his household, and appointed officials, so that from the moment when he opened his eyes he saw
himself crowned and enthroned. He did not think that kingship came by an act
of God, but that it was peculiarly his own attribute. He neglected to seek light
from the counsel of men of intelligence and understanding and from those of
whom he would one day have need. To himself he said: *From father to son, kingship is mine. The Sun and the sown, the fowl and the fish, all are mine'* " (§ 37).

Here again is a specific form of a debate that was not confined to the political thought of Iran. On the contrary, it brings to mind Greek and Hellenistic
discussions of the respective qualities of the "king, son of a king" and of the
"king born of an ordinary subject," which Plato conducted in his overview of
Persian dynastic history. Plato denounces Cambyses and Xerxes, "kings, the
sons of kings," made soft by the care of the women and eunuchs of the palace.[17]
Similarly, Dārā, reared in purple, honors, and flattery, was spoiled from the
start by a whole set of flaws that would prove fatal to him and to his people.

To illustrate his thesis, the author of the *Letter of Tansar* depicts two advisers, opposites in every way (§§ 36–38). One, by the name of Bīrī, is a young page
of Dārā the Younger. Lacking lucidity, Dārā yields to his adviser, whose name,
among the Iranians, became synonymous with an unhappy fate. The other,
Dārā Toyūlšāh's secretary and adviser Rastīn, was "broken to work and galled
in harness, tried and trusted in his service, wise, of sound judgment, pious and
faithful, of pleasing appearance and acclaimed character, with a virtuous disposition and auspicious temperament." Against the increasing attacks and slan-
derous public denunciations of Bīrī, Rastīn requests a secret audience with
Dārā the Elder: "At that time, if people could not tell the King of kings a matter
plainly, they would invent fictitious anecdotes and tales out of their own heads."
That is what Rastīn does. He tells the story of the monkey king who, unable to
convince his personal attendants of a looming danger, preferred to leave his
kingdom on his own initiative. Of course, the anticipated danger became a catastrophe for the inhabitants. The author draws the following lesson: "Truly
revolt against the counsel of a compassionate, wise and experienced man be-
queathes sorrow and leaves behind remorse." Too late, then, the monkeys regret not having followed the advice of "a king, wise and sagacious, virtuous

and learned, who knew the wonders of the world and the marvels of the heavens" and had a "powerful intellect." Rastīn soon leads Dārā the Elder to understand the meaning of the apologue. Some time later, Bīrī dies, "and it was said that Toγūlšāh had had him poisoned at the house of a general."

Then comes the death of Dārā the Elder. Dārā the Younger "seated himself on his father's throne and the peoples of the world offered him felicitations. From India and China, from Greece [*Rum*] and Palestine they gathered at his court with presents and offerings, fair women and tokens to be remembered" (§ 37).

Alas, Dārā understood nothing about politics: "Dārā could not forbear first granting the vazirship to Bīrī's brother. . . . When Bīrī's brother had acquired absolute authority over the realm of Dārā, in revenge for his brother he carried fabrications to the king concerning the famous men and leaders, the rulers and commanders who had been associates and friends of Rastīn. Since the king was young and arrogant and lacked training in affairs, he would not sanction the pardon of transgressions, till it came about that throughout the world the coinage of men's hearts was debased for him and hatred of him became fixed in men's innermost thoughts and trust in his words and deeds vanished. He abandoned the customs of the ancients and adopted this secretary's new ways" (§ 37).

It is easy to imagine what happened upon Alexander's arrival: "When tidings came that Alexander was in the field on his western borders, the king was set on the steed of foolhardihood and the reins of presumption were given into his hand. When the encounter took place, some deserted him, one group set about making terms with the enemy, and others flung themselves upon him and slew him. They repented thereafter, but it was when repentance for that wickedness was without avail" (§ 38).

As a function of that example, the king of kings (Ardašir) "made this a rule, that none who comes after him should name his heir."

It is clear that Dārā the Younger is, first and foremost, a representation of the "bad king," reared to be arrogant, a mindless young man contemptuous of the advice of the elders. When Ardašir sets out to restore Iranian might, he does so with the reign of Dārā Toγūlšāh in mind, not that of his son. But Toγūlšāh is no more a historical figure than is his son. The memory of both, entirely reconstituted, is put to use in what is nothing but an exemplum composed as a panegyric of Ardašir, the only real hero of the story.

From Alexander to Iskandar

Narratives, annals, and poems from the medieval period, constructed around an epic representation of the different Iranian dynasties from the foundation of the world, also regularly insert one or several chapters on Iskandar's conquest of Iran and on his later adventures. The figure of the conqueror from Macedonia (Rūm) has been abundantly studied and continues to produce studies of the greatest importance. Because it would be absurd to attempt to study the figure of Dārā without at the same time identifying the characteristic traits attributed to Iskandar, I shall make ample use of these specialized studies in the following pages. But my intention here is not to present a synthesis of that now well-known theme. Rather, I wish to open the discussion of a particular aspect that has been oddly neglected, no doubt because it is judged both subordinate and less captivating: that of the figure and role of Dārā in the books published in Iran between about the ninth and twelfth centuries. I shall also allow myself to delve into works dating to a later era.

Among the storytellers of yore, as they would be called, the first was the Persian Dīnawarī, who lived between 894 and 903. Of the fifteen or so works attributed to him, one is preserved almost in its entirety: a history of Islam written from the Persian point of view. Foremost among the annalists are Tabarī (839–923) and Tha'ālibī (961–1038). Tabarī, "the supreme universal historian" to borrow C. E. Bosworth's expression (1998a), wrote a history in which he made use of many readings. He traced that history from the Creation of the world and the prophets, and then, in the form of annals, up to 915. Several chapters are devoted to the ancient kings of the Persians, including a history of Bahman and his children (chap. 109), the reign of Dārā, son of Bahman (chap. 111), and the confrontation between Dārā, son of Dārā, and Iskandar (chap. 113). Tha'ālibī was the author of *Universal History,* published in 1021. The first part is devoted to the kings of Persia and is written in a style generally judged more precise than Tabarī's. He traces that "Persian history" from the first man, Gayomard, to the last Sassanid king, Yazdegerd. Many traditions about the kings appear in this book, but Tha'ālibī also quotes a number of apothegms and aphorisms drawn from collections of exempla. There is also a report on the Persian dynasties in al-Ma'sūdī's *Meadows of Gold,* also based on "the Persians' attachment to their traditions, which they transmit from one generation to the next and from father to son." That book begins with Gayomard, the first man, and goes to "Dārā, son of Dārā, son of Bahman, who, in the ancient language of Persia, is named

Daraïous, and who was killed, after a thirty-year reign, by Iskandar son of Fili-
bus the Macedonian" (21). Later, in about 1110, Ibn' Bakhlī composed *Fārs-nāmeh,*
two-thirds of which deals with the pre-Islamic period. The Sassanid period is
discussed at length, but the author also speaks of the first mythic dynasties of
Iran, attributing, for example, the construction of the city of Istakhr to the first
king, Gayomard.

Tha'ālibī was writing at about the same time that Ferdowsī was preparing
his monumental *Book of the Kings,* which is both a museum of sorts, devoted to
Iranian memory, and a collection of archetypes of the ideal monarch. Born in
Tus (in ancient Parthia) in about 939/940, Ferdowsī wrote a *Shāh-nāmeh* for Sultan Mahmūd. In it he gives his epic account, from the first man to the death of
the last Sassanid king, Yazdegerd III, defeated by Sultan 'Umar's armies. Figures and events already briefly glimpsed reappear: Bahman (16), succeeded by
his daughter and wife Homai (17); Dārā the Elder (also called Dārāb) and his
battle against Pheïlekous, whose daughter Nahid he married and then repudiated; and the birth of Iskandar and of Dārā, son of Dārā (18), who soon succeeded his father and who fought Iskandar (19). Then comes a very long book
(20) devoted to the legendary and wondrous adventures of Iskandar, and finally
to his death in Babylon.

Foremost among the great Persian poets is Nizāmī (ca. 1141–1217). He wrote
five long epic poems collected in the *Khamsa (Quintet),* or *Pandj gandj (Five Treasures).* Influenced by Ferdowsī's reading but treated in a specific mode, the account of the adventures of Iskandar *(Iskandar-nāmeh)* is divided into two parts:
the *Sharaf-nāmeh (Book of Honor)* and the *Ikbal-nāmeh (Book of Wisdom).* The first
part is devoted to an account of the conquest, whereas the second presents Iskandar as a wise man and prophet, a true archetype of the ideal sovereign and
an inspired prophet.

To assess that body of literature properly, one needs to realize from the
start that the struggle between Iskandar and Dārā generally occupies only a
few sections or a few chapters in it. As in the *Alexander Romance,* most of the
narrative has to do with the adventures after Dārā's death, during which Iskandar was led to discover the world and its wonders, and to discover himself.
Over time, that tendency would only become more prominent. Centered on
extolling wisdom and religion, the Islamic literature would increasingly give
precedence to philosophical reflection. It would make Iskandar and certain episodes the basis for collections of exempla. For example, in Jāmi's *Kerad-nāmeh-ye
eskandarī (Book of Alexandrian Wisdom),* completed in 1484, the reader can peruse

twenty-seven sections, each of which is introduced by a short narrative and followed by a philosophical apologue, an anecdote, and a final comment. As C.-H. Fouchécour rightly remarks, "Jāmi condensed the story of Alexander, so as to insert it into a book of wisdom for the use of the prince and his court."[18] There is no longer a continuous narrative strictly speaking. Tastes had evolved: "We did not read the story of Iskandar and Dārā," the poet Hāfez had already said. Jāmi, of course, represents the end of a literary and intellectual development. But the works of his great predecessors—Ferdowsī, and especially, Nizāmī—though devoted to narration, were also books of wisdom and advice, whose purpose was to define good kingship. The story of Iskandar and Dārā always constituted a source of examples with a moral value. To borrow the words of al-Ma'sūdī (21:102), "a society can live only under the aegis of a king who leads and who imposes respect for justice and obedience to the laws dictated by reason."

Brother, Enemy, Hero

From the Sassanid period to the Islamic period, the image of Dārā stood opposed to the figure of Alexander. But the image of Alexander in Persian and Arabo-Persian changed significantly in the shift from Aliksandar to Iskandar. It has long been noted that, unlike the image of Aliksandar in the Pahlevi tradition, that of Iskandar is positive overall. In fact, he became a hero of Iran. Here, for example, is how Nizāmī introduces the figure, having reconstituted him to fit his own vision of a Muslim and a poet:

> When I cast my lot in the labyrinth of history to find a hero for my book, all of a sudden the image of Iskandar appeared before me and could no longer be dismissed. Do not be confused by the sight of that sovereign, who could wear a sword as well as a crown: some call him lord of the throne, conqueror of empires; others praise his wisdom because of his just reign; still others consider him a prophet for his purity and piety. Of the three seeds sown by that wise man, I myself would like to make a tree grow. First, I shall speak of kingship and conquest. Then I shall adorn my words with wisdom, reviving his old battle. Finally, I shall knock on the doors of prophecy, since God himself calls him a prophet.[19] (Sharaf-nāmeh, trans. J.-C. Bürgel [1995], pp. 65–66)

Nizāmī's book displays undeniable singularities within the Persian cultural and literary traditions. But the opposition—though real—between the Pahlevi tradition and the Persian and Arabo-Persian tradition must not be pushed too far. There is also a continuity between them. Despite what some have supposed, it is not impossible that the *Alexander Romance* was already translated, known, and adapted during the Sassanid period. It may then have been integrated into a first "book of kings," the *Kvadāy-nāmāg*, which ought to be considered the prototype for the *Shāh-nāmeh* of the Islamic period. Ferdowsī himself may be laying claim to just such a tradition in his preface: "There was a book from ancient times in which many stories were written. All the mobeds possessed parts of it, every intelligent man carried a fragment with him. There was a noble [*pehlewān*][20] from a family of *deqqans*,[21] brave and mighty, full of intelligence and very illustrious. He liked to seek out the deeds of the ancient kings and to collect the narratives of past times. He summoned from each province an old mobed who had assembled the parts of that book. He asked each one for the origin of the illustrious kings and warriors and how they had organized the world at the beginning."

Then a particularly gifted young man, Daqiqi, began to collect the traditions in a book. But he was murdered, "and his poem was not completed." One day, a friend of Ferdowsī's told him: "I shall bring you the Pahlevi book. Don't fall asleep! You have the gift of speech, you have youth, you know how to tell a heroic tale. Recount that royal book again, and seek through it glory with the great. Then he brought that book to me." Later, Ferdowsī was fond of quoting the "book of the *deqqan*." Did the author really have a book in Pahlevi in his hands, or does the reference rather allow him, by means of a literary ruse encountered many times, to easily authenticate his narrative? That is still a matter of intense debate, the traces of oral transmission being persistent and recurrent. In any event, Ferdowsī's *Book of the Kings* is certainly not the first of its kind, though it is the most impressive and the most accomplished.

There is no doubt that the versions transmitted by the Pahlevi sources were not lost. In the chapter of the *Fārs-nāmeh* that Ibn' Bakhlī devotes to "Dārā the Great, son of Bahman," we learn that "Dārā had a vizier by the name of Rechtan, wise, prudent, and discerning." This is clearly the same individual who is depicted in the *Letter of Tansar* under the name "Rastīn." As for al-Ma'sūdī, he knows of the existence of Ardašir's *Kar-nāmeh*, "in which the king himself recounted his wars, his expeditions, and everything concerning his reign." He also refers to the *Testament of Ardašir* (24: 162). In medieval literature, Dārā's palace is situated in Istakhr, which, built very close to Persepolis, was the capital of the Sassanid kings. Ferdowsī calls it the "glory of the Persians' country"

and the "diadem of the kings and glory of Fārs" (bk. 19, lines 195, 250). It is there
that Dārā takes command of his armies, and there that he seeks refuge after his
defeats. It is also there that Iskandar comes in triumph "to place on his head the
glorious crown of the Keyānids" (bk. 19, lines 456–457). Dārā is thus quite naturally placed within the nearest and best-known context, that of the glorious
Sassanid period.

Several characteristics of the Sassanid Aliksandar are also found in the Persian and Arabo-Persian Iskandar.[22] Even in Ferdowsī's book, Iskandar appears
as a destroyer of Iranian traditions, associated with two other maleficent kings
of Iranian history, Zahhāk and Afrāsiyāb (bk. 43, lines 873–874). In a letter to the
Roman emperor, which the poet attributes to the Sassanid king Khōsrau Par-
viz, he is also denounced as "an old wolf, hungry for vengeance" (bk. 21, lines
646–651). Even more significant are the words attributed to Dārā after his defeat: "The Rūmi [Iskandar] became Zahhāk, and we are Jamshid" (bk. 19, lines
212–213). Dārā was thus identified with Jamshid who, though later corrupted by
pride, was a great royal hero. He brought peace and civilization to his people
and was dethroned by the monstrous usurper Zahhāk, under whose reign "the
customs of noblemen disappeared, and the wishes of the wicked were fulfilled"
(bk. 5, lines 1–2). One cannot imagine a more scathing condemnation of the invader, come to destroy the foundations of the Iranian monarchy and society.

According to Tabarī, "Iskandar summoned all the sages of Persia, had their
books of wisdom assembled, and had them copied out and translated into
Greek. Then he sent them to Greece, to Aristotle, the greatest of the Greek
sages" (p. 516). Tha'ālibī does not acknowledge that Alexander preserved the
traditional books. Rather, he attributes evil acts to him, which the Pahlevi literature had already denounced. Contrary to Dārā's last wishes, Iskandar actually "gave the order to destroy the temples of fire; he killed the magi who served
them and burned the books of Zardusht [Zoroaster], written in gold ink. He
left no beautiful monument standing, no solid fortress, no high castle—not in
Iraq, Fārs, or the other provinces of Ērānšār" (p. 414). That destruction is also
attested by Tabarī, who adds that Iskandar "had Dārā's administrative collections destroyed" (p. 517). According to Nizāmī, it was at the moment Iskandar
refused to pay Dārā tribute that he swore to destroy the temples of fire, as if,
from that date onward, he was a faithful servant to the one and only God.
Later, Nizāmī quite naturally credits him with the decisions made in pursuit of
that aim. Not content to destroy the sites of the old superstitions, Iskandar abolished the New Year's festival (Nawruz), became a convert to the true faith, and

incited the people to live according to God's ways, even decreeing that all women henceforth had to veil their faces.

These authors also show the conqueror taking measures to prevent any return to a unified Iranian monarchy. According to Tabarī, "In every city a leader was set up as governor and king, so that each would be independent and there would be no supreme king who would protect them from the enemy, and so that these governments would perish more quickly by destroying one another. . . . These 'provincial kings' existed for four hundred years" (p. 517).

Tha'ālibī uses nearly identical expressions, and Nizāmī adds that it was following the advice of Aristotle (Aristalis) that Iskandar divided power between myriads of tribal kings. According to Ferdowsī, Aristotle's advice was followed by Iskandar when he was on the brink of death. Aristalis advises Iskandar that, rather than execute the last representatives of the Keyānids, as he had planned to do, he ought to let them live and distribute powers and territories among them: "Each was assigned a place according to his rank, and he drew up a document by which each pledged not to increase even slightly the share attributed to him in the world. These grandees, who had obtained the object of their desire, were given the name 'tribal kings.' . . . Two hundred years passed in that manner, during which it was as if there were no king in the land. The tribal kings paid no attention to one another, and the land enjoyed a long rest. And that occurred in accordance with the plan Iskandar had imagined, in order that the prosperity of Rūm not be in danger" (bk. 21, lines 45–52).

Basing himself on "several historians who did a special study of antiquity," al-Ma'sūdī presents the origin of those he calls "the heads of the satrapies": "Each governor seized the province that had been entrusted to him. Alexander entered into correspondence with these leaders, some of whom were Persians, others Nabateans or Arabs. His policy tended to divide and isolate them, encouraging local usurpation, so that the empire, falling prey to anarchy, could not recover the unity it enjoyed under the power of a single and absolute king" (22:133).

The emphasis on the evolution that Iskandar encouraged, on the advice of Aristotle, can be explained by the fact that, like the Sassanid sources, this body of literature gives great importance to Ardašir's accomplishments, the work of restoration attributed to him. His victory over Ardawān "made all the satraps subordinate to him and assured the unity and stability of his power" (al-Ma'sūdī 22:135). It was Ardašir "who took the Persians' empire away from these provincial kings" (Tabarī, p. 517). "They reigned until Ardašir, son of Pāpak, became king of the Universe" (Tha'ālibī, p. 416). Ferdowsī's book 21, on the Askhanian dynasty, is dedicated in great part to Ardašir's origins, his family connections to Dārā through Sāsān, a son of the last Keyānid king, and to his wondrous adventures and his victory over Ardawān. The following book (22) is devoted entirely to his reign, marked by the birth and education of his son Šapur, who succeeds him. This history is punctuated by apothegms and exempla. Books 25–50 take us to the last descendant of Ardašir, Yazdegerd III.

At the same time, there is a notable difference between the two traditions. To take one example, Dīnawarī recalls elements of the reign of Dārā, son of Bahman. The elder Dārā waged war against Philip of Rūm (Macedonia), was victorious, and brought Macedonia to heel: "Every year Philip would give a tribute of one hundred thousand golden eggs (each weighing a hundred mesqāls [500 grams])." Although the *Alexander Romance* says nothing about a victorious expedition by a Persian king against Macedonia, the practice of paying tribute was already known there. An embassy came to find Philip and to demand payment of the tribute "for the country of King Darius": "one hundred golden eggs . . . each weighing 20 pounds of solid gold." It was then that, for the first time, Alexander intervened directly and sent the ambassadors back to their master Darius, refusing to pay the tribute (1.23.2–5).

By contrast, the rest of Dīnawarī's narrative has no parallel in the Greek legend of Alexander: "Moreover, Dārā [the father] took the king of Rum's daughter to be his wife and returned to Iran." Then the author recounts the story of that Irano-Macedonian marriage: offended by his wife's bad breath, Dārā sends her back to her father. She is pregnant and soon gives birth to the child who will be known by the name "Iskandar." Then Dārā has a son by an Iranian princess: this is Dārā, son of Dārā. The story is found in practically all the other authors. In book 18, which Ferdowsī devotes to Dārā(b), that king demands that Pheïlekous give him his daughter who, curiously, bears the lovely Iranian name "Nahid." The morning after their first night of love, Dārā(b) is disgusted with the fetid exhalations he breathes in while trying to kiss his wife:

> He sent her back to her father. She was pregnant by him but told no one in the world. . . . Then she brought forth a son like the shining moon. His mother named him Iskandar. . . . The caesar told all the grandees that there had been born a caesar of his own race, and no one uttered the name of Dārā(b). Iskandar was taken for the son, and the caesar for the father, since Pheïlekous was ashamed to admit that Dārā(b) had repudiated his daughter. . . . Dārā(b) married another woman after Nahid re-

turned to her father; another son was born to him, full of majesty and
strength, but younger by a year than Nahid's son. On the day of his birth,
he was given the name Dārā. (bk. 18, lines 90–128)

Widely disseminated in Islamic Iran, the idea of a partly exogenous origin
for Alexander is absent from the Pahlevi tradition. That origin is also presented
very differently in the *Alexander Romance* and in the Arabo-Persian tradition. In
the Romance, Alexander is the fruit of a secret union between the Macedonian
princess Olympias, wife of Philip, and the Egyptian pharaoh Nectanebo. In the
Arabo-Persian tradition, Iskandar stems from a diplomatic marriage arranged
between Dārā, son of Bahman, and the daughter of Philip of Macedonia. In a
fictionalized version, the *Dārāb-nāmeh*, written by Abū Tāher Tarsusi in the
twelfth century, Iskandar even has a dual Iranian ancestry: his grandfather Philip
is considered a descendant of the mythic king Feridun. Iskandar's Iranian origin
sets a particular tone for his confrontation with Dārā, and then for the scene
of fraternal recognition beside the dying Dārā. It also attributes an altogether
original place to Iskandar within Iranian history: "Having become king, Iskandar considered nothing greater than the conquest of the country of his father,
Dārā, son of Bahman, and that is why he marched on his father's country, and,
to appropriate power, waged battle with his brother" (Dīnawarī). The meaning
of the invention is clear: "Iran can take pride in having produced the conqueror
of the world, rather than being aggrieved at having succumbed to him."[23]

It should be noted, however, that the story was not favorably received by
everyone. Dīnawarī specifies that "the learned men of Rūm did not accept that
affair and thought that Iskandar was the son of Philip and his descendant." Al-
Ma'sūdī believed that Iskandar was actually the "son of Philip," and he reported
several hypotheses tracing Alexander's origins back to either Noah or Abraham
(22:133; 25:248). Tha'ālibī (p. 399) and Dīnawarī (p. 31) insist on the disagreements
among historians regarding Iskandar's personality and express identical reservations about what they have read regarding his origins: "The Persians claim that
Iskandar was the son of Dārā the Elder." Nizāmī mentions three versions. One
makes Iskandar the king of Persia through one of Philip's daughters. The other
is part of a well-known schema, that of the foundling: during a hunt, Philip supposedly discovered a nursling sucking its thumb near the body of a recently deceased woman. He ordered that the child be raised at court, then adopted him
and made him his successor.[24] But it is the third version that Nizāmī chooses: he
judges that Alexander is actually the son of Philip and a lady of his court. In

Nizāmī, contrary to Ferdowsī, Alexander, though portrayed as a hero, is less a hero of Iran than of Islam. To that end, Nizāmī does not need to claim any biological connection to Iran: on the contrary, the hero's foreign origin illustrates with particular force the universality of the Prophet's religion.

The Reasons for the Defeat

Whether Dārā finds himself facing a "demonized" Aliksandar or a "heroized" Iskandar, the memory of the king remains burdened with the crushing responsibility for the defeat of Iran.

Unlike the Greco-Roman texts, the Persian and Arabo-Persian writings take little interest in the military aspect, except in very literary terms, largely uninformed and uninformative. They are fond of insisting on the unprecedented number of soldiers of both kings. These figures may be as extravagant as those found among the Greco-Roman authors, or they may be metaphorical and poetic expressions:[25] "From Rūm to Misr [Egypt], Iskandar led an army so large that the ants and flies could not find a way through" (Ferdowsī, bk. 19, lines 55–56). As for Dārā, upon learning of his adversary's approach, "he brought from Istakhr an army so large that spears blocked the wind's path. . . . These two armies were without number" (lines 67, 154). The army Iskandar commands to wage the third battle "had neither middle nor end"; and, "as for the army Dārā commanded, you would have thought the earth unable to bear it, you would have believed that heaven would be hindered in its movement" (lines 221–224). That is the significance of the sesame ball sent to Iskandar: Dārā thereby made him to understand that "he would lead on his campaign troops as numerous as sesame seeds" (Tha'ālibī, p. 403).

Furthermore, the strategies of the two camps are never mentioned precisely, and the number and location of the battles are vague and changeable. Dīnawarī announces the existence of "many battles" but does not provide any description of them. Tabarī (p. 514) and Tha'ālibī (p. 408) report a single battle, which unfolded near Mosul—"between Iraq and Syria"—after the two armies had been facing each other for a month (Tabarī), or "on the banks of the Euphrates. . . . It lasted a week" (Tha'ālibī). Nizāmī simply mentions two battles lasting two full days in succession and reports the bravery of the kings.

Here and there echoes can be heard of the Greco-Roman traditions. Dīnawarī presents the royal army's route: "When the news of it reached

Dārā, son of Dārā, he placed his wives, his children, and his treasures in the citadel of Hamadān, which he himself had established." That expression can be seen as a distant and distorted echo of the depositing of Darius's treasures in Damascus. When the two armies fight on the banks of the Euphrates, Alexander receives the advice to "surprise the enemy in a night attack." He replies: "Night attacks are robbery and robbery does not befit kings." The expressions Tha'ālibī uses here (p. 408) are reminiscent of the reply to Parmenion's advice, attributed to Alexander, on the eve of the Battle of Gaugamela.[26]

Ferdowsī, closer to the *Alexander Romance,* describes a first battle on the right bank of the Euphrates: "For seven days, the zealous heroes fought face to face." Then "Dārā, master of the world, turned his back" and crossed over the Euphrates, leaving a number of his soldiers to be massacred by the enemy (lines 150–174). A second battle occurred in the same place, and, after three days of intense battle, "Dārā, whose ambition was to possess the world, left the battlefield filled with sorrow." He returned to Istakhr, "which was the glory of the Persians' country," and there he attempted to form another army. Then came the third Persian defeat and Darius's flight to Kerman. The grandees, addressing their king, describe the scale of the disaster: "All the veiled women of your palace, who feared for your life, all the treasures of your mighty ancestors, which had come into your possession without obstacle, all the daughters of the grandees, all the riches of the Keyānids, are now in the hands of the Rūmi" (lines 254–255).

Then Dārā sends a letter, in which he proposes to exchange "family, women with veiled faces, and children" for treasures from his Keyānid ancestors Guštasp and Isfendiyar. Iskandar's response is favorable, provided that Dārā come to see him in person and willingly hand over, in Istakhr, the "diadem of the kings and the glory of Fārs," which the Rūmi had seized (lines 265–290). Once more desperate, Dārā asks for the aid of Fūr (Porus). Iskandar, learning of this, again takes the offensive at the command of an army, "so large that the sun lost its way in the sky." The result is catastrophic: "Dārā brought his army, an army with no desire to fight, heartbroken and war-weary, for the fortunes of the Iranians were declining. They attacked the Rūmi, but that day, the furious lions acted like foxes. The grandees asked only for protection, and from pride of power they fell into humiliation. Seeing that, Dārā turned his back and fled wailing. Three hundred horsemen accompanied him, a troop composed of the most glorious men in Iran" (lines 305–315).

Dārā and His Men: The Theme of Betrayal

Ferdowsī then recounts the act of treason by two ministers close to Dārā, which will lead to the king's assassination. These two *dastūrs* Mahiar and Dja-nousipar, stand at the king's right and left hands, one as his adviser, the other as his treasurer.[27] Understanding that the situation is hopeless, they resolve to kill the king and to negotiate their fate with Iskandar. This they do: "In the dark of night . . . Djanousipar seized a dagger and struck his master in the chest. The illustrious king's head fell forward, and his entire escort abandoned him" (lines 323–325). Then the two murderers seek out Iskandar and take him to Dārā, who has not yet succumbed to his wounds.

Apart from the geographical location (in Media in the *Alexander Romance,* in Persia for the Arabo-Persian authors), the scene narrated by Ferdowsī was clearly taken from the corresponding passage in the Romance. After he learned "from one of Darius's men who had crossed over to his side" that the Great King had sent a letter to Porus, "king of the Indians," Alexander, who had lived in Persia since his victory, again took the offensive against Media. "He heard that Darius was at Batana, near the Caspian Gates. He continued the pursuit immediately and with all his energy." The Great King was soon betrayed by two "satraps," Bessus and Ariobarzanes, easily recognizable as the two leaders of the plot, as narrated by the Greco-Roman historians: Bessus, satrap of Bactriana, and Nabarzanes, the chiliarch. "For, they said to each other, 'If we kill Darius, we shall receive a great deal of money from Alexander for destroying his enemy.' So with this evil plan they went to Darius, swords in hand. . . . When the traitors heard that Alexander was coming, they fled, leaving Darius dying" (2.20).

That version is fairly kind toward the Great King's memory. The Romance emphasizes the physical courage of Darius, who defends himself vigorously against the two satraps' attack: "Darius defended himself with both hands: with the left he held off Ariobarzanes so that he could not bring his sword close to him, and its blows fell aslant. The traitors found they could not finish him off, however much they struggled; for Darius was a strong man" (2.20.3).

In addition, for the author of the *Book of the Kings* the act of treason is unique. Ferdowsī does not fail to point out that, during the final battle, Dārā's soldiers had lost faith in the future, and that "the grandees asked only for protection." That protection could come from Iskandar alone. The grandees had undoubtedly learned that, after his second victory, Iskandar had promised to spare the lives of those who surrendered voluntarily: "The inhabitants of Iraq were reassured, they all turned toward the Rūmi" (lines 185–190). But overall, the Persian nobles had remained loyal to the king until that moment, even in the near-desperate circumstances. And the two *dastūrs* do not seem to have recruited other conspirators.

The Iranian tradition consistently elaborated a delegitimating discourse about Dārā: the king had been betrayed and defeated because he did not conform to the model of the good king. The betrayal was caused less by an innate vice in Dārā's lieutenants than by the king's inattention to his intimate circle. In some sense the misuse of kingship sowed the seeds of treason. Those who abandoned Dārā, therefore, also acknowledged Iskandar's kingly virtues.

The accusations were made upon Dārā's accession, even by Ferdowsī, who denounces the king's haughty and authoritarian arrogance: "He was a young man, severe and choleric; his tongue was sharper than a sword." The first letter he sent to his loyal supporters was also trenchant: "Whoever deviates from my will and my commands will see how I make heads roll. Obey my orders, all of you, to take others' lives or to give your own" (bk. 19, lines 1–15). That is also the case for Dīnawarī: "When the country's reins fell into the hands of Dārā, son of Dārā, he took the path of oppression, pride, and excess, and he wrote the governors of his country: 'From Dārā, son of Dārā, who shines like the sun on the inhabitants of his country, to so-and-so.'"

From that standpoint, there is a sharp contrast between Dārā and his father, Dārāb. The royal legend of Dārāb, known to Ferdowsī and to many other authors, resembles one of the legends of Cyrus the Great. Dārāb's mother, Homai, widow of Bahman Ardašir, wanted above all to exercise royal power. She abandoned the child at birth, entrusting him "to a freeborn nurse, a holy woman, modest and beautiful." When questioned, Homai responded that "her son was dead." Then she ordered a carpenter to build a wooden basket, which was left in the current of the Euphrates: the child was wearing a precious stone on his arm, and a letter was attached to him. Soon taken in by a pair of launderers (or millers) who had recently lost a child, he was raised by his adoptive parents and "became a noble and strong young man." Then, after many adventures, there is the anticipated scene of recognition between mother and son. Homai seated Dārāb on a golden throne, "and she put the royal crown on her son's head." The conqueror of Rūm, which he compels to pay a tribute, and (secretly) Iskandar's father, he is unanimously acknowledged to be a king at once just, humane, and powerful. It is that image that was passed on to posterity. The only *Dārāb-nāmeh* known to us, that of Abū Tāher Tarsusi, is named for Dārāb the

Elder: a third of the romance is devoted to him, while the rest recounts the adventures of Iskandar and also of Burān-Dokht, daughter of Dārā the Younger,
the latter being a very undeveloped character. And when Saadi, in a monarchical
exemplum from the *Bustan* (pp. 35–46), depicts "Dārā, the illustrious king," one
is tempted to think that it is the image of the father, not that of Iskandar's
adversary, that is implicitly being evoked.

Dārā the Elder's only weakness, no doubt, is the immoderate and therefore
blind love he has for his son, which is why he gave him his own name (Tha'ālibī,
p. 399; Tabarī, p. 511). Everything indicates, in fact, that the young king does not
have his father's positive qualities. When Dārā succeeds his father, Ibn' Bakhlī,
taking the Sassanid writings as his model, sees it as a fateful change in the exercise of royal power. He repeats the story of the royal advisers Rastīn and Bīrī, as
it was introduced in the *Letter of Tansar*. In that text, the decisive betrayal takes
place at the time of battle between the two kings, but it is anticipated in the
first lines: "A band of Dārā's own nobles used guile and treachery to behead
him and brought the head to Alexander. . . . Some [in Dārā's intimate circle]
deserted him, one group set about making terms with the enemy, and others
flung themselves upon him and slew him" (§ 1:38). Here is how Ibn' Bakhlī presents the matter:

> When Dārā the Great went away, he entrusted the kingdom to his son.
> And that Dārā, son of Dārā, was driven by resentment toward his father's
> vizier, Rechtan, for the following reason. There was a child by the name
> of Bīrī, the same age as Dārā, whom he loved a great deal; and that Bīrī
> was on poor terms with the father of Dārā's vizier, whom he intended to
> kill. Then the vizier fed Bīrī poison and killed him. Dārā, son of Dārā,
> was told of it and revenge entered his heart; and his father's vizier began
> to hate Dārā. The vizier, secretly afraid within the depths of his soul,
> conspired with Iskandar of Rūm and incited him against Dārā, son of
> Dārā. The reason for Dārā's inaction lay in the disorder [aroused by] that
> vizier. Dārā, son of Dārā, entrusted the viziership to Bīrī's brother, who
> was an unjust man lacking in wisdom. Dārā, son of Dārā, proved to be
> evil, and his vizier displayed malevolence toward the army and the sub-
> jects, so much so that he had a number of renowned men in his own army
> killed, and he confiscated the nobles' property. Everyone became un-
> happy with him, and when Alexander of Rūm arrived, most of those peo-
> ple asked him to spare their lives and formed an alliance with him.[28]

The relationship Dārā maintained with his advisers is also at the heart of Nizāmī's portrayal, which contrasts Iskandar to his adversary.[29] Nizāmī too specifies that, because of his harshness, Dārā was hated by his subjects, who wanted nothing more than to see him leave the throne. The author explains the reasons for such a fraught situation. As in the *Alexander Romance,* Dārā reproaches Alexander for his youth, treats him as an "immature child, his mind still green," even though they are the same age. The opposition set up by Nizāmī is played out in the behavior of each of the kings toward his elders. Dārā does not listen to Farīburz, "an old man pure of spirit," who advises him not to wage battle and to avoid a disastrous war: it would be better, he says, to conclude an immediate truce. The king is contemptuous of the advice and calls the adviser a "senile old man." After his victory, by contrast, Iskandar showers Farīburz with marks of respect. He simply reproaches Farīburz, before receiving an explanation, for not having given Dārā good advice. Iskandar thereby demonstrates his capacity to became a good king of Iran, a better king than Dārā had been.

Tha'ālibī uses more violent turns of phrase: "When he succeeded his father, he was in the first fire of youth, a time of dreadful aberrations and fearsome flaws. . . . He became haughty and prideful, he spilled a great deal of blood and terrorized the innocents in every way. He dismayed his army chiefs and his subjects and had no use for the kings. They protected themselves from hostilities by sending him tributes" (pp. 401–403).

Tabarī is even harsher. The discontent caused by the king's conduct incites Iskandar to take the offensive: "That Dārā was an evil king, evil toward his subjects and toward the army. He reduced a number of his soldiers to slavery and had them put to death. An enormous number of his subjects were hostile toward him and sought to be delivered from him. . . . When Alexander learned that Dārā's subjects were hostile toward him and sought to be delivered from him, and that, if a foreign king attacked that kingdom, the inhabitants would accept him and Dārā would be left there with no power . . . he resolved to attack Dārā's kingdom. He therefore refused to pay Dārā his tribute" (p. 513).

These accounts, unfavorable to Darius/Dārā, do not necessarily give a correspondingly positive image of Iskandar. Unlike the scene portrayed several times in the *Alexander Romance,* Iskandar does not systematically reject the Persians' offers of collaboration. This is clear in Tha'ālibī:

Dārā's loss was caused by the bad feelings harbored toward him by his officers, who betrayed him by no longer fighting in earnest. Two of his

chamberlains, men from Hamadān, brought Iskandar a message and
pledged to kill Dārā on the battlefield. Alexander promised to shower
them with property and wealth if they carried out what they were proposing. When the two armies resumed battle and the fighting was at its
most heated, Dārā, located in the center, kept guard against the enemy,
but not against his own men. Death therefore took the king by surprise
from the side he believed was safe. He suspected nothing, but suddenly,
his two chamberlains from Hamadān stabbed him twice with spears. He
fell from his horse, mortally wounded. Shouts rose up from within the
army. His companions were in a state of confusion: some took flight, others surrendered, asking to be spared. Alexander, informed of what had
happened to Dārā, ran with a few of his men to the place where he had
fallen. (pp. 408–409)

Abū Tāher Tarsusi's *Dārāb-nāmeh* tells the same story. After the first battle,
a man arrives in Iskandar's camp and reveals that two of Dārā's emirs, named
Mahiar and Janusipar (as in Ferdowsī), "were the object of accusations from
Dārā and contemplated killing him." The messenger comes to Iskandar to offer
to kill Dārā during the battle. Iskandar, delighted, gives the emissary a certain
precious stone. The next day, during the battle, the two emirs stab Dārā.

Sometimes Iskandar himself directly incites the betrayal. The reason most
often advanced is that he has encountered many difficulties in securing victory
on the battlefield. According to Tabarī, it is Iskandar who questions the deserters, who have come to his camp because of the "poor treatment and violence
imposed by Dārā." "Iskandar asked the deserters: Who in Dārā's army can get
closest to him? They replied: Dārā has two chamberlains in his entourage; both
are ill disposed toward him because of the many violent acts. Iskandar sent someone in secret and offered them great wealth if they could assassinate Dārā by
ruse. The two chamberlains consented and agreed to kill him on the day of the
battle, when he would be on horseback. Then Iskandar set a day for the battle"
(pp. 514–515).

The rest of the narrative is not particularly laudatory of Iskandar. Attacked
during the battle by "a man from the Persian army," the king "showed great
fear of him." Furthermore, upon seeing that the two chamberlains had not per-
petrated their crime, Iskandar, according to Tabarī, is ready to give up the enterprise of conquest: "He thought they had changed their minds: it was decided
to conclude peace the next day and to turn back. . . . Dārā, for his part, fearing
Alexander's army, also intended to conclude peace." But, persuaded by the two

chamberlains, the Persian king returns to battle, which surprises and panics Iskandar, "who unexpectedly saw Dārā's army attacking. . . . He was frightened and wanted to take flight." It is then that the two chamberlains strike Dārā from behind: "They went to Alexander's camp and announced that they had knocked Dārā off his mount and that his army was in flight" (pp. 514–515).

Ibn' Bakhlī also points out Iskandar's inability to gain the upper hand and the providential role of the traitors: "Nevertheless, the war between them lasted a full year, and Dārā kept Iskandar from advancing, until, after that, two men from Hamadān joined together, stabbed Dārā with a weapon between his two shoulders in the midst of battle and fled into Iskandar's army."

The causal connection is made even more clearly by Dīnawarī: "Many battles took place between Dārā and Alexander, but in none of these did Alexander obtain any reassuring result. After that, Alexander confidentially encouraged two men from the people of Hamadān to kill Dārā, trusted men at court and Dārā's personal guard. These men committed an act of treason and carried out Dārā's murder. For one day, on one of the battlefields, they suddenly attacked Dārā from behind and brought him down. That event caused Dārā's army to disperse."

Nizāmī, by contrast, without denying the intentional collusion between Iskandar and Dārā's ministers, wishes to absolve Iskandar. According to him, the first battle was particularly bloody and its outcome indecisive. When night had fallen, two of Dārā's high dignitaries came to talk secretly with Iskandar, proposing to assassinate their king. Their proposal scandalized Iskandar, who did not understand how such methods could be employed. He thought about it, however, and finally agreed. The reason? To end a war that was causing so much bloodshed.[30] During the next day's battle, the two ministers killed Dārā. Only then did Iskandar regret his decision and decide to punish the assassins.[31]

Like Nizāmī, most of the other authors certify that Iskandar immediately regretted what he had done, and, to maintain the coherence of the narrative, they allow him to protest his good faith and integrity before the dying Dārā. At the same time, however, they choose not to praise excessively his military victory. Some even opt to devalue it, because, according to them, he never would have defeated Dārā without the agreement he made with the traitors. In twice pointing out that Iskandar was frightened by battle and thought of fleeing, Tabarī even presents a shabby image of the conqueror, comparable to the one the Greco-Roman sources give of Darius. That ambivalence reveals the difficulty the Persian and Arabo-Persians authors encountered in their efforts to make compatible what in fact was not: to explain the defeat without affronting Iranian sensitivities, and to integrate Alexander into the history of Iran even while maintaining their distance. Nizāmī resolves the contradiction by making Iskandar a hero of Islam, anxious not to spill blood, and who regrets after the fact that he used treachery.

The differences between the *Alexander Romance* and the Persian and Arabo-Persian tradition thus come into sharper focus. Granted, the Romance already denounces the arrogance of Darius, not only toward Alexander, whose youth the Persian king looks upon with contempt, but also and especially toward the Persian dignitaries. The theme of betrayal is introduced from the start. Darius's first couriers, who brought the king's letter demanding the delivery of tribute, make a first offer to Alexander: the messengers "proposed to tell him how he could capture Darius in an ambush." Alexander refuses (1.37.7–8). Later, after a second defeat, one of Darius's satraps comes looking for Alexander and offers to seize Darius, a proposal once again rejected by the Macedonian king, who declares he does not trust a man ready to betray his own people (2.10.1–2).

The episode of the two ministers' betrayal is similarly borrowed from the *Alexander Romance* (2.9.6–9) but is twisted around at Iskandar's expense. In the Romance it is Darius who is denounced for attempting to have Alexander assassinated. The Great King, the would-be assassin says, "promised to give me part of his kingdom and his daughter in marriage." In the end, Alexander draws a lesson from the episode before his assembled soldiers: "Men of Macedon, you too must be as brave in battle as this man." In addition, though Bessus and Ariobarzanes have hopes of being rewarded by Alexander, no bargain with the Macedonian camp is mentioned (2.20.1). After Darius's death, Alexander declares he knows nothing about the murderers. If he issued a proclamation that he would reward them, it was solely as a ruse, so that they would come find him and be put to death. And that is obviously what happens (2.21.7–11). Once again, the author attributes to Alexander a line serving to defend against accusations that were probably made against him. The king claims he had planned to punish them harshly from the start. For, he exclaims before Bessus and Ariobarzanes, who are outraged at such disloyalty, "How could I suppose that those who killed their own master would spare me?" (2.21.10).

The Recurrence of the Model

Despite the hesitations and contradiction of the poets and chroniclers, the meaning of the opposition between the two kings leaves little room for doubt. Because the act of treason is unanimously explained—even from the Persian point of view—in terms of Dārā's harshness, Dārā is the one really responsible for the disaster. Because of their king's unjust conduct, the Persians turned away from him and rallied behind Iskandar. Thus Dārā himself provided his enemy brother with the trump card that allowed him to prevail, less by his conduct on the battlefield, which is sometimes less than heroic, than by the boon of the treasonous act in his adversary's camp. On this point, there is a great continuity of inspiration and themes between the Sassanid writings and the Persian and Arabo-Persian literature. Dārā's reign, when compared to that of his father, is a living illustration of the bad king. A good king like Dārāb, conqueror of Philekoüs, would never have been defeated by Iskandar, quite simply because his intimate circle, the nobles, and the common people would have remained faithful to him without restriction or exception.

To Dārā's great historiographical misfortune, it is the negative image that was transmitted over the *longue durée* of Iranian memory. A good example is provided by a work written by Mīrkwhānd (1433/4–1498), a native of Central Asia who was Iranian by culture. He devoted his life to writing a universal history in Persian, which "enjoyed exceptional popularity throughout the Turco-Iranian regions, was used in many later historical compilations and translated several times into Turkish."[32] Book 1 takes the reader "from the creation to Yazdagird III," that is, to the last Sassanid king, defeated by Sultan 'Umar. Well-known figures also appear, namely, the Keyānid kings, including Dārā(b) and his son Dārā. The elder king is presented in a very laudatory manner, as "a sovereign of great splendor, and a conqueror of extensive sway." The author recalls his resounding victory over Filikus of Rūm, the imposition of a tribute, marriage to Filikus's daughter (who is soon repudiated), and the secret birth of Iskandar. Then comes the succession, entrusted to a "son whom he loved exceedingly, and called after his own name," that is, Dārā. The reign of little Dārā, afflicted with disastrous flaws, is harsh and unjust. As a result, "most of the princes and nobles of Irán, being hurt at his conduct, addressed Letters to Iskander, promising him their unanimous support, and thus inciting him to claim the kingdom. . . . On the day of his escape from the field of battle . . . two persons of Hamadán, of the number of his chamberlains, who were distinguished by confidential intercourse and accumulated honours . . . rent his bosom with their traitorous poniards and fled to Iskander's army."[33]

Mīrkhwhānd's reputation extended beyond the borders of the Iranian and Turkophone lands and, from the seventeenth century on, reached far into Europe. In fact, it remained a major source for the history of medieval Iran until the end of the nineteenth century. It is cited, for example, in Gobineau's *Histoire des Perses* (*World of the Persians* [1869]: 1:268; 2:361). Gobineau declares that "the history [he] tends to favor is much less that of the facts . . . than that of the impression produced by these facts on the men in whose midst they manifested themselves" (1:265–266). He explains at length why, in his opinion, one ought not to have contempt for Iranian writings, for "authors of the Namehs" and other annalists, "who vied to unite, coordinate, and assemble in an order provided by the tradition an enormous mass of facts dating back to the most remote eras and progressively coming down to them" (1:263). That is why, when Gobineau discusses Iskandar and Dārā (2:361ff.), he makes ample use not only of Ferdowsī's *Book of the Kings* but also of Abū Tāher Tarsusi's *Dārāb-nāmeh*. Behind Gobineau's Darius, the Sassanid and Arabo-Persian Dārā is easily recognizable:

> He began to persecute the great families . . . [so that], when Alexander appeared at the border, many of the vassals went over to his side. According to the chronicler [Abū Tāher Tarsusi], that explains the extreme ease with which Alexander conquered the vast empire of Iran, where he found no serious resistance from the landowners and where, on the contrary, he had been solicited. . . . These grandees of the empire, so long disgusted, accustomed to every sort of intrigue, constantly prepared to revolt, unable to be at peace with their master's justice—any more than that master could count on their loyalty—had conceived the plan, hatched the plot, to substitute for the ruling family the hero of the West: young, brilliant, strong, backed by an authority that was already much more substantial. . . . Alexander, summoned by the grandees and the common people, was initially much more the leader of a conspiracy against the Achaemenids than a conqueror in the true sense of the word. (2:369–370; 463)

One of the last incarnations of that figure is found in an Arabic opuscule, the *Annals of Oman*, set down in writing in 1728.[34] The first chapter tells how members of the el-Azd tribe, led by Màlik, went to settle in Oman. Under the leadership of Màlik's son Honàt, an advance guard of two thousand elite horsemen clashed with the Persian forces occupying the region "in the name of Dārā, son of Dārā, son of Bahman." The genealogy leaves no doubt: this is our Dārā. He had a lieutenant there, called the marzaban, who also maintained surveillance over the Persian settlers in the region. The term *marzpān* (border guard), well known in the Sassanid Empire, clearly suggests that elements of the oral transmission date back to that period. The Persian leaders refused the request the Màlik and his people had made to obtain lands and pastures. At this juncture, war erupted. In accordance with a narrative model encountered many times in the *Book of the Kings,* the battle unfolds over three successive days. It ends with the Persians' defeat, "the Persian leader having been killed by Màlik in single combat."

The Persians wrote to Dārā-bin Dārā, asking for his permission to return to their own country. Learning of this, Dārā was overcome by anger and the desire to take his revenge. He therefore sent one of the most renowned of his *marzpāns,* giving him 3,000 of his most remarkable warriors. The Persians, upon receiving a letter from Màlik, and trusting in the superiority of their forces against the minuscule Arab army, were contemptuous of him and gave an insolent and haughty reply. Unsurprisingly, Màlik won the battle. Two of his sons even managed to kill a huge elephant: "The rest of the Persian army set off in ships and went to Persia, crossing the sea. So it was that Màlik conquered the entire country of Oman and seized all the possessions of the Persians." Later, he agreed to send the Persian prisoners back to their own country.

The author declares that he has summarized what he learned of the "many poems and traditions that celebrated the expedition of Màlik and his sons, and their battle against the Persians." All the same, it is not easy to know precisely at what date and by what stages the epic of Oman was constituted around recurrent themes (the powerful Persian king and the small enemy army, the fight between leaders that puts an end to the battle, the departure of the defeated Persian army and its return to Persia, and so on). Let me simply observe that the figure of Dārā is once again that of a prideful king incapable of maintaining his ancestors' imperial legacy.

ᶓ[11]ᶒ

Death and Transfiguration

The Different Versions of Darius's Death

When last seen, Darius was mortally wounded and dying of thirst. He was being assisted by a certain Polystratus, who brought him a little water in his helmet, drawn from a nearby spring. Shortly before, the Great King had been deposed at the instigation of two top officers, Bessus, satrap of Bactriana, and Nabarzanes, the chiliarch (their names are "Bessus" and "Ariobarzanes" in the *Alexander Romance*). While Alexander was giving chase via a forced march from Ecbatana through Parthian country, the Great King was struck dead by two conspirators. The sources occasionally differ on the identity of the assassins, though they agree on Bessus's political responsibility. The account, written along fairly similar lines, can be found in Arrian, as well as in Plutarch and in the Vulgate authors. Bessus, after reaching Bactria in his own governorship, proclaims himself Great King and takes the name "Artaxerxes." It is only several months later that he is captured by Alexander, then executed, under conditions that vary a great deal from one author to another.

The episode was the object of a great deal of commentary in antiquity and gave rise to many contradictory versions. The existence of a conspiracy by the kingdom's two top officers was known to all the Persian and Arabo-Persian authors: in Ferdowsī and in Abū Tāher Tarsusi's *Dārāb-nāmeh*, they bear the names "Janusipar" and "Mahiar." The Iranian tradition displays notable particularities: on one hand, the murder of the king does not occur in Parthia but in Persia, and not during a retreat but in the heat of a decisive battle; on the other, the punishment of the regicides ordered by Iskandar is carried out in Persia itself and immediately follows the previous story (the same is true in the Romance).

Another version clearly suggests that Darius was killed by Alexander.[1] It was presented for the first time by Manetho and was adopted by several authors in late antiquity, then in the medieval West.[2] According to the *Chronicon Paschale,* a Mesopotamian stronghold called Doras, disputed by the Byzantines and Persians, acquired that name because it was there that Alexander stabbed Darius to death with his spear (in Greek, *doru*).[3] It is possible that the story grew out of the tradition of a single combat between Darius and Alexander. It may also be that, in the interest of better expressing the Egyptian point of view, some wanted to attribute to the "son" of Nectanebo the feat of personally eliminating the last representative of a foreign dynasty that had ruled Egypt. Although mention of this version is also found in the Arab authors al-Maʿsūdī and Ibn Khaldūn, that way of portraying Darius's death remained unusual.[4]

There are other discrepancies within the Greco-Roman tradition. A Greek inscription of 264/263 speaks of "Alexander's capture of Darius," though no one knows what is meant by that.[5] Does the terminology imply that Darius was alive when Alexander reached him? The same characterization is found in Malalas, who wrote a universal history during the Byzantine period.[6] But the dominant thesis is that Darius was dead when Alexander finally reached him: "Darius died from his wounds soon after, before Alexander had seen him."[7] The bluntness of Arrian's declaration seems to be directed implicitly against a different view, known from Diodorus's time onward and set out as follows: "Just after his death, Alexander rode up in hot pursuit with his cavalry, and, finding him dead, gave him a royal funeral. Some, however, have written that Alexander found him still breathing and commiserated with him on his disasters. Dareius urged him to avenge his death, and Alexander, agreeing, set out after Bessus, but the satrap had a long start and got away into Bactria, so Alexander suspended the chase and returned" (Diodorus 17.73.3).

Mentioned only by Diodorus in the Greco-Roman sources, the story of Alexander receiving Darius's last words and witnessing his last breath is the one depicted in the *Alexander Romance* and in the entire Persian and Arabo-Persian literary and iconographic tradition.

Polystratus between Darius and Alexander

The scenario adopted by the Greco-Roman authors produces a kind of narrative disappointment in the reader. We know that Alexander was anxious and in a hurry to find the fleeing Darius, that he had not given up his desire to fight man to man, and that he had persisted unflaggingly from the start of the campaign. Darius was no less impatient. "Consigned to his fate," "oppressed by the isolation" in his tent, deprived of all the pomp of kingship and a prisoner of his own men, the Great King was now ready, after slipping from Alexander's grasp for years, to welcome the one he recognized as his conqueror.[8] When told that the Macedonian's arrival is imminent, Darius refuses to give in to the pressures of Bessus and the conspirators, who try to persuade him to continue his eastward march: "Darius . . . declared that the gods had come to avenge him and, calling for Alexander's protection, refused to go along with the traitors."[9] It is then that he is shot through with arrows and abandoned bleeding. The encounter between Alexander and Darius, anticipated and foreshadowed in that way, ought to have represented symbolically the end of the war of movement between lower king and upper king, its narrative and emotional denouement. But it does nothing of the sort: Darius's death makes any exchange or conversation between the two kings impossible.

But the ancient authors, anxious to depict the voluntary transmission of power from Darius to Alexander, resort to a literary device that allows them to establish an almost direct communication between the two kings before Darius's death. Because it is difficult to imagine that a deposed king, deprived of everything and close to death, would send a letter, an ordinary individual has to be brought on stage, someone who will serve as an agent to transmit Darius's message to the Macedonian king, who arrives at the side of an enemy already dead and therefore mute. The ancient authors could thereby make the two accounts congruent: Darius died before Alexander's arrival and therefore could not address him directly; and Darius transmitted a message to Alexander. A simple and effective means is used to that end: a go-between receives the royal message and transmits it to Alexander.

That role is played by a Macedonian soldier belonging to the advance guard. He is anonymous in Justin but bears the name "Polystratus" in Curtius and Plutarch. The ancient texts perfectly evoke the search conducted by the first detachments of Alexander's army to locate the Great King. Initially the search is fruitless; then Polystratus discovers the king in a squalid chariot. In giving a few drops of water to Darius, consumed by a raging thirst, the soldier easily establishes a personal relationship with the Great King, particularly because, according to certain authors, the king knew the soldier's language. The tradition cited by Plutarch and Justin render Darius's last words. The Great King thanks Polystratus for his gesture and entrusts him with a message for Alexander: "Just breathing his last . . . he was able to ask for drink, and when given some cold water by Polystratus, he said to him, 'My good sir, this is the worst of all my misfortunes that I am unable to recompense you for your kindness to me; but Alexander will reward you, and the gods will reward Alexander for his courteous treatment of my mother and wife and daughters. I give him my right hand through you.' With these words he took Polystratus by the hand and died" (Plutarch, *Alexander*, 43.3–4).

Justin obviously used the same source but introduced new motifs:

> One of the soldiers, going to a neighbouring spring, found Darius in the vehicle, wounded in several places, but still alive. One of the Persian captives being brought forward, the dying prince, knowing from his voice that he was his countryman, said that "he had at least this comfort in his present sufferings, that he should speak to one who could understand him, and that he should not utter his last words in vain." He then desired that the following message should be given to Alexander: that "he died without having done him any acts of kindness, but a debtor to him for the greatest, since he had found his feelings towards his mother and children to be those of a prince, not of a foe; that he had been more happy in his enemy than in his relations, for by his enemy life had been granted to his mother and children, but taken from himself by his relatives, to whom he had given both life and kingdoms; and that such a requital must therefore be made them as his conqueror should please. For himself, that he made the only return to Alexander which he could at the point of death, by praying to the gods above and below, and the powers that protected kings, that the empire of the world might fall to his lot. That he desired a legitimate and not a burdensome favour, a sepulchre; and, as to avenging his death, it was not his cause alone that was concerned, but precedent, and the common cause of all kings, which it would be both dishonourable and dangerous for him to neglect; since, in regard to vengeance, the interests of justice were affected, and, in regard to precedent, those of the general safety. To this effect he gave him his right hand, as the only pledge of a king's faith [*unicum pignus fidei regiae*] to be conveyed to Alexander. Then, stretching out his hand, he expired. (11.15.5–13)

The declaration attributed to Darius is a long panegyric of his adversary, constructed around the theme of the gratitude the Great King owes Alexander because of the mercy he showed toward members of the royal family. The theme was not new; it was introduced even before Gaugamela, when the eunuch Tyriotes came to announce to Darius that his wife Stateira was dead and that Alexander, who held her in respect, had had an official funeral in her honor and memory. That is the meaning of the prayer that Darius addressed to his gods: "Parent gods, who watch over the Persian throne, grant that I may again restore the fortune of Persia to its former state, in order that I may have an opportunity of repaying Alexander in person the kindness which he has shown to those whom I hold dearest; but if indeed the fated hour has arrived, and the Persian empire is doomed to perish, may no other conqueror than Alexander mount the throne of Cyrus." (30.12–14). Plutarch adds: "The above is the account given by most historians of what took place on this occasion."

That beautiful declaration is also found, almost word for word, in Arrian and Curtius. Plutarch repeats it elsewhere in a similar form: "If then the Fates have otherwise determined as to me and mine, O Jupiter preserver of the Persians, and you, O Deities, to whom the care of kings belongs, hear your suppliant, and suffer none but Alexander to sit upon the throne of Cyrus."[10] The scene, obviously invented, shores up the ancient discussions of Alexander's continence; in addition, it belongs to the narrative context of an anticipated harmonious succession from Darius to Alexander, which Darius accepts and desires.

The Great King proclaims that he is in Alexander's debt. The terminology is well known, appearing in a multitude of Greek texts that evoke the gift/countergift system of the Persian court and the obligation of subjects to always render service to the Great King, who, in return, will reward them. The very logic of (unequal) exchange is that, in the last instance, the king is never the obligee of anyone: though the beneficiary of services rendered by his subjects, he is the donor par excellence, thanks to the gifts he makes or promises to make in the future.[11] Here, by contrast, Darius is a donee, dually so, vis-à-vis Polystratus *and* vis-à-vis Alexander. Unlike all the other exempla that show a Great King receiving water from a common soldier or subject, Darius is in the position of obligee, because, having lost everything and close to death, he cannot make a countergift that would in turn oblige Polystratus. Hence the remark Plutarch attributes to him: "This is the worst of all my misfortunes that I am unable to recompense you for your kindness to me." By contrast, the king proclaims his debt toward the soldier and promises him a countergift: "Alexander will reward you [*apodōsei soi tēn kharin*], and the gods will reward Alexander for his courteous treatment of my mother and wife and daughters." In other words, Alexander will settle the account—which amounts to his being designated Darius's successor. That is the real meaning of the story Plutarch sets out in another of his works: "Darius adopted Alexander, after he had called the Gods to witness the act."[12]

Then Darius, about to give up the ghost, gives his "right hand" to Polystratus, telling him to transmit it to Alexander. The custom is well known and of-

ten attested in the Greek authors, including in the context of Darius III's court
and then of Alexander's.[13] In Diodorus's telling, in about 350 Tennes, leader of
the rebels of Sidon, facing the threat of the offensive conducted by Artaxerxes III,
sent Thettalion, one of his close circle, on an embassy to the Great King, promising to hand over the city and even to aid the king in the planned reconquest of
Egypt. The Great King was delighted and promised to reward him with great
gifts *(megala dōra)*. But Thettalion was also charged with obtaining guarantees:
the Great King had to "confirm his promise by giving his right hand." Furious
that no one trusted him, Artaxerxes decided to have Thettalion put to death.
Then, persuaded by the condemned man that he was making a mistake, he accepted the request and "gave him his right hand, which is the surest pledge
amongst the Persians."[14] Then there is the example of the rebel Mithridates,
who agreed to betray the satrap Datames on the condition that Artaxerxes II
"give him his pledge in accordance with the Persian custom, with his right
hand. He received that guarantee sent by the king."[15]

In each of these three cases (many others could be cited), the two contract-
ing parties are not in each other's presence, and the guarantee (the right hand)
is transmitted through an intermediary. This may mean either that the intermediary quite simply shakes the recipient's right hand, as the Great King had
shaken his, or that he transmits an object in the shape of a hand.[16] Note Justin's
expression: Darius "gave him his right hand . . . to be conveyed to Alexander
[*dextram se ferendam Alexandro dare*]," which is comparable to Nepos's expression regarding Artaxerxes II: "Guarantee sent by the king [*a rege missam*]."
These words seem to refer to the sending of an object, but other formulations
by Plutarch and Justin leave room for doubt: "I give him my right hand through
you"; "he gave him his right hand . . . to be conveyed to Alexander. Then,
stretching out his hand, he expired." In any event, whatever its concrete expression, the custom authenticated an oral message from the king, just as the royal
seal authenticated a letter. According to Nizāmī, a contract was concluded with
this gesture: "And the old man grasped his hand—hard!—in his own, to seal
thereby the oath, the agreement, and the pact."[17]

Darius's gesture therefore constitutes a dual guarantee: on behalf of Polystratus, who can use it to his advantage with Alexander, in order to receive the
gift promised by Darius; and also on behalf of Alexander, who, though he could
not witness the Great King's final moments in person, can legitimately stand as
his designated successor, particularly in the eyes of the Persians, who are familiar
with the custom. Furthermore, in entrusting to Alexander the task of punishing
the regicides, Darius justifies in advance the continuation of the expedition.

All the authors mention that Alexander made the decision to give his enemy a royal funeral. By contrast, the Macedonian's arrival at the site of Darius's mortal remains is not described in great detail. It is simply pointed out that Alexander feels pain both at the defeated man's personal fate and at the fragility of all things human and royal, which that fate brings to the conqueror's mind: "Alexander . . . showed great grief at the sight" and "wept at the thought of Darius' succumbing to a death so unworthy of his exalted position."[18] Only Plutarch, even while making the usual reflections on Fortune, adds a symbolic detail to the image, one intended to increase the dramatic and emotional tension of the scene: "Beholding Darius struck to the heart with several arrows, he did not presently sacrifice to the Gods or sing triumphal songs to celebrate the end of so long a war, but unclasping his own cloak from his shoulders he threw it over the dead corpse philosophically, as it were to cover the shame of royal calamity."[19]

That royal gesture is also attested in the *Alexander Romance,* but there it is performed prior to Darius's death. In all cases, it is easy to understand its popularity among painters: they were fond of illustrating the particularly unfortunate fate of Darius, betrayed and assassinated by his intimate circle, and even more, the moral elevation and piety of the Macedonian king (Fig. 48).

48. *Alexander arriving at the dead Darius (G. Piazzetta).*

Alexander beside the Dying Darius

Although the *Alexander Romance* also highlights Alexander's compassion, the scene takes on a special cast, quite simply because the narrative is constructed on the basis of a scenario known to Diodorus: "Alexander found him still breathing and commiserated with him on his disasters. Dareius urged him to avenge his death, and Alexander, agreeing, set out after Bessus."[20]

After his defeat, the Persian king hastily crosses the Stranga River (frozen at the time) and takes refuge in his palace, where he laments having been the cause of Persia's misfortunes and reflects out loud on the whims of Fortune. Then, as Alexander is himself arriving in Persia, Darius reaches Media. It is there, in one of his palaces, that he is assassinated by two of his satraps, Bessus and Ariobarzanes, and left to die. Alexander, having reached Darius's side, "cried out and began to shed tears, lamenting him as he deserved; then he covered Darius' body with his cloak. Placing his hands on Darius' breast, he spoke these words, pregnant with pity: 'Stand up, King Darius. Rule your land and become master of yourself. Receive back your crown and rule your Persian people. Keep your kingdom to its full extent. I swear to you by Providence above that what I say is honest and not feigning. Who was it who struck you? Tell me their names, so that I may give you peace'" (2.20.5–6).

At that moment, "Darius groaned and stretched out his hands to Alexander." The Persian king, clutching at Alexander "and drawing him to himself," then gave a speech punctuated by appropriate reflections on the whims of Fortune. He also asked Alexander to look after his family and to marry his daughter Roxana: "With these words, Darius laid his head on Alexander's breast and died."

Dārā Dying in Iskandar's Arms

The Persian tradition borrowed the scenography of the *Alexander Romance,* but it also adapted it to its own imagery and specific preoccupations. According to Ferdowsī, "Swift as the wind, Iskandar dismounted and placed the wounded man's head on his thigh. He looked to see whether Dārā was able to speak and massaged his face with his two hands, took off the royal diadem from his head, undid the cuirass covering his chest, and shed many tears, seeing that there was no doctor near the wounded man" (bk. 19, lines 553–556).

Each of the kings wept a great deal, so much so that, in the vivid expression of Abū Tāher Tarsusi, "had they been able to learn of his condition, Iskandar would have made the stone, the bird, and the fish weep!" The two kings, though causing each other distress, exchange words, the substance of which already appears in the Romance: Iskandar promises to "return the empire and the throne" to Dārā if he recovers his health; as for Dārā, he speaks interminably of the whims of Fortune: "I am a great example of what I am saying, and my story is a warning to all." Then he communicates his last wishes: that Iskandar take care of his family and marry his daughter Rouschenek. In Tha'ālibī, Dārā also recommends that Iskandar "not let the small dominate the great, not destroy the temples of fire, and avenge him of his assassins" (p. 411; see also Tabarī, p. 516).

There is an essential difference between the *Alexander Romance* and the Persian tradition: the Alexander of the Romance is reputed to be the son of Olympias and Nectanebo and has no kinship ties to Darius. The Persian tradition is completely different, because of the shared ancestry of Dārā and Iskandar through their father, Dārā(b), son of Bahman. Hence the words uttered by Iskandar: "We are of the same branch, the same root, the same family; why would we destroy our bloodline with our ambition?" (bk. 19, lines 343–344). "My brother," replies Tha'ālibī's Dārā: "Listen to your brother's last wishes" (p. 410).

For the scene of fraternal recognition to unfold, however, Iskandar must be declared worthy of his Iranian family. But because he had actively participated in the plot against Dārā, he was not really worthy. Hence the speech he gives at the bedside of his dying brother, in Dīnawarī, for example. After telling of the two ministers' betrayal, that author writes: "That event caused Dārā's army to disperse, and Iskandar advanced on Dārā, who was swimming in his own blood. Immediately he dismounted, sat at the bedside of Dārā, who had one last gasp of air left, and placed his head on the tail of his garment. Weeping for him, he said: 'Brother, if you escape death, I shall give you back your country, and I pledge to keep my promise. Ask me, then, as your last wish, for anything you want, so that I may do those things.'"

Dārā replies, reflecting aloud on the whims of kings' fates and adding: "'For my part, I commend my remaining wives and children to you and ask you to marry my daughter, because she was the light of my life and the apple of my eye.' Alexander said: 'I will do so. Now tell me who is responsible for the act of treason against you, so that I may take my revenge.' Dārā could not reply to Alexander. His tongue was now forever silenced."

The scene concerns the forgiving or forgetting of the treachery of Iskandar who, according to Dīnawarī—and also to Tha'ālibī, Tabarī, and Nizāmī, as

well as Abū Tāher Tarsusi in the *Dārāb-nāmeh*—had accepted the two traitors'
initial offers. Nizāmī says that Iskandar regretted his attitude as soon as he
learned of Dārā's murder. And in general, Iskandar, upon arriving at Dārā's
bedside, declares, not without apparent hypocrisy, that he had no role in the
recent events: "O most noble and illustrious of men, O you who are the king of
kings, I am sorry for what has just happened to you! But thanks to God, I am
not the cause of the blow that struck you. God knows the good intentions I had
toward you. He knows that I offered, were I to seize the victory, to behave
kindly toward you and to respect our bonds of kinship" (Tha'ālibī, pp. 409–410).
"I would not have wanted to see you in this state; but I did not do it, it is your
own people who have treated you this way" (Tabarī, pp. 515–516).

In accordance with Dārā's wishes, "the two men were hanged, and stones
and arrows flung at them, so that their flesh and their bones were reduced to
shreds. Alexander said: 'Such is the punishment of those who make an attempt
on the lives of kings'" (Tha'ālibī, p. 411). That formulation recalls the words
Darius transmits to Alexander via Polystratus: "It was not his cause alone
that was concerned, but precedent, and the common cause of all kings."[21] In
Dīnawarī and Tabarī, the execution is preceded by a conversation between Iskandar and the two treacherous ministers. The king speaks in such a way as to
clear himself of any accusation of treason toward the man he has come to comfort on his deathbed. Not without some rhetorical audacity, Iskandar justifies
both the agreement he made with Dārā's ministers and the punishment he is
now imposing on them: "He sent for them to come and gave them all the
riches he had promised. Then he told them: 'I pledged not to kill you, and I did
not guarantee your life. In the interest of justice, it would not be fair if I were
to let you live, in view of your treason against your king, and if the king's
blood were to remain unavenged. Anyone who kills a king must be killed on
the spot.' Then he had them crucified and sent out the following proclamation: 'Let everyone see these two and let no one betray his king!'" (Tabarī,
p. 516).

The scene and the lines are nearly identical in Dīnawarī. The two assassins,
attached to the gibbets, are astonished to be so treated, because Iskandar had
promised them promotions in his army: "'Yes,' replied the king, 'here's the promotion I give you.' Then he gave the order to stone them."

Ferdowsī, for his part, does not need to justify Iskandar's conduct. In his account, the two *dastūrs* hoped that Iskandar would reward them, but they acted
alone, without making any proposition to the king of Rūm and without receiving

any pledge on his part. After their crime, they come looking for Iskandar. He immediately arranges to be taken to Dārā and orders the two assassins put under guard. After the Persian king's funeral, he goes forward with the punishment: "Iskandar had set up raised gibbets opposite [the royal tomb], one of which bore the name of Janusipar and the other of Mahiar, and he hung the two wretches to them, still alive; he had these king-killers attached upside down. The soldiers came out of the camp, each with a stone in his hand, and they killed them on the gibbets, pathetically and shamefully. Cursed be anyone who kills a king! When the Iranians saw what Iskandar had done to avenge the death of the free people's king, all offered him their homage and proclaimed him king of the land" (bk. 19, lines 400–407).

Nevertheless, in a letter he sent "to each illustrious man, to each grandee in each province, and also to the mobeds," Iskandar judged it necessary to exonerate himself, as if the matter were not self-evident: "I swear by the master of the sublime sun that I did not want to place Dārā's life in danger. The enemy of that king came from his own palace, it was one of the servants and not a stranger. . . . My pure heart is filled with grief for Dārā, and I will do everything to carry out his last wishes" (bk. 19, lines 449–450).

Iskandar is now considered worthy of succeeding Dārā and of being integrated into the glorious lineage of the Keyānid kings—either because he is reputed to bear no responsibility for Dārā's death or because he has been absolved of having used trickery to win the victory. In reality, he already displayed proof of his Keyānid ancestry during an earlier episode, inspired by the *Alexander Romance*. To learn who his adversary was, Iskandar disguised himself, was admitted to Dārā's court, and took part in a grand dinner. Everyone was struck by his extraordinary charisma: "All the grandees were speechless with admiration and secretly exalted him for his beauty, his majestic bearing, his prudence, his stature, [the strength] of his limbs, and his splendor. . . . Dārā observed the courage and wisdom, the eloquence, the dignity, and the stature of the envoy; it was as if that man were Dārā himself. . . . He asked him: 'What is your name? For in your bearing and on your forehead you bear the mark of the Keyānids. You appear to be greater than a mere subject, and I believe you are Iskandar. Clearly, heaven prepared you for a crown by giving you that bearing, that stature, that speech, and those characteristics'" (Ferdowsī, bk. 19, lines 66,68, 81–82, 94–98).[22]

In the *Alexander Romance*, by contrast, "The Persians looked in amazement at Alexander because of his small stature" (2.15.1). Implicit in several Greco-

Roman texts, Alexander's small stature is also indicated by Tha'ālibī, who says that "the historians report that Iskandar was small of stature" (p. 443). There is, of course, no reason to worry about these trompe-l'oeil contradictions. In the passage Ferdowsī cites, the description is not at all realistic: elaborated by Dārā himself, it is an exposition of the royal virtues associated with the lineage of the Keyānids, a "mirror of the prince," which Dārā holds out to the man he does not yet know is his brother and successor.

Texts and Images

Beyond the influence of the *Alexander Romance,* the profoundly Iranian character of Dārā's death scene must be evaluated in terms of the graphic and pictorial expressions to which it gave rise. In the Iranian world, narratives, tales, and stories are not only transmitted in writing but are also read out loud and constantly reinvented by bards and minstrels. In addition to speech, they readily use paintings, which noninitinerant storytellers place permanently in coffeehouses, and as painted canvases, which itinerant minstrels transport with them everywhere and unroll in front of their listeners.[23] These paintings represent the most famous scenes evoked in the recitation, especially the scenes drawn from the *Shāh-nāmeh.* A few years ago, Michael Wood took a photo in an Iranian village: speaking in front of a semicircle of assembled villagers, the storyteller uses a large canvas to shore up the narrative. In front of the painting, the book is set on an easel. The canvas depicts the famous scene of Dārā's death in the arms of Iskandar, who is shown in all his glory, as the "Two-Horned One." The Persian king, with an oddly "Christ-like" face, is recumbent, his head supported by Alexander's arm, as Alexander places his right hand in that of his "brother." Armies are visible in the background; in the foreground, a horse (Fig. 49).

All in all, the representation reproduces a composition adapted many times by miniaturists (Figs. 50–54). This is in fact one of the most frequently represented scenes in Ferdowsī and Nizāmī manuscripts.[24] The two kings are usually placed in the middle of the miniature, Iskandar seated or kneeling on the ground, supporting Dārā, who is lying in Iskandar's lap and leaning toward him. To the right and left are the two armies, which had been fighting until the moment Dārā was stabbed; the two murderers are in the foreground, prisoners, or sometimes already hanging on gibbets. The background depicts a landscape of mountains, at the summit of which horsemen also represent

49. *In present-day Iran, a* Shāh-nāmeh *storyteller presenting the death of Dārā in
     Iskandar's arms.*

the armies of each camp. In the foreground are two horses: that of Dārā, who
was unseated by his assassins, and that of Iskandar, who, as soon as he learned
of the assassination, came in haste and leapt to the ground to comfort his
"brother."

Sometimes accompanied by an explicit legend (Fig. 53; Richard 1999, p. 82),
the image closely follows the text. It is not unique, however. The exact same
scenography can be found in other paintings, including coffeehouse paintings,
which represent a different episode from the *Book of the Kings*. This is the death
of Sohrab in the arms of Rustam, a great mythic hero of Iran. Rustam is likened
to his horse, Raksch, which possesses uncommon strength and intelligence.
After a hunt, Rustam falls asleep, and "Turks," taking advantage of the situation, capture Raksch. Rustam, searching for his horse, heads for the city of Se-
mengan, where the king offers him hospitality. During the night, the king's
daughter Tehmineh, who has fallen in love with Rustam based solely on his
renown, comes to join him; the king subsequently give his consent for them to
marry. Rustam finds Raksch and, before leaving for further adventures, gives
his wife an onyx that she must put on the arm of the child she is expecting.
That child is named Sohrab and, like his father, is very close to the horse he has

50–53. Persian miniatures: Dārā dying in Iskandar's arms (BnF, Oriental manuscripts, Persian supplement 1617/89v).

chosen for himself. That relationship is somewhat reminiscent of Alexander's rapport with Bucephalus: "Mounted on that horse, he resembled Mount Behis-tun!" (bk. 12, line 197).

After many adventures, the father and son, who do not know each other, find themselves fighting a pitched battle in opposing armies. Because the winner of

51. Persian supplement 1307/77.

52. Persian supplement 1111/234.

the conflict remains in doubt, the outcome of the war will be decided in single combat. Of course, it is Rustam and Sohrab who face off. During the fighting, Rustam mortally wounds Sohrab. It is then that, thanks to the onyx, father and son recognize each other. But it is too late: Sohrab dies, and Rustam builds a magnificent tomb for him.[25]

53. *Persian supplement 332/132.*

In these paintings (Fig. 54), the scene is depicted as the painters imagined it, clearly on the basis of a canonical cartoon (Fig. 55). The resemblance to the scene of Dārā's death is striking: again there is a mountainous background; Sohrab, lying on the ground and losing blood, rests in the arms and against the knees of Rustam, who is kneeling in front of him. The son's torn tunic reveals the identifying onyx. The two horses are also shown, the famous Raksh and Sohrab's horse. Although the representations differ in their specific narrative details (the two traitors, for example), the resemblance between the graphic compositions is remarkable, whether between the two protagonists (Rustam/ Iskandar; Sohrad/Dārā); the horses; or even in the relationship between the central scene and the background. Through the preexisting model, the painters could integrate perfectly into Iranian memory a scene invented by Alexandrian writers, while adding to it a specific and distinctive element. For, unlike the romance, Iranian legends place the protagonists together in a scene of recognition (father and son; brother and brother). It is this characteristic, in fact, that creates the narratological connection between each of the two couples, who can also be distributed as follows: Rustam/Iskandar and Sohrab/Dārā, plus Raksch/ Bucephalus.

54. Sohrab's death in the arms of Rustam, Iranian coffeehouse painting.

55. Sohrab's death in the arms of Rustam: painting by an Iranian artist.

The Last "Speech from the Throne"

To return now to the last wishes expressed by Dārā, as he lay dying in Iskandar's arms: the scene resembles other scenes that Greek authors from the classical age put into words. Xenophon introduces the most famous one at the end of the *Cyropaedia* (8.7). Feeling his strength declining, Cyrus "summoned his children . . . but also his friends and the Persian dignitaries. When everyone was present, he began the speech something like this." He asks his two sons, Cambyses and Tanyoxarkes, whom he (rightly) senses might fight each other for supreme power, to remain faithful to the division of responsibilities he proposes: the kingship to Cambyses, a large governorship to Tanyoxarkes. He also explains how he wishes to be buried. Then, having bid everyone farewell, "he held out a friendly hand, covered his face, and died." It is also on his deathbed that Darius II establishes the division of power between the elder son (the future Artaxerxes II) and the younger (Cyrus the Younger), and that he transmits a few moral precepts to the son who is supposed to succeed him: "I practised justice before all men and before the gods."[26]

As A. Christensen has rightly pointed out, it is likely in this case that Xenophon and the other Greek authors knew of Iranian narratives and adapted the motif to their own.[27] These last declamations, frequently seen in the Sassanid literature, belong to a particular literary and moral genre, the *andarz* (both "precept" and "word of wisdom"), often developed through a narrative, as with the *exempla*.[28] One of the most famous writings is the *Testament of Ardašir*, known through its Arabic translation, which opens with these words: "Greetings from Ardašir, son of Pāpāk, king of kings, to those of the Persians who will succeed him." The king explains "the qualities belonging to the king" and offers a series of reflections and advice on the proper administration of the state, including a discussion of the crown prince. He explains: "I have left my discernment as my inheritance, since I cannot leave you my body."[29] The ceremony allows the king to make official the transition of power to the designated heir and to transmit rules and teachings.

Ferdowsī, himself greatly inspired by Sassanid literature, punctuates his *Shāh-nāmeh* with many such precepts and discourses, which, once collected, constitute a sort of Mirror of Princes. The book has a recurrent motif: the king, sensing the approach of death, summons the grandees and his own family to his deathbed and transmits to them his last counsels and instructions. To take merely two examples, Dārā(b) and Ardašir:

When twelve years had gone by, Dārā(b)'s strength and fortunes de-
clined. Homai's brilliant son wasted away and sensed he was being called
to another dwelling. He assembled the grandees and sages, and spoke to
them at length of the throne of power, adding: "Now it is Dārā son of
Dārā(b) who will be your benevolent guide. All of you, listen to his opinions, obey him, have joy in your hearts in the performance of his orders.
This royal throne does not remain long with anyone; when good fortune
arrives, it disappears very quickly. Strive to be good and just, remember
me with pleasure." He uttered these words, heaved a sigh, and that pome-
granate petal became like a fenugreek flower. (bk. 18, lines 130–137)

The same was true for Ardašir: "When seventy years had passed over him,
the enlightened master of the world became ill. He felt his death approaching,
the green leaf of his life about to turn yellow. He summoned Šapur to him and
gave him countless pieces of advice" (bk. 22, lines 545–546).

Apart from repetitive reflections on the fragility of a king's condition,
Ardašir also gives his son the benefit of his experience. He recommends that
his heir promote religion, because religion and royal power are intimately
linked—a theme already developed with particular insistence in the *Testament
of Ardašir* and in the *Letter of Tansar,* which, moreover, probably inspired
Ferdowsī. Ardašir warns his son against the dangers he needs to watch out for
on the throne: injustice, favor given to lowborn men, and the hoarding of money,
in other words, a lack of generosity. He also recommends that his son choose
his adviser well and avoid any man who is "quick-tempered and haughty, who
finds pleasure in reproaches and quarrels." And in fact, Šapur "governed with justice and wisdom. . . . But after thirty years and two months had passed, he summoned Ormūzd to him and told him . . ." And so on.

There is no doubt that the accounts of Dārā's death themselves belong to
that context, at once literary, moral, and political. The remarks he makes to Iskandar are truly those of a Keyānid king about to die, conversing with his successor and transmitting his message to him. Beyond the apparent banality of
the words, the scene is directly inspired by a model of advice (the *andarz*) that
expresses Sassanid reflections on kingship, society, and religion. Soon it will be
Iskandar, presenting himself as "the new Dārā," who will propagate the royal
Keyānid teachings, in a letter he sends to all the prominent men in each province: "Seek justice and be obedient. . . . Whoever presents himself at my court
will receive gold, slaves, crowns, and thrones. . . . Send to my treasury everything

you owe. . . . You will maintain the palaces of the previous kings in accordance with the ancient custom; you will not leave the markets unattended . . . the border unguarded" (lines 432–440).

The Funeral of Darius/Dārā

According to Justin, among the last wishes that Darius transmitted to Alexander was "a legitimate and not a burdensome favour, a sepulchre." In fact, after copiously weeping over the enemy's remains, Alexander "also directed [Darius's] corpse to be buried as that of a king, and his relics to be conveyed to the sepulchres of his ancestors."[30] Plutarch specifies that Alexander spent considerable sums toward that end.[31] The funeral ceremonies and their location are confirmed by Diodorus, and even more clearly by Arrian: "Alexander sent the body of Darius to Persepolis, with orders that it should be buried in the royal sepulchre, in the same way as the other Persian kings before him had been buried."[32]

In the absence of indisputable archaeological evidence and of texts describing an actual ceremony, it is difficult to determine whether such a funeral actually took place, or whether it is merely a declared intention that was never followed through. At this point the discussion of the *realia* is not conclusive. But, if the ceremony did take place, it was not conducted personally by Alexander, who was in a hurry to resume his march eastward, at a time when Bessus had just proclaimed himself Great King in Bactria. That is the essential difference between the version in the *Alexander Romance* and the Persian tradition.

After describing Darius's death in the arms of Alexander, the Romance reports his decision to have Darius buried "in the Persian manner." A description follows of the cortege that formed at the time: "He had the Persians march in front, followed by the Macedonians in full armour. Alexander put his own shoulder to the carrying of the bier, along with the other satraps. They all wept and mourned, not so much for Darius as for Alexander, at the sight of him shouldering the bier. After the burial had been carried out in the Persian manner, he dismissed the crowds" (2.21.1–2).

Note that the author says nothing about the burial site. A difficulty arose on that point, in fact, because Darius's final moment were set very realistically in Parthia ("near the Caspian Gates"). But because the rest of the narrative implies that Alexander is in Persia, where he makes decisions (2.22), the suggestion is that the funeral ceremony also took place there. It is only too easy to leap to that conclusion, given that Bessus and Ariobarzanes came to surrender to Alexander, who "ordered them to be . . . crucified on the grave of Darius," and that Darius's death and the assassins' punishment in essence mark the end of the expedition. At that moment the account of the conquest is over and the narrative of Alexander's extraordinary adventures begins.

Iskandar's participation is a recurrent feature of the Persian and Arabo-Persian accounts. Tabarī simply mentions that "Dārā died, then Iskandar buried him" (p. 516), and Tha'ālibī writes, without further details: "Iskandar held his funeral and followed his body to the site of the sepulchre, along with his army officers" (p. 411). Both writers locate the battle on the banks of the Euphrates. The same is true for the author of the *Dārāb-nāmeh,* the only one to provide the following precision: "Dārā was wrapped in a shroud, his weight in musk and camphor was placed in his coffin, and he was sent to Iran." In Ferdowsī, the final battle is set in Carmania, on the Persian border, and it is apparently before the journey to Istakhr [Persepolis] that the dead king is buried. Here is the description of the tomb and the ceremony:

> Iskandar built a tomb in the manner of the Persians, worthy of Dārā's rank and in accordance with the rules of his religion. That bleeding body was washed with rose water, since the time of eternal slumber had come to it; it was dressed in Rūm brocade, embroidered with stones and pure gold. His body was covered with camphor, and from that moment on, no one ever saw Dārā's face again. Iskandar placed a gold dais in the tomb and a musk crown on the king's head; he laid Dārā in a gold coffin and shed a flood of tears over him. When the coffin was taken away, all the grandees carried it in succession. Iskandar walked in front, on foot, followed by the grandees, whose eyes were awash in blood. Thus he walked to the tomb of Dārā: it was as if his skin were splitting open from pain. He placed the king's coffin on the dais and followed in every detail the customs of the Keyānids. (lines 390–400)

The resemblance to the *Alexander Romance* is obvious, but the differences are no less noteworthy. In the Greek text, the ceremony is placed under the sign of collaboration between the Macedonians and the Iranians, whereas in Ferdowsī it is a specifically Persian ceremony, conducted by the man who had proclaimed himself "the new Dārā." As for the internal layout of the tomb, it is described in accordance with canonical traits—compare, among other examples, the tomb of Khōsrau Anuširwān, built and decorated in keeping with the king's own prescriptions: "You will embalm the body with camphor, you will place a musk crown on the head, you will bring from the treasury five untouched robes in gold brocade that have never been used, and you will dress me in them, in the manner of the Keyānids and the custom of the Sassanid kings" (bk. 41, lines 4594–4595).

Dārā's Succession

One of the last wishes that Darius whispered in Alexander's ear was that the young conqueror should care for the defeated man's family and should be joined in marriage to his daughter. Here are Darius's words, "reconstituted" by the Romance: "I commit my mother to you as if she were your own, and I ask you to sympathize with my wife as if she were one of your relatives. As for my daughter Roxane I give her to you for a wife, to start a line of descendants that will preserve your memory. Be proud of them, as we are of our children, and, as you grow old together, preserve the memory of your parents—you of Philip, and Roxane of Darius" (2.20.8–9).

As far as we know from the "historical" sources, Darius never had a daughter by the name of Roxana. It is clear how that story came into being: first, as a result of Darius's proposal to make Alexander his son-in-law, in exchange for an end to war; and second, because of the marriage Alexander later celebrated with Roxana, daughter of a Sogdian noble, whose beauty, according to Arrian, was comparable only to that of Darius's wife.[33]

This scene, inherited from the Romance, is recounted by all the Arabo-Persian authors. Here is Ferdowsī's account: "Take care of my children, my allies, and my women, full of wisdom and with veiled faces. Ask me for my daughter in marriage, she of pure body, and give her happiness on the throne. Her mother named her Roushenek and made the world happy and content through her. My child will not make people speak ill of you, even our worst enemies will not slander her. She is the daughter of a king; by her wisdom she will be the diadem on the forehead of illustrious women" (bk. 19, lines 370–375).

The character of the scene, apart from obvious resemblances, varies from one tradition to the other. Alexander's marriage to Roxana does not consecrate and broaden an already-existing alliance but supposedly creates it from whole cloth: the union thus blessed by Darius will allow Philip's lineage to be united with that of Darius himself. The symbolism here is comparable to the joint participation of the Macedonians and the Persians in the cortege taking Darius to his tomb (2.21.1). The narrative unfolds against the backdrop of a policy known to Greek readers in antiquity, namely, Irano-Macedonian marriages, celebrated in great pomp in Susa in 325 at the initiative of Alexander (himself joined in marriage to one of Darius's daughters; another daughter of the deceased Great King married Hephaestion).[34] No doubt the children born of such unions would feel marked by their mother's origins, but they would in the first place be the sons and daughters of Macedonian nobles.

It was a completely different matter within the context of the history revised and corrected by the Iranian tradition. Once Iskandar was reputed to be Dārā's half-brother, the proposed union was not really a mixed marriage to create family ties between Iranians and Macedonians. It was an endogamic union (between uncle and niece) typical of the Iranian traditions and which frequently occurred in the Achaemenid period. For example, according to the Greek sources, Darius III himself was the offspring of a marriage between a brother and a sister and had married his sister Stateira. Nevertheless, the marriage between Iskandar and Roshanek has a certain specificity, because endogamic marriages are practically never found in the Iranian legends reported by the *Shāh-nāmeh*, which are founded on exogamy.[35]

In any event, the foreseeable future for such a marriage is part of the context of Iranian history. That is how Ferdowsī's Dārā understands it in addressing his brother: "I hope she will give you a glorious son, who will revive the name Isfendyār, will make the fire of Zerdousht glow, will take the Zend Avesta in his hand, will observe the oracles, the feast of Sedeh and that of the New Year, will honor the temples of fire, Ormūzd, the moon, the sun, and Mihr, will purify his soul and his face with the water of wisdom, will reestablish the customs of Lohrasp and the cult of the Keyānids that Guštasp followed, will treat the great as great, and the small as small, will make religion thrive and will be well-off" (bk. 19, lines 376–380).

That anticipated grandson may be considered the successor of the great names of the Keyānid dynasty designated by Dārā. He will be the depository of the virtues and dispositions that allow a good king to establish relations both intimate and respectful with the gods. He will be able to maintain the Right Religion, to sacrifice before the fire altars, and to ensure the country's social and political cohesion, a country where each class (the "great" and the "small") must remain in its place, as the monarchical writings of the Sassanid period so clearly express it. In other words, the future of Iran looks grand:

thanks to Iskandar, the glorious lineage of the Keyānids will continue after Dārā's death.

Matters are more complex than they may seem, however. Marriage is only one of the provisions by which the dying king hopes that his kingdom will be maintained: "I give you my daughter Roushenek in marriage: display toward her the consideration she merits, treat her with kindness as your wife and give her a generous station. Honor the nobles and grandees of Persia, do not let the small dominate the great, do not destroy the temples of fire and avenge me of those who killed me" (Tha'ālibī, pp. 410–411).

Yet the entire Sassanid tradition, adopted in large part by the Arabo-Persian tradition, made Alexander the destroyer of the Holy Books and of the sacred fires. It also attributed to him the plan to put to death the grandees of Iran: only the intervention of Aristalis (Aristotle) led Iskandar to abandon his initial idea. But Aristalis's own proposal was not particularly generous, given that its aim was to weaken Iran by dividing it among many dozens of "tribal kings." As a result, the roles played by Iskandar and Dārā are contradictory. Iskandar is nothing but a transitional king whose primary function is, so to speak, reduced to that of siring an "Iranian Keyānid." And that is not all. In reality that marriage, planned and performed, was childless. Ferdowsī tells us that the wedding was celebrated in accordance with royal pomp and specifies that Iskandar "remained with his wife for seven days." Then, very quickly, he left Iran and began his extraordinary adventures, with an expedition to India (bk. 20, lines 45–270).

Roushenek does not see Iskandar again until his return to Babylon, where she receives his last wishes, expressed in a letter to his mother: "If Roushenek brings a son into the world, he will perpetuate his father's glory, and none but he must be king of Rūm, since he will bring prosperity to the country. But if, at the hour of her distress, she brings a daughter into the world, marry her to the son of Pheïlekous, whom you shall give the title of my son and not my son-in-law, and through whom you will keep my memory fresh in the world" (bk. 20, lines 1800–1804).

In other words, the Macedonian/Rūmi side of Iskandar/Alexander has taken the upper hand. He makes no plans to hold on to the country of Iran but is concerned simply with Rūm. Roushenek, after wailing and shedding tears, disappears from the narrative. According to other authors, Iskandar sent her just after the wedding to live in the country of Rūm, and it was by letter that he made his last wishes known (Tabarī, p. 517; Tha'ālibī, p. 449). And when, after his death, the Persians asked that he be buried in Persia, in "the land of kings," a leader of the Rūmi responded: "Iskandar must return to the land from which he came." Soon the Persians themselves had to face the facts, for they heard a wise old man tell them: "The land of Iskandar is in Iskandarieh, which he founded when he was alive" (bk. 20, lines 1851–1866). According to Tha'ālibī (p. 449), Iskandar was actually buried in Alexandria; according to Tabarī, his body "was transported to Greece . . . and Lagos-Ptolemy succeeded him" (p. 524).

It is altogether striking that no "hidden king" legend ever depicts a son born of the marriage between Iskandar and Roushenek. The only known son of Iskandar is the one to whom Tabarī alludes, a certain Alexander, who, raised by Aristotle in the land of Rūm, refuses to succeed his father, preferring "to withdraw from the midst of men and devote himself to the worship of God" (p. 524). Iskandar does not even perform the role that the dying Dārā assigned him: that of giving Dārā a successor.

At the same time, Dārā's historical role is significantly enhanced by the familial relationship with Ardašir, founder of the Sassanid dynasty, which one current of the Iranian tradition attributes to him. The royal legend of Ardašir, also known to Ferdowsī and reported by him (bk. 21, lines 62ff.),[36] is actually transmitted by the king himself:

> Of the 240 petty kings installed by Alexander, the region of Fārs and nearby regions were under the authority of Ardavān. Pāpāk was the border governor *(marzapān)* of Fars, and one of the representatives whom Ardavān had named. He had his seat in Istakhr and had no son to perpetuate his name. Sāsān was a shepherd employed by Pāpāk, who always stayed with the king's horses and livestock. He was descended from the line of Dārā, son of Dārā. During Alexander's accursed reign, Dārā's descendants had settled privately in the remote regions, traveling with the Kurdish shepherds. But Pāpāk did not know that Sāsān was descended from the family of Dārā, son of Dārā. . . . Then the secret was revealed]. Later, Pāpāk gave his daughter in marriage to Sāsān. . . . She was soon pregnant and gave birth to Ardašir. (*Testament of Ardašir*, §§ 1–18)

In reestablishing Iran's unity, in restoring the Right Religion *(dēn),* in reattributing to each group the place it was supposed to occupy in the social organization, Ardašir ended the unfortunate aberration introduced by the defeat of Dārā, whom he avenged: "Today the King of kings [Ardašir] has cast the shadow of his majesty over all who have acknowledged his pre-eminence and service and have sent him tribute. . . . Thereafter he has devoted all his thoughts to attacking the Greeks [Rūm] and pursuing his quarrel against that people; and he will not rest till he has avenged Dārā against the successors of Alexander, and has replenished his coffers and the treasury of state, and has restored . . . the cities which Alexander laid waste in Iran" (*Letter of Tansar*, § 42).

That same inspiration is behind Ferdowsī's overview of Iranian history after Dārā and Iskandar, and the return to the unity and greatness of Dārā's time. Even while attributing the measure to the "wisdom" of Iskandar, he reports that the king acted "so that at least one country [Rūm] would remain a cultivated and prosperous country." That required weakening and dividing up Iran: "Two hundred years have thus passed, during which it is as if there were no king in the land. They paid no attention to one another, and the land enjoyed a long rest; and that happened in accordance with the plan Iskandar had come up with, so that the prosperity of Rūm would not be in danger" (bk. 21, lines 49–52).

There follows the legend of Sāsān, son of Dārā/Darius, and of his descendants, up to the birth of Ardašir, then his ascent to the throne: "He girded himself with the girdle and took in his hand the club of kings. He readied the palace where he resided and henceforth was called king of kings; no one could have distinguished him from Guštasp" (bk. 22, lines 1–2).

The very outcome of the story admirably reveals Iskandar's dual nature and the dual figure of Dārā. Iskandar became part of dynastic history, but at the price of genealogical acrobatics and after a marginal and contradictory assimilation process. Recall that, after his defeats, Ferdowsī's Dārā (bk. 19, lines 212–213) identified his adversary with Zahhāk (a particularly evil king) and assimilated himself to Jamshid (the prototype of the good, beneficent king). In reality, Ferdowsī's book shows that, over the *longue durée* of the Iranians' imaginary memory, Iskandar was by turns and simultaneously Zahhāk and Jamshid. As for Dārā, though denounced as a "bad king" incapable of inspiring his people's devotion, and as a result defeated by his half-brother Iskandar, he plays his role as the transmitter of the "royal glory" proper to the Keyānids: not thanks to his daughter Roushenek but thanks to his brother and his brother's descendants. They, at the cost of suffering and sacrifice, were able to perpetuate the Keyānids' bloodline and transmit it to Ardašir.

Iskandar and Dārā's "Other" Daughter

The Arabo-Persian authors, after noting, even emphasizing, the active complicity between Iskandar and Dārā's assassins, attempted with greater or lesser conviction to clear Iskandar of all responsibility in the murder of the Persian king.

At stake was the credibility of the scene of fraternal recognition, linked to the harmonious transfer of power. There is an exception that deserves to be noted, however: the account given by Abū Tāher Tarsusi in the *Dārāb-nāmeh*, a sort of popular romance dating to the eleventh to twelfth centuries, where the figure of Iskandar is infinitely less radiant than in many works of that period.[37]

And yet Iskandar's Keyānid ancestry is more marked there than elsewhere. He is born of Dārāb, the eponymous hero, whose life takes up a third of the romance. Dārāb had married Nahid and had spent a brief wedding night with her. Furthermore, Philip, father of Nahid, is reputed to be descended from a mythic king of Iran. The conflict between the two half-brothers is also rendered in an original manner. It results from a debate about Iranian identity: Dārā makes it known to Iskandar that he does not acknowledge his Iranian roots; in response, Iskandar orders Dārā to give him half of Dārāb's inheritance. Dārā of course refuses. War follows, including the battle near the Euphrates, then the agreement between Iskandar and the two emirs (Jānusyār and Māhyār), Dārā's assassination, and the scene of reconciliation, when Dārā asks Iskandar to marry his daughter Roushenek.

She is "extremely beautiful." Her only flaw—if it is one—is the presence of peach fuzz on her lip. Better known by her other name, Burān-Dokht ("girl with the rosy complexion"), she not only has the advantages of charm in her favor but is also "accomplished," as a result of the scrupulous education her father has given her: "He taught her all the arts useful to a prince," horsemanship and the handling of heavy weapons. As she will abundantly prove over the course of the romance, and even several times at Iskandar's expense, she is perfectly capable of fighting and even of winning a single combat to decide a victory: "She was intimidated by no man." She thus belongs to a well-known literary and human type, that of the woman warrior, also familiar to the Greek authors.[38] It is easy to associate Roushenek/Burān-Dokht with another Roxana, this one from a great Persian family from Darius II's time, as Ctesias describes her: "She was very beautiful and among the most skillful with the bow and javelin."[39] Then there is Rhodogune, as depicted by Polyaenus. She quells the rebellion of one of the empire's tribes.[40]

Burān-Dokht quickly demonstrates her energy and independent spirit against Iskandar. She even manifests a true spirit of revolt against the fate that had been dealt Dārā and Iran:

When the news of Dārā's death reached her, the bright world grew dark in her eyes. She threw herself down from the throne onto the dark ground and fainted. Someone sprinkled her face with rose water until she came to. . . . Letting out a howl, she rent her clothing, tore out her hair, clawed her beautiful moon face, bit her forearm, and ripped her own flesh with her teeth, until the announcement came that someone had brought her father's body. . . . Seeing the coffin, she threw herself from Dārāb's mount, rolled in the dust and blood, and seemed to be out of her mind. . . . She said, in tears: "O my father, my soul's strength, what is the point of living without you? And yet I swear to you on my soul and on that of my noble ancestor Dārāb, son of Ardašir, in attendance here, to demand vengeance for you from Iskandar, descendant of Philip, for I know it is he who commanded Jānusyār and Māhyār to treat you that way."

We shall not follow the heroine in all her adventures, which are in great part indistinguishable from those of Iskandar in India, Ceylon, and beyond. Not only is she the opposite of the "true" Roushenek (she follows Iskandar, fighting him and supporting him by turns), she is also the only figure depicted as a rival in Iskandar's bid for power. Because of the intimacy of her bond to her father and grandfather Dārāb, it is possible that, deep down, she considers herself perfectly worthy of ascending to the throne of the Keyānids, as her grandmother Homai had done. Whereas Iskandar is regularly called "king of Rūm" and is certainly not depicted as a hero, she is frequently designated the "queen of Iran," dressed in "royal glory." She alone has access to King Jamshid's hiding places in the underground passages of the city of Istakhr. Iskandar, by contrast, is unable to force his way in. And so on. It is tempting to conclude that the opposition between Burān-Dokht and Iskandar is not merely personal. To be sure, as a woman she is attached to the man who is her half-brother and who has become her husband: she grieves him, wears mourning for him for forty days, and does not survive him for more than a year. At the same time, however, one may wonder whether the fictionalized introduction of that character did not also make it possible to express, in Dārā's name, some of the contradictory feelings the Iranians had toward the conqueror and toward their vanquished king.

V

A FINAL ASSESSMENT
AND A FEW PROPOSALS

❧ 12 ❧

Darius in Battle

Variations on the Theme "Images and Realities"

Darius, Alexander, and Discourses on Kingship

In the end, the overall judgment of Darius III by the Greco-Roman authors does not allow for much nuance. The last Great King never embodies the foremost quality of the ruler: to be a leader of men, that is, someone who can do without his usual comfort and live like the common soldier, who can make the right tactical and strategic decision whenever a new situation arises, and who leads the charge and mounts the assault from the front line. On the contrary, Darius was the first to turn tail, and his "shameful" flight led to his own army being routed. He took advantage of his own people's sacrifice to elude his fate.

The success of such a portrayal lies, first, in a systematic opposition to Alexander the Great, who is himself erected into the emblematic figure of a heroic ethos, with which he is closely identified. It lies, second, in the literary talent of the authors, who throughout their discourses were able to skillfully set out a series of rhetorical snares, one inside the other, into which the memory of Darius vanishes. And finally that success lies in the character's insertion into the all-embracing imagery of the "Persian Great King" that had been constructed throughout the classical period. This imagery was easily recycled within the continuity of the Hellenistic Roman period and was reinstrumentalized in the modern and contemporary periods, borne on the "Orientalist" wave. Collections of exempla, particularly numerous in the Roman period, certainly played a major role in the diffusion of the model. In the exempla, therefore, Darius III, though he has a relatively minor role in specific anecdotes and fabliaux,

corresponds perfectly to a negative image, illustrated primarily by his predecessors. The persistence of that imagery explains why judgments of the Great
King are just as disparaging among those Roman authors who tend to emphasize Alexander's serious flaws and vices.

The royal figure is really treated no better in Iran. Especially in comparison
to his father, Dārā(b), the good king, Dārā does not govern by the traditional
rules accepted by all. That is the principal cause of the defeat, which results directly from the support afforded Iskandar by a number of Darius's intimates,
worn down and exasperated by the king's conduct. The deadly and cutthroat
treason of his two "ministers" is condemned, of course, but is at the same time
reinterpreted within the context of a broader political reflection that makes Dārā
the one truly responsible for the disunity that weakens his camp.

The negative judgment thus rendered is all the more striking in that Alex-
ander/Iskandar is not praised unreservedly in the Persian and Arabo-Persian
tradition. Not only do the Sassanid texts violently and irrevocably condemn
him for the destruction and misfortune he brought to Iran, but the Persian and
Arabo-Persian texts themselves also express reservations, at least for the phase
when Iskandar was contending with Dārā. In particular, it is altogether noteworthy that a number of authors do not make Iskandar a hero of the battles but,
on the contrary, attribute his victories to the deliberate use of the betrayals
occurring in Dārā's camp. By virtue of his fictive kinship with the last Great
King, which justifies the final fraternal scene of recognition, Iskandar is in some
sense integrated into Iranian history, but he is still an "outsider." The royal legend of Ardašir spreads the fiction of a direct kinship tie between Dārā and the
first Sassanid and, as a result, eliminates Iskandar from the royal succession over
the long term. At the very least, it considers his reign a digression.

The parallels and similarities that can be identified in each of the traditions
are not reducible, therefore, to the known influence of the *Alexander Romance*
on Persian literature. The convergences stem in the first place from the very
nature of the narratives depicting Alexander and Darius, and from the politico-
philosophical reflections associated with them. The writings of Arrian, Curtius, and their colleagues are not the result of historical research conducted on
the basis of identified and authenticated documents, interpreted in accordance
with a critical method whose rules and procedures are accepted by all. In the
part of their works devoted to the war and battles between Alexander and Darius, the objective of the authors of the Roman period was not so much to analyze events as to make a moral (or moralistic) judgment, based on a codified

representation of the good king and exceptional leader. Less works of history than handbooks with illustrative anecdotes, they could be titled "On the Kingship of Alexander in Action."

Beyond the internal contradictions that the genre generates from one author to another, there is a constant opposition between a hero of history, the good king, fearless and beyond reproach on the battlefield, and an antihero, the bad king, judged incapable of carrying the banner of monarchical values. Darius, rather than being placed within a continuous, exhaustive, and precise narrative that would assign a meaning and an identity to his character, is depicted within an incomplete and fragmentary narrative framework, constructed for the most part from exempla and apothegms that illustrate his shortcomings. These appear all the more contemptible in that they are constantly set in radical opposition to the incomparable virtues of the "Macedonian hero."

It is no different in the Iranian traditions. The *Letter of Tansar* indicates that, even in the Sassanid period, the "exemplary" story of Dārā was instrumentalized within a discourse on good kingship. The monarchical fable that grew up around Dārā the Elder and Dārā the Younger in their relations with good and bad royal advisers (Rastin and Bīrī) originated in Iran and was later adopted in Ibn' Bakhlī's *Fārs-nāmeh:* it is found nowhere in the history of Darius. To be sure, Dārā's historical fate suffered greatly from the defeat at Alexander's hands, but the writers primarily judge the king as a function of an intangible image of Iranian kingship, to which he reputedly did not conform. It is not so much with respect to his military abilities or failings that Dārā's acts are assessed as in terms of the qualities that a good king must know how to deploy within his close circle, within society as a whole, and vis-à-vis the gods. Because of his inability to control his passions and drives (especially anger), to listen to the wise counsels dispensed by the elders, and to secure his people's loyalty, Dārā was condemned from the start to an unhappy but foreseeable fate, and he dragged Iran along with him.

To bring those charges, the writers had no need to borrow slavishly from the Greco-Roman literature. It is not really surprising that Arrian, the *Alexander Romance,* and the Sassanid and Persian literature all characterize the good king and the bad king in the same way, at least in one respect: within the context in which Alexander and Darius are introduced, the key to success or failure lies to a great degree in the common destiny that the king was or was not able to weave with his immediate circle and his subjects. As Plutarch writes: "For it is not Fortune that overrules men to run the hazard of death for brave princes;

but the love of virtue allures them—as natural affection charms and entices bees—to surround and guard their chief commander."[1]

The good king is quite naturally a conqueror; the conquered sovereign, abandoned by his own people, is quite naturally a bad king. Monarchical morals, universal in their essence, are therefore secure.

What Is to Be Done?

In the introduction to this book, I wondered to what extent the ancient sources dealing with Darius/Dārā are still usable for the historian of today. The final assessment can be expressed in two parts. On one hand, the analysis I have conducted has proved fruitful for the history of images and representations; on the other hand, it does not provide any great hope for those who would like to get back to "reality." Even taking into account a preliminary observation, namely, that any attempt at biographical reconstitution would be spurious, we need to note that, at the end of our journey, we still do not know who Darius was. And our uncertainty about the "real" Alexander has also increased—because it appears to be such a tricky matter to establish a methodological and cognitive link between images and realities.

Are we therefore condemned to discern only a depersonalized silhouette of Darius, created from whole cloth by the admirers and adulators of Alexander, himself reduced to the status of an icon? For the most part, yes, without a doubt: the absence of solid documentation remains an insurmountable obstacle. To understand the decisions attributed to Darius during the pitched battles, the ideal would be to possess sources that make explicit the conduct that a Great King ought to adopt in all circumstances of wars and battles. We are not in possession of such sources. For though the famous inscription of Darius I in Naqsh-e Rustam (DNb)—a true mirror of Achaemenid princes—exalts the royal virtues of commander and leader, it offers no key that would tell us concretely and realistically about the place that one Great King or another occupied in the battles. From the ideal Darius I of Naqsh-e Rustam to the unreal Darius III of the Greco-Roman sources, we simply move from a canonical royal image to its inverted reflection in a different mirror.

I have brought to light the literary and ideological biases of the ancient sources, but that does not mean I am justified in proposing a counterimage. That would merely be the absurd and unacceptable result of a particularly simplistic mechanical reversal. Moreover, though I have teased out the contradictions between Arrian and one or another Vulgate author, that does not permit me to advance a firm conclusion about the "true" Darius. It is clearly possible to cast into relief the suspect character of the portrayal in the Greco-Roman sources; but strictly speaking, it is not possible to infer therefrom the extent to which the image misrepresents the truth of the historical figure, because we possess no indisputable marker of that "Achaemenid reality."

The matter is not definitively settled, however. By means of a final reflection on method, I should like to show, on the basis of a recurrent motif—"Darius's flight"—that, beyond the glaring inadequacy of the ancient tradition, a path for reflection is possible. It takes the form of comparative history. This method may suggest an interpretation other than that put into words and images by a hegemonic Greco-Roman current and, in a certain way, "confirmed" by the view from Iran.

To return, therefore, to the problem of models: the heroic model, inherited by mimesis from Homer—usually via Xenophon—became the hegemonic principle for describing and explaining Alexander and his adventure but also an interpretive framework for understanding Darius's "shameful" defeats. In antiquity this model was called into question, in both narrative practice and in terms of rhetoric. For example, Arrian was adept at showing, in the invented dialogues with Parmenion, that Alexander could display circumspection when the moment required caution. The model was also contested more formally, more theoretically even, within Alexander's entourage. The debate can be linked to a discussion conducted within Cyrus the Younger's close circle, but it does not directly concern Achaemenid monarchical practice or theory. I am convinced, however, that it can shed light on the reflections to be made about the Achaemenid warrior king, particularly because, on this point, Byzantine sources echo identical debates in the Sassanid court.

I therefore propose to set out the premises and conclusions of the debate in question, then to compare it to a debate of the same type that unfolded in modern France and that was decided in the age of Louis XIV. That foray into comparative history will, I hope, in its turn justify my initial hypothesis, namely, that there was a code specifically conceived for the Great King at war, and that Darius's conduct, including his successive retreats from the battlefield, can therefore be explained with reference to a specifically Persian royal ethos.

The King's Life and the Survival of the World

This "initial hypothesis," as I have called it, was already suggested in a book on Iranian religions, published in 1965 *(Die Religionen Irans)*.[2] The author, Geo

Widengren, addresses the problem within the Indo-Iranian context and proposes the following solution: according to him, the Persian king never participates in combat. By way of example, he refers to Xerxes, who, "seated on a high throne, oversaw the Battle of Salamis," but also to Darius III: "Darius III followed the battles of Issus and of Gaugamela as they unfolded, calmly installed in his war chariot. When the battle was lost, he fled, because his duty was not to fight but simply to survive in order to rule. It was a great mistake to see that as cowardice. Such is absolutely not the case. In the Māhabharāta, Yudishthira, the model for rulers, does not participate in the battle; he merely supervises and directs it" (1968, p. 179).

Introduced as an interpolated clause, the discussion lacks a preliminary analysis of Darius's situation during the battles.[3] But all in all, Widengren's hypothesis is appealing, as C. Nylander ("The Coward King," 1993) has also pointed out. At best, it allows us to understand certain information provided by the Vulgate authors, which Widengren does not reproduce: Darius supposedly agreed to leave the battlefield at Gaugamela only at the insistence of his immediate circle, who were anxious to protect the king's life.

That is because the king is not merely the head of state. He assumes an importance that extends beyond his person, because of his role and his place in the general regulation of the world. In describing the organization of the royal procession leaving Babylon, Curtius gives precise indications on the robe Darius wore on that occasion: "The sumptuous attire of the king was especially remarkable. His tunic was purple, interwoven with white at the centre, and his gold-embroidered cloak bore a gilded motif of hawks attacking each other with their beaks. From his gilded belt, which he wore in the style of a woman, he had slung his scimitar, its scabbard made of a precious stone. His royal diadem, called a 'cidaris' by the Persians, was encircled by a blue ribbon flecked with white."[4]

Georges Dumézil has provided a commentary on this text.[5] The author begins with the premise—whose validity can be easily conceded—that the choice of colors bears a meaning: this was not a sartorial whim on the part of the last Darius. The three colors refer to the three functions of the Indo-European (Indo-Iranian) king: priest, soldier, and peasant. In support of his interpretation, Dumézil refers to another Iranian text, in which Ohrmūzd puts on a white garment, which is that of the priesthood. A second figure is wearing a gold and silver garment decorated with precious stones: this is the uniform of the warrior. Then a dark blue garment is mentioned, the uniform of the farmer. These three functions are an expression of the social body as a whole; and the king combines all three in his person. That is also attested by a famous inscription of Darius I, in which the king utters a "trifunctional" prayer addressed to Ahura Mazda, asking him to divert from Persia "the enemy army, the bad year [that is, the bad harvest], and lies [*drauga*] [that is, disloyalty and rebellion]."[6] The king is not simply a warrior. As the representative on earth of the great god Ahura Mazda, he is the one who maintains the *arta*, the overall organization of the world here below, in a direct relationship with the divine world. He has a cosmological function. In some sense, the global balance depends on the royal person and his privileged connections to the gods. In wartime as well, the king is the intermediary between the lower world and the higher world: at one point, a Greek text depicts Darius I uttering a prayer to the Iranian storm god, who then sends a beneficent rain to save the army from dying of thirst in the middle of the desert.[7]

Military Expeditions and the Itinerant State

Like Xenophon's Cyrus and Herodotus's Xerxes, Darius III is accompanied by images of the gods:[8] "Above the tent . . . a representation of the sun gleamed in a crystal case. . . . In front, on silver altars, was carried the fire which the Persians called sacred and eternal. Next came the Magi, singing the traditional hymn." Also in the cortege was the chariot dedicated to Ahura Mazda and the chariot consecrated to the Sun.[9] These are the ancestral deities, whose assistance Darius invokes before the battles.[10]

The presence of the gods, their altars, and their priests in Xerxes's army in 480, and in Darius III's in 333—but also the presence of the royal princesses with Darius, and with King Khōsrau Anuširwān marching against Armenia in 576 C.E.—highlights a specific feature of the Great King at war. This characteristic completely eluded the ancient authors, who were primarily concerned with denouncing the cumbersomeness of the royal retinue, for reasons both moral and logistical. Xerxes's march toward Greece and Darius's toward the Mediterranean cannot be reduced to a military expedition in the narrow sense of the term. In accordance with a notion of political space found in many societies, both Western and Middle Eastern, a military expedition is one occasion among others for the king to visit the peoples of his empire and to renew the bonds of authority and submission, even to collect the gifts, taxes, and tributes that are due him, while at the same time engaging in an ostentatious redistribution of wealth.[11]

Apart from the voluminous documentation on "royal entrances" in medieval and modern France, which may suggest a number of comparatist

reflections, both the principle and the practice were known in the Sassanid period and were expounded with a great deal of clarity in a text attributed to King
Khōsrau Anuširwān (Chosroes) himself:

> I wanted the kings of those [traversed] regions, who had their investiture
> from us, to know that we were ready to face journeys; that we had the
> means to do so, whenever we judged it necessary. [I wanted] them to be
> impressed by the spectacle of the majesty of kings, the large number of
> soldiers, their preparation and their weapons in good condition. They
> would have been encouraged by that spectacle to fight enemies and would
> have assessed the power of the man who named them his regents, if ever
> they needed to call on him. We would like to take advantage of that jour-
> ney to distribute gifts and lambs with our own hands; to give them the
> chance to approach the throne and granting them the honor of speaking
> to them, in such a way that all these favors might increase their affection
> and devotion for us and their desire to fight our enemies. Furthermore, I
> wished to inform myself about the condition of their fortresses and to
> question [the taxpayers] on these problems during our journey.[12]

Such practices signified to everyone that, for a few months, the court had
become an itinerant state, one whose power became inscribed in the landscape
and in collective mentalities by virtue of its periodic wanderings. When the Great
King took command of his armies, his pomp was no different from that which
accompanied him during the annual migrations that took him from one residence to another. All the royal services (including the royal stable, the kitchens,
the chariots transporting water in silver vessels, the royal concubines, scribes,
secretaries, and so on) took part in a migration, that of the court, the palaces,
the army, and the state as a whole. Every body occupied a space meticulously
defined in the official cortege that formed at sunrise, when the royal caravan
left the city that had just lavishly welcomed it.[13] That also explains why Darius
was accompanied by his immediate family, and why there were customs governing the place that the royal tent was to occupy in the center of the camp and
also the place of the blood princesses in the camp and during the marches.[14]
Curtius claims that, during the Battle of Issus, "the king's wife and mother and
a crowd of other women" were placed "in the centre of the force," by which he
obviously means at the center of the marching army and the camp, and not in
the center of the contingents arrayed on the battlefield.[15] This implies that,
even when a displacement of the court was combined with a military expedi-

tion, the Great King could not be reduced to his function as a war leader. The royal person was surrounded at that time by the same ceremonial and the same protection he enjoyed when the court was at its fixed residence in Persepolis, Susa, Babylon, or Ecbatana.

Darius's Mare

Now that I have put forward my hypothesis and developed it in a preliminary manner, it remains to be tested with the aid of texts. Their suspect ideological orientation does not necessarily mean that they are devoid of all informative value. I therefore return to a few passages that, beyond the burden they impose on the memory of Darius, offer concrete information—masked by the interpretive deadwood—about the decision the Great King made to leave the battlefield.

Arrian says that, at Issus, Darius fled in his chariot, before abandoning it and leaping onto a horse. The king then continued his flight, changing his mount from time to time.[16] Curtius provides comparable information but adds an important nuance: "Frightened that he might fall into his enemy's hands alive, Darius jumped down and mounted a horse which followed his chariot for this very purpose [ad hoc]." And Plutarch, describing the Battle of Gaugamela, specifies the animal's sex: "Darius, we are told, left his chariot and his arms, mounted a mare which had recently foaled, and rode away." That precision is repeated by Aelian, an author from the Roman period, in a moralistic tale included in a work that collects anecdotes related to animals. In that case, it is the mare's attachment to her foal that the author intends to illustrate: "When the battle being fought near Issus turned badly for the Persians, and when Darius was defeated, he mounted on a mare, anxious as he was to escape and save his life as quickly as possible. Remembering the foal she had left behind, the mare is well known to have saved her master, with all the speed and care possible, from such a critical moment of danger."[17]

That exemplum was used in antiquity, and has been used in contemporary historiography, to condemn even more harshly the Great King's cowardice. But if the interpretation imposed by the Greco-Roman authors is hypothetically set aside, the documentation may give rise to another reading. It is just as likely that Persian monarchical values required, in cases of extreme danger, that the king be able to leave the battlefield to escape death and capture. In that sense, the king's departure from the battlefield was actually planned not by the personal decision of a panic-stricken king but simply in conformance with well-established customs—hence the presence of a horse "for that very purpose," to borrow Curtius's expression. In that respect, despite its apparent absurdity (but the historian cannot choose his documents), Aelian's little story, or rather the original piece of information on the basis of which it is constructed, serves to confirm the information transmitted by Curtius and Plutarch and used in part by Arrian and Diodorus.

From Darius to Chosroes

Widengren's hypothesis, arising from an intuition shored up by Indo-Iranian comparatism, would apparently make it possible to reconcile contradictory information about Darius III's conduct and to analyze it in terms of Iranian religious and political notions or, if one prefers, in terms of the rules and practices of "good kingship." Although the specifically Achaemenid documentation offers no possibility of conducting any "experimental verification," Iranian history provides an interesting parallel, even given that it was transmitted through Greek sources of the Byzantine period.

At that time, the Hellenophone authors were very fond of "Persian customs." Take the case of Agathias, or Procopius of Caesarea, who somewhat earlier had devoted several books to the wars between Justinian and the Persians of his time. The number of references to the customs and laws of the Persians is very high in these sources.[18] One example (situated outside the chronological parameters of Procopius's *Wars*) is altogether typical. In 576 King Khōsrau I Anuširwān (Chosroes) conducted a campaign in Armenia. He soon met strong opposition and lost his entire baggage train, including the royal princesses, and even the fire altar that followed him everywhere. He was reduced, therefore, to a situation close to that of Darius III after his defeats. Chosroes was forced to withdraw and pass back over the Euphrates. According to three authors, he made a decision at that time that would have repercussions for his successors. According to Evagrius, "he erected an immortal stela in memory of his flight. Inscribed on it was the law he had proposed, that no king of Persia should ever again wage a campaign against the Romans." The same information is found in Theophylactus, who mentions that the king "published in the form of a law the shame resulting from his defeat. . . . In the future, it will no longer befit the king of the Persians to take the path of war." According to John of Ephesus, the decision stipulated more specifically that the king would not leave on a campaign except to fight another king.[19]

The "law" in question, as the Byzantine authors retransmitted it—using expressions that do not coincide exactly—may seem scarcely credible, especially its postulated causal relationship to a defeat at the hands of the Byzantines. At the very least, even if the texts cited refer to a reality, the formulations the Byzantine authors use do not really allow us to reconstitute either the original text or the conditions of its elaboration and application. That does not mean, however, that the information must be purely and simply rejected. On the contrary, a very simple interpretation may be drawn from these texts: at the time, the Sassanid court was pondering the question of the king's participation in military operations. For reasons that may well belong to Widengren's hypothesis, it was decided that the king was not to place his person in danger (or a royal custom to that effect, long known but fallen into disuse, was promulgated anew).

The Debates in the Immediate Circles of Alexander and Cyrus the Younger: Two Models of the "Warrior King"

I will now leave the Iranian realm and attempt to broaden the comparatist perspective to the Macedonian camp. In the long passage he devotes to the heroic conduct of Alexander during the siege of a fortified Indian city, Arrian reports that the grave wounds the king had received during the previous siege had alarmed all his men, but for reasons specific to each class of soldiers. Among the enlisted men, "when they ceased their lamentation, they became spiritless, and felt perplexed as to the man who was to become the leader of the army; for many of the officers seemed to stand in equal rank and merit, both in the opinion of Alexander and in that of the Macedonians. They were also in a state of perplexity how to get back in safety to their own country, being quite enclosed by so many warlike nations. . . . Besides, they seemed then at any rate to be in the midst of impassable rivers, and all things appeared to them uncertain and impracticable now that they were bereft of Alexander" (6.12.1–2).

Here again, in Arrian's words, are motifs frequently advanced by the ancient authors to explain the Greek soldiers' fear of moving deeper into the Great King's territories, and their panic at not knowing how to find their way out again, given the many natural obstacles and the known or postulated hostility of "so many warlike nations." Coming shortly after the mutiny at the Hyphasis, where they had already expressed the wish to return to their country and see their wives and children again, these fears also demonstrated the desire to return to Macedonia guided by the king, in whom they had complete confidence.[20]

Alexander had to organize an entire scenario to reassure his soldiers, so that they would have proof before their eyes that their king was still alive and ready to lead them. He had a boat brought down the Hydraotes River in view of everyone, then disembarked and mounted his horse: "When he was seen again mounting his horse, the whole army re-echoed with loud clapping of hands."[21]

As Arrian presents them (based on Nearchus's statements), the reasons invoked by the king's friends are both more specific and more political: "Nearchus says that some of his friends incurred his displeasure, reproaching him for exposing himself to danger in the front of the army [*pro tes strateias*] in battle; which they said was the duty of a soldier [*stratiōtes*], and not that of the general [*strategos*]. It seems to me that Alexander was offended at these remarks, because he knew that they were correct, and that he deserved the censure. However, like those who are mastered by any other pleasure, he had not sufficient self-control to keep aloof from danger."[22]

This was certainly a classic debate in antiquity. Polybius, for example, illustrates the specific duties of the general *(strategos)* compared to the ordinary soldier *(idiōtēs):* whereas the soldier is not obliged to show any restraint in looting the enemy camp, the general must not give in to his impulses.[23] The opposition also appears in Curtius. When Alexander tried to engage in single combat with Darius, he acted more like a soldier than a commander, writes Curtius, meaning by that that the Macedonian king was prepared to take risks that ought not to be taken by the leader.[24]

In one of Lucian's *Dialogues of the Dead,* in which the author contrasts Alexander and his father, he too illustrates the idea that the general must calculate risks wisely. Not only does Philip devalue Alexander's victories over Darius and the Persians; he also expresses reservations about the personal feats his son is boasting about. Alexander is fond of pointing out that he is "in love with danger" and likes to "face danger at the head of his army." Philip concedes that it can be glorious for a king to be wounded, but he also judges that his son's feat of leaping all alone onto a fortification is not necessarily praiseworthy.[25] Traces of this view can be found between the lines of Plutarch's panegyric as well: the author believes it necessary to defend Alexander for having been "rash and daringly inconsiderate."[26]

The reproaches that the king's immediate circle makes of Alexander are more or less reminiscent of the deadly quarrel he had in Samarkand a few years earlier with his foster brother Kleitos. At a banquet, Kleitos opposes Alexander's adoption of the Achaemenid court ceremonial. He criticizes him for moving away from the traditional Macedonian mores and of personally taking credit for victories that were those of the entire army. In particular, he reminds Alexander that, at the victory of the Granicus, if he, Kleitos, had not been there, Alexander would have been mortally wounded by the Persian who attacked him.[27] Apparently, therefore, Kleitos calls into doubt the "monomachic" version that had already gained the ascendant through the writings of the flatterers surrounding the king.[28]

In India, the tone of the reproaches of Alexander is different. The Macedonians do not call into question the reality of the individual feat—even though, as all the ancient authors confirm, there were subsequently a multitude of diverging accounts about the identity of the companions who played a role in the story, and even though certain narratives call into doubt one or another part of the official version.[29] The substance of the debate was that those close to the king disputed the legitimacy of the individual feat, when weighed against the collective interest. The definition of the army leader that emerges is no longer that of a Homeric hero, waging a personal battle so that the memory of his great deeds will be celebrated in the future. It is that of a leader responsible for the army's survival and obligated toward the collectivity. The leader must not expose himself on the front lines.

The object of debate is also the king's very function vis-à-vis the Macedonians. Although the ancient sources exalt him first and foremost as a strategos and elite soldier, and though that was certainly the image Alexander himself sought to impose, the Macedonian king was not simply a war leader. He had a fundamental religious role, and in extreme cases the function of strategos could, if necessary, be separated from the king function. Furthermore, even though Alexander's campaign marked a noticeable evolution in Macedonian monarchical theory and practice, throughout the expedition Alexander continued to perform his ritual and religious duties: he sacrificed every day to the traditional gods, in keeping with Macedonian practices, and thus summoned their protection over his people. That explains, on one hand, why after Alexander's death his half-brother Arrhidaeus was chosen to succeed him, even though he was reputed to be incapable of leading an army. It was because Arrhidaeus "accompanied the king in performing . . . religious ceremonies."[30] The responsibility for military operations fell to companions close to Alexander. The panic of the Macedonian soldiers after Alexander's death in Babylon is therefore understandable: in the absence of a direct and capable heir, the Macedonians no longer had either a strategos who could lead them to Macedonia or a high priest who could intervene with the deities. They had lost all protection. As the soldiers noisily reminded Alexander in India, the expedition he was conducting was not a personal adventure; he was also in charge of a collectivity. Just as, in normal times, the Macedonian king did not exercise absolute power, so too the king ought not to have believed he was released from his customary obligations when the kingdom had become itinerant.

In this case, Arrian does not comment on the reaction of Alexander's lieutenants, though he irrevocably condemned the reproaches Kleitos had made: Arrian believes that Kleitos deeply offended his king. Does that silence indicate that, deep down, Arrian admits the validity of the reproaches made by Alexander's lieutenants? According to traditional Roman values, the individual feat was not to be rejected, and there was even a tradition of single combat. In fact, it is with the aid of a specifically Roman vocabulary *(opimum decus)* that Curtius alludes to the single combat that, according to him, Alexander engaged in with Darius.[31] Polybius, for his part, explains that "many Romans voluntarily engaged in single combat to determine the outcome of a decisive battle, and a not negligible number chose sure death in advance, either in wartime to save others or in peacetime to ensure the defense of public affairs."[32] But in reality, the rite of consecrating an enemy's armor in the Temple of Jupiter Feretrius was performed only on very rare occasions and did not have its roots in Rome's remote past.[33] In addition, to borrow Marrou's words, "the feat never had the character of an individual epic [in Rome]; it was always carefully subordinated, as to its purpose, to the public good and public safety. . . . The Roman hero . . . by his courage or wisdom, saved the nation in danger. . . . The choice of examples available to the young Roman were borrowed from national history and not from heroic poetry" (*Histoire de l'éducation* [1950], p. 320).

Is Arrian's understanding of the reaction of Alexander's lieutenants based on an implicit reference to these collective Roman values? That is possible, but one cannot say for certain. Arrian's reservations are indicated, however. Being overcome by his pleasure and unable to stay away from danger, Alexander deviates from the royal virtue with which Arrian and the entire panegyric tradition repeatedly credit him, namely, a close and harmonious union between boldness and circumspection. The same appears to be true for Curtius: "Alexander made an incredible and phenomenal move which added far more to his reputation for recklessness than to his glorious record."[34] One senses here both admiration and reservations; and in another passage, the same author seems to express some hesitation about Alexander's mad pursuit during the Battle of Gaugamela. "While the outcome of the fight was still undecided, he conducted himself like a conqueror." Given his impulsiveness, it seems highly unlikely that he pursued the fugitives at the time "with caution rather than eagerness."[35] That somewhat bombastic expression, used in a very defensive discursive context, seems to echo criticisms from the Macedonians against a leader who, in this case, had allowed himself to be swept along by his rashness (an irrepressible desire to lay his hands on Darius) instead of displaying circumspection (gnōmē).

The debate also recalls one that took place before the Battle of the Granicus. Parmenion had advised waiting until the next day before attempting to cross the river. Alexander responded that adopting such a tactic "would be in accordance neither with the fame of the Macedonians nor with my own eagerness for encountering danger."[36] In reporting the same dialogue, Plutarch comments on Alexander's maneuver: "It seemed the act of a desperate madman rather than of a general to ride thus through a rapid river, under a storm of missiles, towards a steep bank where every position of advantage was occupied by armed men."[37]

These situations and debates bring to mind the exchanges that, according to Plutarch, took place between Cyrus the Younger and Clearchus before the Battle of Cunaxa. Clearchus strongly advised Cyrus not to expose himself personally to the danger of the front lines; rather, he ought to "remain behind the combatants." Hence Cyrus's scathing reply, somewhat comparable to those attributed to Alexander in response to Parmenion: it would be unworthy of his royal ambitions to adopt such a tactic. And even while denouncing Clearchus for refusing "to array his Greeks over against the king" and exempting Cyrus from responsibility for the defeat, Plutarch nevertheless acknowledges that "it was a great mistake for Cyrus to plunge headlong into the midst of the fray, instead of trying to avoid its dangers."[38] Diodorus expresses the criticism even more clearly: "Cyrus, being elated by the success of his forces, rushed boldly into the midst of the enemy and at first slew numbers of them as he set no bounds to his daring; but later, as he fought too imprudently, he was struck by a common Persian and fell mortally wounded."[39]

Here again is the inverted image of the ideal leader, who must be full of courage and daring and at the same time full of discernment and good sense. Arrian knows to contrast that image to Parmenion, when the needs of the argument require it: it is not enough to be prepared to run toward danger, it is also necessary to display judgment.[40] Between Plutarch's lines, one also senses a clear reproach of Alexander: he was "forced to fight, pell-mell, man to man, before he could put those who had followed him over into battle array."[41] But

Arrian defends the king: whether concerning the Granicus or Gaugamela, he is intent on pointing out that Alexander is not unduly rash. At the Granicus River, Alexander "entered the ford, keeping his line always extended obliquely in the direction in which the stream turned itself aside," so as not to arrive on the other bank in complete disarray.[42] The same is true at Issus, but there, "the Macedonian phalanx had been broken."[43] That is no doubt why Polybius, contesting Callisthenes's version of the Battle of Issus, is also intent on defending Alexander: "Such extravagance cannot be imputed to Alexander, when everyone acknowledges his expertise and experience in the art of war from childhood on. It must rather be imputed to the historian."[44]

From Parmenion to Cardinal de Richelieu

This is an important debate, and it was not only elaborated, in the Greek manner, within the intimate circles of Alexander the Great and Cyrus the Younger or in the court of the Sassanids. It was also conducted in almost identical—or, in any case, comparable—terms by French jurists and theorists during the medieval and modern periods.

Although the idea of a king fighting for the common good was widespread in the Middle Ages, it was also debated, even contested. In about 1300, Pierre Dubois defended the reverse thesis. His argument is presented by the great medievalist and historian Ernst Kantorowicz in his famous book *The King's Two Bodies*: "[Dubois] declared that in case of war the king should not expose himself or even join his army. The king, wrote Dubois, was to remain 'in his native land and indulge in the procreation of children, their education and instruction, and in the preparation of armies—*ad honorem Dei*.' That is to say, whereas the ordinary citizen was expected and even obliged to sacrifice fortune and life for the *patria*, the head of the body politic was not expected to bring the same sacrifice but supposed to submit to another patriotic occupation after the model, as Dubois added, of some Roman emperors and of the Khans of the Tartars, 'who rested quietly in the middle of their kingdoms' while sending their general out to wage war" (p. 262).

Kantorowicz emphasizes that Dubois's idea was not new: "In fact, a new ideal of kingship is found sporadically in the later Middle Ages: the Prince who did not himself fight, but stayed at home while generals fought his wars" (pp. 262–263). Kantorowicz believes that Dubois may be thinking of Justinian's model. It is also imaginable that the themes developed in the philosophical romance *Sidrach* had made an impression on readers: "The wise Sidrach, asked by his interlocutor, a fabulous king of the Levant, whether the king should go to battle, gave the advice that the king himself should not fight, but stay in the rear of his army; for 'if the army is lost and the king escapes, he can recover another army; but if the king is lost, all is lost.' We cannot tell whether Pierre Dubois was influenced by the *Sidrach*. However, the idea of the 'non-fighting king' gradually gained ground. . . . In the case of Dubois it was obviously the continuity of the dynasty which, for the sake of the whole body politic, appeared more important than the king's exposure to the contingencies of warfare" (pp. 263–264, 265).

Kantorowicz adds: "Nor is it impossible that the Pseudo-Aristotelian tractate *De mundo,* which was twice translated into Latin during the thirteenth century, bears some responsibility for that new vision of kingship" (p. 263). The treatise contains a portrait of the all-powerful Persian king ensconced within his sumptuous palaces of Susa and Ecbatana, a "celestial Versailles," to borrow Kantorowicz's expression. There the Great King, identified with God, is "invisible to all" but "he sees all and hears all," thanks to multiple go-betweens and monitors.[45] That image is the one Plutarch chose in the *Life of Agesilaus* (15.9) and the one that grew up around Darius III: enjoying every delight in his palaces of Susa and Ecbatana, refusing to personally do battle, choosing to wage war by means of his gold and his generals. For Dubois, in any case, the reference to the Roman emperors and Tartar khans "who rested quietly in the middle of their kingdoms" while sending their general to wage war strangely evokes the judgments made in antiquity of the Great Kings in general and of Darius III in particular.[46]

It would not be surprising if the Greek representation of the Persian king inspired, albeit only in part, the reflections of a French jurist at the very start of the fourteenth century. When one reads the works of these theorists and the reflections of historians of today, one has the impression that the situations depicted, the commentary put forward, and the apothegms invented are extraordinarily similar to those found in the Greco-Roman authors. This is certainly no mere coincidence: directly inspired by their readings of ancient works, the authors of collections of exempla and the theorists of the modern age readily found in their ancient colleagues the means for bolstering and illustrating the courage and exploits of their monarchs. Similarly, Budé (1965, 53r–v–54r) and Gentillet (1968, pp. 100–101), holding forth on the relationship that the king must maintain with his immediate circle, within the context of reflections on the king's two bodies in particular, do not fail to refer to Alexander and his two friends Hephaestion and Craterus.

Even so, the doctrine of a warrior king legitimated by victory, and even by wounds received on the battlefield, remained very much alive.[47] In opposition to the Spanish "hidden sovereign," who never appears on the battlefield, kings of France were portrayed as fighting and conquering. That is the image the royal panegyrists wanted to impose. In 1560, at the siege of Jarnac, the future Henry III fought on the front lines of his squadron: "He ran a great risk of losing his life. . . . [He had to defend himself] against the fury of enemies who, fighting around him, made courage of despair." In 1573, at the siege of La Rochelle, he spared "no expense or fatigue or danger, not relaxing the violent zeal that took him into battle." According to his biographer Hardouin de Péréfixe, Henry IV liked to be recognized on the battlefield, and, like a Homeric hero or like Alexander as portrayed by the rules of Homeric mimesis, he wore a cluster of white feathers on his helmet "to attract notice."[48] During the siege of Paris (1589), "he was seen at all times in the most dangerous places, making the work go faster, motivating the soldiers."

Conversely, the king who did not correspond to the model was judged harshly. For example, Henry III, according to the polemicist Pierre de l'Estoile, instead of overrunning the kingdom's enemies, "held tournaments, jousts, and ballets and many masquerades, where he could usually be found dressed as a woman. He opened his doublet and uncovered his throat, wearing a pearl necklace and three cloth collars, two ruff collars and one reverse collar, like those worn by the ladies of the court of that time." In short, that king was quite similar to the caricature of the Persian king, confined within his palaces, effeminate, refusing the call to arms, while indulging in the delicacies of his table and the pleasures of his harem.[49]

Consider more particularly the resounding defense by François La Mothe Le Vayer (1588–1672) of the image of a king leading the assault at the head of his troops. A philosopher and scholar, La Mothe published an impressive number of essays and treatises. Although his *Instructions de Monsieur le Dauphin* (1640) attracted the attention of Richelieu (to whom the book was dedicated), it was only belatedly that La Mothe was entrusted with Louis XIV's education, up until the coronation of his royal student (1652–1654).[50] A renowned Hellenist, he was a refined connoisseur of the ancient authors, whom he portrayed in a work titled *Jugement sur les Anciens et principaux historiens grecs et latins* (*Judgment on the Ancients and Principal Greek and Latin Historians;* 1646). It contains, among other things, very laudatory entries on Arrian and Curtius. In addition, his essays are filled with exempla borrowed from the ancient authors, in accordance with a rule he set, that of "adjusting a few parallels of ancient history to the circumstances of our time" (*Oeuvres*, 2:69).

Like many of his contemporaries, La Mothe was a great admirer of the man he called "the Swedish Hercules," Gustav II Adolf, an ally of France (1631) who conducted a long-victorious campaign against the Austrians on behalf of the German Protestants. Gustav was killed at the Battle of Lützen on November 6, 1632. That event provided the impetus for La Mothe Le Vayer's *Discours sur la bataille de Lützen* (*Discourse on the Battle of Lützen*, 2:65–81). He returned to the subject in a digression introduced into the chapter of his *Instructions* devoted to a prince's duties during a war (1:111–135). Anxious to respond vigorously to the detractors of the late king of Sweden, he framed the problem as follows: "What is of foremost important during war . . . is to know, not so much whether [the prince] must make war in person as whether he ought to expose himself to the perils of battle, leaving to chance a life on whom so many others depend and to whose preservation that of the state is often bound" (1:105).

La Mothe marks his disagreement with those who, with reference to the king of Sweden, "call his valor pure recklessness" (1:110) and judges, conversely, that what they call "prudence is often only an essential cowardice" (2:77). "But I maintain that, after all, when the security of the state, the interests of the Crown, and especially, some glorious and important conquest are at stake, come what may, there is no monarch who must not spill what blood he has in his veins, rather than betray his honor and fall short of what all the great princes have judged to be their duty" (1:113–114).

La Mothe contrasts the glory of the warrior king to the self-effacement of the "cabinet kings" and pursues his argument by turning to the "ancient originals of heroic virtue," from which the king of Sweden "had been cast" (2:78–79): "And if Alexander had not shown the Macedonians, through all his wounds, that he was taking cities and doing battle—since he asked for no courage on their part with which his own would not share the difficulties—he would not have led them as he did as far as the banks of the Ganges (1:109). . . . How many times did Caesar dash to the front lines of his armies, so exposed that he was compelled to take his first legionnaire's shield?" (2:77).

Not surprisingly, the author turns to his own advantage the distinction between soldier and general so often drawn from the ancient texts. He maintains that only the hero inspired by Homer (2:74) is able to unite the two in his person: During the Battle of Pharsalus, "Caesar made an appearance at almost every battle site and behaved as much as a soldier as an army general (1:117). . . .

[The king of Sweden] knew very well that if Alexander had not fought as a soldier on the banks of the Granicus, he would never have been victorious as a monarch on the plain of Arbela" (2:80).

La Mothe does not fail to cite Xerxes as a perfect counterexample to the model whose virtues he celebrates. During the Battle of Salamis, Xerxes chose "an advantageous place rather than risk, along with [his soldiers], the fate of so many provinces" (1:108). But the examples of Caesar and Alexander are also brought to bear at this point, because their deaths are judged less than heroic: "Caesar was stabbed in the Roman Senate; and Alexander perished from overeating or from poison, in Babylon (1:122). . . . It is more honorable for a prince to die fighting and to make his grave on the field of his victory than to be stabbed in the Roman Senate or to perish, either by poison or by bingeing in Babylon" (2:81).

The king of Sweden's feat during the siege of Frankfurt-am-Oder, where he personally mounted the assault of the wall, climbing one by one the rungs of the ladder he had put up (1:79), may bring to mind the exploit attributed by all the ancient authors to Alexander, mounting on his own the assault of the walls of the fortified town in India. The risks taken are identical and the consequence is the same: the king's body becomes covered with scars. The apothecary who embalmed Gustav Adolf's body reported no fewer than nine open wounds and thirteen old scars. La Mothe Le Vayer does not fail to mention the report (2:80) and clearly establishes a direct relationship to Plutarch's declaration about Alexander's body:[51] "[Plutarch] shows that there was no part of his body, from the top of his head to the soles of his feet, that did not have some honorable scar remaining from an infinite number of other battles" (2:78).

Death in battle is therefore the outcome expected of the warrior king portrayed by La Mothe. The king himself announces as much to his nobles, when he takes command of the great expedition that will end tragically at Lützen: "I, who have exposed my life amidst so many dangers and who spilled my blood for the homeland so many times—without being mortally wounded, thanks be to God—I must ultimately make the sacrifice of my person; that is why I bid you farewell, hoping to see you again in a better world."

These words, spoken by the king of Sweden, define the sacrificial king: "When the king takes on the sins and redeems the misfortunes of his people, he is only taking to the extreme the original vocation of personalized power, which is to embody the collective fate and thus to take upon oneself, to shift onto one's own head, the ordeals of one's nation.' "[52]

La Mothe Le Vayer was not the only one to defend that theory. In 1646, when his contemporary Nicolas Perrot d'Ablancourt translated Arrian's *Anabasis* into French (under the title *Les guerres d'Alexandre,* or *Alexander's Wars*) and dedicated it to the "duc d'Anguien," Perrot praised the courage and war heroism of the young Macedonian king, "who conquered two thousand countries in a row; all the states of the great lord and king of Persia, along with part of those of Mogor and the great Cam of Tartaria." He also exalted the ethos of the nobility of his time, especially that of Condé. Nicknamed "the New Alexander," the dedicatee, in accordance with the immutable rules of flattery, is even considered more valorous than his model, who "conquered effeminate peoples softened by a long peace and by the delights of Asia." It is especially interesting to see again an expression already used by La Mothe Le Vayer against those who, unable to "understand such a high value, have called it recklessness."[53]

Neither La Mothe nor Ablancourt reports the debate, retransmitted by Arrian, that unfolded on the same subject within Alexander's entourage. From the ancient authors, they draw arguments they can exploit within the context of the defense and illustration of their thesis; but they do not intend to offer ammunition to their opponents.

In fact, there was far from widespread agreement on that position. The debate continued at the highest echelons of the state, between the king and his principal advisers. In 1635 it pitted Louis XIII against Richelieu, who was aware of the risks with respect to what we would call the continuity of the state. While diplomatically acknowledging that the king's courage was above suspicion, the cardinal pointed out that war could be waged by valiant lieutenants. In addition to the risk of having the king die in battle, Richelieu emphasized that a defeat, always possible, would hurt the king's prestige and the monarchy. The argument did not have the expected effect: Louis XIII took command of the army on the Lorraine front. Joël Cornette sees that debate as the mark of an evolution in the conception of the state. On one hand, the monarchy was still entirely pervaded by the spirit of feudalism, which required that the king be the first among nobles and that the nobles perform the most extravagant feats before the king's eyes. Nobles and kings shared the same ideal, the "utopian chivalrous *fraternitas* of royal war." On the other hand, the king performed duties other than those of a war leader; he had to oversee the administration of the kingdom, the exercise of justice.

Hence the ineluctable choice made by Louis XIV in 1693, to the amazement and even indignation of many: the king abandoned the Flanders campaign and decided henceforth to run everything from Versailles. Nevertheless, he did not lose the prestige born of war leadership: quite simply, thanks to images, paintings, and feasts, it was in the representation of war and not in war itself that power and charisma now found expression. That included the instrumentalization of scenes drawn from the history of Alexander.[54] The king could "make war" without being present on the front with the troops, and without risking his life by being the first to face enemy fire. Artists, rather than depict the battles and the violent taking of cities, represented the king himself, reflecting on the plans for the campaign: "Less prestigious measures, you will say. Nothing of the sort. These royal actions are as much a part of the king's job as the others. Moreover, they constitute its essence. That is the very act of governing. They determine the success of the war."[55]

Return to Darius III

The arguments exchanged among Alexander's companions, in Sassanid power circles, and among the advisers of Louis XIII and Louis XIV, serve as a reminder that, despite its obsessive presence in the ancient writings (and in a number of works of courtier chroniclers in modern France), the heroic model is not a universal interpretive key.[56] As recent and less recent debates have shown, the battles waged in the *Iliad* must not be confused with tournaments of knights facing off in any number of single combats. In that work, monomachia might be more a literary theme than an analytical tool.[57] From a methodological standpoint, it would be paradoxical at the very least to evaluate the attitude and decisions of Darius III as a function of the royal and aristocratic ethos that the Greek poet had wanted to glorify a few centuries earlier—and as a function of the requirements of mimesis, a procedure used systematically by the admirers of Alexander's epic.

The skewed nature of the interpretation that the ancient authors give does not require that one call into doubt the factual historicity of the royal councils convened by Darius III, which met to deliberate on the measures to be taken in the face of Alexander's offensive and then of his first successes in Asia Minor. In a situation unprecedented in Achaemenid history, when an external enemy was moving constantly toward the interior of the empire, it would not have been unusual for a debate to have unfolded on the role the Great King ought to play in the counterattack. Granted, we cannot be satisfied with the repeated use of the stock explanation that capable generals were lacking.[58] Furthermore,

Diodorus, who advances that interpretation, explains in the same breath that Darius "canvassed his Friends and Relatives and selected those who were suitable, giving to some commands suited to their abilities and ordering others to fight at his side."[59] The formulation recurs in Diodorus whenever he evokes the Great Kings' military preparations.[60] It expresses the idea that the right to name generals fell to the king alone and that these choices were made as a function of the sovereign's personal confidence and not as a function of a (nonexistent) hierarchical grid supposedly imposed on him. And yet the subsequent operations clearly show that the Great King had no lack of Persian nobles trained in the military arts and completely devoted to his person. It is therefore not impossible that, beyond the topos, this debate also signifies that the king did not normally have to take command of the army.

Other important indications need to be recalled at this point. A tradition about Gaugamela, transmitted by Curtius and Justin and then by Orosius, provides food for thought. Curtius reports the Great King's shame upon having to flee, and his desire to voluntarily put an end to his life: "Highly visible as he was in his chariot, he felt ashamed to abandon his forces."[61] Orosius repeats the statement, and Justin adds a clarification, whose meaning cannot escape anyone: "Darius . . . was compelled by his officers to flee."[62] His close circle, primarily concerned with preserving their king's life, prevented him from committing suicide, then obliged him to retreat.

It would be perfectly understandable if advisers had argued before the battle about the considerable risks the Great King would be taking by exposing himself in person. It would also be comprehensible if they had taken all the measures necessary to get him to leave the battlefield safe and sound, once the fate of the Persian armies was judged hopeless or, even more simply, once the fighting came dangerously close to the king. The famous "mare" makes her appearance once again: she is supposed to allow the Great King to return to the base camp in the rear and, above all, to keep him from falling into the hands of an adversary resolved to pursue him unflaggingly.

One last "statistical" observation will serve to illustrate, if not to reinforce, the image of kings who do not fight on the front lines. Only one Great King (Cyrus the Great) is reputed to have died during a military expedition; and in reality, the diversity of traditions and legends leaves that question entirely open.[63] Among his successors, only one died of a wound (Cambyses), and it was purely accidental, not received in battle. By contrast, no king is reputed to have been wounded during a war, even though most of them are known to have headed military expeditions (Cambyses, Bardiya/Smerdis, Darius I, Xerxes I, Artaxerxes I, Darius II, Artaxerxes II, Artaxerxes III, and Darius III). Four died of old age or illness (Darius I, Artaxerxes I, Darius II, and Artaxerxes II); seven died as a result of assassination plots (Bardiya/Smerdis, Xerxes I, Xerxes II, Artaxerxes III, Arses/Artaxerxes IV, and Darius III). From that standpoint as well, Darius III is no exception: he clearly occupies a place in the continuity of the turbulent history of the Achaemenid dynasty.

It is clear that Widengren's hypothesis has gradually taken on a conceptual consistency and a documentary density, which flesh out the sketch proposed by the author. In the course of my discussion, that hypothesis has been supported by closely related contributions from comparative history and from fragments of Greco-Roman texts, which, though not abundant or absolutely indisputable and univocal, are coherent and concordant. Comparative history suggests an interpretive model whose validity is illustrated by the ancient texts. These texts inscribe it in Achaemenid history, if only in the guise of a plausible hypothesis. It can be formulated as follows: If, on two occasions, Darius left the battlefield before the end of the battle, he did so in conformity with Achaemenid monarchical theory and practice.

Was the Great King "courageous" or "cowardly"? It is possible to believe—to conclude if not to close the debate opened in antiquity—that the question and answer(s) have, strictly speaking, no relevance with respect to the problem raised. After all, among the historians of the modern period, no one has ever wondered whether, in making the decision to no longer fight at the head of his troops, Louis XIV displayed "cowardice."

ABBREVIATIONS

GREEK AND ROMAN SOURCES

GENERAL BIBLIOGRAPHY

NOTES

THEMATIC NOTES BY CHAPTER

ILLUSTRATION CREDITS

INDEX

Abbreviations

1. Works Cited in Abridged Form

Atkinson, *Commentary I*	J. E. Atkinson, *A Commentary on Q. Curtius Rufus' Historiae Alexandri Magni, Books 3 and 4.* (Amsterdam: Gieben, 1980).
Atkinson, *Commentary II*	J. E. Atkinson, *A Commentary on Q. Curtius Rufus' Historiae Alexandri Magni, Books 5 to 7.* (Amsterdam: Hakkert, 1994).
Baynham, *Quintus Curtius*	E. Baynham, *Alexander the Great: The Unique History of Quintus Curtius.* (Ann Arbor: University of Michigan Press, 1998).
Berve, *Alexanderreich*	H. Berve, *Das Alexanderreich auf prosopographischer Grundlage.* Vols. 1 and 2. (Munich, 1926; repr. New York: Arno Press, 1973).
BHAch 1	P. Briant, *Bulletin d'histoire achéménide Topoi, Supp.* 1 (Paris: De Boccard, 1997): 5–125.
BHAch 2	P. Briant, *Bulletin d'histoire achéménide 2* (Paris: Ed. Thotm, 2001).
Bosworth, *Commentary I*	A. B. Bosworth, *A Historical Commentary on Arrian's History of Alexander,* vol. 1: *Commentary on Books I–III* (Oxford: Clarenden Press, 1980).
Bosworth, *Commentary II*	A. B. Bosworth, *A Historical Commentary on Arrian's History of Alexander,* vol. 2: *Commentary on Books IV–V* (Oxford: Clarendon Press, 1995).
Hamilton, *Commentary*	J. R. Hamilton, *Plutarch, Alexander: A Commentary* (Oxford: Clarendon Press, 1969).
Heckel, *Commentary*	J. C. Yardley and W. Heckel, *Justin: Epitome of the Philippic History of Pompeius Trogus,* vol. 1: *Books 11–12: Alexander the Great.* Translation and appendices by J.-C. Yardley with commentary by W. Heckel (Oxford: Clarendon Press, 1997).
HEP	P. Briant, *Histoire de l'empire perse: De Cyrus à Alexandre* (Paris: Fayard, 1996).

HPE   P. Briant, *From Cyrus to Alexander: A History of the Persian Empire* (Winona Lake: Eisenbrauns, 2002).

KCP   P. Briant, *Kings, Countries, Peoples: Selected Studies on the Achaemenid Empire* (Leiden, forthcoming).

RTP   P. Briant, *Rois, tributs et paysans* (Paris: Les Belles Lettres, 1982).

2. Acronyms and Abbreviations for Reviews and Periodicals

AAH   *Acta Antiqua Academiae Hungraricae* (Budapest)

AchHist *Achaemenid History* (Leiden)

AHB   *Ancient History Bulletin* (Calgary)

AHR   *American Historical Review*

AION   *Annali dell'Istituto Orientale di Napoli*

AJAH   *American Journal of Ancient History*

AJPh   *American Journal of Philology*

AMI   *Archäologische Mitteilungen aus Iran*

AncSoc   *Ancient Society* (Brussels)

ANRW   *Aufstieg und Niedergand des romischen Welt*

ARF   *Ruralia: Revue de l'association des ruralistes français*

BAGB   *Bulletin de l'Association Guillaume-Budé*

BAI   *Bulletin of the Asia Institute*

BCH   *Bulletin de correspondance hellénique*

BIFAO   *Bulletin de l'Institut français d'archéologie orientale* (Cairo)

BSOAS   *Bulletin of the Society of Oriental and African Studies* (London)

CAH   *Cambridge Ancient History*

CdE   *Chronique d'Égypte* (Brussels)

CPh   *Classical Philology*

CQ   *Classical Quarterly* (Oxford)

CRAI   *Comptes rendus de l'Académie des inscriptions et belles-lettres* (Paris)

CW   *Classical World*

DHA   *Dialogues d'histoire ancienne* (Besançon-Paris)

EncIr   *Encyclopaedia Iranica* (New York)

EncIs   *Encyclopaedia of Islam*

GIF   *Giornale Italiano di Filologia*

GJ   *Geographical Journal*

HSClPh   *Harvard Studies in Classical Philology*

IA   *Iranica Antiqua*

IJAIS   *Nāme-ye Irān-e Bāstān: The International Journal of Ancient Iranian Studies*

INJ	*Israel Numismatic Journal*
JAOS	*Journal of the American Oriental Society*
JHS	*Journal of Hellenic Studies* (London)
JJP	*Journal of Juristic Papyrology*
JNES	*Journal of Near Eastern Studies* (Chicago)
JRAS	*Journal of the Royal Asiatic Society* (London)
JRS	*Journal of Roman Studies* (London)
MDAI(A)	*Mitteilungen des Deutschen Archäologischen Instituts: Athens*
NC	*Numismatic Chronicle*
QdS	*Quaderni di Storia*
RAC	*Reallexicon für Antike und Christentum*
RdE	*Revue d'égyptologie*
REA	*Revue des études anciennes*
REG	*Revue des études grecques*
REL	*Revue des études latines*
RhM	*Rheinisches Museum*
RSA	*Rivista Storica Italiana*
SELVOA	*Studi Epigrafici e Linguistici sul Vicino Oriente Antico*
SEPOA	*Société pour l'étude du Proche-Orient ancien* (Paris)
STIR	*Studia Iranica*
Trans.	*Transeuphratène* (Paris)
ZDPV	*Zeitschrift der Deutsche Pälastina-Vereins*

Greek and Roman Sources

The life dates of the authors are often approximate because unknown. Only those studies and commentaries (abbreviated below as ST. COMM.) that have informed this book are mentioned, by author's name and year of publication; they are cited in more complete form in the alphabetical bibliography that follows. In the French original, quoted passages from Greco-Roman sources were usually taken from the Collection des Universités de France (CUF) edition (Paris: Les Belles Lettres) and were sometimes modified.

Aelian (165/170–230/5 C.E.). *Varia historia*. Edited and translated into French as *Histoires variées* by M. Dacier (Paris, 1827). Also translated into French as *Histoires variées* by A. Lukinovitch and A.-F. Morand (Paris: Les Belles Lettres, 1991).

———. *De natura animalium*. Translated into French as *La personnalité des animaux* by A. Zucker. Vols. 1–2 (Paris: Les Belles Lettres, 2001–2002).

ST. COMM.: Kindstrand 1998.

Agathias (ca. 532–ca. 580 C.E.). "Agathias on the Sassanians." Edited and translated into English by A. Cameron. *Dumbarton Oak Papers* 23–24 (1969–1970): 67–183.

Ammianus Marcellinus (ca. 338–395 C.E.). *Historiae*, books 23–25. Edited and translated into French as *Histoires* by J. Fontaine. Vol. 4 (CUF, 1987).

Appian (late first century C.E.–ca. 160 C.E.). *The Mithridatic Wars*. In vol. 2 of *Appian's Roman History*, translated into English by Horace White (London: W. Heinemann, 1913). Translated into French as *Guerre de Mithridate*. Vol. 12 of *Appien: Histoire romaine* (CUF, 2001).

Arrian (ca. 80–160 C.E.). *Arrian's Anabasis of Alexander*. Translated into English by P. A. Brunt (Cambridge, Mass.: Harvard University Press, 1976); also translated into English by P. Mensch, in J. Romm, *The Landmark Arrian* (New York: Pantheon, 2010); also translated into English by Edward James Chinnock (New York: G. Bell & Sons, 1893). Translated into French as *Anabase d'Alexandre* (with *Inde*) by P. Savinel (Paris: Éditions de Minuit, 1984). Edited and translated into Italian as *Anabasi di Alessandro*, by F. Sisti (Rome: Fondazione Lorenzo Valla, 2001).

ST. COMM: Bosworth 1976, 1981, 1988a, 1995; Brunt 1976, I:ix–lxxxvi; Fears 1977; Gorteman 1958; Gray 1990; Schepens 1971; Stadter 1980; Tonnet 1979, 1987, 1988; Vidal-Naquet 1984; Romm (ed.), 2010.

Athenaeus (written about 200 C.E.). *Deipnosophists*. Edited and translated into English by C. B. Gulick. 7 vols. (London: W. Heinemman, 1927–1941). Edited and translated into Italian. 4 vols. (Rome: Ed. Salerno, 2001).

ST. COMM.: Braund and Wilkins 2000; Gambato 2000; Jacob 2001.

Aulus Gellius (b. ca. 125–128 C.E.). *Noctes atticae*. Translated into French as *Les nuits antiques*, by R. Marache (vols. 1 and 2) and by Y. Julien (vol. 3). 3 vols. (CUF, 1967, 1978, 1998).

Caesar (100–44 B.C.E.). *De bello gallico*, book 3. Edited and translated into French as *Guerre civile* by P. Fabre (CUF, 1959).

Chariton of Aphrodisias (between the first and second century C.E.). *De Chaerea et Callirhoe*. Translated into French as *Chairéas et Callirhoè* by G. Molinier (CUF, 1985). Also translated into French in P. Grimal as *Romans grecs et latins* (Paris: Gallimard, 1958), pp. 379–513.

ST. COMM.: Baslez 1992; Daude 2002; Luginbill 2000; Salmon 1961.

Chronichon Paschale (seventh century C.E.). Translated into English by M. Whitby and M. Whitby (Liverpool: Liverpool University Press, 1989).

Cicero (106–43 B.C.E.). *Disputationes tusculanae*. Edited and translated into French as *Tusculanes* by G. Fohlen and J. Humbert. In *Cicéron: Oeuvres philosophiques*. Vols. 1–2 (CUF, 1931, 1960).

Claudian (about 370–404 C.E.). *De consulatu Stilichonis*. Edited and translated into French by V. Crépin in *Oeuvres complètes*. Vols. 1–2 (Paris: Librairie Garnier, n.d).

Cornelius Nepos (about 110–24 B.C.E.). Edited and translated into French by A.-M. Guillemin in *Oeuvres* (CUF, 1961).

ST. COMM.: Geiger 1979, 1985; McCarthy 1974.

Ctesias (late fifth century to mid-fourth century B.C.E.). *Persica*. Translated into French as *Histoires de l'Orient* by J. Auberger (Paris: Les Belles Lettres, 1991); also edited and translated into French by D. Lenfant as *Ctésias: Témoignages et documents* (CUF, 2003).

Dio Cassius (164–229 C.E.). *Dio's Roman History*. Translated into English by Earnest Cary. 9 vols. (Cambridge, Mass.: Harvard University Press, 1960–1990).

Dio Chrysostom (40/50–100 C.E.). *Discourses*. Edited and translated into English by H. L. Crosby (London: W. Heinemann, 1932–1952).

Diodorus of Sicily (first century B.C.E.). *The Library of History*, book 17. In vol. 8 of *Diodorus of Sicily*, translated into English by C. Bradford Welles (London: G. P. Putnam's Sons, 1963). Edited and translated into French as *Bibliothèque historique, livre XVII: Histoire d'Alexandre* by P. Goukoswky (CUF, 1976).

ST. COMM.: Hamilton 1977; Prandi 1996, 2013.

Diogenes Laertius (first half of the third century C.E.). *Vitae philosophorum*. Translated into French as *Vies de philosophes illustres*, under the editorship of M.-O. Goulet-Cazé (Paris: Librairie générale française, 1999).

Dionysius of Halicarnassus (late first century B.C.E.–mid-first century C.E.). *The Roman Antiq-uities.* Translated into English by Earnest Cary and Edward Spelman (Cambridge, Mass.: Harvard University Press, 1937).

Eusebius of Caesarea (260–339 C.E.). *Praeparatio evangelica.* Translated into French as *Préparation évangélique* by J. Sirinelli. Vol. I. (Paris: Éditions du Cerf, 1974).

Frontinus (first century C.E.). *Strategemata.* Edited and translated into French as *Les strat-agèmes* by D. Nisard. In *Ammien Marcellin. Jornandès. Frontin (Les stratagèmes). Végèce. Modestus* (Paris: Firmin Didot, 1885).

Herodotus (fifth century B.C.E.). *The Histories.* Translated into English by Aubrey de Sélin-court (London: Penguin, 1972). Edited and translated into French as *Histoires* by P.-E. Legrand (CUF, 1956–1964).

Historiens d'Alexandre. Edited and translated into French by J. Auberger (Paris: Les Belles Lettres, 2001). Fragments of ancient historians of Alexander.

> ST. COMM.: Pearson 1960; Pédech 1984; Robinson 1953.

Itinerarium Alexandri. Edited and translated into English as *Alexander's Itinerary,* by I. Da-vies. *AHB* 12, nos. 1–2 (1998): 29–54.

> ST. COMM.: Tabacco 1992; Tonnet 1979.

Justin (second or third century C.E.?). *Epitome of the Philippic History of Pompeius Trogus.* Translated into English by John Selby Watson (London: Henry G. Bohn, 1853). Edited and translated into French as *Histoires philippiques* by E. Chambry and L. Thély-Chambry. Vols. 1 and 2 (Paris: Ed. Garnier, n.d.).

> ST. COMM.: Yardley and Heckel 1997.

Livy (50 B.C.E.–12 C.E.). *Ab urbe condita libri.* Edited and translated into French by D. Nisard. Vols. 1 and 2 (Paris, 1882); also translated into French by G. Walter (Paris: Gallimard, 1968).

> ST. COMM.: Chaplin 2000; Mahé-Simon 2001; Morello 2002.

Lucan (39–65 C.E.). *De bello civili (Pharsalia).* Edited and translated into French as *La guerre civile (la Pharsale)* by A. Bourgery. Vols. 1 and 2 (CUF 1927, 1930).

Lucian (b. ca. 120 C.E.). Complete works translated into French in *Oeuvres complètes* by E. Talbot (Paris: Hachette, 1866).

———. *Navigium.* Translated into French with notes as *Le navire, ou les souhaits* by G. Hus-son. Vols. 1 and 2 (Paris: Les Belles Lettres, 1970.)

> ST. COMM.: Bompaire 1958.

Orosius (fifth century C.E.). *Historiae adversus paganos,* books 1–3. Edited and translated into French as *Histoires (contre les païens)* by M.-P. Arnaud-Lindet (CUF, 1990).

Plato (about 429–347 B.C.E.). *Leges.* Translated into French as *Lois* by L. Robin. In vol. 2 of *Oeuvres complètes* (Paris: Gallimard, 1950), pp. 635–1131.

Pliny the Elder (23/4–79 C.E.). *Historia naturalis,* book 31. Edited and translated into French as *Histoires naturelles* by J. Serbat (CUF, 1972).

———. *Historia naturalis,* book 36. Edited and translated into French as *La peinture* by J.-M. Croisille and P.-E. Dauzat (Paris: Les Belles Lettres, 1997).

Plutarch (before 50–ca. 120 C.E.). *The First Oration of Plutarch concerning the Fortune or Virtue of Alexander the Great* and *The Second Oration of Plutarch concerning the Fortune or Virtue of Alexander the Great.* In vol. 1 of *Plutarch's Morals,* translated by William W. Goodwin et al. (Boston: Little, Brown, 1878). Edited and translated into French as *De fortuna Alexandri* by F. Frazier and C. Froidefont. In vol. 5, pt. 1, of *Plutarque: Oeuvres morales* (CUF, 1990), pp. 68–156.

————. *Life of Agesilaus.* In vol. 5 of *Plutarch's Lives,* translated into English by Bernadotte Perrin (London: W. Heinemann, 1917). Edited and translated into French as *Agésilas* by R. Flacelière and E. Chambry. In vol. 9 of *Plutarque: Vies* (CUF, 1975).

————. *Life of Alexander.* In vol. 3 of *Plutarch's Lives,* translated into English by Aubrey Stewart and George Long (London: George Bell and Sons, 1892). Edited and translated into French as *Alexandre* by R. Flacelière and E. Chambry. In vol. 9 of *Plutarque: Vies* (CUF, 1975).

————. *Life of Artaxerxes.* In vol. 11 of *Plutarch's Lives,* translated into English by Bernadotte Perrin (London: W. Heinemann, 1926). Edited and translated into French as *Artaxerxès* by R. Flacelière and E. Chambry. In vol. 9 of *Plutarque: Vies* (CUF, 1975).

ST. COMM.: Duff 1999; Hamilton 1969; Pelling 2002; Stadter 1965; Tatum 1996.

Polyaenus (second century C.E.). *Strategemata.* Edited and translated into English by P. Krentz and E. L. Wheeler as *Polyaenus: Stratagems of War.* Vols. 1 and 2 (Chicago: Ares, 1994).

Polybius (about 200–118 B.C.E.). *Historiae.* Edited and translated into French as *Histoire* by Paul Pédech (CUF, 1969–1995). Also translated into French by D. Roussel (Paris: Gallimard, 1970).

ST. COMM.: Pédech 1964.

Porphyry (234–ca. 305 C.E.). *De abstinentia,* 1–3. Edited and translated into French by J. Bouffartigue and M. Patillon. Vols. 1–2 (Paris: CUF, 1977, 1979).

Procopius (fifth century C.E.). Books 1–2. Edited and translated into English by H. B. Dewing. Vol. 1 (London: W. Heinemman, 1914).

Pseudo-Callisthenes. *The Greek Alexander Romance.* Translated by Richard Stoneman (London: Penguin, 1991). Translated into French as *Le Roman d'Alexandre: La vie et les hauts faits d'Alexandre de Macédoine* by G. Bounoure and B. Serret (Paris: Les Belles Lettres, 1992).

ST. COMM.: Bridges and Bürgel 1996; Finazzi and Valvo 1998; Franco 1999; Gaullier-Bougassas 1990; Harf-Lancner, Kappler, and Suard 1999; Ieranò 1996; Jouanno 2002; Merkelbach 1977, 1989; Pfister 1958; Polignac 2000; Suard 2001.

Quintus Curtius Rufus (first century C.E.?). *The History of Alexander.* Translated by John Yardley (London: Penguin, 1984); also edited and translated into English by J.-C. Rolfe. Vols. 1 and 2 (Cambridge, Mass.: Harvard University Press, 1946). Edited and translated into French as *Histoires* by H. Bardon. Vols. 1 and 2 (CUF, 1961).

ST. COMM.: Atkinson 1980, 1994, 1998; Baynham 1998; Blaensdorf 1971; Bossuat 1946; Dempsie 1991; Devine 1971; Dosson 1887; Fears 1974, 2001; Koch 1999, 2000 (bibliography); MacCurrie 1990; McKechnie 1999; Minissale 1983; Moore 1995; Rutz 1984; Spencer 2002, 2009.

Seneca (first century C.E.). *De ira.* Edited and translated into French by A. Bourgery in *Sénèque: Dialogues.* Vol. 1 (CUF, 1961).

————. *De beneficiis*. Edited and translated into French by F. Préchac as *Des bienfaits*. Vols. 1 and 2 (CUF, 1926, 1928).

ST. COMM.: Fillion-Lahille 1989 *(De ira)*; Helm 1939.

Strabo (ca. 64 B.C.E.–21 C.E.). *The Geography,* books 15–16. Edited and translated into English by H. L. Jones. Vol. 7 (Cambridge, Mass.: Harvard University Press, 1966).

Suetonius (ca. 70–130 C.E.). Complete works edited and translated into French in *Oeuvres* by M. Cabaret-Dupaty (Paris: Librairie Garnier, n.d).

Tacitus (ca. 56–120 C.E.). *Annales*. Edited and translated into French as *Annales* by J.-L. Burnouf and H. Bornecque. Vols. 1 and 2 (Paris: Ed. Garnier, n.d.).

————. *Historiae*. Edited and translated into French as *Histoires* by J.-L. Burnouf (Paris: Ed. Garnier, n.d.).

Valerius Maximus (first century C.E.). *Facta et dicta memorabilia*. Edited and translated into French as *Actions et paroles mémorables,* by P. Constant. Vols. 1 and 2 (Paris: Ed. Garnier, n.d). Also edited and translated into French as *Faits et dits mémorables,* by R. Combès. Vols. 1 and 2 (CUF, 1995, 1997).

ST. COMM.: André 1965; Helm 1939; Maslakov 1984.

Velleius Paterculus (ca. 20 B.C.E.–ca. 30 C.E.?). *Compendium of Roman History*. Edited and translated into English by F. W. Shipley (London: W. Heinemann, 1955).

ST. COMM.: André 1965; DeMonte 1999.

Xenophon (ca. 430–ca. 360 B.C.E.). *Anabasis*. Edited and translated into English by Carleton L. Brownson, revised by John Dillery (Cambridge, Mass.: Harvard University Press, 1998). Translated into French as *Anabase* by P. Masqueray. Vols. 1 and 2 (CUF, 1961).

————. *Cyropaedia*. Edited and translated into French as *Cyropédie* by M. Bizos. Vols. 1–3. CUF, 1972, 1973, 1978. [ST. COMM.: Nadon 2001; Tatum 1989.]

————. *Oeconomicus*. Edited and translated into French as *Économique* by P. Chantraine (CUF, 1949).

Zosimus (between the fifth and the sixth century C.E.). *Historia nova*. Edited and translated into French as *Histoire nouvelle* by F. Paschoud. Vol. 1 (CUF, 1971).

General Bibliography

Abel. A. 1955. *Le Roman d'Alexandre: Légendaire médiéval*. Brussels: Office de Publicité.

———. 1966. "La figure d'Alexandre en Iran." In *La Persia e il mondo greco-romano*. Rome: Accademia nazionale dei Lincei, pp. 119–136.

———. 1975. "Iskander Nāma." *EncIs* 4, no. 2: 133–134.

Aerts, W. J., and M. Gosman, eds. 1988. *Exemplum et similitudo: Alexander the Great and Other Heroes as Points of Reference in Medieval Literature*. Groningen: E. Forste.

Ahl, A. 1922. *Outlines of Persian History*. New York: Lemcke and Büchner; Leipzig: O. Harrassowitz.

Alpers, K. 1969. "Xerxes und Artaxerxes." *Byzantion* 39:5–12.

Alram, M. 1993. "Dareikos und Siglos: Ein neuer Schatzfund achaimenidischer Sigloi aus Kleinasien." In *Circulation des monnaies, des marchandises et des biens,* edited by R. Gyselen, pp. 23–46. Bures-sur-Yvette: Groupe d'études pour la civilisation du Moyen-Orient.

Altheim, F. 1954. *Alexandre et l'Asie: Histoire d'un legs spirituel,* translated from the German by H. D. del Medico. Paris: Payot.

Amouzgar, J., and A. Tafazzoli. 2000. *Le cinquième livre du Dēnkārd: Transcription, traduction et commentaire*. Paris: Association pour l'avancement des études iraniennes.

Andrae, B. 1977. *Das Alexandermosaik aus Pompeji*. Reklinghausen: Verlag A. Bongers.

André, J. M. 1965. "L'otium chez Valère Maxime et Velleius Paterculus ou la réaction morale au début du principat." *REL* 43:294–315.

Arjomand, S. A. 1998. "Artaxerxes, Ardašīr, and Bahman." *JAOS* 118, no. 2: 245–248.

Ash, R. 1999. "An Exemplary Conflict: Tacitus' Parthian Battle Narrative." *Phoenix* 53:114–135.

Assimacopoulou, F. 1999. *Gobineau et la Grèce*. Frankfurt: Peter Lang.

Atkinson, J. E. 1980. *A Commentary on Q. Curtius Rufus' Historiae Alexandri Magni, Books 3 and 4*. Amsterdam: Gieben.

———. 1994. *A Commentary on Q. Curtius Rufus' Historiae Alexandri Magni, Books 5 to 7*. Amsterdam: Hakkert.

———. 1998. "Q. Curtius Rufus' 'Historiae Alexandri Magni.'" *ANRW* 34, no. 4: 3447–3483.

Atkinson, J. E., and J. C. Yardley. 2009. *Curtius Rufus: Histories of Alexander the Great. Book 10*. Introduction and historical commentary by Atkinson, translation by Yardley. Oxford: Oxford University Press.

Auberger, J. 2001. *Historiens d'Alexandre*. Paris: Les Belles Lettres.

Auerbach, E. 1963. *Mimesis: The Representation of Reality in Western Literature*. Princeton, N.J.: Princeton University Press.

Babelon, E. 1907–1910. *Traité des monnaies grecques et romaines*. Vol. 2: *Descriptions historiques*. Paris: E. Leroux.

Badian, E. 1958. "The Eunuch Bagoas: A Study in Method." *CQ* 8:144–157. Repr. in Badian 2012, pp. 20–35.

———. 1977. "The Battle of Granicus: A New Look." In *Ancient Macedonia*, 2:271–293. Thessaloniki: Hidryma Meletōn Chersonēsou tou Haimou. Repr. in Badian 2012, pp. 224–243.

———. 1994. "Darius III." *EncIr* 6, pt. 1: 51–55.

———. 1999. "A Note on 'Alexander Mosaic.'" In *The Eye Expanded: Life and the Arts in Graeco-Roman Antiquity; A Festschrift for Peter Green*, edited by R. F. Morton, pp. 77–92. Berkeley: University of California Press. Repr. in Badian 2012, pp. 404–419.

———. 2000. "Darius III." *HSClPh* 100:241–268. Repr. in Badian 2012, pp. 457–478.

———. 2012. *Collected Papers on Alexander the Great*. New York: Routledge.

Bailey, H. W. 1943. *Zoroastrian Problems in the Ninth-Century Books*. Oxford: Clarendon.

Baragwanath, E. 2002. "Xenophon's Foreign Wives." *Prudentia* 34, no. 2: 125–158.

Barbier de Maynard, A. C., trans. 1880. *Sa'adi, Le Boustan ou Verger*. With an introduction by the translator. Paris: E. Leroux.

Barbier de Meynard, A. C., and Pavet de Courteille, eds. and trans. 1868. *Maçoudi: Les prairies d'or*. Vol. 2. Paris: Imprimerie nationale.

Baroin, C. 2002. "Les cicatrices ou la mémoire du corps." In *Corps romains*, edited by P. Moreau, pp. 27–46. Grenoble: J. Million.

Barry, M., trans. 2000. *Nezâmi: Le pavillon des sept princesses*. With an introduction and annotations by the translator. Paris: Gallimard.

Baslez, M.-F. 1992. "De l'histoire au roman: La Perse de Chariton." In *Le monde du roman grec*, edited by M.-F. Baslez et al., pp. 199–212. Paris: Presses de l'École normale supérieure.

Baynham, E. 1995. "Who Put the 'Romance' in the Alexander Romance? The Alexander Romances within Alexander Historiography." *AHB* 9, no. 1: 1–13.

———. 1998. *Alexander the Great: The Unique History of Quintus Curtius*. Ann Arbor: University of Michigan Press.

———. 2001. "Alexander and the Amazons." *CQ* 51, no. 1: 115–126.

Beelaert, A. L. 1999. "Alexandre dans le discours sur les âges de la vie dans l'Iskandernāmā de Nīzamī." In *Alexandre le Grand dans les littératures occidentales et proche-orientales*, edited by L. Harf-Lancner, C. Kappler, and F. Suard, pp. 43–252. Paris: Université de Paris X Nanterre.

Beneker, J. 2002. "No Time for Love: Plutarch's Chaste Caesar." *Greek, Roman and Byzantine Studies* 43, no. 2: 13–29.

Benjamin, S. 1888. *Persia*. New York: G. P. Putnam.

Benveniste, E. 1938. "Traditions iraniennes sur les classes sociales." *Journal Asiatique* 230:529–549.

Bercé, Y.-M. 1990. *Le roi caché: Sauveurs et imposteurs, mythes politiques populaires dans l'Europe moderne.* Paris: Fayard.

Berlioz, J., and J.-M. David, eds. 1980. *Rhétorique et histoire: L'exemplum et le modèle de comportement dans le discours antique et médiéval.* Paris: École de Rome.

Bernard, P. 1990. "La campagne de Gaugamèles et l'entrée d'Alexandre à Babylone." *BCH* 114:515–524.

Berve, H. 1926. "Dareios." In *Das Alexanderreich auf prosopographischer Grundlage.* Repr. New York: Arno Press, 1973, pp. 116–129.

Biasutti, F., and A. Coppola, eds. 2009. *Alessandro Magno in età moderna.* Padua: Coop. Libraria Editrice Università di Padova.

Billault, A. 1991. *La création romanesque dans la littérature grecque à l'époque impériale.* Paris: Presses universitaires de France.

———. 1995. "Peut-on appliquer la notion d'asianisme à l'analyse de l'esthétique des romans grecs?" *AAH* 36:107–118.

Birt, T. 1925. *Alexander der Grosse und das Weltgriechentum bis zum Erscheinen Jesu.* 2nd rev. ed. Leipzig: Quelle & Meyer.

Bischoff, H. 1932. "Der Warner bei Herodot." Inaugural dissertation, Marburg. Leipzig: n.p.

Bittner, S. 1985. *Tracht und Bewaffnung der persischen Heeres zur Zeit der Achaimeniden.* Munich: Verlag Klaus Friedrich.

Blaensdorf, J. 1971. "Herodot bei Curtius Rufus." *Hermes* 90, no. 1: 11–24.

Blair, S. S. 1992. *The Monumental Inscriptions from Early Islamic Iran and Transoxiana.* Leiden: Brill.

Bloedow, E. F. 1995. "Diplomatic Negotiations between Darius and Alexander: Historical Implications of the First Phase at Marathus in Phoenicia in 333/332 B.C." *AHB* 9, nos. 3–4: 93–110.

Blois, F. de. 1998. "Eskander-Nāma of Nezāmī." *EncIr* 8:612–614.

Bompaire, J. 1958. *Lucien écrivain: Imitation et création.* Repr. Paris: Les Belles Lettres, 2000.

Bontems, C., L. P. Raybaud, and J-P. Brancourt. 1965. *Le Prince dans la France des XVIe et XVIIe siècles.* Paris: Presses universitaires de France.

Bordreuil, P. 1996. "Une nouvelle monnaie babylonienne de Mazday." In *Collectanea Orientalis: Histoire, arts de l'espace et industrie de la terre; Études offertes en hommage à Agnès Spycket,* edited by H. Gasche and B. Hrouda, pp. 27–30. Neuchâtel: Recherches et publications.

———. 1998. "La fin de la carrière du satrape Mazday d'après une monnaie araméenne." *CRAI* (January–March): 219–227.

Borzsák, S. 1966. "Der weinende Xerxes: Zur Geschichte seines Ruhmes." *Eos* 56:39–52.

Bossuat, R. 1946. "Vasque de Lucène, traducteur de Quinte-Curce (1468)." *Bibliothèque d'humanisme et de renaissance: Travaux et documents* 8:197–245.

Bossuet, J.-B. 1691. *Discours sur l'Histoire universelle à Monseigneur le Dauphin pour expliquer la suite de la Religion et les changemens des Empires: Depuis le commencement du monde jusqu'à l'Empire de Charlemagne.* 1st ed., 1681. Paris.

Bosworth, A. B. 1976. "Arrian and the Alexander Vulgate." in *Alexandre le Grand: Image et réalités*, by A. B. Bosworth, E. Badian et al., pp. 1–33. Geneva: Vandoeuvres.

———. 1980. *A Historical Commentary on Arrian's History of Alexander, I: Commentary on Books I–III*. Oxford: Clarendon.

———. 1983. "The Impossible Dream: W. W. Tarn's *Alexander* in Retrospect." *Ancient Society: Resources for Teachers* 13, no. 3: 131–150.

———. 1988a. *From Arrian to Alexander: Studies in Historical Interpretation*. Oxford: Clarendon.

———. 1988b. *Conquest and Empire*. Cambridge: Cambridge University Press.

———. 1988c (1996). "Ingenium und Macht: Fritz Schachermeyr and Alexander the Great." *AJAH* 13, no. 1: 56–78.

———. 1995. *A Historical Commentary on Arrian's History of Alexander, II: Commentary on Books IV–V*. Oxford: Clarendon.

———. 1996. *Alexander and the East: The Tragedy of Triumph*. Oxford: Clarendon.

———. 1997. Book review of Prandi 1996. *Histos*, http://www.dur.ac.uk/Classics/histos /1997/bosworth.html.

———. 2003. "Plus ça change . . . Ancient Historians and Their Sources." *Classical Antiquity* 22, no. 2: 167–197.

Bosworth, C. E. 1998a. "Al-Tabarī." *EncIs*, 2nd. ed., 10:11–16.

———. 1998b. "Ebn Al-Balkhī." *EncIr* 8:4.

Bounoure, G, and B. Serret, trans. 1992. *Pseudo-Callisthène: Le roman d'Alexandre; La vie et les hauts faits d'Alexandre de Macédoine*, with commentary by the translators. Paris: Les Belles Lettres.

Boutier, J., A. Dewerpe, and D. Nordman. 1984. *Un tour de France royal: Le voyage de Charles IX (1564–1566)*. Paris: Aubier.

Boyce, M. 1954. "Some Remarks on the Transmission of the Kayanian Heroic Cycle." In *Proceedings of the Twenty-Third International Congress of Orientalists: Cambridge, 21–28 August, 1954*, edited by Denis Sinor, pp. 45–52. London: Royal Asiatic Society.

———. 1955. "Zariadres and Zarēr." *BSOAS* 17, no. 3: 464–477.

———. 1957. "The Parthian Gōsān and Iranian Minstrel Tradition." *JRAS* 1, no. 2:10–45.

———. 1968a. *The Letter of Tansar*. Rome: Istituto Italiano per il Medio ed Estremo Oriente.

———. 1968b. "Middle Persian Literature." In *Handbuch der Orientalitisik*, vol. 4: *Iranistik*, pp. 31–66. Leiden: Brill.

Braund, D., and J. Wilkins, eds. 2000. *Athenaeus and His World: Reading Greek Culture in the Roman Empire*. Exeter: University of Exeter Press.

Bravo, B. 1968. *Philologie, histoire, philosophie de l'histoire: Étude sur Droysen, historien de l'Antiquité*. Wroclaw: Zaklad Narodowy Imienia Ossoliskich.

Brelich, A. 1961. *Guerre, agoni e culti nella Grecia arcaica*. Bonn: R. Habelt.

Briant, P. 1973. *Antigone le Borgne*. Paris: Les Belles Lettres.

———. 1982a. *Rois, tributs et paysans [RTP]*. Paris: Les Belles Lettres.

———. 1982b. *État et pasteurs au Moyen-Orient ancien*. Paris: Maison des Sciences de l'Homme; Cambridge: Cambridge University Press.

———. 1988. "Le nomadisme du Grand roi." *IA* 33:253–274.

———. 1994. "De Samarkand à Sardes et de la ville de Suse au pays des Hanéens." *Topoi* 4, no. 2: 455–467.

———. 1996. *Histoire de l'empire perse: De Cyrus à Alexandre [HEP].* Paris: Fayard.

———. 1997a. "Bulletin d'histoire achéménide I [BHAch 1]." *Topoi. Supp.* 1. Paris: De Boccard, 5–125.

———. 1997b. "Note d'histoire militaire achéménide: À propos des éléphants de Darius III." In *Esclavage, guerre, économie en Grèce ancienne: Hommages à Yvon Garlan,* edited by P. Brulé and J. Oulhen, pp. 177–190. Rennes: Presses universitaires de Rennes.

———. 1999a. "Alexandre à Babylone: Images grecques, images babyloniennes." In *Alexandre le Grand dans les littératures occidentales et proche-orientales,* edited by L. Harf-Lancner, C. Kappler, and F. Suard. Paris: Université de Paris X Nanterre.

———. 1999b. "The Achaemenid Empire." In *Society and War in the Ancient and Medieval World,* edited by K. Raaflaub and N. Rosenstein, pp. 105–128. Cambridge, Mass.: Harvard University Press.

———. 2000a. *Leçon inaugurale (10 mars 1999).* Paris: Collège de France.

———. 2000b. "Numismatique, frappes monétaires et histoire en Asie Mineure achéménide: (Quelques remarques de conclusion)." In *Mécanismes et innovations monétaires dans l'Anatolie achéménide: Numismatique et histoire (Acte de la Table ronde internationale d'Istanbul, 22–23 mai 1997),* edited by O. Casabonne, pp. 266–274. Istanbul: Institut français d'études anatoliennes; Paris: Diff. de Boccard.

———. 2000c. "Darius III face à Alexandre: Mythe, histoire, légende." *Annuaire du Collège de France* 100:781–792.

———. 2001a. *Bulletin d'histoire achéménide [BHAch 2].* Vol. 2. Paris: Ed. Thotm.

———. 2001b. *Darius, les Perses et l'empire.* 2nd ed. Paris: Gallimard.

———. 2001c. "Darius III face à Alexandre: Mythe, histoire, légende (suite.)" *Annuaire du Collège de France* 101:707–723.

———. 2002a. *From Cyrus to Alexander: A History of the Persian Empire [HPE].* Winona Lake, Ind.: Eisenbrauns.

———. 2002b. "Perses et Iraniens après la disparition de l'empire achéménide: Histoire et historiographie." *Annuaire du Collège de France,* http://www.college-de-france.fr/me dia/pierre-briant/UPL52050_BriantR01-02.pdf.

———. 2002c. "Guerre et succession dynastique chez les Achéménides: Entre 'coutume perse' et violence armée." In *Army and Power in the Ancient World,* edited by A. Chaniotis and P. Ducrey, pp. 39–49. Stuttgart: Steiner Verlag.

———. 2002d. "History and Ideology: The Greeks and 'Persian Decadence.'" In *Greeks and Barbarians,* edited by T. Harrison, pp. 193–210. New York: Routledge.

———. 2003a. "Milestones in the Development of Achaemenid Historiography in the Times of Ernst Herzfeld (1879–1948)." In *Ernst Herzfeld and the Development of Near Eastern Archaeology, 1900–1950,* edited by A. Gunter and S. Hauser, pp. 263–293. Leiden: Brill.

———. 2003b. "La tradition gréco-romaine sur Alexandre le Grand dans l'Europe moderne et contemporaine: Quelques réflexions sur la permanence et l'adaptabilité des modèles interprétatifs." In *The Impact of Classical Greece on European and National Identities,* edited by M. Hagsma et al., pp. 161–180. Amsterdam: Gieben.

———. 2005a. "Alexandre et l'hellénisation de l'Asie: L'histoire au présent et au passé." *Studi Ellenistici* 16:9–69.

———. 2005b. "The Theme of 'Persian Decadence' in Eighteenth-Century European Historiography: Remarks on the Genesis of a Myth." In *The World of Achaemenid Persia*, edited by J. Curtis and St John Simpson, pp. 3–15. London: Tauris.

———. 2009a. "The Empire of Darius III in Perspective." In *Alexander the Great: A New History*, edited by W. Heckel and L.-A. Trittle, pp. 141–170. Oxford: Wiley-Blackwell. Repr. in *Alexander the Great: A Reader*, edited by I. Worthington. 2nd ed., pp. 152–195. London: Routledge, 2012.

———. 2009b. "Alexander and the Persian Empire, between 'Decline' and 'Renovation.'" In *Alexander the Great: A New History*, edited by W. Heckel and L.-A. Trittle, pp. 171–188. Oxford: Wiley-Blackwell.

———. 2009c. "Le passé réutilisé dans les cours hellénistiques." In *The Past in the Past: Concepts of Past Reality in Ancient Near Eastern and Early Greek Thought*, edited by H. Barstand and P. Briant, pp. 21–36. Oslo: Novus Forlag.

———. 2010. *Alexander the Great and His Empire*, translated by A. Kuhrt. Princeton, N.J.: Princeton University Press.

———. 2011. *Alexandre le Grand*. 7th rev. ed. Paris: Presses universitaires de France.

———. 2012. *Alexandre des Lumières: Fragments d'histoire européenne*. Paris: Gallimard-Essais.

———. Forthcoming a. *Kings, Countries, Peoples: Selected Studies on the Achaemenid Empire* [KCP], translated by A. Kuhrt. Leiden.

———. Forthcoming b. "George Grote on Alexander the Great." In *George Grote and the Classical Heritage*, edited by K. Demetriou. Leiden: Brill.

Bridges, M., and J.-C. Bürgel, eds. 1996. *The Problematics of Power: Eastern and Western Representations of Alexander the Great*. Bern: Peter Lang.

Brosius, M. 1996. *Women in Ancient Persia*. Oxford: Clarendon.

Browne, E. G. 1893. *A Year amongst the Persians*. London: Black.

———. 1908. *A Literary History of Persia from the Earliest Times until Firdowsi*. London: T. Fischer.

Brulé, P. 1989. "Des femmes au miroir masculin." *Mélanges Pierre Lévêque*. Vol. 2: *Anthropologie et société*, pp. 49–61. Paris: Les Belles Lettres.

Brunt, P. A. 1962. "Persian Accounts of Alexander's Campaigns." *CQ* 12, no. 1: 141–155.

———, trans. 1976. *Anabasis Alexandri*, by Arrian. Cambridge, Mass.: Harvard University Press.

Brutter, A. 1997. *L'Histoire enseignée au Grand Siècle: Naissance d'une pédagogie*. Paris: Belin.

Budé, G. 1965. *L'institution du Prince*. Text introduced, edited, and annotated by C. Bontems. In C. Bontems, L. P. Raybaud, and J. P. Brancourt, *Le Prince dans la France des XVIe et XVIIe siècles*, pp. 1–143. Paris: Presses universitaires de France.

Bürgel, J.-C. 1991. *Das Alexanderbuch, Iskandarnāme*. Zurich: Manesse Verlag.

———. 1995. "Conquérant, philosophe et prophète: L'image d'Alexandre le Grand dans l'épopée de Nezâmi." In *Pand-o Sokhan: Mélanges offerts à Ch.-H. de Fouchécour*, edited by C. Balaÿ et al., pp. 65–78. Louvain: Peeters.

————. 1996. "Krieg und Frieden in Alexanderepos Nizamis." In *The Problematics of Power: Eastern and Western Representations of Alexander the Great,* edited by M. Bridges and J.-C. Bürgel, pp. 91–107. Bern: Peter Lang.

Burstein, S. 2000. "Prelude to Alexander: The Reign of Khababash." *AHB* 14, pt. 4: 149–154.

Bury, Sieur de. 1760. *Histoire de Philippe et d'Alexandre le Grand, rois de Macédoine.* Paris: Chez l'auteur, chez d'Houry, and chez Dubure l'aîné.

Callu, J.-P. 1999. "Alexandre dans la littérature latine de l'Antiquité tardive." In *Alexandre le Grand dans les littératures occidentales et proche-orientales,* edited by L. Harf-Lancner, C. Kappler, and F. Suard, pp. 33–50. Paris: Université de Paris X Nanterre.

————. 2010. *Julius Valère: Roman d'Alexandre.* Turnhout: Brepols.

Calmard, J. 1999. "Flandin and Coste." *EncIr* 10, no. 1: 35–39.

Calmeyer, P. 1990a. "Das Persepolis der Spätzeit." *AchHist* 4:7–36.

————. 1990b. "Die Orientalen auf Thorwaldsens Alexanderfries." *AchHist* 5:91–119.

————. 1992. "Zwei mit historischen Szenen bemalte Balken der Achaimenidenzeit." *Münchener Jahrbuch der bildenden Kunst* 43:7–18.

————. 2009. *Die Reliefs der Gräber V und VI in Persepolis.* Mainz: von Zabern.

Cameron, A. 1969–1970. "Agathias on the Sassanians." *Dumbarton Oak Papers* 23–24:67–183.

Camerotto, A. 2001. "*Aristeia:* Azioni e tratti tematici dell'eroe in battaglia." *Aevum Antiquum,* n.s. 1: 263–308.

Cardascia, G. 1995. "La ceinture de Parysatis: Une *Morgengabe* chez les Achéménides?" In *Hommage à Guillaume Cardascia,* pp. 137–146. Paris: Université de Paris X Nanterre.

Carlson, M. L. 1948. "Pagan Examples of Fortitude in the Latin Christian Apologists." *Classical Philology* 43:93–104.

Carney, E. D. 1993. "Olympias and the Image of the Virago." *Phoenix* 47, no. 1: 29–55.

————. 1996. "Alexander the Great and Persian Women." *AJPh* 117:563–583. Repr. in Carney 2000b, pp. 82–113.

————. 2000a. "Artifice and Alexander History." In *Alexander in Fact and Fiction,* edited by A. B. Bosworth and E. Baynham, pp. 263–285. Oxford: Oxford University Press.

————. 2000b. *Women and Monarchy in Macedonia.* Norman: University of Oklahoma Press.

————. 2006. *Olympias, Mother of Alexander the Great.* New York: Routledge.

Carradice, I. 1987. "The 'Regal' Coinage of the Persian Empire." In *Coinage and Administration in the Athenian and Persian Empires,* edited by I. Carradice, pp. 73–95. London: British Archaeological Reports.

Cary, G. 1956. *The Medieval Alexander.* Cambridge: Cambridge University Press.

Casari, M. 1999. *Alessandro e Utopia nei romanzi persiani medievali.* Rome: Bardi Ed.

Ceaucescu, P. 1974. "La double image d'Alexandre à Rome: Essai d'une explication politique." *Studi Clasice* 16:153–158.

Chaplin, J. D. 2000. *Livy's Exemplary History.* Oxford: Oxford University Press.

Chardin, J. 1711. *Voyages de Monsieur le Chevalier Chardin en Perse et autres lieux de l'Orient.* 10 vols. Amsterdam.

————. 1735. *Voyages du Chevalier de Chardin en Perse et autres lieux de l'Orient.* New ed. Amsterdam.

———. 1830. *Voyages du Chevalier de Chardin en Perse et autres lieux de l'Orient*, vols. 1–20. In *Nouvelle Bibliothèque des voyages ou choix des voyages les plus intéressants*. Vols. 30–49. Paris: Lecointe éditeur.

Chaybany, J. 1971. *Les voyages en Perse et la pensée française au XVIIIe siècle*. Paris: Geuthner.

Chelkowski, P. 1977. "Nīzamī's Iskandarnāmeh." In *Colloquio sul Poeta persiano Nizāmī e la leggenda iranica di Alessandro Magno*, pp. 11–53. Rome: Accademia Nazionale dei Lincei.

———. 1995. "Nīzamī Gandjawī." *EncIs*, pp. 78–83.

Christensen, A. 1930. "La légende du sage Buzurjmihr." *Acta Orientalia* 8:81–128.

———. 1931. *Les Kayanides*. Copenhagen: Andr. Fred. Høst & søn.

———. 1934. *Le premier homme et le premier roi dans l'histoire légendaire des Iraniens*. Vol. 2. Berlin: Harrassowitz.

———. 1936. *Les gestes des rois dans les traditions de l'Iran antique*. Paris: Librairie orientaliste Paul Geuthner.

———. 1944. *L'Iran sous les Sassanides*. 2nd ed. Copenhagen. Repr. Osnabrück: O. Zeller, 1971.

Chronicon Paschale (284–629 A.D.). 1989. Translated with notes and introduction by M. Whitby and M. Whitby. Liverpool: Liverpool University Press.

Ciancaglini, C. A. 1997. "Alessandro e l'incendio di Persepoli nelle tradizioni greca e irancia." In *La diffusione dell'eredità classica nell'età tardoantica e medievale: Forme e metodi di trasmissione*, edited by A. Valvo, pp. 59–81. Alexandria: Edizioni dell'Orso.

———. 1998. "Gli antecedenti del *Romanzo* siriaco di Alessandro." In *La diffusione dell'eredità classica nell'età tardoantica e medievale: Il "Romanzo di Alessandro" e altri scritti*, edited by R. B. Finazzi and A. Valvo, pp. 65–92. Alexandria: Edizioni dell'Orso.

Clarke, H. W. 1881. *The Sikander Nāmae Bará*. New Delhi: V. I. Publications.

Cohen, A. 1997. *The Alexander Mosaic: Stories of Victory and Defeat*. Cambridge: Cambridge University Press.

Cornette, J. 1993. *Le roi de guerre: Essai sur la souveraineté dans la France du Grand Siècle*. Paris, Payot. Repr. 2000.

Croiset, A., and M. Croiset. 1938. *Histoire de la littérature grecque*. Vol. 5: *Période alexandrine* [A. Croiset], *Période romaine* [M. Croiset]. Paris: Les Belles Lettres.

Croisy-Naquet, C. 1999. "Darius ou l'image du potentat perse dans le roman d'Alexandre de Paris." In *Alexandre le Grand dans les littératures occidentales et proche-orientales*, edited by L. Harf-Lancner, C. Kappler, and F. Suard, pp. 161–172. Paris: Université de Paris X Nanterre.

Curteis, A. M. 1886. *Rise of the Macedonian Empire*. New York: C. Scribner's.

Curtis, V. 1998. "Minstrels in Ancient Iran." In *The Art and Archeology of Ancient Persia: New Light on the Parthian and Sasanian Empires*, edited by V. Curtis, R. Hillenbrand, and J. M. Rogers, pp. 182–187. London: Tauris.

Curzon, G. N. 1892. *Persia and the Persian Question*. Vol. 2. London. Repr. New York: Frank Cass and Co., 1966.

Dakhlia, J. 1998. *Le divan des rois: Le politique et le religieux dans l'Islam*. Paris: Aubier.

Dalby, A. 2000. *Empire of Pleasures: Luxury and Indulgence in the Roman World*. London: Routledge.

Darmesteter, J. 1878. "La légende d'Alexandre chez les Parses." In *Mélanges publiés par la Section historique et philologique de l'École des hautes-études*, pp. 83–99. Paris: Champion.

———. 1885. *Coup d'oeil sur l'histore de la Perse.* Paris: E. Leroux.

———. 1894. *Lettre de Tansar au roi de Tabaristan.* Paris: Imprimerie nationale.

Daryaee, T. 1995. "National History or Keyanid History? The Nature of Sasanid Zoroastrian Historiography." *Iranian Studies* 28, nos. 3–4: 129–141.

———. 2001–2002. "The Construction of the Past in Late Antique Persia." *IJAIS* 1, no. 2: 1–14.

Daude, C. 2002. "Le personnage d'Artaxerxès dans le roman de Chariton, *Chairéas et Callirhoè: Fiction et histoire.*" In *Les personnages du roman grec*, edited by B. Pouderon, pp. 137–148. Lyons: De Boccard.

David, R. 1994. "Sa'adī." *EncIs*, 2nd ed., 8:740–743.

Davidson, O. 1985. "The Crown-Bestower in the Iranian Book of Kings." In *Papers in Honour of Professor Mary Boyce*, 2:61–148. Leiden: Brill.

———. 1994. *Poet and Hero in the Persian Book of Kings.* Ithaca, N.Y.: Cornell University Press.

Davies, I. 1998. "*Alexander's Itinerary:* An English Translation." *AHB* 12, nos. 1–2: 29–54.

Davis, D. 1992. *Epic and Sedition: The Case of Ferdowsi's Shāhnāmeh.* Washington, D.C.: Mage.

———. 1996. "The Problem of Ferdowsî's Sources." *JAOS* 116:48–57.

———. 2002a. "Greek and Persian Romances." *EncIr* 11, no. 4: 339–342.

———. 2002b. *Panthea's Children: Hellenistic Novels and Medieval Persian Romances.* New York: Bibliotheca Persica.

———, trans. 2006. *Shahnameh: The Persian Book of Kings.* New York: Viking.

De Bruyn, C. 1711. *Reizen over Moskovie, door Persie en Indie.* Amsterdam: Hendrik van de Gaete.

Del Monte, G. 1997. *Testi della Babilonia ellenistica.* Vol. 1: *Testi cronografici.* Pisa: Istituti editoriali e poligrafici internazionali.

———. 2001. "Da 'barbari' a 're di Babilonia': I Greci in Mesopotamia." In *I Greci: Storia, Cultura, arte, Società.* Vol. 3: *I Greci oltre la Grecia*, edited by Salvatore Settis, pp. 137–166. Turin: Einaudi.

DeMonte, J. 1999. "Velleius Paterculus and 'Triumphal' History." *AHB* 13, no. 4: 121–135.

Dempsie, W. A. R. 1991. "A Commentary on Q. Curtius Rufus, *Historia Alexandri*, Book 10." Ph.D. diss., St. Andrews University.

Devauchelle, D. 1995. "Réflexions sur les documents égyptiens datés de la deuxième domination perse." *Trans.* 10:35–43.

Devine, A. M. 1979. "The Parthi, the Tyranny of Tiberius, and the Date of Quintus Curtius Rufus." *Phoenix* 33, no. 2: 142–159.

Dīnawarī, Abu Hanīfa (Dinavarī). 1888. *Kitāb al-akhbār al-tiwāl*, edited by V. Guirgass. Leiden: Brill.

Di Vita, A., and C. Alfona, eds. (n.d.) *Alessandro Magno: Storia e mito.* Exh. cat. Rome: Leonardo Arte.

Dosson, S. 1887. *Étude sur Quinte-Curce: Sa vie et son oeuvre.* Paris: Hachette.

Dover, K. J. 1982 (1978). *Greek Homosexuality*. Cambridge, Mass.: Harvard University Press.

Drews, R. 1973. *The Greek Accounts of Eastern History*. Cambridge, Mass.: Harvard University Press.

Drijvers, J. W., et al., eds. 1997. *De reizen door het Nabije Oosten van Cornelis de Bruijn*. Leiden: Ex Oriente Lux.

Droysen, J.-G. 1833. *Geschichte Alexanders des Grossen*. Berlin: Fincke.

———. 1883. *Histoire de l'hellénisme*. Vol. 1: *Histoire d'Alexandre le Grand*. Translated from the second German edition [1877] under the direction of A. Bouché-Leclercq, with a foreword by the translator (pp. iii–xxxvi). Paris: E. Leroux.

———. 1935. *Histoire d'Alexandre le Grand*. Translated from the German with an introduction by J. Benoist-Méchin. Repr. Paris: Club du meilleur livre, 1957.

Dubel, S. 2002. "La beauté romanesque ou le refus du portrait dans le roman grec d'époque impériale." In *Les personnages du roman grec*, edited by B. Pouderon, pp. 29–58. Lyons: De Boccard.

Duff, T. 1999. *Plutarch's Lives: Exploring Virtue and Vice*. Oxford: Clarendon.

Duleba, W. 1995. *The Cyrus Legend in the Šāhnāme*. Kraków: Enigma.

Dumézil, G. 1985. "Le costume de guerre du dernier Darius." In *Mélanges Tucci*, 1:261–265. Rome: Istituto Italiano per il Medio ed Estremo Oriente.

———. 1986. *Mythe et épopée*. Vol. 5. Paris: Gallimard.

Dupont, F., and T. Éloi. 2001. *L'érotisme masculin dans la Rome antique*. Paris: Belin.

Duruy, V. 1862. *Histoire de la Grèce ancienne*. Vol. 2. Paris: Hachette.

———. 1889. *Histoire des Grecs depuis les temps les plus reculés jusqu'à la réduction de la Grèce en province romaine*. New ed. Vol. 3. Paris: Hachette.

Eddy, S. 1961. *The King Is Dead: Studies in the Near Eastern Resistance to Hellenism, 334–31 B.C.* Lincoln: University of Nebraska Press.

E. Flandin: Voyage en Perse (1840–1841). 1995. Exh. cat. Le Blanc: Amis de la Bibliothèque municipale du Blanc.

Egger, B. 1994. "Looking at Chariton's Callirhoe." In *Greek Fiction: The Greek Novel in Context*, edited by J. R. Morgan and R. Stoneman, pp. 31–48. London: Routledge.

El-Sayed, M. G. 2012. "Al-Tabari's Tales of Alexander: History and Romance." In *The Alexander Romance in Persia and the East*, edited by R. Stoneman, K. Erickson, and I. Netton, pp. 219–231. Groningen: Barthuis.

Emerson, J. 1992. "Chardin." *EncIr* 5:369–377.

Engels, D. W. 1978. *Alexander the Great and the Logistics of the Macedonian Army*. Berkeley: University of California Press.

Erasmus. 1992. *Oeuvres*. Paris: R. Laffont.

Facella, M. 2009. "Darius and the Achaemenids in Commagene." In *Organisation des pouvoirs et contacts culturels dans l'empire achéménide*, edited by P. Briant and M. Chauveau, pp. 379–414. Paris: Les Belles Lettres.

Faure, P. 1982. *La vie quotidienne des armées d'Alexandre*. Paris: Hachette.

Fears, J. R. 1974. "Parthi in Q. Curtius Rufus." *Hermes* 102:623–625.

———. 1977. Book review of P. A. Brunt, *Arrian. Anabasis*. I, 1976. *AHR* 82:1220–1223.

———. 2001. Book review of E. Baynham, *Alexander*, 1998. *AJPh* 122, no. 3: 447–451.

Fehr, B. 1988. "Zwei Lesungen des Alexandermosaiks." In *Bathron: Beiträge zur Architectur und verwandten Künster; Festchr. H. Dremp*, pp. 121–134. Saarbrücken: Saarbrücker Druckerei und Verlag.

Ferdowsī [Firdowsī]. 1836. *Le livre des rois*. Edited, translated, and annotated by J. Mohl. Vols. 1–7. Paris. Repr. Paris: J. Maisonneuve, 1976.

———. 2006. *Shahnameh: The Persian Book of Kings*, translated by D. Davis. New York: Viking.

Ferrier, R. W. 1996. *A Journey to Persia: Jean Chardin's Portrait of a Seventeenth-Century Empire*. London: Tauris.

Fillion-Lahille, J. M. 1989. "Le *De ira*." *ANRW* 36, no. 2: 1616–1638.

Finazzi, R. B., and A. Valvo, eds. 1998. *La diffusione del'eredità classica nell'età tardoantica e medievale: Il "Romanzo di Alessandro" et altri scritti*. Alexandria: Ed. dell'Orso.

Flacelière, R., and E. Chambry, ed. and trans. 1975. *Plutarque: Vies*. Paris: CUF.

Flandin, E. 1851. *Voyage en Perse de MM. Eugène Flandin, peintre, et Pascal Coste, architecte: Relation de voyage par M. Eugène Flandin*. Vols. 1 and 2. Paris: Baudry.

Flandin, E., and P. Coste. 1851. *Voyage en Perse pendant les années 1840 et 1841*. Vols. 1–3. Paris: Gide et Baudry.

Flower, H. 2000. "The Tradition of the *Spolia Opima*: M. Claudius Marcellus and Augustus." *Classical Antiquity* 19, no. 1: 34–64.

Foss, C. 1977. "The Battle of Granicus: A New Look." In *Ancient Macedonia*, 2:495–509. Thessaloniki: Hidryma Meletōn Chersonēsou tou Haimou.

Fouchécour, C.-H. 1976. "Une lecture du *Livre des rois* de Ferdowsi." *STIR* 5, no. 2: 171–202.

———. 1986. *Les notions morales dans la littérature persane du IIIe/IXe au VIIe/XIIIe siècle*. Paris: Ed. Recherches sur les civilisations.

———. 1999a. "Jâmi, conseiller des Princes ou Le Livre de la sagesse d'Alexandre." *Kâr-Nâmeh* 5:11–28.

———. 1999b. "Alexandre le Macédonien iranisé: L'exemple du récit de Nézâmi (XIIe siècle) de la visite d'Alexandre à la grotte de Key Khosrow." In *Alexandre le Grand dans les littératures occidentales et proche orientales,* edited by L. Harf-Lancner, C. Kappler, and F. Suard, pp. 227–241. Paris: Université de Paris X Nanterre.

Franco, C. 1999. "Il Romanzo di Alessandro." *QdS* 49, no. 1: 45–102.

Frye, R. 1976. *The Heritage of Persia*. 2nd ed. Guernesey: Cardinal.

Fuhrmann, H. 1931. *Philoxenos von Eretria: Archäologische Untersuchungen über zwei Alexandermosaike*. Göttingen: Dieterich Universität-buchdruckerei W. F. Kaestner.

Fusillo, M. 1993. *Naissance du roman*. Paris: Le Seuil.

Gabrielli, F. 1971. "L'epopea firdusiana e la letteratura araba." In *La Persia nel Medioevo*, pp. 209–213. Rome: Accademia nazionale dei Lincei.

Gaillard, M. 1999. "Alexandre dans la littérature 'semi-populaire' de l'Iran médiéval (le *Dârâb nâmeh d'Abu Tâher Tarsusi*)." In *Alexandre le Grand dans les littératures occidentales et proche-orientales,* edited by L. Harf-Lancner, C. Kappler, and F. Suard, pp. 367–369. Paris: Université de Paris X Nanterre.

———, trans. 2005. *Alexandre en Iran: Le Dârâb-nâmeh d'Abu Tāher Tarsusî*. With commentary by the translator. Paris: de Boccard.

Gambato, M. 2000. "The Female-Kings: Some Aspects of the Representation of Eastern Kings in the *Deinosophistae*." In *Athenaeus and His World: Reading Greek Culture in the Roman Empire*, edited by D. Braund and J. Wilkins, pp. 227–230, 559–562. Exeter: University of Exeter Press.

García Sánchez, M. 2002. "Miradas helenas de la alteridad: La mujer persa." In *La mujer en la Antigüedad*, edited by C. Almaro Giner et al., pp. 45–76. Valencia: Seminario de Estudios sobre la Mujer en la Antigüedad.

Garvin, E.-E. 2003. "Darius III and Homeland Defense." In *Crossroads of History: The Age of Alexander*, edited by W. Heckel and L. A. Tritle, pp. 87–111. Claremont, Calif.: Regina.

Gauger, J.-D. 2000. *Authentizität und Methode: Untersuchungen zum historischen Welt der persisch-griechischen Herrscherbriefe in literarischer Tradition*. Hamburg: Kovač.

Gaullier-Bougassas, C. 1998. *Les Romans d'Alexandre: Aux frontières de l'épique et du romanesque*. Paris: Ed. Champion.

———, ed. 2011. *L'historiographie médiévale d'Alexandre le Grand*. Turnhout: Brepols.

Geiger, J. 1979. "Cornelius Nepos, De regibus exterarum genitum." *Latomus* 38:662–669.

———. 1985. *Cornelius Nepos and Ancient Political Biography*. Wiesbaden: F. Steinter Verlag.

Gentillet, I. 1968. *Anti-Machiavel*. Edition of 1576, with commentary and notes by C. Edward Rathé. Geneva: Librairie Droz.

Geyer, A. 1992. "Alexander in Apulien." In *Kotinos: Festschrift für Erica Simon*, pp. 312–316. Mainz: Verlag Philipp Von Zabern.

Ghirshman, R. 1951. *L'Iran des origines à l'Islam*. Paris: Payot. Repr. Paris: A. Michel, 1976.

Gignoux, P. 1984. *Le livre d'Ardâ Virâz.: Translittération, transcription et traduction du texte pehlevi*. Paris: Ed. Recherches sur les civilisations.

———. 1994. "Dēnkard." *EncIr* 7:284–289.

———. 2007. "La démonisation d'Alexandre le Grand d'après la littérature pehlevie." In *Iranian Languages and Texts from Iran and Turan: Ronald E. Emmerick Memorial Volume*, edited by M. Macuch, M. Maggi, and W. Sundermann, pp. 87–97. Wiesbaden: Harrassowitz.

Gillies, J. 1786. *History of Ancient Greece, Its Colonies and Conquests, from the Earliest Accounts till the Division of the Macedonian Empire in the East*. Vol. 2. London.

Giuliani, L. 1977. "Alexander in Ruvo, Eretria und Sidon." *Antike Kunst* 20:26–42.

Glassner, J. J. 1993. *Chroniques mésopotamiennes*. Paris: Les Belles Lettres.

Glück, J. J. 1964. "Reviling and Monomachy as Battle Preludes in Ancient Warfare." *Acta Classica* 7:25–31.

Gnoli, G. 1989. *The Idea of Iran: An Essay on Its Origin*. Rome: Istituto Italiano per il Medio ed Estremo Oriente.

———. 1995. "La demonizzazione di Alessandro nell'Iran sassanide (III–VII secolo d.C.) e nella tradizione zoroastriana." In *Alessandro Magno: Storia e mito*, edited by Antonino Di Vita and Carla Alfona, p. 175. Rome: Leonardo Arte.

Gobineau, Comte A. de. 1869. *Histoire des Perses d'après les auteurs orientaux, grecs et latins, et particulièrement d'après les manuscrits orientaux inédits, les monuments figurés, les médai-*

lles, les pierres gravées, etc. Vols. 1–2. Repr. Tehran: Imperial Organization for Social Services, 1976.

Goldman, B. 1993. "Darius III, the Alexander Mosaic, and the *Tiara Ortho.*" *Mespotamia* 28:51–69.

Goldstein, M. 1912. *Darius, Xerxes und Artaxerxes in Drama der neuerer Literaturen.* Leipzig: A. Deichert.

Gorteman, C. 1958. "Basileus Philalèthès." *CdE* 22:256–267.

Goukowsky, P. 1976. "Notice." In *Diodore de Sicile: Bibliothèque historique livre XVII,* pp. ix–lviii. Paris: Les Belles Lettres.

———. 1998. "Le cortège des 'rois de Babylone.'" *BAI* 12:69–77.

Gray, V. J. 1990. "The Moral Interpretation of the 'Second Preface' to Arrian's Anabasis." *JHS* 110:180–186.

Grayson, A. K. 1975. *Assyrian and Babylonian Chronicles.* Locust Valley, N.Y.: J. J. Augustin. Repr. Winona Lake, Ind.: Eisenbrauns, 2000.

Green, P. 1974. *Alexander of Macedon.* London: Pelican.

———. 1978. "Caesar and Alexander: Aemulatio, imitatio, comparatio." *AJAH* 3:1–26.

Grell, C. 1993. *L'Histoire entre érudition et philosophie: Étude sur la connaissance historique à l'âge des Lumières.* Paris: Presses universitaires de France.

Grell, C., and C. Michel. 1988. *L'École des princes ou Alexandre disgracié: Essai sur la mythologie monarchique de la France absolutiste.* Paris: Les Belles Lettres.

Grenet, F. 2003. *La geste d'Ardashir fils de Pâpag.* Die: Ed. A. Die.

Grignaschi, M. 1966. "Quelques spécimens de la littérature sassanide conservés dans les bibliothèques d'Istanbul." *Journal Asiatique* 254:1–142.

———. 1996. "Un roman épistolaire gréco-arabe: La correspondance entre Aristote et Alexandre." In *The Problematics of Power: Eastern and Western Representations of Alexander the Great,* edited by M. Bridges and J. C. Bürgel, pp. 109–123. Bern: P. Lang.

Grimal, P. 1958. *Romans grecs et latins.* Paris: Gallimard.

Gropp, D. G. 2001. *Wadi-Daliyeh II: The Samaria Papyri from Wadi-Daliyeh.* Oxford: Clarendon.

Grote, G. 1856. *A History of Greece from the Earliest Period to the Close of the Generation Contemporary with Alexander the Great.* 12 vols. London: J. Murray.

Gruen, E. S. 1998. "Rome and the Myth of Alexander." In *Ancient History in a Modern University,* 1:178–191. Grand Rapids, Mich.: Eerdmans.

Guenée, B. 1967. "Les entrées royales françaises à la fin du Moyen Âge." *CRAI* 2:210–212.

Guenée, N, and F. Lehoux. 1968. *Les entrées royales françaises de 1328 à 1515.* Paris: Ed. du Centre National de la Recherche Scientifique.

Guirgass, V, ed. 1888. *Kitāb al-akhbār al-tiwāl,* by Abu Hanīfa Dīnawarī. Leiden: Brill.

Guyot, P. 1980. *Eunuchen als Sklaven und Freigelassene in der griechischrömischen Antike.* Stuttgart: Klett-Cotta.

Habby, J. 1998. "Alessandro incendio di libri?" In *La diffusione dell'eredità classica nell'età tardoantica e medievale: Il "Romanzo di Alessandro" e altri scritti,* edited by R. B. Finazzi and A. Valvo, pp. 135–140. Alexandria: Edizione dell'Orso.

Hägg, T. 1983. *The Novel in Antiquity.* Berkeley: University of California Press.

Hall, E. 1993. "Asia Unmanned: Images of Victory in Classical Athens." In *War and Society in the Greek World*, edited by J. Rich and G. Shipley, pp. 108–133. London: Routledge.

Hamilton, J. R. 1969. *Plutarch, Alexander: A Commentary*. Oxford: Clarendon.

———. 1977. "Cleitarchus and Diodorus 17." In *Greece and the Eastern Mediterranean in Ancient Prehistory and History: Studies Presented to F. Schachermeyr*, pp. 126–146. Berlin: W. de Gruyter.

Hammond, N. G. L. 1978. "A Note on 'Pursuit' in Arrian." *CQ* 28:336ff. Repr. in Hammond 1994, pp. 59–63.

———. 1980. "The Battle of the Granicus River." *JHS* 100:73–88. Repr. in Hammond 1994, pp. 93–108.

———. 1994. *Collected Studies*. Vol. 3. Amsterdam: Hakkert.

———. 1997. *The Genius of Alexander*. London: Duckworth.

Hanaway, W. L. 1970. "Persian Popular Romances before the Safavid Period." Vols. 1 and 2. Ph.D. diss., Columbia University.

———. 1971. "Formal Elements in the Persian Popular Romances." *Review of National Literature* 2, no. 1: 139–160.

———. 1974. *Love and War: Adventures from the Firuz Shāh Nāma of Shikh Bighami*, translated from the Persian. New York: Delmar.

———. 1982. "Anāhitā and Alexander." *JAOS* 102:285–295.

———. 1994a. "Dārāb-Nāma." *EncIr* 7, pt. 1: 8–9.

———. 1994b. "Dāstān-Sarā'ī." *EncIr* 7, pt. 1: 102–103.

———. 1998. "Eskandar-Nāma." *EncIr* 8:609–612.

Hansen, M. H. 1993. "The Battle Exhortation in Ancient Historiography." *Historia* 42:161–180.

———. 1998. "The Little Grey Horse: Henry's Speech at Agincourt and the Battle Exhortation in Ancient Historiography." *Histos* 2: 46–63, http://research.ncl.ac.uk/histos/documents/1998.02HansenTheLittleGreyHorse4663.pdf.

Harf-Lancner, L., C. Kappler, and F. Suard, eds. 1999. *Alexandre le Grand dans les littératures occidentales et proche-orientales*. Paris: Université de Paris X Nanterre.

Harrison, C. 1982a. "Persian Names on Coins of Northern Anatolia." *JNES* 41, no. 3: 181–194.

———. 1982b. "Coins of the Persian Satraps." Ph.D. diss., University of Pennsylvania.

Hatzopoulos, M. 1994. *Cultes et rites de passage en Macédoine*. Paris: De Boccard.

———. 1996. *Macedonian Institutions under the Kings: A Historical and Epigraphic Study*. Vols. 1 and 2. Athens: Kentron Hellēnikēs kai Rōmaïkēs Archaiotētos.

Heckel, W. 1983. "Alexandros Lynkestes and Orontas." *Eranos* 81:139–143.

Heeren, A. 1846. *Historical Researches into the Politics, Intercourse, and Trade of the Principal Nations of Antiquity*. Vol. 1: *Asiatic Nations: Persians, Phoenicians, Babylonians*. Vol. 2: *Asiatic Nations: Scythians, Indians*, translated by D. A. Talboys. London: H. G. Bohn.

———. 1854. *A Manual of Ancient History, Particularly with Regard to the Constitutions, the Commerce and the Colonies*, translated from the German. 6th ed. London: H. G. Bohn.

Hegel, G. W. F. 1899. *The Philosophy of History*; translated by John Sibree. New York: Colonial.

Helm, R. 1939. "Valerius Maximus, Seneca und die 'Exemplasammlung.'" *Hermes* 74:130–154.

Henkelmann, W. 1995–1996. "The Royal Achaemenid Crown." *AMI* 28:275–293.

Hériché, S. 2000. *"Les Faicts et les conquestes d'Alexandre le Grand" de Jean Wauquelin (XVe siècle): Édition critique.* Geneva: Droz.

Herzfeld, E. 1929–1930. "Rapport sur l'état actuel des ruines de Persépolis et propositions pour leur conservation, avec 30 planches et une carte." *AMI* 1:17–40.

Hillenbrand, R. 1996. "The Iskandar Cycle in the Great Mongol *Šahnāma.*" In *The Problematics of Power: Eastern and Western Representations of Alexander the Great,* edited by M. Bridges and J. C. Bürgel, pp. 203–229. Bern: P. Lang.

Hogarth, D. G. 1897. *Philip and Alexander of Macedon: Two Essays in Biography.* New York: C. Scribner's Sons.

Holm, A. 1896. *The History of Greece from Its Commencement to the Close of the Independence of the Greek Nation.* Vol. 3: *The Fourth Century up to the Death of Alexander,* translated by Frederick Clarke. London: Macmillan.

Hölscher, T. 1973. *Grieschische Historienbilder des 5. und 4. Jahrhunderts v. Chr.* Würzburg: K. Triltsch.

———. 1981–1983. "Zur Deutung des Alexandermosaiks." *Anadolu (Mélanges E. Akurgal)* 22:297–307.

Holt, F. 1999. "Alexander the Great: In the Interests of Historical Accuracy?" *AHB* 13, no. 3: 111–177.

———. 2000. "The Death of Coenus: Another Study of Method." *AHB* 14, nos. 1–2: 49–55.

Hornblower, S. 1994. "Persia." *CAH* 6, no. 2: 45–96.

Horworth, H. 1903. "The History of Coinage of Artaxerxes III, His Satraps and Dependents." *NC,* 4th ser., 3:95–159.

Huss, W. 1994. "Der rätselhafte Pharao Chababasch." *SELVOA* 11:97–112.

Huyse, P. 2002. "La revendication de territoires achéménides par les Sassanides: Une réalité historique?" *STIR* 24:294–308.

Ibn Baklhī. 1921. *Fārs Nāmeh,* edited by G. Le Strange and R. A. Nicholson. London: Luzac and Co.

Ibn Khaldūn. 1967–1968. *Discours sur l'histoire universelle (Al-Muqaddinm),* translated with preface and notes by Vincent Monteil. Vols. 1–3. Paris: Ed. Sinbad.

Ieranò, G. 1996. "Il barbaro in fuga: Un'eco dei *Persiani* di Eschilo nel *Romanzo di Alessandro.*" *Aevum Antiquum* 9:217–234.

Jackson, A. V. W. 1920. *Early Persian Poetry, from the Beginnings down to the Time of Firdausi.* New York: Macmillan.

Jacob, C. 2001. "Ateneo, o il dedalo delle parole." In *Ateneo: I Deipnosphisti; I dotti a banchetto traduzione italiana commentata,* 1:xi–cxvi. Rome: Salerno Editrice.

Jacques Gamelin, 1738–1803: Les collections du Musée des Beaux-Arts de Carcassonne. Exh. cat. Carcassonne.

Jamzadeh, P. 2012. *Alexander Histories and Iranian Reflections: Remnants of Propaganda and Resistance.* Leiden: Brill.

Joannès, F. 1982. *Textes économiques de la Babylonie récente.* Paris: Editions Recherche sur les civilisations.

———. 1994. "L'eau et la glace à Mari." In *Florilegium Marianum II: Recueil d'études à la mémoire de Maurice Birot.* Paris: SEPOA, pp. 151–157.

————. 2001. "Les débuts de l'époque hellénistique à Larsa." In *Études mésopotamiennes: Recueil de textes offerts à Jean-Louis Huot,* edited by C. Breniquet and C. Kepinksi, pp. 249–264. Paris: Diff. de Boccard.

————. 2006. "La Babylonie méridionale: Continuité, déclin ou rupture?" In *La transition entre l'empire achéménide et les royaumes hellénistiques, c. 350–300,* edited by P. Briant and F. Joannès, pp. 101–135. Paris: de Boccard.

Jouanno, C. 2002. *Naissance et métamorphose du Roman d'Alexandre: Domaine grec.* Paris: Ed. Centre National de la Recherche Scientifique.

————, trans. 2009. *Histoire merveilleuse du roi Alexandre maître du monde.* Toulouse: Anacharsis.

————, ed. 2012. *Figures d'Alexandre à la Renaissance.* Turnhout: Brepols.

Justi, F. 1879. *Geschichte des alten Persiens.* Berlin: G. Grote.

————. 1884. *Geschichte der orientalischer Völker im Altertum.* Berlin: G. Grote.

Kallet, L. 2001. *Money and the Corrosion of Power in Thucydides.* Berkeley: University of California Press.

Känel, F. von. 1984. *Les prêtres-ouab de Sekhmet et les conjurateurs de Serket.* Paris: Presses universitaires de France.

Kantorowicz, E. 1957. *The King's Two Bodies: A Study in Mediaevel Political Theology.* Princeton, N.J.: Princeton University Press.

Kappler, C. 1996. "Alexandre dans le *Shāh Nāma* de Firdousi: De la conquête du monde à la découverte de soi." In *The Problematics of Power: Eastern and Western Representations of Alexander the Great,* edited by M. Bridges and J. C. Bürgel, 22:165–190. Bern: P. Lang.

Ker Porter, R. 1821–1822. *Travels in Georgia, Persia, Armenia, Ancient Babylonia . . . during the Years 1817, 1818, 1819 and 1820, with Numerous Engravings of Portraits, Costumes, Antiquities, etc.* Vols. 1 and 2. London: Longman, Hurst, Rees, Orme Brown.

Khaleghi-Motlagh, D., and C. Pellat. 1985. "Adab I, II." *EncIr* 1:431–444.

Kienast, D. 1996. "Der Wagen des Ahura-Mazda und der Ausmarch des Xerxes." *Chiron* 26:285–313.

Kindstrand, J. K. 1998. "Claudianus Aelianus und sein Werke." *ANRW* 34, no. 4: 2954–2996.

Kleiss, W. 1992. "Beobachtungen auf dem Burgberg von Persepolis." *AMI* 25:155–167.

Kleiss, W., and P. Calmeyer. 1975. "Das unvollendete achaemenidische Felsgrab bei Persepolis." *AMI* 8:81–98.

Knipfing, J. R. 1921. "German Historians and Macedonian Imperialism." *AHR* 26:657–671.

Koch, H. 1999. Book review of E. Baynham, *Quintus Curtius,* 1998. *Histos* 3:140–146, http://research.ncl.ac.uk/histos/documents/1999.RD02KochonBaynhamAlexander140146.pdf.

————. 2000. *Hundert Jahre Curtius-Forschung (1899–1999): Ein Arbeitsbibliographie.* St. Katharinen: Scripta Mercaturae.

Kolata, A. 1996. "Mimesis and Monumentalism in Native Andean Cities." *Res* 29, no. 30: 233–236.

Konuk, K. 2000. "Influences et éléments achéménides dans le monnayage de la Carie." In *Mécanismes et innovations monétaires dans l'Anatolie achéménide: Numismatique et his-*

toire, edited by O. Casabonne, pp. 171–183. Istanbul: Institut français d'études anatoliennes; Paris: De Boccard.

Koulakiotis, E. 2006. *Genese und Metamorphosen des Alexandermythos im Spiegel der griechischen nich-historiographischen Überlieferung bis zum 3. Jh. n. Chr.* Constance, Germany: Universitätverlag.

Kuhrt, A. 1990. "Alexander in Babylon." *AchHist* 5:121–130.

———. 2007. *The Persian Empire: A Corpus of Sources from the Achaemenid Period.* Vols. 1 and 2. London: Routledge.

Kuhrt, A., H. Sancisi-Weerdenburg et al., eds. 1987–1994. *Achaemenid History.* Vols. 1–10. Leiden: Nederlands Instituut voor het Nabije Oosten.

Lambton, A. K. 1971. "Islamic Mirrors for Princes." In *La Persia nel Medioevo*, pp. 419–442. Rome: Accademia Nazionale dei Lincei.

La Mothe Le Vayer, F. 1669. *Oeuvres.* Vols. 1–15. New ed. Paris: L. Billaine.

Lane Fox, R. 1986. *Alexander the Great.* London: Penguin. 1st ed. 1973.

La Taille, J. de. 1992. *Daire*, edited by M. G. Longhi. In *La tragédie à l'époque d'Henri II et de Charles IX.* Vol. 4 of *Théâtre français de la Renaissance*, 1st ser. (1568–1573), pp. 269–350. Paris: Presses universitaires de France; Florence: S. Olschki.

Lattimore, R. 1939. "The Wise Adviser in Herodotus." *CPh* 34:24–35.

Lauffer, S. 1978. *Alexander der Grosse.* Munich: Deutscher Taschenbuch.

Lazard, G. 1972. "*Pahlavi/Pahlvâni* dans le *Šahnâme*." *STIR* 1, no. 2: 25–41.

Le Brun [De Bruyn], C. 1718. *Voyages de Corneille Le Brun par la Moscovie, en Perse, et aux Indes orientales . . . enrichi de plus trois cens vingt tailles-douces*, translated from the Dutch. Vols. 1 and 2. Amsterdam.

Le Goff, J. 1996. *Saint Louis.* Paris: Gallimard.

Lemaire, A. 2000. "Remarques sur certaines légendes monétaires ciliciennes (Ve–IVe siècle av. J.-C.)." In *Mécanismes et innovations monétaires dans l'Anatolie achéménide: Numismatique et histoire*, edited by O. Casabonne, pp. 129–142. Istanbul: Institut français d'études anatoliennes.

Lenfant, D. 2001a. "La 'décadence' du Grand Roi et les ambitions de Cyrus le Jeune: Aux sources perses d'un mythe occidental?" *REG* 114:407–438.

———. 2001b. "De Sardanapale à Élégabal: Les avatars d'une figure du pouvoir." In *Images et représentations du pouvoir et de l'ordre social dans l'Antiquité (Actes du colloque, Angers, 28–29 mai 1999)*, edited by M. Mollin, pp. 45–55. Paris: De Boccard.

———. 2009. *Les 'Histoires perses' de Dinon et d'Héraclide: Fragments édités, traduits et commentés.* Paris: de Boccard.

Le Rider, G. 1998. "Antimène de Rhodes à Babylone." *BAI* 12 (*Studies in Honor of Paul Bernard*): 121–140.

———. 2001. *Naissance de la monnaie: Pratiques monétaires de l'Orient ancien.* Paris: Presses universitaires de France.

———. 2007. *Alexander the Great: Coinage, Finances and Policy*, translated by W. E. Higgins. New York: American Philological Society.

Le Roux, N. 2000. *La faveur du roi: Mignons et courtisans au temps des dernier Valois (vers 1547–vers 1589).* Paris: Champ Vallon.

Le Strange, G., and R. A. Nicholson, eds. 1921. *Fārs Nāmeh,* by Ibn Baklhī. London: Luzac and Co.

Letoublon, F. 1993. *Les lieux communs du roman grec: Stéréotypes grecs d'aventure et d'amour.* Leiden: Brill.

Lewis, F. 2001. "Golestān-e Sa'adī." *EncIr* 11, pt. 1: 79–86.

Lichtheim, M. 1980. *Ancient Egyptian Literature.* Vol. 3: *The Late Period.* Berkeley: University of California Press.

Longhi, M. G. 1992. Introduction to J. de la Taille, "Daire" and "Alexandre." In *La tragédie à l'époque d'Henri II et de Charles IX.* Vol. 4 of *Théâtre français de la Renaissance,* 1st ser. (1568–1573), pp. 271–298, 353–380. Paris: Presses universitaires de France; Florence: Olschki.

Loraux, N. 1980. "Thucydide n'est pas un collègue." *QdS* 12:55–81.

———. 1989. "Blessures de guerriers." In her *Les expériences de Tirésias,* pp. 108–123. Paris: Gallimard.

Loti, P. 1904. *Vers Ispahan.* Paris. Repr. Paris: Calmann-Lévy, 1925; Tehran: Iqbāl, 1978.

Luginbill. R. D. 2000. "Chariton's Use of Thucydides' *History* in Introducing the Egyptian Revolt (*Chaireas and Callirhoe* 6.8.)." *Mnemosyne* 53, no. 1: 1–11.

Lumpe, A. 1966. "*Exemplum.*" In *Reallexikon für Antike und Christentum,* edited by T. Klauser, vol. 6, cols. 1229–1257. Stuttgart: Hiersemann.

Maas, E. 1921. "Eunuchos und Verwandtes." *RhM* 74:432–476.

MacCurrie, H. 1990. "Quintus Curtius Rufus: The Historian as Novelist?" *Groningen Colloquia on the Novel.* Vol. 3, edited by H. Hofmann, pp. 63–77. Groningen: Forsten.

MacKenzie, D. N. 1990. "Bundahišn." *EncIr* 4:547–551.

Maçoudi [a -Mas'ūdi]. 1868. *Les prairies d'or,* edited and translated by C. Barbier de Meynard and Pavet de Courteille. Vol. 2. Paris: Imprimerie nationale.

Mahé-Simon, M. 2001. "L'enjeu historiographique de l'*excursus* sur Alexandre." In *Le censeur et les Samnites: Sur Tite-Live, livre IX,* edited by D. Briquel and J.-P. Thuillier, pp. 37–53. Paris: Ed. rue d'Ulm.

Malcolm, Sir John. 1829. *The History of Persia from the Most Early Period to the Present Time.* Vol. 1. New ed. London: John Murray.

Malloch, S. J. 2001. "Gaius' Bridge at Baiae and Alexander-imitatio." *CQ* 51, no. 1: 206–217.

Mann, K. 2007. *Alexander, a Novel of Utopia,* translated from the German by David Carter. London: Hesperus.

Manteghi, H. 2012. "Alexander the Great in the Shānāmeh of Ferdowsī." In *The Alexander Romance in Persia and the East,* edited by R. Stoneman, K. Erickson, and I. Netton, pp. 161–174. Groningen: Barthuis.

Marincola, J. 1997. *Authority and Tradition in Ancient Historiography.* Cambridge: Cambridge University Press.

Marrou, H. I. 1950. *Histoire de l'éducation dans l'Antiquité.* 2nd ed. Paris: Le Seuil.

Marsden, E. W. 1964. *The Campaign of Gaugamela.* Liverpool: Liverpool University Press.

Martin, A. 1904. "Monomachia." In *Dictionnaire des Antiquités grecques et romaines,* edited by Charles Daremberg and Edmond Saglio. Vol. 3, pt. 2, pp. 1991–1994. Paris: Hachette.

Marx, F. A. 1937. "Tacitus und die Literatur der *exitus illustrium virorum.*" *Philologus* 92:83–103.

Maslakov, G. 1984. "Valerius Maximus and Roman Historiography: A Study of the *Exempla* Tradition." *ANRW* 2.32.1: 435–496.

Maspéro, G. 1890. *Histoire ancienne des peuples de l'Orient.* Vol. 3: *Les empires.* Paris: Hachette.

Massé, H. 1919. *Essai sur le poète Saadi.* Paris: Geuthner.

———. 1935. *Firdousi et l'épopée iranienne.* Paris: Perrin.

McCarthy, T. 1974. "The Content of Cornelius Nepos' *De viris illustribus.*" *CW* 67, no. 6: 383–391.

McKechnie, P. 1999. "Manipulation of Themes in Quintus Curtius Rufus Book 10." *Historia* 48, no. 1: 44–60.

Mederer, E. 1936. *Die Alexanderlegenden bei den ältesten Alexanderhistorikern.* Stuttgart: W. Kohlhammer.

Meeks, D. 2001. "Traitement, conservation et transport de l'eau du Nil: Histoire et problèmes." In *"Tekhnai": Techniques et sociétés en Méditerranée: Hommages à Marie-Claire Amouretti,* edited by J.-P. Brun and P. Jockey, pp. 499–512. Paris: Maisonneuve et Larose.

Meisami, J. S. 1995. "The *Šāh-nāme* as Mirror for Princes: A Study in Reception." In *Pand-o Sokhan: Mélanges offerts à Ch.-H. de Fouchécour,* edited by C. Balaÿ et al., pp. 265–273. Louvain: Peeters.

———. 1999. *Persian Historiography to the End of the Twelfth Century.* Edinburgh: Edinburgh University Press.

Melikian-Chirvani, A. 1971. "Le royaume de Salomon: Les inscriptions persanes de sites achéménides." *Le Monde iranien et l'Islam* 1:1–41.

———. 1988. "Le Livre des rois, miroir du destin." *STIR* 17:7–46.

Menasce, J. de. 1972. *Le troisième livre du Dēnkārt.* Paris: C. Klincksieck.

———. 1983. "Zoroastrian Pahlavī Writings." In *The Cambridge History of Iran.* Vol. 3, pt. 2, edited by Ehsan Yarshater, pp. 1166–1195. Cambridge: Cambridge University Press.

Mendels, D. 1981. "The Five Empires: Notes on a Propagandistic *Topos.*" *AJPh* 102:330–337.

Mensch, P, trans. 2010. *Anabasis Alexandrous: A New Translation.* In *The Landmark Arrian,* edited by J. Romm, pp. 3–315. New York: Pantheon.

Merkelbach, R. 1977. *Die Quellen des griechischen Alexanderromans.* 2nd. ed. Munich: Beck.

———. 1989. "Der Brief des Dareios in Getty-Museum und Alexanders Wortwechsel mit Parmenion." *Zeitschrift für Papyrologie und Epigraphik* 77:277–280.

Messina, G. 1935. "Mito, legenda e storia nella tradizione iranica." *Orientalia* 4:257–290.

Metzger. H. 1967. "À propos des images apuliennes de la bataille d'Alexandre et du conseil de Darius." *REG* 80:308–313.

Mildenberg, L. 1990–1991. "Notes on the Coin Issues of Mazday." *INJ* 11:9–23.

———. 1999a. "Artaxerxes III Ochus (358–338 B.C.): A Note on the Maligned King." *ZDPV* 115, no. 2: 201–227.

———. 1999b. "A Note on the Coinage of Hierapolis-Bambyce." In *Travaux de numismatique grecque offerts à G. Le Rider,* edited by M. Amandry and S. Hurter, pp. 277–284. London: Spink.

Miller, D. A. 2000. "Other Kinds of Hero: The Coward Knight and Intelligence Embattled." *Journal of Indo-European Studies* 28, nos. 1–2: 221–235.

Milns, R. D. 1966. "Alexander's Pursuit of Darius through Iran." *Historia* 15, no. 1: 256.

Minissale, F. 1983. *Curzio Rufo, un romanziere della Storia.* Messina: Peloritana Ed.

Mīrkhond [Mīrkhwānd]. 1832. *History of the Early Kings of Persia from Kaiomars . . . to the Conquest of Iran by Alexander the Great,* translated by D. Shea. London.

Mitford, W. 1835. *The History of Greece from the Earliest Period to the Death of Agesilaus, Continued to the Death of Alexander the Great by R. A. Davenport.* Vols. 7–8. London.

Mohl, J. 1836. Preface to Firdousi, *Le livre des rois.* Vol. 1, pp. iii–xcii. Repr. Paris: Maisonneuve, 1976.

Molé, M. 1953. "L'épopée iranienne après Firdūsi." *La nouvelle Clio* 5 *(Mélanges A. Dupont-Sommer):* 377–393.

———. 1993. *La légende de Zorastre selon les textes pehlevis.* Paris: Peeters.

Momigliano, A. 1942. "Terramarique." *JRS* 32:53–64.

———. 1971. *The Development of Greek Biography.* Cambridge, Mass.: Harvard University Press.

———. 1983 (1971). "Mise au point sur la biographie grecque." In *Problèmes d'historiographie ancienne et moderne,* pp. 104–119. Paris: Gallimard.

Montaigne, Michel de. 1962. *Essais,* edited by M. Rat. 2 vols. Paris: Garnier Frères.

———. 1965. *The Complete Essays of Montaigne,* translated by Donald M. Frame. Stanford: Stanford University Press.

Moore, P. 1995. "Quintus Curtius Rufus' 'Historia Alexandri Magni': A Study in Rhetorical Historiography." Ph.D. diss., Oxford University.

Morello, R. 2002. "Livy's Alexander Digression (9.17–19)." *JRS* 82:62–85.

Moreno, P. 2001. *Apelles: The Alexander Mosaic,* translated by David Stanton. Milan: Skira.

———. 2009. "Iconografia di Alessandro nell'arte antico." In *Alessandro Magno in età moderna,* edited by F. Biasutti and A. Coppola, pp. 373–474. Padova: Cooperativa Libraria Editrice Universita di Padova.

Moret, J.-M. 1975. *L'Ilioupersis dans la céramique italiote: Les mythes et leur expression figurée au IVe siècle.* Vol. 1. Rome: Institut suisse de Rome.

Morgan, J.-R., and R. Stoneman, eds. 1994. *Greek Fiction: The Greek Novel in Context.* London: Routledge.

Morier, J. 1812. *A Journey through Persia, Armenia and Asia Minor to Constantinople in the Years 1808 and 1809.* London.

———. 1818a. *A Second Journey through Persia, Armenia and Asia Minor to Constantinople in the Years 1810 and 1816.* London.

———. 1818b. *Voyages en Perse, en Arménie, en Asie Mineure et à Constantinople faits dans les années 1808 et 1809.* Paris.

Müller, M., ed. 1901. *The Sacred Books of the East,* translated by various Oriental scholars. Vol. 5. Oxford: Clarendon.

Murrison, C. L. 1972. "Darius III and the Battle of Issus." *Historia* 21:399–423.

Nadon, C. 2001. *Xenophon's Prince: Republic and Empire in the "Cyropaedia."* Berkeley: University of California Press.

Neuhaus, P. 1902. "Der Vater der Sisygambis und das Verwandschaftsverhältnis des Dareios III Kodomannos zu Artaxerxes II und III." *RhM* 57:610–623.

Neumann, C. 1971. "A Note on Alexander's March-Rate." *Historia* 20:196–198.

Niccolini, A. 1832. "Musaico scoperto in Pompei il di 24 ottobre 1831." *Real Museo Borbonico* 8:1–50.

Nicolet, C. 1988. *L'inventaire du monde: Géographie et politique aux origines de l'empire romain.* Paris: Fayard.

Nicolet-Pierre, H. 1989. "Les monnaies des deux derniers satrapes d'Égypte avant la conquête d'Alexandre." In *Kraay-Morkholm Essays: Numismatic Studies in Memory of C. M. Kraay and O. Mørkholm*, edited by G. Le Rider et al., pp. 221–230. Louvain-la-Neuve: Institut supérieur d'archéologie et d'histoire de l'art.

———. 1999. "Argent et or frappés en Babylonie entre 331 et 311 ou de Mazdai à Séleucos." In *Travaux de numismatique grecque offerts à G. Le Rider*, edited by M. Amandry and S. Hurter, pp. 285–305. London: Spink.

Niebuhr, B. G. 1847. *Vorträge über alte Geschichte.* Berlin: Reimer.

———. 1852. *Lectures on Ancient History from the Earliest Times to the Taking of Alexandria by Octavianus*, translated by Leonhard Schmidtz. 3 vols. London: Taylor, Walton, and Maberly.

Niebuhr, C. 1780. *Voyage en Arabie et en d'autres pays circonvoisins*, translated from the German. Vol. 2. Utrecht: J. Van Schoonhoven.

Nippel, W. 2008. *Johann Gustav Droysen: Ein Leben zwischen Wissenschaft und Politik.* Munich: C. H. Beck.

Nīzamī [Nezâmî]. 2000. *Le pavillon des sept princesses*, translated from the Persian, edited and annotated by M. Barry. Paris: Gallimard.

Nöldeke, T. 1879. *Geschichte der Perser und Araber zur Zeit der Sasaniden, aus der arabischen Chronik des Tabari.* Repr. Leiden: Brill, 1973.

———. 1887. *Aufsätze zur persischen Geschichte.* Leipzig: T. O. Weigel.

———. 1930. *The Iranian National Epic or the Shahnamah*, translated by L. Bogdanov. Bombay: K. R. Cama Oriental Institute.

Nylander, C. 1982. "Il milite ignoto: Un problema nel mosaico di Alessandro." In *La regione soterrata dal Vesuvio: Studi e prospettive*, pp. 689–695. Naples: Università degli Studi.

———. 1983. "The Standard of the Great King: A Problem in the Alexandermosaik." *Opuscula romana* 19, no. 2: 19–37.

———. 1993. "Darius III—The Coward King: Point and Counterpoint." In *Alexander the Great: Reality and Myth*, edited by J. Carlsen et al., pp. 145–159. Rome: L'Erma di Bretschneider.

Oakley, S. P. 1985. "Single Combat in the Roman Republic." *CQ* 35, no. 2: 392–410.

Ogden, D. 2009. "Alexander's Sex Life." In *Alexander the Great: A New History*, edited by W. Heckel and L. A. Tritle, pp. 203–217. Chichester, UK: Wiley-Blackwell.

———. 2011. *Alexander the Great: Myth, Genesis and Sexuality.* Exeter: University of Exeter Press.

Olmstead, A. T. 1948. *A History of the Persian Empire.* Chicago: University of Chicago Press.

Ouseley, W. 1821. *Travels in Various Countries of the East, More Particularly in Persia.* Vol. 2. London.

Pahlavi, M. R. 1979. *Réponse à l'histoire*. Paris: A. Michel.

Panaino, A. 1987. "La Persia nel pensiero e negli scritti di Hegel." *Paideia* 42, nos. 4–6: 192–213.

Paschoud, F., ed. 1998. *La biographie antique*. Geneva: Vandoeuvres.

Pearson, L. 1960. *The Lost Histories of Alexander the Great*. New York: American Philological Association.

Pédech, P. 1964. *La méthode historique de Polybe*. Paris: Les Belles Lettres.

———. 1984. *Historiens compagnons d'Alexandre*. Paris: Les Belles Lettres.

Pellat, C. 1995. "Dīnavarī." *EncIr* 7, pt. 4: 437.

Pelling, C. 2002. *Plutarch and History*. Swansea: Classical Press of Wales; London: Duckworth.

Perdu, O. 1985. "Le monument de Samtoutefnakht." *RdE* 36:89–113.

Pernice, E. 1907a. "Bemerkungen zum Alexandermosaik." *MDAI* 22:25–34.

———. 1907b. "Nachträgliche Bemerkungen zum Alexandermosaik." *MDAI* 23:11–14.

Pernot, L. 1993. *La rhétorique de l'éloge dans le monde gréco-romain*. Vol. 2. Paris: Institut d'études augustiniennes.

———. 2013. *Alexandre le Grand: Les risques du pouvoir, textes philosophiques et rhétoriques traduits et commentés*. Paris: Les Belles Lettres.

Perrin, Y. 1998. "À propos de la 'Bataille d'Issos': Théâtre, science et peinture; La conquête de l'espace ou d'Ucello à Philoxène." *Cahiers du Centre-Glotz* 9:83–116.

Perrot, G., and C. Chipiez. 1890. *Histoire de l'art dans l'Antiquité*. Vol. 5: *Perse, Phrygie, Lydie et Carie, Lycie*. Paris: Hachette.

Perrot d'Ablancourt, N. 1972. *Lettres et préfaces critiques*, edited by R. Zuber. Paris: M. Didier.

Pertusi, A. 1971. "La Persia nelle fonti bizantine del secolo VII." In *La Persia nel Medioevo*. Rome: Accademia Nazionale dei Lincei, pp. 605–628.

Pfister, F. 1958. "Dareios von Alexander getötet." *RhM* 101:97–104.

Pfrommer, M. 1998. *Untersuchungen zur Chronologie und Komposition des Alexandermosaiks auf antiquarischer Grundlage*. Mainz: P. von Zabern.

Piemontese, A. M. 1995. "La figura di Alessandro nelle letterature d'area islamica." In *Alessandro Magno: Storia e mito*, edited by Antonino Di Vita and Carla Alfona, pp. 177–183. Rome: Leonardo Arte.

Pintard, R. 2000. *Le libertinage érudit dans la première moitié du XVIIe siècle*. Geneva: Slatkine. 1st ed. 1943.

Poirier, G. 1996. *L'homosexualité dans l'imaginaire de la Renaissance*. Paris: H. Champion.

Polignac, F. de. 1999. "Alexandre maître des seuils et des passages: De la légende antique au mythe arabe." In *Alexandre le Grand dans les littératures occidentales et proche-orientales*, edited by L. Harf-Lancner, C. Kappler, and F. Suard, pp. 215–225. Paris: Université de Paris X Nanterre.

———, ed. 2000. *Alexandre le Grand, figure de l'incomplétude*. Rome: École française.

Prandi, L. 1996. *Fortuna e realtà dell'opera di Clitarco*. Wiesbaden: F. Steiner.

———. 2005. *Memorie storiche dei Greci in Claudio Eliano*. Rome: L'Erma di Breschneider.

————. 2013. *Diodoro Siculo, Bibliotheca storica, Libro XVII.* Milan: Vita e Pensiero.

Pritchett, W. K. 1985. *The Greek State at War.* Vol. 4. Berkeley: University of California Press.

Pseudo-Callisthenes. 1991. *The Greek Alexander Romance,* translated by R. Stoneman. New York: Penguin.

————. 1992. *Le Roman d'Alexandre: La vie et les hauts faits d'Alexandre de Macédoine,* translated with commentary by G. Bounoure and B. Serret. Paris: Les Belles Lettres.

Raby, J. 1983. "Mehmed the Conqueror's Greek Scriptorium." *Dumbarton Oaks Papers* 37:15–34.

Radet, G. 1925. "Notes sur l'histoire d'Alexandre. IV: Les négociations entre Darius et Alexandre après la bataille d'Issus." *REA* 27:183–208.

————. 1930. "Alexandre en Syrie: Les offres de paix que lui fit Darius." In *Mélanges R. Dussaud,* pp. 235–247. Paris.

————. 1931. *Alexandre le Grand.* Paris: L'artisan du livre.

Rawlinson, G. 1871. *The Fifth Monarchy.* Vol. 3 of *The Five Great Monarchies of the Ancient Eastern World,* pp. 84–539. New York: Dodd, Mead, and Co.

————. 1900. *Ancient History from the Earliest Times to the Fall of the Western Empire.* Rev. ed. New York: Colonial.

Raynaud, C. 1999. "Alexandre dans les bibliothèques bourguignonnes." In *Alexandre le Grand dans les littératures occidentales et proche-orientales,* edited by L. Harf-Lancner, C. Kappler, and F. Suard, pp. 187–207. Paris: Université de Paris X Nanterre.

Reardon, B. P. 1971. *Courants littéraires grecs des IIe et IIIe siècles après J.-C.* Paris: Les Belles Lettres.

Regards sur la Perse antique. 1998. Exh. cat. Le Blanc: Amis de la bibliothèque du Blanc.

Renault, M. 1972. *The Persian Boy.* New York: Pantheon.

Richard, F. 1995. *Raphaël du Mans: Missionnaire en Perse au XVIIe siècle.* 2 vols. Paris: L'Harmattan.

————. 1999. "L'iconographie se rapportant à Eskandar dans le manuscrit djalâyeride du *Adjâbeh-nâmeh* de Tûsi Salmâni de la Bibliothèque nationale de Paris." In *Alexandre le Grand dans les littératures occidentales et proche-orientales,* edited by L. Harf-Lancner, C. Kappler, and F. Suard, pp. 77–88. Paris: Université de Paris X Nanterre.

Rizzo, G. E. 1925–1926. "La 'Battaglia di Alessandro' nell'arte italica e romana." *Bolletino d'Arte* 12, no. 2: 529–545.

Roaf, R. 1983. *Sculptures and Sculptors at Persepolis.* London: British Institute of Persian Studies.

Robert, L. 1980. *À travers l'Asie Mineure: Poètes et prosateurs, monnaies grecques, voyageurs et géographie.* Athens: De Boccard.

Robinson, C. A. 1953. *The History of Alexander the Great.* Vol. 1: *The Extant Historians.* Providence, R.I.: Brown University Press.

Roisman, J. 1983–1984. "Why Arrian Wrote His Anabasis." *RSA* 13–14:253–263.

Rollin, C. 1817. *Oeuvres complètes: Histoire ancienne.* New ed. Paris: Ledoux et Tenré. 1st ed. Paris, 1731–1738.

Rollinger, R., and K. Ruffing. 2012. "'Panik' im Heer: Darios III, die Schlacht von Gaugamela und die Mondfinsternis vom 20. September 331 v. Chr." *Iranica Antiqua* 47:101–113.

Romilly, J. de. 1988. "Le conquérant et la belle captive." *BAGB* 1:3–15.

Romm, J., ed. 2010. *The Landmark Arrian: The Campaigns of Alexander.* New York: Pantheon.

Ronconi, Alessandro. 1940. *Exitus illustrium virorum.* Florence: Le Monnier.

———. 1966. "*Exitus illustrium virorum.*" *RAC* 6, cols. 1258–1268.

Root, M. 1979. *The King and Kingship in Achaemenid Art.* Leiden: Brill.

Rosivach, V. J. 1984. "The Roman's View of the Persians." *CW* 78:1–8.

Ross, D. J. A. 1963. *Alexander Historiatus: A Guide to Medieval Illustrated Alexander Literature.* London: Warburg Institute.

Ross, E. C., trans. 1874. *Annals of Oman to 1728.* With annotations by the translator. Calcutta. Repr. Cambridge: Oleander, 1984.

Rowson, E. K. 1999. "Al-Tha'alibī." *EncIs.* New ed. 10:425–428.

Rumpf, A. 1926. "Zum Alexandermosaik." *MDAI* 77:229–241.

Rutz, W. 1984. "Das Bild des Dareios bei Curtius Rufus." *WJA* NF 10:147–159.

Saadi. 1880. *Le Boustan ou Verger,* translated with an introduction by A. C. Barbier de Meynard. Paris: E. Leroux.

Sabatier, G. 1999. *Versailles ou la figure du roi.* Paris: Albin Michel.

Sachs, A. J., and H. Hunger. 1988. *Astronomical Diaries and Related Texts from Babylonia.* Vol. 1: *Diaries from 652 B.C. to 262 B.C.* Vienna: Österreichische Akademie der Wissenschaften.

Safa, Z. 1987. "Andarz II." *EncIr* 2:16–22.

Said, E. 1979. *Orientalism.* New York: Vintage.

Sainte-Croix, M. de. 1804. *Examen critique des anciens historiens d'Alexandre-le-Grand.* Paris: Imprimerie de Delance et Lesueur.

Saint-Félix, A. J. M. de. 1839. *Histoire des nations iraniques, Mèdes, Perses, Parthes, Bactriens et Persans.* In *Précis de l'histoire des peuples anciens,* 3:275–448. Paris.

Salazar, C. F. 2000. *The Treatments of War Wounds in Graeco-Roman Antiquity.* Leiden: Brill.

Salmon, P. 1961. "Chariton d'Aphrodisias et la révolte égyptienne de 360 av. J.-C." *CdE* 36:365–376.

Sancisi-Weerdenburg, H. 1983. "Exit Atossa: Images of Women in Greek Historiography on Persia." In *Images of Women in Antiquity,* edited by A. Cameron and A. Kuhrt, pp. 21–33. Detroit: Wayne State University Press.

———. 1985. "The Death of Cyrus: Xenophon's *Cyropaedia* as Source for Iranian History." In *Papers in Honour of Professor Mary Boyce,* 2:459–471. Leiden: Brill.

———. 1987a. "The Fifth Oriental Monarchy and Hellenocentrism." *AchHist* 2:117–131.

———. 1987b. "Decadence in the Empire or Decadence in the Sources? From Source to Synthesis: Ctesias." *AchHist* 1:33–46.

———. 1988. "*Persikon dé karta o stratos dôron:* A Typically Persian Gift." *Historia* 37, no. 3: 372–373.

———, ed. 1989a. *Persepolis en Pasargadae in Wissenlend Perspectief.* Leiden: Ex Oriente Lux and Groningen: Universiteitsbibliothek.

———. 1989b. "The Personality of Xerxes, King of Kings." In *Archeologia iranica et orientalis: Miscellanea in honorem L. Vanden Berghe,* 1:549–561. Ghent: Universiteit Gent.

———. 1993. "Alexander and Persepolis." In *Alexander the Great: Reality and Myth,* edited by J. Carlsen et al., pp. 177–188. Rome: L'Erma di Bretschneider.

———. 1999. "The Persian King and History." In *The Limits of Historiography: Genre and Narrative in Ancient Historical Texts*, edited by C. Shuttleworth Kraus, pp. 91–112. Leiden: Brill.

Sancisi-Weerdenburg, H., and J. W. Drijvers, eds. 1990. *AchHist 5 (The Roots of the European Tradition)*.

———, eds. 1991. *AchHist 7 (Through Travellers' Eyes: European Travellers on the Iranian Monuments)*.

Sanders, D. E., ed. 1996. *Nemrud Dağ: The Hierothesion of Antiochus I of Commagne*. Vols. 1 and 2. Winona Lake, Ind.: Eisenbrauns.

Sanjana, D. D., ed. and trans. 1896. *The Pahlavi Kârnâmê-î Artakshîr î Pâpakân*. Bombay: Education Society's Steam Press.

Savinel, P., trans. 1984. *Arrien, "Histoire d'Alexandre."* Paris: Ed. de Minuit.

Scerrato, U. 1995. "Alessandro-Iskandar dhu'l I-Qarnayn' nell'arte dell'Islam." In *Alessandro Magno: Storia e mito*, edited by Antonino Di Vita and Carla Alfona, pp. 185–191. Rome: Leonardo Arte.

Schachermeyr, F. 1949. *Alexander der Grosse: Das Problem seiner Persönlichkeit und seines Wirkens*. Vienna: Akademie der Wissenschaften. 2nd ed., 1973.

Schäfer, D. 2009. "Ptolemaic Friends? The Persians on the Satrap Stela." *Organisation des pouvoirs et contacts culturels dans l'empire achéménide*, edited by P. Briant and M. Chauveau, pp. 143–152. Paris: De Boccard.

Schepens, G. 1971. "Arrian's View of His Task as Alexander-Historian." *Anc Soc* 2:254–268.

Schmalz, B. 1994. "Ein triumphierender Alexander?" *MDAI* 101:121–129.

Schmidt, E. 1953–1970. *Persepolis*. 3 vols. Vol. 1: *Structures, Reliefs, Inscriptions*. Vol. 2: *Contents of the Treasury and Other Discoveries*. Vol. 3: *The Royal Tombs and Other Monuments*. Chicago: University of Chicago Oriental Institute.

Schmidt, W. 1914. *"De ultimis morientum verbis."* Inaugural dissertation, Marburg.

Schmitt, R. 1982. "Achaemenid Throne-Names." *AION* 42, no. 1: 83–95. Repr. in *Selected Onomastic Writings*, pp. 164–175. New York: Bibliotheca Persica, 2000.

Seibert, J. 1972. *Alexander der Grosse*. Darmstadt: Wissenschaftliche Buchgesellschaft.

———. 1987. "Dareios III." In *Alexander der Grosse: Festschrift G. Wirth*, 1:437–456. Amsterdam: Adolf M. Hakkert.

———. 2001. "Der Streit um die Kriegsschuld zwischen Alexander d. Gr. und Dareios III: Ein überflüssiger Disput?" In *Punica-Libyca-Ptolemaica: Festschrift für W. Huss zum 65. Geburtstag*, edited by K. Geus and K. Zimmermann, pp. 121–140. Leuven: Peeters.

Sekunda, N., and J. Warry. 1998. *Alexander the Great: His Armies and Campaigns, 334–323 B.C.* London: Osprey.

Seux, J. M. 1965. "Les titres royaux *šar kiššati* et *šar kibrāt Arba'i*." *Revue d'Assyriologie et d'Archéologie Orientale* 59, no. 1: 1–18.

Shahbazi, A. S. 1980. "From Pārsa to Taxt-e Jāmšīd." *AMI* 13:197–207.

———. 1990. "Early Persians' Interest in History." *BAI* 4:257–265.

———. 1991. *Ferdowsī: A Critical Biography*. Cambridge, Mass.: Harvard University Press; Costa Mesa: Mazda.

———. 2001. "Early Sasanians' Claim to Achaemenid Heritage." *IJAIS* 1, no. 1: 61–73.

Shaked, S. 1987. "Andarz I." *EncIr* 2:11–16.

Shaki, M. 2000. "Gabr." *EncIr* 10, pt. 3: 239–240.

Sherwin-White, S. 1978. "Hand-Tokens and Achaemenid Practice." *JHS* 16:183.

Simpson, W.-K., ed. 2003. *The Literature of Ancient Egypt: An Anthology of Stories, Instructions, Stelae, Autobiographies, and Poetry.* New Haven, Ct.: Yale University Press.

Sisti, F. 1982. "Alessandro e il medico Filippo: Analisi e fortuna di un anedotto." *Bolletino di Classica,* ser. 3, fasc. 3: 139–151.

———. 1994. "Le proposte di pace di Dario ad Alessandro fra anedotto e verità storica." *Acmè* 1–2:209–215.

———, trans. 2001. *Arriano, Anabasi di Alessandro.* Vol. 1. Milan: Mondadori.

Sisti, F., and E. A. Zambrini, trans. 2004. *Arriano, Anabasi di Alessandro.* Vol. 2. Rome: Fondazione Lorenzo Valla.

Six, J. P. 1884. "Le satrape Mazaios." *NC* 3rd ser., 4:97–159.

Smith, S.-S. 2007. *Greek Identity and the Athenian Past in Chariton: The Romance of Empire.* Groningen: Groningen University Library.

Smoes, E. 1995. *Le courage chez les Grecs d'Homère à Aristote.* Brussels: Ed. Ousia.

Southgate, M. S., trans. 1978. *Iskandarnamah: A Persian Medieval Alexander-Romance.* New York: Columbia University Press.

Spawforth, A. 1994. "Symbol of Unity? The Persian-Wars Tradition in the Roman Empire." In *Greek Historiography,* edited by S. Hornblower, pp. 233–247. Oxford: Clarendon.

Spencer, D. 2002. *The Roman Alexander: Reading a Cultural Myth.* Exeter: University of Exeter Press.

———. 2009. "Roman Alexander." In *Alexander the Great: A New History,* edited by W. Heckel and L. A. Tritle, pp. 251–274. Chichester, UK: Wiley-Blackwell.

Stadter, P. A. 1965. *Plutarch's Historical Methods: An Analysis of the "Mulierum virtutes."* Cambridge, Mass.: Harvard University Press.

———. 1980. *Arrian of Nicomedia.* Chapel Hill: University of North Carolina Press.

Stähler, K. 1999. *Das Alexandermosaik: Über Machterringung und Machtverlust.* Frankfurt: Fischer.

Stevenson, R. B. 1997. *Persica: Greek Writing about Persia in the Fourth Century B.C.* Edinburgh: Scottish Academic Press.

Stewart, A. 1993. *Faces of Power: Alexander's Image and Hellenistic Politics.* Berkeley: University of California Press.

———. 1994. "The Alexander Romance: from History to Fiction." In *Greek Fiction: The Greek Novel in Context,* edited by J. R. Morgan and R. Stoneman, pp. 117–129. London: Routledge.

Stoneman, R., trans. 1991. *The Greek Alexander Romance,* by Pseudo-Callisthenes. New York: Penguin.

Stoneman, R., K. Erickson, and I. Netton, eds. 2012. *The Alexander Romance in Persia and the East.* Groningen: Barthuis.

Strauss, B. S., and J. Ober. 1990. "Darius III of Persia: Why He Lost and Made Alexander Great." In *The Anatomy of Error: Ancient Military Disasters and Their Lessons for Modern Strategists,* pp. 103–131. New York: St. Martin's Press.

Stronach, D. 1989. "Early Achaemenid Coinage: Perspectives from the Homeland." *IA* 24 (*Mélanges P. Amiet.*, 2:255–279).

Suard, F. 2001. *Alexandre: La vie, la légende.* Paris: Larousse.

Swoboda, H. 1901. "Darios III." *RE* 4, no. 1, cols. 2205–2211.

Sykes, P. 1951. *A History of Persia.* Vols. 1–3. 3rd. ed. London: Macmillan.

Sylvestre de Sacy, A. I. 1793. *Mémoire sur diverses antiquités de la Perse.* Paris.

Syme, R. 1988. "The Cadusii in History and Fiction." *JHS* 108:137–150.

Tabacco, R. 1992. *Per una nuova edizione critica dell'"Itinerarium Alexandri."* Bologna: Patron Ed.

Taffazzoli, A. 1994. "Dārā(b) I, II." *EncIr* 7, pt. 1: 1–2.

Tarn, W. W. 1948. *Alexander the Great.* Vol. 1: *Narrative.* Vol. 2: *Sources and Studies.* Cambridge: Cambridge University Press.

Tatum, J. 1989. *Xenophon's Imperial Fiction: On "The Education of Cyrus."* Princeton, N.J.: Princeton University Press.

———. 1996. "The Regal Image in Plutarch's Lives." *JHS* 116:135–151.

Tavassoli, G. A. 1966. *La société iranienne et le monde oriental, vus à travers l'oeuvre d'un écrivain anglais James Morier et d'un écrivain français Pierre Loti.* Paris: Adrien-Maisonneuve.

Thirlwall, C. 1845. *A History of Greece.* Vol. 6. London.

Tilia, A. B. 1972. *Studies and Restorations at Persepolis and Other Sites of Fârs.* Vol. 2. Rome: Istituto Italiano per il Medio ed Estremo Oriente.

Tilliette, J. Y. 1999. "*L'Alexandréide* de Gautier de Châtillon: Énéide médiévale ou 'Virgile travesti'?" In *Alexandre le Grand dans les littératures occidentales et proche-orientales,* edited by L. Harf-Lancner, C. Kappler, and F. Suard, pp. 275–287. Paris: Université de Paris X Nanterre.

Todd, R. A. 1964. "W. W. Tarn and the Alexander Ideal." *Historian* 27:48–55.

Tonnet, H. 1979. "Le résumé et l'adaptation de l'*Anabase* d'Arrien dans l'*Itinerarium Alexandri.*" *Revue d'histoire des textes* 9:243–254.

———. 1987. "La 'Vulgate' dans Arrien." In *Zu Alexander der Grosse: Festschrift G. Wirth,* 1:635–656. Amsterdam: Adolf M. Hakkert.

———. 1988. *Recherches sur Arrien, sa personnalité et ses écrits atticistes.* Vols. 1 and 2. Amsterdam: Hakkert.

Toynbee, A. 1969. *Some Problems of Greek History.* London: Oxford University Press.

Tresson, P. 1931. "La stèle de Naples." *BIFAO* 30, no. 1: 368–391.

Tripodi, B. 1986. "La Macedonia, la Peonia, il carro sacro di Serse (Herodot 8, 115–116)." *GIF* 38, no. 2: 243–251.

Vanden Berghe, L. 1987. "Les scènes d'investiture sur les reliefs rupestres de l'Iran ancien: Évolution et signification." In *Studi Tucci,* 3:1511–1531. Rome: Istituto italiano per il Medio ed Estremo Oriente.

———. 1992. *Reliefs rupestres de l'Iran ancien.* Brussels: Musées royaux d'art et d'histoire.

Van der Cruysse, D. 1998. *Chardin le Persan.* Paris: Fayard.

Van der Spek, R. 1993. Book review of Sachs and Hunger 1988. *BiOr* 50, nos. 1–2: 91–102.

———. 1998. "The Chronology of the Wars of Artaxerxes II in the Babylonian Astronomical Diaries." In *Studies in Persian History: Essays in Memory of David M. Lewis,* edited by

M. Brosius and A. Kuhrt, pp. 230–236. Leiden: Nederlands Instituut voor het Nabije Oosten.

———. 2003. "Darius III, Alexander the Great and the Babylonian Scholarship." *AchHist* 12: 289–346.

Van Wees, H. 1988. "Kings in Combat: Battles and Heroes in the *Iliad*." *CQ* 38, no. 1: 1–24.

Vasileva, N. E. 1994. "About the History of Sir Rober Ker Porter's Album with His Sketches of Achaemenid and Sassanian Monuments." *AMI* 21:339–348.

Vaux, W. S. W. 1850. *Nineveh and Persepolis: An Historical Sketch of Ancient Assyria and Persia, with an Account of the Recent Researches in Those Countries*. London: Arthur Hall, Virtue and Co.

Vickens, G. M. 1990. "Būstān." *EncIr* 4:573–574.

Vidal, G. 1981. *Creation: A Novel*. New York: Random House.

Vidal-Naquet, P. 1983. *Le chasseur noir*. Revised and corrected edition. Paris: La Découverte.

———. 1984. "Flavius Arrien entre deux mondes." In *Arrien, Histoire d'Alexandre*, translated by P. Savinel, pp. 309–394. Paris: Éditions de Minuit.

Villanueva-Puig, M.-C. 1989. "Le vase des Perses: Naples 3253 (inv. 81947)." *REA* 91, nos. 3–4: 277–298.

Volney. 1791. *Les ruines ou méditations sur les révolutions des empires*. Rev. ed. Preceded by "Aperçus sur la vie et les ouvrages de Volney *(Extraits des Causeries du Lundi)*." Paris: Garnier Frères.

Von Stahl, A. F. 1924. "Notes on the March of Alexander the Great from Ecbatana to Hyrcania." *GJ* 64:312–329.

Vuitard, C., trans. 1581. *Les faicts et conquestes d'Alexandre le Grand, Roy des Macédoniens, descripts en grec, en huict livres, par Arrian de Nicomédie surnommé le nouveau Xénophon: traduicts nouvellement de grec en françoys*. Paris: Imprimerie de F. Morel.

Wagner, M.-F., and D. Vaillancourt, eds. 2001. *Le roi dans la ville: Anthologie des entrées royales dans les villes françaises de province (1615–1660)*. With introduction and annotations by the editors. Paris: Honoré Champion.

Weber, G. 1883. *Histoire grecque: Les peuples orientaux*, translated from the 9th German ed. Paris: C. Marpon et E. Flammarion.

Whatley, N. 1964. "On the Possibility of Reconstructing Marathon and Other Ancient Battles." *JHS* 84:119–139.

Whitby, M. 1994. "The Persian King at War." In *The Roman and Byzantine Army in the East*, edited by E. Dabrówa, pp. 227–263. Kraków: Drukarnia Uniwersytetu Jagielloskiego.

Whitby, M., and M. Whitby, trans. 1989. *Chronicon Paschale (284–629 A.D.)*. With notes and introduction by the translators. Liverpool: Liverpool University Press.

Wickens, G. M. 1990. "Būstān." *EncIr* 4:573–574.

Widengren, G. 1960. "La légende royale de l'Iran antique." In *Hommages à G. Dumézil*. Brussels: Latomus, pp. 225–237.

———. 1965. *Die Religionen Irans*. Stuttgart: Kolhammer.

———. 1968. *Les religions de l'Iran*, translated by L. Jospin. Paris: Payot.

Wiesehöfer, J. 1994. *Die "dunklen Jahrhunderte" der Persis: Untersuchungen zu Geschichte und Kultur von Fārs in frühhellenistischer Zeit (330–140 v. Chr.)*. Munich: Beck.

————. 1996. *Ancient Persia from 550 B.C. to 650 A.D*, translated by Azizeh Azodi. London: Tauris.

Wilcken, U. 1952. *Alexandre le Grand,* translated by Robert Bouvier. Paris: Payot.

Winnicki, J. K. 1991. "Militäroperationen von Ptolemaios I und Seleukos I. in Syrien in den Jahren 312–311 v. Chr. (II)." *AncSoc* 22:147–201.

————. 1994. "Carrying Off and Bringing Home the Statues of the Gods: On an Aspect of the Religious Policy of the Ptolemies towards the Egyptians." *JJP* 24:149–190.

Wirth, G. 1971. "Dareios und Alexander." *Chiron* 1:133–152.

————. 1993. *Der Brand von Persepolis: Folgerungen zur Geschichte Alexanders des Grossen.* Amsterdam: Hakkert.

Wiseman, D. 1983. *Nebuchadrezzar and Babylon.* Oxford: Oxford University Press.

Wood, M. 1997. *In the Footsteps of Alexander the Great: A Journey from Greece to Asia.* Berkeley: University of California Press.

Worthington, I. 1999. "How 'Great' Was Alexander?" *AHB* 13, no. 2: 39–55.

Yamanaka, Y. 1993. "From Evil Destroyer to Islamic Hero: The Transformation of Alexander the Great's Image in Iran." *Annals of the Japanese Association for Middle-East Studies* 9:55–87.

————. 1999. "Ambiguïté de l'image d'Alexandre chez Firdawsī: Les traces des traditions sassanides dans le *Livre des Rois.*" In *Alexandre le Grand dans les littératures occidentales et proche-orientales,* edited by L. Harf-Lancer, C. Kappler, and F. Suard, pp. 341–353. Paris: Université de Paris X Nanterre.

Yardley, J.-C., and W. Heckel, eds. and trans. 1997. *Justin, Epitome of the Philippic History of Pompeius Trogus, I: Books 11–12: Alexander the Great.* Translated with appendices by J.-C. Yardley and commentary by W. Heckel. Oxford: Clarendon.

Yarshater, E. 1971. "Were the Sasanians Heir to the Achaemenids?" In *La Persia nel Medioevo,* pp. 517–531. Rome: Accademia Nazionale dei Lincei.

————. 1976. "Lists of Achaemenid Kings in Biruni and Bar Hebraeus." In *Biruni Symposium,* edited by Ehsan Yar-Shater, pp. 49–65. New York: Columbia University Iran Center.

Zaehner, R. C. 1955. *Zurvan: A Zoroastrian Dilemma.* Oxford: Clarendon.

Zecchini, G. 1989. *La cultura storica di Ateneo.* Milan: Vita e pensiero.

Zevi, F. 1997. "Il mosaico di Alessandro, Alessandro e i Romani: Qualche appunto." In *Ultra terminum vagari: Scritti in onore di Carl Nylander,* edited by B. Magnusson, S. Renzetti, P. Vian, and S. V. Voicu, pp. 385–397. Rome: Ed. Quasar.

Zotenberg, H. 1958. *Chronique de Tabari.* Vol. 1. Repr. Paris: Maisonneuve.

————, ed. and trans. 1900. *Histoire des rois des Perses par Al-Tha'alibī.* Paris: Imprimerie nationale. Repr. Tehran: M. H. Asadi, 1963.

Zuber, R., ed. 1972. *Lettres et préfaces critiques,* by Nicolas Perrot d'Ablancourt. Paris: Libr. M. Didier.

————. 1995. *Les "belles infidèles" et la formation du goût classique.* 2nd ed. Paris: A. Michel. 1st ed., Paris: A. Colin, 1968.

Notes

Preface to the English-Language Edition

1. I have attempted to give an assessment in *Alexander the Great and His Empire,* trans. A. Kuhrt (Princeton, N.J.: Princeton University Press, 2010), pp. 159–185 ("The History of Alexander Today: A Provisional Assessment and Some Future Directions"). Among the many publications on different versions of the *Alexander Romance,* see, for example, R. Stoneman, K. Erickson, and I. Netton, eds., *The Alexander Romance in Persia and the East* (Groningen: Barthuis, 2012), where, curiously, the figure of Darius/Dārā is never discussed as such.

2. See my "Empire of Darius III in Perspective," in *Alexander the Great: A New History,* ed. W. Heckel and L.-A. Tritle (Oxford, U.K.: Wiley-Blackwell, 2009), pp. 141–170, repr. in *Alexander the Great: A Reader,* ed. I. Worthington, 2nd ed. (London: Routledge, 2012), pp. 152–195. On the transition, see P. Briant and F. Joannès, eds., *La transition entre l'empire achéménide et les royaumes hellénistiques, c. 350–300 av. J.C.* (Paris: Les Belles Lettres, 2006).

3. In French, see the book reviews by L. Martinez-Sève in *Revue des Études Grecques* 116, no. 2 (2003): 722–724; C. Mossé in *Annales HSS* 5 (2005): 1071–1072; X. Tremblay in *Revue des Études Anciennes,* 109, no. 1 (2007): 381–383; M.-F. Baslez in *Topoi* 14, no. 2 (2006): 515–517; and the review article by P. Payen, "L''ombre' des Grecs," *Revue de Philologie* 78, no. 1 (2004): 141–154; in German, H. Koch in *Orientalia* 74, no. 4 (2005): 440–442; in Italian, D. Ambaglio in *Athenaeum* 93, no. 2 (2005): 707–709; and in English, J.-P. Stronk in *Bryn Mawr Classical Review* (March 10, 2004) (unpaginated: http://bmcr.brynmawr.edu/2004/2004 -03-10.html); R. Stoneman in *Classical Review* 56, no. 2 (2006): 415–417; M. Brosius in *Gnomon* 78, no. 5 (2006); 426–430. In the pages that follow, I will refer to these reviews by the name of the author and the year of publication.

4. *Histoire de l'empire perse* (1996), hereafter cited as *HEP,* translated into English as *From Cyrus to Alexander: A History of the Persian Empire (HPE),* chap. 18: "Darius and the Empire Confront Macedonian Aggression."

5. See, in particular, "'Brigandage,' conquête et dissidence en Asie achéménide et hellénistique," *Dialogues d'histoire ancienne* 2 (1976): 163–259 (prepared in 1972–1974),

whose main arguments are revised and extended in my *État et pasteurs au Moyen-Orient ancien* (Paris: Maison des Sciences de L'Homme; Cambridge, U.K.: Cambridge University Press, 1982); and "Sources grecques et histoire achéménide," in *Rois, tributs et paysans* (Paris: Les Belles Lettres, 1982), pp. 491–506. The latter article, very dated, illustrates the state of the documentation as it existed some thirty years ago. Although the questions raised remain valid, I would now write the article in a completely different way.

6. Since *Histoire de l'empire perse* (1996), I have given two successive assessments in *Bulletin d'Histoire Achéménide* (*BHAch* 1, 1997, and *BHAch* 2, 2001). See, more recently, A. Kuhrt's sourcebook *The Persian Empire*, 2 vols. (London: Routledge, 2007), and the proceedings of many Achaemenid colloquia held in different European countries, in Turkey, or in the United States between 2000 and 2012. See also my "Achaemenid Empire," in *The World around the Old Testament,* ed. Bill T. Arnold and Brent A. Strawn (Grand Rapids, Mich.: Baker Academic, forthcoming).

7. Although they provide nothing about the king's personality and very little about his politics, the primary sources do offer interesting information on the state of the empire on the eve of the Macedonian invasion (cf. Briant 2009, which complements Chapter 1 of this book, "A Shadow among His Own"). By contrast, the revolt of Cyrus the Younger is known primarily through Xenophon's *Anabasis* (*HPE*, pp. 615–634), and any study of the Median Wars must be conducted (albeit very imperfectly) by means of Herodotus's *Histories* (*HPE*, pp. 139–161, 525–542).

8. Within the discursive framework chosen by Tremblay, the use of terminology marked by a totally inappropriate Hellenocentrism (i.e., "Greek Asia") is paradoxical to say the least. On the use that the historian of the Achaemenid Empire makes of certain inscriptions written in Greek (and sometimes in two or three languages), see chaps. 2–4 of my forthcoming collection *Kings, Countries, and Peoples (KCP)*.

9. Although all the classical sources must be used with caution, they are not all "adulterated" in the same way or to the same degree. The best proof of that is the reference Tremblay makes to the letter of Parmenion. He is thinking of the partial inventory of Persian riches done in Damascus after the victory of Issus, a list that Parmenion sent to Alexander. Tremblay thus implicitly acknowledges that some of the classical sources provide real Achaemenid information.

10. D. Ambaglio (2005), p. 709, judged that the book does not increase our knowledge of history ("con questo non aumenta la nostra conoscenza della storia"). But that formulation tends to reduce unduly the "knowledge of history" to the knowledge of the events. I note as well that the author says nothing about chapter 12, where, precisely, I attempt to put forward interpretive proposals within a comparatist perspective.

11. See also my "History and Ideology: The Greeks and 'Persian Decadence,'" in *Greeks and Barbarians,* ed. T. Harrison (New York: Routledge, 2002), pp. 193–210; my "Theme of 'Persian Decadence' in Eighteenth-Century European Historiography: Remarks on the Genesis of Myth," in *The World of Achaemenid Persia,* ed. J. Curtis and St John Simpson (London: Tauris, 2010), pp. 3–15; and my *Alexandre des Lumières: Fragments d'histoire européenne* (Paris: Gallimard, 2012), pp. 513–556 ("Alexandre, l'Europe et l'Orient immobile").

12. B. Lincoln uses this sentence ironically in *Journal of Near Eastern Studies* 72, no. 2 (2013): 264.

13. P. McKechnie, "Manipulation of Themes in Quintus Curtius Rufus Book 10," *Historia* 48 (1999): 44–60; A. B. Bosworth, "Plus ça change . . . Ancient Historians and Their Sources," *Classical Antiquity* 22, no. 2 (2003): 167–197.

14. On the method used, see *HPE*, pp. 693–696 ("Another 'Achaemenid' Source: The Alexandrian Historians"); see also "Greco-Hellenistic Sources, Persian and Macedonian Institutions: Continuities, Changes, and 'Bricolages,'" and "The *Katarraktai* of the Tigris: Irrigation-works in Elam and Babylonia from Darius III to Alexander," in *Kings, Countries, and Peoples* (forthcoming), chaps. 22 and 28.

15. See *HPE*, pp. 697–871, and my "Empire of Darius III in Perspective" (2009), where I was able to use more recently published primary sources.

Introduction

1. Jacques Le Goff, *Saint Louis* (Paris: Gallimard, 1996), pp. 13–27.

2. Pierre Briant, *Histoire de l'empire perse* (1996), translated into English as *From Cyrus to Alexander: A History of the Persian Empire* (2002), pp. 817–878, 1042–1050 (hereafter cited as *HPE*); see the review of criticism in Pierre Briant, *BHAch* 2.

3. Pierre Briant, *Alexandre le Grand* (2011), p. 27; 7th updated edition (2011), p. 27; translated into English as *Alexander the Great* (2010), p. 28.

4. Briant, *Alexandre le Grand* (2011), pp. 39–59; Briant, *Alexander the Great* (2010), pp. 42–66.

5. According to Arrian (3.22.5), Darius was about fifty years old when he died.

6. J.-Y. Tilliette, "*L'Alexandréide* de Gautier Châtillon" (1999), p. 283.

7. Alain Corbin, *Le monde retrouvé de Louis-François Pinagot: Sur les traces d'un inconnu (1798–1876)* (Paris: Flammarion, 1998), p. 8.

8. Alain Corbin, "Recherches pinagotiques (suite et fin)," *ARF* 4 (1999), http://ruralia .revues.org/91.

9. The biographical data, established on the basis of the classical sources, are collected in Berve's entry in *Alexanderreich*, 1:116–129, no. 244; see also entries no. 290 (Drypetis), 711 (Sisygambis), 721 (Stateira, wife of Darius), 722 (Stateira, daughter of Darius), and 833 (Ochus).

10. J.-L. Mayaud, J. Rémy, and C. Boujout, "Recherches pinagotiques: À propos du *Monde retrouvé de Louis-François Pinagot*," *ARF* 3 (1998), http://ruralia.revues.org/60.

11. Arrian, *Anabasis*, 3.11.3.

12. On *The Queens of Persia* after Le Brun and its relation to Alexander and Louis XIV, see C. Grell and C. Michel, *L'École des princes ou Alexandre disgracié* (1988), pp. 108–116, 220–223.

13. Chevalier Andrew M. Ramsay, *Les voyages de Cyrus avec un discours sur la mythologie*, critical edition by G. Lamoine (Paris: Champion, 2002), p. 23; on this book, its author, and his milieu, see also J. Tatum, *Imperial Fiction* (1989), pp. 27–29.

14. On Fréret and his chronological and historical studies, see C. Grell, *L'Histoire entre érudition et philosophie* (1993), pp. 84–93.

15. An exception is C. Croisy-Naquet's article "Darius ou l'image du potentat perse dans le roman d'Alexandre de Paris" (1999).

1. A Shadow among His Own

1. Plutarch, *Alexander*, 69.2.

2. Curtius 3.3.13.

3. Diodorus 17.71.7.

4. Reading of manuscript uncertain.

5. Ctesias, *Persica* 19 = *FGrH* F13.

6. In principle, Dārāb refers to the father, Dārā to the son, but usage varies.

7. Arrian 3.22.1; Diodorus 17.73.3; Justin 11.15.5; Plutarch, *Fortune of Alexander*, 2.12 (= *Moralia*, 343B). Within the context of this discussion, it would be absurd to "collate" the Greco-Roman sources with the Persian and Arabo-Persian sources, or to confirm one by means of the other (the latter sources also describe the funeral ceremonies).

8. Curtius 4.10.23: *patrio Persarum more*; cf. Diodorus 17.54.7; Plutarch, *Alexander*, 30.1; Plutarch, *Fortune of Alexander*, 2.6 (= *Moralia*, 338E).

9. Curtius 3.12.13–14: *patrio more*.

10. Appian, *Roman History: The Mithridatic Wars*, 16.113; cf. Plutarch, *Pompeius*, 42.3–5.

11. Xenophon, *Anabasis*, 1.6.11.

12. Plutarch, *Alexander*, 43.7.

13. Ctesias, § 58; Plutarch, *Artaxerxes*, 17.7; see the critical debate in *HPE*, p. 989, on a hypothesis regarding a "possible" tomb of Cyrus the Younger in Fārs.

14. See, in particular, Arrian 6.29.4–11, 30.1–3.

15. Even if one concedes that the representation of the human figures and of the battle scene on the Naples Mosaic implies the existence of indisputable traits realistically observed, the original painting was the work of a Greek artist: it is not an "Achaemenid" document. It is therefore impossible to prove (despite Badian's forthright declaration in "Alexander Mosaic" [1999], p. 85; [2012, p. 413]) that the face attributed to the Great King was inspired by a "very detailed description of Darius" or that "the artist must himself have seen Darius." The hypothesis is not unthinkable, but in the absence of an authentically "Achaemenid" portrait, one must remain extremely cautious about the postulated realism of said portrait.

16. These documents have now been published in Shaul Shaked and Joseph Naveh, *Aramaic Documents from Ancient Bactria* (London: Khalili Family Trust, 2012), with my own preliminary comments in "The Empire of Darius III" (2009a), pp. 148–151.

17. Justin 10.1.2–5: *Codomannus quidam*.

18. The translation here and below is by R.-K. Ritner, in Simpson, ed., *Literature of Ancient Egypt* (2003), pp. 392–397.

19. Herodotus 7.1.5–8 (*HPE*, pp. 525, 960).

20. Diodorus Siculus 16.47.7; see also 15.42–43, 18.33.2–6, 18.34.6–36; 20.73–76 (see explanations and comments in *HPE*, pp. 685–687).

21. Arrian 1.20.3; cf. Babelon, vol. 2, part 2, cols. 65–68 (the hypothesis dates to Lenormant's article in the *Revue Numismatique* [1856], p. 25); see also K. Konuk, "Influence et éléments achéménides" (2000), p. 179 (following Six, *RN* [1890]: 241–246).

22. Diodorus 17.48.5–6; Curtius 4.1.34–35; 5.13.

23. Nearchus, quoted by Strabo 16.3.7.

24. "The expression "regions beyond the river" refers to Syria, which is beyond the Euphrates River; on this Mazday, see Briant, "Empire of Darius III" (2009a), pp. 160–162.

25. Curtius 3.11.10; cf. Arrian 2.11.8, Diodorus 17.34.5 (with different spellings).

26. Arrian 3.1.2.

27. Translated by M. Lichtheim in *Ancient Egyptian Literature*, vol. 3 (1980): 42–43.

28. Translated in A. Kuhrt, *The Persian Empire* (2007), pp. 447–448. Bracketed ellipses indicate lacunae on the original tablet.

29. Plutarch, *Alexander,* 34.1: *basileus tes Asias.*

30. Curtius 5.1.17.

31. On Thorwaldsen's iconographic program, see P. Calmeyer, "Die Orientalen" (1990b), and my brief remarks in *Alexandre des Lumières* (2012), pp. 448–449 and 691n59 (bibliography).

2. Darius Past and Present

1. In the tradition followed by Boccaccio, Darius immediately succeeds Artaxerxes III; his predecessor Arses is completely ignored.

2. Orosius, *Historiae adversus paganos, 3.7.5; 17.7 (inani misericordia); 18.10; 20.4.*

3. Curtius 5.1.1–16; 5.8–13.

4. Diodorus 17.6.1–2 and Justin 10.3.3. The episode is not included by Orosius, which explains Boccaccio's silence.

5. The linguistic status of Darius's different interlocutors raised a few problems for the ancient authors.

6. As I show in *Alexandre des Lumières* (2012), however, Droysen also owes a great deal to the eighteenth-century authors.

7. See Rollin, *Histoire ancienne,* 4:266–268: "Quel jugement on doit porter sur Alexandre."

8. *Jacques Gamelin, 1738–1803: Les collections du Musée des Beaux-Arts de Carcassonne,* vol. 2 (Carcassonne, 1990), drawings, nos. 36, 40, 44–55, 58–61, 63.

9. Arrian, *Anabasis,* 3.22.2–6.

10. Barthold Georg Niebuhr was the son of the traveler Carsten Niebuhr, who visited and described Persepolis.

11. The same expression appears in Gobineau, *Histoire des Perses,* vol. 2 (1869), p. 357: "Alexander completed the Asiatization of Greece"; cf. my "Alexandre et l'hellénisation' de l'Asie" (2005a), and "Grote on Alexander the Great" (forthcoming b).

12. On Gobineau's method, see esp. Malcolm, *History of Persia,* vol. 1 (1829); on Iskandar and Dārā, pp. 55ff.; regarding Alexander and his succession, however, the author gives priority to the Greco-Roman sources, calling them "more authentic" (p. 64).

13. See F. Assimacopoulou, *Gobineau et la Grèce* (1999), pp. 145–146, and chap. 5 ("Histoire des Perses") as a whole, pp. 123–154.

14. See Toynbee, *Some Problems of Greek History* (1969), pp. 420–440: "If Ochus and Philip Had Lived On"; pp. 441–486: "If Alexander the Great Had Lived On."

15. See my *Alexandre des Lumières* (2012), chap. 16, "Alexandre, l'Europe et l'Orient immobile."

16. The author is making a transparent allusion to the practice of endogamy.

17. His conviction is clearly based on a silent but transparent use of a very disputable interpretation already given in Strabo 15.2.2; cf. *HPE*, pp. 165–166.

18. On the question of the cataracts on the Tigris and on the authors quoted here, see my overview in two parts, "Retour sur Alexandre et les katarraktes du Tigre," *Studi ellenistici* 19 and 20 (2006 and 2008), as well as my *Alexander the Great* (2010), pp. 89–93. Let me add that the opinion expressed regarding the economic importance of the destruction of the cataracts predates Droysen by a great deal. See my *Alexandre des Lumières* (2012), esp. pp. 332–348.

19. See P. Briant, "Impérialismes antiques et idéologie coloniale dans la France contemporaine: Alexandre 'modèle colonial,'" *Dialogue d'histoire ancienne* 5 (1979): 282–293, and esp. *Alexandre des Lumières* (2012), pp. 203–233 (with references).

20. Major Reynaud, "Alexandre le Grand colonisateur," *Revue Hebdomadaire*, April 11, 1914.

21. Duruy acknowledges, however, that Droysen's book "is too favorable toward Alexander" (Duruy 1862, p. 302n1).

22. N. Perrot d'Ablancourt, *Lettres et préfaces critiques* (1972), pp. 137–139.

23. N. Loraux, "Thucydide n'est pas un collègue" (1980).

3. "The Last Darius, the One Who Was Defeated by Alexander"

1. Valerius Maximus 9.3, ext.

2. Plutarch, *De auditu*, 18 (= *Moralia*, 48A).

3. Plutarch, *Apophthegmata* (= *Moralia*, 172D–E).

4. Plutarch, *Fortune of Alexander*, 1.9 (= *Moralia*, 330E).

5. Valerius Maximus 1.1., intro.

6. Suetonius, *Augustus*, 89: *Praecepta et exempla publice vel privatim salubria*.

7. Cicero, *In Verrem*, *Actionis secundae*, 3.90.209: *ex vetere memoria, ex monumentis ac litteris, plena dignitatis, plena antiquitatis*.

8. Quintilian, *Institutio oratoria*, 2.4.20; 3.8.66.

9. Cicero, *Tusculanae disputationes*, 1.44.108: *omni historia curiosus*.

10. Strabo 11.11.3.

11. Porphyrus, *De abstinentia*, 4.21.

12. Plutarch, *Fortune of Alexander*, 2.5 (= *Moralia*, 328C).

13. Eusebius of Caesarea, *Praeparatio evangelica*, 1.4.6–8.

14. Seneca, *De ira*, 3.22.1.

15. Ibid., 3.17.1.

16. Herodotus 1.137.

17. Seneca, *De ira*, 3.22.1.

18. See in particular Plutarch, *Artaxerxes*, 1.1.1; 2.1; 4.4–5 etc.; Plutarch, *Apophthegmata*, 173F–174A. Nepos, *De regibus*, 21.1.4; Aelian, *Varia historia*, 1.32–34.

19. Curtius 3.2.17 *(mite ac tractabile ingenio)*; 3.8.5 *(sanctus et mitis)*.

20. Plutarch, *Moralia*, 458E.

21. Cicero, *Tusculanae disputationes*, 5.34.97; Plutarch, *Artaxerxes*, 12.6.

22. Valerius Maximus 9.2., ext. 5.

23. Ibid., 3.2, ext. 2 (chapter on valor, *virtus*); also 7.3, ext. 2.

24. Ibid., 9.2, ext. 7 and 11 (cf. Plutarch, *Artaxerxes*, 16.2–7).

25. Valerius Maximus, 9.1, ext. 3; see Cicero, *Tusculanae disputationes*, 5.7.20.

26. Athenaeus 12.539b.

27. See, for example, ibid., 4.144b–c, 12.529d, 545f; and Xenophon, *Agesilaus*, 9.5.

28. Arrian 1.12.1: *kerukos es ten epeita mnemen*. The discussion allows Arrian to claim to be the first person to produce such a work.

29. Ibid., 6.9.5.

30. Diodorus 17.99.1.

31. Plutarch, *Apophthegmata* (= *Moralia*, 172D–E).

32. Cf. Nepos, *De regibus*, 21.

33. Lucian, *Alexander*, 2.

34. Valerius Maximus, 9.3, ext.

35. On Voltaire's position, see C. Rhis, *Voltaire: Recherches sur les origines du matérialisme historique*, 2nd ed. (Geneva: Slatkine / Paris: Champion, 1977), pp. 150–162, quotation at p. 152; and Briant, *Alexandre des Lumières* (2012), pp. 239–245.

36. See Alpers, "Xerxes und Artaxerxes" (1969).

37. There are 818 adages in the first edition (Paris, 1500), 4,151 in the definitive edition (Basel, 1533): J.-C. Margolin, *Érasme* (1992), p. 103.

38. Zuber, *Lettres et préfaces critiques* (1972), pp. 216–217 and nn. 21–22.

39. I. Gentillet, *Anti-Machieval* (1968), p. 10 (commentary by the editor C. E. Rathé).

40. I also note in passing that, in the works of jurists in the modern period, similarities between certain institutions of ancien régime France and Persian institutions known through Greek sources are explicitly mentioned: see the interesting notations in Cardascia, "La ceinture de Parysatis" (1995), p. 143.

41. Valerius Maximus 1.1, intro.; Quintilian, *Institutio oratoria*, 2.4.10; 3.8.66; Rollin, *Oeuvres* (1817), 1:566. On that pedagogy, see Brutter, *L'Histoire enseignée au Grand Siècle* (1997), pp. 49–50.

42. Strabo 15.3.24.

43. An allusion to the assassination of Stateira (wife of Artaxerxes II) by Parysatis (his mother), well known through Ctesias, then later through Plutarch *(Artaxerxes)*.

44. Plutarch, *Regum et imperatorum apophthegmata, Alexander,* 11 (= *Moralia,* 180B), 30 (= *Moralia,* 181E).

45. Aelian, *Varia historia,* 12.43.

46. Strabo 15.3.24; Plutarch, *Alexander,* 31.7.

47. Valerius Maximus, 3.8.6, 4.3.4, 4.7.2, 5.1.1., 6.4.3 (exploits of Alexander); 3.3, ext. 1 (a young Macedonian page's resistance to suffering).

48. Polyaenus, *Strategemata,* 4.3.1–32.

49. Arrian 3.22.2–6.

50. "Book 11 contains the acts and deeds of Alexander [*res gestae Alexandri Magni*] up to the death of Darius, king of the Persians [*usque ad interitum regis Persarum Darii*]. In a digression, the origins and the kings of Caria are set forth."

51. Book 11 in Justin includes, in order, the accession of Alexander (1), the restoration of order in Greece (2–4), Alexander's departure (5), the victory of the Granicus and its consequences (6), the conquest of Asia Minor as far as Gordion (7), the campaign of Issus (8–11), the campaign of Phoenicia (10) and of Egypt (11), the negotiations with Darius (12), then the victory of Gaugamela (13–14) and the plot against Darius and his death (15).

52. Curtius 5.1.1–2. The Latin text, translated literally, raises a problem: the expression "Thrace under the supreme command of Alexander" obviously means "other parts of Alexander's empire"; cf. Atkinson, *Commentary II*, p. 29.

53. Diodorus 17.62.1–63.5.

54. Ibid., 17.5.3.

55. Pompeius Trogus, *Prologues of the Philippic Histories,* in Justin 10.3.6.

56. Diodorus 17.3.6 (and chaps. 4 and 8–15); parallel discussion in Justin 11.1.5–10 (and subsequent chapters); a detailed report on Alexander's victories in Europe also appears in Arrian 1.1–10 and in Plutarch, *Alexander,* 11–14.

57. Arrian 2.14.5.

58. Diodorus 17.6.2.

59. Ibid., 17.7.1–3.

60. Arrian 2.14.9: *peri tes basileias* ("on the subject of kingship").

61. Diodorus 17.6.3: the battles would be fought "for the supremacy" *(peri tou prōteiou).*

62. See the long account in Diodorus 16.43–51 (flight of Nectanebo: 41.1).

4. Arrian's Darius

1. Arrian 3.22.2; *malthakos,* soft, effeminate, lacking in vigor; *ou phreneres,* lacking sangfroid, lacking in good sense.

2. Plutarch, *Artaxerxes,* 7.3: *phronein kai makhestai.*

3. Nepos, *Pausanias,* 1.2: *in primis omnium Persarum et manu fortis et consilii plenus;* Diodorus 15.10.4: *en tois polemiois andreia dienegkein . . . kata tas sumboulas outōs eustokhein.*

4. Diodorus 16.47.1: *arētē kai eunoia (eunoia,* "benevolence," refers here to loyalty to the king).

5. Ibid., 16.40.4: *dia tēn kakian kai apeirian.*

6. Ibid., 2.33.1: *andreia kai synesis.*

7. The complete texts of these royal inscriptions, with English translations, can be found in Roland G. Kent, *Old Persian: Grammar, Text, Lexicon* (New Haven, Ct.: American Oriental Society, 1953), pp. 138–140 and 150–152.

8. Plutarch, *Apophthegmata* (= *Moralia,* 172C): *phronimōteros.*

9. Diodorus 17.30.2: *andreia/stratēgia/symboulos.*

10. Ibid., 16.48.1 (leaders in the service of Pharaoh Nectanebo): *arētē kai agkhinoia stratēgikē.*

11. Herodotus 3.25:. . . *emmanes . . . kai ou phrēnērēs.*

12. Arrian 1.13.7.

13. Ibid., 1.18.7 *(gnōmē),* 9 *(kairos,* circumstances).

14. Ibid., 7.28.2.

15. See also Curtius 4.16.29, which gives an implicit negative judgment of Alexander, who set off in pursuit of Darius without reflection: *in illo ardore anima vix credi potest, prudentius quam avidius persecutus est.*

16. Plutarch, *Alexander*, 4.1–3.

17. Ibid., 21.6: *kallistos kai megistos*, and 33.5: *kalon andra kai megan*. On the stereotypical aspect of the terminology, see L. Robert, *À travers l'Asie Mineure* (1980), pp. 423–424.

18. In A. Croiset and M. Croiset, *Histoire de la littérature grecque*, vol. 5 (Paris: de Boccard, 1928), p. 364.

19. Strabo 14.1.41.

20. R. J. Bompaire, *Lucien écrivain: Imitation et création* (1958; repr. Paris, 2000), pp. 13–32.

21. Xenophon, *Oeconomicus*, 1.18: *peri tēs basileias . . . makhoumēnos.*

22. Plutarch, *Artaxerxes*, 6.4 (softness: *malakia*; Arrian uses the same term in its adjectival form to characterize Darius).

23. Ibid., 6.1: *polemikos, philetairos; basileōs phronēma kai philotimia ekhontos.*

24. Just like Alexander (Plutarch, *Alexander*, 6; the taming of Bucephalus).

25. Arrian 7.28.2 (Alexander); 2.11.10 (Darius).

26. See R. Drews, *The Greek Accounts of Eastern History* (Cambridge, Mass.: Harvard University Press, 1973), pp. 47–69.

27. M. H. Hansen, "The Battle Exhortation" (1993) and "The Little Grey Horse" (1998), a response to W. K. Pritchett's argument in *Essays in Greek History* (Amsterdam: Gieben, 1994), pp. 27–109.

28. Diodorus 17.6.1–2; Justin 10.3.3–5.

29. Lucian, *Dialogus quomodo solus nudus per Acheronta transvehi potest*, 14.1 (Alexander and Philip); 15.3 (Alexander, Hannibal, Minos, Scipio).

30. Plutarch, *Fortune of Alexander*, 2.6 (= *Moralia*, 338E).

31. Xenophon, *Anabasis*, 1.9.25–26.

32. Plutarch, *Alexander*, 23.10 (also 50.3).

33. Ctesias, *Persica*, 58. On the question of defectors from Cyrus the Younger and Artaxerxes II, see *HPE*, pp. 622–627.

34. Ptolemy's denunciation: Diodorus 18.33.2–4.

35. Aelian, *De natura animalium*, 6.25.

36. Arrian 7.14.5.

37. Plutarch, *Alexander*, 8.2.

38. Dio Chrysostom 4.30.

39. Arrian 1.11.7–8.

40. Ibid., 1.14.5–7 and 15.

41. Diodorus 17.20.3–6.

42. Arrian 1.14.4.

43. Plutarch, *Alexander*, 16.7.

44. Ibid., 32.9.

45. Arrian 1.15.3.

46. Ibid., 2.8.11: *to mēson tēs pases taxeōs epeikhe, kataper nomos tois Persōn basileusi tetakhtai.*

47. Ibid., 3.11.3–4.

48. Xenophon, *Anabasis*, 1.8.21–23: *kai pantēs d'oi tōn barbarōn arkhontes meson ekhontes to autōn hēgontes.*

49. See Callisthenes's harsh criticism in Polybius 12.22.2–3.

50. See esp. Xerxes's example (480): Herodotus 7.56, 212; Diodorus 11.7.1; 18.3 and *passim* (cf. *HPE*, p. 227).

51. An aulic title (*Syggeneis* in Greek: see *HPE*, pp. 309–311).

52. Curtius 4.4.11 (Tyre); 4.6.14 (Gaza).

53. Ibid., 4.6.29.

54. Arrian 6.7.5–6.

55. Diodorus 17.99.1.

56. Ibid., 17.99.3; see Curtius 9.5.3.

57. Arrian 1.14.4.

58. Diodorus 17.21.2.

59. Justin 12.8.1: the term *pariter* clearly establishes a relation to Alexander, whose merits the author has again just celebrated, linking his feats to those of Heracles (12.7).

60. Plutarch, *Alexander*, 60.12. That is, about 6 foot 7 inches tall.

61. Ibid.; Diodorus 17.88.5.

62. Curtius 8.14.14.

63. Lucian, *Quomodo Historia conscribenda sit*, 12.

64. Curtius 8.14.45.

65. Arrian 5.19.1: *hyper basileais hēgōniasmenos.*

66. Diodorus 17.30.7: *eis ton hyper tēs basileias kindunon.*

67. Arrian 5.19.3.

68. Ibid., 2.14.3.

69. Ibid., 2.14.8–9: *peri tes basileias . . . agōnisai.*

5. A Different Darius or the Same One?

1. Curtius 3.2.14–19, 3.8–25, 5.1.3–9.

2. Ibid., 1.3–9, 1.8–11, 13.13–15.

3. Plutarch, *Alexander*, 1.2–3.

4. Curtius 5.11.4: *haud rudis Graecae linguae erat.*

5. Justin 9.15.6: "One of the Persian captives being brought forward, the dying prince, knowing from his voice [*vox*] that he was his countryman [*civis*], said that 'he had at least this comfort in his present sufferings, that he should speak to one who could understand him.'" The expressions used are intentionally ambiguous; the reader does not know in what language the king and the soldier will converse. What is clearly suggested at least is that it is not Greek.

6. Curtius 3.12.6–7: *Mithrenem, qui Sardis tradiderat . . . proditor;* cf. the narrative and the report on the terms of the agreement of Sardis in Arrian, *Anabasis*, 1.17.3–4, along with my study "Alexander at Sardis" (*KCP*, chap. 5), and *HPE*, pp. 842–852, on other cases of Persians going over to the Macedonian side.

7. Curtius 5.1.44: *Mazeam transfugam . . . Bagophanem, qui arcem tradiderat . . . Mithreni Sardium proditori.*

8. Ibid., 3.7.11–15 (Sisines):. . . *inter socios fideles;* 4.10.16 (Greek soldiers):. . . *benevolentia ac fides.*

9. Arrian 1.25.3: *pistos.*

10. Curtius 3.6.17:. . . *ingenitam* . . . *erga suos reges suos venerationem.* On the many ancient narratives, see F. Sisti, "Alessandro e il medico Filippo" (1982); also Atkinson, *Commentary I* (1980), pp. 163–169, Heckel's commentary in J.-C. Yardley and W. Heckel, *Justin, Epitome of the Philippic History of Pompeius Trogus, I* (1997), pp. 128–131, and Baynham, *Alexander the Great* (1998), pp. 141–144.

11. Curtius 5.8.3: *fidelitate erga regem ad ultimum invicta.*

12. Ibid., 5.9.1; 6.5.1–2.

13. Ibid., 5.9.16: *nefas esse deseri regem.*

14. Ibid., 5.10.2.

15. Ibid., 4.6.5–6.

16. Ibid., 3.13.17: "respect for the king's station": *memoria majestatis suae.*

17. Ibid., 4.6.7 *(eximiae in regem suum fidei),* and 4.6.29 *(iam tum peregrinos ritus nova subeunte fortuna).*

18. Ibid., 4.6.4: *perfidia* . . . *proditio.*

19. Ibid., 5.11.6 and 5.12.5: *proditio.*

20. Ibid., 3.6.11: *crimen parricidi* (Philip); 6.7.7 (Dymnus); 5.9.9; 12.4 (Bessus against Darius).

21. Ibid., 5.8.12.

22. Ibid., 5.8.9: *proditores et transfugae.*

23. Ibid., 5.8.3: *fidelitate erga regem ad ultimum invicta;* 10.7:. . . *Graecorum quoque fides;* 11.6: *fides invicta;* 11.11: *Graecorum militum fides timebautur;* 5.11.12: *omnia pro fide experiri paratus;* 5.11.2.

24. Ibid., 3.3.1: *in quis plurimum habebat spei;* 8.1: *praecipua spes et propemodum unica.*

25. See the detailed critical analysis and alternative proposals in *HPE,* pp. 783–800.

26. Diodorus 17.29.7.

27. Cf. also ibid., 17.73.1–4.

28. Ibid., 17.5.3–6.

29. Arrian 2.14.5 and many other texts (Curtius 6.3.12; Strabo 15.3.17, etc.), quoted and analyzed in *HPE,* pp. 769–780.

30. Diodorus 17.5.6.

31. *Ut post mortem Ochi regnari Arses, deinde Darius, qui cum Alexandro, Macedonum rege, bello conflixit.*

32. Justin 10.3: *In eo adversus provocatorem hostium Codomannus quidam cum omnium favore processit.*

33. Valerius Maximus 3.2.24: *fuisse cum quibus inspectante utroque exercitu ex provocatione dimicasset;* see also Aulus Gellius 2.11.2–3.

34. Arrian 1.15.4.

35. Curtius 3.11.5: *quasi singuli inter se dimicarent.*

36. Diodorus 17.20; cf. Arrian 1.15.6–8.

37. Diodorus 17.21.4 *(tēs andragathias to prōteion apēnēgkato);* cf. ibid., 6.1 *(to prōteion tēs andreias apēnēgkato).*

38. Ibid., 17.83.5–6: *protokalēsato . . . monomakhēsai.*

39. Curtius 7.4.35 (cf. §33: *provocavit ad pugnam*).

40. Ibid., 7.4.40.

41. See also ibid., 3.111.7: Alexander at Issus sought for himself "the rich trophy of killing the king" *(opimum decus caeso rege expetens).* That also explains the desire of the Macedonian soldiers at Gaugamela: "Each soldier sought for himself the glory of killing the enemy king" (4.15.25). Famous instances of this practice, by Manlius Torquatus, Valerius Corvinus, and Scipio Aemilianus, are also cited in Valerius Maximus (2.3.6), who explains: "But since they were placed under the auspices of another, they did not present the spoils to Jupiter Feretrius to consecrate them to him."

42. Plutarch, *Marcellus,* 7.1–2.

43. Aulus Gellius 9.11. This barely qualifies as a single combat, given that Valerius is assisted by a raven (hence the name "Corvinus"), a "sign of divine power," which attacks the Gallic leader and blinds him.

44. Ibid., 9.13.

45. For the battle of David and Goliath, see 1 Samuel 17:4–51.

46. Plutarch, *Pyrrhus,* 24.3–6.

47. Strabo 13.2.3.

48. Procopius, *De bellis,* 1.13.29–39.

49. Ferdowsī, *Book of the Kings,* bk. 8, lines 180–181, 205–210.

50. Ibid., bk. 12, lines 1050–1052.

51. See Plutarch, *Artaxerxes,* 24.5–9: *philia kai symmakhia.*

52. Arrian 3.19.4: *symmakhoi;* cf. *HPE,* pp. 765–768.

53. M. Mauss, "Essai sur le don," repr. *Sociologie et anthropologie* (Paris: PUF, 1950), pp. 150–152.

54. Nepos, *Datames,* 1.1–2.

55. Plutarch, *Artaxerxes,* 24.9.

56. Herodotus 3.30. On the warrior function among the Persian kings, see *HPE,* pp. 225–230.

57. Ctesias, quoted in Diodorus 2.33.4.

58. Strabo 11.13.11.

59. Nepos, *De regibus,* 1.2: *quorum uterque privatus virtute regnum est adeptus.*

60. Aelian, *Varia historia,* 12.43.

61. Athenaeus 14.633d–e.

62. Xenophon, *Cyropaedia,* 1.2.1; Strabo 15.3.18 (*HPE,* pp. 329–330).

63. Athenaeus 13.575f.

64. Curtius 3.9.4: *Ipsum regem in eodem cornu dimicaturum.*

65. Ibid., 4.14.8; also Diodorus 17.59.2: "Darieus . . . commanded his own left."

66. Plutarch, *Alexander,* 21.6; 33.5.

67. Justin 10.3.6.

68. Curtius 3.11.7 (Issus).

69. Diodorus 17.60.2 (Gaugamela).

70. Curtius 4.15.28–29; Diodorus 17.60.2.

71. Curtius 4.15.30.

72. Arrian 1.16.3.

73. Orosius 3.17.3: "But since Darius saw that his men were defeated, though he was ready to die on the battlefield, he was forced to flee on his own men's insistence [*persuasu suorum fugere compulsus est*]"; Justin 11.14.3 *(sed a proximis fugere compulsus est).*

74. Curtius 4.16.9; the anecdote is also reported in Justin 11.14.4.

75. Procopius, *De bellis,* 2.12.3–5.

76. Diodorus 17.7.1–3; Justin 11.6.8–10 (on this passage, see *HPE,* pp. 821–823).

77. Diodorus 17.1.1; Curtius 3.3.6 and 4.9.3; and Diodorus 17.39 (Darius after Issus): "He was not crushed in spirit in spite of the tremendous setback he had received" (cf. *HPE,* pp. 823–832).

78. Diodorus 17.48.5–6; Curtius 4.1.34–35; 5.13.

79. Curtius 3.9.4 and 4.14.8; Diodorus 17.59.2; Arrian 2.11.8; Xenophon, *Anabasis,* 1.8.21.

80. Plutarch, *Fortune of Alexander,* 2.11 (= *Moralia,* 342B); not mentioned in *Alexander,* 5.1–3.

81. *FGrH* 90, F66.34: *en mesois.*

82. Lucian, *Navigium,* 31: *kata mēson, ōs nomos basileusi tōn Persōn.*

83. Similarly, Diodorus, borrowing from Xenophon the schema of Charidemus's condemnation, adds the expression "according to the custom of the Persians": Diodorus 17.30.4; Xenophon, *Anabasis,* 1.6.10.

84. See Polybius 12.18.9–10 and 22.2–3.

85. Agathias 113B–125B; see A. Cameron's edition in *Dumbarton Oaks Papers* 23 (1969): 74–89.

86. See "Persian customs" cited in Procopius, *De bellis,* 1.3.17; 1.5.1; 1.5.2; 1.5.8–9, 40; 1.6.13; 1.11.3–4; 1.11.34, 37; 1.17.28; 1.18.52–54; 2.28.25–26; and my remarks in "Perses et Iraniens après la chute de l'empire achéménide: Histoire et historiographie" (2002b).

87. See esp. Arrian 2.14.5, the "quotation" from a letter Alexander sent to Darius: "You unjustly seized the throne contrary to the law of the Persians [*oudē kata ton Persōn nomon*]"; see other texts and commentaries in *HPE,* pp. 770–794, and in "Guerre et succession dynastique chez les Achéménides: Entre 'coutume perse' et violence armée" (2002c).

88. Curtius 3.11.11.

89. Diodorus 17.1.3–5.

90. Plutarch, *Fortune of Alexander,* 2.13 (= *Moralia,* 343E).

91. Ibid., 2.10 (= *Moralia,* 341B), with a quotation from Homer, *Iliad,* 11.265, 541.

92. Plutarch, *Fortune of Alexander,* 1.9 (= *Moralia,* 331C).

93. Plutarch, *Coriolanus,* 14.2: *symbola tes andreias; Moralia,* 276D.

94. Valerius Maximus 3.2.24; see also Aulus Gellius 2.11.2.

95. Curtius 4.16.31: *indicia virtutis.*

96. Ibid., 4.15.31: *adversa . . . terga.*

97. Ibid., 3.11.9: *adverso corpore vulneribus acceptis.*

98. Ibid., 4.6.24: *obducta cicatrice inter primores;* and the same theme in 7.9.11.

99. Ibid., 4.14.6: *cicatrices, totidem corporis decora.*

100. Plutarch, *Fortune of Alexander,* 1.9 (= *Moralia,* 331C): *eikonas . . . aretēs.* Cf. the speech in which Marcus Servilius proudly evokes his wounds: "Then, it is said, he bared his chest and told in what war he had received each of his wounds" (Livy 45.39.13).

101. Plutarch, *Fortune of Alexander,* 1.2 (=*Moralia,* 326E, 237A).

102. Ibid., 2.8 (=*Moralia,* 340B); Plutarch was obviously confused, giving Darius the name of his predecessor, Arses; the title *astandes* (head of the royal mail office) shows that Plutarch is actually thinking of Darius and not Arses (*HPE,* pp. 771–772).

103. Plutarch, *Alexander,* 5.3; Plutarch, *Fortune of Alexander,* 2.11 (=*Moralia,* 342C).

104. Plutarch, *Fortune of Alexander,* 1. 41.8–10.

105. This is also a recurrent theme in the Persian and Arabo-Persian authors.

106. Texts quoted and translated in Stewart, *Faces of Power* (1993), pp. 376–378.

107. Curtius 3.11.11; *ad hoc.*

108. Ibid., 4.15.24; 28; on the courage of the Persian troops surrounding the king, see also Diodorus 17.59.1–4.

109. On this theme, see *HPE,* pp. 210–216, 227–230.

110. See Calmeyer, "Historischen Szenen" (1992). On this documentation, see A. von Kienlin and L. Summerer, *Tatarlı: The Return of Colours* (Istanbul: T. C. Kültür ve Turizm Bakanlığı, 2010).

111. *Eminens:* Curtius 3.3.15–16; 3.11.7; 4.13.26; 4.15.30; 5.10.12.

6. Darius between Greece and Rome

1. Plutarch, *Fortune of Alexander,* 1.8 (=*Moralia,* 330B–C).

2. Velleius Paterculus, *History of Rome,* 2.41.1–2: *in vitam, non in voluptatem uteretur.*

3. Lucan, *Pharsalia,* 9.46–53 (*sarissa* = Macedonian weapon; *pilum* = Roman weapon).

4. Lucian, *Quomodo Historia conscribenda sit,* 2.

5. Arrian 3.11.4.

6. Ibid., 3.22.1.

7. Polybius 10.28.3.

8. Justin 12.3.2–12; 4.1; also Plutarch, *Alexander,* 45.1.

9. Justin 11.15.2.

10. Curtius 4.12.11; 5.7.9; 5.8.1; 6.2.11–15.

11. Dio Cassius, *Roman History,* 40.14.2–3.

12. Ammianus Marcellinus 23.6.2; Justin 41.4.

13. Pliny 31.21.35; on this custom, see *KCP,* chap. 11.

14. Strabo 16.1.16.

15. Athenaeus 12.513f.

16. Curtius 5.8.1.

17. Dio Chrysostom, *Orationes,* 6.17.

18. Lucian, *Navigium,* 28–29.

19. Lucian, *De domo,* § 5 (*HPE,* pp. 236–237).

20. Livy 34.6.7–9: *luxuriae enim peregrinae origo ab exercitu Asiatico invecta in urbem est.*

21. Ibid., 9.17: *iam in Persarum mores adduxisset; superbia mutatio vestis.*

22. Diodorus 17.77.4–7: *persikē tryphē . . . polyteleia tōn Asianōn basilēōn.*

23. Justin 12.3.8–12: *degenerasse;* also 12.4.2: "to adopt the manners of the Persians, whom, from the effect of such manners, he had overcome."

24. Ibid., 12.4.1.

25. Ibid., 9.8.4, 20–21.

26. Curtius 4.6.29: *peregrinos ritu* (punishment inflicted on Batis).

27. Diodorus 17.64.4 and 17.112.6: *pros anēsin kai tryphēn*.

28. Curtius 5.1.4–6.

29. Ibid., 5.2.8.

30. Ibid., 5.1.36–38.

31. Valerius Maximus 9.1.3 (chapter titled "De luxuria et libidine").

32. Ibid., 2.6.1.

33. See Curtius 4.8.4; 5.2.2; 6.2.15.

34. Livy 23.18.12.

35. Valerius Maximus 9.1, ext. 1.

36. Curtius 6.2.1–2.

37. Ibid., 6.6.1–2.

38. Same expression in Diodorus 17.77.6.

39. Curtius 6.6.4, 6, 8, 10.

40. Ibid., 10.1.42.

41. Arrian 3.2.9.

42. Plutarch, *Fortune of Alexander,* 1.8 (= *Moralia,* 330IA–D); also *Alexander,* 47.5–8.

43. Arrian 3.22.5.

44. Velleius Paterculus, *History of Rome* 1.6.1–2 *(summa imperii; imperium Asiaticum);* 1.6.6 *(Assyrii principes omnium gentium rerem potiti sunt).*

45. Zosimus, *Historia nova,* 1.2.5.

46. Orosius 1.4; 1.19; 3.6–11; 3.7.5.

47. Arrian, *Anabasis,* 2.6.7.

48. Arrian, *Indica,* 1.3.

49. Curtius 4.14.24.

50. Lucian, *Charon sive Contemplantes,* 9.

51. Plutarch, *Pompeius,* 34.7.

52. Plutarch, *Fortune of Alexander,* 1 and 2.

53. Plutarch, *De fortuna Romanorum,* 2 (= *Moralia,* 317B–C).

54. Plutarch, *Fortune of Alexander,* 1.5 (= *Moralia,* 328E): *eudaimonein.*

55. Eusebius, *Praeparatio evangelica,* 1.4.6–8. The literary topos of cultural norms disseminated by the dominant power at the expense of the practices and customs of the subjugated peoples persisted with little or no variation for more than seven centuries.

56. See also Polybius 10.28.3: in reporting the existence of privileges in Parthia granted to the local peasants, Polybius specifies that they had been promulgated "during the time when the Persians ruled Asia" (cf. my analysis in *KCP,* chap. 12).

57. Plutarch, *De fortuna Romanorum,* 4 (= *Moralia,* 317F–318A).

58. Claudian, *De consolatu Stilichonis,* 3.159–167.

59. Dionysius of Halicarnassus, *Roman Antiquities,* 1.2.1.

60. Ammianus Marcellinus 23.6.7.

61. Ibid., 23.6.1.

62. Herodotus 1.201–214.

63. Strabo 15.3.24.

64. Diogenes Laertius, *Vitae philosophorum*, 5.94; *Persika idiōmata*.

65. Tacitus, *Annales*, 3.61–63.

66. Dio Cassius 80.4.1; Herodian 6.2.2.

67. Appian, *Roman History: The Mithridatic Wars*, 116.

68. Ibid., 108, 117.

69. Diodorus 40.4; Appian, *The Mithridatic Wars*, 117.

70. Dio Cassius, *Roman History*, 49.17.5.

71. Valerius Maximus 3.3., ext. 3e; 8.7, ext. 15; 1.6, ext. 1; 2.10, ext. 1; 3.2, ext. 3.

72. Ibid., 5.3, ext. 3g; cf. 6.5, ext. 2; 1.6, ext. 1; 3.2, ext. 2; 9.13, ext. 1.

73. Ibid., 1.6, ext. 1.

74. Ibid.

75. Ibid., 9.5, ext. 2: *cujus in nomine superbia et impotentia habitat*.

76. Ibid., 9.1, ext. 3.

77. Claudian, *In Rufinum*, 2.105–107; 120–123.

78. During the Battle of Gaugamela, the Achaemenid contingents were arrayed "by nation" (Diodorus 17.58.1), which accounts for the reflection attributed to Darius: "He was most concerned lest some confusion should arise in the battle from the numerous peoples assembled who differed in speech" (17.53.4).

79. Seneca, *De ira*, 3.13, 3.20.

80. Ibid., 3.16.3.

81. Ibid., 3.16.4.

82. Ibid., 3.21.1–4. The anecdote is recounted much more fully in Herodotus 1.189–190.

83. Ammianus Marcellinus 23.6.36 (with inaccuracies regarding the history of the magi's usurpation).

84. Arrian 4.11.6, 9.

85. Strabo 15.3.4 and 3.8; Curtius 3.3.1 (reference to the war against Croesus, with a brief confusion with Cyrus the Younger; 4.14.24).

86. Curtius 6.6.11; 7.3.1; Arrian 4.3.1; Strabo 11.11.4.

87. In reality, founded by Darius; same confusion in Aelian, *De natura animalium*, 1.59.

88. Diodorus 17.71.1.

89. See the contradictory information about his tomb collected in Strabo 15.3.7–8; see also Curtius 5.6.10; Arrian 6.29–30.

90. Curtius 10.1.32.

91. Plutarch, *Fortune of Alexander*, 2 (= *Moralia*, 343A).

92. See Plutarch, *Artaxerxes*, 3.1–2 (cf. *HPE*, pp. 523, 969).

93. On the line of Cyrus's successors, see Strabo 15.3.24.

94. Arrian 6.29.9.

95. Plutarch, *Alexander*, 69.4. The tradition appears again (with variants) in Arrian (6.29.8) and Strabo (15.3.7). But is it necessary to point out that there was never any inscription on the tomb, in Persian or in Greek?

96. Strabo 11.11.4; Arrian, *Anabasis*, 4.3.1.

97. Arrian, *Indica*, 9.10; *Anabasis*, 6.24.2–3 (the author claims that Cyrus brought back only seven soldiers from that disastrous expedition).

98. Being "descended from one of the seven Persians," that is, from one of the seven conspirators who, under Darius I's leadership, put an end to the usurpation of the magus Smerdis in 522 B.C.E., was a sign of distinction still embraced within the Persian nobility in Darius III's time (*HPE*, pp. 97–114).

99. Curtius 4.12.8; 10.1.22.

100. Ibid., 4.14.24.

101. Ibid., 6.3.12. Here the reference is to Bagoas the Elder, not to the man supposed to have been Darius's and then Alexander's lover.

102. Ibid., 3.10.8.

103. Ibid., 4.1.10–11.

104. Ibid., 5.6.1.

105. Ibid., 10.6.14 (Ptolemy's discourse in Babylon after Alexander's death).

106. Ibid., 7.5.28.

107. Diodorus 17.72.6.

108. Arrian 3.16.7; 7.19.2.

109. Diodorus 17.72.6.

110. Curtius 5.7.11; Plutarch (*Fortune of Alexander*, 1.7 [= *Moralia*, 429D], and *Alexander*, 37.7) speaks of the "throne of Darius," apparently thinking of Darius III.

111. Plutarch, *Alexander*, 37.5: *megalosophrosynē, aretē*.

112. Arrian 4.11.6. The terrible reputation of Cambyses in the classical sources (beginning with Herodotus) can be attributed to the accusation that he had destroyed the Egyptian temples and had ridiculed the rites and beliefs of the inhabitants: see *HPE*, pp. 55–61.

113. Arrian 3.16.4.

114. Ibid., 7.17.3.

115. Ibid., 7.14.5.

116. Plutarch, *Fortune of Alexander*, 1.7.

117. In his long narrative on Darius's accession, Herodotus (3.84–87) recounts that Darius's groom, in a charming ruse, succeeded in making his master's horse whinny first, thus deciding which of the conspirators would be recognized as king. The episode is repeated often by the ancient authors (for example, Valerius Maximus 7.8.2 and Ammianus Marcellinus 23.6.36, who thought that "seven descendants of that race of magi usurped the Persian crown after Cambyses' death").

118. The decisive interference of Atossa, one of Darius's wives and the mother of Xerxes, is also borrowed from Herodotus (7.2–4): see the discussion in *HPE*, pp. 518–522 and 958–960.

119. Plutarch, *Fortune of Alexander*, 2.8 (= *Moralia*, 340B).

120. "Ochus" was the name borne by both Darius II and Artaxerxes III before their accession to the throne. Plutarch, *Fortune of Alexander*, 1.2 (= *Moralia*, 327A), also 2.3 (= *Moralia*, 336E).

121. Ibid., 2.9 (= *Moralia*, 341A).

122. Aelian, *Varia historia*, 12.43.

123. Valerius Maximus 3.4.

124. Herodotus 3.139–140 and 7.3 *(idiōtes)*; cf. Valerius Maximus 5.2.1 *(privatus)*.

125. Nepos, *De regibus*, 21.1.2.

126. See Plato, *Leges*, 3.693–696: "Darius was not the son of a king; there was no soft-ness in the upbringing he received," unlike Cambyses and Xerxes, who were reared by women and eunuchs, far away from men.

127. Plutarch, *Fortune of Alexander*, 1.2 (=*Moralia*, 326E).

128. Ibid., 2.3 (=*Moralia*, 336C).

129. It is cited by Strabo (15.3.8) but, rather oddly, in a discussion of Cyrus's tomb. The forgery was probably inspired by Herodotus's famous declaration (1.136), repeated almost word for word by Strabo (15.3.18), that Persian children "are taught three things only: to ride, to use the bow, and to speak the truth" (cf. *HPE*, pp. 327–330). The classical texts them-selves echo the Mirrors of Princes in a muted and Hellenized form, particularly the in-scription that appears on Darius's tomb in Naqsh-e Rustam, where, however, hunting is not mentioned (*HPE*, pp. 210–216).

130. Justin 10.3.5.

131. Without omitting to recall that heroic deed (in a peculiar form: he speaks of a "dynasty of seven magi kings" that Darius supposedly overthrew), Ammianus Marcelli-nus adds a digression on Hystaspes, father of Darius, who was considered a religious re-former in the tradition of Zoroaster (23.6).

132. Strabo 15.3.24.

133. In reality, Babylonia and Susiana are also discussed in bk. 15.

134. That is, in accordance with a practice well known to the Greek authors, the rev-enues taken from the village were theoretically to be used for that purpose.

135. Strabo 16.1.3. See also the description of the same region in Ammianus Marcel-linus (23.6.22): "Ecbatana, Arbela, and Gaugamela, where Alexander made Darius eat dust in a lightning-fast war, following battles with various outcomes"; in Dio Cassius, *Roman History*, 68.26: "Arbela and Gaugamela, near which places Alexander conquered Darius."

7. Upper King and Lower King

1. Diodorus 17.7.2; 18.2.

2. Justin 11.6.8 (cf. Arrian 3.10.2).

3. In Greek: *anō/katō* (up/down); *anabainein/katabainein* (ascend/descend); *anōtērō/anōtatō* (higher, highest); *ai anō satrapeiai* (High Satrapies).

4. Arrian, *Anabasis*, 1.12.4.

5. Quotations: Nepos, *Agesilaus*, 4.1–2; Xenophon, *Hellenica*, 4.1.41.

6. Diodorus 17.54.6, where luxury *(tryphē)*, associated with the easy life (Darius), stands opposed to glory *(doxē)*, acquired in battle (Alexander).

7. Plutarch, *Fortune of Alexander*, 1.10 (=*Moralia*, 332A), where Darius's luxury *(tryphē)*, linked to structural inactivity *(apraktos/apraxia)*, stands opposed to the multifarious achievements of a conqueror-civilizer (Alexander).

8. Justin 11.5.10 and Diodorus 17.7.2.

9. Plutarch, *Alexander,* 17.3 *(anebainō).* The author thus accounts for Alexander's decision to first seize the Mediterranean countries: Arrian 1.20.1.

10. Curtius renders this as "Alexander had now determined to attack Darius wherever he was" (3.1.19).

11. Plutarch, *Alexander,* 18.5–6.

12. Diodorus 17.30; Curtius 3.2.10–19.

13. See also Arrian 2.1.3, who uses more measured words.

14. Ibid., 2.6.3–4; cf. also Curtius 3.8.1–9 and Plutarch, *Alexander,* 20.1–4.

15. Curtius 3.8.1–11.

16. Ibid., 3.2.1; Diodorus 17.30.6.

17. Arrian 1.16.3.

18. Ibid., 1.20.3; 2.1.1 ("commander of the whole fleet and of the entire sea-coast"); Diodorus 17.23.5–6.

19. Curtius 5.1.39; 5.8.517; 9.1–8.

20. Ibid., 5.11.

21. Herodotus 3.80–84.

22. Ibid., 7.8–13; cf. *HPE,* pp. 518–522.

23. Ibid., 7.8–18.

24. Ibid., 9.41–42; *nomos tōn Perseōn.*

25. See Diodorus 17.18.2–4; Arrian 1.12.9–10.

26. See Diodorus 17.29.4.

27. Curtius 3.4.3.

28. Diodorus 17.18.3: cf. *HPE,* pp. 822, 1043.

29. Justin 11.6.8: *occulta consilia victoriae furtivae convenire;* Arrian 3.10: *aiskhrōs klepsai tēn nikēn, alla phanerōs kai aneu sophismatos . . . nikēsai.*

30. Curtius 3.8.11: *haec magnificentius iactata quam uerius.*

31. Curtius commonly uses the term *purpurati,* "those who wear purple," to designate court nobles.

32. Herodotus 7.59–100; Xerxes-Demaratus discussion, 7.101–104; reference to Xerxes in Curtius 3.2.2: "[He] began a numerical review using Xerxes' method" (cf. Herodotus 7.60).

33. Herodotus 7.45 *(makarizō; makarios* means "lucky"); Curtius 3.2.10 *(laetus:* lucky).

34. Herodotus 5.24: *syssitos kai symboulos.*

35. Ibid., 7.2–4: Plutarch, *Artaxerxes,* 2.4–5.

36. Diodorus 17.30.2: *symboulos.*

37. Arrian 1.12.10.

38. Diodorus 17.30.4.

39. Curtius 3.8.3.

40. Diodorus 15.43.2.

41. Plutarch, *Themistocles,* 29.5–6.

42. Daniel 6:3–4 (King James Version; the story of the lion's den follows).

43. Curtius 3.2.17–18.

44. Diodorus 17.30.4: *kata tōn Perseōn nomon.*

45. Xenophon, *Anabasis,* 1.6.10.

46. Curtius 3.2.19.

47. Xenophon, *Anabasis,* 1.6.11.

48. Curtius 3.8.14–15; see also Arrian 2.7.1.

49. Curtius 5.10.14: *natura simplex et mitis;* 3.8.5: *sanctus et mitis.*

50. Ibid., 3.8.5.

51. Ibid., 3.2.17: *mite ac tractabile ingenium.*

52. Ibid., 3.8.6.

53. Diodorus 17.30.4.

54. Curtius 3.8.3.

55. Ibid., 3.2.10: *solita vanitate.*

56. See, for example, Plutarch, *Alexander,* 23.7; *Moralia,* 65C–D; Arrian 4.8.3, 8.6, 9.9; Lucian, *Quomodo Historia conscribenda sit,* 12.

57. Arrian 2.6.4 (Darius prior to Issus); 4.8.3 (Alexander and the Kleitos affair: "Such men have always destroyed and will never cease to ruin the interests of those who happen to be reigning.")

58. Athenaeus, *Deipnosophists,* 6.234c–262a.

59. Plutarch, *Moralia,* 54–56.

60. Seneca, *De beneficiis,* 6.30–31.

61. Diodorus 17.30.6.

62. Ibid., 17.30.5.

63. See Herodotus 5.24.

64. Curtius 3.8.6.

65. Diodorus 16.40.4–6: *tous hyper tēs basileias agōnas.*

66. Ibid., 15.29.2.

67. See, in particular, ibid., 15.41.2,5; 16.46,7; 49.7.

68. See *HPE,* pp. 595–596.

69. Diodorus 17.23.5.

70. Plutarch, *Agesilaus,* 15.1.

71. Diodorus 17.30.1.

72. See Diodorus's rendering, 17.29; 31.3.

73. Arrian 2.14.6.

74. Plutarch, *Agesilaus,* 15.8; Plutarch, *Artaxerxes,* 20.6, where the author gives the explanation: "for the Persian coin has the figure of an archer stamped upon it."

75. Arrian 2.14.5.

76. Ibid., 1.25.

77. Ibid., 2.4.9–11; Curtius 3.6.4–17.

78. Valerius Maximus 3.8.6.

79. Curtius 4.9.13.

80. Ibid., 3.8.7.

81. Diodorus 17.30.7 *(anagkazō).*

82. Curtius 3.8.7–9: *mos maiorum* (custom of the ancestors).

83. Ibid., 3.8.10.

84. Arrian 2.6.4.

85. Curtius 3.8.2: "They strongly urged Darius to retreat and head for the plains of Mesopotamia once more"; Arrian 2.6.6–7.

86. Arrian 2.6.3–4.

87. Curtius, 3.8.8.

88. Xenophon, *Anabasis*, 2.2.10–11, repeated in Diodorus 14.25.8.

89. Plutarch, *Agesilaus*, 15.1.

90. Curtius 3.2.10–16.

91. Arrian 1.13.2–6 (before the Battle of the Granicus); 1.18.6–9 (outside Miletus); 2.25.2–3 (diplomatic offers from Darius after Issus); 3.10.1–2 (prior to Gaugamela); 3.18.11–12 (in Persepolis).

92. Polybius 10.26.9.

93. Arrian 7.29.1.

94. Ibid., 3.22.2.

95. See Plutarch, *Artaxerxes*, 6.2 *(oi anō)*.

96. On the scarcity of valorous generals, see Diodorus 16.40.4–6 and 17.30.7.

97. Xenophon, *Anabasis*, 1.6.5: *symboulos*.

98. Plutarch, *Artaxerxes*, 8.3–6. The term *eulabeia*, translated as "circumspection," also connotes a defensive position and even fear.

99. Diodorus 14.22.2 (citing his source, Ephorus); see also Cyrus's own declarations as expressed (or rather, compiled) by Xenophon, *Anabasis*, 1.5.9; Curtius 3.2.9.

100. Lucian, *Navigium*, 35, then 34.

101. Plutarch, *Artaxerxes*, 7.1–2.

102. Xenophon, *Anabasis*, 1.7.17, 19.

103. Arrian 2.10.1: *tei gnōmēi dedoulōmenos*.

104. Ibid., 7.7.8. See *KCP*, chap. 28: a summary can be found in my *Alexander the Great* (2010), pp. 89–93.

105. Arrian 2.6.4 ("he came to the conclusion that Alexander was no longer desirous of advancing further"); Curtius 3.8.10–11.

106. Arrian 2.10.2.

107. Curtius 3.11.7: *opimum decus caeso rege expetens* (Issus).

108. Diodorus 17.34.4.

109. Ibid., 17.20.3: "He hoped that by his individual gallantry Asia might be relieved of its terrible menace."

110. Ibid., 17.60.1.

111. Plutarch, *Alexander*, 20.2; see also the ambiguous passage in Plutarch, *Fortune of Alexander*, 2.9 (= *Moralia*, 341C).

112. Curtius 3.11.10; Diodorus 17.34.5.

113. Arrian 2.12.1.

114. See, for example, Curtius 3.11.5: *collato pede, quasi singuli inter se dimicarent* ("foot to foot, as for a series of duels").

115. Arrian 2.14.9.

116. Curtius 4.11.21: *praemia esse belli*.

117. See in particular the expressions in Diodorus 14.23.25: *tous hyper tēs basileias agōnizomenous* (Cyrus against Artaxerxes II; with an explicit comparison to the monomachia between the two brother Eteocles and Polynices, known through tragedy); 16.40.6: *tous hyper tēs basileias agōnas* (Artaxerxes III); 17.30.7: *tous hyper tes basileias agōnas* (Darius III), cf. Arrian 2.14.9: *agōnisai per tes basileias* (Alexander's response to Darius), and Xenophon, *Economics*, 4.18: *peri tēs basileias . . . makhoumenos* (Cyrus the Younger); Diodorus 14.54.6: *diamakhestai pros auton peri tēs tōn olōn monarkhias* (Alexander's response to Darius).

118. Lucian, *Navigium*, 37: *peri tēs arkhēs makhomenon*.

119. Plutarch, *Artaxerxes*, 10–11; see *HPE*, p. 630.

120. Arrian 3.14.2.

121. Diodorus 17.33.5.

122. Plutarch, *Alexander*, 20.8.

123. Justin 11.9.9.

124. Arrian 3.14.2–3, 6.

125. Curtius 4.15.27–29.

126. Plutarch, *Alexander*, 20.8: *en prōtois agōnizomenos*.

127. Arrian 2.25.3.

128. Diodorus 17.39.1.

129. Ibid., 17.54.6.

130. Ibid.

131. Texts cited: Arrian 3.17 (Alexander and the Uxians); Diodorus 19.19.3–8 (Antigonus and the Cosseans); on the status of the populations of the Zagros Mountains, their relations with the Great King, then with Alexander and his successors, see my studies and analyses (with assembled documentation): *État et pasteurs* (1982b), pp. 57–112; *HEP*, pp. 747–753, 1045–1046, 1048–1049.

132. Plutarch, *Agesilaus*, 15.1.

133. See Arrian 2.14.9: *agōnisai* (first embassy); Curtius 4.11.21; *praemia belli* (third embassy).

134. Diodorus 17.55.1.

135. Curtius 4.6.1; also Justin 11.12.5.

136. Curtius 3.12.5.

137. Plutarch, *Alexander*, 21.1.

138. Diodorus 17.37.3.

139. Arrian 2.12.5.

140. Diodorus 17.38.2.

141. Curtius 4.11.6.

142. Ibid., 4.14.22.

143. Arrian 2.11.9–10; Plutarch, *Alexander*, 20.11–13; Curtius 3.11.23 ("it being their tradition to welcome the conqueror in the tent of the conquered king"); Diodorus 17.36.5 (Alexander might "take it as an omen for his conquest of the empire of all Asia").

144. Arrian 3.11.5.

145. Ibid., 5.18.4.

146. Ibid., 6.11.4.

147. Justin 11.9.9.

148. Curtius 4.15.30.

149. Diodorus 17.60.3–4; 64.1.

150. Arrian 2.11.4–5.

151. Curtius 3.11.11 *(qui ad hoc ipsum sequebatur)*; see also Curtius 3.11.26: "Darius' flight had taken him far away with frequent changes of horses"; cf. Diodorus 34.6–7 (another chariot is brought to Darius), and 37.1 (the Great King hastily flees by mounting his best horses one after another).

152. Plutarch, *Alexander*, 33.8.

153. *Alexander Romance*, 2.39.8–9; cf. A. Beelaert, "Alexandre dans le discours sur les âges de la vie" (1999), p. 247.

154. For example, H. Fuhrmann, *Philoxenos* (1931), p. 146.

155. Arrian 3.10.

156. Ibid., 3.10.2: *phanērōs kai aneu sophismatos*.

157. Justin 11.6.8.

158. Valerius Maximus 9.1, ext. 1 (Xerxes); Athenaeus 12.539b (Darius).

159. Aeschylus, *Persians*, 492–512; *Roman*, 2.16.7–8.

160. Herodotus 7.40 (Xerxes); Curtius 3.3.11 (Darius).

161. Justin 2.10.21–24: *Ipse autem primus in fuga, postremo in proelio* (same expression concerning Darius III in Arrian 2.11.4).

162. Caesar, *Civil War*, 3.96; cf. Plutarch, *Pompeius*, 72.3: "He put on a garment befitting his present misfortune and stole away."

163. Lucan, *Pharsalia*, 8.35–40.

164. Cf., for example, Plutarch, *Alexander*, 20.9: *en prōtois agōnizomenos* (Alexander).

165. Arrian 2.11.4: *xyn tois prōtois epheugē* (Darius at Issus); cf. Justin 2.10.20–24: *primus in fuga* (Xerxes).

166. Plutarch, *Alexander*, 17.3; 18.5; Curtius 3.1.19.

167. Arrian 2.6.6.

168. Ibid., 2.14.9.

169. Curtius 4.5.8.

170. Ibid., 4.13.9.

171. Plutarch, *Alexander*, 32.3: *phygomakhounta Dareion*.

172. Curtius 4.14.2.

173. Ibid., 4.15.25.

174. Diodorus 17.33.5 and 34.4.

175. Plutarch, *Alexander*, 20.10; Diodorus 17.37.2 (200 stadia is about 22 miles).

176. See also Diodorus 17.25.1; Curtius 3.12.1 and 4.1.1–3.

177. Curtius 4.15.32–33.

178. Ibid., 4.16.28–29.

179. Ibid., 4.16.9 (and the arrival of Alexander's troops, 16.16–18): cf. Justin 11.14.4.

180. See the account in Arrian 3.14.4–6; 15.1–6 (quotation at 15.5).

181. Curtius 4.16.3: *Dareum felicius fugere quam se sequi*.

182. Plutarch, *Alexander*, 33.9–11, records the different versions.

183. Diodorus 17.37.3.

184. See in particular Plutarch, *Marcellus, 6–8.*

185. Curtius 3.1.17; the same expression is found at 7.4.40, to designate a defeated ene-my's head, which Erigyius, the victor in single combat over an Iranian leader, comes to offer Alexander.

186. Curtius 5.1.3–9; cf. Arrian 3.16.1–2.

187. Diodorus 17.64.1–2; cf. 17.73.2.

188. Arrian 3.21.1–5.

189. Curtius 5.8.2: *itaque proelio magis quem fugae se praeperabat.*

190. Ibid., 5.9.1.

191. Ibid., 5.8.1.

192. Ibid., 5.10.12–13: *Alexandri manus, quas solas timebat, effugere properabat.*

193. Ibid., 5.13.4: *in illo corpore posita est nostra victoria.*

194. Ibid., 5.13.5.

195. That is, about forty-five miles (on horseback).

196. Arrian 3.22.5.

197. Aelian, *De naturum animalium, 6.25.*

198. Ferdowsī, *Book of the Kings,* bk. 1, lines 660–750; this comparison was previously proposed by B. G. Niebuhr (1852, 2:390–91): "Darius fled before [Alexander] as Yazdegerd did before the Arab conquerors."

199. In the version transmitted by Diodorus (17.73.4), Alexander promises Darius, still alive, to avenge him: "Alexander . . . set out after Bessus, but the satrap had a long start and got away into Bactria, so Alexander suspended the chase and returned."

8. Iron Helmet, Silver Vessels

1. Curtius 3.3.8–25. On that custom, there is also a text by Iamblichus, recently trans-lated into French and annotated by P. Goukowsky in "Le cortège des 'rois de Babylone,'" *BAI* 12 (1998): 69–77.

2. See the example of the speech delivered by Barère, a member of the National Con-vention, before the Committee of Public Safety on July 26, 1793, when the Vendean rebels ("the brigands") were making light work of the revolutionary army: "Your army resem-bles that of the king of Persia. It is dragging along 120 carts of baggage, while the brigands are marching with their weapons and a piece of bread in their sacks. You will never man-age to defeat them so long as you do not adopt their way of fighting." Barère seems to be imitating Charidemus, who pointed out to Darius that Alexander's soldiers were subject to a "discipline . . . due to poverty's schooling" (Curtius 3.2.12–15). Barère may have learned of Charidemus's speech through the long quotation and commentary Rollin pro-vides (4:42–46). See also Briant, *Alexandre des Lumières* (2012), pp. 534–538.

3. Curtius 3.11.20: *non belli, sed luxuriae apparatus.*

4. Ibid., 5.1.23: *ad luxuriam magis quam ad magnificentiam.*

5. The image of shoes trimmed with nails made of precious metals also appears in Plutarch, *Alexander,* 40.1. To better praise the simplicity of Alexander's life, Plutarch cites

several of his companions as countermodels. For example, "Hagnon of Teos had his shoes fastened with silver nails"; the exemplum is repeated in Athenaeus 12.539c (citing Phylarchus and Agarchides of Cnidus) and in Aelian, *Varia historia*, 9.3. The expression *avaro potius hosti praeda optabilis* ("booty offered up to the enemy's greed") originates, once again, in the exemplum and illustrates it: cf. Livy 9.17: *praedam verius quam hostem* (Darius's army); Curtius 5.1.6: *mox futura praeda sibi* (Alexander's army gorging on booty and Darius lying in wait).

6. See Plato, *Leges*, 6.777–780.

7. Valerius Maximus 3.7, ext. 8: to a friend who praised the strength of his city's walls, a Spartan replied: "If you made them for women, well done! If for men, shame on you!"

8. Arrian 2.11.9–10: *es polytelē diaitan*.

9. Curtius gives a list a little later on (3.13.12–15), a veritable Who's Who of Persian high society.

10. Athenaeus 11.781f–782a. The figures are impressive: they add up to four metric tons.

11. See also Heracleides quoted in Athenaeus 4.145d: "Throughout the [king's] dinner his concubines [*pallakai*] sing and play the lyre; one of them is the soloist, the others sing in chorus."

12. Athenaeus 12.545f.

13. Aelian, *De natura animalium*, 1.10.

14. Lucan, *Pharsalia*, 8.397–399.

15. Ammianus Marcellinus 23.6.76.

16. Diodorus 17.77.6–7; cf. Curtius 6.6.8 (*HPE*, pp. 280–283).

17. Athenaeus 13.557b.

18. See Tacitus, *Historiae*, 3.40.

19. Livy, *Historia romana*, 9.17: *mulierum ac spadonum agmen trahentem . . . praedam verius quam hostem*.

20. Herodotus 3.17–26.

21. See *HPE*, pp. 286–297, esp. 286, 289 (delicate birds) and 294–297 (dishes).

22. A prestigious aulic title granted to a few dozen individuals, to whom the Macedonian king thereby indicated his favor.

23. Caesar, *De bello civili*, 3.96: *miserrimo ac patientissimo exercitu . . . luxuriem*.

24. Plutarch, *Alexander*, 24.3: *diaitēs barbarikēs . . . ton tōn Persōn plouton*.

25. Ibid., 22–23.

26. The term used *(anandria)* designates cowardice on the battlefield.

27. Plutarch, *Fortune of Alexander*, 2.11 (= *Moralia*, 342A); cf. *Alexander*, 23.9.

28. Strabo 15.3.22; see also Valerius Maximus 9.1, ext. 3.

29. Diodorus 17.108.4; Valerius Maximus 9.1.2.

30. Plutarch, *Alexander*, 23.9; Xenophon, *Anabasis*, 1.9.20–28, esp. 25–26.

31. Frontinus 4.1.6.

32. See Athenaeus 12.539d–f; Aelian, *Varia historia*, 9.3; Polyaenus 4.3.24.

33. Plutarch, *Alexander*, 57.5: *o epi tōn strōmatophylakōn tetagmenos*.

34. Arrian, *Anabasis*, 6.25.5: *tēn kataskeuēn tēn basilikēn xumpasan*.

35. Plutarch, *Eumenes*, 2.6–7.

36. Polyaenus, *Strategemata*, 4.3.10.

37. Curtius 6.6.14: *cum grave spoliis apparatuque luxuriae agmen vix moveretur.*

38. Plutarch, *Paulus Aemilius,* 12.11–12.

39. Curtius 6.6.15–16.

40. See Arrian, *Anabasis,* 3.14.4–6; Curtius 4.15.9–12.

41. Curtius 4.16.28: *iacturam saecinarum inpedimentorumque . . . in ipsa acie.*

42. Ibid., 4.15.12.

43. Frontinus, *Strategemata,* 4.3 *(De continentia),* 1 (Cato), 9–10 (Scipio, Alexander).

44. Plutarch, *Artaxerxes,* 24.9–10.

45. Frontinus, *Strategemata,* 4.6.3.

46. Lucan, *Pharsalia,* 9.590–594; 616–618.

47. Arrian, *Anabasis,* 6.25.3.

48. Curtius 7.5.9–10; Plutarch, *Alexander,* 42.6–10; Frontinus, *Strategemata,* 1.7.7.

49. Curtius 4.7.5–16; Plutarch, *Alexander,* 26.10–13; 27.1–4; Arrian 3.3.3–6.

50. Polyaenus, *Strategemata,* 4.3.25. His account seems quite clearly inspired by Arrian's.

51. Plutarch, *Alexander,* 40.1, 41.1.

52. Curtius 3.6.19–20.

53. Plutarch, *Alexander,* 42.6–10; but during the final pursuit of Darius, it is true that Alexander surrounded himself with a troop of battle-hardened horsemen (Arrian 3.20), turning even the foot soldiers into horsemen in the last stage, when he took a route lacking resupplies of water (21.8).

54. Curtius 7.5.12; cf. Plutarch, *Alexander,* 42.8–9: "He took the helmet into his hands; but seeing all the horsemen around him eagerly watching him and coveting the water, he gave it back without tasting it. He thanked the men for offering it to him, but said, 'If I alone drink it, all these soldiers will be discontented.'"

55. Athenaeus 2.45a–b *(basilikon hydōr . . . elaphrotaton kai hēdiston).*

56. Curtius 5.2.9 *(delicata aqua).*

57. Strabo 15.3.22 *(elaphrotaton).*

58. Athenaeus 2.45c, quoting Polybius.

59. Ibid., 2.41f, quoting Theophrastus.

60. Pliny, *Historia naturalis,* 31.21.35.

61. Athenaeus 2.46b.

62. Pliny, *Historia naturalis,* 31.23.401; see also the rich explanations of J. Serbat, French translator of Pliny in the Collection des Universités de France (Paris: Les Belles Lettres, 1972), pp. 126–137.

63. Xenophon, *Cyropaedia,* 1.3.9.

64. Diodorus 17.5.6.

65. Plutarch, *Artaxerxes,* 19.9.

66. The discussion of "water drinkers" is included in *Les nuits de Ramazan (Voyage en Orient* [Paris: Garnier Flammarion], vol. 2 [1980], pp. 215–221, quotation at p. 216). The stopover in Constantinople occurred in 1843.

67. Plutarch, *Alexander,* 36.4.

68. In *De consulatu Stilichonis* (3.157–158), written in 400 C.E., Claudian repeats a comparable expression that includes the image of consumption: among the markers of Roman

territorial domination was the capacity "to partake of the Rhone and to drink from the Orontes."

69. Herodotus 7.83.

70. Aelian, *De natura animalium*, 17.36, and Seneca, *De ira*, 3.20 (Cambyses in Egypt); cf. Herodotus 7.128 (Xerxes's army).

71. Strabo 16.1.3; Plutarch, *Alexander*, 31.6–7.

72. See, for example, Curtius 5.6.3, describing the wealth of Persepolis, including royal furnishings accumulated "not to be functional but to be ostentatiously ornate [*supellex non ad usum, sed ad ostentationem luxus comparata*]." For *tryphē* as softness, see Plutarch, *Alexander*, 40.2: *doulikōtaton . . . to tryphan . . . basilikōtaton dē to ponein*. See also *HPE*, pp. 299–301.

73. *Moralia* 342A.

74. Aelian, *Varia historia*, 12.40: *polyteleia kai alazoneia*.

75. Diodorus 18.26.6 and 27.5.

76. Seneca, *De ira*, 3.20.

77. See Arrian 6.26.1.

78. See also Plutarch, *Artaxerxes*, 4.4–5 (identical to Aelian 1.33) and 5.1 (identical to Aelian 1.32 and to the story recounted at the beginning of the *Apothegms*). The story also enjoyed great success in the Byzantine period: cf. K. Alpers, "Xerxes und Artaxerxes" (1969).

79. Plutarch, *Artaxerxes*, 14.1.

80. In my opinion, the detail of the "water of the Choaspes" is an addition by Aelian, following the logic of his introduction: the other stories show that the kings are ready to drink any water whatever if they are in need.

81. Plutarch, *Artaxerxes*, 12.4–6.

82. Aelian, *Varia historia*, 12.40: the term used (the verb *kērussō* in the passive voice) allows for either translation, but both the narrative and the syntactical context clearly introduce a notion of obligation.

83. On the term *nomos (persikos)* in Greek literature, and on possible equivalents in Elamite and Babylonian, see *HPE*, pp. 510–511, 520, 777–778, 956–957; on the expression *kata tēn (eautou) dynamin* (Aelian, *Varia historia*, 1.31), see the examples in *HPE*, p. 931. Aelian's text provides particular support for the discussion of the differentiation between gifts and tributes in the Achaemenid Empire (see *HPE*, pp. 394ff.). On the Persian system of royal gifts and the status of benefactors, see the many discussions in *HPE*, pp. pp. 301–336, 347–354, 923–925.

84. See Theopompus quoted by Athenaeus 4.145a (*HPE*, pp. 402–403).

85. Plutarch, *Apothegmata*, 184D–E.

86. Y.-M. Bercé, *Le roi caché* (1990), p. 276, and chap. 6 as a whole ("Le roi avisé").

87. Nizāmī, *Haft Paykar*, quoted from the French translation by M. Barry, *Livre du pavillon des sept princesses* (Paris: Gallimard, 2000), pp. 439–446.

88. Saadi, *Bustān (The Fruit Orchard)*, quoted from the French translation by Barbier de Meynard, *Le Boustan ou Verger* (Paris: E. Leroux, 1880), pp. 35–46, 60–64.

89. J. Dakhlia, *Le divan des rois* (1998), pp. 166–167, 266.

90. Plutarch, *Artaxerxes*, 12.6.

91. Plutarch, *Moralia*, 174A.

92. Cicero, *Tusculanae disputationes*, 5.33.97 (with many other exempla meant to illustrate a lesson on the limits of the pleasure to be drawn from food).

93. On Alexander, Arrian 6.26.1: *en isoteti;* cf. Curtius 3.6.19–20: *inter ipsos*. On Artaxerxes, Plutarch, *Artaxerxes*, 24.6.

94. Athenaeus 545d, f.

95. Cicero, *Tusculanae disputationes*, 5.33.97.

96. Ibid., 5.32.92: *quibus nunquam satiari ille posset.*

97. The encounter between Alexander and Diogenes, probably fictional, was a very popular story and often cited: see Hamilton, *Commentary* (1969), 32.

98. Xenophon, *Agesilaus*, 9.3–5.

99. See Athenaeus 4.144b–f; 145a; 12.529d.

100. Justin 9.8.4, 20–21.

101. Strabo 15.3.22.

102. Plutarch, *Fortune of Alexander*, 2.11 (= *Moralia*, 342A).

103. Athenaeus 12.539b; the exemplum is repeated by Valerius Maximus (9.1., ext. 3), but its subject is Xerxes, not Darius III. On Clearchus, a disciple of Aristotle, and his interest in "barbarian wisdom," see L. Robert, *Opera minora selecta*, vol. 5 (Amsterdam: Hakkert, 1989), pp. 441–454.

104. Cicero, *Tusculanae disputationes*, 5.33.97: *negavit unquam se bibisset iucundius.*

105. Plutarch, *Artaxerxes*, 12.6, where *hēdeōs* closely corresponds to *iucundius.*

106. Curtius 4.16.15: "From the villages closest to the road old men and women could be heard wailing [*ululatus*], still calling on Darius as their king [*Dareum adhuc regem clamantium*] in the barbarian fashion [*barbaro ritu*]." The term used *(ululatus)* can also suggest that, on the contrary, the population was lamenting the battlefield deaths.

107. Curtius 5.13.23.

108. Arrian 3.20–21 (excerpts).

109. On the passage from Polybius, see my article in *KCP*, chap. 13.

110. See Arrian 3.21.10: "Darius died from his wounds soon after, before Alexander had seen him."

111. Justin 11.15.5.

112. Seneca, *De ira*, 3.20; Strabo 16.1.3; and Plutarch, *Alexander*, 31.6–7.

113. Polyaenus 7.11.12. Here, Apollo is the Greek equivalent of the Iranian god of storms (*HPE*, pp. 239–240, 915).

114. Cicero, *Tusculanae disputationes*, 5.33.97; cf. Curtius 4.16.12–13. In his *Daire* (1561), Jean de la Taille "quotes" Darius's reply: "Ô breuvage mille fois savoureux, / Je n'avalai jamais boisson si délicate" (O drink a thousand times savorous, / never did I swallow a drink so delicate; lines 1644–1645). The author, not being a historian, was unfamiliar with Cicero's text. No doubt wishing to introduce that nice reply at a moment well suited to his stagecraft, he sets the exchange at the moment Darius is dying in the arms of Polystratus.

115. Suetonius, *Nero*, 48.5.

116. Pliny, *Historia naturalis*, 31.23.40.

117. Plutarch, *Pompeius*, 73.3.

118. Ctesias, quoted by Athenaeus 11.464a: *kerameois potēriois*.

119. Aelian, *De natura animalium*, 6.25.

120. Plutarch, *Alexander*, 43.2.

9. The Great King's Private and Public Lives

1. Curtius 3.11.21–23 *(vis ac libido; crudelitas ac licentia)*; Diodorus 17.35–36.1; Justin 11.9.10–12.

2. Artaxerxes III, who was assassinated by the chiliarch Bagoas.

3. Curtius 3.11.23.

4. Plutarch, *Alexander*, 20.11–13; Diodorus 17.36.5; 37.2.

5. Curtius 3.12.3 *(lugubris clamor barbaro ululatu planctuque)*. Curtius uses the same term in his description of the Battle of Gaugamela, to characterize the despair of Darius's squires, convinced that the king had been killed (4.15.29: *lugubri ululatu*); similarly, in 4.16.15, during the king's flight, "from the villages closest to the road old men and women could be heard wailing [*ululatus*], still calling on Darius as their king in the barbarian fashion [*barbaro ritu*]"—unless these were howls of grief uttered by the parents, mothers, and wives of the soldiers who had died in battle.

6. See Arrian 4.19.4–6; 20.1–4.

7. Ibid., 7.28.2.

8. Plutarch, *Fortune of Alexander*, 2.5 (= *Moralia*, 338C).

9. Plutarch, *Alexander*, 22.4.

10. Diodorus 17.38.3–7.

11. Plutarch, *Alexander*, 21.3–7; 11 *(egkrateia; sophrosynē)*.

12. Arrian 4.19.6 *(sophrosynē)*.

13. Curtius 3.12.18–23.

14. Arrian 2.11.9.

15. Xenophon, *Cyropaedia*, 4.2.2.

16. Ibid., 4.3.1.

17. Ibid., 3.3.67.

18. 3.11.23: cf. Diodorus 17.36.5 and Plutarch, "Alexander," 20.11 (cf. *HPE*, p. 188).

19. Xenophon, *Cyropaedia*, 4.6.11 *(mousourgoi* are also recorded in the booty taken in Damascus: *HEP*, p. 306).

20. Ibid., 4.11.47.

21. Ibid., 7.13.15.

22. Xenophon, *Anabasis*, 1.8.28–29.

23. Athenaeus, *Deipnosophists*, 12.609a: *kallistē*.

24. Aelian, *Varia historia*, 12.1: *kallistē*; cf. also Athenaeus 13.576d: *kallistē*.

25. Diodorus 17.77.6; Plutarch, *Artaxerxes*, 27.2; cf. *Esther*, 2.2–3 (*HEP*, pp. 289–203).

26. Athenaeus 13.575b: *kallistē tōn kata tēn Asian gynaikōn*.

27. Xenophon, *Cyropaedia*, 4.3.1.

28. Curtius 3.11.24: *haec formae pulchritudine nec illa quidem sorte corruptae*.

29. Ibid., 3.12.21–22: *virgines reginas excellentis formae . . . suae pulchritudine corporis*.

30. Plutarch, *Alexander*, 21.6: *poly pasōn tōn basilidōn euprestatēn*.

31. Ibid., 21.10.

32. Ammianus Marcellinus 24.4.27 *(in Perside, ubi feminarum pulchritudo excellit)*.

33. Arrian 4.19.5.

34. Athenaeus 13.609a.

35. Ctesias, *Persica*, 28, 42.

36. Plutarch, *Artaxerxes*, 6.5, 6:16–19.

37. Arrian 4.19.5: *kallistēn tōn Asianōn gynaikōn*.

38. Plutarch, *Alexander*, 77.6.

39. In Curtius 3.13.13–14, Artabazus's wife and Mentor's three daughters are cited within a subset that includes the women and children of the great families of Daskyleion.

40. Plutarch, *Quomodo adulator ab amico internoscatur*, 3 (= *Moralia*, 50E). As J. Sirinelli, translator of the Budé edition, remarks (1989, p. 281), "the play on words between flattering women [*kōlakides*] and "step stools" [*klimakides*] is impossible to translate, similar to *encenseur/ascenseur* [flatterer/elevator]." See Montaigne's rendering of Plutarch: "And were there not the Climacides, women in Syria who, crouching on all fours, served as a footstool and a stepladder for ladies to climb into their coach?" (*Essays* 2.12, Frame trans. [1965], p. 337).

41. Athenaeus 6.256c–d. "Female despots" is a translation of the term *anax*, in the rare feminine form. The word was also used by Aeschylus to characterize Atossa in *The Persians*.

42. In 343, Artabazus and Mentor, having broken away from Artaxerxes III, went into exile in Macedonia.

43. Valerius Maximus 9.1: *De luxuria et libidine*, ext. 7: *effeminatior . . . delicato imperio*; 9.1.3.

44. Plutarch, *Alexander*, 21.5.

45. Aelian, *Varia historia*, 12.1: *dia to kallos to tou sōmatou, kai eti mallon dia tēn eugeneian tēs psykhēs*.

46. Diodorus 17.35.4–7; Curtius 3.11.21–22.

47. Plutarch, *Artaxerxes*, 27.1; cf. *Themistocles*, 26.4–5, and the story repeated in *Chaereas and Callihroe* (5.3).

48. Aelian, *Varia historia*, 12.1.

49. Plutarch, *Alexander*, 21.7: *apsykhous eikōnas agalmatōn*.

50. S. Dubel, "La beauté romanesque ou le refus du portrait" (2002), pp. 47–48; on the term *agalma*, see also my pages in *KCP*, chap. 2, §3.

51. Homer, *Iliad*, 1.323, 23; 2.689; 19.246, 282; 24.676.

52. Aelian, *Varia historia*, 12.1.

53. Diodorus 17.67.1.

54. Curtius 5.3.12–15; cf. Arrian 3.17.5.

55. Plutarch, *Alexander*, 43.7.

56. Livy 1.57.9; Suetonius, *Augustus*, 64.

57. See inscription SEG 4:634, translated and annotated by A. Bielman, *Femmes en public dans le monde hellénistique (IVe–Ie s. av. J.-C.)* (Paris: SEDES, 2002), no. 44, pp. 224–229.

58. Polyaenus 8.53.2 and 5.

59. Athenaeus 12.528f.

60. Compare, for example, Voltaire, *Essai sur les moeurs,* ed. René Pommeau (Paris: Classiques Garnier, 1990), 2:774: "It was the fate of Persia that all its dynasties began in strength and ended in weakness. Almost all these families met the fate of Serdan-pull, whom we call Sardanapalus."

61. Plutarch, *Fortune of Alexander,* 1.2 (= *Moralia,* 326F).

62. Herodotus 4.162.

63. Ibid., 9.108–111.

64. Ibid., 112: "Amestris . . . had Masistes' wife horribly mutilated. Her breasts, nose, ears, and lips were cut off and thrown to the dogs; then her tongue was torn out and, in this dreadful condition, she was sent home."

65. Arrian 2.12.6; Plutarch, *Fortune of Alexander,* 2.6 (= *Moralia,* 338E).

66. Curtius 6.2.6; Chariton, *Chaereas et Callihroe,* 6.1.

67. Plutarch, *Alexander,* 22.5.

68. Arrian 4.19.5.

69. Livy 36.49; Polybius 10.18.3–15.

70. Andobales's name is given as "Indibilis" in Livy; the Ilergetes were one of the Iberian nations.

71. Livy 26.60: *captiva . . . adulta virgo, adeo eximia forma.* The identical description is found in Valerius Maximus 4.3.1 *(eximiae inter eos formae virginem aetatis adultae)* and Frontinus 2.11.5 *(inter captivas eximiae formae virgo nubilis).*

72. Plutarch, *Alexander,* 21.5 *(en hiērois kai hagiois).*

73. Ibid., 22.1–6; Polybius 10.19.3; cf. Livy 26.50; Frontinus 2.11.5; Valerius Maximus 4.3.1.

74. Plutarch, *Alexander,* 21.4; cf. Curtius 3.12.23.

75. Diodorus 17.38.1; Justin 11.9.16.

76. Valerius Maximus 4.3.1; see also Frontinus 2.11.5.

77. Curtius 6.2.9.

78. Among the paintings commissioned for the Salon de Peinture in Paris in 1777, one bore the following title: "The Chevalier de Bayard Returns His Prisoner to Her Mother and Gives Her a Dowry." C. Grell, *Le dix-huitième siècle et l'Antiquité en France,* vol. 1 (Oxford: Voltaire Foundation, 1995), p. 636.

79. Frontinus 2.11.25.

80. Valerius Maximus 4.3.1.

81. Plutarch, *Alexander,* 30.1; Justin 11.12.6; see discussions in Bosworth, *Commentary I,* p. 321; Heckel, commentary in Yardley and Heckel's edition of Justin's *Epitome* (1997), pp. 160–161; Atkinson, *Commentary I* (1980), p. 392.

82. Curtius 4.10.19.

83. Plutarch, *Fortune of Alexander,* 2.6 (= *Moralia,* 338E); see Curtius 4.10.18–24.

84. Curtius 4.10.25–26; cf. Plutarch, *Alexander,* 30.2 (Tireos).

85. Curtius 4.10.13–34; Plutarch, *Fortune of Alexander,* 2.6 (= *Moralia,* 338E–F), *Alexander,* 30; Justin 11.12.6–8; Arrian 4.20.1–3.

86. Curtius 4.11.1–6; Justin 11.12.9–16.

87. Plutarch, *Alexander*, 21.6 and 33.5 (*Kalos/kallistos* and *mēgas*); the same terminology is used in Diodorus 17.37.5, with reference to Hephaestion. On the vocabulary of praise in the Roman imperial period, see the examples regarding Lucian in L. Robert, *À travers l'Asie Mineure* (1980), pp. 423–424. Robert points out that the same stock phrases are also found on inscriptions from the same period (second century c.e.).

88. See Diodorus 17.38.2; Curtius 3.12.26.

89. Plutarch, *Artaxerxes*, 1.1 (*praotēs kai megalopsykhia); cf. 2.1 (proateros) 30.9 (praos).*

90. Aelian, *Varia historia*, 12.1.

91. 3.2.17 (*mitis et tractabilis); 3.8.5 (sanctus et mitis); 5.8.1 (simplex et mitis).*

92. Chariton, *Chaereas et Callihroe*, 6.1, 3.

93. Plutarch, *Alexander*, 22.6; for a comparison between Plutarch's *Life of Alexander* and *Life of Caesar*, see J. Beneker's interesting article "No Time for Love" (2002).

94. Xenophon, *Cyrus*, 5.1.8.

95. Polybius 10.19.4. The distinction *idiōtēs/stratēgos* exactly coincides, in a military context, to the distinction between the ordinary subject *(idiōtēs)* and the king *(basileus)* so often used in the monarchical literature.

96. Frontinus 2.11.5.

97. Livy 26.50.

98. Aelian, *Varia historia*, 12.1; the story and its variants are also in Xenophon, *Anabasis*, 1.10.2; Justin 10.2, and Plutarch, *Artaxerxes*, 26.5–8, 27.15.

99. Plutarch, *Artaxerxes*, 30 (last years of the reign); 23 (marriage between Artaxerxes and Atossa); 26.2–3 and 30.1 (relations between Ochus and Atossa).

100. Plutarch, *Alexander*, 21.9 (*kalēs kai gennaias . . . gunaikos).*

101. Justin 11.10.2: *captivam . . . propter formae pulchritudinem coepit.*

102. Plutarch, *Alexander*, 30.1 (the fictive third embassy is also at issue here).

103. See Arrian 4.19.5: "Though he was in love with her, he refused to offer violence to her as a captive, and did not think it derogatory to his dignity to marry her."

104. Valerius Maximus 4.3.1: *veneris pecuniaeque cupido.*

105. Curtius 6.4.14.

106. Ibid., 6.4.23.

107. Ibid., 6.5.24.

108. According to Arrian (3.23.4), Nabarzanes and Phratapherncs go to Alexander together, followed shortly thereafter by Artabazus and his sons (23.7); then comes the campaign against the Mardi (24.1–3) and the arrival in "Zadracarta, the largest city of Hyrcania, where the royal residency in Hyrcania was located" (25.1).

109. Curtius 6.5.22–23: *specie singulari spado atque in ipso flore pueritiae.*

110. Ibid., 4.12.8.

111. Ibid., 10.1.37.

112. Plutarch, *Quomodo adulator ab amico internoscatur* (= *Moralia*, 65C–D).

113. W. W. Tarn, "Alexander's Attitude to Sex," in *Alexander*, 2:319–326: "I regret having to write this Appendix, for the title might suggest the worst kind of popular historiography" (p. 319); cf. Curtius 5.1.38, regarding the unseemly conduct of women at the banquets in Babylon: "I beg my readers' pardon for saying it."

114. I note in passing that Tarn was not the first author to have been profoundly shocked by the story Curtius tells. La Mothe Le Vayer, in the foreword (laudatory, in fact) that he devotes to the Latin author in 1646 (*Oeuvres*, vol. 4, pt. 2, pp. 222–232), denounces both Alexander and Curtius: "Alexander used the eunuch Bagoas for the very purpose that made him all-powerful over Darius's affections. . . . It is strange that [Curtius] later had the effrontery to write that Alexander's sensual pleasures were all natural and licit. . . . Certainly Alexander's flaw cannot be mitigated, whatever licence can be adduced on that matter among the Gentiles, both Greek and Latin" (pp. 228–229).

115. Diodorus 17.77.4 *(tryphē kai polyteleia);* Curtius 6.2.1.

116. See the case of Tyriotes, "one of the eunuchs who had attended the king [*e spadonibus, qui circa reginam erant*]" (Curtius 4.10.25; cf. Plutarch, *Alexander,* 30.2 and 11: *thalamēpolos,* "chamber servant").

117. Curtius 6.5.23: *specie singulari spado atque in ipso flore pueritiae.*

118. See Pliny, *Historia naturalis,* 13.41; Ovid, *Amores,* 2.2.1.

119. Aelian, *Varia historia,* 12.1.

120. Athenaeus 4.145b.

121. *Kallistos tōn en tēi Asiai kai ōraiotatos genomēnos.*

122. Curtius 10.1.38.

123. Ibid., 3.3.23: *spadonum grex haud sane illis gentibus vilis.*

124. Tacitus, *Historiae,* 3.40: *multo ac molli concubinarum spadonumque agmine;* 2.71: *histrionum et spadonum gregibus.*

125. Curtius 6.6.8: *quas spadonum greges . . . sequebantur.*

126. *Et ipsi muliebria pati adsueti.*

127. Athenaeus 13.603b; Plutarch, *Moralia,* 65C–D, and *Alexander,* 6.7.7–8.

128. Curtius 10.1.26: *mares, qui stupro effeminarentur.*

129. Ibid., 10.1.29: *importunissimum scortum, ne in stupro quidem et dedecoris patientia fraudis oblitum, quotiens amorem regis in se accenderat.* The term *scortum* is also used a few lines earlier (10.1.26).

130. Ibid., 6.7.2: *amore flagrabat, obsequio uni sibi dedita corporis vinctus.*

131. Ibid., 6.7.11: *effeminatum et muliebriter timidum, alias proditorem amatoris appelans.*

132. Ibid., 6.7.13.

133. Ibid., 5.2.17–22.

134. Ibid., 10.1.26: *moris esse Persis.*

135. In addition to Tacitus, *Historiae,* 2.71 and 3.40, see Suetonius, *Titus,* 7: "His penchant for debauchery was feared as well, when he was seen surrounded by a herd of debauchees and eunuchs [*propter exoletorum et spadonum greges*]."

136. Curtius 6.5.23: "It was Bagoas' pleas that did most to influence Alexander to pardon Nabarzanes."

137. Curtius 10.1.42 *(scortum).*

138. Plutarch, *Alexander,* 22.1–2.

139. There were also collections of exempla devoted specifically to the deaths of illustrious people *(exitus illustrium virorum).*

140. Curtius 5.1.24; 7.6.20; 9.6.23; 10.1.37: *regnare castratum.*

141. Diodorus 17.5.3–6; he was called "Bagoas the Elder" in Theophrastus, *De causis plantarum*, 2.6.17.

142. Arrian 2.14.5; Curtius 6.3.12; Plutarch, *Moralia*, 337E; cf. *HEP*, pp. 789–799.

10. Dārā and Iskandar

1. Persia proper, which Alexander turned into a satrapy, later became part of the Seleucid kingdom (founded in 311 by Seleukos, one of Alexander's successors). Then (as Strabo 15.3.24 had learned), the local petty princes (whose succession is attested by coinage from between the late second century B.C.E. and the early third century C.E.) were subject to the Parthians (the kingdom of the Arsacids, founded by Arsakes in the last third of the third century B.C.E). The Arsacid dynasty ("Askhanian" in the terminology of the Iranian sources) itself marked the restoration of Iranian independence after Alexander. It was in turn overthrown by Ardašir, in about 240 C.E. He founded another Iranian dynasty, that of the Sassanids, to which the Arab conquest put an end (642: Battle of Nihāvand; 651: death of Yazdegerd III).

2. A. Melikian-Chirvani, "Le royaume de Salomon" (1971), p. 1. "Buyid" is the name of a dynasty that ruled the southern and western parts of Iran and Iraq between the mid-tenth and the mid-eleventh century.

3. Quoted from J. Mohl's French translation (1836). Since the publication of the French edition of the present book, a new English translation has appeared: *Shahnameh: The Persian Book of Kings*, trans. D. Davis (New York: Viking, 2006).

4. Niẓāmī, *Haft Paykar*, quoted from M. Barry's French translation, *Le pavillon des sept princesses* (2000), p. 132 (with different transcriptions).

5. Bīrūnī spent part of his life at the court of Mahmūd of Ghazna, Ferdowsī's patron; cf. C. E. Bosworth, *EncIr* 4 (1990): 274–276.

6. E. Yarshater makes this argument in "Lists of Achaemenid Kings" (1976).

7. Niẓāmī, *Haft Paykar*, p. 194.

8. Xenophon, *Cyropaedia*, 1.2.1; Dinon, quoted by Athenaeus 14.630–633; Strabo 15.3.1; cf. *HPE*, pp. 329–339.

9. On this term, see M. Shaki, "Gabr" (2000), and the very interesting article on "Guèbre" in Diderot and d'Alembert's *Grande Encyclopédie*.

10. I note in passing that, in a letter to his sister written from Tehran on January 20, 1856, Gobineau, then secretary of the mission extraordinaire to Persia, boasted that his daughter Diane "professes reservations about Alexander, despite his glory, because he had to ruin Persepolis" (*Lettres persanes* [Paris: Mercure de France, 1957], pp. 41–42).

11. The accounts are quoted in J. Darmesteter, "Légende d'Alexandre" (1878), pp. 86–88.

12. Quoted from M. Grignaschi's French translation (1966).

13. Quoted from P. Gignoux's French translation.

14. Translation in R. C. Zaehner, *Zurvan* (1955), pp. 7–8.

15. See the doubts already expressed by Ibn Khaldūn, *Muqquadimma*, 3:1044–1045.

16. On that aspect, see esp. H. W. Bailey, *Zoroastrian Problems* (1943), pp. 156–175.

17. Plato, *Leges*, 3.693–696.

18. C.-H. de Fouchécour, "Jâmi, conseiller des princes" (1999a).

19. Allusion to the designation "Dhu'l Qarnayn" ("the Two-Horned One") in the eighteenth sura of the Koran, generally acknowledged to refer to Iskandar (see, for example, Tabarī, p. 511; contrary views cited by Tha'ālibī, pp. 400, 442, and by al-Ma'sūdī, 25:248–249); cf. Southgate, trans., *Iskandarnamah* (1978), pp. 196–201.

20. The term "designates a valiant knight of ancient Iran, a warrior of noble birth, and an army leader" (G. Lazard, *"Pahlavi"* [1972]).

21. The term refers to the representatives of the rural aristocracy (cf. A. Taffazzoli, *EncIr* 7 [1994]: 223–225).

22. On this theme, see esp. two studies by Y. Yamanaka, "From Evil Destroyer to Islamic Hero" (1993) and "Ambiguïté de l'image d'Alexandre chez Firdawsī" (1999).

23. See C. Kappler, "Alexandre dans le *Shāh Nāma* de Firdousi" (1996).

24. In Abū Tāher Tarsusi's *Dārāb-nāmeh*, Nahid gives birth to Iskandar in secret, near Aristotle's cloister. Abandoned, the young child is nursed by a nanny goat. Between the ages of four and ten, he is raised by Aristotle. Then Nahid acknowledges him, and Philip names him as his successor. See the annotated M. Gaillard translation (2005).

25. According to Tabarī (p. 514), Dārā's army had 600,000 men, Iskandar's 800,000. Although no more reliable, Tha'ālibī's figures (pp. 404–405) are more reasonable: 80,00 and 12,000, respectively.

26. Arrian 3.10.1–2: "They say that Parmenio went to him in his tent and advised him to attack the Persians at night; they would be surprised, confused and more prone to panic in a night attack. Alexander, however, replied, since others were listening, that it was dishonourable to steal the victory, and that Alexander had to win openly and without stratagem" (Brunt trans.).

27. In Middle Persian, the term *dastūr* designates a learned individual vested with authority; within the context of state institutions (as here), the term can also be translated as "minister": cf. M. Shaki, *EncIr* 7/1 (1994):111–112.

28. Quoted from M. Gaillard's French translation.

29. See A. L. Beelaert, "Alexandre dans le discours sur les âges de la vie" (1999).

30. On Nizāmī's position regarding war and peace, see J.-C. Bürgel, "Krieg und Frieden" (1996).

31. In *Haft Paykar*, Nizāmī roundly condemns those who betrayed Dārā, in a discussion devoted to praising the good king and denouncing bad ministers: cf. M. Barry trans. (2000), p. 435, with brief commentary p. 727.

32. *Encyclopédie de l'Islam*, s.v. "Mīrkwānd."

33. Mirkhond (Mīrkhwānd), *History of the Early Kings of Persia*, trans. D. Shea (London, 1832), pp. 358–364.

34. *Annals of Oman to 1728*, ed. and trans. E. C. Ross (1874; repr. Cambridge: Oleander, 1984), pp. 3–7, for the events cited. On some erroneous conclusions drawn from a passage on the destruction of 10,000 underground canals by Dārā's troops (p. 6), see the remarks by several authors in P. Briant, *Irrigation et drainage* (Paris: Thotm, 2001), p. 13n26 and p. 163n12 (*KCP*, chap. 13).

11. Death and Transfiguration

1. On this version, see F. Pfister, "Dareios von Alexander getötet" (1958).

2. Manetho was an Egyptian priest from the Lagid period (third century B.C.E.) who wrote—in Greek—a history of the Egyptian dynasties from mythic times to 342 B.C.E.: cf. *Aegyptiaka (Epitomè)*, ed. Waddel (Loeb Classical Library), p. 187, F75: "Darius reigned for six years, he was put to death by Alexander," with Pfister's discussion of the vocabulary used in Greek *(katheīlē)* and Latin *(interfecit)*.

3. The *Chronicon Paschale* is a universal history of sorts, set between the Creation and 630 C.E. The text is cited from the edition annotated by M. Whitby and M. Whitby (1989), pp. 100–101.

4. Al-Ma'sūdī, *Meadows of Gold*, pp. 247–248: "Iskandar invaded Syria and Iraq, weapons in hand, annihilated all the kings who were there, and killed Dārā son of Dārā, king of the Persians"; Ibn Khaldūn, *Discours*, 3:1044: "at the time Iskandar killed Dārā and seized the Achaemenid Empire" (Barbier de Meynard and Pavet de Courteille trans.).

5. Marble of Paros B.6 (M. N. Tod, *Greek Historical Inscriptions* 2 [1948], no. 205, p. 310).

6. Malalas, *Chronographia*, 399.13–20, quoted in Whitby and Whitby (1989), p. 101n317, in conjunction with a passage from Theophylactus (150.24–29).

7. Arrian 3.21.10 and 6.11.4 ("Darius was . . . put to death at Alexander's approach"); also Justin 11.15.14; Plutarch, *Alexander*, 43.5; the Great King's death scene is absent from Curtius, because of a lacuna in the manuscripts.

8. Curtius 5.12.8–9.

9. Ibid., 5.13.16: *et Alexandri fidem implorans.*

10. Arrian 4.20; Curtius 4.10.22–34; Plutarch, *Fortune of Alexander*, 2.6 (= *Moralia*, 338F).

11. See *HPE*, chap. 8: "The King's Men."

12. Plutarch, *Fortune of Alexander*, 2.6 (= *Moralia*, 338F).

13. For Darius III's court, see the example of the eunuch Tyriotes, whom Darius urges to pledge before "the name of great Mithras our lord, and by the right hand of a king, which I give you" (Plutarch, *Alexander*, 30.8). For Alexander's court, see esp. the surrender of Nabarzanes: "Alexander did not hesitate to give Nabarzanes an assurance [*fides*], using the Persian conventions [*quo Persae modo accipiebant*], that he would be unharmed if he came" (Curtius 6.4.14). That is what the author, upon Nabarzanes's arrival, calls "the offer" (4.5.2: *accepta fide*). Similarly, when Artabazus comes to surrender, he has his sons "brought to Alexander's right hand" (6.5.4).

14. Diodorus 16.43.

15. Nepos, *Datames*, 10.1–2: *fidemque de ea more Persarum dextra didisset. Hanc ut accepit, a rege missam.*

16. On this point, see S. Sherwin-White, "Hand-Tokens" (1978) (the example of Polystratus is not cited).

17. Nizāmī, *Haft Paykar*. Barry trans., p. 350.

18. Plutarch, *Alexander*, 43.5; Justin 11.15.14.

19. Plutarch, *Fortune of Alexander*, 2.11 (= *Moralia*, 332F); cf. *Alexander*, 43.5.

20. Diodorus 17.73.3.

21. Justin 11.15.12; cf. also *Letter of Tansar*, §1.

22. See C. Kappler, "Alexandre dans le *Shāh Nāma*" (1996), pp. 171–173. I borrow from Kappler the translation of the lines from Ferdowsī.

23. On the coffeehouse paintings, see the detailed studies in L. Summerer and A. von Kienlin, eds., *Tatarlı: The Return of Colours* (Istanbul: T.C. Kültür ve Turizm Bakanlığı, 2010).

24. See R. Hillenbrand's remarks in "The Iskandar Cycle" (1996), pp. 209–210; and F. Richard, "L'iconographie se rapportant à Eskandar" (1999), p. 83.

25. The "Story of Sohrab" appears in Ferdowsī, *Book of the Kings*, bk. 2, lines 75–185.

26. Athenaeus 12.548e; Xenophon, *Anabasis*, 1.1.9; cf. *HPE*, pp. 615–617; 986–987.

27. A. Christensen, *Les gestes des rois* (1936), pp. 126–136.

28. See S. Shaked, "Andarz I" (1987), and Z. Safa, "Andarz II" (1987); also C.-H. de Fouchécour, *Notions morales* (1986).

29. Text translated by M. Grignaschi in "Quelques spécimens" (1966), pp. 68, 83; see also Fouchécour, *Notions morales* (1986), p. 85ff.

30. Justin 11.15: *corpusque regio more sepeliri et reliquias ejus majorum tumulus inferri jussit.*

31. Plutarch, *Fortune of Alexander*, 2.12 (= *Moralia*, 348B).

32. Diodorus 17.73.3: *basilikē taphē;* Arrian 3.22.1.

33. Arrian 4.20.5.

34. Ibid., 7.4.4–8.

35. On this point, see R. Davis, "Greek and Persian Romances" (2002a), p. 339: "We may take this concern with exogamy as emblematic of the political relationships espoused by a national epic."

36. See also al-Ma'sūdī (23: 149–151) (which makes Sāsān a devout Muslim coming to offer precious gifts at the Kaaba). Particularly murky at the chronological level, another tradition known to Tabarī (pp. 526–527) and Tha'ālibī (p. 526), makes Aschk, founder of the Askhanian (Arsacid) kingdom, the son of Dārā the Elder. He supposedly killed his brother Dārā the Younger, "in Alexander's time," then killed Antiochus, before being attacked by the Roman emperor Constantine. While emphasizing that the Askhanians undoubtedly belonged to the royal (Keyānid) race, Tha'ālibī rightly insists on the uncertainty of the many dynastic legends.

37. My warm thanks to Marina Gaillard, who made available to me her unpublished French translation of the romance. I have used it systematically here and have also greatly benefited from the introduction she prepared; see also Gaillard, *Alexandre en Iran* (2005).

38. See Plutarch's *Mulierum virtutes* 3 (cf. P. A. Stadter, *Plutarch's Historical Methods* [1965], pp. 53–56); this collection of exempla later inspired Boccaccio in his *De mulieribus claris*.

39. Ctesias, *Persica*, 54.

40. Polyaenus, *Strategemata*, 8.27. Warned of the revolt of a subject people while she is taking her bath, Rhodogune hastily ties back her hair and swears not to wash it again so long as she has not defeated the rebels. After her victory, she takes a bath and carefully washes her hair: "The royal seal of the Persians bears an image of Rhodogune with her hair attached" [*sic*].

12. Darius in Battle: Variations on the Theme "Images and Realities"

1. Plutarch, *Fortune of Alexander*, 2.13 (= *Moralia*, 344D–E).

2. I quote from the French translation (1968).

3. For example, regarding the "Naples Mosaic."

4. Curtius 3.3.17.

5. G. Dumézil, "Le costume de guerre du dernier Darius" (1985).

6. Inscription of Darius in Persepolis (*DPd; HPE*, pp. 182, 241, with commentary by E. Benveniste, "Traditions iraniennes" (1938), pp. 538–543, and G. Dumézil, *Mythe et épopée*, vol. 5 (1986), pp. 617–621.

7. Polyaenus 7.11.12. See my comments in *HPE*, pp. 239–240 and the bibliographical note, p. 914–915.

8. Xenophon, *Cyropaedia*, 1.5.14; 8.3.11–12; Herodotus 7.40–41.

9. Curtius 3.3.8; cf. *HPE*, pp. 189–190.

10. Curtius 4.13.11 ("the Sun, Mithras, and the sacred, eternal fire"); 4.14.24 ("By our country's gods, by the eternal fire . . . by the bright sun"); see also Plutarch, *Alexander*, 30.5–8 (Oromazdes/Ahura Mazda; Mithra).

11. On the displacements of the Achaemenid court and their political significance, see my "Le nomadisme du Grand roi" (1988) and *HPE*, pp. 183–195, which draws a comparison with the "royal entrances" studied by B. Guenée (1967) and Guenée and Lehoux (1968), then by J. Boutier, A. Dewerpe, and D. Nordman in *Un tour de France royal* (1984), and by M.-F. Wagner and D. Vaillancourt in *Le roi dans la ville* (2001); for the Islamic societies and kingdoms, see J. Dakhlia, *Le divan des rois* (1998), pp. 308ff.; the model was also used within the context of the Inca empire: cf. A. Kolata, "Andean Cities" (1996).

12. Quoted from the French translation of M. Grignaschi (1966), p. 19.

13. Herodotus 7.39–41 (Xerxes leaves Sardis); Curtius 3.3.8–25 (Darius III leaves Babylon); see also Goukowsky, "Le cortège des 'rois de Babylone'" (1998).

14. Diodorus 17.35.3; Curtius 3.3.22–23; 3.8.12; 3.9.6; the famous story of the captive Persian princesses implies that their tent was located near the royal tent (Curtius 3.11.3).

15. Curtius 3.9.6: *in medium agmen* (in Latin, *agmen* designates "the army on the march," in opposition to the "fighting army").

16. Arrian 3.11.5; likewise, apparently, in Diodorus 17.34.6–7 (Darius is brought another chariot) and 37.1 (he flees in haste, riding his best horses one after another); also Curtius 3.11.26 (the king in flight constantly changes horses); on the horse relays in the royal post system, see *HPE*, pp. 369–371.

17. Curtius 3.11.11; Plutarch, *Alexander*, 33.8; Aelian, *De natura animalium*, 6.48.

18. See Agathias's opuscule on the history and institutions of the Sassanid Persians (A. Cameron's edition, 1969–1970); "Persian customs" cited in Procopius, *De belli*, 1.3.17, 20; 1.5.1–2, 8, 40; 1.6.14; 1.9.7; 1.11.3–4, 34–35, 37; 1.16.28; 1.18.52; 2.28.25–26; see P. Briant, "Perses et Iraniens" (2002b).

19. Evagrius, *Historia ecclesiastica*, 212.15: *gegraphé nomon;* Theophylactus, *Historiae*, 3.14; *epoiēsato nomōi . . . thesmothetei;* John of Ephesus, *Historia ecclesiastica*, 6.9. The texts are presented and subtly analyzed by M. Whitby in "The Persian King at War" (1994).

20. See Koinos's speech at the Hyphasis, Arrian 5.27.5–6; on the reactions of the Macedonian soldiers, see my remarks in *Rois, tributs et paysans* (1982a), pp. 36–39, 73–81; cf. the fears expressed by the Greek mercenaries after Cyrus's death: Xenophon, *Anabasis*, 3.1.2–3; also Tissaphernes's speech to the Greek mercenaries, 2.5.16–22; as H. Tonnet notes in *Recherches* (1988), 1:256–257, Arrian was also inspired by Xenophon.

21. Arrian 6.13.1–3.

22. Ibid., 6.13.4.

23. Polybius 10.19.4; cf. also Arrian 5.18.4–5 (Porus).

24. Curtius 3.11.7: *Alexander non ducis magis quam militis munia exequebatur.*

25. Lucian, *Dialogi mortuorum*, 12.5: *philokindynos . . . prokindyneuein tou stratou.*

26. Plutarch, *Fortune of Alexander*, 1.4 (= *Moralia*, 327E): *aboulos, propētēs.*

27. Arrian 4.8.5–6; cf. 1.15.8; Kleitos cut off the arm of Spithridates, who was preparing to strike Alexander from behind.

28. On the importance of the theme of monomachia in the flatterers' writings, see the anecdote reported (in the form of a monarchical fable) by Lucian, *Quomodo Historia conscribenda sit,* 12; during a journey on the Hydaspes in India, Alexander throws into the river a manuscript in which Callisthenes reported a duel between the king and Porus.

29. Arrian sought to resolve these disputes: "Let me mention these facts as a digression from the main narrative, so that the correct account of such great deeds [*erga*] and calamities may not be a matter of indifference to men of the future" (6.11.8).

30. Curtius 10.7.2; on that discussion, see my analysis in *Antigone le Borgne* (1973), pp. 323–327, and my note in *HPE,* p. 1050 and *Alexander the Great* (2010), pp. 143–144; on the relationship between the monarchy and the people in Macedonia, see M. Hatzopoulos, *Macedonian Institutions* (1996), 1:261–322.

31. Curtius 3.11.17; see also Diodorus 17.38.3.

32. Polybius 6.54.4: *tes tōn koinōn pragmatōn aphaleias.*

33. See H. Flower, "The Tradition of the *Spolia Opima*" (2000).

34. Curtius 9.5.1: *magis ad famam temeritatis quam gloriam insignem.*

35. Ibid., 4.16.29: *in illo ardore animi vix credi potest, prudentius quam avidius persecutus est.*

36. Arrian 1.13.6.

37. Plutarch, *Alexander,* 16.4: in Greek, the opposition is between *manikōs* (insanely) and *gnōmē* (reason, intelligence).

38. Plutarch, *Artaxerxes,* 8.2–3: *mē kindyneuein auton . . . mē phylaxasthai ton kindynon* (Clearchus's reproaches).

39. Diodorus 14.23.7: *prokheiroteron kindyneuōn.*

40. Arrian 1.18.6–9: *gnōmē.*

41. Plutarch, *Alexander,* 16.5.

42. Arrian 1.14.7.

43. Ibid., 2.10.5.

44. Polybius 10.22.5–6.

45. [Aristotle], *Peri Kosmou* 399a (*HPE,* pp. 259–261); on the theme of the "invisible prince" in a completely different chronological and cultural context, see also the reflections of J. Dakhlia, *Le divan des rois* (1998), pp. 238–242.

46. See Diodorus 17.54.6, and Plutarch, *Fortune of Alexander*, 1.10 (= *Moralia*, 332A).

47. My discussion on the warrior function of the king in modern France is inspired by J. Cornette's *Le roi de guerre* (1993), esp. chap. 6, "Un roi présent à la tête de ses armées?" pp. 177–207.

48. See Plutarch, *Alexander*, 16.7: "Alexander himself . . . was made a conspicuous figure by his shield and the long white plume which hung down on each side of his helmet."

49. On the polemical attacks against Henry III and his *mignons*, see G. Poirier, *L'homosexualité* (1996), pp. 109ff., quotation at p. 111; N. Le Roux, *La faveur du roi* (2000), pp. 622–629, on lampoons directly denouncing the feminization of mores under the combined influence of bad princes and their unworthy favorites; see also pp. 276–270.

50. On this individual, in addition to the entry in the *Nouvelle biographie universelle* (1862), vol. 22, col. 255–261, see esp. R. Pintard, *Libertinage érudit* (2000 [1943]), pp. 127–148 (on his moral and philosophical positions); and Cornette, *Roi de guerre*, pp. 182–184. Quotations taken from F. La Mothe Le Vayer's *Oeuvres* (1669 edition).

51. Plutarch, *Fortune of Alexander*, 1.9 (= *Moralia* 331C): Every part of his body "called to his remembrance the conquered nation and the victory, what cities he had taken, what kings had surrendered themselves; never striving to conceal or cover those indelible characters and scars of honor . . . he always carried [them] about him as the engraven testimonies of his virtue and fortitude."

52. J.-M. Bercé, *Le roi caché* (1990), p. 226.

53. N. Perrot d'Ablancourt, *Lettres et préfaces critiques* (1972), pp. 131–135; see R. Zuber, *Les "belles infidèles"* (1955), pp. 165–279, esp. pp. 206–214.

54. See C. Grell and C. Michel, *L'École des princes* (1988), esp. pp. 64–70 and 220–223 (analysis of one of the paintings commissioned from Le Brun).

55. G. Sabatier, *Versailles ou la figure du roi* (1999), p. 341, and all of chap. 8, "Le roi de guerre," pp. 334–397; see also J. Cornette, *Roi de guerre*, chap. 8, "Versailles, temple du roi de guerre." Much later, Napoleon would also judge that "the presence of the general is indispensable, he is the head, the totality of an army. . . . It is not the Macedonian army but Alexander that was on the Indus. . . . It is Caesar who conquered Gaul" (*Mémoires*, 1935), 3:90.

56. I mention in passing the figure of the "coward knight," which existed alongside the dominant figure of the hero of the "Homeric" type in medieval literature: cf. D. A. Miller, "Other Kinds of Hero" (2000).

57. See the helpful clarification by H. Van Wees, "Kings in Combat" (1988).

58. It is also expressed in Procopius 1.17.29–30, within the context of the Sassanid court.

59. Diodorus 17.30.7, 17.31.1.

60. Ibid., 11.71.2 (satraps named by Artaxerxes I: cf. *HEP*, p. 588); 17.7.2 (Darius himself in 334).

61. Curtius 4.15.30: "It is said that Darius drew his dagger and considered avoiding ignominious flight by an honourable death"; Justin 11.14.3: "Darius, when he saw his army repulsed, wished himself to die"; Orosius 3.17.3.

62. Justin 11.14.3 *(sed a proximis fugere compulsus est)*; Orosius 3.17.3: "He was forced to flee on the insistence of his people [*persuasu suorum fugere compulsus est*]."

63. See H. Sancisi-Weerdenburg, "The Death of Cyrus" (1985).

Thematic Notes by Chapter

N.B. The full titles of the studies cited in abridged form below can be found in the general bibliography.

Notes to Chapter 1. A Shadow among His Own

∞ In 1787 Volney published *Voyage en Égypte et en Syrie (Travels through Egypt and Syria,* translated from the French in 2 volumes; New York, 1798), then, in 1788, *Considérations sur la guerre des Turcs (Considerations on the War with the Turks,* translated from the French, London, 1788); he is also the author of *Chronologie d'Hérodote, conforme à son texte* (Paris, 1809).

—On Hegel and Persia, cf. Panaino's "La Persia nel pensiero" (1987).

—On the expectations for the mission that the Russian minister set for Ker Porter, see N. E. Vasileva, "About the History of Sir Robert Ker Porter's Album" (1994). On the investiture reliefs, see L. Vanden Berghe, "Scènes d'investiture" (1987) and *Reliefs rupestres* (1992), particularly pp. 64–67 on the relief of Ardašir in Naqsh-e Rustam; see also E. Schmidt, *Persepolis*, vol. 3 (1970), pp. 122–123 and photographic plates 81 (relief) and 82 (inscriptions).

—On the different editions of Chardin's *Voyages* and on the other publications, see D. Van der Cruysse, *Chardin le Persan* (1998), pp. 517–520, as well as R. W. Ferrier, *A Journey to Persia* (1996), and J. Emerson, "Chardin" (1992). Chardin visited Persepolis three times, in 1666, 1667, and 1674, the third time accompanied by the draftsman Grelot (Van der Cruysse, pp. 102–104; 207–212).

—On Flandin, see the two exhibition catalogs *Regards sur la Perse antique* (1998), and E. Flandin: *Voyage en Perse (1840–1841)* (1995), as well as J. Calmard's recent summary "Flandin and Coste" (1999).

—On the figure of De Bruyn and his travels, see J. W. Drijvers et al., eds., *De reizen door het Nabije Oosten* (1997).

—On the journeys of Loti and Morier in Iran, see G. A. Tavassoli, *La société iranienne* (1966), particularly the remarks on Loti's visit to Persepolis (pp. 42–54).

∽ English translations of the royal inscriptions can be found in R. G. Kent, *Old Persian: Grammar, Texts, Lexicon*, 2nd ed. (New Haven, Ct.: American Oriental Society, 1953), and in A. Kuhrt, *The Persian Empire*, 2007. The nonnarrative aspect of the royal inscription has often been analyzed, especially in several innovative studies by H. Sancisi-Weerdenburg, most recently, "The Persian King and History" (1999); a number of comments can also be found in *HPE*, pp. 114–128, 212–216, 518–520, 550–554; on the builder-king, see ibid., pp. 165–171, 554, 573, 675–676. On the passage from Plutarch, *Alexander*, 69.2, see my remarks in "Empire of Darius III" (2009a), pp. 164–165.

∽ On the stages of the rediscovery of Persepolis and on the travelers, see in particular H. Sancisi-Weerdenburg's introduction in *Through Travellers' Eyes* (1991), pp. 1–35, as well as the articles collected in that volume; see also the catalog of the exhibition that Sancisi-Weerdenburg held in Groningen in 1989 on that theme *(Persepolis en Pasargadae)*, with an extremely useful list of travelers and their publications, pp. 96–104. Many quotations from travelers in Persia appear in Vaux's very helpful *Nineveh and Persepolis* (1850), pp. 286–437. See also E. Herzfeld, "Rapport sur l'état actuel des ruines de Persépolis" (1929–1930); the last part of the report deals with the "scope and duration of the clearing work and the discoveries to be expected" (pp. 36–38). The chronology of the works projects conducted in Persepolis in the time of Artaxerxes III and subsequently raises many problems, some of which have remained unresolved since the halting of the planned excavations. In addition to the indications to be found in Schmidt, *Persepolis*, 1:279–280 and 3:99–107 (royal tombs of Persepolis) and 3:162–163 (reliefs of Artaxerxes III), see especially A.-B. Tilia's innovative *Studies*, vol. 2 (1972), pp. 243ff.; also M. Roaf, *Sculptures* (1983), pp. 140–141, and P. Calmeyer, "Das Persepolis der Spätzeit" (1990a), pp. 7–36 (p. 12, on the number 12 in Persepolis and in Darius III's cortège), as well as P. Briant, *Darius, les Perses et l'empire* (2001b), p. 106. Initially the displacement of blocks in the southwest region of the terrace of Persepolis was attributed to the measures of Darius III, but it is now certain that it must be dated to the post-Achaemenid period (cf. Schmidt 1:279). As for the archaeological traces of the fire in certain palaces of Persepolis in Alexander's time, there are no truly exhaustive analyses on the question; see H. Sancisi-Weerdenburg's "Alexander and Persepolis" (1993), though I do not agree with her on the question of Alexander's policy and plans.

∽ On the royal tombs of Naqsh-e Rustam and Persepolis, the American excavations (begun by E. Herzfeld and continued by E. Schmidt) have made exhaustive studies possible: see the meticulous descriptions in Schmidt, *Persepolis*, vol. 3 (1970) (attributing tomb V to Artaxerxes II). Iranian archaeologists have continued the excavations; cf. A. Sami, *Persepolis* (Shiraz: Musavi Printing Office, 1975), pp. 81–86; see also M. Root, *King and Kingship* (1979), pp. 73–76; Calmeyer, "Das Persepolis der Spätzeit" (1990a), pp. 10–14 (tomb V: Artaxerxes III), and Kleiss and Calmeyer, "Das unvollendete achaemenidische Felsgrab bei Persepolis" (1975). The most recent study on the inscriptions on tomb I (Naqsh-e Rustam) and tomb V (Persepolis) is R. Schmitt's *Beiträge zur altpersischen Inschriften* (Wiesbaden, 1999), pp. 1–25 (arguing that tomb V is that of Artaxerxes III, hence the initials adopted, A^3Pb; cf. also pp. 91–104); see also Schmitt, *The Old*

Persian Inscriptions of Naqsh-i Rustam and Persepolis (Corpus Inscriptionum Iranicarum, part 1, vol. 1, Text 11) (London, 2000), pp. 119–122, and P. Calmeyer's *Reliefs* (2009), published posthumously.

—The lack of precision in Diodorus's description has already been pointed out several times, for example, in Perrot and Chipiez, *Histoire de l'art*, vol. 5 (1890), pp. 617–618, 627–628.

∞ Royal "portraits" on coins: the drawing of a daric is taken (with minor modifications) from T. Hyde, *Veterum Persarum et Parthorum et Medorum religionis historia*, 2nd ed. (Oxford, 1770), table 2, facing p. 113, and commentary p. 311. A discussion appears in Babelon, vol. 2, part 1 (1907), on "the Median daric and siglos," pp. 250–257, then another on "the numismatic iconography of the Achaemenid kings" (pp. 258–263), where the author makes explicit the basis of his argument. He applies his theory in vol. 2, part 2 (1910), where, after a "general introduction" (pp. 2–31), he passes in review "the kings of Persia of the Achaemenid dynasty" (pp. 38–72). It is there (p. 70) that the drawing I reproduce in the text (Fig. 18) can be found. On the assumptions guiding the portraits of Darius II and Cyrus the Younger, see my remarks in *Rois, tributs et paysans* (1982a), pp. 273–274, with note 37, in *HPE*, p. 1021, and in my *Leçon inaugurale* (2000a), pp. 15–16; see also "Darius III face à Alexandre" (2000c). On the typology of Achaemenid coins, see esp. I. Carradice, "The 'Regal' Coinage" (1987), table of types, p. 78; D. Stronach, "Early Achaemenid Coinage" (1989), table of types, p. 260, repr. here fig. 20; and finally, M. Alram, "Dareikos und Siglos" (1993), analysis of a treasure of 1491 siglos from Asia Minor, and presentation of type IV/3–5, which may date to Artaxerxes III and Darius III. For darics and double darics struck in Babylon after Alexander's death, see. H. Nicolet-Pierre, "Argent et or frappés en Babylonie" (1999), pp. 296–305, and G. Le Rider, *Alexander the Great: Coinage, Finances and Policy* (2007), pp. 201ff.

∞ The "discovery" of an Arses/Artaxerxes IV in the Xanthos trilingual inscription can be credited to E. Badian: see bibliography in *HPE*, pp. 1011–1012, and in my article in *CRAI* (1998): 305n1, translated into English in *KCP*, chap. 3, n. 2.

∞ Administrative Documents
  —Thebes papyrus dating to Darius: D. Devauchelle, "Réflexions sur les documents égyptiens" (1995), p. 43;
  —Bucheum stela: ibid., p. 37 (referring to the original English publication of 1934); Wadi-Daliyeh papyri: Cross, *Eretz-Israel* 8 (1985): 7–17; and D. G. Gropp, *Wadi-Daliyeh*, vol. 2 (2001);
  —On the Babylonian documentation from the end of the Achaemenid period, see the explanations by A. Kuhrt in Kuhrt, Sancisi-Weerdenburg et al. (1987), vol. 1, pp. 147–157; by G. Van Driel, ibid., pp. 159–181 (p. 164, on a tablet from Ur perhaps dating to Darius III), and by M. Stolper in *CAH* VI² (1994): 234–260, esp. pp. 240–241; a number of recent publications have appeared in that field. The Babylonian list of rations was published in F. Joannès, *Textes économiques* (1982), pp. 331–336 (cf. pp. 331–332 on dating criteria: "a cluster of presumptions [more] than indisputable proof"; cf. Stolper's reservations in *CAH* VI², p. 240n23); the Larsa texts are published and

annotated in Joannès, "Les débuts de l'époque hellénistique à Larsa" (2001), and Joannès, "La Babylonie méridionale" (2006). Several Babylonian chronicles are available online at http://www.livius.org/babylonia.html.

—Astronomical tablets: The texts were edited (in three volumes) by A. J. Sachs and H. Hunger, *Astronomical Diaries*, vol. 1 (1988); the introduction, pp. 11–38, has many explanations that I have adopted in part; the numbering adopted by the editors, -330, -322, etc., raises a few problems, well explained by R. Van der Spek in his long and important book review (1993, esp. pp. 92–93). Twenty-seven texts date to the Achaemenid period: three (actually, only two) by Artaxerxes I: one by Darius II; fifteen (in fact, sixteen) by Artaxerxes II; five by Artaxerxes III; and three by Darius III. Several of the tablets dating to Artaxerxes II have been edited and studied by R. Van der Spek, "The Chronology of the Wars of Artaxerxes II" (1998) (see also my remarks in *HEP*, pp. 633–634, 1010–1011, and *BHAch* 2:93–94); see also his "Darius III, Alexander the Great" (2003), where the astronomical tablets and the cuneiform literary texts from that period are assembled and analyzed; and also G. del Monte, *Testi della Babylonia ellenistica* (1997), pp. 1–17. On the difficulties in interpreting certain information, particularly prices and their variations, see several studies in J. Andreau, P. Briant, and R. Descat, eds., *Prix et formation des prix dans les économies antiques* (Saint-Bertrand-de-Commingnes, 1997), esp. pp. 313–356, and *La guerre dans les économies antiques* (Saint-Bertrand-de-Commingnes, 2000), pp. 293–313. On the date of Alexander's death in tablet -322, cf. L. Depuydt's study in *WO* 28 (1997): 117–135, and R. Van der Spek's remarks in *Orientalia* 69/4 (2000): 435.

∞ The question of reign names among the Achaemenids (*HPE*, pp. 777 and 1033), with references to earlier studies, was first discussed by A. J. Sachs in *AJAH* 2 (1977): 129–147, then in R. Schmitt, "Achaemenid Throne-Names" (1982), where the Greco-Roman documentation and the Babylonian documentation are presented side by side; on Artašata/Darius/Codomannus, see pp. 86 and 90–91. Despite Badian's denials ("Darius III" [2000], pp. 247–249 = [2012], pp. 460–461), Codomannus may very well have been (as Schmitt proposed in n. 34, following Harmatta) a nickname given to Artašata, comparable to the case of Bardiya/Smerdis, also known in Xenophon by the name "Tanyoxarkes," which (perhaps like Codomannus) refers to his physical strength. As for the hypothesis presented by Badian concerning a possible Semitic origin of the anthroponym, it should be carefully examined by specialists.

∞ The bibliography on the Satrap Stela has grown considerably since it was first published. I provide a summary of the discussions in *HPE*, pp. 1017–1018 (also p. 959 regarding the expression "eldest son"); see also Devauchelle's subsequent "Réflexions sur les documents égyptiens" (1995); Burstein, "Prelude to Alexander" (2000); Badian, "Darius III" (2000), pp. 252–254 = (2012), p. 463–464 (which neglects most of the more recent studies); see also D. Schäfer, "Ptolemaic Friends?" (2009), and esp. the new translation (quoted here) by R. K. Ritner in Simpson, ed., *Literature of Ancient Egypt* (2003), pp. 392–397, which includes an updated bibliography. On the documents dating to Khababash, see the list drawn up in Huss, "Der rätselhafte Pharao Chababasch"

(1994). On Ptolemy's expedition to Syria, which preceded the confirmation of the donation in Buto, see Winnicki, "Militäroperationem in Syrien" (1991), and, on the Ptolemaic motif of the return of the statues deported by the Persians, an important study by the same author, "Carrying Off and Bringing Home the Statues of the Gods" (1994), about which, however, I expressed a few reservations in an article published in French (2003c) and translated into English as "When Kings Write History," chap. 8 of *KCP*. The connection to Darius's strategic and logistical problems has been argued several times, as has the link with a "Babylonian revolt" (Uruk King List: cf. English translation at http://www.livius.org/k/kinglist/uruk.html); see the discussion and bibliography in *HPE*, pp. 818–820, 1032, 1042–1043.

∞ War and coinage: The hypothesis about the coinage of Sinope was proposed by Harrison, in *Coins of the Persian Satraps* (1982b), pp. 266–284, and "Persian Names on Coins" (1982a); see bibliography and summary in *HPE*, pp. 828–829 and 1043–1044. On the literary sources that make it possible to retrace the career of Mazday (rendered as "Mazaios" in Greek), see Berve, *Alexanderreich* (1926), no. 484, and many occurrences in *HPE* (for example, pp. 845–846 and 1046); and Briant, "Empire of Darius III" (2009a), pp. 160–162, with a comprehensive bibliography. On Mazday's new coinage, see a final assessment of the most recent discussions in *BHAch* 1:62 and *BHAch* 2:99. On the coins of the Egyptian satraps, see especially H. Nicolet-Pierre, "Les monnaies des deux derniers satrapes d'Égypte" (1989), whose conclusions I have adopted.

∞ The inscription of Semtutefnakht has been the occasion for several publications: the most recent and the most precise is Perdu, "Le monument de Samtoutefnakht" (1985), the second part of which was never published; it may be complemented by Tresson, "La stèle de Naples" (1931), and von Känel, *Les prêtres-ouab de Sekhmet* (1984), no. 56, pp. 120–125. Note that, as Bosworth clearly saw (*Classical Philology* 78 [1983], p. 159), the document certainly does not allow us to deduce that Semtutefnakht "collaborated" with Alexander against the Persians: cf. *HPE*, p. 1049.

∞ The tablet mentioning the Persian defeat at Gaugamela and its repercussions is numbered −330 in the Sachs-Hunger collection (1:177–179); it already occasioned the publication of Wiseman's *Nebuchadrezzar and Babylon*, pp. 116–121; the English translation adopted here is provided by A. Kuhrt in her *Persian Empire* (2007), pp. 447–448; an annotated Italian translation also appears in G. Del Monte, *Testi della Babylonia ellenistica* (1997), pp. 1–6. The tablet has given rise to a long and important study by Bernard, "La campagne de Gaugamèles" (1990), pp. 515–529; see also Kuhrt, "Alexander in Babylon" (1990), and my commentary in *HPE*, pp. 828–842, 845–850, and 1043–1050 (reflections on possible archaeological traces near Sippar, of Alexander's campaign after Gaugamela); a new analysis of terminology (concerning the "panic") has recently been proposed by R. Rollinger and K. Ruffing, "'Panik' im Heer" (2012). On the titulature "king of the totality," see Seux, "Les titres royaux" (1965), esp. p. 7, table of occurrences. The Babylonian chronicle mentioning Darius III and the battle against the Haneans was published in Grayson, *Chronicles* (1975), p. 112 (chronicle 8); the identification of Darius III is confirmed by Glassner, *Chroniques* (1993), p. 206; on the appellation "Haneans," see

Briant, "De Samarkand à Sardes" (1994). Based solely on the Greco-Roman sources, and placing my interpretation within the framework of "royal entrances," I previously proposed the existence of a negotiation between the Babylonian authorities and Alexander, on one hand, and between Alexander and Mazday, on the other, in "Le nomadisme du Grand roi" (1988), pp. 255–263; see the new arguments advanced in Kuhrt, "Alexander in Babylon" (1990), and, on an identical practice in Sardis in 334, see another of my articles, "Alexandre à Sardes" (1993), English trans. in *KCP*, chap. 23.

∞ I have eliminated from the discussion a Babylonian text that, following the analyses of Sherwin-White and Kuhrt, I used in *HPE*, pp. 863–864, 1049–1050 (while noting the difficulties of the text) and most recently, in "Alexandre à Babylone" (1999a), pp. 30–32 (quoting a recent French translation by P. Tallon). This is a difficult cuneiform text called "Dynastic Prophecy," which some have wanted to see as a Hellenistic reference to the fight between Alexander and Darius. Rather curiously, the writer seems to present Darius, in the form of a prophecy *ex eventu,* as reconstituting his army and winning the victory over Alexander, thanks to the aid of the Babylonian deities. It was tempting to see that as a Babylonian representation of the transitional period and as evidence of a deterioration in relations between the Macedonian leaders and the Babylonian elites at the time of the wars between Alexander's successors. But, combined with criticism and counterproposals already made after Grayson's publication, the recent reexaminations have now persuaded me not to use this text, which is being read in a completely different manner: see Del Monte, "Da 'barbari' a 're di Babilonia'" (2001), and Van der Spek, "Darius III, Alexander the Great and the Babylonian Scholarship" (2003).

Notes to Chapter 2. Darius Past and Present

∞ The chapter "De Dario Persarum rege" from Boccaccio's *De casibus* is quoted from the P. G. Ricci and V. Zaccarior edition (with Italian translation), in *Tutte le opere di Giovanni Boccacio,* vol. 9 (Milan, 1983), pp. 316–323; on its influence, see G. Cary, *Medieval Alexander* (1956), pp. 252–257, 265 (on Lydgate), 266–267 (on Petrarch). The theater devoted to Darius III (and other Persian kings) was surveyed and introduced in the very useful essay by M. Goldstein, *Darius, Xerxes und Artaxerxes* (1912). On Jacques de la Taille's *Daire* and *Alexandre,* see M. C. Longhi's introduction in *La tragédie à l'époque d'Henri II et de Charles IX* (1992). On the influence of the authors of the Vulgate and of Orosius, see the well-researched pages in Ross, *Alexander historiatus* (1963), p. 18 *(Histoire ancienne jusqu'à César),* 67–80, and 80–83 for the first translations of Arrian, Diodorus, and Plutarch; on Orosius, see M.-P. Aranus-Lindet's introduction in *Histoires (contre les païens),* vol. 1 (Paris, 1990), pp. vii–xcix; on the use of Orosius and Justin in the *Roman de Toute Chevalerie* by Thomas de Kent (about 1175), see Gaullier-Bougassas, *Les romans d'Alexandre* (1998), pp. 187–188, 221. On the popularity of Curtius in the medieval and modern periods, see S. Dosson, *Étude sur Quinte-Curce* (1887), pp. 357–380; more recently, see M. G. Longhi, *La tragédie* (1992), p. 274n3 (list of French translations published in the first decades of the sixteenth century), and Raynaud, "Alexandre dans les bibliothèques bourguignonnes" (1999); on Vasque de Lucène, see also R. Bossuat, "Vasque de Lucène" (1946), and Hériché, *Édition critique* (2000), pp. xxxv–xxxvi, who points out that, from 1180 onward, Gautier de Châtillon followed Curtius rather than Pseudo-Callisthenes's romance. On the first translations of Arrian, see Ross, *Alexander historiatus* (1963), pp. 80–81; on Perrot d'Ablancourt's translation, see R. Zuber, *Les "belles infidèles"* (1995), and *Lettres et préfaces critiques* (1972), pp. 131–144 (the fawning dedication is addressed to "Monseigneur le duc d'Anguien"); on Mehmed the Conqueror's reading of Arrian, see J. Raby, "Mehmed the Conqueror's Greek Scriptorium" (1983), pp. 18–19 (my thanks to Gilles Veinstein for this reference). On images of Alexander in the Middle Ages and Renaissance, see the books edited by C. Gaullier-Bougassas (2011) and by C. Jouanno (2012).

∞ On Rollin, see my study "La tradition gréco-romaine sur Alexandre le Grand dans l'Europe moderne et contemporaine" (2003b), which includes a bibliography. Neither of the two German editions of Droysen's *Geschichte Alexander des Grossen* (1833 and 1877) has been translated into English. Droysen's work has often been analyzed; the most useful study is still Bravo's *Philologie, histoire, philosophie de l'histoire* (1968), along with the recent intellectual biography by W. Nippel, *Droysen* (2008). Bravo's book also has a number of interesting discussions of Droysen's contemporaries and predecessors, such as J. Gillies, G. Grote, and B. G. Niebuhr; on these authors see Briant, *Alexandre des Lumières* (2012); on B. G. Niebuhr and German historiography, see also J. R. Knipfing, "German Historians and Macedonian Imperialism" (1921). On Rawlinson, see Sancisi-Weerdenburg, "The Fifth Oriental Monarchy and Hellenocentrism" (1987a). The literature on Grote is vast: most of the references are cited in my "George Grote on Alexander" (forthcoming b) .

—On the Alexander of Tarn and that of Schachermeyr, see, respectively, two studies by A. B. Bosworth, "The Impossible Dream" (1983) and "Ingenium und Macht" (1988c); on Tarn's book, see also R. Todd, "W. W. Tarn" (1965), and, on Schachermeyr's work, R. Andreotti, *RFIC* (1951). On Alexander historiography in the nineteenth and twentieth centuries, see Briant, "Alexandre et l'hellénisation de l'Asie" (2005a) and "Alexander and the Persian Empire" (2009b).

∞ On the historical novel *The Persian Boy* by Mary Renault and its relation to the ancient sources, see Spencer's interesting remarks in *The Roman Alexander* (2002), pp. 212–213.

∞ Return to the sources. I have addressed elsewhere certain themes treated in these pages. Because my aim here is not to conduct a detailed or exhaustive historiographical analysis of recent works on the Persian Empire and on the history of Alexander (because they are both so repetitive and unoriginal on Darius), I have simply indicated in the text (implicit) references to a few very traditional historiographical orientations, which—despite firm, convincing, and repeated warnings (see also Nylander, "Darius III" [1993])—have remained particularly durable and persistent:

—The often glaring and increasingly incomprehensible inadequacy (with respect to the progress in Achaemenid history) of the portrayals of Darius III's empire could be illustrated by many examples. To be persuaded, you need only consider, one by one, the books that have appeared on Alexander over a period of twenty years (cf. Briant, *Alexander the Great* [2010], pp. 153–174), though some are more cartoonish than others. It is rather distressing to observe how absent the Achaemenid context continues to be in the reflections proposed by several authors in the most recently published works (ibid., pp. 174–185);

—The topos of Achaemenid decadence has persisted since Xerxes, resulting in a simplistic explanation for Alexander's conquest: see bibliography, comments, and suggestions in Briant, "History and Ideology" (2002d), "The Theme of 'Persian Decadence' " (2005b), "Alexander and the Persian Empire" (2009b), and *Alexandre des Lumières* (2012), esp. chap. 16 ("Alexandre, l'Europe et l'Orient immobile").

—That topos is also linked to overt claims about the economic and commercial development spurred by Alexander: see Briant 2009b, and 2010, pp. 83–100.

—On the recurrent judgments of Artaxerxes III's reign, see, e.g., Lauffer, *Alexander* (1978), p. 8; A. B. Bosworth, *Conquest and Empire* (1988b), p. 17; and finally, Mildenberg, "Artaxerxes III" (1999a), which is based on the coinage attributed to the king. But Mildenberg seems not to know (p. 200) that, in reality, the favorable portrait of Artaxerxes III he is proposing is not really new (cf. for example, H. Horworth, "The History and Coinage of Artaxerxes III" [1903], p. 3, following Nöldeke);

—The (no less traditional) physical and moral portrait of Darius III also persists, combined with a reference to his Cadusian exploit, but without any literary or anthropological analysis of the narrative;

—on his ability to oppose Alexander: see, e.g., Green, *Alexander* (1974), p. 102;

—on his overwhelming personal responsibility at the military and strategic levels: see, e.g., Worthington, "How 'Great' Was Alexander?" (1999), pp. 46–47; and, even though his personal courage is acknowledged, Strauss and Ober, *The Anatomy of Error* (1990), pp. 112–113, 124–131; and Hornblower, *CAH* 6, no. 2 (1994): 53;

—Then there are those, more circumspect but disappointing, who judge that nothing reliable can be said: e.g., Lane Fox, *Alexander* (1986), p. 100.

—The well-worn thesis of the impossibility, even for a courageous and intelligent man such as Darius, to come out the victor against Alexander, already argued by Bossuet and endlessly repeated since then, has again been adopted very recently by Badian ("Darius III" [2000], p. 265 = [2012], p. 470), in a rather disappointing conclusion to his study of the last Great King: "He found himself facing one of history's greatest military leaders. What might have sufficed against an Agesilaus proved totally inadequate against Alexander."

∽ Among the Iranists, the most notable effort to reassess Darius is Nylander's "Darius III" (1993), which resituates the Naples Mosaic within the recent Achaemenid Studies movement (see in particular, pp. 145–147 and nn. 3–9). Of the classicists, J. Seibert, following Wirth's "Dareios und Alexander" (1971; reprinted and further developed in *Der Brand von Persepolis* [1993], pp. 33ff.), pointed out that the history of Darius has been seen unilaterally from the European point of view (*Alexander der Grosse* [1972], p. 80) and sought to adopt another view in a specialized article ("Dareios III" [1987]), but in it he adopted a quite traditional method, and the results are therefore rather disappointing. Badian's "Darius III" (1994) is merely a summary and, though helpful, his more recent study (2000) is infinitely less innovative than the author—who shows little regard or consideration for his predecessors—complacently wants to suggest. I attempt a new assessment in "The Empire of Darius III" (2009a) and in *Alexander the Great* (2010); cf. the first edition (1974) of *Alexandre le Grand* (7th ed. 2011).

ç⁄o On the recent renewal of (ancient) debates about the consequences of Alexander's conquests and the judgments to be made about the individual and his methods, see the polemic that has unfolded, for example, in *Ancient History Bulletin* 13, nos. 2–4 (1999): 39–55, 111–117, 136–140, with respect to and on the basis of A. B. Bosworth's *Alexander and the East* (1996). I note in passing that Worthington's "How 'Great' Was Alexander?" (1999), pp. 39–55, which is supposed to revise downward Alexander's "greatness," relies on an extraordinary number of hackneyed topoi and methodological errors, which Holt's responses ("Alexander the Great: In the Interests of Historical Accuracy?" [1999], and "The Death of Coenus" [2000]) analyze in only a very partial manner. I shall not insist on that problem here, as this is not the place to develop my own views; I shall return to it elsewhere, in dealing more specifically with the history of Alexander: cf. "Alexandre et l'hellénisation de l'Asie" (2005a), esp. pp. 42–62.

ç⁄o Concerning the reexamination of Darius's qualities as a leader and strategist, note that one of the first in the recent period to attempt to reevaluate Darius was Marsden, *Gaugamela* (1964), pp. 5–6, then Murrison, "Darius III and the Battle of Issus" (1972), and more recently, E. Badian, "Darius III" (2000) and E. E. Garvin, "Darius III and Homeland Defense" (2003). I shall not deal here with controversies between specialists on the reconstruction of battles. By way of example, I refer to two articles on the Battle of the Granicus published in the same collection (and under the same title, as a result of an error on the part of the publishers), by two authors, Badian and Foss ("The Battle of Granicus: A New Look" [1977]). The debate is interminable, and since then Hammond's own reconstruction ("The Battle of the Granicus River" [1980]) has shown that the side taken is based on a (rather unconvincing) choice that he and many others make between one of the two versions, with respect to the trust to be granted to the postulated source. Badian concludes that, as is often the case, the heroization of Alexander prevents us from doing an adequate analysis of his plan, and hence of his success. He adds, however (in opposition to the doubts strongly expressed by Dellbrueck, n. 58): "We need not despair of all understanding" (pp. 292–293). Of course! But is it not appropriate from time to time to admit as well that the state of the documentation prevents us from going further, as least in the factual reconstitution of the topography and of the events? As for the complicated diagrams, filled with colored arrows that supposedly reconstitute in great detail the movements of the different contingents (cf. Hammond's article but also several articles by A. M. Devine— published in *AncW* 12 [1985]: 25–59; 13 [1986]: 87–115; 15 [1988]: 3–20—and Sekunda and

Warry's *Alexander the Great* [1988], or Hammond's *The Genius of Alexander* [1997], pp. 88, 107, 165), is it impertinent to observe that they are not necessarily convincing? On this point I refer to the still-relevant reflections on the Persian Wars in Whatley ("On the Possibility of Reconstructing Battles" [1964]): "I am afraid that the more I study the subject the more sceptical I become about the possibility of reconstructing the details of these battles and campaigns. . . . Of most of the propositions [concerning Marathon] advanced, I feel myself compelled to repeat 'It is probable and the contrary is also probable'" (pp. 119 and 139).

Notes to Chapter 3. "The Last Darius, the One Who Was Defeated by Alexander"

∾ On the birth of the genre of biography and its development in the Hellenistic period, see the always stimulating studies of A. Momigliano, *The Development of Greek Biography* (1971) and "Mise au point sur la biographie grecque" (1983 [1971]); see also the studies in the collection edited by F. Paschoud (1998).

—On Cornelius Nepos and his work, see Geiger, "Cornelius Nepos, *De regibus exterarum gentium*" (1979); and McCarthy, "The Content" (1974).

—The bibliography on Plutarch is too vast to list; in addition to J. R. Hamilton, *Commentary* (1969), I note only two recent books (in which, however, Alexander and Darius are hardly discussed), T. Duff, *Plutarch's Lives* (1999), and Pelling, *Plutarch and History* (2002; collection of eighteen articles by the author).

∾ To my knowledge, there is no recent overview of the literature of exempla in antiquity. The best introduction is still Lumpe, *"Exemplum"* (1966). A great deal of information and many reflections can also be found in Bompaire, *Lucien* (1958), pp. 162–191, 333–378, 443–468; see also the proceedings of the colloquium edited by Berlioz and David (1980), where, compared to antiquity, the Middle Ages is, not surprisingly, particularly well represented, because of the abundance of research in that field: cf., for example, Le Goff, *Saint Louis* (1996), esp. part 2, chap. 4, pp. 363–387: "Le roi des 'exempla,'" with bibliography; on the "deeds and sayings of Alexander," used as exempla in medieval and modern literature, see Cary, *The Medieval Alexander* (1956), pp. 143–162 ("The Conception of Alexander in the Books of 'Exempla' and in Preachers"); and the proceedings of the colloquium published in Aerts and Gosman, eds., *Alexander the Great and Other Heroes* (1988); on the use of ancient exempla by the church fathers, see Carlson, "Pagan Examples" (1948). The study of the exemplum has been less innovative among specialists in antiquity, as J. M. David noted in 1980 in Berlioz and David, *Rhétorique et histoire* (1980), p. 23: "It is only in recent years that interest has grown in what should be a means for better understanding certain kinds of transference from myth to behavior and from behavior to myth."

∾ See the French editions of the various authors cited in the text, plus a few specialized studies, primarily dedicated to the authors of the principate, especially Valerius Maximus and his contemporaries: in addition to the introduction and copious notes of

Combès in the Collection des Universités de France (Belles Lettres) edition, vols. 1 (1995) and 2 (1997), see Helm, "Valerius Maximus" (1939); André, "*L'otium* chez Valère Maxime et Velleius Paterculus" (1965); Maslakov, "Valerius Maximus and Roman Historiography" (1984); on Seneca, see also Fillion-Lahille, "Le *De ira*" (1989). On the use of exempla in Livy, see Chaplin, *Livy's Exemplary History* (2000); on the work of Velleius Paterculus and its objectives, a recent overview and bibliography can be found in DeMonte, "Velleius Paterculus and 'Triumphal' History" (1999). On Aelian, see J. K. Kindstrand, "Claudianus Aelianus und sein Werke" (1998), and L. Prandi, *Memorie storiche*, (2005), pp. 81–90 ("L'Alessandro di Eliano"). On the Deipnosophists by Athenaeus, see Zecchini, *La cultura storica di Ateneo* (1989), and Braund and Wilkens, eds., *Athenaeus and His World* (2000); there is now an edition with an annotated Italian translation, *Ateneo: I Deipnosophisti*, 4 vols. (2001), including a remarkable introduction by Jacob ("Ateneo, o il dedalo delle parole" [2001]), which merits an attentive reading.

⚭ On the genre of exempla concerning the deaths of famous men and/or the last words pronounced on their deathbeds, see Ronconi, *Exitus illustrium virorum* (1940), and his overview, "*Exitus illustrium virorum*" (1966) as well as—much earlier—W. Schmidt, *De ultimis morientium verbis* (1914) and Marx's more specific "Tacitus und die Literatur der *exitus illustrium virorum*" (1937).

⚭ For the Vulgate authors, in addition to Tarn's pages in *Alexander*, 2:1–133, and Goukowsky's introduction to book 17 of Diodorus of Sicily ("Notice," 1976), see, within a vast bibliography, Hamilton, "Cleitarchus and Diodorus" (1977), Bosworth, "Arrian and the Alexander Vulgate" (1976), and Tonnet, "La 'Vulgate' dans Arrien" (1987), as well as his *Recherches*, 1:107–132 (1988); see also Prandi, *Fortuna e realtà dell'opera di Clitarco* (1996), along with D. Asheri's book review, *QdS* 48/2 (1998): 229–233 and the long review article by Bosworth in *Histos* (1997 = http://research.ncl.ac.uk/histos/documents/1997.RD08BosworthPrandiClitarco211224.pdf).

—On Curtius, see Dosson's classic but dated *Étude sur Quinte-Curce* (1887). Works on Quintus Curtius have multiplied in recent years: see the essays by Dempsie (1991), Moore (1995), and Spencer (2002), the historical commentary by Atkinson (1980, 1994), the translation and commentary on book 10 by Atkinson and Yardley (2009), and the very helpful critical bibliography by Koch, *Curtius-Forschung* (2000). On the composition of the book, see Baynham, *Quintus Curtius* (1998), esp. chap. 5 (pp. 132–164), titled, "*Regnum* in the First Pentad: Alexander and Darius"; see also Atkinson, "Q. Curtius Rufus' 'Historiae Alexandri Magni'" (1998). On his methods and on the limits of his credibility as a historian, see Atkinson's account in *Commentary I* (1980), and Bosworth (1983): 150–161; the long book reviews of Baynham's book by Koch, *Histos* (1999 = http://research.ncl.ac.uk/histos/documents/1999.RD02Kochon-BaynhamAlexander140146.pdf), and Fears, *AJPh* 122, no. 3 (2001): 447–451; as well as McKechnie's very interesting article "Manipulations of Themes" (1999).

⚭ The *Alexander Romance* is the name given to a diverse set of texts, each version (the technical term is "recension") differing from the others in content. The history of the text is very complicated: see Franco (1999), pp. 47–56, and the variants presented and translated by Bounoure and Serret (1992), pp. 151–225, and Stoneman (1991), p. 1–32. For a more complete account, see Jouanno (2002), pp. 13–55 and 247–462. A large number of studies and commentaries have been and continue to be written on these documents. It would be pointless, however, to give a complete list of them, because the figure of Darius is regularly missing from the analyses. Vast bibliographies can be found in the proceedings of the specialized conferences held in recent years: Bridges and Bürgel, eds., *The Problematics of Power* (1996); Finazzi and Valvo, eds., *La diffusione dell'eredità classica* (1998); Harf-Lancner, Kappler, and Suard, eds., *Alexandre le Grand* (1999); and Polignac, ed., *Alexandre le Grand* (2000). Among the most noteworthy recent publications, see the collections edited by Stoneman and Erikson (2012), Gaulier-Bougassas (2011), and Jouanno (2012). On the relation between history and fiction, see Abel, *Roman* (1995), pp. 37–46; Franco, "Romanzo" (1999), pp. 57–65; Baynham, "Who Put the 'Romance' in the Alexander Romance?" (1995); and Jouanno, *Naissances* (2002), pp. 127–190 and 57–125 (on the Romance's Egyptian roots). I have consulted several translations of the *Alexander Romance:* G. Bounoure and B. Serret's French translation of 1992 is quoted in the French version of the present book (2003); R. Stoneman's English translation (1991) is quoted here. Both translators use version L of the *Alexander Romance,* but Stoneman has inserted chapters from version A in square brackets. Version γ was translated into French by C. C. Jouanno (2009) and into English by Stoneman (1991), pp. 161–188. *Alexander's Itinerary* has been translated into Italian with a commentary by R. Tabacco (1992) and into English by I. Davies (1998), the translation used here. Davies mentions the hypothesis that attributes its authorship to Julius Valerius, which Callu rejects in "Alexandre dans la littérature latine" (1999); on the *Itinerarium,* see especially Tabacco, *Per una nuova edizione critica,* with a partial annotated Italian translation (1992); and, on Arrian's influence, Tonnet, "Le résumé et l'adaptation de l'*Anabase*" (1979). Julius Valerius's *Res gestae Alexandri Macedonis* was recently edited and translated into French by J.-P. Callu (2010), with a very rich introduction (pp. 5–37) and an abundance of explanatory notes (pp. 219–264). The Callu edition also includes three other texts from the same era (fourth century c.e.): *Alexander's Itinerary* (pp. 266–319), *The Epitome of the History of Alexander* (*Alexandri Magni Macedonis epitoma rerum gestarum,* pp. 319–343), *The Book of the Death and Testament of Alexander* (*De morte testamentoque Alexandri Magni Liber,* pp. 347–359), and the *Letter from Alexander the Macedonian to His Master Aristotle* (*Epistula Alexandri Macedonis ad Aristotelem magistrum suum,* pp. 361–375). My summary of the Romance follows the Bounoure and Serret translation, pp. 1–122 (Alexander's youth up to his accession to the throne, pp. 1–26; the military expedition up to Darius's death, pp. 27–70; Eastern adventures, pp. 75–146).

Notes to Chapter 4. Arrian's Darius

∞ The bibliography on Arrian is enormous: see, for example, P. A. Stadter, *Arrian of Nicomedia* (1980), and A. B. Bosworth, *From Arrian to Alexander* (1988a), not neglecting his *Commentary I* and *II*); see also P. Vidal-Naquet, "Flavius Arrien" (1984), and F. Sisti's introduction to *Arriano* (2001), pp. xi–lxv; on Arrian's objectives and methods in the *Anabasis,* see also Roisman, "Why Arrian Wrote His Anabasis" (1983–1984), and esp. Schepens, "Arrian's View of His Task" (1971). On what Arrian borrowed from Xenophon, I have greatly benefited from H. Tonnet's *Recherches sur Arrien* (1998), which remains fundamental; see in particular 1:225–282, "L'imitation de Xénophon" (pp. 253–254 on the portraits); see also B. P. Reardon, *Courants littéraires* (1971), pp. 210–216; "Arrian is not really a historian. His work came into being not from any interest in politics but from a literary frame of mind" (p. 210). Of the English translations, P.-A.Brunt's *Anabasis* and *Indika* (in 2 vols.) in the Loeb Classical Library should be noted, as well as P. Mensch's version in J. Romm, ed., *The Landmark Arrian* (2010), which also includes a number of assessments of various problems by distinguished scholars.

∞ The fragments of the lost Alexander authors have been edited by F. Jacoby, *Die Fragmente der griechischer Historiker,* part 2b (1926), and translated into English by C. A. Robinson, *The History of Alexander the Great,* vol. 1 (1953); they are now available in a bilingual (Greek and French) edition, thanks to J. Auberger, *Histoires d'Alexandre* (2001); see L. Pearson, *Lost Histories* (1960), and P. Pédech, *Historiens compagnons d'Alexandre* (Paris, 1984). The fragments edited by Jacoby, accompanied by an English translation, are now available online on the Brill website: http://www.brill.com/publications/online-resources/jacoby-online (work in progress).

∞ On the physical portrait of the two king, it is noteworthy that Plutarch (*Alexander,* 4.1–3) grants much less space to Alexander's physical portrait than he grants, for example, to that of Demetrius Poliorcretes (cf. P. Wheatly, *AHB* 13/1 [1999]: 5–12); on this subject, see also the ancient evidence collected by A. Stewart, *Faces of Power* (1993), pp. 341–350. On Alexander's stature, see Curtius 7.8.9; the Scythian ambassadors, ushered in to see Alexander, were confused since, according to the author, "they judged a man's courage according to his physique [*magnitudo corporis*], and they thought Alexander's slight build [*modicus habitus*] entirely at odds with his reputation." That is also implied in the famous scene where Alexander and Hephaestion go to visit the Persian princesses in their tent, and Sisygambis throws herself at the feet of Hephaestion, who, "while he was the king's age, in stature he was his superior [*corporis habibu praestabat*]"; Curtius 3.12.16); "Hephaestion was taller and more handsome" (Diodorus 17.37.5). In the *Alexander Romance,* "the Persians looked in amazement at Alexander because of his small stature" (2.15.1); see, similarly, the fairly complete portrait found in a branch of the *Alexander Romance,* where the Macedonian king is called "of average size" (*Itiner. Alex.* 14: *Statura juvenis mediocris*); Tha'ālibī (961–1038) repeats the romance motif in his *History of the Kings of Persia,* in which he writes: "The historians report that Iskandar was small of stature" (Zotenberg ed., p. 443).

∞ On mimesis, in addition to E. Auerbach's *Mimesis* (1963), quoted in the text, see A. Croiset and M. Croiset, *Littérature grecque* (1938), 5:356–370, and especially Bompaire, *Lucien* (1958), particularly the first part, "La doctrine de la *mimèsis*," pp. 11–159; the book's subtitle aptly expresses the notion that mimesis is not necessarily confined to literary invention alone; see also Reardon, *Courants littéraires* (1971), chap. 1: "*Paideia* et mimèsis," pp. 3–10, which explicitly follows Bompaire's arguments and interpretations.

ᴄᴘ The ancient evidence and the fragments from Hegesias of Magnesia are collected in Jacoby, *FGrH* 2b, no. 142. On his treatment of the story of Batis in Gaza, see J. E. Atkinson, *Commentary I,* pp. 341–342, which, following L. Pearson, *Lost Histories* (1960), pp. 247–248, points out that the Homeric influence is mediated in Curtius by a Virgilian mimesis. As I note in the text, contemporary historians have also succumbed to the passion for mimesis: Georges Radet (*Alexandre le Grand* [1931], pp. 104–106), spurred by Homeric enthusiasm—which he make his explanatory principle for the expedition and the figure of Alexander—does not fail to treat the episode (also using Hegesias) and to see the epilogue (rather incomprehensibly) as "an inspiration of a completely different nature, which, three and a half centuries before Christ, in that corner of the world near Jerusalem, seems to be a distant prototype for the exquisite scene in which Mary of Bethany pours an abundance of perfumes over Jesus' feet." The "Asianism" denounced by Dionysius of Halicarnassus lives on.

ᴄᴘ On the glorification of Cyrus the Younger's memory in antiquity, see the analysis in *HPE,* pp. 621–627, 630–631, as well as D. Lenfant, "La 'décadence' du Grand Roi" (2001a). On the opposition between Agesilaus and the Great King (anonymously designated by that term), see my remarks in *AchHist* 2 (1987): 8–10. On the payment for services among the Persians, and the Great King's *polydōria,* see *HPE,* chap. 8: "The King's Men."

ᴄᴘ According to Plutarch (26.2), the casket in which Alexander placed his copy of the *Iliad* was part of the plunder from Darius's baggage train in Damascus. On the place of Homer in education during the Hellenistic and Roman periods, see H. I. Marrou, *Histoire de l'éducation* (1950), p. 228: "He did not lose favor over the entire Hellenistic period. . . . Homer dominated all of Greek culture . . . [until] the Byzantine Middle Ages." See also pp. 355 and passim.

Notes to Chapter 5. A Different Darius or the Same One?

ᴄᴘ On single combat, in addition to A. Martin's "Monomachia" (1904) and the pages in W. K. Pritchett's *Greek State at War* (1985), 4:15–20, see J. J. Glück, "Reviling and Monomachy" (1964) (the author, however, situates his exposition within a questionable evolutionist view, considering the custom of the duel archaic, having disappeared in the course of the first half of the first millennium). The relation between duels and battle in the *Iliad* has in fact been reinterpreted in H. Van Wees, "Kings in Combat" (1988); see also A. Camerotto, "*Aristeia*" (2001). On single combat in the Roman tradition, see (part of an extensive bibliography) the good overview by S. P. Oakley, "Single Combat in the Roman Republic" (1985). The question of the tradition of *opima spolia* and its development in Rome has recently been revisited in great detail by H. Flower, "The Tradition of the *Spolia Opima*" (2000). For ritualized duels and fighting in the Greek tradition, see A. Brelich, *Guerre, agoni* (1961).

∞ On the Cadusian duel specifically, I have already undertaken a preliminary analysis in *HPE*, p. 771. The hypothesis of a Persian version encountered a very determined opponent in E. Badian, "Darius III," pp. 241–268, esp. p. 243n10 (adopting a rare discourteous tone); note that the author bases himself solely on the name "Codomannus" and on the (acknowledged) contradiction with the name "Artašata," certified for Darius in the Babylonian astronomical diaries before his accession—a contradiction that does not seem prohibitive to me. Whatever the solution, it does not affect the historical and anthropological interpretation of Justin's and Diodorus's texts that I propose (but at which Badian does not even hint).

∞ The ancient sources on the Cadusians have been collected in R. Syme, "The Cadusii in History and Fiction" (1988); see also R. B. Stevenson, *Persica* (1997), pp. 96–100. On the status this people had in the empire, see my reflections and hypotheses in *HPE*, pp. 726–733 and 767–68. On the theme of the king's military virtues, see *HPE*, pp. 225–230; the inscription of Darius on his tomb *(DNa)* is presented and discussed ibid., pp. 210–213. Regarding Justin's expression "Persian people," rather than see it as a reflection of Iranian notions (for example, Badian, "Darius," [2000], p. 246n12=[2012], p. 473n.12), I should like to link its usage, on one hand, to a practice specific to Justin (cf. P. Briant, *Antigone le Borgne* [1973], pp. 291–292, 303–307, 316–317) and, on the other, to a comparable expression *(demos/*people) in Pausianas (2.5), in reference to the accession of Darius II (*HPE*, pp. 590–591). In general, it is impossible to say to what Persian international realities that terminology corresponds, if, in fact, the authors were themselves aware of it or granted it any importance—which can legitimately be cause for doubt.

∞ The hypothesis of the "mercenaries' source" was developed in W. W. Tarn, *Alexander the Great* (1948), 1:58; 2:72; for opposition to that hypothesis, see, for example, Pearson, *Lost Histories* (1960), pp. 78–81; P. A. Brunt, "Persian Accounts" (1962); Briant, *Antigone le Borgne* (1973), pp. 97–118.

∞ On Darius's place in Curtius, cf. W. Rutz, "Das Bild des Dareios" (1984), and E. Baynham, *Quintus Curtius* (1998), pp. 132–164. For Curtius, Diodorus, and the ancestral customs of the Persians, see, e.g., Diodorus 17.30.4 (*kata ton tōn Persōn:* Charidemus's death sentence); 17.35.3 (*kata ti patrion nomon ethos tōn Persōn;* the princesses accompany the army on campaign); Curtius 3.3.8 (*patrio more Persarum:* the royal cortege sets off at sunrise); 3.8.9 (*more maiorum:* the king at war); 3.8.12 (*more patrio:* the king's wives accompany him to war); 3.12.13 (*patrio more:* funerary customs); 3.12.17 (*suo more:* the Persian princesses perform proskynesis); 4.6.5 (*more Persarum:* they know how to keep a secret); 4.10.23 (*patria Persarum more:* funerary customs); 4.14.25: (*patrio more:* the king in his chariot); 4.16.15 (*barbaro ritu:* cheers directed at the royal chariot); 5.10.12 (*pristino more:* the king in his chariot). On them, see the commentary in *HPE*, pp. 518–522, 772, 774, 777–778, and index, p. 1177, s.v. *nomos persikos*. On the life and (little-known) work of Dinon, see R. B. Stevenson, *Persica* (1997), pp. 9–15, and Lenfant, *Histoires perses* (2009), pp. 51–253.

∞ On the fictionalized biographies of Persians in relation to royal favor, see *HPE*, pp. 319–323. On the passage from Aelian (12.43) and how the qualifier *doulos* (slave) applied to Darius III should be understood, see *HPE*, pp. 770–772 (and in conjunction with my

Antigone le Borgne [1973], pp. 19–24, regarding the qualifier *autourgos,* which Aelian applies to Antigonus I Monophthalmus in the same passage).

—Odatis and Zariadres: there are a great many studies on oral transmission among the Iranians (I have dealt with the literary texts relating to the Achaemenid period in *HPE,* pp. 329–330, 924). One of the best-known is M. Boyce's "The Parthian Gōsān and Iranian Minstrel Tradition" (1957); the author considers the story of Odatis and Zariadres and comparable stories found in the Iranian traditions; see also her more specialized article "Zariadres and Zarēr" (1955).

∞ On the value of exempla on wounds and scars, see N. Loraux, "Blessures de guerriers" (1989, archaic and classical periods in Greece); inspired by Loraux's studies but more specific, see C. F. Salazar, *The Treatments of War Wounds* (2000), esp. chap. 8, *Alexander the Great,* pp. 184–208; and lastly, C. Baroin, "Les cicatrices ou la mémoire des corps" (2002). It should also be noted that the scars received during particularly dangerous hunts were also displayed as proof of valor: see, for example, Cyrus the Younger and the bear hunt (Xenophon, *Anabasis,* 1.9.6) or the use Lysimachus made of the many scars acquired during lion hunts (Plutarch, "Demetrius," 27.6, and other texts I explicate in *DHA* 17/1 [1991]: 222–223).

∞ Since its discovery, the Naples Mosaic has been the occasion for a huge bibliography, which cannot be cited exhaustively here. See, first, the original publication by A. Niccolini, "Musaico scoperto a Pompei" (1832), with many plates and drawings; the analysis of the document is followed by two complementary studies, one by F. M. Avellino, pp. 51–54 (proposing that it represents the Battle of the Granicus), the other by D. B. Quaranta, pp. 55–68 (judging that it concerns Issus, and that the creator of the original painting might have been Apelles); on the interpretation Goethe proposed in March 1832, see quotations and critical comments in B. Andrae, *Alexandermosaik* (1977), pp. 29–36. The other representations of the "Battle of Alexander" in Italy are presented and analyzed in G. E. Rizzo, "La 'Battagli di Alessandro,' " (1925–1926); see also Pfrommer, *Alexandermosaik* (1998), pp. 146–160, and P. Moreno, *Apelles* (2001), pp. 83–96.

—It would be easy to compile a bibliography on the question and acquire an overall sense of the discussions through recent books: T. Hölscher, *Historienbilder* (1973), pp. 122–169; A. Stewart, *Faces of Power* (1993), passim (see index, p. 503); A. Cohen, *Alexander Mosaic* (1995); M. Pfrommer, *Alexandermosaik* (1998); F. Stähler, *Alexandermosaik* (1999); P. Moreno, *Apelles* (2001) and "Iconografia di Alessandro" (2009). Among the studies that have influenced the historiography of the question, let me mention especially C. Nylander, "Il milite ignoto" (1982), "Standard of the Great King" (1983), and "Darius III" (1993); and also E. Badian's recent article, "Alexander Mosaic" (1999). Nylander's viewpoint was vigorously disputed by T. Hölscher, "Zur Deutung" (1981–1983) and more recently by M. Pfrommer, *Alexandermosaiks* (1988) and B. Goldman, "Darius III" (1993) (Goldman, like Pfrommer, doubts the accuracy of the details concerning the Great King's head covering and clothing). Among other recent studies, see Y. Perrin, "À propos de la 'Bataille d'Issos' " (1998) (which is particularly concerned with considerations about the painting's composition).

Notes to Chapter 6. Darius between Greece and Rome

∞ The Roman view of Alexander is frequently treated as a historiographical theme: see P. Ceaucescu, "La double image d'Alexandre" (1974); P. Green, "Caesar and Alexander" (1978); P. Vidal-Naquet, "Flavius Arrien entre deux mondes" (1984); E. S. Gruen, "Rome and the Myth of Alexander" (1998); S. J. Malloch, "Gaius' Bridge at Baiae and Alexander-imitatio" (2001); see also *Neronia IV: Alejandro Magno, modelo de los emperadores romanos* (Brussels, 1990), as well as D. Spencer's *The Roman Alexander* (2002). On the moralistic view of authors of the principate (following Cicero), see J.-M. André, "L'otium" (1965). Many interesting comments and ideas can also be found in E. Koulakiotis, *Alexandermythos* (2006), both on Alexander as exemplum among philosophers during the late classical period and the Hellenistic period (pt. 3), and on the views elaborated by moralists and rhetors during the Roman imperial period (pt. 4).

∞ The Romans and Persia: The modest nature of the Romans' knowledge of Achaemenid Persian history has been judiciously argued in V. J. Rosivach, "The Romans' View of the Persians" (1984); I am not convinced by the reverse thesis recently advanced as an established fact by P. Goukowsky, *BAI* 12 (1998): 73. On *inventio* in the Roman narratives of wars against the Parthians, see the very interesting article by R. Ash, "Tacitus' Parthian Battle Narrative" (1999). On the Roman view of luxury among the Parthians (who are frequently called "Persians" or "Medes"), see A. Dalby, *Empire of Pleasures* (2000), esp. pp. 186–191. Mentions of the Parthians were regularly used, and continue to be used, in an attempt to fix the date (still very controversial) of Curtius and his work: see, for example, R. Fears, "Parthi in Q. Curtius Rufus" (1974); A. M. Devine, "The Parthi, the Tyranny of Tiberius" (1979); and Atkinson's overview of the question, "Q. Curtius Rufus' 'Historiae Alexandri Magni'" (1998), pp. 3452–3455; on the context, see also E. Baynham, *Quintus Curtius* (1998), pp. 15–35.

∞ On the use of exempla in Livy and on his view of the "Asian" evolution of Rome, see J. D. Chaplin's excellent *Livy's Exemplary History* (2000), though the passage on Alexander is not mentioned (recent clarifications can be found in M. Mahé-Simon, "L'enjeu historiographique de l'*excursus* sur Alexandre" (2001), and R. Morello, "Livy's Alexander Digression" (2001).

∞ On the episode of the Amazons, see E. Baynham's "Alexander and the Amazons" (2001).

∞ The theory of the successive five empires, also illustrated by the famous passage in the Book of Daniel (2:21–45), has given rise to a large number of studies, for example, D. Mendels, "The Five Empires" (1981); see also L. Pernot, *La rhétorique de l'éloge* (1993), 2:747–762. On the Roman expansion "on land and sea," see A. Momigliano, "Terra marique" (1942), and C. Nicolet, *L'inventaire du monde* (1988), pp. 53–64 (and the entire discussion, pp. 27–68).

∞ On the "letter from Darius to Gadatas," see my recent analysis (2003; English version in *KCP*, chap. 3), where I propose that it is very likely a forgery from the Roman period. The question of whether the Parthians and Sassanids were aware of the Achaemenid past has given rise to a great many contradictory studies: see the convincing summation of P. Huyse, "La revendication de territoires achéménides par les Sassanides" (2002). On the dynasty of the kings of Commagene and its "gallery of ancestors" (from Darius I and Xerxes) in the mountain sanctuary of the Nemrut Dağ, see D. E. Sanders, ed., *Nemrud Dağ* (1996), and M. Facella, "Commagene" (2009).

∾ On Cyrus's popularity in the Roman period, see, for example, Ammianus Marcellinus 23.6.10 (Cyrus, "that good king, supplied with strength like the river of the same name") or Dio Chrysostom, *Discourse*, 25.4 (opposition between an inspiring royal virtue [*daimōn basilikos*] and the flaws of his successors Cambyses and Darius), or Plutarch, *Fortune of Alexander*, 2.12 (= *Moralia*, 343A): foremost among all the models for Alexander was Cyrus, whose lofty vision and intelligence *(phronēma)* he shared. On the instrumentalization of the Median Wars in the Roman period, see A. Spawforth, "Symbol of Unity" (1994). On the portrait of Xerxes in Roman moralistic literature, see also S. Borzsák, "Der weinende Xerxes" (1966).

∾ On the references to ancient documents (Ammianus Marcellinus's *antiqui libri*): in the fourth century B.C.E., Ctesias—cited by Diodorus—claimed to have consulted "the royal parchments" *(basilikoi diphterai)* of the Persian court; that is merely a literary topos, repeated ten centuries later by Agathias (*HPE*, pp. 6, 889) in his book on the Sassanids, which also invokes the authority of the *basileioi diphtērai* (A. Cameron, *Dumbarton Oaks Papers* 23–24 [1969–1970]: 74, 88, 162–163). On that well-known method of validation in ancient historiography, see J. Marincola, *Authority and Tradition* (1997), pp. 103–117 and 280–282.

Notes to Chapter 7. Upper King and Lower King

∾ The aim of this chapter is not to reconstitute the strategies or military operations, but rather to analyze clearly the construction of the literary portrait of Darius; on Darius's strategy, see my analysis in *HPE*, pp. 817–842.

∾ On the theme (known from Homer's time on) of the adviser who delivers warnings to the king, see H. Bischoff, "Der Warner bei Herodot" (1932), and R. Lattimore, "The Wise Adviser" (1939). On what Curtius borrowed from Herodotus, see, for example J. Blaensdorf, "Herodot bei Quintus Rufus" (1971). On kings' advisers in Polybius, see P. Pédech, *La méthode historique de Polybe* (1964), pp. 230–235. On the Charidemus affair, Baynham's analysis in *Quintus Curtius* (1998), pp. 136–140, is not without interest, but in my view it remains incomplete because of the author's inadequate attention to literary analysis. On the competitions between courtiers, see *HPE*, pp. 319–323. On the relation between kings and the leaders of expeditions, see *HPE*, pp. 340–343; on financial organization, see, in *HPE*, pp. 595–596, my comments on a passage from the *Hellenica Oxyrhynchia* (§19.2); see also *HPE*, p. 327 on the hostages left at the central court; *HPE*, pp. 823–828, for what one ought to think of the plans to take the war to Europe that Diodorus attributes to Memnon and to the Great King. On the gift and prevarication, see D. Lewis's remarks in *REA* 91/1–1 (1994): 227–234.

∞ There is a large bibliography on the Vase of the Persians and on its painter. I refer merely to one of the recent studies that gives a nuanced overview of the question and which cites and analyzes the earlier bibliography: M.-C. Villanueva-Puig, *REA* (1989). The date now accepted for the vase is "330 or thereabouts"; Villanueva-Puig does not fail to recall (p. 286) that exegetes had formerly proposed it was the representation of the council at which Charidemus took the floor, but the image of the Great King and of Asia (king's council, scene of the tribute) is actually constructed on schemata used throughout the fifth and sixth centuries; it therefore certainly does not designate a specific king or reign. In passing, the author also addresses (p. 293) a hypothesis based on the story Aelian recounts in the *Varia historia*, 12.64 (quoted in the text), namely, the royal adviser's obligation to stand on a gold plinth; on the Darius vase, some have wanted to see the small round platform on which the adviser is standing as he addresses the king, seated on his throne, as the graphic illustration of that "gold plinth": Villanueva-Puig rightly points out that this is a hypothesis, nothing more.

On the matter of Sisines and Alexander of Lyncestis, see Bosworth, *Commentary I*, pp. 59–164, and Atkinson, *Commentary II*, pp. 248–250. On the similarities of situations and terminologies between Arrian and Xenophon, see W. Heckel, "Alexandros Lynkestes and Oronta" (1983); Diodorus (17.30.4) also borrowed from Xenophon the template for the condemnation of Charidemus.

∞ On Parmenion and Alexander, passages parallel to those in Arrian can be found in other authors, especially regarding the responses to Darius's embassy: the dialogue held on that occasion was turned into a very popular exemplum (Valerius Maximus 6.4, ext. 3). But comparisons do not add very much to the analysis, except perhaps by confirming the use of literary motifs. Parmenion's repetitive introduction has long been noted, but historians are usually interested above all in two questions (the first being pointless in my opinion, the second badly phrased), namely, Arrian's sources, on one hand, and the historicity of the dialogues, on the other: see, for example, A. B. Bosworth, "Arrian and the Alexander Vulgate" (1976), pp. 30–32 (also *Commentary I*, pp. 114–116, 137–138); P. Pédech, *Historiens-compagnons* (1984), pp. 63–64, who also notes, briefly but correctly, that Alexander's replies are presented "with a perseverance that resembles the repetition of an intentional literary device"; on this, see also Baynham, *Quintus Curtius* (1998), pp. 146, 154–155, and lastly, E. Carney's judicious remarks on method, "Artifice and Alexander History" (2000a), pp. 264–273.

∞ On the slowness in the preparations that the Greek authors regularly attribute to the Achaemenid armies, see my discussion in *HPE*, pp. 652–654. On Artaxerxes II's preparations and those of Darius III, see *HPE*, pp. 616–619 (Artaxerxes II), pp. 688–690, 818–832, 1042–1044 (Darius III). Concerning the use of the motif in Darius's time, four remarks are in order. First, many of the attestations about an earlier age are polemical in nature, intended less to inform than to denounce and caricature (see, for example, Diodorus 15.21;15.9.2; 15.41.2; 16.44.5; 46.7, and Isocrates, *Panegyricus*, 140, 164–165). Second, the mustering of all the contingents between the Indus and Mediterranean was in no way obligatory; the reviews held by Xerxes in 480 allowed him to put the ceremonial army on display, that army itself being a metaphorical representation of the greatness of the empire and the diversity of the populations—hence Xerxes's (and Darius III's) extreme satisfaction in seeing their power thus theatricalized (Herodotus 7.45 and Curtius 3.2.10); these reviews provide no understanding of the makeup of the fighting army, which certainly rested on a much smaller and much more professionalized base than is generally believed. That remark is also valid for Darius III's army. Third, it is altogether obvious that Artaxerxes' preparations against Cyrus were used as a convenient reference, as shown by the active mimesis at work between Xenophon and the authors of the Roman period, especially Arrian. Finally—and not least important— the reference implied that, in both cases, the central authorities were surprised by the enemy offensive, which is certainly wrong in Artaxerxes II's case and in that of Darius III.

∞ On Darius's army and its meticulous preparations before Gaugamela, see *HPE*, pp. 832–842 (and corresponding notes in the bibliography, pp. 1044–1045), and my "Note d'histoire militaire achéménide" (1997b) and "The Achaemenid Empire" (1999b). According to Bosworth (*Commentary I*, pp. 209–210), Arrian's expression (2.10.1) was borrowed from Thucydides; it certainly entails a negative judgment, but less in itself than because of the context in which it is used.

∞ On the tradition of the duel between the two kings, the most complete analysis is E. Mederer, *Die Alexanderlegenden* (1936), chap. 3, pp. 15–36. As was common at the time the book was written, Mederer is especially interested in identifying the primary sources and, within that reductive framework, contrasts "the credible sources" (Arrian) to the legends disseminated by Callisthenes (pp. 17–18).

∞ The question of the diplomatic negotiations between the two kings has generated a flood of studies and publications. In addition to chapter 8 as a whole in his *Alexandre le Grand* (1931) ("Le grand débat sur la question de l'empire," pp. 73–91), G. Radet devoted specific studies to the subject: "Notes sur l'histoire d'Alexandre" (1925) and "Alexandre en Syrie" (1930). I already indicated my great skepticism in an article published in 1977 and reprinted in *Rois, tributs et paysans* (1982a), pp. 357–403, esp. pp. 371–384 (certain formulations would now need to be corrected or qualified). I gave an additional assessment in *HPE*, pp. 832–840, which also has an annotated bibliography (pp. 1044–1045); in that passage I develop the idea that not only are the letters forgeries but that the scope of the territories the Great King is said to have ceded in no way corresponds to the strategic situation of the Persian camp during the dates considered or to his own decisions between Issus and Gaugamela. Since then, several studies have appeared, but they have not led me to modify my point of view, at least overall: see F. Sisti, "Proposte di pace" (1994) (which remains very cautious on the historical kernel of a tradition marked by "anecdotal construction"); E. F. Bloedow, "Diplomatic Negotiations" (1995), which postulates that Arrian's report on Darius's first overtures is a reliable source; Baynham, *Quintus Curtius* (1998), pp. 150–155; in modifying a thesis he had previously defended, E. Badian, "Darius" (2000), p. 257, also concedes that these are texts with a propagandistic value. On the many letters represented in the ancient traditions on Alexander and on the caution required in dealing with them, see J.-D. Gauger,

Authentizität und Methode (2000), pp. 221–257 and 364–365. On the Alexander-Darius letters, see lastly, J. Seibert, "Der Streit und die Kriegsschuld zwischen Alexander d. Gr. und Dareios III" (2001), which, without postulating that they are counterfeits, maintains that the original documents were rewritten by an author (Callisthenes, according to Siebert) inspired by a Herodotean mimesis.

∽ On the opposition between daytime and nighttime battles in the Greek traditions, see, for example, P. Vidal-Naquet, *Le chasseur noir* (1983), pp. 162ff. On possible connections between an episode of Xerxes' flight in Aeschylus (*Persians*, 492–512; the frozen river Strymon) and a passage from the *Alexander Romance* (the frozen river Stranga), see G. Ieranò, "Il barbaro in fuga" (1996); on the loss of the chariot of Zeus/Ahura Mazda, see B. Tripodi, "Il carro sacro di Serse" (1986), and D. Kienast, "Der Wagen des Ahura-Mazda" (1996).

∽ Since a first, groundbreaking article by Heydemann in 1883, the representation of flight/pursuit on the Apulian vases has given rise to a large body of literature, from which I have selected a few particularly noteworthy studies: J.-M. Moret, *L'Ilioupersis* (1975), esp. pp. 155–159, which insists above all on "the indifference and neglect of the painters . . . accustomed to reproducing the same mythological scenes without respite. . . . They worked from preestablished formulas"; L. Giuliani, "Alexander in Ruvo, Ereteria und Sidon" (1977); A. Geyer, "Alexander in Apulien" (1992). Analyses also appear in the books dealing with the Naples Mosaic, because the possible genetic relationships between the two sets of works have often been discussed: A. Stewart, *Faces of Power* (1993), pp. 150–157 (bibliography, pp. 431–432); A. Cohen, *The Alexander Mosaic* (1997), pp. 64–68; M. Pfrommer, *Alexandermosaik* (1998), pp. 173–198 (appendix on "the Great King in flight"). On the relationship between these paintings and the Darius vase, see H. Metzger, "À propos des images apuliennes de la bataille d'Alexandre" (1967), and M.-C. Villanueva-Puig's overview, "Le vase des Perses" (1989), esp. pp. 285–289; lastly, see F. Zevi, "Alessandro e i Romani" (1997), who argues that these funerary vases developed within the context of the expedition of Alexander Molossus (brother of Olympias and king of Epirus) in Taranto between 334 and 331; arguing against that date is, for example, M. Pfrommer, *Alexandermosaik* (1998), p. 178.

∽ On affairs in Darius's camp as seen by Curtius, see also J. E. Atkinson, *Commentary II*, pp. 133–154. The pace and the stages of Alexander's forced marches in pursuit of Darius have always raised many topo-geographical and logistical problems (which do not affect the argument set out here): among other studies, see A. F. von Stahl, "Notes on the March of Alexander the Great" (1924); R. D. Milns, "Alexander's Pursuit of Darius" (1966); C. Neumann, "A Note on Alexander's March-Rate" (1971); N. G. L. Hammond, "A Note on 'Pursuit' in Arrian" (1978); D. W. Engels, *Logistics* (1978), pp. 78–83; see also Bosworth, *Commentary I*, pp. 338–345; and J. E. Atkinson, *Commentary II*, pp. 154–163.

Notes to Chapter 8. Iron Helmet, Silver Vessels

∽ On the court's displacements and the notion of the softening effect of luxury in the classical authors, see my discussions in *HPE*, pp. 183–195 and 286–297 (with annotated bibliography, pp. 910–911 and 921–922). On "those who are in the baggage train" and the well-known problems of discipline, particularly in the Hellenistic armies, see esp. M. Holleaux's studies published in 1922 and 1926 and later collected in *Études d'épigraphie et d'histoires grecques,* vol. 3 (Paris, 1942), pp. 1–26; see also M. Launey, *Recherches sur les armées hellénistiques,* 2 vols. (Paris, 1949; repr. 1987), 2:785–790. The factual reality of the episode analyzed in the text is postulated by D. Engels, *Logistics* (1978), pp. 13 and 86–87, and by P. Faure, *Vie quotidienne* (1982), p. 62. Engels, without discussion, chooses to situate the "fact" before the campaign of Bactria (following Plutarch); Faure maintains that the "fact" was repeated, without even mentioning the problems of method raised by the repetition of the motif in three different circumstances.

∽ On the king's water, see Briant, "The Drinking Water of the Great King," in *KCP*, chap. 12); see a later article by D. Meeks (which overlooks my study), "Traitement, conservation et transport de l'eau du Nil" (2001) (the author asks whether the water of the Nile thus transported remained potable). It is surprising that such a custom was not instrumentalized more in the polemical texts on Persian luxury, though one passage from Valerius Maximus (9.1, ext. 4) denounces the luxury of Antiochus's army and the resulting military weakness. Among the indicators are "the silver vessels used as cooking implements" *(argenta vasa ad usum culinae);* but it does not seem to be a precise reference to the Persian royal custom. On the texts of Mari, I have used F. Joannès' "L'eau et la glace à Mari" (1994) and its conclusions.

Notes to Chapter 9. The Great King's Private and Public Lives

∽ The sources on the members of the royal family who fell into Alexander's hands after Issus are collected in Berve's *Das Alexanderreich,* vol. 2 (1926), no. 290 (Drypetis), no. 711 (Sisygambis), no. 721 (Stateira the mother), no. 722 (Stateira the daughter), and no. 833 (Ochus); see also the interesting presentation and analysis in E. Carney, "Alexander the Great and Persian Women" (1996), the substance of which is repeated in her *Women and Monarchy in Macedonia* (2000b), pp. 95–113 (presentation of Darius's wife Stateira, pp. 94–96; of his daughter Stateira, pp. 108–109); on women of the court, see, in addition to *HPE,* pp. 277–286, M. Brosius, *Women in Ancient Persia* (1996), and M. García Sánchez, "Miradas helenas de la alteridad" (2002).

∽ Studies on the Greek romance have multiplied in recent years: in addition to the proceedings of colloquia, see T. Hägg, *The Novel in Antiquity* (1983); M. Fusillo, *Naissance du roman* (1993); A. Billault, *La création romanesque* (1991); and F. Letoublon, *Lieux communs* (1993); J. R. Morgan and R. Stoneman, eds., *Greek Fiction* (1994). None of the authors directly addresses the so-called historical texts I am discussing, because specialists in literature rightly emphasize the specific identity of the romance genre (see, for example, Billault, pp. 10–17, 47ff.). It is true, however, that, as understood in antiquity, history writing is related to fiction or, at the very least, can introduce literary episodes: "In the classical world, the writing of history was not categorically linked to real referents as it is in the modern period: the historical work, originating in rhetoric, followed a literary code, and the borders that separated it from literary fiction were not clear. . . . History [remains] the primary form of narrative prose, and one of the intertextual models for the romance" (Fusillo, pp. 56–57). Everyone agrees that the "Panthea-Abradatas-Cyrus" episode constitutes a fictionalized episode within the *Cyropaedia* (cf., for example, E. Baragwanath, "Foreign Wives" [2002]). In Curtius particularly, but also in Plutarch, such fictionalized, literary ruses are also numerous in the "Stateira-Darius-Alexander" episode, from the introductory *ekphrasis* (the description of the group of women in the tent plundered by the Macedonian soldiers), so typical of writing in the romance (Billault [1991], pp. 245–265; Fusillo [1993], pp. 81–88), to the physical and moral characterization of the principal heroes and the way time and place are treated.

—Curtius's "history of Alexander" is obviously not a Hellenistic romance (it is missing two elements essential to the story of Stateira, the meeting of gazes and the happy ending), but the development of some of the characters and the writing in certain episodes are very similar to literary writing and inspiration, for example, the large number of declamations delivered theatrically by the characters, their heart-felt vehemence, and their redundancy (see A. Billault, "Notion d'asianisme" [1995], but without reference to Curtius). On the "romance" and fictional invention in Curtius, see H. MacCurrie's important "The Historian as Novelist?" (1990), and P. McKechnie's inspiring "Manipulation of Themes" (1999), despite the counterarguments put forward in A. B. Bosworth, "Plus ça change" (2003); see also F. Minissale's *Un romanziere della Storia* (1983).

—On the romance of Panthea in the *Cyropaedia,* see J. Tatum, *Xenophon's Imperial Fiction* (1989), pp. 21–27, 163–188; and C. Nadon, *Xenophon's Prince* (2001), pp. 152–160; see also E. Baragwanath, "Foreign Wives" (2002), which "analyses the particular narrative patterns that envelop Xenophon's depictions of women through the filter of his wider leadership pattern, with the aim of reaching a deeper understanding of how he envisaged women fitting into his theory of human relations, and of how he used narrative patterning" (p. 127).

—On the similarities (and differences) between the *Cyropaedia* and Chariton's romance, see Tatum (1989), pp. 166–172; Chariton's borrowings from historiographical models has long been pointed out, see, for example, T. Hägg (1983), pp. 5–17, 111–117; on the influence of Ctesias and works dedicated to the history of Alexander (Clitarchus), see M.-F. Baslez, "La Perse de Chariton" (1992), pp. 201–202; on "Chariton and the history of Alexander," see also C. Daude, "Le personnage d'Artaxerxès" (2002). On the revolt of Egypt in that same romance and on the use of Greek historiography from the classical age, see P. Salmon, "Chariton d'Aphrodisias" (1961), who, however, has a questionable tendency to see the history behind the romance everywhere; and lastly, R. D. Lugginbill, "Chariton's Use of Thudycides' *History*" (2000), with a large bibliography, notes 1–5), and S. S. Smith, *Greek Identity* (2007); on the date of the romance (early second century C.E.), see the converging hypotheses of M.-F. Baslez (1992), pp. 202–203, and C. Daude (2002), p. 140 and n. 8. The literary techniques governing the depiction of the heroines' "beauty" have recently been analyzed in S. Dubel, "La beauté romanesque" (2002); see, in the same volume, pp. 329–346, C. Jouanno's "Les jeunes filles dans le roman byzantin du XIIe siècle"; see also F. Letoublon, *Lieux communs* (1993), pp. 119–124, and B. Egger, "Looking at Chariton's Callirhoe" (1994).

—On the relationship between medieval Iranian romances and Hellenistic romances, and their influence on each other, see R. Davis, "Greek and Persian Romances" (2002a), though I am not sure that the story of Panthea and Abradatas "is of course Persian in every detail" (p. 340), and *Panthea's Children* (2002b), where he remarks that "the plots of the Greek novels of late antiquity tend generally to unfold within the territorial and temporal confines of the Achaemenid empire" (p. 2).

—The tragedies *Panthée* (C. Jules de Guersens) and *Alexandre* (Jacques de la Taille) were edited, respectively, by Enea Balmas and Maria Guilia Longhi in *La tragédie à l'époque d'Henri II et de Charles IX*, vol. 4 (1568–1573) in vol. 4 of *Théâtre français de la Renaissance*, 1st ser. (Florence and Paris, 1992), pp. 86–132 and 351–436.

∞ Concerning the exchange that Curtius attributes to Alexander and Sisygambis, I introduced the discussion in a note to an article published in *AchHist* 8 (1994): 286n9, English trans. in *KCP*, chap. 22, in the course of an argument on the relationship between Persian and Macedonian institutions; E. Carney (1996, p. 566 and n. 15) shares my skepticism (also M. García Sánchez [2002], pp. 71–72); it is altogether strange that M. Brosius (*Women* [1996], p. 21n.11) takes Curtius at face value.

∞ On Sardanapalus and the feminization of the palaces of the kings of Asia: P. Briant, "History and Ideology" (2002d); E. Hall, "Asia Unmanned" (1993); M. Gambato, "The Female-Kings" (2000); D. Lenfant, "De Sardanapale à Élégabal" (2001b). On the distaff as a symbol for effemination in Mesopotamian texts, see J. Bottéro's entry on "Homosexualität" (in French) in the *Real-Lexikon der Assyriologie*, p. 465. On the tradition of the woman warrior in the Persian and Iranian tradition, see, for example, Polyaenus 8.27 (Rhodogune); Ctesias, *Persica*, 54 (Roxana), and W. L. Hanaway, "Anāhitā and Alexander" (1982). On the story of Xerxes and Amestris, see esp. Sancisi-Weerdenburg's "Exit Atossa" (1983) and "A Typically Persian Gift" (1988).

∞ On the importance of the "first glance" in triggering love, and hence in the love story, see in particular M. Fusillo, *Naissance du roman* (1993), pp. 212ff., F. Letoublon, *Lieux communs* (1993), pp. 137–145, and E. Baragwanath, "Foreign Wives" (2002), pp. 132–133. The connections between the episodes of Panthea, Stateira, and the Hispanic princess have often been pointed out: see, for example J. de Romilly, "Le conquérant et la belle captive" (1988).

∞ The disastrous image of Parysatis in the classical sources finds a (methodological) parallel in the image elaborated since antiquity of Olympias of Macedonia: see E. D. Carney, "Image of the Virago" (1993) and *Olympias* (2006).

∞ Apart from the studies of Tarn and Badian (1958) cited in the text, the Bagoas episode has elicited little interest in the Alexander historians (some say not a word about it). See, for example, Lane Fox, *Alexander the Great* (1973), pp. 274–275 and 402. Taking the ancient sources at face value, Lane Fox attributes an important role to Bagoas vis-à-vis Alexander; the character is rarely present, he judges, precisely because Alexander's friends observed a "decent silence" about the affair (p. 257); see also the useful pages in Dempsie, "Commentary" (1991), pp. 57–76 (word-for-word commentary on the passage), and J. Atkinson, in Atkinson and Yardley (2009), pp. 93–97 (a commentary on Curtius' story); the author admits that "the tale of Bagōas might belong to the same category [of] apocryphal tales that Plutarch would admit as revealing something of Alexander's character" (p. 16). Although I agree with many of the criticisms that have been made of Tarn's study, I am not tempted to follow the very enthusiastic view of Badian's 1958 article recently expressed by F. Holt ("Another Study of Method," 2000). In reality, the issue at hand is neither to impose a personal view of Alexander nor to succumb to hypercriticism: it is simply to find one's way out of a dead-end discussion, thanks to the technique of literary analysis. See, lastly, P. McKechnie's interesting remarks on the subject, "Manipulations of Themes" (1999). In analyzing book 10 (without, unfortunately, addressing the Bagoas episode), McKechnie comes out in support of Tarn's point of view (though he does not conceal the errors in perspective); he maintains (rightly, in my view) that a number of stories told by Curtius belong to "imaginative fiction," and he judges (not without perspicacity) that such a conclusion can disturb only those "scholars whose wish is to build up the most detailed account possible out of what little there is in the sources" (p. 60): the author's target is explicitly Bosworth, but Badian and his article on Bagoas can easily be added. Bosworth's counterargument in "Plus ça change" (2003) did not persuade me. Without being aware of the analyses I develop in this book, D. Ogden recent discussed the history of Bagoas within the context of a general reflection on Alexander's sexuality ("Alexander's Sex Life" [2009], pp. 213–217; *Alexander the Great* [2011], pp. 167–170). One of these comments is particularly noteworthy: "The story, I submit, is simply too good, and should not be used to draw any conclusions about the nature of the relationship with Bagōas, or about the development of it" (2009, p. 216–2011, p. 170; see also 2011, pp. 187–188, regarding the literary devices used by Curtius).

On eunuchs in the Persian court, see texts and discussions in *HPE*, pp. 268–277, 919–920, and the historical overviews in *BHAch* 1:67–68 and 2:109–110; the many studies published since that time have never addressed the Bagoas affair. On Bagoas's almost generic name, see E. Maas, "Eunuchos und Verwandtes" (1921), pp. 458–459. On the beauty of young boys *(puer delicatus)*, the playthings of their masters in Rome, see F. Dupont and T. Éloi, *L'érotisme masculin* (2001), pp. 207–260 (but without reference to the episode), also pp. 115–137 on cross-dressing, but only with examples of "transvestites," that is, of "effeminate" males who dressed in women's clothes *(vestis muliebris);* on the sexual representation of the eunuch in Rome, see, lastly, P. Cordier, *"Tertium genus hominum"* (2002), pp. 61–75.

🖎 The story of Aspasia (mentioned several times in this chapter) has not given rise to specialized studies, with the exception of P. Brulé's "Des femmes au miroir masculin" (1989), but Brulé does not specifically place the story within the totality of Greek representations of the world of "Oriental" palaces.

∞ The biographical markers for Bagoas are almost negligible (see entries in Berve, *Alexanderreich* [1926] no. 195, and in P. Guyot, *Eunuchen* [1980], p. 190). A Bagoas, son of Pharnakes, is known to have been one of the trierarchs of the Indian fleet (Arrian, *Indica*, 18.8), but there is nothing to suggest that it is the same young eunuch under discussion here (cf. Berve, *Alexanderreich*, vol. 2, nos. 194–195). It is also known that Alexander, in the last days of his life in Babylon, went to dine with Bagoas, "whose house was ten stadia from the palace" (Aelian, *Varia historia*, 3.23: *oikos*). Here again the uncertainty persists, because the only concordant text is a passage from Theophrastus's *Enquiry into Plants* (2.6.7), which alludes to "a garden of Bagoas the Elder [*o palaios*] in the vicinity of Babylon [*peri Babylōna*]." It does seems that this is the same piece of property, and one has the impression that this Bagoas the Elder was the chiliarch whom Darius executed at the start of his reign (*HPE*, p. 902), who apparently owned another residence (Plutarch, *Alexander*, 39.10: *oikos*)—unless this is the same one (Plutarch does not locate it precisely). All in all, then, nothing is certain.

∞ Orxines's career and his execution are also known through Arrian 6.29: he took command of Persia after the death of the satrap named by Alexander, who had several satraps suspected of treason put to death; he also subjected the magi assigned to guard Cyrus's tomb to torture, then released them because they were cleansed of all suspicion and did not denounce anyone else; it was on the road between Pasargadae and Persepolis that Alexander decided to have Orxines executed, because the Persians had accused him of many instances of misappropriation and looting (6.30.1–2). The story of Bagoas is grafted onto that narrative framework: see Berve, *Alexanderreich*, vol. 2, no. 592. E. Badian's article in A. B. Bosworth and E. J. Baynham, eds., *Alexander the Great in Fact and Fiction* (Oxford, 2000), pp. 92–93 [2012, pp. 420–456], offers nothing new.

∞ On the question of homosexuality among the Persians: Herodotus (1.135) and Xenophon (*Cyr.* 2.2) claim that the Persians had learned the love of boys from the Greeks; Plutarch vigorously opposes that view (*On the Malice of Herodotus*, 13 [857B–C]). There is no doubt that the practice was also widespread among the Persians: see the brief discussion in *HPE*, pp. 919–920. The polemic was revived in the modern period, especially between Voltaire and some of his contemporaries (J. Chaybany, *Les voyages en Perse* [1971], pp. 257–259): see J.-M. Gesner's interesting little book *Socrates sanctus paederasta*, published in 1752 in the papers of the Göttingen Academy and translated into French by A. Bonneau; the translation has been reissued by Éditions Paris-Zanzibar, 1998; it is followed (pp. 50–69) by the "Polémique entre Voltaire et Larcher à propos de Gesner," in which Voltaire and Larcher engage in a spirited debate about Sextus Empiricus's text on homosexuality among the Persians. On the Greek conception of homosexuality, see K. J. Dover, *Greek Homosexuality* (1982); on the importance of the kiss between the *erōmenos* and the *erastēs*, see F. Dupont and T. Éloi, *L'érotisme masculin* (2001), pp. 244–260; on pederasty among the Macedonians, see Berve's remarks, *Alexanderreich* [1926 (1973)] 1:10–11, and M. Hatzopoulos, *Cultes et rites de passage* (1994), pp. 93–97.

∞ Regarding translations as *mignon*: on Perrot d'Ablancourt, see R. Zuber's splendid *Les "belles infidèles"* (1968 [1995]), as well as his edition of N. Perrot d'Ablancourt, *Lettres et préfaces critiques* (Paris, 1972). The discussion of *mignons* and the representations associated with them in Henry III's time is indebted to G. Poirier's *L'homosexualité* (1996) and N. Le Roux's recent *La faveur du roi* (2000), quotations pp. 9–11, 263–270, 621ff. On pp. 264–265, Poirier mentions the use of *mignon* in Amyot's translations; the term *mignon* in the sense of "faithful companion" is used, for example, by Budé, when he speaks of Alexander's relationship with Hephaestion and Craterus (*Institution du Prince* [1965] 53r; cf. also Gentillet, *Anti-Machiavel* (1968) p. 100: "Two gentlemen among his most special friends and servants." In addition, more recent translations of Plutarch continue to use the term in reference to Bagoas (cf. *Alexander*, 67.8, where *erōmenos* is translated in that way by R. Flacelière (Flacelière and Chambry, *Plutarque: Vies* [1975], 9:114). It must be acknowledged that the translation of *erōmenos* as *mignon* is common (cf. Hatzopoulos, *Cultes et rites de passage*, p. 96, translating Diodorus 14.37.6): it is nonetheless questionable. The English translator for the Loeb Classical Library translates Diodorus more accurately as "whom he loved"; similarly for the translation of Curtius in the same collection: "Bagoas . . . who had been loved by Darius and was afterwards to be loved by Alexander" (on the vocabulary, cf. Dover, *Greek Homosexuality* [1982], pp. 31–32). As for translations of Curtius, H. Bardon's French translation in the G. Budé collection, *Quinte-Curce*, 1:181, has: "Bagoas had been Darius's *mignon* before becoming that of Alexander"; similarly Dymnus, "who burned with love for a *mignon* called Nicomachus" (p. 188). The English "minion" is also found in Tarn, *Alexander* (1948), 2:320 (I note in passing that a polemic also erupted in England in the sixteenth century around minions and bad advisers to the king: see Le Roux, *La faveur du roi* [2000], p. 662). By contrast, Vaugelas, a rival of Perrot d'Albancourt and translator of Curtius, uses the following formulation in reference to Bagoas: "having been greatly loved by Darius and soon by Alexander," and this expression, referring to Dymnus, "who greatly loved a young man" (*Quinte-Curce, De la vie et des actions d'Alexandre le Grand*, new edition, Lyons, 1774, 2:52). It is also true that Vaugelas at times prefers to replace the precise crudeness of the Latin with euphemisms: cf. p. 461, his translation of Curtius 10.1.26: instead of, "He replied that he paid his respects to the king's friends, not his whores [*scorta*], and that it was not the Persian custom to regard as men [*mares*] those who allowed themselves to be sexually used as women [*qui stupro effeminarentur*]" (John Yardley trans.), one finds this wonderful "belle infidèle": "He replied that he honored the king's friends but not his eunuchs; that the Persians used such people differently from the Greeks." Probably anxious first and foremost not to shock his readers, Vaugelas also seems thereby to take sides in the polemic between Herodotus and Plutarch on the origin of homosexuality among the Persians.

Notes to Chapter 10. Dārā and Iskandar

∞ On the history of Persia and Iran between the conquest of Alexander and the Arab conquest, see R. Ghirshman's chapters in *Iran: L'Iran des origines à Islam* (1951/1976), pp. 200–350, R. Frye's *Heritage*, 2nd ed. (1976), pp. 143–292, and lastly, the excellent overview by J. Wiesehöfer, *Ancient Persia* (1996), pp. 105–121; on the period between the conquest of Alexander and the establishment of the Parthian dynasty, see J. Wiese-höfer, *Die "dunklen Jahrhunderte" der Persis* (1994); see also A. Christensen, *L'Iran sous les Sassanides* (1944).

∞ Medieval and modern Arab and Persian inscriptions were recorded by several travel-ers (Chardin, Niebuhr, and others); a French translation of them appears in Sylvestre de Sacy, *Mémoires* (1793), pp. 125–165 ("Mémoire sur les inscriptions arabes et persanes de Tchéhel-Minar"), with revision of the dates: cf. E. G. Browne, *A Year among the Per-sians* (1893), pp. 352–354 (with translations into English of two inscriptions); several engraved in Persepolis by different individuals were published in S. S. Blair, *The Mon-umental Inscriptions from Early Islamic Iran* (1992), nos. 6–7, 43–44; quotations and com-mentary in A. S. Melikian-Chirvani, "Le royaume de Salomon" (1971); the English translation of the inscription of Šapur II in Persepolis is taken from J. Wiesehöfer, *Ancient Persia* (1996), p. 223 [all other inscriptions in this chapter are my translation—trans.]; Wiesehöfer's book has dense and well-informed pages on what has survived and what has been forgotten of the ancient periods in modern Iran (pp. 223–242). On the history of the site's name, see esp. S. Shahbazi, "From Pārsa to Taxt-e Jāmšīd (1980).

∞ The question of the "Achaemenid memory" in Parthian and Sassanid Iran has given rise to a number of studies. The most important is still E. Yarshater, "Were the Sasa-nians Heirs to the Achaemenids?" (1971), which concludes that they were not and speaks of "amnesia." T. Daryaee's point of view in "National History or Keyanid His-tory?" (1995) did not convince me, and it also seems to me that G. Gnoli's arguments in *The Idea of Iran* (1989), pp. 115–128, about the preservation of an Achaemenid memory of the Parthian period in Fars needs to be considered with reservations (cf. my re-marks in "Le passé réutilisé" [2009c]); on the supposed Sassanid claims to Achaeme-nid territories, see, lastly, the discussion in P. Huyse, "La revendication de territoires achéménides" (2002) and, in counterpoint, S. Shahbazi, "Sasanians' Claims" (2001), and T. Daryaee, "Memory and History" (2001–2002).

∞ The Iranian royal legend (origin, development, and dissemination) has often been studied: in addition to T. Nöldeke's *Iranian National Epic* (1930), which remains funda-mental, see A. Christensen's *Les Kayanides* (1931), *Le premier homme* (1934), and *Les gestes des rois* (1936).

∞ On the oral transmission of legends, see A. S. Shahbazi, "Early Persians' Interest in History" (1990), and M. Boyce, "Some Remarks on the Transmission" (1954), "Zariadres and Zarēr" (1955), and "The Parthian Gōsān" (1957); see also V. Curtis, "Minstrels" (1998); on the itinerant minstrels in medieval and modern Persia, see esp. W. L. Han-away, "Dāstān-sarā'ī" (1994), and O. M. Davidson, *Poet and Hero* (1994), pp. 56–60 (espe-cially on Ferdowsī's *Book of the Kings*); on the "reciters of the books of kings" from the time of Mahmūd of Ghazni, see A. S. Melikian-Chirvani, "Le livre des rois" (1988), pp. 8, 19, 33.

∞ On Pahlevi literature in the Sassanid period generally, see E. G. Browne, *Literary His-tory* (1908), pp. 103–110, M. Boyce's overview, "Middle Persian Literature" (1968b), and the (posthumous) chapter by J. de Menasce, "Zoroastrian Pahlavī Writings" (1983). Concerning the different works cited in the chapter:

—on the *Dēnkard* and the *Bundahišn,* see the excellent introductions by P. Gignoux, *Dēnkard* (1984a), and D. N. MacKenzie, *Bundahišn* (1990); book 3 of the *Dēnkard* was edited and translated into French by J. de Menasche as *Troisième livre* (1972), book 5 by J. Amouzgar and A. Tafazzoli as *Cinquième livre* (2000), and book 7 by M. Molé as *Légende de Zorastre* (1993). Many translated and annotated passages can also be found in the following studies: G. Messina, "Mito, legenda e storia" (1935); H. W. Bailey, *Zoroastrian Problems* (1943), esp. pp. 149–175; and R. C. Zaehner, *Zurvan* (1955).

—The *Letter of Tansar* was translated into French with an introduction by J. Darmesteter, *Lettre de Tansar* (1894); see by preference the English translation annotated by M. Boyce, *Letter of Tansar* (1968a), and quoted here; see also Christensen, *Iran* (1944), pp. 63–66, and the important remarks of C.-H. de Fouchécour in *Notions morales* (1986), pp. 89–93.

—The Arabic version of the *Testament of Ardašir* was published by M. Grignaschi, "Quelques specimens" (1966), pp. 1–3 (introduction), pp. 8–9 (relationship to the *Letter of Tansar*), pp. 68–83 (French translation), pp. 84–90 (explanatory notes); on this text, see also C.-H. de Fouchécour, *Notions morales* (1986), pp. 87–89.

—The *Kārnāmē ī Artakšīr ī Pāpakān* is quoted from the old edition-translation of D. D. P. Sanjana (1896); it has recently been translated into French by F. Grenet as *La Geste d'Ardashir* (2003).

—The *Ardā Vīrāz Nāmag* was edited and translated by P. Gignoux, *Le livre d'Ardâ Virâz* (1984).

∽ In the absence of references to (nonexistent) studies on the figure of Dārā, see the many studies devoted to the figure of Alexander in Pahlevi literature; it would be helpful, to gain a knowledge of this literature, to consult the appendix that Southgate devoted to "Alexander in Pahlavi Literature" (*Iskandarnamah* [1978], pp. 186–189); see also C. A. Ciancaglini, "Alessandro e l'incendio di Persepoli" (1997), esp. pp. 66–77 (with an Italian translation of the pertinent passages from the *Ardā Vīrāz Nāmag*, pp. 69–70); G. Gnoli, "La demonizzazione di Alessandro" (1995); I have also used the translations and commentaries of G. Messina, "Mito, legenda et storia" (1935); many texts are introduced, translated, and annotated in H. W. Bailey, *Zoroastrian Problems* (1943), esp. pp. 149–175, and in R. C. Zaehner, *Zurvan* (1955). Lastly, P. Gignoux was kind enough to share with me a study, unpublished at the time, which is now available: "La démonisation d'Alexandre le Grand d'après la littérature pehlevie" (2007).

∽ There is a significant body of literature on the legend of Alexander in Persian and Arabo-Persian. Its scope can be ascertained by consulting recent collections: M. Bridges and J. C. Bürgel, eds, *The Problematics of Power* (1996); L. Harf-Lancner, C. Kappler, and F. Suard, eds., *Alexandre le Grand dans les littératures* (1999); see also A. Abel, "La figure d'Alexandre en Iran" (1966), M. S. Southgate, *Iskandarnamah* (1978), pp. 190–201 ("Alexander in the Works of Persian and Arab Historians of the Islamic Era"), as well as the helpful overview by W. L. Hanaway, "Eskandar-Nāma" (1998), with bibli-

ography; and finally, the collection (rather disappointing overall) edited by Stoneman, Erickson, and Netton, *The Alexander Romance in the East* (2012).

—Tabarī's chronicle is quoted from the H. Zotenberg translation, *Chronique de Tabari*
(1958); on the individual and his work, in addition to T. Nöldeke's introduction
(*Tabari* [1879], pp. xiii–xxviiii), see the excellent and informative overview by C. E.
Bosworth, "Al-Tabarī" (1998a); on the image of Alexander, see El-Sayed, "Al-Tabari's
Tales of Alexander" (2012) (which takes no note of my chapter).

—Tha'ālibī is quoted from the Zotenberg translation (*Histoire des rois des Perses* [1990;
1963], which includes a long introduction (pp. i–xlv); see also E. K. Rowson, "Al-
Tha'alibī" (1999).

—Al-Mas'ūdī is cited from the translation by A. C. Barbier de Meynard and Pavet de
Courteille (1868).

—the (unpublished) translation of Dīnawarī was very kindly provided to me by Marina Gaillard, who prepared it based on the V. Guirgass edition (1888). On the author, see C. Pellat, "Dīnavarī" (1995). M. Gaillard also supplied me with a translation of the pages of Ibn' Bakhlī's *Fārs-nāmeh* (ed. G. Le Strange and R. A. Nicholson,
1921) that concern the history of Dārā; on the authors, see C. E. Bosworth's entry
"Ebn Al-Balkhī" (1998b).

—For Ferdowsī, I have used the famous translation by J. Mohl (Paris, 1836; books 1–7
reprinted in 1976). A new English translation by D. Davis appeared after the French
edition of the present book was published: *Shahnameh: The Persian Book of Kings*
(New York: Viking, 2006). On Ferdowsī and his work, in addition to the lengthy
introduction by J. Mohl, see (among others) H. Massé, *Firdousi et l'épopée iranienne*
(1935), A. S. Shahbazi, *Ferdowsī* (1991), D. Davis, *Epic and Sedition* (1992), O. M. Davidson, *Poet and Hero* (1994); on the composition of the *Shah-nameh,* see also C.-H. de
Fouchécour, "Une lecture" (1976); on its influence as a mirror of princes, see A. S.
Melikian-Chirvani, "Le livre des rois" (1988), and J. S. Meisami, "The *Šah-nāme*"
(1995). The problem of the sources that Ferdowsī used and that of the connections
with Pahlevi literature have often been discussed, with contradictory results: see
T. Nöldeke, *The Iranian National Epic* (1930), esp. pp. 9ff., Shahbazi, *Ferdowsī* (1991),
pp. 33–38, and lastly, D. Davis's stimulating article, "The Problem of Ferdowsī's
Sources" (1996), which tends to insist on the importance of oral transmission via the
minstrels; on that question, see the well-known study by M. Boyce, "The Parthian
Gōsān" (1957); see also V. Curtis, "Minstrels" (1998), and W. L. Hanaway, "Dāstān-Sarā'ī"
(1994). On the ambiguous figure of Alexander in Ferdowsī's work, see esp. Y. Yamanaka's "From Evil Destroyer to Islamic Hero" (1993) and "Ambiguïté de l'image
d'Alexandre" (1999); see also C. Kappler, "Alexandre dans le *Shāh Nāma*" (1996); H.
Manteghi's "Alexander the Great in the Shānāmeh of Ferdowsī" (2012) neglects
many of the recent studies (including those by Kappler, Melikian-Chirvani, and
Yamanaka), and offers nothing new. In her recent book *Alexander Histories and Iranian Reflections* (2012), P. Jamazdeh unconvincingly takes up her favorite theme,
that of the Persian and "Zoroastrian" echoes in the classical texts dealing with Alexander, but she does not raise the specific question of the figure of Alexander in
Iranian literature.

—For Nizāmī's *Iskandar-nāmeh,* see H. W. Clarke's English translation, *Sikander Nāmae* (1881), and J. C. Bürgel's German translation, *Alexanderbuch* (1991); see, lastly, a paraphrase of the *Sharafnāmeh* by P. Chelkowski, "Nizāmī's Iskandernāmeh" (1977), pp. 27–35 (the chapters dealing with the fight between Iskandar and Dārā are presented on pp. 26–32). On the author, see P. Chelkowski, "Nizāmī" (1995), W. L. Hanaway, "Eskandar-Nāma" (1998), and M. Barry, Nezâmî" (2000), pp. 507–705; on the representation of Iskandar, see also J. C. Bürgel, "Conquérant, philosophe et poète" (1995), and A. L. Beelaert, "Alexandre dans le discours sur les âges de la vie" (1999).

—On the other authors cited in the text: Abū Tāher Tarsusi's *Dārāb-nāmeh* is presented at length in W. L. Hanaway, "Persian Popular Romances" (1970), who also devotes a specific study to the heroine Burān Dokht, ibid., pp. 29–54, and in "Anāhitā and Alexander" (1982). I have used a French translation by M. Gaillard; my warm thanks to the author for her kindness in making the manuscript available to me before its publication in 2005. On the medieval Persian romances and their relationship to the Hellenistic romances, see D. Davis, "Greek and Persian Romances" (2002) and *Panthea's Children* (2002).

—Saadi's *Bustan* is quoted from the Barbier du Meynard French translation (1880); on the author, see H. Massé, *Saadi* (1919); R. Davis, "Sa'adī" (1994); G. M. Vickens, "Bustān" (1990); F. Lewis, "Golestān-e Sa'adī" (2001); C.-H. de Fouchécour, *Notions morales* (1986), pp. 311–355 ("La réussite du genre: L'oeuvre morale de Sa'adī").

—On Jāmi's *Kerad-nāme,* see C.-H. de Fouchécour, "Jāmi, conseiller des princes" (1999a).

Illustration Credits

Index